# GOVERNORS
# *of*
# WASHINGTON

GEORGE W. SCOTT, PH. D.

To order additional copies of this book, contact
www.civitaspress.net


Library of Congress Control Number 2010904652
ISBN: Hardcover


This book was printed in the United States of America.

Governors listed on the cover, clockwise from top.

1. Isaac Stevens
2. Eugene Semple
3. Elisha Ferry
4. Watson Squire
5. John R. Rogers
6. Marion Hay
7. Ernest Lister
8. Clarence D. Martin
9. Arthur B. Langlie
10. Daniel Evans
11. Dixie Lee Ray
12. Gary Locke

## *Acknowledgments*

Historians rely on the institutional memories of archivists as well as their inventories. State Archivist Sid McAlpin, his deputy David Owens, and senior archivists Pat Hopkins and Dave Hastings drew on full careers to bring me buried jewels. Lupita Lopez found hundreds of boxes and Mary Hammer diligently sought out 80 photos. Ed Nolan at the Washington State Historical Society, Laura Arksey at the Eastern Washington State Historical Society, Cheney, Larry Stark, senior archivist at Washington State University, Karyl Wynn and Karla Rickerson, successively heads of Special Collections at the University of Washington, oriented me to dozens of collections. Nicolette Bouchet and Gary Lundell of their staff were patient beyond the call of duty. Archivists Deb Kennedy of King County, Scott Cline of the City of Seattle and Susan Karren of the National Archives and Records Administration's Northwest Regional Branch were unfailingly responsive. Carolyn Marr, the photographic archivist at the Museum of History and Industry, knew what I needed and uncovered a large segment of the photos.

Professors Bill Rorabaugh, Arther Ferrill, John Findlay, and the late Hugh Bone of the University of Washington, Brewster Denny, founding Dean of its Institute of Public Affairs (now the Evans Graduate School of Public Affairs), read and critiqued. Professors David Stratton and Richard Hume of Washington State University, Charles Mutchler and Jay Rea of Eastern Washington University, and Carlos Schwantes of the University of Missouri sliced imagined "pearls" onto the cutting room floor. A special salute is owed Don Burrows, former director of the Washington State Department of Revenue, who created the crucial Appendix 3. Richard Rodger, Director of Senate Committee Services, Olympia, facilitated Cheri Randich's charting hundreds of vetoes (Appendix 7). Grant Kelly, a master of computerdom, gently lifted me out of innumerable cul-de-sacs. Veronica Velasco patiently did the layout graphics and configured the appendices. Wendi Lindquist deligently proof read. My wife Ruth and our daughter Courtnay, communications major, rescued me from prose foibles and as usual got the last word.

Only one in 20,000 citizens, has the honor of state office. I had the privilege of serving with over 500 legislators over 14 years and knowing seven of the last nine governors (Governor Gregoire excepted). They, their senior staff and peers in the Third House candidly collaborated in creating 1,600 pages of oral history. My legislative leader colleagues, intelligent public servants in office at considerable cost to their families and professional lives, leavened this politician's leanings with different perspectives. They are the state's lifeblood.

*"To describe the beauties of this region, will, on some future occasion, be a very grateful task to the pen of the skillful panegyrist. The serenity of the climate, the innumerable pleasing landscapes, the abundant fertility that unassisted nature puts forth require only to be enriched by the industry of man, with villages, mansions, cottages, and other buildings, to render it the most lovely country that can be imagined."*

*Captain George Vancouver, 1792*

# *Prologue*

Edmond Meany, then the Northwest's foremost historian, published his cameo *Governors of Washington* in 1915 in less than 100 pages. At the time, the state's annual budget was under 15 million and it had 500 employees. The same figures in 2007 were $46 billion (half federal dollars) and 110,000 (including 70,000 public school teachers largely paid for by the state). The state is the largest "corporation" in Washington, with one million clients. Being governor is the most demanding, diverse and vulnerable of tasks, one done on the shifting sands of public opinion. The ego satisfactions are undeniable, but a job well done never assures reelection. The real rewards of public service are just that, together with an unmatched opportunity for personal growth from exposure to Washingtonians in every walk of life.

Winston Churchill famously said, "History is going to be kind to me, because I intend to write it." Governors work 60- to 80-hour weeks. Once out of office, and especially if they have a long tenure, their historical residue is voluminous enough to daunt almost anyone less talented, or who is not a trained, tenured, specialized historian. But the papers of an administration are an excellent gauge of the state's evolution and the energy and imagination of the executive. Several of the territorial governor's papers are housed in a single carton, and only the most conspicuous of them are evaluable. The average for the nine governors since World War II is 250 boxes. Governor Evans left 810. More than 30 dissertations and theses have been written on the executives or their eras since Professor Meany put pen in hand, but this is the first single volume synthesizing all the research.

My intent is to intrigue the lay reader, upperclassmen and graduate students, political aficionados, and those thinking of public service or politics. Governors and legislators are the last generalists and rewarded with an unequalled kaleidoscopic engagement with their time. For an overall assessment see Appendix X.

Politicians are regularly damned as "compromisers," that is, they did not take "my" prescription. A healthy democracy is the quintessence of compromise. Democracy is a *reflection* of the level of engagement of its citizens, and cannot rise far above them. Congresswoman Barbara Jordan put it succinctly: "The greatest threat to liberty is inattention." Informed voters elect the best politicians who are society's middlemen, charged with finding ways to deliver the greatest good for the greatest number and prevent the state or the nation from sundering into competing factions. What greater privilege exists?

George W. Scott, Ph.D.

Seattle, September, 2012

## *The Evolution of the Executive*

I. In the *Territorial-Colonial Period (1853 to 1889)*, the governor and four other statewide elected officials (we now have nine) and a few aides were the state. As late as 1877 Governor Elisha Ferry pled unsuccessfully for a full-time secretary. Governors were appointed by the president, needed a month to get here, and were ousted if the opposition won. Tenures averaged 2.7 years. The territory depended on Congress for dollars. Its chief roles, education, roads, and local law enforcement (the militia excepted), fell to the counties. The executive and the legislature were savaged by a partisan press and increasingly pressured by timber companies and the railroads.

II. *The Populists and Progressives.* From statehood to the end of World War I (1889 to 1919), reaction to the Gilded Age set in, aggravated by accelerating urbanization. Tensions rose as agricultural, small government Jeffersonian values and the needs of the rising working class in Tacoma, Spokane, and Seattle for organization and protection conflicted with commerce and industry. The Populists defined the issues and, after 1901, the Progressives regulated the railroads, passed workmen's accident compensation, the initiative, referendum, and recall, took the first steps toward land use planning, and granted women the vote eight years before the nation. Individualism and "progressivism" became part of the state's identity.

III. *The early 1920s and the 1930s* were not as dissimilar as assumed. Progressivism lingered as Governor Hart consolidated the proliferating agencies into nine "Code" departments, an infrastructure that still exists. Reactions to the disappointments of WWI, labor unrest, a "general strike," and a passing "Red scare" stalled reform. Lingering small-government ideas left Democrats impotent and Republicans the benefactors of prosperity until the Depression began in 1929. Washington, Oregon, and

Idaho elected "conservative" Democratic governors unwilling to fully embrace Franklin Roosevelt's New Deal. "States' rights" stands echoed as mandates for "matching dollars" from the state to share in the federal cornucopia drove budgets and reconfigured departments.

IV. *World War II and the Cold War (1941 to 1964)* ended the Depression, saw the peak of the extractive industries, and drew a second more diverse wave of immigrants to major military installations, the shipyards, Boeing, and its suppliers. Republicanism revived in 1940 in the person of Arthur Langlie (1941-45, 1949-57), the first three-term governor. He and other "Eisenhower Republicans" affirmed the New Deal, but overgenerous welfare initiatives left him struggling to keep the state solvent. Mon Wallgren's intervening term (1945-49) saw the apex and waning of the intense partisan politics of the 1930s, fed by the hardships of the Depression. Albert D. Rosellini (1957-65) was a transitional figure, practicing old politics and avoiding new taxes, while bringing in contemporary management methods and restoring the state's social institutions to health.

V. *The Dan Evans Era (1965 to 1977)*. The House Republican Leader quickly turned into the epitome of '60s activism. Washington's budget nearly tripled in 12 years. Evans' aggressiveness and path breaking environmental laws fueled expectations, but the distractions of the Vietnam War, Watergate, a third term, and the loss of the GOP majority in the House in 1972 slowed his pace. Tax reform fell a second time, and voters resisted a constitutional convention and structural reforms. However, the states, long the reflexive backwaters of Congress, reasserted themselves and became the fastest-growing and most dynamic tier of government.

VI. *Consolidation and Centrism (1977 to 2005)*. The legislature responded to Evans' ascendancy by arming itself with over 200 full-time staff. Lobbyists and the bureaucracy grew apace. (The new Department of Ecology, for instance, expanded to 900 staff by 2000). The state supreme court ventured into "dual sovereignty," reconsidering policies as well as the constitutionality of laws, as seen in the Seattle School District's successful suit mandating "full" funding of public schools. Governor Dixy Lee Ray (1977-81), a "Democrat" with Republican leanings, an outsider and accident of her time, enlarged public frustrations. Former county executives John Spellman, Booth Gardner, and Gary Locke returned the state to its centrist traditions. Congressman Mike Lowry (1993-97), one of only three avowed liberals to sit in the governor's chair since statehood, was trapped by the recession of the early '90s and tripped by his lack of discretion.

VII. *The Prospect: An Age of Overriding Urbanism and Overreach.* A massive inflow of over a million new residents since the 1980s, most of them to Puget Sound, completed Seattle's conversion to a liberal "San Francisco of the North." Unprecedented technology based affluence enriching districts east of Lake Washington overturned the GOP's historic hold on them by 2006, ending its chance of regaining legislative majority until the they are reclaimed or extraordinary leadership emerges. Republicans will continue to have almost all the legislators from Eastern Washington, but this quarter of the state's population offsets only Seattle's like share, and Left-tending King County is growing much faster.

The fate of Christine Gregoire, who was elected Washington's second woman governor in 2004, is indicative. She too was a centrist, but more than her predecessors governors Booth Gardner and Gary Locke, has been pulled left by the liberals leading nearly two to one majorities in the House. Since "the worst recession the Great Depression" began in 2007, despite shifting fund balances to the General Fund, passing over pension payments and absorbing a federal "stimulus," a quarter of an unsustainable budget has been excised only because of the consititutional mandate the budget be balanced, the public's paralysis in the frozen economy, and a tax system at its limits, and despite the House's liberal orientation. The 2012 legislature found itself against the wall. Even if initiatives do not reduce revenue or impose fresh obligations, forecasts dictated squeezing out ten percent more from the remaining $36 billion. A weary governor announced a year ahead she would not seek a third term in 2012, as doubt about the economy deepened, unemployment was unmoved at 9.1 percent, and another $2 billion gap forced the calling of an unprecedented special session between Thanksgiving and Christmas.

In the last 30 years Republicans have elected no more than three of the nine statewide elected officials. The outcome of the centerpiece governorship contest of 2012 between Attorney General Rob McKenna and First District Congressman Jay Inslee is competitive because of the wider exposure and campaign talents of the former. Given that liberal King County will cast an increasing share of the vote, the now "Democratic leaning," state is likely to revert to where it was in FDR's last election in 1944, predictably Democratic.

*Contents*

Chapter 1

# The Territorial Executive: Responsibility without Authority

*(1853-1889)*

## "The Real Washington" or Just "The Other Washington"?

The Western territories formed by the Northwest Ordinance of 1787 were "colonies," more than the original 13 states.[1] Their governors were torn between presidents and congresses vying to keep control, and legislatures trying to enlarge their power by making the presidential appointees dependent on them.[2] In the Organic Act passed March 2, 1853 creating Washington Territory, its chief executive was also given command of the militia and was Superintendent of Indian Affairs. The president also chose the Secretary [of State], Attorney [General], and Marshal. The governor might pick lesser territorial officers and grant pardons. Congress paid the bills, about $1 million a year in each of the first six years. Congress could void any territorial law. Washington Territory's citizens had less, not more self- governance.[3]

Gubernatorial tenures were short, changing when the president did, and a round-trip from Olympia to "Washington City" might take 90 days. In the interims, secretaries (of state) who were second in importance dispensed Congress's funds and often acted as the governor's alter ego.[4] The first, Charles H. Mason, a capable 23 year-old Brown University graduate was acting governor for 30 months, half of first Governor Steven's term. Like other lonely men in the wilderness, he succumbed at

30 to John Barley Corn. Mason's estate contains copies of Tacitus, Livy, and McCauley's *England* and an unpaid bar bill of $33 (over $300 today).[5] His replacements were mainly admirable men, but the secretary's status as "first among equals" slid steadily, turning into an incubation station as specialist peers took over his tasks. Still, as the territory expanded with "jumbled and chaotic growth," they were essential bridges in the transit from appointive to bureaucratic government.[6] Washington's governor was weaker than those in the Midwest, initially lacking the veto, and soon lost the Indian superintendency. Still forceful leadership at the beginning and end of the period, and the legislature's loss of it due to the Civil War, combined with the deprecating effects on elective politics of the Gilded Age, insured the governor the highest profile.[7]

Isaac Stevens, an engineer who was first in his class at West Point, saw no future in the army after the war with Mexico in 1845. Fired with ambition, he also persuaded President Pierce to have him map the best rail routes west of the Missouri. This first achievement, carried off by three teams of less than 100 archeologists, biologists, geologists, and cartographers in five and a half months, is arguably Stevens' best. Secretary of War Jefferson Davis, the future Confederate president, preferred a southern route and countered with negative reports on Snoqualmie and "Stevens" passes, but had to accede. In defining the nature of the Northwest in some detail, the Pacific Railroad Surveys filled in Lewis and Clark's sketches of a half century earlier. The region's interior was no longer largely terra incognita. The legislature chartered its own never-realized Northern Pacific Railroad in 1857, with the governor as chief executive. A real one, like the settler's other prime goal, statehood, was still three decades off.

The survey manifested Stevens' incredible energy, capacity for detail, tenacity — and a critical flaw. The new governor "commanded best" when subordinates shared his viewpoint. He seemingly gave latitude for independent judgment to his colleagues — then castigated them for not adhering precisely to instructions. "Misunderstandings and clashes of will" were laid to their character faults.[8] Better suited to the army than the rocks, shoals, and compromises of politics, Stevens enjoyed the advantage of Washington's first and finest legislature. It convened February 27, 1854, in a wooden building fronting the bay. The Parker and Coulter General Store occupied the first floor. Legislators accessed the "chambers" on the second by an outside stairway. The average age was 28, but at least nine of the 27 members were professionals, comparing well with the 147 legislators 150 years later, especially in light of how many fewer of them were in the populace. One died of apoplexy the day after his swearing in, perhaps sent off by the enormity of their tasks. The lawmakers wrote civil and criminal codes, probate and justice practice laws, created eight counties, memorialized Congress for ports of entry, lighthouses and land rights for George Bush the territory's first black man, and adjourned in 64 days.[9] Governor Stevens got what he asked for: a functioning government, election laws, a commission to shape public schools, and land for a university. Joint resolutions to annex Hawaii, settle the San Juan boundary dispute with Britain, bring mail service to Puget Sound, conduct more surveys, build roads, and equip and arm the militia went to Congress. A strong legislative leadership cadre collaborated with him to preempt sectional struggles and controversies, like the location of public buildings.[10] The drafters of the first laws were indeed "citizen-legislators," practical men, not parliamentarians, unpaid and eager to get back to making a living. Their priorities were clear, there were fewer voices to be heard, and they faced only a handful of lobbyists.

Predictably, politics bloomed in the second session in December 1854, where buildings and appropriations were dealt out. The legislature voted to locate the territorial penitentiary in Clark County (at Vancouver) and the capitol at Olympia. Seattle got the territorial university and was sure it had "lost." The perennial fights over patronage, the scourge of the federal government long after the Pendleton Act of 1888, harassed the territory and state until fixed by initiative in 1961. They seem petty, even outrageous, until one realizes that apart from farming, being a town merchant or in the small cadre of lawyers, there were few outlets for the ambitious. The governor controlled just three dozen jobs. The $10,000 given the state printer (in 1860) to publish new statutes was a prize that sent the legislature into partisan spasms before any other business could be conducted. The Democratic legislature gave the job to the (Olympia) *Pioneer and Democrat* until 1861. The paper, which was profitable, paid part of the party's bills and was Stevens' mouthpiece more than a vehicle for educating citizens put off by the incessant partisanship. The territory escaped the midcontinent plagues of the Jacksonian Era, where the executive's work was taken over by legislative committees. Only when this became transparently impracticable did a true executive and a distribution of power to other statewide officials emerge. Stevens' kinetic and assertive personality guaranteed he would be "first among equals," but the legislature of 18 representatives (rising to 30 as population grew) and the Council (Senate) of nine, elected to one and three-year terms, could and did ignore the governor. In the first 11 years, no bills were submitted to him but were forwarded directly to Congress. He was empowered to fill vacancies in the new offices of auditor, treasurer, and librarian in the 10 months a year the legislators were in recess. One-year terms kept them on short leashes.

The lawmakers effectively controlled the militia, choosing its brigadier, commissary, and quartermaster generals every three years.[11] Roads were designated by their select commission and maintained by county commissioners, as were schools. The *Organic Act* and infrequent congressional nullifications of laws reminded the legislature who was really in charge as court decisions hemmed them in.[12] It could not dispose of public land, tax U.S. property, assess taxes other than on value, discriminate against nonresidents, borrow, fix unequal levies, incur debt, incorporate banks, or offer a means of exchange. To discourage "logrolling" [vote trades for bills], every law had to have one "object." The judiciary was a supreme court of three, one justice heading each district court, supplemented by probate courts, and justices of the peace.

## The Indians, Impatience, Injustice

Stevens stumbled badly as Indian Superintendent. Congress' passage of the Donation Land Act started a stampede of settlers toward the coast as gold rushes harried the tribes east of the Cascades. There was room for all, but most pioneers saw themselves as belonging to a superior civilization and the virtual invitation to seize land without title made "extinguishing" the Indian claims and relocating them onto reservations difficult.[13] The governor hired a Harvard lawyer to draw a uniform treaty and quickly got tribes on Puget Sound to sign. Threats were necessary at Walla Walla to get a convocation of 5,000 from tribes east of the Cascades to concur and he overplayed his hand at Medicine Creek on the Nisqually Flats in 1854, provoking the Indian Wars of 1855-56. There were 350 natives and just 14 whites present, and "the best feelings prevailed among all." The Indians resented giving up their ancestral homelands for reservations, but seeing the inevitable, several tribes consented. Then Stevens became "incensed" at Chehalis Chief Tleyuk, who insisted relocation be to their land and that he be named the Grand Tyee. The meeting dissolved after the governor reprimanded and insulted him by tearing up the paper on which the government recognized him as chief — in front of the assembled.[14]

Whatever "possessory rights" the Indians supposedly had were suborned to Congress' underlying assumption it was the ultimate owner and arbiter of the land. The village tribes of the coast had no better places to go, but the semi-nomadic ones on the Great Columbia Plain saw their fate if their range of motion was lost. Stevens took the settler's view. Natives who did not cooperate, assimilate, and become farmers were "enemies." Determined to "direct and follow the public will," he sent word to the peaceful Nez Perces inviting them to "submit to the justice and mercy of the government."[15] He refused to heed the "go slow" advice or cooperate with General John E. Wool, commanding the army in the Northwest, who viewed the governor's undisciplined militia as a greater threat than the Indians.

The Native Americans knew the "turf" and were better armed. Two separate military operations and defeats in the Yakima Valley and at Steptoe Butte (between Spokane and Pullman) delayed Congress's approval of the treaties and pay for the militia.[16] The governor proclaimed martial law to circumvent habeas corpus and try "miscreants" like Chief Leschi, the governor's leading antagonist on Puget Sound. Proper punishment could be meted out promptly in military courts. Stevens lost in Judge Lander's Pierce County courtroom and was fined $50 for contempt. The legislature divided into pro- and anti-Stevens factions. Congress passed a joint resolution chastising the governor for suspending habeas corpus, interfering with the courts, and assembling a military commission (which found it lacked authority), to try those who he thought unwilling to force Indians onto reservations for treason. The president issued a reprimand through his secretary of state.[17] When Chief Leschi's brother Queimuth was murdered in Stevens's office, the killers – who were known – were not prosecuted. The governor was upset only because it happened there. Nothing could have prevented the small surprise attacks of the Indian Wars, nor did anything positive come of them unless it was the creation of rudimentary military roads. General Wool was recalled by the army. His ban on settlement east of the Cascades was officially retained — until Congress confiscated the trespassed land. Native Americans were ignored, submerged and partitioned off, not "assimilated."

Politics in the Northwest mirrored national trends more than the forging of the frontier. Starting with the primary election of 1856, the unavoidable slavery issue realigned the parties, shoving the Whigs off the scene. "Free Soilers" joined newly minted Republicans to form legislative majorities opposed to Democrat Stevens.[18] Needing a change of venue and to repair his image on the Potomac, Stevens became the territory's delegate to Congress, only to be denied nomination for a third term in 1861 by internal party chicanery. President Lincoln and the Republicans were now in charge, the Civil War was on, and patriotic resolutions rushed through the legislature. Stevens, a Massachusetts native who opposed secession in 1860 and unrealistically pursued a "compromise" — to the point of rewriting the Constitution — was a liability to the Democrats.

The isolated territory was least affected by the war. A few frontiersmen took sides after the passage of the Kansas-Nebraska Act of 1854, to make it a slave or Free State. But in 1861, there were just 64,000 whites in the entire Northwest, scrabbling for existence with a negligible number of blacks. The settlers were still overwhelmingly farmers from the Ohio and Missouri valleys. The territory had "the characteristics of a transplanted border state," one steeped in conservatism and nationalism. The few New Englanders among them were also "Jeffersonians," averse to being "dictated to" and to political extremes. "Independence" from the federal government's "foreign appointments," not slavery, was the burning question. Before leaving, Stevens helped raise a territorial regiment to guard the coast. It was crumbling when the governor-cum major general was shot in the temple leading the charge of his brigade at Chantilly, Virginia in 1861.

## Legislative Legerdemain

The legislators overreached in 1855, "repealing" the Organic Act. Congress reacted by combining all territorial statutes into one, requiring preapproval of all expenditures, making territorial offices gubernatorial appointees and critically, vesting the executive with the veto.[19] The overnight need to officer a huge army stripped the legislatures of leaders, though many would return as governors. The loss of a professional cadre, particularly lawyers (from seven in 1854 to three in 1879), deprived the legislature of leaders, despite its expansion to 24 and 12 members respectively. In the industrializing Gilded Age, lawmakers were buffeted by and often beholden to stronger corporate powers, the railroads (welcomed at almost any price), and lumbermen, while being ignored by the widely dispersed pioneers hacking out homesteads.

Lacking the means for tackling large tasks, the legislators fell on discrediting ones like patronage seeking. In 1862-63, the lawmakers passed 150 private acts, most of them "exclusive monopolies" for ferries, bridges, and never built railroads, but "almost no general laws." Sectional and personal struggles recurred over the location of the capitol, penitentiary, university, and other institutions.[20] "Legislative divorces" were broadly condemned and frequently used. The vitriolic partisan press jaundiced the most generous reader against the legislators, further discouraging the talented that might have entered politics.

Congress had strengthened governors during the Civil War to curb local indulgences, beginning with the veto in 1864. And in the mid-1870s, the legislature gave the executive new appointments like the trustees of the insane asylum, the State Board of Education, and logging district commissioners. The governor and the chief justice were designated to inspect the auditor's books. A true executive had emerged whose status no longer hinged on force of personality. If the afflictions of legislators were not understood, conventional wisdom on the territorial executives was equally disparaging. Despite howls they were "carpetbaggers" and "presidential cronies," the 14 governors before 1889 almost without exception had resumes attractive in any generation. Four were exceptionally able, only one incompetent, and one corrupt. Four had been legislators, one a governor of New Jersey (twice), six congressmen, and one became a two-term U.S. senator. Eight had been government administrators, 11 officials in local or state government. There were two major generals, brigadier generals, colonels, and a captain in the Civil War. Seven were lawyers, one a physician, another a civil engineer, and five graduates of the best Eastern universities.[21] Time to get to station, brevity of tenure, congressional contortions, dependency on the president, and the patronage maladies of the nineteenth century diluted their strengths.

Stevens' successor Fayette McMullin (1857-59) was a political hack. The unimposing ex-congressman from Virginia and slavery advocate lacked spine. He was expected to pardon officers from Fort Steilacoom who exposed perjured testimony and made a strong defense and at Chief Leschi's second trial. Then 150 Puget Sounders threatened the governor with corporal punishment, and he demanded the War Department censure the officers. Hubert Howe Bancroft the monumental Northwest historian of the time wrote, his "chief objective in coming to Washington seems to have been to get rid of one wife and marry another."[22] U.S. Secretary of State Lewis Cass, with Stevens' impetuosity in mind, tried to impress upon McMullin that he had a sensitive task. "The remoteness of the Territory … the sparseness of the White population, the … turbulent character of the settlers, the Indians and … contiguity to the British possessions … call for great firmness and discretion." Apart from mimicking Stevens' views, McMullin did little but demonstrate pettiness. He argued with Mason as to who should go on leave, then tried to bar dancing from the capitol, the only suitable place. When Mason ignored him, McMullin reported Mason's "habit of indulging too freely in the social glass" to Cass.[23] On returning to the territory in August 1858, Mason found the governor had left a month earlier. McMullin's days were numbered when he got a legislative divorce, despite criticizing the hypocrisy of granting them to others. He went on to be a member of the confederate congress, his vanity intact.

The first photograph of Governor Richard Gholson, another Virginian, was recently discovered. His father was Welsh and English, his mother English and Cherokee. Educated in Virginia, he read law in Kentucky, where he ardently campaigned for President Buchanan. Tall, lean, and eloquent, with black hair parted in the middle and falling over his ears, he looked like an Indian. His byword was, "Politics was first, and business afterward." Gholson left his small grist mill in the hands of farmers, expecting to be left a portion. He was in office when the army landed on San Juan Island in July 1859, precipitating the Pig War and the territorial standoff with Great Britain over the San Juan Islands, and when gold rushes briefly returned the population east of the Cascades to parity. With war in the balance, Gholson adopted the truculent stance of junior army officers, offering his military might, "In view of the excited state of a portion of the people on Vancouver Island ... and from a judicious regard for the welfare of the populace should a collision occur."[24] When General Winfield Scott was rushed to the Northwest and began talks with Britain's Governor Douglas of Vancouver Island, Gholson complained of the "anomalous state of affairs here"; he was being left out of decisions made in his jurisdiction. To his credit, he asked the county assessor who had tried to collect taxes to make reparations and to observe a "scrupulous regard" for their rights of all British subjects."[25] In January 1860, he petitioned for leave if the union fell apart. "Unwilling to serve a day under a so-called Republican president," Gholson resigned a month before Lincoln's inauguration, went to Texas to gather his family of 12, and back to Kentucky to campaign against the "Black Republicans."[26]

Lincoln's appointment of Ohioan William H. Wallace, who studied law in Indiana, moved to Iowa in 1835, and to Washington Territory in 1853, evidenced a willingness to grant western positions to a "western" man. Wallace had earned the favor as director of the coalition against Stevens' Democratic "machine" since 1854.[27] He was in the First Legislature and became president of the Council. Wallace was the first resident and Republican elected congressional delegate after being governor, the former being considered the better station. His ambition was Lincoln's affliction. Before taking the qualifying oath as governor, Republicans made him their nominee for delegate.[28] Having helped gerrymander Idaho's boundaries to split the Democratic leaning miner's vote between the two territories in the interest of Olympia friends, the president named Wallace the first governor of Idaho and elected its first delegate. Washington Territory was left in the tender hands of Secretary L. Jay S. Turney, an Illinoisan, who was "not familiar with your statutes, local interests and local prejudices." When not on leave, Turney refused to give opinions and practiced "absolute inactivity."[29]

## Surviving the Gilded Age

English-born William Pickering (1862-66), an Oxford graduate of integrity, brought a reverse temperament. He had known Lincoln in the

Illinois legislature, where he served (1842-52). A civil engineer, Pickering's interests were federal assistance for roads and obliterating enemies of the president and the GOP. He worked to firm the Republican allegiances of radicals opposing slavery. Democrats, the governor said, were "secesh" [secessionists.] "Everybody knows that ... Democracy means opposition to the government, and nothing but that." Two contrasting outcomes underlined the governors' dependency on the president. Within a month, the collector of customs at Port Townsend, protected by Treasury Secretary Salmon P. Chase, trained the guns of his revenue cutter on the town to remove the Customs House to another site he was promoting. Pickering melodramatically rushed to the "theatre of war." Victor Smith, the collector, declared war on all territorial appointees and persisted. Ungrateful Port Townsendites blamed the governor, supplying the margin that elected a Democratic delegate in 1863.

The Smith fiasco evolved into a permanent breach between President Lincoln and Chase.[30] Wallace had installed attorney Elwood Evans to replace Turney as secretary.[31] Pickering's mediation failed and Evans had to fight for five months to get into his office. When he turned printing over to a Union Democrat newspaper and had it affirmed by a legislative coalition, the governor protested he "bit the hand that fed him" and claimed that Evans was "part of the Executive office." Wallace took the matter to the president. Lincoln told Secretary of State Seward that Evans had "gone over to the enemy using the patronage to establish and uphold a paper to oppose and embarrass the Administration." The State Department returned printing to the governor, who began his own newspaper.[32]

Pickering's problems illustrated the limitations of his office. The gold rushes in Northeastern Washington and in Idaho's Salmon River Country were enticing an impatient and unruly horde of men. Establishing law and order was a special challenge to the Republicans, who had labored long to disassemble the Stevens' "Democratic machine." But Pickering mirrored his generation's faith in self-government and politics came first. He took no interest in bringing territorial authority to the mines. After all, only the army had the power to quash the anarchy. Lincoln was shot before Pickering's pledged reappointment was signed.[33] The war added to the destabilization of government at every level. A rush of soldiers eager for new adventures, tradesmen, "mule skinners," and cattlemen surged into the vacuum. Only on Puget Sound did the "truck" gardeners, merchants, lumbermen, fisher and oystermen, loggers, and real estate "boomers" enjoy a semblance of civil government. Contrary to Idaho, Washington suffered from revolving governorships, as well as from politics and patronage.

The upsets peaked in the Grant administration. George Cole was a New York teacher disappointed as a '49er in California. In a year, he was in the Oregon legislature and chaired a committee petitioning Congress for a "Columbia Territory." In 1860, he was in Walla Walla and back to prospecting. In 1863-65, he was the first resident of eastern Washington to be seated in Congress. Cole was never officially governor, for the U.S. Senate in its jousts with President Johnson, refused to ratify him. The Washington Legislature's first memorial to become a state was passed and ignored by Congress. Cole later served as postmaster in Portland for Presidents Grant and Hayes and as a contractor for the Northern Pacific along Pend Oreille Lake. By 1883, he was a farmer in Spokane County and served two terms as its treasurer.

The Senate could not refuse Johnson's next New Yorker, Marshall Moore (1867-69). The Yale graduate, lawyer, former prosecuting attorney, and judge stood out as a brigadier in the war. Moore understood the need for new institutions and communications (mail routes and roads) as perquisites of progress. He died in 1870 before his efforts bore fruit.

Alvan Flanders of New Hampshire, lured to the gold fields in 1851, was twice a California legislator and a businessman in Wallula prior to his election as a delegate in 1867. Acting on the unanimous motion of the West Coast Republican congressmen, in 1869 Grant named him executive (1869-70). Strong evidence suggests his appointment was a trade to install opportunist nonpareil Selucius Garfielde as delegate. Eight months later, Flanders was removed with no complaint of record and without being told why. Influential German-Americans in the Midwest coveted his chair as a scalp for one of their flock. Garfielde and Senator Williams of Oregon signed off. Congressmen again had the whip hand. There was no complaint to what was standard practice.[34] Flanders legacy is a prediction: "On Puget Sound will be built a city from whose wharves ships will sail to every port on the Coast … the Pacific islands and … Asia."[35]

Garfielde's machinations divided the GOP in Washington more than usual. Installing a German-born former general from Wisconsin, Edward S. Salomon (1870-72), ensured enough unity to reelect the devious delegate in 1870.[36] An unexpected visit by a Treasury Department auditor in the summer of 1871 found $30,500 in public money missing. The receiver of funds, who was installed at the behest of Salomon, had loaned the money without security to him and a few associates.[37] Everyone else confessed. Salomon scurried to Portland and British Columbia raising money and replaced the funds in a week. He stayed in office five more months, until U.S. Secretary of State Fish noticed his requests through influential friends for leaves. Grant asked for Salomon's resignation "owing to recent occurences."[38] Salomon went onto two terms in the California legislature and as a district attorney.

## Mainstays

Three bona fide administrators at the close of the territorial period brought a measure of prominence and dignity to the executive office. Once Salomon was discredited, Elisha P. Ferry (1872-80), fought the ever-expedient Garfielde for control of the party.[39] Ferry, who had lived in the territory for 26 years, had no illusions: Garfielde represented "the worst of a class ... the corrupt carpetbagger who took office for the spoils." Territorial governors could align with the "ins" or face abuse and extinction. He astutely built the Republicans' most formidable political team, which along with a close association with Garfielde formed out of necessity gave him the security to be what the delegate was not.[40] Ferry's other paradox was that he was both the last Jeffersonian executive and the chief transfer agent to urban society.[41]

A lawyer, he was the first mayor of Waukegan, Illinois, in that state's constitutional convention, its bank commissioner, and colonel-adjutant general on the governor's staff, where he raised and equipped regiments for the war. Ferry came to Washington in 1874 as a surveyor. This prudent, first fully professional manager brought fiscal stability in the five lean years after the Northern Pacific defaulted in 1873. The next year, Congress again stifled the legislature by adding the auditor, librarian, school superintendent, and university regents to the governor's patronage, while tactlessly giving the militia the right to elect its officers. The petulant Council [Territorial Senate] retaliated by rejecting Ferry's appointments. Republicans argued for acquiescing to the fount of all favors; Democrats cried "tyranny." Ferry ran an administration free of upheaval and President Hayes renamed him to a second term in the face of disgruntled federal office holders and the chief justice, who came out against him. On leaving office, the governor joined Northern Pacific Railroad's law firm and in 1884 managed to derail an antimonopoly bill aimed at the railroad's land grants and to win nomination of its preferred nominee for delegate.

William A. Newell (1880-84), another Ohioan, had a degree from Rutgers and an MD from the University of Pennsylvania in 1839. Elected to Congress from New Jersey in 1846 and 1848, he began the Coast Guard and was its first superintendent. Newell was elected governor of New Jersey in 1857, went to Congress from 1860 to 1864, and then was beaten in a second run for governor in 1877 by General McClellan (who had surveyed Stevens Pass for Stevens, his subordinate in the Civil War).

The Northern Pacific (NP) reached Puget Sound in Newell's term, three decades after Stevens had proven it practicable. Henry Villard had just become president of the NP and moved to get coal mines in the foothills of the Cascades held by his adjunct, the Oregon Improvement Company.[42] The legislature anointed an inspector of mines to enforce a ventilation code. Newell countered with the nomination of the lawyers representing the NP, bringing a workers' revolt.[43] Despite explosions at the Carbonado and Newcastle mines, Newell did nothing. His contribution to democracy was the first affirmation and definition of the veto power. Until 1881, the legislators bypassed the executive by passing joint resolutions with the effect of law. The governor reminded the secretary of state that the resolutions were void without his signature and made it stick.[44]

Urbane businessman Watson C. Squire (1884-87) was a Wesleyan University and Cleveland Law School graduate, a colonel in the Civil War and the second executive in the closing period demonstrating character. He had traveled internationally as a supervisor for the Remington Arms Company. It fell to him to protect the Chinese, who descended into coastal cities after the completion of the Great Northern, from the nativist Knights of Labor. In October 1885, when an "immense mob" gathered in Seattle, he declined to send in the militia on the advice of King County sheriff and future governor John McGraw who wanted no "military interference." Squire did not want "the name of our territory ... disgraced by the attempt to root out [the] Chinese by force."

November brought new large gatherings of irate workmen in Seattle and Tacoma. McGraw pleaded with the governor to "send troops here at once." Squire appealed to the rioters "to array yourselves on the side of law." If the territory was to become a great self-governing state, it must "assert" the "power of self-control and self-preservation" and not "suffer the fate of Wyoming and the speedy interference of United States troops." On November 7, Tacomans drove virtually every Chinese out of town. Three months later, 196 Chinese "voluntarily" left Seattle for San Francisco by ship, in fear of their lives. Squire declared martial law, and had to reverse himself as McGraw had asked President Cleveland for federal troops. In three days, both cities were calm.[45] Few were convinced that both officials were "deliberately exaggerating" the situation. The governor won praise for declaring martial law, the same assumption of authority for which Stevens was damned and McGraw was voted out of office. Squire's reluctance to use force also spoke to his desire not to stall statehood, and was a measure of progress from Stevens' treatment of Native Americans.[46]

Migration surged as Squire was seated as governor. Washington's population billowed 40 percent in the second half of his term and property tax assessments (for a 2.5 mill tax) yielded another $181,000, turning the territory's biennial deficit of $22,000 into a $72,597 surplus in 1885-86. The state of public education, where the bulk of the money went, can be neatly summed. Teachers' salaries in the 858 mostly one-room districts averaged $45.38 a month. Three-fourths of the eligible children or 37,256 attended — but only 17,501 on a given day. The University's library had 2,500 volumes. In Squire's last year, the legislature appropriated $80,000 for a permanent prison at Walla Walla, but neither he nor they supplied operating funds or rules. Rather than lose the institution no one else wanted, locals came up with $25,000 for food and striped overalls and ran the prison by a commission they controlled. The eight-by-eight-foot cells having nothing but a hole in the floor were closed in the 1970s.

The rest of Squire's reputation as "constructive and conservative" rests on his elaborate reports to the Secretary of the Interior, "the best ... that has ever been given by a governor of any territory." Reprinted by the Northern Pacific, they reached Europe, stimulating new waves of immigrants and capital.[47] By the time he left office in 1887, the territory was home to a quarter million souls, enough to become a state. He then served two admirable terms as U.S. senator.

In 1884, Grover Cleveland reclaimed the presidency for the Democrats for the first time in 24 years. The President was determined to weaken the spoils system. Western Democratic governors backed Cleveland's pledge to select "federal officers for the territories" from residents there, making good Grant's intent of 1873. Cleveland too was forced to balance their demands for patronage against his pledge to mitigate partisanship. He tried to find other even handed conservatives to compete with those who did not share his values.[48]

The irrepressible Eugene Semple (1887-1889) was the embodiment of versatility, the common characteristic of the territorial executives. On leaving Cincinnati Law School, he set up shop in Portland, became the Oregon state printer, a farmer, circuit court clerk, and Portland Police Commissioner. In Vancouver, Semple was a lumber dealer, amateur engineer, and organizer of the Columbia Waterway Association fighting the Oregon Steam Navigation Company's monopoly. Seattleites who wanted their own road were behind an anti-monopoly bill aimed at the Northern Pacific, which had so long "slighted" them. They touted former mayor Beriah Brown for governor, as did Delegate Charles Voorhees. Vancouver's Semple had the support of southwest Washington and businessmen along the NP line. Cleveland's attorney general aligned with him, correctly believing Semple was beyond the reach of the NP.[49]

The patronage of scores of inspectors, surveyors, revenue officers, and commissions spawned by the legislature and the now decided Republican lean of the territory brought on immediate agitation by the GOP for election of the governor. Semple's firm law and order stance in the face of new anti-Chinese outbreaks, his decision to join against the incinerative battle for forfeiture of the Northern Pacific's land grants, and his belief in woman suffrage further narrowed his base of support, but testify to his courage.[50] He knew "this martial law and Chinese business will control the next territorial election, and if the action of the governor is sustained by the president, it will be Republican by a large majority."[51] The women's suffrage movement was activated in 1887 when the territorial supreme court denied women the right to vote. The legislature passed a new act granting them suffrage. The governor stood behind the law despite a nearly even division of public opinion, only to have the new state constitution omit and thus override the Suffrage Act. Semple was the territory's only "liberal" governor, a prologue to a Populist-Progressive heritage that would last 90 years. He voice was of "some significance" in urging "greater government activity for the in-rushing waves of settlers," hospitals, asylums, and charitable institutions.[52]

Disappointment over "delayed" statehood, prohibition, and woman suffrage raged on. The governor, a businessman who appealed to business Democrats, did not share their views on labor. His worst impasse underscores the limits of the territorial executive and tells of the changing times. Unrest among Seattle laborers, fishermen on the Columbia, and the risings of the coal miners at Newcastle and Roslyn, were part of the national pattern of resistance to the excesses of laissez-faire engulfing the Gilded Age. As the Knights of Labor stood off Pinkerton's private detectives at Newcastle, the militia's loose chain of command made it "not practicable to maintain a proper degree of discipline." Armed men hired by a Portland detective agency were deputized as U.S. Marshals, but in fact arrived at Roslyn to escort black strike breakers. They were arrested and let go by the straddling Kittitas County sheriff.[53] Semple took a narrow view of his legal powers and stayed neutral on the matter despite his private beliefs. At Newcastle, the brigadier in charge of the territorial guard took it upon his own authority to settle new outbreaks. The King County sheriff ordered strikebreakers to leave. Semple was no longer neutral, but "amazeful." He countermanded the order, fired his officers, and lectured the company of the proper uses of the guard. Management won, but the governor's legislation to outlaw private armies became law.[54]

Semple was in the minority of those faithful to President Cleveland's intent to blunt the wholesale use of patronage and empower the wing of the Democratic Party that overthrew its Eastern leaders. Ironically, Cleveland lost in 1888, opening the way for admission of the new "Republican" states. Elisha Ferry narrowly beat the Democrats led by Semple. His charm, confidence, glibness, and endless urgings to engage and invest mirrored the speculative boom and bust years. The former governor's Lake Washington Waterway Company filled Seattle's Duwamish tide flats in attempting to connect the south end of Lake Washington to saltwater by cutting through Beacon Hill, but the effort ruined him financially.[55]

## Failed Executives?

The omnibus bill that admitted North and South Dakota, Montana, and Washington to the union in 1889 favored the GOP.[56] Whether the end of territorial tutelage or "vassalage," only four territories had yet to become states. The territorial governors were the face of the federal government and the minions of parties too much beholden to corporate America. Most were politicians, not career administrators, with little sympathy lost on the Eastern "carpetbaggers" by the newly self-conscious, destined-for-independence Westerners.[57]

It is hard for the three generations since the New Deal, inured to an expanding panoply of public services, to grasp the nineteenth century's minimalist attitudes about the nation's collective life. "Government" was the teacher, the sheriff, a rare road crew, all paid by the county, and later a handful of cities large enough to own utilities. In 1890, the agrarian life beloved of Jefferson and the sons of the "Wild West" was being overwhelmed. The territory's governors and legislators are to be judged in the light of a "from scratch" start, in an untamed land, as dependents of the president, as congressional orphans with no final authority, with limited resources and delayed communications, where patronage was the coin of politics and partisanship perennial. Stevens set the benchmarks for leadership and rash behavior. Four others (Rogers, Ferry, Squire, and Semple) surpassed their era. Washington Territory was not so much ill governed as ungoverned.

Long after the Civil War, Democrats were the leading advocates of Manifest Destiny, order, and private property. As late as the constitutional convention of 1889, they led in cutting state officials' salaries, as both parties fought for a frugal image.[58] It was not until the industrial revolution overtook Jefferson's America in Washington in the 1880s that they began to move left of their heritage to find a new base among the urban underclass. The structure of state government changed little between 1889 and 1921. The differences included dropping the constraints of the Organic Act, the election of statewide officials, the reaction to and refutation of the Gilded Age known as Populism, and the work of the Progressives who expanded and realized their agenda in the next 20 years. It took the Great Depression to finally convince voters beyond doubt that the doctrines of minimal government were archaic.

## Land's End?

Frederick Jackson Turner's famous claim that the westward movement from the Missouri River to the Pacific "closed" with the end of "free land" in 1890 falls short in the Northwest.[59] In the 1840s a widening stream of pioneers crossed the lower Columbia before reaching the Pacific, turning more north than west or south. What pioneers absorbed on the way was soon submersed by the telescoped rush that transformed Oregon Country in one generation. Nor was this the finale. The Great Northern Railway locomotives laboring through Stevens Pass after 1887 carried an envelopment of immigrants from the north, flooding Everett, Seattle, and Puget Sound. The largest contingents were Scandinavians and farmers from the Old Northwest longing for a land that looked like what they left in Europe, or simply relief from grass hoppers and 100-degree summer-to-winter climate changes.[60] New Englanders envisioning a space both fresh and "civilized," for their comfortable years were ahead of time. Both were vanguards and ballasts for an emerging society struggling for steadiness.

The end of arable and almost "free" land in 1890 was a myth projected from the Midwest. The new state then had four "urban" clusters (Walla Walla, Spokane, Tacoma, and Seattle). The 28 counties created by the territorial legislators were soon divided 11 more times. Vegetable gardening extended from the Nisqually Flats to the Duwamish Basin. The berry, pea, legume, and bulb patches in the Skagit Valley were still being cleared. Canals and flumes on the benches of the Okanogan, Wenatchee, Yakima, and Columbia rivers were just being surveyed, dug or built. Cattle ranches were small-scale. The experiment in dry land wheat farming across the 200 square miles northwest of the Palouse to Ritzville was uncertain and experimental. Good land was available in quantity; the expense was the hard labor and risks in cultivating it.

Historians bent on critique often impose contemporary mores on the past, forgetting it is circumstances not human nature that changes. A new cohort of revisionists, the "New" Western Historians reared in the uproar of the 1960s that came of age professionally in the 1980s, scolded Turner for his optimism. With 20-20 hindsight, they damned the degrading of Native Americans, the decimation of forests, fish, and animals, pollution, and the general lack of foresight. Having made these points, they do not say how it might have been otherwise. A current school of historians favors "place" or locality as the primer to the past, stamping updated or derived identities on the Northwest as fast as it socially re-contours. This ignores the ever more urban, detached, and disparate lifestyles in the "Empire of the Columbia." Its outposts were differently hewn, dependent on natural resources, and subject to the nation's most diverse geography and climates. Cities and "place" came later.[61]

A century on, we should be impressed that Washington, despite the pall-mall rush from the frontier to freeways has had an orderly evolution, until recently avoiding the congestion, cultural and racial separatism afflicting older and larger metropolitan areas. Until the 1980s, Washington enjoyed a leading edge reputation as a "progressive" state. The Northwest corner is still a relatively unspoiled. Now with seven million residents and growing, its environmental thrust seems spent, its constitution and infrastructure visibly dated, its tax system grossly unfair and its voters bent on governing by initiatives that limit public resources on the one hand and add obligations with the other. Washingtonians will have to pay more attention to their state if the "promised land" is not to become a plundered one.

Chapter 2

# Populism Made Manifest: The New Nationalism, The New Freedom

*(1889-1919)*

## A Convoluted Constitution

The 1878 constitutional convention convened in Walla Walla to win northern Idaho, keep southeast Washington from Oregon, and gain statehood. The Republican *Walla Walla Union* felt the less than 20 percent turnout to select delegates evidenced a lack of popular interest in statehood. Its political opposite, the *Walla Walla Statesman*, rejoiced in the proposed constitution's defeat: there would not be another "Republican" state.[1] The referendum was approved by the voters and snubbed by Congress. Washington Territory's second and successful version of 1889 sums fin de siècle sentiment: need of a strong executive to thwart legislative intrigue, and dispersing executive authority to what are now eight other statewide elective officials to check any abuses on his part. "Pluralized" control left the first state governor with less power than the last territorial one.[2] There are no restrictions on the governor, whose power is now greater than the other eight state offices combined. The constitution simply says, "He shall see that the laws are faithfully executed."[3] Debate centered on the ["item"] veto, what became a Damocles' sword was implanted in the Constitution: "He [the governor] may object to one or more sections *or items* [emphasis added], while approving other portions of the bill." Some delegates thought the two-thirds vote to override was too liberal! The first real evidence as to how policy could be impacted came in 1893, when instead of vetoing a bill on the mining bureau the governor killed the entire budget.[4]

Constitutions, often the best guides to a state's history, became more curious as they moved west. Turner's thesis is valid here, to the extent that 28 of the constitution's articles are borrowed from at least ten states. Language from California, Oregon, and Wisconsin is conspicuous in the 1878 Constitution as well as takings from Colorado, Missouri, Indiana, Illinois, Pennsylvania, Texas, and Ohio. A draft prepared by W. L. Hill for the *Oregonian* caught the mood: it "was not so much if the corporations were going to control the new State government as how many concessions they could gain." Loans and gifts to the private sector were verboten. A century later, lawyers had to be very creative in structuring joint private-public ventures like the Mariners ballpark and the Seahawks football stadium in Seattle.[5] A crucial fight on the last day in 1889 was over leasing choice tidelands on Puget Sound. In a close-run vote, state ownership was assured when the legislature was directed to form a commission to "establish harbor lines in all the navigable waters … harbors, estuaries, bays and inlets of the states.. The [state] shall never give, sell or lease to any private person, corporation or association any rights whatsoever in the waters beyond such harbor lines." Reactions to the Gilded Age prompted the state's first regulatory and "environmental" impulse, just in time to gain a modicum of control over city waterfronts.[6] Distrusting authority, the constitutional convention began a pattern of overcompensation to dilute it.[7] Restraints belonging in statutes went into the constitution. Lotteries were forbidden. Legislative divorces were barred and a utilities commission was formed to keep the railroads from making the lawmakers a caboose.

In 1880, one city had over 5,000 inhabitants: now three had 25,000. Local governments were declared to be "creatures" of the state, their operations defined and revenue capped. Amidst the flotsam were arcane references like, "A frequent recurrence to fundamental principles is essential to the security of individual right and the perpetuity of free government." The Washington State Constitution is longer than the Magna Carta and the Constitution of the United States, was amended 96 times as of 2005, and stretches across 212 pages of the legislative manual.[8] Three major attempts to clarify and compress it over a half century have been defeated by major interests fearing loss of protections (e.g., the 1 percent property tax lid, and the prohibition against an income tax), or advantages (like dedication of the gas tax to "highways"), or by those who simply fear change more than embarrassment.[9]

## Elisha Ferry: Hail and Farewell to the Jeffersonian West

In the 1880s, the pioneers were still present, but soon submerged by a larger wave of immigrants coming on the new northern transcontinental railways. They were more prosperous and abundantly optimistic; but industrialization, competition in a larger market, higher carrying costs than in other regions, and cheap labor led to overproduction and lower wages. The myth of the superiority of farm life lived on as the backbone of a moral crusade to set the evils of the Gilded Age right. The territory's growth was so explosive before 1889 (from 75,116 to 357,000), it created a statewide brick shortage. The time the executive had to make statehood a success was telescoped. Fortunately, history repeated itself, and the steady hand of the popular Elisha Ferry was returned to the rudder as the state's first elected governor.[10] His "Admission Day" address of November 11, 1889 reached the hyperbolic levels expected on such occasions. The day was of "transcendent interest" for "those who ... had crossed the Continent [to plant] ... the standard of civilization and Christianity .... It marks the end of one form of government and the beginning of another."[11] This was not so structurally; there was more continuity than change.

The crucial difference for the new states was being out from under the patronage-pressed president, congresses only erratically engaged with the territories, and in the hands of their own statewide elected officials.[12] Ferry's inaugural message diagrammed state government, focused on implementing the legislature's constitutional obligations in statutes, and sketched Congress' magnanimous grants of land to fund the new tasks. For labor, this meant ending contracts for convicts as well as augmenting and extending mining law to include other industries. In declaring "the citizen has a right to look for the fullest protection against bodily injury," Ferry set the stage for an inclusive workmen's compensation system 20 more years in the making. A "uniform system" for counties and municipalities of over 5,000, and "home rule" (for those over 25,000) meant spelling out the strata, organization, elections, and compensation of officials. The constitution dictated superior courts and a five-person supreme court. The federal judge for Washington was part of the federal Ninth Circuit Court.

The constitution was "very explicit" as to corporations and "no subject ... more worthy." A means had to be found to prevent "the unjust use of the great powers" conferred on them, while avoiding the "tendency to prevent ... foreign capital [from outside the state] ... and discourage the inception of large enterprises." The legislature mandated what became a public service (now the Utilities and Transportation) commission to regulate rates and conditions for common carriers (and soon utilities). In 1880, there had been only a few miles of railroads within Washington's borders; now they crisscrossed the state. The Great Northern had reached Seattle and the state was being linked to two other transcontinental roads. The commission was empowered to fix rates, together with fees on forestry and fisheries, lest both resources be "irredeemably devastated." Free railroad passes (largely for legislators) were no more. The Australian (direct) ballot was adopted for local elections, but not for U.S. senators.[13]

The First Legislature (1889-91) met three consecutive years. Ferry called a special session in 1890 to reconfigure departments to meet the new demands and inventory natural resources so they could be exploited and taxed to pay for infrastructure. Like their territorial counterparts, the legislators had "a high order of practical intelligence," and more familiarity with their turf.[14] Over half had been in the new state since 1854. They passed most of what the governor wanted. Washington was Republican, with but one Democratic state senator and six representatives. The administrative primacy of the Superintendent of Public Instruction was strengthened at Ferry's urging, by making all agency heads report to him. This did nothing to sort two enduring puzzles — uneven funding of school districts based on their property wealth and the damage done to quality by the pervasive American fetish that schools, however small, must be "locally" controlled. Of the 1,044 schoolhouses at statehood, only 49 were broken into grades. There were so many districts that 117 had no housing. The 1,349 teachers instructing 45,757 pupils were paid an average of $42 a month. A state property tax, one on cities, and interest from the "irreducible fund" from land sales supplied only $6 a year per student from the state. [See Appendix 3 for relative values]. "Self-interest being deemed sufficient to provide for local educational opportunities" this, school district levies and private subscriptions it was felt, were enough.[15] The question of whether parents should pay for textbooks was left hanging.[16]

The pivotal question was whether the "munificent endowments" of federal lands would be well managed or misused. Sections 16 and 36 were set aside for schools. Another 132,000 acres were granted for the legislative, executive, and judicial buildings; 100,000 for starting and sustaining a scientific school [i.e., a "university"]; 100,000 for normal [teacher training] schools and 200,000 for charitable, educational and penal institutions. Ferry saw an "indirect duty" to create a reformatory for "depraved and vicious youth." As it was, judges had the choice of putting them in the penitentiary with "hardened criminals," or letting them off, too leniently in his opinion, with a reprimand. "There is to be found in all our large cities a class of young boys who defy parental authority, and have little regard for the rights of property."[17]

The 36-year-wait for statehood, optimism, and the "cult of success" encouraged pork barrelling.[18] Every community wanted one of the new institutions. Vancouver got the School for Defective Youth (the blind and deaf), Chehalis got a reformatory, and Steilacoom the mental asylum. Four faculty members staffed the normal school at Ellensburg underway in 1891, the year the other at Cheney burned down. Seattle was sure it had "lost" in landing the university. All were overseen by a short-lived State Board of Higher Education, a mechanism which might have curtailed many of the institutions' intramurals for resources.

Receipts at the end of the first biennium (ending October 31, 1891), were $607,419, disbursements $603,274, and bonded debt $234,658, a meager beginning by standards even a half century later. One could not be too frugal. The *Spokane Chronicle* laid the state's debt at the governor's feet, charging "extravagance." Apart from his appointees, the Ferry team was two men. "Nearly nineteen months ago," he penned John McGraw, "the legislature allowed me a Private Secretary at $1,800 per year, and a stenographer at $1,200 a year. My private secretary being a stenographer and typewriter, I have not employed another." His other expenses [over 19 months] were $656.72, or $38.23 a month. "Isn't this awful extravagance?"[19]

Ferry predicted "Washington will [soon] be universally recognized as one of the greatest of the American states." In reality, in 1889 there was no capitol or offices for the statewide elected officials, who were "scattered about the highways and byways of the City of Olympia." "The dignity of the State…[was] compromised by the humiliating spectacle of the Supreme Court being obliged to hold its sessions wherever chance of accident of location permits." Harvests continued to outpace consumption and the overbuilt railroads with their unbridled competition, manipulative managements, and watered stock rang in the crash of 1893. Construction of a dignified capitol was halted indefinitely.[20] The emotional wear of Ferry's office was palpable: "I cannot hope that my administration has come up to the expectations of my friends," he wrote Henry Landes, "The state of my health has prevented me from doing many things which I would have done." He had come to "appreciate the more highly the few instances of true and disinterested friendship … prevent[ing] us from losing all confidence in … human nature … . I fear I am growing to be pessimistic in my view of mankind."[21]

## The Many Lives of John McGraw

Governor John McGraw (1893-97) spent his term as a placeholder, balancing the state's books and broadening its tax base. What he lacked in charisma, McGraw more than made up in tenacity, native agility, and resilience, overcoming five major defeats. He left for the West after losing his Maine general store in the depression of 1873. Arriving in Seattle penniless in 1876, he clerked at the Occidental Hotel, and then owned the American House near Yesler's Wharf — until it burned. He became a policeman, city marshal, and was reelected King County Sheriff — until he tried to protect the Chinese in the 1886 riots. A man of little education, McGraw studied law, joined a prestigious firm, was again elected sheriff, and by 1888 was president of the Seattle First National Bank.

The legislature's generosity had to be reined in by vetoes. Empathizing with the pains of the recession, the legislators passed a deficiency judgment bill, compelling creditors to refund the debtor's equity on foreclosure. McGraw saw it leading massive repudiation of debt and a chilling of capital inflow. His popularity once more depleted and with the clashes of the anti-Chinese mobs ringing in his ears the governor stood firm, blocking another mob ready to hijack a train in Puyallup to join Jacob Coxey's Army on the Potomac to protest federal inaction on veteran's pensions. Broke when he left office, McGraw received a small grubstake loan, sailed with his son for the Klondike, and returned with enough gold to erase his debts. He was a realtor and insurance broker and eager to complete the Lake Washington Ship Canal while president of the Seattle Chamber of Commerce from 1905 to 1909.[22]

McGraw was a proto-Progressive, a leading indicator Republicans were to have dramatic divisions over how to react to rapid urbanization. "I hope the ticket is entitled to the active, earnest support of the liberal sensible people who want nothing for themselves but insist on clean government," he wrote Erastus Brainerd, editor of the Republican oriented *Post-Intelligencer* at the outset of the 1896 campaign. "I'm for Teddy" he affirmed in 1904. He had his "differences" with GOP U.S. Senator George Turner and a positive view of the patriarch of the Bullitt family, which was to bulk large in gubernatorial elections and Democratic politics for a century. Prosperity agitated McGraw's frustrations at having been straight-jacketed in his four years as governor. "Kind things should be said concerning us while we are on earth and I have no use for the lying [sic] eulogies like the one pronounced upon the late Governor Rogers by the present governor." The good-natured, rebounding Irishman could not help being envious.[23]

## Ideology Meets Reality

The economy improved erratically, not at the speed an impatient electorate expected, and its oscillations became more dramatic as the cities grew. Farmers hurt as logging and shipbuilding boomed. The rail net was now complete, but long-haul charges to the East meant they could never compete with Midwest growers. Conspiracy theories blossomed, monopoly practices were blamed, and a "fair" (forced reduction) in rates by regulation demanded. The free school textbooks issue, the initiative and referendum, woman suffrage, and direct election of U.S. senators were unresolved, as reactions to unbridled corporatism climaxed. All of these nostrums were in the Populist Party's platform in 1896, with the key economic remedy: fixing the value of silver at 16 to 1 to gold to induce inflation.

The "Fusion" ticket of Populists, Democrats, and "free silver" Republicans elected with formidable Democrat turned Populist governor John R. Rogers (1897-1901) was a shaky combination.[24] "Fusion is repugnant to all the better class of Democrats" one admitted, but the new governor was not the "wild man" conservatives decried. It can be argued he was an "ultra-conservative ... agrarian Democrat," a Jeffersonian fixated on the idea of the "inalienable right" to hold land. Agriculture was more than a living; it was a way of life, a basis for society. He was a "Thomas Paine" battling the corporate powers that would destroy this lifestyle. "The very ambiguity gave ... the appearance of novelty, of radicalism. These are the conditions," he had written in 1883, "The great plain people ... are to unite against the organized aggression of the privileged few, or they are to become helpless servants of a poorly concealed plutocracy."[25]

In Boston, Rogers had apprenticed as a pharmacist. In Jackson, Mississippi, he managed a drugstore until 1860, and then decided it was safer in Illinois where he taught school as well. In Kansas after 1876, he opened a hardware store, built a sod house on the plains, and was an organizer for the Farmer's Alliance, forbears of the Populists. For several years he was the editor of the *Kansas Commoner*, serializing his hopes into a novel, *Looking Forward: Or the Story of an American Farm*. In 1895, five years after moving to Puyallup, he was celebrated as the Representative-father of the Barefoot Schoolboy Law (universal grade school education). This first try to "equalize" made the more affluent cities bear part of the cost of funding country schools, a problem aggravated by the reluctance of rural assessors, given their proximity to the taxpayers, to keep valuations current.

Rogers was seated as governor six years after his arrival, by 12,000 votes. The Populist's margin in the 1897 legislature was greater: in the House 45 of them faced 10 Democrats, 11 Silver, and 11 regular Republicans. In the Senate it was 15, 4, 2, and 13. But they were inexperienced, faction ridden, lacked leadership or the temperament to be led, and had an over wide agenda from prohibition to barring state ownership of banks. The Populists were undone on the first vote, to choose a U.S. senator. They split down the middle, "Old Line" ideologues versus the Fusionists, Silver Republicans, and practical Democrats who had joined the ticket as the only way out of obscurity. Neither of the latter joined to caucus and the regular Republicans withheld the votes needed for two-thirds on key constitutional referenda. Roger's core ideas foundered in a moiling sea. He pleaded, "Gentlemen … if quarreling is essential, let your quarrels be settled within the next seven days."[26] Rail rate regulation lost by a vote. The able executive had moderated — and was on his own. He was able to consolidate the education and institutions' boards, extend regulation to savings and loans, and abolish the fish wheels scooping the life out of the Columbia.

Rogers poured his disillusionment into letters to Midwestern friends. "I stand now for precisely the same principles … I have battled for over 20 years" (perpetuating Jeffersonian Democracy), he wrote the editor of the *Farmer's Sentinel* in Chicago. Bringing the "late war" and the "single tax question" up was "idiotic." The 1897 session remains the state's best epigram of how ideologues damage democracy. The "very large majority," a seemingly "ideal combination of affairs," had turned produced a "peculiar condition." A few "impracticables" and "corrupt men" denied appointments were slaying all before them. The governor told another editor, "One of the most disheartening revelations … has been the duplicity, the utter worthlessness and the criminality of loud shouters for 'Reform' and the 'Rights of Humanity,' when placed in positions of trust. I had an unwieldy mass of supporters at my back." He despaired, "I do not believe that our forces can be got together with perfect harmony … which is absolutely essential." "They proved to be just as weak as the Republicans when they heard the siren song of the lobbies."[27]

Too many of Washington's Populists were true believers, undone by a lack of direction, naïveté, inexperience, unruliness, and inability to agree on a program. The patronage malady salted the wound. The man who might possibly have made a janitor wanted to be prime minister: "I was amazed," Rogers fumed. "There was hardly a Pop in the whole state who did not think that now that we had a Populist governor, he was fully entitled to whatever might be in the line of political favor lying around loose. Dissatisfaction, discontent and general political riot were all inevitable."[28] Rogers implemented McGraw's idea of centralizing patronage in a State Board of Control (now the Office of Financial Management, the governor's budget arm) to run the five largest operations — health, the mental hospital at Steilacoom, the penitentiary, the reform school at Chehalis, and the soldiers' home at Orting. He appointed Ernest Lister, chair of the Pierce County Populists, as secretary of the board.

The hard-liners were certain democracy had been compromised. The Populists on the board wanted two more of their breed to ensure a majority so they could give two superintendents patronage. When the governor fired them,[29] the schism was complete. "The matter of appointments is one of the most troubling things I have ever had to attend to. Whoever is appointed, those who are not appointed are certain to feel that great injustice has been done .... I wish I had not an appointment to make."[30] The governor's enemies claimed he was keeping the patronage for himself. The state treasurer, whom Rogers had removed for "misconduct," ran against him.

The Populists did agree on fiscal conservatism. McGraw's 1895 budget was $1,272,328. Roger's first, with a consolidation of state boards and vetoes of dollars for the normal schools at Ellensburg and Bellingham, was $1,117,568. His explanations set the bar for vacuity. The schools "opposed ... a just public policy at the present time." In July, the steamer *Portland* arrived in Seattle with a "ton of gold," setting off the Klondike Gold Rush. The anemic economy revived overnight as Seattle became supplier and point of departure for hordes of prospectors. Rogers was the only Populist reelected in 1900 — of necessity as a Democrat — with a plurality of 2,000 in the face of 13,000 majorities for the state and national GOP tickets. He died of pneumonia 15 months later, his dream of prolonging agricultural America intact.

The Populist rhetoric of the 1890s is found in *Looking Backward*, the title of Henry George's famed testament to the "single tax." Rogers was more complex than his cohorts, yet essentially "a secular theologian who ... preached the old mythic religion ... Arcadian republicanism." His Populist-themed books of the 1890s dwelt not on economic values, but on the social morays preeminent before 1870 — the independence, security, and warmth of the close-knit family and the salubrious effects of outdoor living. The farmers' paranoia over urbanization and productive success had driven them to desperation. Their assumption in 1896 that consumers would join the producers was wrong. The just gestating Labor Movement proved "profoundly indifferent" and weak, and not a few of those in the 50-year fight against plutocracy were now drained and ambivalent. Others had seen and sought the luxuries of urban life and saw their futures there. The Populists had failed to grasp the art of compromise, the crux of legislative politics. Their triumph was in educating and arousing the voters to use the power of government to keep corporations at bay, setting the scene for the twentieth century. John Rogers, the only Populist in state office and their "most distinctive personality," endured as an administrator by moderating, despite being at odds with his party and the onrushing age.

## The Progressives: Republican Successes, Democratic Successors

By 1901, the capitalists widely credited until the 1890s with the country's rise to greatness, were in new President Teddy Roosevelt's phrase and in the public mind, "malefactors of great wealth." If only because Washington's prosperity was now doubly dependent — on wheat railed to Chicago and logs sailed to San Francisco — its politics continued to twin the nation's. For the first time since the Civil War an urban political elite the Progressives mediated politics, enacting most of the Populist agenda.

## Henry McBride: Coping with the Deluge

Capable, colorless, and deliberate Lieutenant Governor Henry McBride (1901-1905), completed Roger's term and began the emancipation of Republicans from the thrall of the railroads. The first governor born in the West, in Utah, was educated at Trinity College in Connecticut and admitted to the bar in 1884. He was Skagit County Prosecuting Attorney in 1888 and a superior court judge in 1891. McBride's reputation as an able and judicious administrator resounded in his 1903 message to the legislature, highlighting educational opportunities beyond the eighth grade and keeping the institutions free of politics, an urban view.[31] In-migration surged and Washington's population again tripled in two decades. Farmer militancy and surpluses fell in tandem as prices rose 90 percent between 1899 and 1910. Turner's thesis had given great weight to the environment. Newcomers came by rail and settled in or near the cities aggregating around Puget Sound seeking a "home community," not a farm.[32] Cultural influences, specialization, and materialism became more obvious. The shipbuilding industry matured in 1904 with the launching of the battleship *Nebraska* in Seattle. Automobiles appeared, Andrew Carnegie's libraries were built, the legislature funded "bookmobiles," and the Seattle Symphony gave its first performance.

McBride, the public's careful quiet custodian, respected and liked by those who worked with him, was defeated, never having been elected in his own right. It was a reminder that the presumption in politics that prosperity is the first step to reelection is just that: public service often has to be its own reward. He went into lumbering in Snohomish County, then banking and law in Seattle.

## Albert Mead: In Over His Head?

Mead (1905-1909), a former mayor of Blaine, legislator, and Whatcom County Prosecutor was the last party-nominated governor. In 1905, Roger's established a railroad rate-setting commission, regulated industry, appointed a bank examiner, a board of tax commissioners, an oil inspector, and a highway board, the nation's first state industrial insurance, and improved care for the mentally impaired. In 1907, an elected insurance commissioner extended oversight to that industry. An institution for the "feeble-minded," a second reformatory for males at Monroe, indeterminate sentencing of convicts (variable terms suiting the situation), were crowned by a direct primary. Mead's most conspicuous triumph was the first civil service law, for institutions. His Progressive side was revealed as the first vigorous wielder of the veto. As early as January 9, 1905, he sent back ten bills, among them two for the "relief" of individuals, one enabling the Puget Sound Mill Company to make a "corporate appropriation of private property," to squelch the building of highways amended in by log rolling and to head off a referendum on the "liquor question," a trigger for more turmoil. Sadly, he also sidelined a tax commission, aimed at doing for revenue collection what the Board of Control accomplished for "efficiency."[33]

In 1905, Washington became the nation's lumber capital: nearly four billion board feet were cut. Resentment of the federal government rose as President Theodore Roosevelt moved to exercise federal oversight of natural resources. Mead told the *P-I's* editor Erastus Brainerd, "I sympathize thoroughly" with Roosevelt's water and forest policies. "A great improvement is being worked," but withdrawing large swaths of land into the public domain was "making it too difficult to secure title…which really belongs to [the state]."[34] Worry about becoming a "plundered province" (in Bernard Devoto's phrase) directly conflicted with cutting forests to fuel an urban economy. Washington's chronic ambivalence toward the federal government had begun. Mead's frustration was of a nineteenth-century man powerless to stop new assertions of national power to reign in an out-of-control industry stripping the state's mountainsides, and that of a modest Progressive also voicing the sentiments of those mourning the death of laissez-faire, as the Populists had their lifestyle.

The Panic of 1907 ended eight years of prosperity. Half as much lumber was milled, yet the economy still broadened. The Lake Washington Ship Canal was being dug, raising the Port of Seattle to international class, the first National Apple Show was held in Spokane, and 763 automobiles were registered — a larger augury of the future. Thwarting the last attempt to move the capitol to Tacoma without the constitutional mandate for a two-thirds vote or a referendum may have been the last nail in Mead's coffin. It was "absolutely unjustifiable" to leave the building they had just moved into in downtown Olympia before completion.[35]

Mead was being "assaulted" for mediocre appointments. "I think I have been able to accept with becoming philosophy the vociferous and even hysterical declarations of my enemies that I am untrustworthy and disloyal," he wrote Brainerd, who was behind many appointments.[35] He wisely retired to Bellingham, leaving farewell requests to the legislature implying he knew state affairs had become too complex for his managerial abilities. A spate of investigations of his nominees soon confirmed his policy instincts stronger than his judgment. President Theodore Roosevelt's New Nationalism transformed many Republicans into reformers and government toward being society's protector. Unrest among miners, loggers, farmers (who were still overproducing), and shipyard workers through World War I, rooted a progressive strain in the state's politics for 60 years. The tenures of Marion Hay, (1909-13) and Ernest Lister (D), (1913-19) peaked Republican progressivism, and transferred the torch of reform to Wilsonian Democrats.

## The Ambiguous Marion Hay

In 1908, Samuel Cosgrove of Pomeroy won the GOP nomination and election as governor and ruined his health. He was belatedly carried into the capitol on a stretcher on January 27, 1909, gave an inaugural speech and asked for a leave of absence to regain his balance. A special railroad car took him back to California, where he died on March 18.[36] Lieutenant Governor Marion Hay had been a land developer since 1889, owned a mercantile store in Wilbur, and was Lincoln County Republican chairman (1898-1902). He was aggressive enough to be elected in a three-week campaign with the support of just one daily newspaper.[37] The businessman throve as an administrator where Mead had miscarried, but was "ignorant of Western Washington politics and politicians" and obsessed with the Progressive nostrum of "efficiency," instituting a "Bureau of Inspection of Public Offices" (soon the Efficiency Department). This partly explains his over expectations, equivocations, and often "irritating righteousness." He was assertive, hesitant and critical by turns, outspoken, but a weak speaker. Hay, a "reformer on the right," exemplified his divided party as progressivism was sapped by renewed prosperity and the nationalism of World War I.[38]

The 1909 Alaska-Yukon-Pacific Exposition at the University of Washington buffered damage lingering from the Panic of 1907, and punctuated Washington's emergence from the wilderness in eastern eyes. To his credit, Hay was first to bring the full powers of the governorship to bear. Sickened by the spoils system, he ordered that anyone discharging his office in a "reasonably efficient manner" was not to be "molested."[39] The new statutes of that year ran 1,000 pages, including woman's suffrage (effective in 1910), a new criminal code, and a public service (utility regulating) commission passed with his backing. Hay led in mediating the now-full-blown antagonisms between labor and business. A first-in-the-nation state run workmen's accident fund was his premiere achievement. "It [workmen's compensation] is working out far more satisfactorily," the governor rejoiced. In 1910, companies paid $600,000 for insurance to protect them against suits and just $100,000 to the injured. In the first half of 1911, they paid the state $511,000; $127,000 went to the injured and $111,000 to their widows and orphans, leaving $273,000 in the fund.[40] On moral issues, Hay could be taciturn and evasive: his veto of Sunday liquor sales in hotels pleased the Progressives. Then he took up the cudgel for local option, upsetting "wets" and "drys."

The governor, who had given little thought to conservation, became a defender of natural resources. Yet Washington became the only Republican state to disagree with Roosevelt on conservation in the Progressive Era. He was not alone. Selfish interests resisted mightily, but the federals came on so fast that not a few Westerners began to believe they were seeing too much of a good thing. Lumber was now over a third of the economy and others reasoned disposal of the public domain and exports, now capitalized on a large scale, were perquisite to growth. In August 1909, Hay sided with Interior Secretary Richard Ballinger in his battle with Chief Forester Gifford Pinchot, Roosevelt's point man. The high-handed refusal to let a delegate from the state present Hay's viewpoint at a presidentially convened governors' conference on conservation at St. Paul in September 1910 completed the conversion of an ally into an antagonist. "The conservation movement as…initiated, was a timely and good thing for the country, but a few of the leaders have become so intoxicated with the power they once possessed that they will brook no interference."[41] The eight Western governors meeting at Hay's call on August 2 at Salt Lake demanded greater state control. Then Hay hesitated again, realizing he was in bed with bitter enemies like Land Commissioner E. W. Ross and the *Seattle Times* redoubtable Colonel Alden Blethen.[42]

Hay was convinced that Washington State was ahead of the Potomac, and pointed to the railway and fish commissions as proof. The governor convoked investigative commissions as no one had, to make the Forestry Department a model for state control, preempt Congress, reorganize, fashion fish and game laws, give protection to shellfish, and create a water code.[43] He offered concrete "state's rights" alternatives, assistance for "private" forests, reforestation, state control of water power sites, and a 50-year limit on leases and compacts between the states that reverberated until the 1950s.[44]

Hay could not overcome the research of Eastern conservationists, and lacked the confidence and presence to challenge a national movement. His offer to mediate was ignored as the combatants saw there was no middle ground. His 1910 commission on forest needs molded a "comprehensive, orderly and economic plan" for the State Forest Bureau, predecessor to the Department of Lands. He enforced conservation practices but forfeited his last opportunity to integrate his ideas before the 1911 legislature. Frustrated, he made foolish statements on conservation and castigated its advocates. Moderates, among them who feared "special Interests" more than "Pinchotism," jumped his ship.[45]

Personalities overtook issues. Hay's stand and predicament in the great GOP confrontation of 1912 can be laid to his early backing of President Taft and Ballinger on states' rights as much as his initial attitudes. The high-water mark of reform, passage of the initiative, referendum, and recall in 1912, undid him. Caught between President Taft's unforgiving regulars and Roosevelt's Bull Moosers, the governor again temporized. He was "a great believer in the direct primary," it "tended to destroy bossism and corporation control of politics. A few years ago it was almost impossible, if not entirely so to secure the passage of any kind of a bill without it first having received the approval of the two large transportation companies [James J. Hill's Great Northern and Henry Villard's Northern Pacific]. These men seemed to hold the legislature in the hollow of their hands."[46] In 1911, Hay noted train lawyers now came to Olympia only to testify before committees, sensing continuous on-site lobbying hurt their cause.

Hay now sounded the tocsin for the regulars. The open primary also tended "to destroy political parties and breaks down party loyalty." He heard legislators say they owed nothing to their party. Direct elections should apply only statewide to the municipal level, where candidates had visibility. The judiciary and all statewide elected officials, except the lieutenant governor, should be appointed by the chief executive. Hay was definite on the item veto. Legislators "put appropriation bills up to the governor to veto and then go home…and say, 'I did my best but the governor vetoed it. Much trading has been done.'"[47]

He even considered "ducking" the state convention. "Many Roosevelt leaders are Hay supporters and I think it is better that I have an urgent call to other regions along about that time." He valued loyalty and cooperated with regulars who had voted against his legislation and were to control the GOP convention, ostensibly to avoid chaos. Hay ingenuously expected the Progressives to do the same, only to see them bolt to the Bull Moose Party.[48] With Taft's renomination to the presidency came self-justification: Roosevelt's candidacy had been "purely a selfish and personal ambition and no principle involved … I cannot follow him."[49]

Washington was now in the advance guard of reform, its governance practices the state of the art. Success was bought with fatigue. The Progressives wanted more of the New Nationalism in 1912, but little else, leaving the impression they had done what they could and all the public expected. Marion Hay was in significant ways the "true Progressive" he believed himself to be. He was also a party-loyal instinctual conservative, who underestimated the revolt against the old order, lacked "political sophistication," and leapt the wrong way. His casuistry and the GOP's enmities precluded survival.[50] "I know I do not have the ability of some of my predecessors," he told Brainerd in 1908, but "I can leave … with a clean record."[51]

## Ernest Lister and The New Freedom

Democrat Ernest Lister (1913-19) was the first of the state's three genuinely liberal executives.[52] His whirlwind gubernatorial canvassing paralleled Hay's. Everett's Judge W. W. Black won the Democratic primary but was declared ineligible by the Supreme Court because he had not resigned.[53] Lister, the runner-up, was left with three weeks to campaign. The question was Hay or Lister, Rogers' protégé, the real reformer. Tellingly, the Socialists and Prohibitionists jointly polled 16 percent. Disappointed Progressives decided the outcome. Half their votes now came from "urban" Snohomish, King, and Pierce counties and on balance went to Lister, the only statewide Democratic winner. He took the governor's chair by 600 tallies as Roosevelt carried Washington by 35,000 votes. The GOP split put New Jersey Governor Woodrow Wilson in the White House.[54]

This first "man of the city," a Tacoma iron molder with a business college education, was a councilman at 23. His statewide reputation grew after Governor Rogers put him in charge of the state's largest agency, the Board of Control, coordinating all social services. Lister was also the last chief executive to carry rural values into the urban era. In 1913, he began as a supervisorial conservative who would now be known as a "neo-liberal" and a "micro-manager." "I urge upon you the necessity of holding down appropriations to the lowest possible point consistent with proper management," he admonished the legislators. "In our endeavor to be progressive, there is often a tendency to go too far. It is well at all times to follow safe and sane lines, to follow public opinion rather than rush in advance of it."

The governor also insisted on continuing "progressive lines," and was willing to spend money and innovate. His transparent sincerity often persuaded the Republican legislature. In 1913, he signed a minimum wage for women and children into law. The governor repeatedly asked for a presidential primary, abolition of the straight ticket, the short ballot, and amendments to the initiative, referendum, and recall to make them more viable, as well as direct election of U.S. senators, redistricting, and a renovating constitutional convention.[55] He was the first executive to realize the possibilities of the veto, if not the first to pen ruses obscuring his motives. A half million dollar levy for the permanent road fund was too high; a Board of Land Commissioners meant to advance property tax equalization was killed because his bill substituting a tax commissioner for the tax commission fell by the wayside.[56] Hay's Bureau of Inspection and Supervision was slated for abolition and the auditor was given several more assistants.

President Wilson's reforms, apparently over in 1914, resumed in 1916 with rural credits, workmen's compensation for federal employees, the Child Labor Act, and the appointment of Louis Brandeis to the Supreme Court.[57] Lister's liberalism became unabashed: here was a chance to make Democrats the majority and inheritors of the Progressive agenda.[58] When a "federal brigade" led by Spokane conservative Roscoe Drumheller broke a pledge to install an agreed on chair at the state Democratic convention, the governor ignored the state organization and campaigned with the "Wilson Independent" and with the Nonpartisan League, ejecting an uncooperative member of the Industrial Insurance Commission to reinforce the point. The 1917 Republican legislature predictably refused to eliminate half its membership as the governor recommended, mounted new hurdles to the initiative, referendum and recall over his veto, and passed a law prohibiting picketing within 500 feet of a business or interference in an employer's hiring practices.[59] Progressivism was not dead and the New Freedom had superseded the New Nationalism.[60] But America had entered World War I. Patriotic exhuberance and a pacifying prosperity competed with it.

Labor strife was Lister's particular hell. His cross, as a union man, was keeping the lid on in the roiling labor strife threatening war production.

Fish, wheat, lumber for ships and spruce-framed "aeroplanes" must get to Europe. He refused the Left's demands for a special session in 1918, citing the state's prodigious contributions and knowing that legislative refusals of labor's demands might incite riot.[61] The Russian Revolution in 1917, strikes at the Ruston (Tacoma) and Everett lumber mills, a new "massacre" at Centralia and "Wobbly" (The Industrial Workers of the World) union's incitements to "revolution" kept the propertied classes on edge. The Army set up a Spruce Corps and the Loyal Legion of Loggers and Lumbermen (a 'company union') to assure supply, and the governor established a state secret service to infiltrate the most volatile organizations.[62]

Lister's strenuous efforts to lessen the chance of an outbreak of inflammatory industrial clashes and his managerial style wore him down. Though no stranger to the bureaucracy, his fatal fault was immersion in detail; everything from policy decisions to orders for paper crossed his desk. The governor collapsed, and soon died June 14, at age 48, from heart and kidney disease, never to enjoy the relative calm that followed.[63] The finale of the War to End All Wars, the Treaty of Versailles, imposed retributions begetting another and gave the U.S. Senate an excuse to abort American entry into the League of Nations. Washingtonians, eager to forget two decades of class tensions and bloodletting, preferred peace at no further price. In one of its periodic swings, the nation turned from internationalism back to insularity and self-indulgence, to be paid for at an outrageous expense after 1929.

Chapter 3

# Between the Wars: The Twenties and Thirties

*(1920-40)*

Washington's youth was compressed by the onrush of immigrants, urbanism, and war. The population grew from 349,390 in 1890 to 1,356,622 in 1920. If drink, dance, Darwinism, and isolationism were hallmarks of the twenties, it was not just World War I weariness or prohibition or the ruins of the Treaty of Versailles. Some heard the footfalls of the Russian Revolution in the disorganized and short-lived Seattle General Strike (February 6-11, 1919). Shipyards and spruce mills on the coast fell silent in 1919, yet Puget Sound continued to prosper, as the falling price of wheat presaged a 20-year recession-cum-depression in the Inland Empire.[1] The clash of "two Washingtons," which began with the territorials resisting "colonialism" by "Washington City" (on the Potomac) mutated into fear of the impact of conservation on the forest economy in the Progressive period and resentment of the strings attached to federal aid after 1932. Analogously, the regional anxieties evident at the 1879 constitutional convention and the contests over placing the capitol now became a pervasive, ongoing internecine East-West schism between urban and rural cultures. For Eastsiders, it was no longer a matter of getting protection from Indians. They had lost population parity. How were they to counteract Puget Sound's crushing political weight?

The most dramatic impact of the return to "normalcy" in the 1920s was loss of the two-party system. Wartime patriotism had throttled dissent and Progressivism and united Republicans. By 1924, Democrats east of the mountains were split between largely impotent farmer movements and many moderate conservatives among Democrats were only a shade away from Progressives reabsorbed into the GOP. Some King County Democrats fled to the banner of Robert La Follette's late-blooming Progressive Movement. The Democratic Party fell to third-party status. Seattleite A. Scott Bullitt, the party's only talented gubernatorial contender in the 1920s, was unable to bridge these gaps in 1928.

In the twenties, the voters turned to Republicans to sustain prosperity as they did to the Democrats after 1932 to relieve austerity. The coming of the New Deal seated Clarence D. Martin of Cheney, a moderate who had led the party in the 1920s in the governor's chair. Symbolically, he was the last executive from Eastern Washington. While struggling to keep up with President Franklin Roosevelt's persistent experimentation, Martin tussled with the Democratic Left's more radical agendas. One-party domination in both decades made compromise and progress harder.

The labor turmoil of Governor Ernest Lister's years made it clear the state could not be a distant arbiter in an urban society. Some of Washington's vast acreage of logged-off lands was given to veterans, but "stump farms" were mere survival. Unions were legalized and, in 1921, a Department of Labor and Industries created. Completion of the Snoqualmie Pass highway in 1915 heralded the automobile age and focused farmers' demands for "farm to market" roads. In ten years, transportation was taking 40 percent of state revenue. Highways beached Puget Sound's "mosquito fleet," and the Seattle-Tacoma Interurban died in 1928. Railroading literally passed its crest with the completion of the Cascade Tunnel a year later. "Air passenger services" were aloft, coastal trade via the Panama Canal opened, and in 1917 the Lake Washington Ship Canal validated Seattle as an "international class port." An entrepôt economy irrevocably linking the dry side of the state to Puget Sound and Asia was all that strengthened the often tenuous ties of the "two Washingtons."[2]

All the essential institutions of state government were in place by the end of the Progressive period: the public schools, the university in Seattle, the land grant college at Pullman, normal schools at Bellingham, Ellensburg, and Cheney, three hospitals for the insane at Steilacoom, Medical Lake, and Sedro Woolley, a school for the deaf and blind at Vancouver, a training (juvenile reform) school at Chehalis, one for girls at Grand Mound, the Soldiers' Home and Colony at Orting, a veterans' home at Retsil, a custodial school for the mentally retarded at Medical Lake, a reformatory at Monroe, and the penitentiary at Walla Walla. They housed 7,267 persons between 1922 and 1924. The state had become a significant provider of social services, in need of chief executives with skills well beyond those of the territorial and Populist-Progressive periods. For the executive's third incarnation In the twenties, the voters hired a moderate and consolidator, then a reactionary.

## The Executive in the Twenties: The Remainder of Reform, the Drift to Deadweight

### Louis Hart: The Residue of Reform

"Lodges" boomed in the twenties. Louis F. Hart (1919-25), an attorney and "joiner," was elected Lieutenant Governor in 1913 largely on fame gained on his tours as Grand Secretary of the Washington Grand Lodge, International Order of Odd Fellows. He became chief executive on Ernest Lister's death and was returned in his own right in 1920. The centrist had a low enough profile to survive the GOP's factional fights.[3] A biographer's verdict that "he never exerted a strong, dominating influence over the Republican party" and that "many of the most significant events of the era happened without the active participation of the governor"[4] needs revision in the second respect. Hart's attainments came from collaboration and shared decision making with the talented House Majority Leader, Mark Reed (Shelton), and Senator P. H. Carlyon (Olympia), who shepherded a volatile coalition of Southwest Washington "cow counties" and east of the Cascades legislators determined to neutralize Seattle. The governor clearly grasped the need for restructuring, convened and studied reconfiguration and set the stage with his public and legislative testimony. "Business administration, everywhere in vogue," Hart reminded the legislators, "[is] none too good for adoption and use in our public affairs." The "executive branch" now comprised 60 officials and agencies.

The landmark Administrative Code of 1921, to which he gave "twenty months … all my spare effort and time," compacted the agencies, boards, and commissions into ten "code departments" under governor appointed directors (see Appendix 2). An "Administrative Board" (the first "cabinet") started gathering twice a month on his call. The other operations were delegated to equalization, finance, highways, archives, parks, the state capitol, voting machine and state library committees, and the state law library. The governor served on the first, last, and highways boards. Reed pushed the bill through the house 89 to 5. Carlyon snuffed out any further amendments and got a 32-3 vote (with two absent) in the senate.

Hart also enhanced the executive in surmounting the legislator's preference for having all agencies come to it separately for money. The coalesced "governor's budget" confirmed the governor as the state's linchpin.[5] The critics, who were soon charging that although "efficiency" may have improved, "savings" had not, were wrong. The State had $500,000 on hand at the end of 1924 compared to an overdraft of $1.02 million when the code took effect.[6]

Third, quadrupling of the state's population since 1890 and the near tripling of property taxes since 1910 forced the tax reform question. Real estate produced 70 percent of state intake, though it was no longer the basic form of wealth. "Our … high rate of taxation is not so much due to the high cost of government as … the cost of high government," the governor contended to 20-year State Senator Alex Polson. There was "constant agitation" for new government activities. Having taken little notice, the taxpayer "suddenly wakes up … [and] condemns" the collectors.[7] Once the obligatory "Governor's Conference on Retrenchment" for gathering "constructive criticism" was over, Hart unveiled the first full study of taxation "to distribute the burdens of government more equitably."[8] At the end of the 1921 session, he ordered the Board of Equalization to immediately update and make uniform property tax assessments, to square the budget.[9] "The condition of our public schools is almost, if not quite as deplorable as the institutions of higher learning. Hundreds of teachers are quitting … by reason of meager wages." And local government was using just four and a half of the five mils granted by the legislature.[10]

Hart forthrightly came out for an inheritance tax. "Our community property law makes the spouses equal owners. But the third agency, the State, has been largely ignored. I know of no form of taxation that can bring in so large a fund with so light a burden as a properly adjusted inheritance tax." He advocated one of up to 50 percent on "large" estates over $50,000. "When a man dies he cannot take his property with him. He cannot give it away to strangers, regardless of the rights of the surviving spouse or … dependents. He should not be permitted to disregard the interests of the State which has protected him … and made possible its accumulation." Alternatively, the governor was willing to have a "small sales tax."[11]

Fourth, Hart initiated the "user pays-dedicated fund" principle enshrined in 1944 by initiative, setting the gas tax aside for highways, and chastised Standard Oil's publicizing of the two-cent tariff. It was after all, "for the construction of highways, which makes greater consumption of gasoline necessary."[12] The General Fund must be relieved of "carrying special and local departments that ought to pay their own way." Floating the "fish tax" to meet that Fishery's losses, "owing to the smallness of the salmon run for the last two years," was a left-handed recognition of ecological decline. "A careful revision of all fee lists" to make other bureaus self-supporting became standard practice. In 1923, the legislators also heeded the governor's call for a "Blue Sky" law to protect investors "from the machinations of … corrupt and fraudulent vendors of stocks." In stark contrast to his successor, Hart commended the university's regents for "fearless … performance of duty" in tying up its original downtown tract with a 50-year lease in the face of "importunings," preventing its sale "before the people learned of the great value of the property."[13]

The governor's request for supplemental spending from a projected surplus of $2 million stands as a poignant example of the state's new social commitments. The custodial school for the mentally deficient just built at Medical Lake had a waiting list of 200, a 35 percent increase. "While I appreciate the demands for economy, I cannot believe these demands justify us in ignoring the humane duty of care of these unfortunate children."[14] His traditional side is seen in signing "an Act to prevent the Procreation [sic] of Feeble Minded," to combat the "divorce evil" by restricting grounds and in an infrequent veto of a bill regulating real estate brokers. "We have about reached that point in regulating the affairs of society where it would be well to stop and consider the limits to which we may go. We should still be allowed to travel the highways and streets … without an enamel and numbered license plate on our collar."[15]

"The political situation in Washington is chaotic," Hart confirmed to U.S. senator Wesley Jones in the summer of 1913, as the GOP's wrangle of the wings raged on. He pled for a "quiet conference with a few Republicans who are more interested in defeating the Democratic Party than they are in controlling the party machinery." If the GOP was to win in 1926, Hart believed "it will be by keeping some of the same old line managers in the background and by a number of others of us making some self-sacrifice."

Postwar cynicism was in full bloom. H. L. Mencken, the *American Mercury's* satiric icon of the 1920s, was not the only curmudgeon mocking "uplifters." ("If I am convinced of anything, it is that Doing Good is in bad taste.") Progressivism did linger until 1925, as Washington's twentieth-century governors sought to subdue the class antagonisms that rose after statehood. Hart's collaboration with strong legislative leaders was critical. Moderate businessmen like Speaker Mark Reed and the conservative leaders of the Washington State Federation of Labor (WSFL) negotiated agreements. In return for an anti-syndicalism bill, employers raised workmen's compensation benefits, encouraged accident prevention, and agreed to limit the courts' power to enjoin trade-union actions. In 1923, Hart allied with the WSFL to raise benefits, lobbied Congress for a child-labor amendment to the federal Constitution and for a state minimum wage. In the 1920s this was indeed "social vision" and "pioneering industrial legislation," considering that the "Red Scare," Klu Klux Klan nativism, and "normalcy" were suffocating reform.[16]

Many of the New Deal's conservation tenets were anchored in the 1920s. Hart realized "our forests are being denuded ... and commercial interests are demanding their further destruction." He found the "influence of commercialism in our governmental agencies" distasteful.[17] It was the 1921 legislature that first sanctioned a feasibility study of what became the Columbia Basin Project. By making property tax collection more equitable and broadening the tax base, Hart lowered the state's share of millage 30 percent and rebalanced the budget, reflecting his moderation and realism. Merging departments recognized greater complexity and the costs of urbanization. Ninety years on, the "code" departments" are still the nucleus of executive power, although by 1972, the accretion of new agencies again put 60 percent of state employees outside his ambit. (See Appendix 2). Hart declared a victory for "efficiency" in 1925. In fact, the governor's struggle for authority and accountability had just begun.[18]

## Roland Hartley: Oblivious to the End

The state's worst governor, the incorrigible Roland Hill Hartley (1925-33), is a standing argument against one party control. His "confused"[19] grade school education left an unformed mind unable to distinguish large issues from small ones, or those of principle from parliamentary maneuvers. Running the family-owned Clough-Hartley shingle mills in Everett (and lesser enterprises), did not induce tolerance for those not sharing his opinions. His time in 1878 as secretary to the mayor of Brainerd, Minnesota, and exposure to Governor David Clough, a contentious single term as mayor of Everett (1909-11), "one of the most ... tempestuous ever experienced by an executive officer," and as a state representative (1915-17), did nothing to alter his mind set. "Our administration must be Progressive, but it must be economical," he averred in a phrase du jour.

In 1924, the time had arrived for the man who had come close in the gubernatorial primaries of 1916 and 1920. The nineteenth century capitalist and penultimate miscast as a public administrator was swept in by the temper of the time and a gift for showmanship. The first governor to win two full terms tried to impose simple business methods on an apparatus being reconfigured to deliver education and social services without a sense of proportion, the ability to compromise, or social grace.

The *Seattle Argus* read the 1924 election as "the great opportunity of the business interests for years have been crucified upon the cross of the direct primary. This year … the business interests have but one candidate." Labor was supine, and Hartley toned down his negativism. He sidestepped a Ku Klux Klan bill to destroy Catholic schools and the "Bone bill," widening the reach of public power.[20] In a 10-man field he edged out Edward L. French by less than 2,000 votes. The press had its doubts, except for the quirky *Seattle Times*, whose publisher "Colonel" Alden Blethen was soon promoted to brigadier and made Commanding General of the State Guard. He had a new flag officer's uniform tailored, strode into Hartley's office, and snapped a salute: "General Blethen reporting for duty, sir." The governor, in his shirt sleeves and armbands, looked up. "Jesus Christ, Alden, have we been attacked?" Blethen was right to be warily optimistic.[21] The only governor to enjoy unchallengeable public and legislative majorities and an able legislative leadership wasted it all by taking on everyone else.

Hartley, a "supplicant at the shrine of rugged individualism," told the 1925 legislature the state was "a business institution" one "too much governed." He had made but one promise — leaner government — a declaration of belief searching for a basis in fact. Three weeks into session he got the legislators to agree to an unprecedented request that they adjourn till fall when findings of his "survey" of state operations would be available. The pungent phrases in his inaugural, like "pusillanimous blatherskites" (those who disagreed), were still entertaining. By October, any gilding was off the lily. "Political dopesters and … rumor spreaders" were speculating "what the legislature is going to do to Hartley. The legislature can't do anything to Hartley, because Hartley doesn't want anything." He had "great confidence" in it. "Washington has never had a better [one]. All realize we hold our mandates, not from the self-constituted political bosses who do the talking, but from the people who do the voting and pay the taxes … I don't give a whoop how the legislature organizes, so long as it … organizes for work and not for horse play."[22]

His first target was Majority Leader Reed, now in a fierce and ultimately successful struggle with the governor's old guard. When the legislators were recalled in November, the only reason given was the necessity for a budget for the rest of the biennium. The governor's "survey," which he claimed was the most "comprehensive program ever developed," was an incomplete, amateur, solo act. There was grumbling that the new tax commission amounted to "centralization." Open insurgency broke out in the house when Hartley vetoed HB 40, $400,000 for revolving loans to farmers to purchase seed wheat, as paternalism.[23]

Hartley did nothing to assuage his critics. By midsummer his directors were complaining that the cabinet had yet to meet. The governor isolated himself from the other statewide elected officials, questioning what he could not control. His bitter critique of the two other members of the Land Commission was plausible. As he explained to Vice President Charles Dawes, timber was two-thirds of the state's industrial payroll — and taxes. "We are cutting three trees where we should be cutting but one, and [in] … twenty years will see the end of this great industry. Timber owners and mill operators are engaged in a competitive orgy of cutting, slashing, and waste. In the end, those who will suffer most are … the general public." The Commission, he complained, was abetting the lumber and education lobbies who were colluding to liquidate the state's largest asset for quick cash.[24] The governor gets credit for a weak but improved timber law.

Hartley's megalomania bloomed. A lay board of five had been named to investigate what he termed the "disproportionate and alarming cost" of public education. Ignorance could not keep him off the "forbidden ground." Education was "the biggest business in the State," and the most mismanaged. "It is time somebody defined public education. Don't misunderstand me. I am not contending for less education, but for more education for less money."[25] His answer was a constitutional amendment abolishing the office of Superintendent of Public Instruction and calling in the best available administrator (appointed by the governor). Tactless attacks exhausted the House's patience.[26] Child welfare advocates' new law and labor legislation were dismissed as "altruistic twaddle." The problems of youth were "attributable to poverty … or enforced neglect. I will cite you dozens of such cases due to willful, inexcusable neglect of child-petting, joy-riding, jazz-seeking parents who do politics, society, and uplift," the governor pontificated, offending the PTA and women's clubs.[27] The press had faulted his killing of the Kittitas (County) Reclamation project to discredit his economies. "The howl of those whose selfish schemes have been thwarted, and of those whose hands have been stricken from the people's pockets is music to my ears. May their numbers increase."[28] The WSFL took exception to Hartley's charges there were "bolshevists" and of course "pusillanimous blatherskites" among the backers of the child labor amendment, and pledged his recall.

The brasher the governor was, the more the contrarian voters heard a man speaking his mind and applauded. Emboldened, he replaced university regents, who fired its president Dr. Henry Suzzallo, on the governor's 'list' since he advised an eight-hour day as chair of Governor

Lister's timber team. In 1926, Hartley told the regents to keep their budget requests for the next biennium identical to the prior one. Suzzallo had kept lobbying for more money. Hartley informed Columbia University president Schuyler Wallace, "The tendency ... among the special-privilege seekers is to dwarf and minimize the authority of the Executive. If representative government is to live, there must be an executive power sitting yonder, detached and aloof from political chicanery and scheming. The judges' decisions reach only so far as the executive. A mob calls on the legislative branch ... and attempts to destroy it. Who stops it? The executive, if need be, to protect the peace and dignity of the State." The bitter rivalry between the president of the university and the state college (at Pullman) could be ended only one way, by a lay board of nine (appointed by the governor), in control of higher education. "Presidents would be taken out of politics."[29] It was Hartley or chaos in higher education. House Floor Leader Mark Reed and 60 of his majority chose passive resistance. To the end, the governor could not imagine why he was "misrepresented, lied about and abused" by the Republican legislature. "What's all the fuss about anyway? We must all surely want the same thing in the final analysis."[30]

In 1928, Hartley campaigned with a quartet from a flatbed truck loaded with "wasteful" accessories from the new capitol, like a $100 hammered brass cuspidor. The "Cuspidor Caravan" entertained while the disorganized anti-Hartley groups' protests fell on deaf ears, despite the hostile dailies trumpeting his recall. By 1931, executive-legislative relations had reached an all-time low. Not one of the 22 bills from a Tax Investigation Commission was enacted, "Thanks to the Senate majority. These malcontents have spent their time abusing the governor." He vetoed everything important: personal and corporate income taxes, the "Showalter" school bill, child welfare and malpractice bills. His striking of one on abandoned horses is peerless. "Even nature fakers can make no one believe a 'mule' is a 'horse.' A horse might make a 'jackass' out of itself, as did members of the present senate, but I would still be unwilling to convert a state senator into a 'jackass' by legislative enactment."[31]

Roland Hill Hartley entered office with more advantages than anyone who has held it, but the political misanthrope's maladroitness and misfeasance brought state government to near standstill. He "detested everyone who opposed his views." The executive rule desirable in business was inimical to delivering diverse social services. The departmental restructuring of 1921, the independence of the other statewide-elected officials, and legislative leaders who knew better were saving graces. Hartley was immersed in detail, unclear on anything but austerity, identified with no particular group, indiscriminate in his charges about his peers, and trailed more than a whiff of megalomania. His legacies were calling attention to the forest industry that was bringing on its own demise by failing to replant, tightening the budget law, and having the director of the Highways Department named by the governor. A 1927 audit had disclosed "irregularities" and the "prevalence of graft running to large sums." The chief highways engineer went prison for refusing to turn over his books.

As the Depression deepened, so did the governor's asceticism. "I made one promise, and one promise and only one, that if elected, I would use my every effort to reduce the cost of government, by the simple standard of plain business." The contradictions and necessary compromises of politics were lost on him. The cry of the "whole citizenship" was for reduced taxes, but he had "encountered the most insidious and bitter opposition ever faced by a governor." A "closely knit fraternity" of demanders that opposed to his "rigid policy of retrenchment" was being abetted by "powerful newspapers" printing "misrepresentation unparalleled in this or any other state."

In 1932, there was a balance of $1,369,747; his directors and vetoes had saved $36 million. Initiative 64, limiting all property tax levies to 40 mills, "must be enforced." "Laxness in control" and "nonessentials" were to blame for inflation in education costs. "Centralized control of all school budgets might be necessary if outright bankruptcy is to be averted." The answer was to replace professional educators on the State School Board with laymen. It was a "pleasure" to see the University of Washington regents had cut $1 million "without reducing in any way the efficiency of the institution." Two of the three normal schools should be closed. Like the Bourbons, Hartley learned nothing and forgot nothing. The persevering provincial, performer and artifact was unaware that the politics of governance should have been the first, not the last thing on his mind.[32]

## The New Deal: A House Divided

The prolonged fourth incarnation of the governorship began on the upended economic terrain of the Depression. Over 20 years, two moderate governors parried a resurgent legislative Left and mounting social welfare groups who wrote initiatives to get what executive-senate coalitions denied them. Clarence D. Martin (1933-41) and Arthur B. Langlie (1941-45, 1949-57) were of different parties, but of one mind. Martin, a conservative Democrat and wheat miller from Cheney, west of Spokane, was a palliative echo of the party he had chaired in the 1920s.

Langlie, a reformist councilman and mayor of Seattle (1935-40), was the Western incarnation of the emergence of "eastern liberal establishment" Republicans led by New York's Governor Tom Dewey. The circumstances and temper of America two decades later under Dwight Eisenhower's "Modern Republicanism" were vastly different, but both governors concentrated on sustaining balance by restraining the Left and its radical allies.[33]

Nowhere in the West was the coming of the New Deal more dramatic. In 1932, Democrats in Washington went from one U.S. Senator, and a single Representative, and less than ten state legislators to winning every congressional chair, all but one of the nine statewide offices, 70 of the 98 seats in the State House, and a 25-to-21 edge in the State Senate, despite GOP holdovers.[34] Clarence Martin had neither threatened nor condemned in his 750 speeches for the Democratic nomination, vowing "Decency in politics, honesty in government," unemployment relief, an income tax, "a fresh economic deal, a different social order, and a new political spirit."[35] Early on, the New Deal was strongest on his home turf, long-stricken northeastern Washington, and weakest on Puget Sound. His intense campaigning, a 75 percent vote from Spokane County, and a near-even split of King County primary votes between Socialist judge William Pemberton and liberal lawyer Lewis Schwellenbach ensured his victory.[36]

Over 100,000 people in the state were unemployed by 1931 and 287,000 in 1933, when the legislature created the Washington Emergency Relief Administration (WERA) to allocate food, clothing, and government jobs. The governor's appointment of social worker Charles Ernst, manager of Seattle's relief efforts as Director of Unemployment, was telltale.[37] In effecting Martin's modest welfare and pension proposals, Ernst quickly became both a lightning rod and a bulwark against those seeking partisan spoils from his burgeoning bureau. The governor was deluged with job seekers and fierce Democratic internal strife first surfaced over the governor's refusal to clean house: "I did not get all my majority from Democrats and I think both parties should be represented" shocked the regulars. "Capable" Republicans were retained.[38] In 1934, the State Democratic Central Committee asked that Ernst and four others be dismissed; Martin replied that party leaders were acting "like a lot of school children."

Given the unprecedented pressure to act, the governor's intention to hold "intra-governmental hearings" on the "Preliminary Budget" assembled by the Department of Efficiency, which he then might adjust as he pleased, went the way of the Administrative Board.[39] Overnight, the state assumed daunting financial burdens. Martin saw no alternative to a new Department of Public Welfare as controller for all kinds of grants if the state paid for them too, bringing more umbrage down on Ernst.[40] The 1933 session made the state a more-than-an-equal partner with the counties in public education. Olympia was also obligated to the $30-per-month old-age pensions (contingent on need), partly to keep the destitute out of county "poor farms." These funding shifts and the control that came with them further centralized governance and indeed transformed local governments into "creatures of the state."[41]

Property values fell by half and were capped in 1932 at 40 mils by initiative. Martin pressed for income, business and occupations and luxury taxes as temporary expedients expiring in two years, and for a $10 million bond issue for local projects to "match" federal funds. He cut salaries 15 to 25 percent. Dreaming of a major federal initiative, legislators set aside $377,000 for the Grand Coulee Dam authorized by Congress in the winter of 1933, to show the state was serious, and sanctioned the Columbia Basin Commission the Northwest states' feeble coordinating body.[42]

Martin tried to stave off a special session in 1933: "It would be almost impossible to handle the majority of these people, who are desirous of a $5 [legislator's] per day job and almost every type of legislation would be considered." The Left amended the governor's bill to reduce mortgage foreclosures into one affecting all kinds of credit, and vainly joined to co-opt a veto. "Ruinous delays in the collection of all debts … would jeopardize extension of credit," he reproved the House. Proposals like having the state take over the distribution of gasoline, which Martin favored, passed the House 83-10, only to fall two to one in the senate.

The state's finances deteriorated as the Depression dropped to its nadir. In June 1933, the state Supreme Court felled the Business and Occupations tax and in September the bond issue, a victim of the $400,000 debt limit embedded in the constitution in 1889. Its Fourteenth Amendment, dictating uniform tax rates, stymied the graduated income tax. The Left, disillusioned with the governor's economies from the outset, noted the fifth and deciding vote on the supreme court was cast by Spokane's John Geraghty, whom Martin had moved from the Department of Efficiency to the high bench.[43]

In February 1934, commissaries and food vouchers redeemable at grocery stores were substituted for food depots, and the first direct uprising arrived in Olympia. Not a few of the members of the Seattle Unemployed Citizens League were living in the scrap and cardboard shacks of "Hooverville" on the Duwamish tide flats filled by Governor Eugene Semple 30 years earlier.

Martin shouldered more resentment as federal relief administrator Harry Hopkins interred the Civilian Works Administration, which President Roosevelt deemed too costly, shifting 32,000 of the unemployed in the state to other projects, or to relief. Seventy-eight percent of the $31 million spent by the Washington Emergency Relief Administration was federal. Hopkins' threat to cut off funds if the state did not meet its "match" ratcheted up pressure on the governor.[44]

As the malaise deepened, labor unions gained 5,000 members in March, April, and May 1934, tilting the State Labor Council away from its traditional craft-based conservatism. Martin shared Labor's doubts about the efficacy of the National Recovery Act's price control mechanisms also disliked by consumers, but threatened to place "price gouging" gasoline companies under the Department of Public Works so they could be regulated as utilities. The Left was nonplussed. It captured the King County Democratic convention in May, splitting the state party in half and turned down a motion to endorse the governor while laying hands on the rest of the 1934 slate. Nationalization of banks, state takeover of fuel suppliers, and the Bone Power Bill allowing public utility districts to extend services beyond their counties were acclaimed. The Grange's blanket primary initiative permitted cross voting, Martin's salvation in 1936, to the disdain of those who had long walked in the wilderness.[45]

The governor embarked on a study to reorient Olympia towards unfinished business, issued the second call for a constitutional review, and went on the radio in August to prepare the 1935 legislators and the public for new extensions of state power. He now hedged on how it was to be financed. A flat income tax was desperately needed to pick up the loads, but Martin was now only "inclined to agree" with putting the soon-to-fail measure on the fall ballot. He was "reluctant" to turn to a sales tax, unless the constitution was amended "to permit specific property tax relief for the small home owner." Critics interpreted his tepidity as a characteristic "lack of clear and forceful leadership."[46] And the volatile freshmen who were the majority in the House in both 1933 and 1935 were ever more eager to act. The Left's tactic in 1935, to redistribute the governor's new powers among the statewide officials, almost undid the 1921 Reorganization Act. Senator James A. Murphy's bill stripped the governor of appointive power, abolished the "Code" departments, and shifted authority from second-rank officials to the directors of several independent boards the legislature had birthed. The administration's new Department of Welfare was to be under the State Finance Committee, where the treasurer and auditor could outvote Martin and name a new director. Three days later, this was rescinded 56-41 and the governor's bill passed 64-33.[47] The best measure of left-wing strength was on the recast "Production of Use" initiative, authorizing a commission to expend $5 million to acquire idle farms and factories, tabled 48-44 — with the few Republican votes.[48]

Martin still happily identified with the New Deal and its largesse, as did the legislators, enabling a state NRA, AAA, and ownership of power distribution. A bill giving the governor carte blanche authority to set competitive codes for business passed the House 88-11 and squeezed by the Senate.[49] The cleavages were now plain and the governor and conservative senators positioned to block anything more. The first intimations of a coalition of conservative Eastern Washington Democratic senators and Republicans that tipped the close division in the "majority" caucus and left liberals in the "minority" after 1939 had appeared. The coalition of up to eight of mostly east of the Cascades Democrats that stood by Martin and then Langlie made the urban-rural schism transparent, and was the balance wheel in legislative politics for 20 years.

Pensions joined relief as the set-piece controversies and the chief challenges to the state's credit. When 40,000 — not the projected 12,000 — qualified, the only choice was to prorate checks from $30 to $21 a month, despite Martin's protestations he would not be satisfied until they were $40. The Communist-influenced Washington Commonwealth Federation (WCF), the umbrella pressure group that had carried the flag for state-owned cooperatives, soon spun off the Washington Old Age Pension Union (WOAPU). None of these left-liberal organizations achieved the "mass movement" status the latter claimed, were able to unify the Left in Olympia, or offer creditable statewide candidates between 1932 and 1940; they did become the governor's ongoing nemeses.[50] At the end of a tumultuous 24-hour sitting at Aberdeen in May 1936, the Left was in control of the State Democratic convention, and endorsed takeover of idle factories ("Production for Use") and state ownership of natural resources. The governor attributed this to "leaders of the Communist Party" and ran for reelection on fiscal prudence, advertising profits from the state's new liquor monopoly. He had "cooperated at every turn with President Roosevelt on economic recovery," balanced the budget with $9 million less taxes, initiated a flood-control program, and increased game and commercial fishing licenses.[51] Martin anticipated the large infusions of eastern investment capital — if radicals did not upset recovery.

The WCF aided him by nominating King County Commissioner ("Radio Speaker") John C. Stevenson, of whom anything might be expected, after he endorsed its new initiative. State Auditor Otto Case did the governor's primary work, carving up Stevenson's more generous pension plan, and the Seattle Central Labor Council laid hands on the entire Democratic ticket before the WCF could find a substitute for Stevenson. The "spoils men of King County" were behind it all. The governor fumed, firming up his eastern base against the now-liberal west side. Aghast at Roland Hartley's reappearance, 50,000 Republicans crossed over under the new blanket primary passed by initiative in 1935 to re-nominate and thus reelect Martin.[52]

Like Woodrow Wilson in 1914, in 1936 Martin assumed reform was past. The object was to augment recovery. "The people had pointed the way" for the 1937 session. He quickly treated the last-resort 1935 sales tax as a many-virtued thing, "It has reached many who never contributed to the upkeep of government" and made them realize "that state government is not a detached, distant and indifferent agency. It is everybody's business."[53] Payrolls in Washington had doubled between 1933 and 1936, and revenue gains would pay for pensions. FDR's second pullback of federal dollars in 1937 shattered Martin's prognosis and triggered a new recession. The Left was resuscitated in the House and the senate's presiding officer, Lieutenant Governor Victor Meyers, gave lie to the governor's dream of ample pensions without new taxes.[54] The body's conservative coalition rescued Martin by taking away Meyers' ability to make committee assignments keeping key committees out of the Left's hands. In the House, the Left's Jurie Smith got 39 votes (of the 49 needed) for Speaker on the first ballot. The WCF's three-man lobbying team with its chronic disorder helped little.[55]

The president reminded the governors yearly after 1933 that failure to pay their share of Civilian Conservation Corps dollars for use in state parks and forests meant loss of Congress' benevolence. His intention to greatly expand the boundaries of the new Olympic National Park, which he visited in the summer of 1938, was even more worrisome to Martin. "Having satisfied myself (via a Forest Service study) it would not harm the pulp and paper industries of the Peninsula," FDR continued to act as if there "was an agreement in principle between all of us as to the proposed extensions" and added the rain forests of the Hoh and Bogaschiel valleys treasured by loggers, securing them in the Olympic National Park, rather than a national forest. Martin, who had fought strenuously for smaller additions, was thanked for his "cooperative attitude."[56]

Public resentment of the West Coast Maritime Strike of 1934, lumber strikes in 1935, and the Newspaper Guild's three-month shutdown of the *P-I* in 1936, prompted the governor to take the offense with a labor disputes bill, the first attempt to modify a New Deal statute. The Washington State Industrial Tribunal curtailed rights guaranteed under the 1935 Wagner Act, anticipating the Taft-Hartley Act of 1947 by a decade. Three gubernatorial appointees were given broad discretion to intervene in disputes and order 30-day "truces." Detractors imagined a Martin move to consolidate power, as any of the appointees could be dismissed for "inefficiency, neglect of duty or malfeasance." It passed the Senate 35 to 9 and even if enraged house radicals and the reserved AF of L tradesmen were not ideal partners, it approved Labor's counter measure, 77-22. It was a draw; both bills died.[57]

By 1938, the governor was openly hostile to the militants and chafing at federal economic intervention. "Please don't send any more no good Democrats down to Olympia and expect us to do anything for them," he pled at Seattle's University Christian Church. "If you must send worthless men ... send no-good Republicans because they are not quite so bad." Martin men formed a purge committee to oust "irresponsible radicals." Half the 43 were from King and Pierce counties. The governor did not want to see "men and women ... who don't believe in profit ... in Olympia."[58] Defeat of the private power utilities' I-130 forcing referendums on proposed PUD takeovers and the return of the entire congressional delegation in November pleased the Left, but the "purge" restored Martin's edge in Olympia. The governor anchored to starboard: "economic security ... [was] as important as social security." Unemployment compensation further complicated Charles Ernst's tasks. The county commissioners who dispensed relief were given lists to choose their managers from, to tighten rules and equalize pension payments. To bring pensions to $30 a month, $36 million was needed; Martin offered $20 million, the status quo. The WCF took to arms, but was unable to raise taxes.[59]

An opera bouffe' climax to the family feud occurred when Vic Meyers tried to call a special session while the governor was in New York. He was compelled to charter a plane and arrived in Spokane at 7:58 am, preempting his surrogate. The 30 progressive legislators who came to Olympia for an audience on April 25, left at the end of the day without seeing him. The refusal of WCF leaders to disavow Soviet Russia after the Nazi-Soviet Pact and its invasion of Finland in 1939, imprinted on many what Martin argued: "Communists," not humanitarians, were at its helm. The broad-based left-liberal coalition of convenience of the 1930s crumbled.[60]

Ernst's dropping of 1345 pensioners in King County upset Democratic moderates and sealed the governor's fate by the time he welcomed new Seattle Mayor Langlie in March of 1938: "Seattle will not have to apologize for an unbalanced budget or uncashable warrants much longer. You are to be congratulated on the election of a mayor like Arthur S. [sic "B."] Langlie. There is now an open door between him and the capitol." Langlie quickly strode through it. A federal Reconstruction Finance Corporation (RFC) loan and a state tax diversion backed by Martin replaced the city's dilapidated "Street Railway" with electric trolleys, engines of popularity. Langlie was reelected mayor in April 1940 with 80 percent of the vote, allowing him to break even in Seattle in November despite being a Republican and capture the governor's chair over former U.S. Senator Clarence Dill by 6,000 votes. Martin, who had lost the primary, was plainly relieved.[61] "The people seem to be well satisfied with his election," the governor wrote his son Frank, "It is obvious that there was a strong undercurrent against the Spokane candidate. The Mayor told me … that it is evident that the Democrats did for him what the Republicans did for me in 1936."[62]

Martin can only be roughly compared to his peers in Idaho and Oregon, Democratic governors whose enthusiasm for the New Deal "turned to grudging acceptance, then to suspicion."[63] Independence was the Western tradition and resistance to urban-eastern experimentalism, neither as uniform nor "nationalized" as it seemed, was predictable. Martin's uninspiring task as state Democratic chair in the 1920s had been to keep a dispirited and impotent party intact. In the 1930s, his aggravations came less from the New Deal than trying to restrain the clamorous left wing of a majority from adopting the impossible. He was not as conservative as critics claimed. Even in the crisis of 1937-38, Washington spent more on general relief per capita than the majority of states. His farewell address to the 1941 session asked for a return to a "$100 million standard" for the state, a budget just $12 million above where it stood a decade earlier. (See Appendix 4, for effects of population and inflation) "We who step aside … will proudly remember we held the line when the going was hardest."[64]

## *Pictorials, Section One*

*Isaac Stevens: Soldier, Surveyor, Governor, WSA*

*Chief Seattle, the exceptional leader of the Indians. MHI*

*The Parker and Colter General Store. The second floor was home to the Washington Territorial Legislature in 1854. WSCM*

*This photo was recently found and is the only known one of Richard Gholson, who could not wait to get out of Olympia once Lincoln was elected. WSA*

*Governor Elisha Ferry*

*Governor John McGraw, survivor. WSA*

*Bridging the Territory and Statehood: Governor Elisha Ferry's inaugural in 1889 at the first state capitol . WSA*

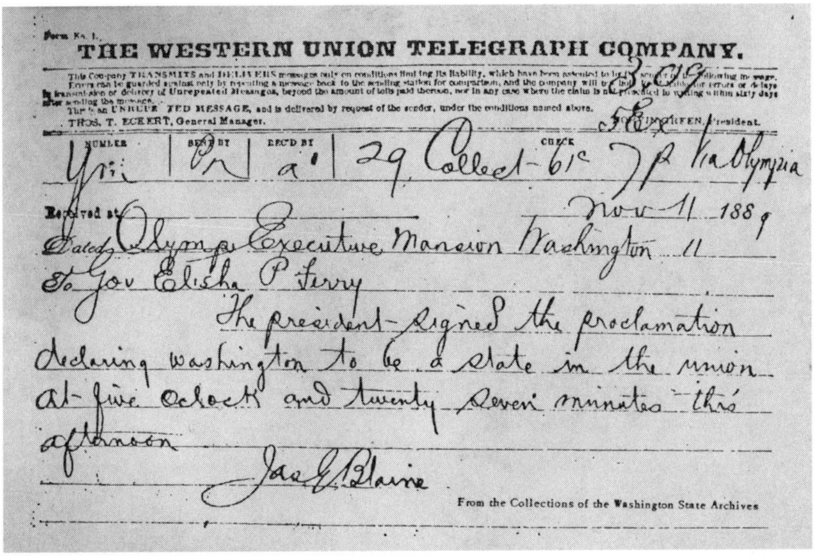

Form No. 1.

THE WESTERN UNION TELEGRAPH COMPANY.

This Company TRANSMITS and DELIVERS messages only on conditions limiting its liability, which have been assented to by the sender of the following message. Errors can be guarded against only by repeating a message back to the sending station for comparison, and the company will not hold itself liable for errors or delays in transmission or delivery of Unrepeated Messages, beyond the amount of tolls paid thereon, nor in any case where the claim is not presented in writing within sixty days after sending the message.

This is an UNREPEATED MESSAGE, and is delivered by request of the sender, under the conditions named above.

THOS. T. ECKERT, General Manager. [illegible] GREEN, President.

309

5 Ex

| NUMBER | SENT BY | REC'D BY | | CHECK |
| --- | --- | --- | --- | --- |
| Yri | Pr | a' | 29 Collect 61c | 7p Via Olympia |

Received at Nov 11 1889

Dated Olympia Executive Mansion Washington 11

To Gov Elisha P Ferry

The president signed the proclamation declaring washington to be a state in the union at five Oclock and twenty seven minutes this afternoon

Jas G Blaine

From the Collections of the Washington State Archives

*Proclamation making Washington a State, 1889. WSA*

*The Neo-Georgian Governor's Mansion, built in 1909*

*Governor Albert E. Mead: misunderstood or misfeasant? WSA*

*The last of the Jeffersonians: Governor John R. Rogers. WSA*

*Governor Watson Squire, industrialist, United States Senator. WSA*

*Governor Marion E. Hay: Progressive or straddler? WSA*

*Governor Ernest Lister: The Wilsonian Democrat faced WWI tensions. WSA*

*Governor Louis Hart: clubman and reorganizer.*

*The Second State Capitol, Olympia (1907), ca 1917. It now houses the Superintendent of Public Instruction. WSA*

*The Alaska Yukon Pacific Exposition on the grounds of the University of Washington, Seattle, 1909. The climax of Gold Rush prosperity and the Progressive era. MHI.*

*Governor Hart, left, Dr. Henry Suzzallo, Jim Gallagher and a model of Husky Stadium, 1920. WSA*

*Rolland Hill Hartley artifact. WSA*

*Topping off the dome. 1928. Governor Hartley at peak.*

*Seattle's Hooverville on the Duwamish Flats during the Great Depression.* WSL

*Clarence Martin as State Democratic Chair, and candidate for the State House of Representatives in the 1920s. He returned in the House Minority for the 1947-49 biennium.*

*Governor Martin campaigns on a horse at the Ellensburg Rodeo in 1936. PI*

*Comedic relief or pain in the posterior? Band leader Vic Meyers lost for mayor of Seattle in 1932, but became Lieutenant Govenor for five terms, and later as Secretary of State. WSHS*

*Just in time for WWII: President Franklin D. Roosevelt (center) dedicates the Grand Coulee Dam in 1939. PI*

*Lacey V. Murrow, Governor Martin's Director of Highways at the west entrance to the new Lake Washington Floating Bridge, 1939. PI/MHI*

*A meeting of the minds: Governor Clarence D. Martin, left, and Governor-Elect Arthur Langlie confer in November 1940.*

Chapter 4

# Arthur B. Langlie: Republican Governor in a Democratic Age

*(1941–45, 1949–57)*

## Mugwump

Arthur B. Langlie (1900–66) was the first three-term governor of Washington, the only man to regain the chair, and the sole Republican to hold statewide office in the New Deal. The westward odyssey of Bjarne Langlie's family from Norway to Minnesota, North Dakota, and ending in 1905 on the Olympic Peninsula, mirrored that of the large Scandinavian community. The grocer's son spent six years at the University of Washington between being a rigger in Clallam Bay logging camps, running planers in mills on the shores of Lake Union, and a summer working as a "bindle stiff" in the Palouse wheat fields at $6 a day. In high school he played tennis and captained the baseball team. At the university, Langlie led the Tubby Graves nines that took three regional crowns, and the tennis team that captured the Northwest Intercollegiate singles tournament in 1923. Sports, Fir Tree, Oval Club, and two years as president of Phi Kappa Sigma also eroded his grade point, but he graduated in the law honorary in 1926.[1]

Seattle was still coping with its gold rush hangover when the Great Depression brought in uprooted loggers and farmers and radicals beset city hall. The tempestuous coast wide strike by Harry Bridge's longshoremen in 1934 and his clashes with Dave Beck's teamsters compounded the tumult. Langlie's nine years of quiet civil practice with Shank, Belt, and Rode ended abruptly when he became the third city council nominee of the New Order of Cincinnatus. The municipal reform movement was a vehicle for professionals, progressive Republicans, and bourbon Democrats, either left out of or uncomfortable with partisan politics in the New Deal. "Replace the political racketeers with the Cincinnatus musketeers of good government," was the cry.[2] The King County Labor Council and the vociferous Washington Commonwealth Federation (a "triple alliance of liberals, labor and farm,")[3] labeled he and running mate Fred Hamley "tools of a fascist dictatorship," but they led the ticket. North End burghers wanting the city to adopt their lifestyle had outvoted the city's southern commercial and industrial sectors. The demographic shift spurring a four-year crusade for fiscal accountability, police integrity, and administrative "cleanliness" presaged Seattle's conversion to three decades of municipal peace and being the sedate "Queen City of the Northwest."[4]

County Prosecutor Warren Magnuson ignored evidence on 66 whorehouses, gambling dens, and speakeasies Hamley's Efficiency Committee uncovered. The city's budget had been trimmed 54 percent in two years, and in trying to get it to balance, the three Cincinnatans (David Lockwood had been elected in 1934) solidified the opposition: recall petitions were circulated in the north end. Despite membership declines in outlying chapters, centralization, and internal strife in the Seattle post, Cincinnatus contested for mayor in 1936. Langlie bested four other civic leaders to be nominated on the fifth ballot.[5] Demagogic former mayor John Dore caught the drift and reversed his frugal views of 1932–34. "You can't attract tourists to a Sunday school town," he thundered, "I'll make a San Francisco out of it. "Langlie? "He's a nice boy …a nice clean boy, whatever that may be. But that is no reason any sensible mother would want to see him become mayor …"[6] Cincinnatus's theme, "They Kept Their Promises," and endorsements from all three metropolitan dailies met a crescendo of innuendo. Langlie spent half his time explaining "The Truth about Cincinnatus." He drew 21,290 votes, his three primary opponents 44,000.

Dore became the other finalist — by 110 votes. Dave Beck was the reason, and now the fulcrum on which the general election hung. Langlie told his emissary he would be in his office afternoons four to five, though he knew a meeting of minds with Beck meant his election was "right in the bag."[7] Cincinnatus endorsed a merit system, Hamley's plans to remodel the dilapidated Street Railway, Lockwood's central garaging plan, and the trio's referendum for a purchasing officer. The order's election eve rally at the Moore Theater for 1,200 was tame compared to Dore's 90-minute tirade at the Ballard Eagles Hall. Langlie lost, as vote margins above the ship canal slipped to three to one. Changes to the city charter became the order's legacy. The other upshot was an enduring enmity. Langlie reflected at the end of his career that of the three elections he lost, two were when he was not attacking Dave Beck.[8]

## Mayor of "The Queen City of the Northwest"

By 1939, FDR's preparations for war were pumping tens of millions of dollars into the state's economy, which in two years was lifted out of the Depression as fast as it had gone in. Seattle started a three-decade reign as a calm, culturally laggard regional center, proud of its WASP values and respectably conservative in its politics. The core Langlie team appeared: Hamley as Water Superintendent and his "Colonel House." Lockwood chaired the Civil Service Commission, and Evro Beckett, managing director of the Edmond Meany Hotel, went on the park board. Chief William Fitzgerald set out to "remove politics" from the fire department. The budget was ratcheted down another $616,000 (on a total of less than $7 million). Water rates were raised and Martin's nod got the legislature to raise the cities' share of the gas and liquor taxes. The banks resumed cashing payroll warrants. It was the New Deal's Reconstruction Finance Corporation that financed the "trackless trolleys" first seen in January 1940. Seattle emerged from the Depression with the lowest General Fund debt of any city over 300,000.[9] Dave Beck had power and wanted respect; Labor went off the front page. Defense work muted the longshoremen's militancy. Seattle settled back to its traditional if tightened "tolerance policy" on vice. Langlie was reelected mayor in 1940 with 76 percent of the vote, still a record.[10]

## 1940: Go East, Young Man

His Seattle base buttressed, in April Langlie decided to run for governor. An orchestrated "campaign of importunings" began with Spokane Republicans caravanning west. In July, politicos from every urban area east of the Cascades laid 25,000 signatures on his desk. His car top speaker played a Sousa march or "God Bless America" in towns from Cle Elum to Kettle Falls, as he darted into stores and restaurants, then back to a crowd to talk about "honest non-partisan government." Governor Martin was anathema to left-wing Democrats and caught in the controversy over third terms (for both he and President Roosevelt).

When Clarence C. Dill of Spokane entered the contest, his conservative base was split two ways. The last governor from Eastern Washington was through.[11]

C. C. Dill, congressman from the Fifth District (Eastern Washington) from 1914 to 1918, was defeated for voting against World War I. In 1922, those with serious reservations about the Great Crusade and the farm depression narrowly elected him U.S. senator. By the time he resigned in 1935, some Democratic regulars saw his "independent" stance as expediency. By the time Dill announced for governor in 1940, he was a shopworn foil for Seattle's youthful mayor at the peak of his popularity. As Dill and Langlie raked the beleaguered Martin on his home turf, the governor tagged Dill a "dangerous man" trailing extremists, to Langlie's ultimate benefit. Dill expected to ride in with Roosevelt, but as he ran to the right in the general election mimicking the mayor's calls for economy by reform, west side liberals found "no outstanding progressive" in the race.

The two differed on public power and welfare (the Commonwealth Federation's new Initiative 141) with its $80 million in unfunded costs. Beck tried to lead Labor to Dill and turn the mayor's theme of "bossism" against him. "I got a break," Langlie reminisced. "I didn't run against C. C. Dill, I ran against Dave Beck. The respectable people of organized labor … is what elected me." Martin cross-backs, "non-partisanship" name familiarity in Seattle kept him from being drowned in the awesome King County Democratic reservoir. He won by 5,816 of the 777,844 votes cast, by getting 50,000 more votes there than any other Republican.[12]

## On His Own: The First Administration

The nation's second youngest governor,[13] and the first in 28 years of a different persuasion than the legislature, startled Democrats hearing him for the first time with a "frank and rather progressive" inaugural address. He advocated new departments of the budget and Employment Security, extension of the definition of "injury" to occupational diseases, and broadening civil service. In 1938, Oregon had overtaken Washington as the nation's prime timber producer, and by 1940, the state was cutting more timber than it was growing. The proceeds of state forests, which went to building schools, were supervised by three boards and five different elected officials. Langlie's "Comprehensive Forest Preservation Act" with a Forestry Board of two forestry deans and seven gubernatorial appointees picked from various associations trod on their turf and was repeatedly felled by partisanship in 1941 and 1943. Instead, Democrats caucused on shifting "code" (gubernatorial) departments to the state officials.[14]

The cabinet met for the first time in 12 years. Fred Hamley, a Jeffersonian Democrat, was director of Public Service (utility regulation) and the governor's idea man. Lockwood, 34, took Finance that included Institutions and was to become the Department of General Administration.[15] Labor leader Robert

Harlin, a Republican Langlie had met on the city council, headed Labor and Industries. Evro Beckett came to Olympia to oversee the Liquor Board. This nucleus of the "administrative board" replicated the Seattle efficiencies: record keeping was formalized, purchasing centralized, autos pooled, and blanket insurance bought. The counties were no protection against the avalanche of patronage seekers and partisan pressure on departmental directors. Seattle Times reporter Ross Cunningham, 33, now the governor's special assistant, was the eye of the needle through which they had to pass.[16]

Langlie's intense dislike of partisan politics now turned into a liability as well. Veteran King County Republican Chair Ralph Horr chafed for patronage, blamed the governor for appointing former Democrats and too many Cincinnatans, and edged closer to Beck.[17] In October, district leaders' petitions appeared asking for Horr's removal and the GOP convention agreed on a cooperative chair. Langlie's aloofness from the Republican State Central Committee caused its executive Tom Oakshott to resign, alleging "one man was superior to a great political party." Legislative Democrats, put on the defensive by their first programmatic challenges, were sorely aware their patronage had evaporated and passed only two of Langlie's four bills for a merit (civil service) system in the Unemployment Compensation and Social Security departments. When classification (defining positions and equalizing salaries) was also closeted, the governor created a "joint system including only the half of state employees in his" ambit by administrative fiat. There the matter rested for two decades.

A "Standards Committee" of executive insiders centralized the amount and quality of patronage and, as importantly, imposed cost control to all agencies beginning in 1944, which was quickly resurrected in April 1949. It "resolved itself into a permanent organization" the first meeting, imposed pre-audits (cash flow monitoring) on the departments, became the clearinghouse for salaries, ordered the State Personnel Office to begin classification studies elsewhere as recommended in a four-year-old consultant's study, and seized all "procurement and personnel problems." In two hours, nine other tighteners were adopted, most unanimously.[18] If Langlie could not get civil service, stop unfunded initiatives, or the legislature from shifting the onus on him to balance the budget as the constitution required, he had to have a choke hold on expenditures and a device for quality control.

## War Comes to the West Coast

Arthur Langlie was the only governor to face two wars, the first against the Axis, the second, its extension, the Cold War. War started during the

1941 legislature and overshadowed all else in the first administration. Isolationism reigned even as rails from the street railway were being shipped to Japan and made into rifles. FDR prepared for war as quietly as he could. In August, Langlie informed federal director of Civilian Defense, Fiorello LaGuardia, that a State Emergency Commission for National Defense had formed under the adjutant general of the state guard for "civilian protection." Industrial and economic planning was also to be done by a state bureau.[19]

After December 7, LaGuardia ordered all Japanese to "remain in their homes pending determination of status." Those who have been apprehended have been carefully selected" by the FBI, he wrote. The state's 15,470 Germans, 8,853 Italians, 5,683 Issei (foreign-born Japanese), and 8,882 Nisei (naturalized Americans), were now suspect as "enemy aliens." Ten days later, a nervous Lieutenant General J. L. Dewitt, commanding the Western Defense Command, said it "did not appear that the FBI was keeping aliens and sympathizers still at large under surveillance." Nor was the bureau giving instructions. "Our common interests are to leave nothing undone to prevent sabotage. At the same time we do not wish any group of loyal citizens to be subjected to any action that might tend to alienate their loyalty."[20] The president signed notorious Federal Executive Order 9066 of February 1942, subjecting all Japanese to relocation inland. Langlie ordered them to turn their firearms in to the State Patrol and declared the entire state a "Protective Defense Area." He was the first to tell Congress' Tolan Committee in Seattle "an overwhelming majority of Washingtonians believe total evacuation …is necessary immediately. Every precaution should be made to be humane …but the people feel this is no time to worry about hurt feelings." These sentiments were echoed by the state's congressional delegation.[21]

Of the 14,400 "Japanese" in the state, 12,892 were incarcerated, 8,600 were American-born, and 5,600 "aliens," of which 9,660 lived in King County. Two-thirds of 110,000 detained on the West Coast were American citizens. Authors have dwelt on the abridgment of civil rights and spoken of "concentration camps."[22] Living in thin-walled tar-papered barracks like the Minidoka Relocation Center southeast of Boise, Idaho, was close quarters and uncomfortable during winter and summer. None of the other conditions describing abusive "camps" existed. War hysteria did obscure the Constitution. But Westerners had never faced war and King County, where nearly all the Japanese lived, was closest to Pearl Harbor and the Land of the Rising Sun. Nor should the pervasive fear be overlooked that took hold after two-man Japanese submarine was sighted in Elliott Bay and the army base at Adak in the Aleutians bombed in 1942.

The West Coast governors were appointed as property custodians and loss of it, largely for inability to pay mortgages or rents, was for many internees as great a sacrifice as the taking of freedom. Truck garden produce fell a quarter. Under a "Food Will Win the War" banner, the governor's Farm Labor Committee mobilized 250,000 man-hours work from students, work-release inmates, and off-hours state employees for the banner harvests of 1942 and 1943. Air raid blackout protocols were not "fully approved" by the Office of Civilian Defense until March 1943, which had "neither the power of enforcement or compulsion." Everything except protection of defense plants fell to the states and communities. The legislature created the Washington State War Council, a more potent successor to the 1941 State Defense Council.[23] The council had no budget, but its regulations for "civilian protection," limiting public gatherings, blackouts, and the like had the force of law. In two years, 218,000 auxiliary police, firemen, and air raid wardens were "trained." Whether they afforded practical protection or were mostly paper enlistments can be questioned. There were warnings of sabotage, submarine and "limited" air attacks, commando raids, and incendiary balloons as late as April 1944. All but the last were unlikely as a relaxation of restrictions in late 1943 indicated.[24] Three-quarters of the governor's time went to preparedness — rubber, salvage, blood, and bond drives, gas rationing, and victory gardens. An impressive amount of scrap was recycled into war materiel. War bonds ("the safest investment and most certain income yet devised by man") sustained the country but proved bad investments.[25]

## The Eclipse of the Extractive Economy

Washingtonians had long complained they were an economic "colony of the East." World War II made them a protectorate of a dominant federal government. Its 15,520 employees in Washington in 1938 rose to 100,359 in 1945, exceeded only by California.[26] As Langlie left Seattle, B-17s were rolling out of Boeing's assembly lines. Flashes from welding torches were reviving the shipyards. As the Reconstruction Finance Corporation redirected its searches to sites for new defense plants, the importance of the cheap electricity just on line from the Grand Coulee Dam was plain. Manufacturing soared by half between 1938 and 1949 and the rest of the economy by 70 percent. Washington moved from twelfth or thirteenth among the states in per capita income to fourth or fifth. Population and industry grew more in the war years than in the prior 25. Boeing expanded a hundred times, drawing aluminum and magnesium plant investments of $215 million. Electro chemicals and the shipyards led the demand for power, fusing a climatic fight in the 1950s.

Langlie expected postwar employment to be his problem and enlisted the State Planning Council's research. By 1942, the possibility of extracting aluminum from Eastern Washington clays, glucose from wheat, and utilizing wood waste were underway. A six-year, 12-million-man-hour public works agenda was ready by February 1944. To co-opt the East from reaping the benefits of early conversion, the governor combined 107 business, farm, and labor leaders lured by the prospect of "limitless" foreign trade, as the Washington World Trade Commission.[27] Pat Heatherton, executive officer of the Washington State Progress Commission, told the 1945 legislature, its "Post-Victory employment [program] ... now reaches more than 85 percent of the state." This claim must be taken in the same vein as the number of civil defense persons "trained." "Local communities" were to tell the legislature and Congress what they needed.[28] But the state's role in keeping its economy from reverting to recession was tertiary and the governor's stands for "states' rights" overwhelmed by the now-dominant federal government.

In 1946, Boeing went from 40,000 to 11,000 employees as sales slumped from $600 to $14 million. To the surprise of most, the economy absorbed 182,000 veterans and 40,000 others and readjusted in five years. The Glider Factory survived by gambling on jet aircraft and corralling Cold War defense contracts. Plutonium production at Hanford supported Richland, Pasco, and Kennewick. Building the massive dams that turned the Columbia River into a series of lakes in 20 years, reclamation of the Great Columbia Basin and farm subsidies, and after 1956 an interstate highway system buoyed Central Washington as below-market mortgages did the burgeoning western suburbs. Federal employees fell in half by the mid-1950s. In essence, Congress poured a comparable investment into private sector jobs. The state that had supplied the East lumber, fish, and wheat at unfavorable rail rates diversified its economy and reached critical mass — just in time to underwrite the kind of government that eluded the Left in the 1930s.[29]

The last prewar budget (1939–41) of $98 million is the benchmark to measure the expansion of the welfare state in Washington. Initiative 141of 1940, boosting monthly pension payments to $40 and adding 65,000 to the welfare rolls, opened the new era. In "voluminous correspondence and innumerable conferences," Langlie tried to get the federal Social Security Board to accept revisions and have every applicant be cleared on "need." The war-shocked legislators were jolted a second time by an "executive request" to raise the sales tax from 2 to 3 percent to pay for the 15,000 new enrollees, contingent a referendum to the people for a graduated net income tax[30] both passed the House in eight days. In the end, the pre-audits, reversions of up to10 percent from the departments under his control, and the rising tide of defense dollars balanced a budget of $264 million. The governor's "executive requests" died, as did the partisan Democrats' bills.

The Commonwealth Federation filed Initiative 151 in 1942 because the governor had "sought by every means possible to cut down the pittance to which the aged were entitled." Langlie had thought about liberalizing benefits some, but entitling 43,000 more persons was "a fool's paradise." He was destroying unity against "the black fascist tyranny," the WCF retorted. "Astounding impudence" came the reply, from a "clique of promoters, most of whom acquired their zeal [for war] only after Hitler turned on Russia."[31] Initiative 151 was swamped. Weakened further by its pro-Russian foreign policies as the Cold War began in1945, the federation dissolved itself and its leaders transferred their energies to the Washington Old Age Pension Union, the chief agony of Langlie's second administration.

Democratic strategy in 1942 was to call home their majority. The governor and Seattle advertising executive Fred Baker, his legislative liaison and key political advisor, countered with "moderation versus radicalism" and a "progressive program." Baker, now acting national committeeman, presided at the congressional district caucuses held in lieu of a state convention, denying the governor's critics a forum. The GOP picked up three of the state's six congressional seats and rose to a 10-year high of 42 (out of 96) in the 1943 House. Coalitions in both houses continued to stalemate the Left and Langlie predicted GOP majorities in 1944.[32] The special session he had to call in February 1944 for a "few simple changes" to ensure overseas servicemen the franchise ordained the opposite.

Apart from and in anticipation of Beck's roles, the governor was conspicuously cooperative with Labor. Installing former United Mine Workers president Bob Harlin as head of Labor and Industries set a precedent and pleased the rank and file. Claim backlogs vanished and the executive drew a bill for a second injury fund from savings. The Republican State Central Committee endorsed Referendum 22 and increased workmen's compensation to $50 a month, to be paid for by improving industrial safety. President James A. Taylor of the Washington State Federation of Labor told delegates at its 1942 Wenatchee convention that though Langlie was not Labor's choice in 1940, he had signed all 19 WSFL endorsed bills. The administration's policies were consistently and "affirmatively neutral." Union affiliation was "the inherent right of every individual." It did promote or prevent joining a union and "has not and will not use its influence or one in preference to another," nor would one's status in his agency be affected. The sole restriction was that organizing was not to go on "during business hours." Labor had lost one bill in four years. In 1944, labor legislation headed a list of 40 pledges made good. Langlie was endorsed as "outstandingly sympathetic" and Monrad Wallgren, still undecided about the governor's race, was advised to stay in the U.S. Senate "in behalf of labor's interest." Wallgren, an Everett optometrist-jeweler, who swept into Congress by the 1932 landslide and to U.S. Senate in 1940, was "beseeched" to challenge Langlie in 1944 when no one else did. Launching at the Everett Labor Temple, he scorned the governor as "a bystander in Labor's greatest hour of crisis."[33]

Governor Ronald Reagan's "revolution" of 1980 not excepted, the GOP's most appealing presidential choices in the past 75 years[34] have been either governors or nominated by them. Langlie's first taste of national politics was at the Republican governor's conference at Mackinac Island, Michigan in September of 1943. Senator Bob Taft's isolationists had drafted a platform. The governors wrote the Mackinac Charter, echoing Governor Dewey's call for a United Nations. Langlie came away a dedicated Deweyite and internationalist. He was one of nine Republican governors who broadcast nationwide for Dewey, abetting Democratic strategy at home. "Little Arthur has finally thrown off his guises," Mon Wallgren mused. In 1940, "he ran for governor as part Cincinnatus, part Republican, and part non-partisan." He now stood "revealed as a pure unadulterated Republican" placing himself with "the big corporations, the big bankers .... I will protect the little fellow — he needs it."He was asking the electorate to vote first against FDR, then for him, and would be "rejected by thousands who are Americans before they are Republicans."[35]

Langlie, who disdained press relations from his office, was the sole target at the state level and headed a weak ticket. Secretary of State Belle Reeves repeatedly mailed servicemen, who she had found were 71 percent Democratic.[36] The similarly oriented war workers who had flooded in from the South knew nothing of the Seattle Langlie. Outpolling all other candidates in the July primary led him to believe "that we are at last fighting on even ground." On October 30, the *Post-Intelligencer* noted the governor had yet to speak for himself. The turnout swelled from 46.3 percent to 84.5 percent in the general election, still a milestone. In 1940, Langlie had split King County with Dill. Wallgren's advantage was now 22,283 as the GOP's share east of the Cascades fell by a quarter. Dewey lost Washington to FDR by 125,000 votes; Langlie to Wallgren by 28,230.[37]

Langlie spent the rest of the war as staff officer to the commandant of the Fourteenth Naval District in Hawaii and at Norfolk. Then, while senior partner of Langlie, Todd, and Nickell took half of the next 28 months renewing Republican contacts and coaching the Deweyites who captured the state convention in 1948. "Strengthen the Party" was the imperative theme of the primary tour. The "Langlie for Governor Clubs" were to be ancillary. "He has lost his Cincinnatus accent," the *Spokane Spokesman-Review* exulted.[38] The ex-governor's conviction and clarity had their appeal and after three years in the wilderness he knew "no one can afford to run for office on his record alone." Langlie was both more politic and aggressive. Twenty "points and arguments" contrasted conditions before and after 1945. Mon Wallgren defeated himself. His defensiveness and indiscretions and those of aides made charges of "financial irresponsibility" and "mismanagement" believable. "Dave Beck made a marvelous whipping boy," Fred Baker exclaimed, and the electrical workers and the building trades "really backed Langlie."[39] He ruled out a "Little Taft-Hartley act for the state" and raged at "Beck domination," drawing in longshoremen and Boeing Aero Mechanics being muscled by the Teamsters. In the absence of the straight party ballot of 1944, Franklin Roosevelt, and the adverse reaction of conservative Democrats to the WOAPU, Langlie got a second chance. His plurality of 21,714 was again equal to his King County margin.

## Federal Dominion, Damage Control, and the "Baby Boomers": 1949–57

To the surprise of many, there was no postwar recession. World War II in Washington "merely lengthened into the Cold War." But the state was now the junior partner. In 1938, the federal government had 15,520 employees in the state, in 1945, 100,359. The military bases shrank by 1950, but with Boeing's B-52 bomber and weapons systems and its successful gamble on the "707," transportation equipment [aircraft] displaced lumbering as the state's most important industry. Federal largesse flowed instead into private contracts for massive new dams on the Columbia River. Jobs lost to farm mechanization were redeemed by reclaiming 200,000 acres of the Columbia Basin between 1951 and 1955 and by agricultural subsidies. Low-cost suburban mortgages and the interstate highway system kept construction booming. Employers and the workforce doubled to 46,680 and 450,000; payrolls quadrupled to $1.9 billion. In 1955, 59 percent of Washington's workers were unionized, the second highest in the nation. Regular raises, Beck's jostling, the diversification of the economy to exporting and white-collar tasks, and his "neutrality" spared Langlie the wrath of a United Labor Lobby.[40]

Financing the social legislation by which President Harry Truman's "Fair Deal" fulfilled the New Deal was possible because of the war-resuscitated economy. Congress's dictation of state "matching money" for all major "welfare" programs and initiatives absorbed Langlie's last two terms as chief executive. Votes for old-age pensions in 1940s, I-141 metamorphosed into single-interest campaigns for veterans' bonuses, liquor by the drink, and the Old Age Pension Union's repeated attempts to expand welfare.

Langlie knew "the state needed … a heart and a head. It must be both progressive and solvent."[41] Claiming in the 1948 campaign that revenues would be adequate if waste were eliminated, he engaged in the necessary quadrennial ruse to pacify voters who believe it. Cutting "off at the pockets every political leach who today is sucking the life blood of our school children, or our aged, or the imperiled drivers of our highways … [will] save $12 million a year." This was campaign code for countering the Pension Union's successful new Initiative 172, which pushed the state into the red another $55 million.[42] Reelected, the governor advocated a 2 percent flat income tax — as a two-year "emergency" measure. "I am not asking you to take what is normally a fair share of the responsibility. I want you to know I am willing to carry that … I do this … rather than take responsibility for; … further development of disgraceful conditions in our schools and institutions and our failure to meet our obligations to the aged," he told the legislators.[43] Republicans on senate rules reported the bill out as a personal favor; House Democrats killed it 41 to 58 — with just four Republican "ayes." The 1949 legislature walked away March 8, leaving a $73 million hole. Its refusal to take responsibility over the next eight years is chargeable to conservative GOP and Eastern Washington Democratic senators opposed to personal or corporate income taxes and others who, like Senate Majority Leader Albert Rosellini, voted "nay" on partisan rather than philosophical grounds. House Majority Democrats initially tied to avoid the issue by proposing a $100 million bond issue (to be paid over 30 years), and leaving the governor the blame for the necessary administrative excisions.

Langlie's "ratable reductions"[44] lowered welfare costs one-seventh. (More would be "unbearable and indefensible"). Roderic Olzendam, a tough Tacoma businessman, came down as director of Public Assistance to tackle "abuses." Denying the unqualified and overpaid, freezing wages, and reverting 10 percent of department budgets left $60 million uncovered, "a tough nut to crack." The State Democratic Central Committee's call for a special session was ignored; their legislators had refused the governor's call for taxes, and were likely spend more.[45] Faced with a 1951–53 deficit of $47 million he turned the tables on the legislature by offering three alternative budgets, a tactic repeated in the 1990s. Langlie's preferred version left Initiative 178 short $50 million and $34 million elsewhere unsupported — unless a four percent corporation tax was adopted. The carry-forward gap could be covered by having various state funds buy bonds.[46] The senate's conservatives again balked and the legislature adjourned. In "one of the most startling actions in executive-legislative history," Langlie vetoed the entire budget and reconvened the lawmakers.

When the corporation tax fell twice more in the Democratic House, despite strenuous lobbying by the governor's office, Langlie was indignant. It was "unrealistic and unfair to deceive the people" by making commitments and then denying services by "refusing to provide the revenue." The House married a one percent franchise tax and extension of the sales tax to liquor and hotel rentals that the Supreme Court predictably struck down for violating the constitutional stricture of one subject to a bill. At a second special session, a bipartisan group, acting under a "share the blame" agreement, bumped the business and occupations tax 20 percent and the governor, who had presided over the negotiations, declared the budget "approximately in balance."

Langlie continued to be longer on courage than the legislature. The largest displacement of state resources since Clarence Martin's underwriting of schools and social services had taken place as the result of initiatives. "Welfare" rolls rose 45.6 percent between 1939 and 1949 until 98 of every 1,000 people were receiving aid. In 1940, only 51 received similar aid. But by 1951–53 after repeated allotment raises by initiatives, the budget for the Department of Public Assistance was 43.3 percent of all outlays, twice what it would be 30 years later, more than the public schools' 40 percent, and the administrative load had nearly doubled. When Republican leaders waffled, the governor drafted Common Sense Welfare Initiative 178 and stumped the state in 1950 to end to the biennial assault by "guaranteeing" an indexed $60 floor. The son of an alcoholic father and a poor mother sold the initiative with a work ethic that gave "slackers" no slack.[47]

Welfare was no sooner under control than the World War II baby boom entered school. Canny and formidable Pearl Wanamaker, Superintendent of Public Instruction (1941–57), became the governor's gallstone. The last SPI able to coordinate teachers, principals, and superintendents exerted "extreme pressure" to press budget demands up to 40 percent in two years. Even she, in speaking out against federal aid to education and unionization as president of the NEA (1946–47), was falling behind her constituency. The debt-dogged governor argued that the state owed only the "fundamentals," the rest was to be left to local discretion. Thus began the "special (annual) levies that are a quarter of public school funds. Democratic cries for a graduated net were "futility at its worst." His contribution was to be property tax reform, five bills agreed to in his office to force appraisals from an average of 19 percent, to 30 percent of value.(Fifty percent was the ignored constitutional mandate). The threat to equalize or lose liquor profits was castrated, leaving local boards of assessment in charge.[48] When $10 million was taken from pensions to level a compromise budget the governor helped fashion, seniors flared and Langlie vetoed it entirely. He told Republican speaker Mort Frayn that the 1953 session was his most "disastrous"; the Speaker thought the call for a special session was "stupid."[49] There was not a single hand clap when the governor strode down the center aisle to open the session. The governor lost the battle for fair property taxes and won on the 1953–55 budget at the price of upsetting the leadership of his only Republican legislature. The 1955 Democratic edition awaited an amenable governor in 1957.

Denied the legislative offense, Langlie mounted an administrative one. The governor's Industry Utilization Committee diversified the wood products industry. Waste became pulp, paper, and allied products. He oversaw the joining of the American and Canadian natural gas pipeline. The Washington State World Trade Council evolved from a 1944 Langlie executive request, as did the nation's first State Board Against Discrimination in 1947, and the first driver training in schools. Transportation and public utilities regulation were merged into a Public Service Commission. House Democratic partisans and state officials blocked major reorganizations every two years.[50] All else was by executive order: re-imposing a merit system for departments under the executive's control, a personnel agency, industrial and traffic safety conferences, and an international trade fair to coax Pacific Rim nations to the Port of Seattle. Its exhibits attracted 3,000 buyers in three years. The governor backed tha 1955 bill and named Edward E. Carlson, executive vice president of Western International Hotels, to chair the state's first enterprise in collaboration with the private sector. This inspired the Seattle World's Fair of 1962. Seattle Center was born.[51]

## Way Stations to Conservation

The "renewable resource" concept behind the Clemons Tree Farm near Montesano Langlie dedicated in 1941, spread to 41 million acres across the nation by 1956. The 1949 legislature adopted the idea, set aside $100,000 for "Sustained Yield Forest Number 1," and made the governor chair of an implementing committee. The administration's Keep Washington Green campaigns lowered annual fire losses from 90,000 acres a year in the 1930s to 24,000 in 1952. But production and protection could not keep pace with ruinous clear-cutting and loggers' demand for replacement timber kept the state's commanding conservation issue at the forefront. The Olympic National Forest, created in 1905, was widened to 1,594,560 acres with the creation of Theodore Roosevelt's Mount Olympus National Monument in 1909. Half was put into the new national park by FDR in 1938. Langlie's "renewable resource" and "multi-use" mantras dovetailed with his peers and the U.S. Forest Service, the other half's protector and predator. The USFS's claim it had moved from a "custodial and protective type of task …to intensive management …on an integrated basis … [where no] use is permitted to the exclusion or disregard of other uses and values," was derided by ecologists.[52] In naming an Olympic National Park Review Committee in 1953, the governor set off furor not again seen until a federal judge blocked new incursions in favor of the spotted owl in the 1980s.

The survey was triggered by the peninsula's U.S. Representative Russell Mack, who wanted to turn large tracts of most suited timber back to the Forest Service and expected the committee to supply the rationale. The governor had protested President Truman's adding another 48,000 acres of oceanfront to the park in 1948 and plainly favored "multiple use," but was more interested in being "rid of" the endless controversy in a judicious way. His appointees, chaired by University of Washington Forestry dean Gordon Marckworth, were balanced, as was his convoking statement. Contrary to the "hues and cries," he was "not interested "in anyone's enrichment" and would "first to fight" it. He was for "the people …being able to harvest national resources to strengthen the economy of the state." Three hearings, 55 witnesses, and a tour of the disputed areas later the majority concluded, "In comparison with other American and Canadian national parks and monuments it is not too large, being only twelfth in size." Commercial interests had not "satisfactorily demonstrated" logging another 230,000 acres was critical to the peninsula's economy. Timber outside the park had been "underestimated by a fifth" and was "far in excess of any past or foreseeable demands." In a telling prelude to the environmental age, the WSFL, the CIO's Woodworkers, women's and garden clubs were as negative as outdoorsmen.[53] Langlie was not "rid of the issue."

## Ferries, Floating Bridges, Freeways

Neither Mon Wallgren nor Langlie wished to take over the antiquated Black Ball Ferry Line, the nation's largest ferry fleet. The number of voters dependent on them on the west side of the Sound by 1949 made it impossible to avoid. Once the Toll Bridge Authority was empowered to issue revenue bonds, Langlie moved to buy equipment and landing sites at key crossings to break Black Ball's monopoly. Captain Alex Peabody tried to capture traffic from the new bridge to the Olympic Peninsula at Agate Pass by buying property next door at Lofall. The governor then withheld state tidelands as terminal entries, appealed directly to stockholders, and had the Public Service Commission ask the company to "show cause" why it should not be regulated. The game was up in 1950, when his law put county-chartered ferries under state jurisdiction. The state was in the ferry business for $4.9 million, justified as necessary to develop the Olympic Peninsula. In fact, West Sounders had avoided paying market rates by having the system increasingly subsidized from gas taxes as an extension "highway system." Costs surged ahead of customers, rising 30 percent in 5 years. Fares stablilized, but the political liabilities remained. Users continued to complain that they were underserved and overcharged. In his 1952 campaign, Langlie prematurely unveiled a means of relief. "The world's finest bridge over salt water," Seattle to Bainbridge — could be built by 1958. Then parochialism reared its head, as Bremerton sought to be the destination. Bond houses doubted the bridge could pay for itself. Langlie filed the plans "for any future benefits that may accrue" and asked for $10 million to remodel the boats.[54]

Provincialism also stalled a second Lake Washington span. The Mount Baker neighborhood vigorously fought widening the I-90 right-of-way for the parallel bridge that consultants had recommended and the governor initially decided on. The Lake Washington Planning Association and Kirkland Mayor Al Leland wanted to link his city to Sandpoint via a tunnel under the naval base there for $20 million. Seattle's City Council and Mayor Allan Pomeroy agreed, so as not to offend, but North Capitol Hill and Laurelhurst neighborhoods protested bisection of the Arboretum. Langlie and Bellevue-oriented Eastsiders compromised on Evergreen Point to Montlake for $18 million, but he was out of time. Toll Bridge Authority would decide "as soon as we find out what Seattle officials want to do." In 1956, Gordon Clinton, a friend of Langlie's, became mayor. In a month, the TBA came down for Montlake. Langlie had made new enemies from the Kitsap Peninsula to Kirkland and across the Seattle hourglass.[55]

Langlie's triumphs in transportation came in the usual ways: administration, enforcement, and federal aid. In 1949, 52 percent of the state's highways were "deficient." The lawmakers pushed the gas tax from 5 to 6.5 cents and two years later a gubernatorial request for a $66 million bond issue passed. The administration's star was Highways Director William A. Bugge, who served Governor Rosellini and then built San Francisco's Bay Area Rapid Transit. His superb achievement was devising the criteria for "priority programming" and placing it under an independent highway commission, which all but ended pork barreling.[56] The difficulty of this conversion should be measured against the legislature's other enduring vice, redistricting, which was not turned over to a commission until the 1980s. In 1953, the traffic war on "heedless" drivers started by the governor and State Patrol chief James A. Pryde won national honors: 13 percent fewer drivers lost their lives and the death rate per 100 million miles traveled dropped 21 percent. It also angered those caught by State Patrol planes flying over the main arteries, by radar and unmarked cars, so much so that most of the latter were withdrawn. The public wanted safety — to the point of being caught.

Two more bond issues in 1951 and 1953 brought $84 million for highways more than in the previous 44 years. All but 40 miles of Highway 99 (I-5) were four-laned, Snoqualmie Pass (I-90) widened, and farm to market roads crisscrossed the Columbia Basin. Yet, Langlie knew building the proposed $194 million Seattle freeway from state gas tax revenues was "indulging in wishful thinking." President Eisenhower's massive national highways program funded most of it in 1956.[57] The "most impressive support" was from the governor and his peers, forced to confess the states unequal to the task. Critics misunderstood the president when he testified, "There is nothing in it regarding federal domination." States' needs edged ahead of states' rights.

## The Cameo Cold War: Canwell and "Communists"

As the Cold War heated up, domestic politics became nearly as combative as in the 1930s. Washington's cameo premonition of McCarthyism began in 1947 with the legislature's Joint Fact Finding Committee on Un-American Activities, also known as the "Canwell Committee." Hearings at the University of Washington led to dismissal of three professors and the publication of Edwin Guthman's Pulitzer Prize essays in the *Seattle Times*.[58] The governor contained his strong anti-Communist sentiments and kept a relatively low profile prior to 1952, simply concurring with university President Raymond B. Allen. The Canwell Committee's findings, gleaned by extra judicial procedures, were as unsophisticated as the denials of most of those subpoenaed, who were never proven more idealistic, if assiduous, fellow travelers. Canwell's claim to have "established that many of the Washington Pension Union leadership …was definitely Communist" is defensible. Representatives William Pennock and N. P. Atkinson, president of the WOAPU, did "mastermind" I-172, but it was not likely to break a state "acrawl with trained and iron disciplined Communists." On returning to power in 1949, House Democrats killed the committee with lingering the animus. When the vault on the first floor of the legislative building where the testimony was stored was opened in 1955, the tomb was empty. Canwell's evasiveness and quixotic paranoia when questioned by the speaker and the minority leader suggests he destroyed some data and failed to turn over or secreted other data, leaving the greatest unsolved mystery in the state's history.[59]

The Korean War (1950–53) and Russia's explosion of a hydrogen bomb in 1954 prompted Langlie to reactivate the State Defense Council. At his request, the violent overthrow of the government became a felony and the loyalty oath required of state employees was extended to teachers. The state now had a Department of Civil Defense and practice "walkouts" were staged in major cities, supposedly to minimize casualties from nuclear warheads arriving on missiles. Another exercise assumed the breaching of Grand Coulee Dam bringing a flood at Portland 38 feet above the seawall 40 hours later. Householders felt a fatalistic futility as they turned swimming pools into bomb shelters. The quick and uncontested relocations of 1941-42 seemed a simple solution to fright compared to the terrors of the new nuclear age.[60]

## Third Term Blights: Prisons, Pupils, Power, Presidential Politics

News releases and the byline "A Word from the Governor" in weeklies signaled a third-term try to "finish the job of straightening out the state financially." "We can only assume," the Olympia News snorted, "that he uses the term 'straightening out the state' in the same manner an undertaker speaks of 'straightening out' a corpse preparatory to a decent burial."[61] Langlie luckily drew liberal Seattle congressman Hugh B. Mitchell, who pledged "progress," not "negative impulses." Langlie countered, "Don't gamble on progress" by reverting to "Wallgrenism."[62] The public was so plainly on the governor's side on the WOAPU's new Initiative 184, a $75 dollar pension floor and full medical services, that Mitchell felt compelled to come out against it. His mild manners and rimless glasses left the impression of an intellectual in politics by accident. ADA activist aides turned off Magnuson and money, as Langlie conjured a prototype of the "confused intellectual liberals whom the Communists use so effectively. A 'blackout on decency,'" Mitchell spat. "I plead guilty, is it low," Langlie confessed in taping October television spots. "But I think playing footsie ...with subversive elements ... is just about as low as you can get." A stenographer noted, "Applause, yells, whistles, and stuff." Mitchell embodied the state's ills; he was a statist, not a statesman.[63]

Dwight Eisenhower was Mitchell's unshakable millstone. Langlie's King County chair kept his 292 delegates bound as a unit and 20 of 24 delegates to the Republican National Convention went for Ike. In Chicago, 23 of the 25 Republican governors signed a telegram to the national committee asking that disputed delegations be permitted to vote on other contested delegates (mainly Eisenhower's).[64] Senator Robert Taft's regulars could not keep credential committee's decisions from being referred to the convention. Langlie's amendment referred delegates who had not gotten a two-thirds confirmation vote by the panel to the floor. "The rule in the opinion of every Republican governor ...reflects the best standards of fair play." There was "no question" of favoritism, only of an open or closed operation by the committee or the convention. Governor Sherman Adams called the performance "compellingly effective." This test vote undid the illusion that Taft was in complete control. Three Californians who would be vice president then rounded up the waverers. Governor Earl Warren released his delegates. Senator Bill Knowland then cast a ringing 70 votes for Ike, not fast enough for Senator Richard Nixon. Washington's votes, cast by Langlie, sealed the nomination for Eisenhower. Governor Tom Dewey paved the way and the governors decided the fierce contest between Taft's regulars and Eisenhower's upstarts, at least two of whom wanted to be president, determined the GOP's future.[65] Illinois Governor Adlai Stevenson and Hugh Mitchell competed with an "internationally admired and nearly faultless hero." "Korea, Communism, and inflation," and a desire for change after two decades of Democratic presidents lay heavily on the Democrats. Langlie got 567,822 votes, Mitchell 510,675.

Third terms are generally unwise, even for the ablest of governors. The core of the unfinished agenda is bills that have failed for up to eight years. Allies are overexposed or gone, enemies accrue, weariness besets an administration's stars, and the "lame duck" syndrome sets in two years on, when cabinet members begin to leave for their next career. Langlie's attempts to meliorate conditions in the institutions characterize his legislative long suits, limits, and frustrations. He enticed Dr. Richard McGee to be the first professional penologist for the prison at Walla Walla in 1942, only to be plagued by Depression wages and war turnover. McGee quadrupled his salary to $10,000 a year in 1944 by going to California. In 1949, the superintendent of the Monroe Reformatory wrote, "Many guards are retired policemen, crippled loggers, ex-farmers, and men who are 'resting between jobs." A $20 million bond bill built 18 new buildings, but 10 percent of the institutions department's budget was regularly refunded to reduce the legislature's deficit budgets.[66]

## The Prisons Explode

The governor was in Scandinavia in August 1953 when a 300 prisoner riot killed an inmate, wounded three, and set fire to the machine shop, garage, and powerhouse at the Monroe Reformatory causing $1.5 million damage. In September, 800 rioters withstood three volleys of tear gas to set an imitative $465,000 fire at the penitentiary in Walla Walla. "It's going to take time to work the problem out," the governor conceded. Conditions had improved: salaries for guards had gone from $190 to $252 a month, the workweek reduced from six to five and a half days, and 92 percent of the inmates at the reformatory were employed. Still, the building contracts from a 1950 bond issue were not let until the spring of 1952. With two units to separate hardened cons, the riots could have been forestalled.[67]

The "dark outlook" of institutions in 1949 changed after a $20 million bond issue for buildings was spent on 50 new buildings at 13 locations. Accelerated treatment in mental health treatment under qualified administrators faced "almost 30 years of continuous deterioration." Outpatient services began in 1956. Langlie attracted professional penologists, got con bosses out of control of the institutions, occupied 90 percent of the prisoners, and eventually cut the staff workweek to 40 hours. Vocational training in a new minimum-security building at the penitentiary was a prelude to early parole. The legislature largely ignored Langlie's urgings on salaries and staff supervisors.

Prisoners do not vote and the pattern of improvement and setback and replacing directors every three years reflected the frustrations of having marginal resources. For instance, Dr. Thomas A. Harris, "The … [mental] hospital system came through troubled waters to a high peak of development in many respects," but it was never out of the danger of losing accreditation. In 1955, he estimated the cost of staffing the three mental hospitals "up to an effective level" at $300,000 a biennium. Harris was fired when his wife discovered infidelity with the governor's secretary and filed for divorce. The new couple left for California. Dr. Karl Menninger, brought in to consult in 1956, found the institutions "much above average, and surely among the best in the country." This spoke more to where they had come from and the mediocrity in "comparable to the rest of the Western states."[68]

## The Thirty Years War: The Columbia Valley Authority

Grand Coulee Dam was authorized in 1933 and the Northwest became "all-electric" after 1941. Many public power advocates thought the titanic struggle over whether to unify development, production and distribution of Columbia River power was over. "It is no longer a question of private versus public power. We are now on the threshold of a new era."[69] In fact, the culminating events began in 1944, with Hugh Mitchell's bill for a Columbia Valley Authority (CVA), modeled on the Tennessee Valley Authority. His ideological rectitude was as damaging as Langlie's illusions of state takeover: "Your position [that an unelected federal oligarchy would control Northwest power] is unrealistic and without any solid basis in fact," he abrasively wired the governor and the private utilities. "Real progressives," Langlie retorted, wanted to keep the federal government out of people's lives.[70] Labor, the Grange, the Farm Bureau, and Democratic officeholders were pro; four out of five groups in the Columbia Valley, six of the seven Northwest governors, and private power were opposed. The Army Corps of Engineers and the Bureau of Reclamation united behind the Corps' 308 Master Plan. The governors, led by Langlie, claimed it met their goals for full development and that local control should pass and be coordinated by the Columbia Basin Interagency Committee, a clearinghouse centering on the five major agencies involved.

The CVA was not an "un-American ideology." The Commerce Clause of the Constitution gives Congress control of navigable rivers. Mitchell's language did imply power greater than the Tennessee Valley Authority's and much greater than Congress had refused the Department of Reclamation. His revised bill met resistance to "remote control" by making three locals directors. Langlie's call for an interstate compact, payments in lieu of taxes for new dams, and a place for the states on the governing body would have compromised central direction. There was no middle way between the CVA and Congressman Walt Horan's self-funding "Columbia Basin Account."[71] Mitchell was out of Congress in 1953 when Dwight Eisenhower was inaugurated and even Langlie had to admit to a "recurrent lack of unanimity between federal agencies."[72]

As the struggle climaxed, Spokane's Washington Water Power (WWP) tried to take over Seattle's besieged Puget Sound Power and Light to get its credit. Langlie moved to insert a state power commission as arbiter but was out maneuvered in the 1951 session. Its aims were much larger. Holland Houston, the governor's power adviser, imagined the "the badly messed up" situation could be made right by the state's acquisition of all the PUDs and the Bonneville Power Administration's (BPA) distribution grid as well.[73] The State Power Commission (SPC) was sanctioned two years later, a curiosity born of circumstance. Low water and a severe power shortage lent credence to the idea the Northwest "could not safely rely upon the Federal government as the principal supplier of power." A statewide agency might aid the PUDs who carried "the primary responsibility" and "enable them to undertake … construction [that] … could not be [done] by a single agency." The SPC's "higher cost" steam plants (Houston's fetish) were still cheaper than contracted power. In order to get votes for an "operating" agency, three of the five board members had to represent the "publics." The Westside papers were sure Langlie had contributed some "splendid statesmanship" driving WWP off but did not see that now the PUDs were in the catbird seat. The commission had been made a eunuch. Congress had to approve the SPC was as "coordinator" of any excess power to sold to the SPC and integrated with steam electricity, or the use of the BPA's transmission network, all antithetical to the Washington's Democratic U.S. senators Warren Magnuson and Henry M. Jackson.[74]

The SPC met with the Pacific Northwest Governor's Power Policy Committee (chaired by Langlie), its effeminate predecessor the Columbia Basin Interagency Committee, and the Northwest (private) Utilities Conference Committee, for a "controllable agency … a blow for freedom from federal domination." The lie was given that the claim private versus public ownership was "not a primary consideration" but a yardstick for efficient performance … (an ironic inversion of FDR's argument for public power). In July 1952, the SPC moved to compete with the Grant County PUD in applying for a permit to build the Priest Rapids Dam — after preliminary engineering was underway. Langlie urged Congressman Thor Tollefson to block the PUD. It enlisted thirteen others. When the PUDs rejected the SPC's offer of joint application, he exploded, "The Democrats (i.e., PUD managers) are … only trying to obstruct the progress we are making by trying to take on something that is — and they know it — beyond them." This was "carrying the partnership principle too far."[75]

Persistence turned into folly. Olympia's Gerry Kuykendall, whom Langlie got appointed to the Federal Power Commission, was asked not to rule until an injunction against the SPC was cleared. Senators Magnuson and Jackson intervened and in October Magnuson announced the PUDs would be licensed. The governor urged the 1955 legislature to claim prior right. Lastly, the State Supreme Court forbid the commission from superseding the PUDs. Langlie was willing to collaborate with Houston insisting he "carry on to any extent to obtain proper development of the river."[76]

Eisenhower's natural resources speech in Seattle, October 10, 1952, proved the death knell of the CVA. Federal "empire building" and the "whole hog" theories of reclamation officials were to be supplanted by "partnership" among power producers — with minimal interference from the states. This, he gravely advised the National Governors' Conference at the Olympic Hotel in August 1953, or "we will not long retain the American system of government.[77] Pressed by Langlie, Undersecretary of the Interior Ralph Tudor equivocated. For sale signs were not on federal dams, unless "some responsible public body such as a state, comes in with a proposal … Such a proposal will be approached with an open mind." Washington Water Power's president Kinsey Robinson admitted, "We don't know yet what 'partnership' means."[78] It was never defined beyond the president's speech dedicating McNary Dam at Walla Walla in 1954, as projects "freely chosen by the citizens of each area, with the federal government drawn in as cooperating partner where this seems necessary or desirable."[79]

The CVA, the crown jewel of New Deal-Fair Deal public power ambitions and the only means of synchronizing the multiplicity of powerful and jealous agencies, was defeated by them as much as by the division between the Northwest's Republican governors and its Democratic congressmen. "Partnership" was a theory without substance in the name of federalism. The SPC, created to reassert local resourcefulness, blunted it, and might have expedited the demise of the privates. Relating Houston's first findings to Oregon's Governor McKay in 1949, Langlie was astonished to find "people were trying to mix politics and engineering. We found scores of people attempting ...evaluation in the field." He dwelt on "engineering facts" and ignored political ones.[80] Northwesterners, now addicted to federal largesse, also remained attached to "states' rights."

## Hells Canyon

The dramatic national clash was over a 742–foot "high head" dam at Hells Canyon on the Snake River or the three low dams proposed by the Idaho Power Company (IPC). The IPC's dams would cost $133 million versus $356 million and generate 783,000 kilowatts compared to 800,000. Why pay a price double Grand Coulee, Langlie asked, for half as much power? The "politicians' dam," a "monument to government error," was a "grandiose plan to direct water to California." A "high dam" controlling floods would have also wiped out one of America's two great canyons. "There will be no power shortage unless the people who believe that only the federal government should provide power take over," the governor gloated.[81] The tactical victory allowed Republicans to argue for "partnership." Congress could not be expected to invest more in the Pacific Northwest. The FPC licensed Idaho Power two days after congress' summer solstice began. Demand forced the public and private power warriors to a truce. President Kennedy's dedication of Ice Harbor Dam in 1960 can conveniently be taken as the end of the "Great Columbia Power War."

The demand for power directly conflicts with conserving salmon, the ultimate losers. By World War II, runs on the Columbia were one-fifth previous highs. Oregon and Washington gillnetters and Indian dip net fishermen caught 505,686 salmon on the Columbia in 1952, "the lowest production in the commercial fishery ever." Rehabilitation was a major Langlie goal. Five new salmon hatcheries redoubled the output of domestic fish after 1949, from 15 to 37 million, but could not offset damage done by turbines and the boatings of new legions of sport and commercial fishermen. His Fish Sanctuary Act limiting state sanctioned dams to 25 feet killed Tacoma's plans for a dam on the Cowlitz River at

Mossy Rock. The Federal Power Commission trumped "partnership" in licensing it and the state lost in court. Resentment in Thurston and Pierce counties forced the governor on television in 1953. He was uncertain what the answer was, except steam power. "The governor is ill-advised," the Tacoma News Tribune said bluntly.[82]

Pollution control, lately begun in 1942, split between the health, fish, and game departments, was combined under a commission in 1945. Industrial waste was slowly contained as urban pollutants became more pervasive. Of 188 pollution treatment plants, 126 were less than 8-years-old in 1956.[83] As early as 1941, Native Americans sued to gain half the catch guaranteed them under the Medicine Creek Treaty of 1854. The confirming opinion written by State Supreme Court Justice George Boldt (a Langlie appointee) has had a contradictory impacts. On one hand it affirmed the treaty. On the other, Judge Bolt's giving of half the allowable catch to the tribes put them in 'first position' and gave a disproportionate share of salmon to what was now a small portion of the population. What was the state's third largest resource is a shadow of its former self.

## Countering the Welfare State

Just one of his legislatures had a GOP majority and the 1953–55 Senate was held by just one vote and split between competing factions. The governor was denied his "large goals," the structural, tax, and welfare reforms, but showed more courage than the majorities who stymied him and made Langlie responsible for finding dollars the legislators spent without taxing. Every session the merit system failed, and in the end, just 3,200, a diminishing fraction of state employees, were covered by "executive order."

Langlie's advantage was being the only governor until then to enjoy continuous prosperity. Public school students rose 72 percent, dollars to them four times in constant value. In 1940, the income of old-age pensioners was 47 percent of average, in 1955, 58 percent. In 1941, $10 million was spent on 42,000 aged; in 1956, 20 percent more shared five times the assistance. Washington ranked third in aid to the blind, fourth in disability payments, fifth in old-age payments, and eleventh in aid to dependent children in 1955.[84]

In 1941, the governor had but three "personal assistants, his policy advisor, his alter ego, and an office manager." Given the stringencies of his Cincinnatus days and a defensive position, an "accounting" as opposed to the later "program management" approach is understandable.[85] Seven thousand people in 12 departments and 10 commissions were overseen with two small management divisions (Budget and in Institutions).[86] Washington state government was a shadow of its present self in the

1950s, but "flat and conservative"[87] only in comparison to the expansion of the federal "welfare state." Between 1941 and 1957, state outlays adjusted for inflation doubled and "state employees," half now teachers, trebled to 21,000. Realistic accounting, I-178, the death of the WOAPU due to the Cold War, revenue increases of 5 percent a year, modest inflation, and the absence of the spending synergy of the 1960s brought the budget into balance as Langlie left office. The Democratic legislative majorities, despite their proclivity for spending more than they took in, share credit for tackling problems of a different dimension with patronage staff and frozen salaries ($300 a month from 1941 to 1976).

Langlie's successes came from adept use of the executive's inherent power: "A true liberal is one who will accept new ideas and new thought — if they are practical." Much of what legislators initially ignored, like 1953's Little Hoover Commission proposals, the governor instituted administratively, then became statutory. He separated Institutions and General Administration by fiat when the Legislative Safety and Health Conference delayed. The ideas flowing out of the Governor's Annual Industrial Safety and Health Conference were adopted. He started the Council for the Aging Population, was first to embrace resource renewal, evolved an Air Pollution Control Division, and backed METRO (The Municipality of Metropolitan Seattle) and the cleanup of Lake Washington. The "most serious obstacle to the effective exercise of power," Langlie told the American Assembly "are the forces, which are trying, with remarkable success, to turn state government into … loosely-connected semi-autonomous bodies" — the rise of boards and commissions, some with earmarked or "dedicated funds," which grew to 350 in three decades. Given that the price of the state services were up 99 times in 50 years, they were "doing an amazing job in expanding their services."[87]

The governor's growing impediment was the impression that he saw his choices as, if not divinely inspired, immaculate conceptions. A quality "of religious influence created a blind spot that hampered his [otherwise sound] broad judgment." House Majority Leader George Kinnear warned him in 1949 that most GOP House members opposed an income tax and asked him to seek an alternative. The governor "promised" not to introduce it until he had conferred with leadership. When he did, the caucus voted unanimously to resist. Langlie condemned the leaders for failing to deliver in their presence. Kinnear retired to save his job, dignity, and avoid an open conflict. Leading Seattle civic and businessmen were invited down for their opinions, and "cut … off." "He sought the guidance of God … in making decisions, and, in his own mind … he felt he had received some answers. It was a serious weakness in a man who had outstanding ability beyond doubt."[88]

## 1956: The Voice of Political Conscience

The question of who would succeed turned into a quagmire as three allies, two from Tacoma, all Scandinavians, sought the GOP nomination. Attorney General Don Eastvold, 36, squandered national publicity at Chicago in 1952 on liquor and women, seducing a gubernatorial aide. As Langlie turned to five-term Congressman Thor Tollefson, also of Tacoma, Eastvold made a "critical analysis ... [of] failures of certain departments," and preliminary to a "substantial majority" of Langlie's appointees, 90 percent of whom had "out-lived their usefulness." Tollefson's $22,500 salary, seniority, and ambition to be a federal judge kept him on the fence. His Pierce County stalwarts were mad at the governor for "failing to deliver full support ... ." This left Lieutenant Governor Emmett Anderson of Tacoma. State Senator Al Rosellini, aided by Eastvold, relived his "crime investigations," talked against taxes, and on the "principal issue," the "continuation of the Langlie-Anderson administration."[89] It was no match.

U.S. Senator Warren Magnuson, whom Langlie named to Wallgren's place in 1944, lacked stiff opposition in 1950, until the governor drafted Seattle mortgage banker and civic icon Walter B. Williams. Langlie's radio tirade putting "the blood spilled in Korea" on the hands of "those who had condoned appeasement in the Far East" worked better against the Washington Commonwealth Federation. Magnuson deftly denounced socialized medicine, plumped for bipartisanship, and romped to victory.

In December 1954, Langlie was at the White House with 18 of the president's close associates for a stag dinner and was lured by promises of presidential help and patronage if he would take on Magnuson. "If I have my way I will not be running for public office again," he told the press and, after a breath, added, "I would do anything to support the President in his great work." Time thought no one more personified "Ike's kind of candidate."[90] Then the president had his summer 1955 heart attack and Langlie equivocated until February when the president said, "My answer will be positive." In Spokane the next day, Langlie said, "Eisenhower's decision will be my decision," then begged for 45 more days to deliberate. May 2, the *Post-Intelligencer* ran a feature article on his retirement; two hours later the governor announced that he could do no less than the president. With "fair breaks ...we can win," he wrote a $5,000 contributor, "but ... we will have terrific odds to overcome."[91]

At 55, Langlie was the GOP's senior governor, chair of the National Governors' Conference, and now keynoter for the Republican National

Convention. Ex-governor Frank Clement of Kentucky, also seeking a senate seat, spoke for Democrats. The "boy orator … a … dark-eyed, fast-talking, Bible-quoting, spellbinder" counterpunched the "earnest, hardworking, humorless" man who had "made a great point of publicly consulting his conscience."[92] Keynoters cannot be temperate men. "You Republicans," Clement cried hoarsely, "will not crucify the American farmer on a Republican cross of gold." "Oh, precious Lord, take our hand. Lead us on." Red Smith suggested stories start, "The Democratic party smote the Republicans tonight with the jawbone of an ass." The Republicans at San Francisco's Cow Palace had to lay to rest the idea the Democrats were the "party of the common man." Langlie argued they did not exist. "We reject the idea that any American is a 'common man.' No man is 'average' in the sight of God." He finished with the chosen themes, "peace, prosperity, power." The audience sat motionless for a split second. Chief choreographer George Murphy leapt from his seat and began applauding. So did the delegates — for 45 seconds. Langlie was a superb "speech talker," almost always speaking ad lib from notes.[93]

This was the apex and the end of Langlie's political career. Right to Work Initiative 198 fired a COPE [Labor's Committee on Political Education] voter registration drive and Langlie offended the right wing in opposing it. Beck was for Eisenhower and the Teamsters thanked him by staying neutral in an editorial. Magnuson finessed business as Langlie divided Labor. George Eastes "astounded" the governor when he led a delegation of nine major truckers into his office; Magnuson was their champion and the industry trailed them. There was no matching Magnuson's "visible power" and favors. Eastern Washington farmers, who were not sharing in the general prosperity, wanted the full parity the subsidies the Democrats promised. Magnuson's score on the conservative Farm Bureau's ten-core bills was perfect. Langlie had to admit Eisenhower's veto of the omnibus farm bill with its soil bank alternative was "not completely acceptable." Over 12 years he had signed over 100 farm bills, twice Martin and Wallgren, to no avail with those who now expected support.

The Magnuson-Langlie race was the nation's best test of the viability of the politics of the New Deal versus the potency of Modern Republicanism. Both were lawyers and Scandinavians. Rigorous, religious Langlie was sure of his own rectitude. Bachelor about town Magnuson, generous and pragmatic to the point of cynicism, overpowered with largesse. He had won every project sought for Washington and one-sixth of all public works funds. What Langlie called "the myth that is Magnuson" was even larger. He took credit for the National Cancer Research Institute, which begun in 1937 and was sponsored by 94 senators.[94] In the senator's dozen thick scrapbooks are thousands of news releases on deeds done for local communities. Langlie's billboards said, "High office demands high principle" versus "We're stronger with Magnuson." His maxim, the senator replied, ought to be "High principles, high interest, and low dams." The governor's personal attacks eroded his reputation for fairness. "We've got to get down in the gutter a little … how else can you bet a man who has been in so long and can claim so much seniority?" he asked a campaigner. Magnuson was "absolutely Hollywoodian, with guys, and dolls, and gangsters, an unsuccessful marriage and all the other elements of a cheap film production," made box office by press agentry and a strong staff.[95] The "voice of political conscience" did not draw like the "voice of political service."[96] Langlie's asset was Eisenhower, whom he introduced in Seattle on October 16 and on television the next day from Portland. "Operation Coattail" was ephemeral. Langlie carried San Juan County, the state's smallest and most Republican, in the primary. Magnuson got 61 percent of the vote in November. The one-fifth of Washingtonians dependent on federal jobs liked "Ike" — and pork.

Jefferson said, "We are all Republicans, we are all Federalists." This individualistic creed shrank in the desperation of the Depression and government benefits made Democrats the prevailing party. In 1952, Dwight Eisenhower affirmed, "Never again shall we allow a depression in the United States." Langlie and the president were emblematic of the moderate generation in between. For them, Christian morality demanded using the power of a limited government to both offset capitalism's excesses and, as Ronald Reagan later put it, keep a "safety net" under the needy. The 85-page testimonial to his 12 years in office that Langlie delivered to the 1957 legislature was a paean to federalism. Strong state and local governments were within "the comprehension of the people" and willingness to support them prevented "the accumulation of monopoly of … power in one place." Lincolnian self-reliance and avoidance of deficit spending, short of emergencies, rounded out his philosophic trilogy. The New Deal's vast relief program, then a military-industrial-complex, had wrought a second American political revolution. States' rights stances were now subordinate. States' duties meant taxes and, to many, federal money was, if not "free," a way to get more than one gave. Government dominance of the economy could not be reversed and soon accelerated. In telling the legislators "the purpose of Constitution was not to guarantee states' rights, but to secure human rights," Langlie encapsulated the history of his era and anticipated the one about to unfold.[97] By the late 1950s, a "cult of indifference to politics among educated Americans" was afflicting a newly affluent age. It was no milieu for politician with the disposition of a moralist.

Chapter 5

# Monrad C. Wallgren: Rising with the Tide

*(1945-49)*

### Two Tidal Waves

The Galveston flood of 1900, Mon Wallgren said, "washed my family right out of Texas and into Puget Sound." A 1914 graduate of the Washington School of Optometry, he enlisted in World War I, was commissioned as a reservist in the coastal artillery, then set up shop in his father's Everett jewelry store. Impressive in appearance, a forceful speaker, and a master storyteller popular at service and veterans' clubs, Wallgren was a source of local pride after winning the national amateur balk line billiards championship in 1929.[1] A second tidal wave, the New Deal swell of 1932, carried him into Congress from the Second District. Wallgren is the only person to hold the state's three highest offices — congressman, U.S. senator, and governor. It all happened to this scion of the New Deal in 12 years.

His sole memorable achievement in eight years in the House was triggering Washington's first enduring environmental clash over creation of "Mount Olympus National Park" in 1936. Timber men and conservative Democratic governor Clarence Martin wanted to cut old growth stands on the southern and westerly sides of the mountain and stalled the bill once out of committee. Wallgren's amended bill of 1938 excluded 140,000 acres in the Hoh, Queets, and Quillyute valleys, the choice fellable forest — and recreation areas — leaving 600,000 acres in the park. FDR toured the Olympics with Wallgren and then struck a compromise of 640,000 acres with the Forest Service and Martin, while keeping the upper hand. In December 1939, he added another 250,000 acres to the park — by proclamation.[2]

Appointed to a vacant U.S. Senate seat in early 1940, Wallgren rode in with Roosevelt in November.[3] Backing the president's preparations for war, in 1943 he introduced legislation transferring the Japanese relocation authority to the War Department to assure "vigorous military control." Two years later, he was "visibly perturbed" at letting any Nisei (American-born Japanese) come home until the war was over.[4] Wallgren's Alaska Fisheries Act extended exclusive American jurisdiction to 200 fathoms for "conservation." Forty years of over fishing were needed for the idea to become law.

## Echoing the New Deal

In 1944, Democratic strategy focused on Governor Arthur Langlie, the only Republican in state office. Seattle Congressman Warren Magnuson, the most popular congressman in 1942, again held back. Wallgren was pursued by his party, his only real cause. He hesitated, spending April 1944 at home testing the water. Finally, close friend Harry Truman, with whom he had toured with National Defense ["Truman"] Committee inspecting contracting, inserted his announcement for governor in the congressional record, claiming Washington had "no dynamic [postwar] program for aircraft, magnesium, or aluminum."

Wallgren ran because two years were left on his senate term, no chance was being taken, and certainly, "the people of this state will overwhelmingly vote to reelect Franklin Roosevelt." Privately, he was restless and unsatisfied; wife Mabe (Mabel) was homesick. Her allergies and arthritis needed the dry heat of their Soap Lake and Palm Desert haunts.[5] The issues were fighting "economic royalists" and who could best cooperate with FDR. Cheap, abundant electricity was the state's Aladdin's lamp. All Langlie had done was fight Roosevelt on behalf of the private utilities. The incumbent's postwar planning committee was an organization of national manufacturers who wanted to sell Eastern manufactured goods. He was trying to have Washington "secede from the union," a "do nothing" governor who had never been to D.C. for dollars. Coordination was essential for permanent industrial growth. "What this state needs Wallgren can get."[6]

Wallgren got 98,228 votes in the primary, the appealing governor 197,817. This lead and enthusiasm for presidential nominee Tom Dewey led Langlie to be one of nine governors broadcasting for the national ticket and to a partisan identity. "Little Arthur has finally thrown off his disguises," Wallgren mocked. "He ran for mayor as a Cincinnatus. He ran for governor as ... part Republican and part nonpartisan. Finally ... he ... stands revealed as a pure unadulterated Republican leagued with the big corporations, the big bankers. They are the Republican party. I will protect the little fellow."[7] The wartime primary was in July, doubling time for absentee ballots in the general election. Democratic strategists set up a "Non-Partisan Registration Committee" in every county with $10,000 from the Grange, Public Utility Districts, and the CIO. By mid-August, 50,000 servicemen had applied and 500 cards were coming every day. Secretary of State Belle Reeves saw their primary votes in Thurston County (Olympia) were 71 percent Democratic and advertised the new "soldier vote" law in every newspaper in the state. September became Service Vote Month. Wallgren remained at ease, telling a worried backer, "It is still too early for any intensive campaign to start"[8] In the first three weeks of October, 862,000 registrations came in.[9] In November, voting nearly doubled, to a still record 84.5 percent.

Republicans did better than break even east of the Cascades, but the turnout was 75 percent on the Western Slope. Washington was second in migrant war workers, who tended to vote straight Democratic. Few had known Langlie as mayor. In 1940, he had split King County with C. C. Dill. Now three quarters of Wallgren's narrow winning margin of 28,230 came from there.[10]

## Setting Up a Senate Succession

Wallgren's chief legacy as executive was adventitiously setting up the succession of Warren Magnuson and Henry Jackson to the senate. As 1945 closed, Washington seated two new U.S. senators in 45 days. In a generous last act, Langlie appointed Magnuson to U.S. Senator Homer Bone's seat as he left for the Ninth Circuit Court in San Francisco to give him seniority over the class of 1944. Wallgren's surprise appointment of Hugh B. Mitchell, his campaign manager in 1932 and administrative assistant since, made the mild, spectacled Dartmouth grad the youngest senator at 37, and stripped the governor of his intellect and organizer.[11] Mitchell fell in the Republican resurgence of 1946 to Tacoma's bizarre ex-mayor Harry Cain. Congressman Magnuson seized the same opportunity Wallgren had four years before and swept into the senate seat with the backing of the delegation, the advantages of incumbency, and a brief 21-day special election. Wallgren's Second District successor, Congressman Henry Jackson, beat Cain in 1952 and was a U.S. Senator for 31 years. Jackson focused on foreign policy; Magnuson became senate appropriations chair and a champion of domestic issues. Together they 'covered the waterfront' for three decades, becoming one of the most powerful pairs in the history of the body.[12] Magnuson was the senior member of the Senate when defeated in 1980.

## The Sometime Executive

Former governor Martin came in to shake Langlie's hand on January 9, 1945. The old administration left by the back entrance to the legislative building, as Wallgren was inaugurated with flags, formality, and martial music on the northern capitol steps before an over-coated crowd of 7,500.

Wallgren's prime asset was looking like a governor. Twelve years in a comfortably removed federal sinecure had left him plump, handsomely groomed, and grey haired, with a "round eupeptic face, unravaged and unilluminated ... he was a middle-aged man in high office by circumstance rather than force of character." He was unruffled as Langlie was intense, as habituated to life's pleasures as the ex-governor was to austerity. Above all, the *Seattle Times* observed, "He gives the impression he is sincerely seeking the right direction."[13] These were to be the kindest words of a hostile press. "Mon has gone back to the state to place himself in Purgatory," Magnuson had reported to Bone four days before Christmas.[14] Wallgren soon realized he was closer to the voters and the sedate life of U.S. Senator more comfortable than a governor's.

Partisanship hurt Wallgren. He had ignored Langlie's invitations to study the budget. The Democratic State Central Committee chair, with the governor-elect's concurrence, talked of a "complete house cleaning." State employees began leaving in wholesale lots. Wallgren assumed they were Republicans and were leaving to embarrass him. Langlie warned the custodial institutions (especially the mental hospitals and prisons), were at risk. On December 20, the new executive sent Bellingham radio station owner Rogan Jones, his dubious choice for budget director, to Olympia to say there would be no mass firings if Langlie's merit system worked. It had and inhibited Wallgren's reverse intent. For example, up until 1945 the vulnerable Liquor Board held nine-year terms. Wallgren eliminated them, making the members removable at his pleasure. The GOP 1947 legislature and Initiative 171 restored the terms; Langlie's merit system, effected by executive act, covered 2,964 persons in 1942, enclosed 3,284 or 10 percent more six years later, and left undisturbed, continued to tighten and professionalize its approach. Jones lasted ten months and left his department "in a terrific uproar."[15]

The governor's best managerial pick was prison warden Tom Smith. Soon the 450 men in 1887 "bucket" cells at Walla Walla were down to 150, cannery production tripled, and goals for ongoing work and education goals set.[16] A legislative committee recommended civil service for the boys' school at Chehalis and the girls' at Grand Mound. Politics still militated against the recruitment and retention of qualified staff.[17] The governor avoided detail and delegated too much to a cabinet separated as much by ability as ideology. Administrative Assistant Jack Gorrie, a former newspaperman with a congressional staffer's background, ran the office and wrote Wallgren's speeches. Three experienced advisors — former Speaker of the House Ed Reilly of Spokane, ex-State Patrol Chief Harry Huse, and Director of Conservation Art Garton — had less voice than the new head of the State Democratic Central Committee, left-leaning Jerry O'Connell, a former Montana congressman. He pressured Wallgren for patronage and half-convinced the governor a partisan fortress could be built. Others, tasting power for the first time, sought personal gain. Wallgren spent the first two weeks of his term hunting with ex-Land Commissioner "Progressive" Jack Taylor, the expedient head of the Division of Progress and Industry Development.

O'Connell's base dated from his days as a CIO-PAC organizer. They temperamentally clashed with the Teamsters' Dave Beck, the strongest influence in the administration once O'Connell left. Paul Revelle, director of the Teamsters Promotion League, became head of Transportation. Jack Ballew, the union's membership director handled personnel, then the budget. Clarence Shain opened his tenure at Highways by firing four supervisors with 25 years' experience and forcing his employees to switch from the A. F. of L.'s State, County, and Municipal Employees Union to the Teamsters. George Stuntz at Public Service and Don Clark at Game were especially able. Congressman Hugh Mitchell, Wallgren's former administrative aide visiting in April 1945, said he was "discouraged" by the cabinet's factionalism and lack of direction. The House Speaker George Yantis concurred. It was an "unsatisfactory condition … Wallgren seems to be making an awful lot of mistakes … and still some of the screwballs among [the cabinet] … are quite tickled since they think they are going to town."[18]

## The Legislature: Rejecting the Right, Flanked on the Left

Republican leaders who came to the governor's office to offer cooperation were told it would not be needed, even as the Democrats in each house warred with one another. With Martin and Langlie gone, the Left, who dominated the most liberal House Democratic Caucus in the history of the state, saw their main chance. O'Connell was their ubiquitous spokesman. Speaker Yantis banned O'Connell from his office after he bragged how the

Left got key committee chairs and forbade "the organization of goon squads in the House." O'Connell was soon invited to leave town, at the governor's nod.[19] The Commonwealth Federation, home to the Left since 1932, read the conservative trend of the 1944 elections and moved to disband the 3,500-member organization to show Democrats were "working together." Wallgren and the state's congressional Democrats applauded. But some of the left-most legislators were not to be stifled and threatened a new party if their demands were not met.

The governor was "astonished to have to plead with Democrats to be Democrats." O'Connell, "The Mad Russian with the Irish Name," still haunted him.[20] With the CIO's allies in the House and Beck's seconds in the administration, Labor took the offense. The largest lobby's main thrust, a "Little Wagner Act" fell short, but the nation's most liberal unemployment insurance passed. "There were times when I thought Labor ran a little bit too wild" Wallgren later conceded, and then shifted the subject to his eternal opposition to the Taft-Hartley Act.

Contrary to his two predecessors and to the envy of every governor, Wallgren was endowed with an unparalleled financial windfall. Revenues had doubled to $498 million in the four war years and in his four years jumped another 75 percent to $867 million. After the 1944 election, Wallgren naively said there were "too many employees." Directors were told to trim, but did not. Two weeks into the 1945 legislature, the governor canceled his message to a joint session and turned the budget over to them, suggesting 1943 pay levels, except for employees making under $200 a month. "I Don't Want Washington to be a penny-pinching state." The 26-year-old shipyard rigger chairing House Appropriations was happy to accommodate the second wish and write a budget with a 60 percent increase. After shearing in the Senate, education and institutions were up 36 percent and institutions 33 percent. Wallgren excised $3 million by vetoes, leaving it 29 percent out of balance *($85* of 290 million).[21]

Materials were now available and the huge capital budget for buildings and renovations, much of it bonded and paid for over 30 years, carried an extraordinary delegation of power to the governor. Langlie's postwar projects were lumped into a $103 million appropriation be allocated within six months of war's end by a five-man development board headed by Wallgren. Eighty-one million more was available to "match" anticipated federal grants. The WCF's Howard Costigan had come to Olympia as a "planner," but guidelines never emerged. Public works, schools, and colleges jammed with veterans and the Columbia Basin Reclamation Project got the most money. The pace quickened in the fall of 1946. In November, Wallgren and one other member approved a bloc of 35 projects, "subject to final approval by a quorum."[22] The fear of a faltering peacetime economy never materialized. Over 200,000 servicemen returned, 135,000 war jobs were lost, yet new unemployment peaked at 123,000 in 1946. Shipbuilding stayed up, Boeing equipped the airlines, and Columbia Basin exports and housing markets exploded.

## At Loggerheads with the Lobbies

Congressmen are lobbied. Wallgren found governors are pressured. The Washington Education Association (WEA) especially irked him. The WEA joined with PTAs and formidable Superintendent of Public Instruction Pearl Wanamaker as "The United School Forces" to raise teachers' pensions to $75 a month. When "non-certs" (support staff), just 70 of whom were eligible were included, Wallgren felt hoaxed and vetoed the bill. Wanamaker, formerly a Democratic state senator, felt sabotaged for being nonpartisan in 1944. Julia Butler Hansen, the legislature's most prominent woman, whose committee had molded the bill, turned hostile, comparing Wallgren to the miserly governor Roland Hartley: "I'm afraid the gentlemen who come down from Everett to become governors make pressure groups mandatory and inevitable." In a rift that reverberated statewide, O'Connell got the Democratic Central Committee in her Eighteenth District to deny her a place on the ticket. She ran as an "independent Democrat," won, and in two years was returned as Wahkiakum County chair.[23]

The governor salted the school forces' wounds by omitting pension reserves, endorsing bills by the Left to make the SPI and county superintendents partisan, and originating the school budget in a committee headed by him. "If we can get a hold on the schools," Pearl Wanamaker quoted O'Connell, "we can be in power 50 years." She and the PTA killed Wallgren's new State Timber Resources Board, which added the Land Commissioner's office as a second timber-selling agency, with Referendum 27. "Governors may come and governors may go," she said, "but education goes on forever." Under duress, Wallgren got $100,000 for a comprehensive education study and hinted at a special session for teachers in 1946. In August, he recanted: "As far as I'm concerned there were no mistakes made in the [1945] session, nor in my vetoes .... I stand squarely on my original position."[24]

## The Impasse over Empowering the Executive

The governor's vague eleven-page inaugural address identified opportunities, but gave no specifics. ("We must free small business from all red tape ... not absolutely essential ... a better retirement provision for the aged ... this state should go all out on a recreation and tourist program.") Belief in executive authority and in partisan control lay behind Wallgren's only substantive call, for constitutional revision to unsort the "hodge-podge growth of departmental authority," died aborning. The death of the session's longest bill, a rewrite of the insurance code, typified the agonies partisanship created for the governor and the Left. It lost after doubters vainly pleaded for a compromise boosting payments — and retaining civil service — which would foreclose shedding employees hired during the Martin and Langlie regimes. The Game Commission was among those made partisan, with terms reduced to four years. Sportsmen slew this with Referendum 26. Relationships with half the other statewide officials were unsettled. Land Commissioner Otto Case (D) argued for Referendum 27 — and recalling the governor. Attorney General Smith Troy (D) was uncertain about his relationship with the governor.[25] Liberal State Treasurer Russell Fluent split with Wallgren over office insurance and ran against him as a Progressive in 1948.

Twelve executive request bills did pass, including old age pensions and one dividing the Department of Public Service to create a Veteran's Department and a Division of Progress and Industry. The governor vetoed, in full or part, an extraordinary 48 of 310 bills, including the state takeover of Puget Sound ferries. He excised $15 million from the budget and asked department heads to revert 10 percent of their appropriations. Labor and Industries' Earle Anderson complained, "Many divisions, such as Industrial Relations, have been inoperative for twenty-five years." There was no safety program. Like peers, Anderson asked for $140,000 from the governor's contingency fund and got back $97,000. Wallgren suggested operating at a "deficiency within reason" and by September, the department had overspent the law by $18,000. In 1948, the three mental hospitals were overcrowded by 1,500 patients and as many more waited. Despite the pleas of Institutions Director Jack Ballew, the governor refused to commit to architectural fees in his 1949 budget, leaving the matter to the returning Langlie.[26]

Jerry O'Connell's partisanship and ineptness had alienated educators, sportsmen, and seven of eight other state officials and left Wallgren a legislative eunuch. Veterans were added as World War II was ending in August 1945. He doubted many were Republicans, but those who were GOP activists were told not to apply for state jobs, but wait for their own party to get back into power. This was altered to say he would "not appoint the chairman of the Republican State Central Committee, for instance ..." before leaving for the United Nations Conference in San Francisco. "Deplorable" stormed the commander of the Veterans of Foreign Wars. "No more callous statement has ever come out of the state capitol," the

*Post-Intelligencer* fumed.[27] To make amends, in September 1947, the governor advocated a veterans' bonus (earlier defeated in the legislature) but refused to name a sum. Any advantage he had with veterans was gone.

## The Republican Resurgence of 1946

Cyclical sentiment for "change" after 14 years of depression and war under the New and Fair deals and the return of prosperity begot President Harry Truman a Republican House in 1947. Wallgren's political unraveling was hastened by its Olympia counterpart, the onset of the Cold War, and the rise of anti-Communist sentiment. "Communist influence" was the GOP's refrain of choice; the Commonwealth Federation's new pension Initiative 157 the proof. Wallgren's reaction was to impose the rhetoric of the 1930s on the realities of the 1940s: "Anything keeping ... bankers and big businessmen from dictating to the nation ... the Republicans and my opponent call Communists." Other Democrats saw the WCF, especially since its leaders backed the 1940 Nazi-Soviet Pact, was a burden they could not bear. The Left pressed on, putting the outlaw of atomic weapons, rent and price controls, a state housing authority, and $100 teacher pensions in the state Democratic platform. Wallgren was unabashed, "To those who oppose our progress I say: We had an election last November [in 1944]. We won it. To the victor belongs the spoils."[28] In September 1946, he and five members of the cabinet campaigned for 26 days straight. Reality hit in November. The election of 38 new Republican representatives gave the GOP a 72 to 36 majority. Mitchell and all but one of the six Democratic congressmen lost.

O'Connell's office, the Executive Secretary of the State Democratic Central Committee, was "immediately abolished" and mainstreamer Earl Coe made Chairman. The senate's Republican minority cooperated with conservative Eastern Washington Democrats, an alliance that put the nominal majority in the minority for 20 years. Pandemonium reigned as Lieutenant Governor Vic Meyers, the presiding officer, gave "Majority" Leader Al Rosellini's parliamentary maneuvers free play, but the Senate blunted its liberals. In the House, the weakened Left often embarrassed the governor, which he as a partisan loyalist acting from the defense, now backed. He offered a two-year spending plan of $516 million and then divested himself of responsibility, expecting the worst of both allies and enemies. "I'm past the point of recommending. I'm sitting here ready to execute. The burden of writing the laws has shifted to the Republicans. I'll take care of the executive end."[29]

The new chair of the Revenue and Taxation Committee hired Langlie's budget director and started over. Twenty million in construction was erased, but twice that added to the operating side, leaving a $25 million deficit. The budget rose only 13 percent over 1945, and $117 million was left on the table. All three were records. The Republicans implicitly counted on reversions by Wallgren and new auditors to bring a "balance," a tactic that had been used to discomfit Langlie.[30] The GOP had kept the major controversies over labor and power in committee to avoid floor fights. After two hours with the PUDs, the attorney general and bankers, Wallgren blessed the public purchase of Puget Sound Power and Light (Initiative 166). Previously he had said the PUDs had "provoked distress"; now, "I don't want any question raised. I am a public power man." Republicans stalled the initiative. Wallgren later claimed to have "led western governors in urging self-liquidating (state) hydro projects" and in promoting a Columbia Valley Authority. In truth, he was not a player in either of the era's greatest debates.

## Lifestyle Liabilities

Once Hugh Mitchell was absorbed in his successful 1948 race for Congress, Wallgren lost advice superior to what he had in Olympia,[31] and an ever more hostile press tore into the governor's lifestyle and laxities. The GOP launched a Legislative Council of senior members with subpoena authority (something they valiantly resisted in 1943). Attuned to the security of times past, and insensitive to activity less tolerable to the public, the Governor supplied its agenda. The GOP had screamed vote buying when the eight Democratic legislators Wallgren put on state payrolls rose to 19 after the 1945 session. Wallgren responded that none of them should have to resign since no one in private sector had to do so to hold a public office.[32] Wallgren's chief assistant Jack Gorrie was president and Director of Conservation and Art Garton was secretary of the 800-member "Capitol Club." Formed for "entertainment" in July 1945, it collected $18,000 in "voluntary job insurance" from state employees in 18 months. Two treasurers testified there was "no solicitation." Having department heads collect and personnel chiefs forward the funds was motivation enough. The Legislative Council discovered the only regular activity in which all the members participated was the monthly payment of dues. The press scoffed at the governor's explanation this was common practice and a necessary supplement of his maintenance allowance. When Langlie made it standard fare for hecklers, Wallgren responded irritably, "There isn't such a thing. I told the boys to cut it out two years ago."[33]

The lifestyle at the mansion changed overnight in 1945. Legislators came for drinks and pool in the basement. The governor reciprocated by playing an organ over the rotunda at noon, highlighting the fine acoustics of the Legislative Building. But after Labor Day, when the press photographed him sailing into Victoria Harbor on the "governor's yacht," the questions began to stick. Restoration of the "fisheries patrol boat" had cost $45,000, including inlaid teak and an electric toilet. Upkeep for the *Olympus* came from commercial fishing licenses and thus cost the public nothing the governor insisted. President Truman's picture, taken on board and published in the world's newspapers, was worth the expense of the boat. "The governor does not waste money," he told a Thurston County Democratic picnic. "Any expenditures were appropriated by a Republican legislature."[34] There was "not going to be anything cheap or infamous about this administration." As in his congressional days, Wallgren's diligence was questioned. His 400 days out of Olympia in four years hit print.

Dollars from the sale of his Everett home in 1947 made him the second largest shareholder in KIRO, the state's most profitable radio station. The 1948 purchase of a lot "just twelve miles from Washington State's winter capitol in Palm Springs," as the *Post-Intelligencer* sardonically described it, could not have been timed worse.[35] The governor was becoming removed from his roots.

## From the "Wets" to Dry Falls

Ladeling out liquor licenses, failure to reconstruct the Tacoma Narrows Bridge, the decay of state parks, and a ferry crisis brought the press to full cry. Promoting his liquor-by-the-drink referendum in 1945, Wallgren populistically argued the poor should have the privileges of those joining a private club. Stymied by conservatives and rural dry Democrats in the House, he withdrew the bill and told the Liquor Control Board to liberalize club licensing to an "open door" policy. The Legislative Council cited Wallgren for issuing more licenses than Martin and Langlie had in twelve years, over 300. Middleman attorneys were paid from $8 to $244. The council was "satisfied" most of the clubs in Seattle, who denied having slot machines, lied, were not nonprofit, and had abnormal earnings.[36] None were investigated. The Republican-led council canceled hearings scheduled through the 1948 primary, never calling a witness, preferring the malady to a cure. The Republicans wanted Wallgren to win; hoteliers drove the clubs out of business by initiative. They too could now sell booze — and food at cost.

The Tacoma Narrows suspension bridge fell into the sound in a windstorm on November 7, 1940. The administration's inability to finance its reconstruction or buy the Black Ball Ferry system overshadowed the 1947 legislature. Chief Engineer Clarence Shain of the

Toll Bridge Authority began rebuilding in the spring of 1946, speculating if a new bridge were open, doubled traffic would amortize its cost in 12 years. Wallgren found a proposed contract, insurance, and bond issue "controversial" and was "forced to do an about face."[37] Bellingham broadcaster Rogan Jones, his short-lived budget chief, had reappeared and asked Shain, now Director of Highways, to "enlarge" state's "standard clause" for underwriters so insurers would be eligible in proportion to the number of bridge bonds they bought. "This would require the business to be placed through me …" as had the Liquor Board's warehouses when he was finance director. To succeed, the deals must be made "on a most confidential basis."[38] Jones was named the Broker of Record.

In the fall, Bethlehem Pacific Steel was low bidder at $11.1 million, $2.8 million above engineer's estimates eight months earlier. But the bond market was flooded; there were no bids, and it was now debatable whether tolls could meet payments. Wallgren tried again after the Pierce County commissioners created a $1.5 million indemnity fund. In January 1948, the lowest bid was $13.59 million, there being no guarantee of steel. Senator Magnuson met with the RFC, but full coverage insurance was perquisite, which Jones had not delivered.[38] The insurance commissioner coerced Marsh-McLennan and Johnson and Higgins, who had been "importuned by many parties" but "could not accede to [Jones's] …ideas" until they agreed. Jones, who had been allowed to fail the state twice, got 40 percent of the commissions, and his two partners 30 percent each.[39]

The administration knew by November 1946 that the Black Ball ferries serving Puget Sound were losing money. The company asked the Toll Bridge Authority for a 30 percent rise in fares in February 1947, arguing it could no longer operate on 1937 rates without wartime volume. Director of Transportation Paul Revelle cautioned the governor current fares had upped autos and commuters 20 to 40 percent; a new boost meant 50 to 70 percent. Black Ball rejected a quiet state purchase offer and then got a "temporary" raise only by agreeing to bond the raise and refund it if rates were found "excessive." In July, the Toll Bridge Authority, chaired by the governor, rolled the new fares back by two-thirds, cutting the company's return on investment to 6.04 percent.[40] Captain Alex Peabody appealed, lost, and then asked Wallgren to lease the boats for a year. Refused, he tied them up for a week in February 1948. The dispute was public, with 20,000 riders upset and Wallgren stressed.

Every option was explored except the obvious one. "State operation is not the answer," Revelle advised. He was "half …or three-fourths of the way at an equitable settlement." The governor let it be known Henry Kaiser's shipyards could supply eight new ferries in six months, then backed away under protest from local builders. The state threatened Peabody when he contracted with the counties. Then the attorney general told a surprised governor he could condemn the system but doubted the gas tax could be used to pay the bonds.[41] Wallgren asked him to proceed, the maritime commission to run the ferries to relieve the "critical emergency," and the navy for a quick price on surplus sub chasers to run as "sea taxis." In April, the governor made a "verbal agreement" with a Portland firm for three steel hulls. "It is our intention to get into the ferry business. We are proceeding in an orderly manner."[42] As campaign filings neared in July, the King County commissioners rejected a Wallgren-endorsed $30 million solution by Gilman Consultants. Abandoning the Seattle-Winslow run for a floating bridge across the South Sound and one at Agate Pass was "a political ferry ride." The study, under wraps for a month, found ferry rates would have to go up another nine percent for the state to break even. Wallgren allowed "anything that will give the people temporary service is highly satisfactory."

Lieutenant Langlie had come down the ramp of an LST [Landing Ship, Tank] at Sandpoint Naval Air Station late in 1945 and back into politics. The senior partner of Langlie, Todd, and Nickel made clippings for his Olympia file, Lincoln Day speeches, and announced for governor in April 1948. He raged at a "cloak of secrecy" and buying the ferries in a seller's market. Langlie's idea of "good government," Wallgren retorted was "do-nothing government" and letting "corporations and private utilities" keep a stranglehold on the state's resources." "I thought we could be further along by this time," he conceded to a silent Kitsap Improvement Club in October. "In a couple of months we won't have any trouble."[43] Then the supreme court, responding to a Republican suit, found the 1949 legislature had to sanction condemnation. In that action, Captain Peabody's representative turned out to be Wallgren's personal lawyer. Attorney George Boldt, who settled First Narrows Bridge suits for Langlie by 1945, bought the ferries for the new governor and the state in 1949.

The administration was lax. Parks Director Tom Martin exited early in 1948, saying the state's outdoor facilities were a "rundown lot of places, dying of dry rot." Jerry O'Connell had made the "great bulk of the employees … patronage men who spend their time the year around campaigning." In May of 1948, Vic Meyers's favorite park, Sun Lakes, had a payroll of $56,563; the 71 other state parks $11,005. Wallgren, who had named the rascally Meyers chair of the Development Board, once more called on Earl Coe to make things more "businesslike."[44]

## Isms, Schisms, Egos: The Campaign of 1948

After the 1946 debacle, Coe, as state Democratic chair, and Mitchell, as idea man, struggled to rebuild the party and engage state employees. But the Left departed to Vice President Henry Wallace's Progressives after a show of strength at the morale-shaking 1948 state Democratic convention. To Wallgren's embarrassment, the Resolutions Committee's report for an "uninstructed" delegation (not committed to President Truman) got 199 votes. He assured Democrats there were no Communists in the party, or reason for the surging red scare.[45] Langlie conjured "an army of subversive termites swarming about the Capitol." The legislature's Subversive Activities Investigating Committee tagged O'Connell, focal point of the schism as president of the King County Young Democrats and now Executive Director of the Wallace for President Club,[46] and the Progressive slate, featuring WCF doctrinaires Russell Fluent, Senator Tom Rabbitt, and Representative William Pennock.

Clarence Martin bankrolled Wallgren in 1944, hoping to replace him in the Senate. The ex-governor filed on the last day, taking conservative Democrats and much of Eastern Washington, while pleading for Republican votes, as he had in 1940, to "insure good government no matter who wins in November." Martin's censure of "loose methods" reinforced "the feeling all is not well in Olympia." His binding of Beck to a "morally bad" axis "loaded with power politics and all the evils that go hand in hand with machine politics,"[47] set Langlie's stage. Martin's 89,890 votes and Wallgren's 165,775 at least kept the Democratic primary totals above Republicans'.

The executive of the State Labor Council had endorsed Langlie in 1944, saying Wallgren had "two more years to serve (in the Senate)." The defeat, two years later, of 17-year president James Taylor squelched the heresy, despite a strong complement of vociferous Langlie admirers. Dave Beck's attempt to install his man compounded Wallgren's anguish. State Republicans saw their opening, hired a Labor Relations director, urged a "Bill of Rights" for Labor, devised Initiative 160, raised workmen's compensation, and passed compulsory state disability insurance in 1947, while the Left bruised the entrepreneurial Teamsters chief's ego. If "the damnable policy of personalities" by senior Democrats to the detriment of the Teamsters did not stop, he wrote Senator Magnuson, "the quicker we get the hell out of the Democratic party, the better off we are." Understandings would be concrete in the future, or the Teamsters posture would change.[48] The governor, who once waited an hour in Beck's outer office,[49] mollified Beck by making him a university regent. Beck haters were offended at his new prominence and the Teamsters assault on the aeromechanics at Boeing kept Labor's rank and file at odds. "Do you want a Dave Beck dominated governor?" Langlie asked countless crowds.

It took offending statewide officers, interest groups, Democratic and Labor schisms, managerial gaffes, and a wiser opponent to put Wallgren at risk. His indiscretions and a defensive, flaccid campaign evened the playing field. Carelessly candid, he admitted in 1946 to "periods when I've been downhearted, when I've said I would never run again." Reporters' pens scratched and his staff agonized as he roamed from texts. Jack Gorrie, through whom news was to be released, was seen waving a white handkerchief in the background. The press rumored that Wallgren was "unhappy" in his job, would join Truman's cabinet, or face Democratic rivals forced a reelection announcement in October 1947. Simultaneously, the governor said he would accept a vice presidential nod, but soon renounced the idea. He could not afford to be vice president at $15,000 a year, with "Congress looking down my neck."[49]

Wallgren launched his campaign in Chelan and Okanogan counties in mid-August in a sound truck given by Labor and Industries employees. The themes were New Deal activism versus Republican reaction: Langlie's 20-point agenda meant nothing, for he had done nothing when he had the chance. "Touchy" in Spokane, Wallgren decried the investigations, defended the number of state employees, and laid the furor over Sun Lakes State Park to the press. "The editors were just dumb, or …they are trying to fool the public." His administration was "as clean, or cleaner" than Langlie's. A press release proclaimed, "We have done more, built more, served more, and spent more. We owe less … have more cash on hand." Wallgren seemed unable to make a flat claim, saying, "My record is as good or better than that of any other governor not because mine is so good but because the others were so bad."[45] "It was only a 50 percent effort," Hugh Mitchell lamented on hearing his ideas read hurriedly and without practice. "No man can win elections with half-hearted-poorly done radio speeches."[50]

FDR was dead, and the straight party ballot abolished by the 1947 legislature. Sportsmen and educators' animosity emerged in successful referenda to prevent the abolition of the Game Commission and over changing control of school lands. The GOP slate was the best in two decades. Moderate Speaker Herb Hamblen, running for lieutenant governor, helped Langlie in Spokane, where he was weakest. Presidential nominee Tom Dewey dwelt on good government and his running mate, California Governor Earl Warren, cited record amounts for reclamation from the Eightieth Congress to offset Truman's claim that Republicans were "saboteurs of the West." After Beck's Teamsters crossed the machinists' picket lines at Boeing just before the election, polls put the top races even.[51] Reversing 1944, Wallgren lost by 29,000 votes. "Do you know what beat me?" he queried the *United Press'* Leroy Hittle at lunch the next day. "Langlie's last minute ad referring to me as 'Beck's bad boy.'[51] You know Stub" [Nelson], he told the *P-I's* political writer with characteristic candor, "a fellow can get into more trouble in one day in Olympia than he can in a year in Washington D.C."[52]

## Wallgren as Executive

The man who found security without success as a congressman enjoyed neither as an executive. His partisan troubles stemmed from "wild-eye leftists" and "disloyal" associates as much as Republicans. Former representative Robert Waldron, House floor leader in 1945, said, "Mon Wallgren is the worst Democratic governor we have ever had." The *Times'* Ross Cunningham knew him to be a "truly generous and gregarious" man, "who [under pressure from the Left] had become rather conservative on money matters." Charlie Hodde, the soon-to-be Democratic speaker, appraised him an affable nonentity who "never understood the State's government." He "could have picked some of his department heads at random and done as well." Jack Gorrie reasoned he rose too fast.[52] In an unheard-of vote, the Senate Armed Services Committee tabled the president's nomination of his former colleague to chair the National Security Resources Board. Senator Harry Cain led the opposition; Senator Magnuson backed the PUD's Frank Stewart and Virginia's redoubtable Harry Byrd told the Senate the ex-senator was unprepared. Gorrie, who stood in for Wallgren at his hearings, because "Mon couldn't answer the questions," took the NSRB job in 1953.[53] Truman then named Wallgren to the Federal Power Commission. He left in 1951 after serving as chair. The ex-governor was fatally injured directing traffic while tending to a lady motorist's flat on Highway 99 at the Nisqually Bridge in May, 1961.

Chapter 6

# The Ambidextrous Albert D. Rosellini

*(1957-65)*

## Immigrants' Son

The dark-haired son of Italian immigrants John and Annunziata Rosellini was unlike his Scandinavian contemporaries. After his fling in the Klondike, John was joined by brothers Victor and Frank at the Marconi grocery store and saloon at Sixteenth and Broadway in Tacoma. Prohibition forced the family to Seattle in 1917. They lived above John's Restaurant at Second and James, a ringside seat to see the city's doughboys marching to WWI. In two years, the Rosellinis were back in Tacoma. Beginning at nine as a paperboy, Albert "swamped out" floors, delivered for two drugstores, washed dishes, and worked in a door factory and a cannery by the time he graduated from Stadium High in 1927. He played soccer and tennis and boxed, after John leased a gym where world middleweight champion Freddie Steele and Jack Dempsey trained.

Bright and driven, Rosellini decided on the law, transferring from the University of Puget Sound to the University of Washington as a sophomore. The Depression struck, and by 1930, his oldest sister was the only family member working. Loans from her, butchering 12 hours for $7 on Saturdays, two janitorial jobs, and a stint in the Merchant Marine carried him through law school in 1933, at age 23. He kept doing collections from the library of a small firm in the Northern Life [now Seattle] Tower. Rent was $25 a month, income $125.

In 1932, he helped one of the lawyers, Ed Cochrane, win a House seat in Kent during the Roosevelt sweep. Winter found him lobbying at Olympia for the Puget Sound Pilotage Commission on behalf of a girlfriend's father, a pilot. Court referred criminal defense cases took only part-time, and in 1934, he joined the Young Men's Democratic Club. Urged by its liberal faction, Rosellini registered at the home of a girlfriend in the Rainier Valley's ethnic Thirty-third District, but he lost to the county Democratic chair, Senator "Tiger" Jim Murphy, by 120 votes. Warren Magnuson, the Democratic nominee for prosecutor, was impressed by the 24-year-old and made Rosellini one of his four assistants on his first day in office. He won convictions in all but three of fifty-four jury trials.[1]

## The Legislature: The Art of the Maneuver

In 1936, another colleague, Ed Henry,[2] was elected to the House and urged Rosellini to try again. The poor he had counseled from the prosecutor's office remembered. Murphy was dead, and he "out campaigned" the better known John L. O'Brien for the Senate.[3] Rosellini carefully "observed" during the 1939 session, except for a controversial Unfair Practices Act preventing loss leaders on behalf of the smaller Associated Grocers and prevailed in a constitutional challenge in the Supreme Court. Just six of the forty-six senators were Republicans, but they were soon in "majority" with Governor Martin's allies, led by Earl Maxwell and Joe Drumheller, who assumed leadership. As the 1941 session neared, Rosellini proposed each party caucus elect its leaders, as did Congress, denying Langlie the traditional right to name the majority leader in the Senate, regardless of party, beginning an enmity between the two psychological opposites. Judson Shorett made the motion, then nominated him as floor leader.[4] He was in fact Minority Leader in the Senate most of the 16 years he was nominally "Majority Leader" and, according to Democratic Speaker Charlie Hodde, "gave the impression at times that he liked it."[5] Never eloquent, Rosellini was a facilitator more than an agenda setter, an instinctive nose counter, always a parliamentarian on the attack, and a master of the artifice. Washington State Federation of Labor president Joe Davis had him get a vocational education bill out of Rules Committee. "If we don't get this out for them, none of us will ever be back here," Rosellini told the committee, only to vote against it on the floor. "You never asked me to vote for it," he lamely told Davis.[6]

Never an ideologue, Rosellini's early dalliance with the Left, with whom he soon broke, was driven by the need to side with the majority of the "majority" to attain leadership. His chosen closest associates, a record of voting against nearly all taxes as a legislator, and resistance to new revenue as governor suggest his motives were ambition, combined with an immigrant son's belief in "opportunity." Criticized later by liberals for lack of a program, he described his general position as "liberal," adding, "I guess being liberal means spending more money."[7] Rosellini had a classic and not uncommon case of a temperament at odds with his upbringing and the times. The tenor and equivocal course of his administration suggests he might, under different circumstances, have been a Republican.

Clarence Martin might be gone, but his admirers had elected Arthur Langlie, and the ex-governor's coalition inhibiting Olympia's New Dealers remained. Liberals were outraged and argued the ballots of otherwise straight ticket New Deal voters who had written in Langlie in 1940 were bogus. Rosellini, at his most partisan, moved in a joint session to refuse to seat the new governor pending an investigation. "Freshwater" Ed Reilly, the Speaker from Spokane, still smarting over Governor Martin's primary loss, quashed the motion two to one, but Rosellini's assertiveness appealed to most senate Democrats.

The war-harried 1941 legislature passed a $5 per diem (expense money) for members. Attorney Harold Shefelman was retained by Rosellini and paid by a $5 a head collection to defend it in the supreme court. Fearing cost and competition, Langlie and medical professionals delayed Rosellini's 1943 bill for medical and dental schools at the University of Washington until 1945. He "bashed" Langlie at every opportunity, even calling his farewell address a "humble attempt to justify the mistakes of his administration."[8] Republicans swept the House in 1946 and the Senate fell to a 23 to 23 tie. Several Democratic senators disillusioned with Rosellini's partisan tactics and others from east of the Cascades crossed over on crucial votes, leaving him to lead the "Futile Fifteen" and intensely frustrated.

An embarrassing *Post-Intelligencer* series on licensing "bottle clubs" told of profits for a few attorneys, including Rosellini. Bob Cummings its political editor, drinking in "Committee Room X" (a lounge for members and the press supplied with lobbyist liquor), asked Rosellini how he liked the morning article. Cummings lost four teeth and ran from the room bleeding.[9] As majority leader, Rosellini was vice chair of the Legislative Council in 1951-53, when Shefelman was hired to revamp the code-bureau system of 1921. They ran into a stone wall of elected officials. Langlie's merit system, forestry management, and Department of Administration bills were allowed to leave the Senate after he appointed a 35-member Citizens Advisory Committee, diluting any potential credit. Twenty House

Republicans had deserted fearing for the "separation of power." "The Governor is very disappointed in what we did to his program," Rosellini wrote Congressman Magnuson, "we stopped some vicious legislation, and ... enacted several good measures for which the Democrats can take credit." As committee chair, he fought the changes and sidelined them in 1953 by debating each in detail. In the special session, they again died in the House and, in 1955, on partisan House votes. "The theory ... that you're taking politics out of government ... [by boards and commissions] is ridiculous." Rosellini later said, "Government is politics, you can't take politics out of government."[10] As governor, he would seek realignments and suffer the same fate. Partisanship is the most frequent enemy of reform.

## 1952

The coming of television made investigative panels a preferred technique for a run at higher office. After a secret probe found "organized crime" in October 1951, Rosellini chaired a "Little Kefauver Committee," whose hearings were "sensational" for the time. Tolerance of gambling, bookmaking, prostitution, and police paybacks surfaced in Vancouver, Tacoma, and Seattle. The parade of madams, card sharks, and a hooded addict slowed business to where the Seattle Chamber of Commerce called, asking when he would be through.[11] "It is hard to pinpoint results," *The Christian Science Monitor* wrote, but Vancouver got a new city manager, Tacoma a new police chief, and the aspiring governor "tremendous exposure."[12]

Rosellini started from "scratch" and acted as his own manager, barnstorming the state on a flatbed truck with a country band, and "shook more hands than any ten candidates." Liberal Hugh Mitchell, who had by now served two terms in Congress, enjoyed the backing of Democratic regulars and prevailed. But the Cold War was seething; Rosellini labeled Mitchell a "Trojan horse" leftist, tied him to the Americans for Democratic Action, and laid the groundwork for Langlie's third term. Rosellini paid his $40,000 debt out of legal fees over the next three years and managed best friend Hugh Rosellini's (no relation) second and successful try for the supreme court in 1954. "If you can make it, it's probably an indication that the name's being accepted ... and I'll try again in 1956."[13]

The Eisenhower tide of 1952 kept five of the seven congressional seats Republican and left just 14 regular Democrats in the State Senate. Rosellini harassed green Lieutenant Governor Emmett Anderson and the Republicans' divided leadership of conservative Neil Hoff and Langlie's ally Tom Hall, who when they came to a consensus in caucus, were abused and outmaneuvered on the floor. Their disarray was evident in the inquiry into the reformatory and prison riots in the summer of 1953, headed by Rosellini and Hoff. Sixteen bills emerged, with Rosellini co-sponsoring many. The now minority leader gained so much publicity that in 1955 the Republicans tried to keep him off the Legislative Council. They managed to thwart reopening the search for the "lost" Canwell Un-American Activities Committee's papers — with the help of three hostile Democrats. Otherwise, Rosellini kept a "low profile" in the Senate, being "careful to not make any serious mistakes leading up to the election in 1956."[14] The 50 to 49 Democratic House sent proposals they knew the 24 Republicans and 22 Democrats in the Senate would turn down.

Lacking mandates, both parties were setting a record for 1956. Langlie deferred, except for favoring an early House vote to unveil an income tax duly killed by the Senate. Rosellini admitted one was not possible and bore down on branding Langlie as "the most extravagant governor in the history of the state," taking it from $32 million in the black in 1949 to $40 million in the red in 1955. The "bipartisan approach" Rosellini called for as governor was not to be found.[15] Langlie opted for the "minimum necessary," trimming his totals to $40 million below 1951-53. Giving school districts 25 to 75 percent of their budgets "penalized the dutiful ... immobilizing initiative" he argued, in trying to force realistic assessments of local property taxes to help pay for education. Rosellini ignored the means, a seven-man Board of Equalization, and kept calling for an income tax. He asked that $134 million for education be expanded to $169 million, challenged the constitutionality of the special session, and had the Senate move for impeachment proceedings. The senate's internecine wars, combined with Speaker Mort Frayn's pique over the extra session's taking of $7.5 million in teacher pension funds isolated Langlie. All but two of the 440 new laws in the state's most mediocre session were remedial or about minor groups. One banned hunting with a bow and arrow while drunk.

## Tenacity and the Main Chance: 1956

In 1956, Langlie found Attorney General Don Eastvold, his heir apparent, was having an affair with his receptionist and swung the nomination to a colorless clubman, Lieutenant Governor Emmett Anderson, a Republican Mon Wallgren. The embittered attorney general gave insider information on Langlie's campaign to Rosellini, who tied the defenseless Anderson to 12 years of "Langlieism."[16] The street fighter carried by 100,000 votes, despite Ike's reelection. As the first Catholic to become governor, he was four years ahead of John Kennedy's ascension in the "Other Washington."

Rosellini knew Olympia better than any incoming governor but had given little thought to a cabinet: "If it's a choice between a pure expert and an administrator, I'll take an administrator." Warren Bishop, plucked from the University of Washington's Institute for Public Affairs, was his credible chief of staff *and* [italics supplied] budget director, and the governor's "best decision." Lacking a budget or support from Langlie, Bishop and a secretary worked out of the office of the gentlemanly Secretary of State Earl Coe, who went to Natural Resources. Versatile speaker-cum-troubleshooter Charlie Hodde turned the General Administration's Purchasing Division and the Tax Commission around. Dr. Bernard Bucove at Health and Dwayne Kreager at the new Department of Commerce and Economic Development were exceptionally qualified. Half the cabinet members served in more than one post and met weekly with the press invited. For that reason, the meetings were discussions of alternatives, not to set policy. In 1960, the Office of the Governor was still just 12 people — two professional assistants, seven secretaries, an account clerk, a new "press secretary," and a lawyer. Shrewd attorney Max Nicolai, a grey eminence in the legislative building for 25 years, drafted alternatives, speeches, vetoes, and screened judicial appointments.[17]

## Institutions: From Warehousing to Treatment

Rosellini's inaugural speech stressed Institutions, the governor's signal attainment.[18] A nine-month search netted the administration's superstar. Director of Institutions Dr. Garrett Heyns, 65, had earned a national reputation in Michigan. Mental outpatient clinics, a children's ward at Western State Hospital, conversion of Fort Worden for truant boys, a new maximum-security wing at Walla Walla, more space at Lakeland Village and Rainier Schools for the mentally disabled, and an alcoholic rehabilitation department passed. The first diagnostic center for adults at Tacoma, a corrections screening center at Shelton, honor and forestry camps, conversion of Seattle's Firlands Sanitarium, Yakima's school for the retarded, and doubling of child guidance centers followed.

Heyns found 40 percent of the non-supervisory positions and half of medical and psychiatric positions empty because of low pay.[19] Forty percent of the 430 caseworkers in Public Assistance had rotated in a year. A one-step pay increase in March began the road up for state employees. The National Council on Crime and Delinquency analyzed the parole board, and California's Fred Finsley was brought in as executive director to reinforce professionalism. Heyns intensified in-service training in the institutions, raised morale, lowering resistance to change.[20] The 1880s "bucket cells" at Walla Walla, whose effluent flowed in a trough by the kitchen, were vacated. Idleness for lack of work training fell from 50 to 20 percent. Institution's legislative agenda peaked in 1959 at 14 items, from chaplains to the handling of felons under age 16. Staffing at Western State Hospital (Steilacoom) for the mentally ill was up by half; there were 1,000 new beds. New drug therapies and shorter, more intensive treatment freed more space. The lowest rate of juvenile parole violations in the nation testified to the success of rehabilitation and renewal.[21]

## A Contractor's Camelot

The 1957 inaugural was long on "transition": an atomic energy advisory group, multipurpose dams (and an end to the SPC), air pollution controls, annual legislative sessions, "reorganization," and civil rights legislation. Kindergartens and salary boosts for institutions raised his budget by only $50 million and there was no mention of new revenue. Debt had been paid down and the supreme court's sanction of funding the 1949 veterans' bonus by a cigarette tax meant the constitution's unrealistic $200,000 General Fund debt limit could be skirted by paying bonds over 30 years with minor "nuisance" taxes.

Federal highway aid burgeoned under Eisenhower. Rosellini went from his installation to chair the Toll Bridge Authority, which ended the ten-year debate over placement of a second Lake Washington Bridge. The engineers' advice to build at Evergreen Point could be taken, knowing the Federals would pay for 90 percent of it and interstate construction under the Highway Act of 1956. The economic slack tide of 1957 quickly turned into a full one and credit and favorable external events allowed Rosellini to realize aspirations while avoiding major taxation.[22]

The governor's attempt at fiscal oversight and thus more control over the Highway Commission ran into a bipartisan wall, but a signal advance in transportation was under way. "Priority Programming" replaced legislative log rolling (vote trades between legislators) as a means of allocating highway money. Highways director Bill Bugge, the Langlie cabinet's genius and the redoubtable Julia Butler Hansen, House Highways chair, buttressed the new governor's "broader" approach. He lambasted Eisenhower's 1.5 cent gas tax as "an example of the federal government exercising the prerogatives of the states," but three years later pressed for its continuance. The state stayed among the top five takers, which included building the Tacoma to Everett and Spokane freeways, four-laning I-5 from Seattle to Olympia, commencing the North Cross State Highway, and building the Vernita, Biggs Rapid, and Astoria-Megler bridges across the Columbia – a total 724 miles of interstate highway.

The first floating bridge on tidal waters spanned Hood Canal after a questionable engineering faux pas caused several sections to sink.[23] Freeways and the Evergreen Point Bridge worsened ferry woes. Between 1951 — when the state took over the ferries — and 1957, volume rose 48 percent and capacity 7 percent. The fleet and terminals were in "generally good condition," but by the summer of 1956, all 21 vessels were running, leaving no spare boats. The governor's dream of a cross sound bridge was undone by a struggle between those who wanted Fauntleroy-Vashon or Bainbridge as the western terminus, which was as fierce a debate as Bellevue's need for and Seattle's resistance to a second Lake Washington Bridge. Rosellini had to give up when university president Henry Schmitz, chair of his study commission, reported in January 1961 that construction costs were racing ahead of potential tolls.[24] The route of his successors was taken: Seattle's Colman dock and ferries were enlarged.

## Labor: No Love Lost

The state, then second only to Michigan in unionization, had but one avowedly pro-labor governor — Mon Wallgren — between 1933 and 1993. No arena better illustrates Rosellini's essential conservatism and style. His 1956 promise to put someone from Labor on the University of Washington Board of Regents was easily met in John King. He fulfilled a pledge to the WSFL that he would appoint the director the Department of Labor and Industries from its ranks. Joe Davis, its third in command, was offered the job. The Teamsters balked. Not wanting to displease either camp, Rosellini equivocated, and "serious tension" developed. The governor appointed acting directors and later remembered no conflict.[25]

These events coincided with his "anguish" over the Teamsters' pleas for clemency for their West Coast vice president, Dave Beck, in prison for tax evasion, which Rosellini ultimately granted. In an unusual press release, Rosellini deprecated WSFL president Ed Weston as a "disgruntled child" and refused his request for a special session on unemployment compensation. Weston in turn scathed Labor and Industry's "muddled and confused" leadership and "widespread unhappiness with the … administration."[26] A 1959 executive request (HB 84), that fell short of Eisenhower's recommendations to Congress and the 1958 Democratic platform was only reluctantly backed by Labor, but disavowed when "emasculated" in committee in the House. It passed only after Rosellini went to the House Democratic caucus to plead "unity."

Rosellini did come down hard on Labor's greatest threat in two decades, the Right to Work initiatives of 1956 and 1958, which diverted both unions from a civil service initiative.[27] Labor had one party and no choice but to endorse Rosellini in 1960. Joe Davis, now WSFL president, closed some of Labor's divisions and raised pressure in creating the United Labor Lobby in 1957, which nominally encompassed the more conservative construction trades and the Teamsters. The ULL learned self-reliance. The 1961 session, "undoubtedly the most constructive … Labor has ever had," was assuaging, although Rosellini stood fast against collective bargaining for state employees. At the WSFL's 1962 conclave, the governor described himself as "a liberal Democrat and a friend of Labor," while being picketed by the Building Service Employees led by Jim Bender, the erratic head of the King County Labor Council. The irascible Bender erroneously assumed his state peers were trying to change the Democratic Party into the "Rosellini party" and put the governor on the "unfair" list. National AF of L president George Meany threatened to pull King County's charter after the governor's September $100 a plate dinner was picketed.

Davis seconded the crusade of Norm Schut, the canny executive director of the State Employees Union (The Washington Federation of State Employees), for inclusive civil service. Rosellini had to cancel the unbudgeted January 1957 pay raises the Langlie personnel board may have granted to embarrass him. He was now advised by the attorney general (on request), that the executive orders establishing merit were "questionable." Lack of uniformity was the pretext to "disestablish" them in February. Schut, who had heard him promise the transition would not "be … a device to replace veteran employees with political friends," then watched an estimated 5,000 jobs change hands in the first year and Rosellini's "inclusive" executive request for merit die in the House. By June, Schut was complaining of "acts of coercion," which, he diplomatically told the governor, were "without your knowledge or approval."

The incompetent business manager at Western State Hospital at Steilacoom was sentenced to five years for stealing 500 pairs of shoes, and jobs "were being filled from the outside." In mid-July Ben DiJulio, the governor's patronage operative agreed to merit, but then saw him and dropped a "target date."[28] DiJulio wrote Agriculture's Joe Dwyer, "We do not feel every candidate for state employment can be placed, but we do feel … it is necessary for the welfare of this administration to take care of some of our most deserving people." DiJulio's successor told Schut the "patronage side of politics is a healthy part of our two party system." Persons could be found who were qualified and "loyal."[29] Schut demanded a stop to the "wholesale firing of competent career people" in Labor and Industries to make room. Only 10 of 80 were for cause and 20 percent left to avoid being fired. Democratic officials confirmed the administration was stalling on a director to remove political holdovers.[30] On the last day of the year, the governor granted merit standing to Institutions employees

— but not to anyone employed prior to January. The patronage window was not to be closed until all possible changes were made.

The tension between the administration's desire to use time-honored patronage practices and shifting public attitudes grew and the room for maneuver narrowed. The Legislative Council bore down in 1958 with a bill for a statewide human resources system. The standards committee continued to tighten hiring methods for the governor controlled agencies and, in compliance with a 1959 act, issued a "Suggested Code of Ethics." The state employee's Norm Schut played along. The WSEA went on record in 1959 opposing collective bargaining in the public sector to "comply" with the governor's policy against it or union recognition. Rosellini was still stalling in March 1960 when the WSEA circulated Initiative 207 and voted to put the administration on the unfair list, leaving it to Schut's discretion. Its passage was part pyrrhic victory, locking in the administration's patronage, as well as ending a perennial headache for the executive.[31]

The governor reminded state employees that politics in the office and use of state equipment were illegal, and that nepotism must end — underlining it was a citizen's duty after hours. Simultaneously, directors were told to be available in summer of 1960 as mainstays in the reelection campaign. In 1958, a memo went out from central personnel requesting "a list of all state employees and their current mailing addresses." Barely camouflaged collection of "job insurance" continued. "We have received 500 tickets for distribution," Charlie Hodde reported in 1964, for a fundraiser that netted $22,000 between August and November. "I have underlined the names [on a state printout] that I feel did not respond with adequate effort."[32]

## Shadows of the Mind?

"Investigative reporting" by the *Seattle Times* and the *Post-Intelligencer* and a "whispering campaign" finally ended the practice. The Times uncovered the "DFR" ("Democrats for Rosellini") Fund. The largest contributors — as in the past — were estate appraisers doing business with the state.[33] It blitzed Rosellini for staying free at the New Washington and Olympic hotels 119 nights, which he explained as "partly business, partly political, and partly social," something Langlie had done at the Edmond Meany and Olympic. The two *Times* reporters who spent six weeks in the Department of Licenses found nothing awry, yet wrote 220 column inches on it. Ignoring the politician's mandate not to argue with "a man with a barrel of ink at his back," Rosellini counterattacked. The press had been "quite fair," except for the *Times'* "scheme to discredit the administration. I have no quarrel with some of the facts. But I do resent the insinuations and innuendo that I or my associates have done anything unusual or wrong." The "DFR Fund" compensated him for out of pocket expenses." Then he went on the offense: the *Times* had ignored the "misdeeds of the previous administration ... [although] they recognize the weakness of Republican candidates on issues. These expense funds are completely voluntary. The paper had never understood progress. I am extremely proud of the new look in Olympia. I will fight the *Times* every inch of the way."[34] His first point was well taken. The paper's crusade was led by editorialist Ross Cunningham, Langlie's first administrative assistant.

The *Times* could find "nothing particularly illegal," but five buyers purchased $50 million of supplies a month with no way of assessing needs, rules for competitive bidding, consolidation of bids, or adequate record keeping. This typified processes overdue for update. Director of General Administration Lloyd Nelson, whose previous experience was running an Edmonds drugstore, resigned and Charlie Hodde was sent in.[35] The findings of the John Donoho consultants of Baltimore were the basis of an executive request bill cleaning up what had long been a dubious operation.[36] This segued into the administration's third major achievement, comparable to the recreation of Institutions and its part in ending highways spoils. Donoho set out "best practices," and Warren Bishop defined and refined an inclusive Budget and Accounting Act predicated on "program" budgeting. The goals and a strategy were selected first and then dollar allocations applied to the priorities. Standard formulas were created for higher education (student support at the various levels, libraries, and capital investment), minimizing the chronic competition between the schools.

"The last [1957] legislature made 454 separate appropriations," the governor proudly noted, "the new structure will require only 220."[37] "We are going to balance the budget. We are going to wipe out most of the General Fund deficit. We are going to adopt the soundest tax program ... possible within the limits of the existing tax structure and constitutional framework." [That is, without an income tax, or major new levies.][38] The legislature raised the sales tax two-thirds of a cent, contingent on the outcome of a referendum on an income tax. "I never experienced such an adverse reaction," Rosellini remembered.[39] There was a flood of abusive mail and Republicans began taunting him as "Taxallini." He countered with a superfluous expenditure advisory council. To the governor's credit at the end of August 1960 the General Fund was temporarily in the black for the first time since January 1950.[40] He was now forced to withhold $22 million from the departments and the biennium still ended $44 million in the red.

## 1960: An Affirmation of Sorts

Rosellini polled his directors (25 Protestants, 7 Catholics, and a Unitarian) as late as September 1959, saying he was undecided on a second term. He had been campaigning for three months "as if the election were to be held day after tomorrow," and Luke Graham brought the Democratic Party to its highest state of readiness.[41] A testimonial dinner for the governor in early 1957 raised $100,000 and his base broadened; $17,000 came in for $1 memberships in the "Rosellini for Governor Club." When it became obvious former that Spokane state senator and current superintendent of Public Instruction Lloyd Andrews, 40, the only Republican holding statewide office, would be the GOP nominee, Rosellini traveled relentlessly in rural Eastern Washington. A GOP leader claimed, "Al has shaken every hand and crowned every hometown queen East of the mountains."

The *Seattle Argus* saw a "Hobson's choice." If there was any "provable evidence of dishonesty or graft," the editor would present it in the next issue. "Mr. Rosellini's trouble is that he manages to give the impression that things are rotten in Denmark." Patronage was "all important …the hangers on, the petty chiselers give the administration a bad odor and undo all the good resulting from top-level appointees."[42] Rosellini had defended the spoils system early on and ignored the 1959 ethics code forbidding gratuities.[43] The grist for a "whispering campaign" came from cases like Robert Long's. The co-owner of the Jacaranda restaurant (the Worlds Fair's House of Tomorrow barged to the Port of Olympia), claimed he paid $6,000 indirectly to the Rosellini campaign fund to get a liquor license.[44] A memo to directors at the outset of the second term spoke of ambiguity at the top. They were now "required to maintain a steady schedule of public appearances." The charge that "during the campaign some of the administrative work was slighted" stuck. There had been "loose talk about the operations of various departments." Two later executive memos warned use of state cars for politics was ground for dismissal. The governor may have been "too soft," but some had "let the administration down. I urge you to put great emphasis on honesty, integrity, morality and the capacity to do the job. Operations in the next four years of necessity will be tighter than the last four."[45]

Andrews was negative, his accomplishments few, and he was contradictory in out promising the governor.[46] Rosellini was too intense; his anger flaring in a televised debate. He overworked the word "reactionary" and tried to pass off the Hood Canal Bridge's come apart as a "Republican project." "Cronyism" charges were turned on the challenger and "Promises versus Performance" compared, beginning with Institutions. County Democratic organizations held "Kennedy-Rosellini" coffee hours. The governor was never as liberal, but was a convert for a graduated net income tax, collective bargaining for public employees, and a 9.5 percent teacher pay raise. His win by 17,865 of 1,214,446 votes was the narrowest since 1940. Five initiatives, including civil service, daylight saving time, and liquor-by-the-drink in taverns had raised the turnout to 82.3 percent, the highest since 1944, again making the difference.[47] John F. Kennedy lost to Richard Nixon in Washington but took the White House, dispelling the idea a Catholic could not win.

In January, the governor told the legislators, "the will of the people must prevail." Education was the only exception to holding the status quo, though he said to a writer, "we must have more money."[48] What was now unavoidable was best done sooner rather than later. He advocated an income tax peaking at four percent at $1,000 Adjusted Gross Income (after deductions) and lifting the sales tax on food and drugs. Business despised a 43 percent surtax on gross receipts, to be traded for 2 percent of their profits over 12.5 percent. Boeing bought in, but House Republicans denied the 59 Democrats of the two-thirds needed for the necessary constitutional referendum.[49] The result was the usual Band-Aid cuts and $24 million in small excise taxes.

## Caesarean Section: The Bewildering Birth of the Item Veto

Unbeknownst to the governor, the chair of the Senate Ways and Means Committee had introduced and passed a bill to raise state elected officials' salaries. Vetoing his own raise "was a smart political move."[50] The "item" veto, the ability to strike a word as easily as a paragraph, was affirmed by the supreme court. It was a major enhancement of executive power for a decade. Striking a "not" after a "shall" could turn a restrictive law into an affirmative one. Rosellini spent first two days of the 1961 session quietly encouraging legislators to override his veto![51]

## Natural Resources: From Ideology to Output

The birth of King County's METRO and enactment of the governor's Air Pollution Control Advisory panel told of advancing environmental pressures from urbanization. Langlie's fisheries director Milo Moore (a Democrat until 1964) was kept on. The hatchery program begun in 1945 was expanded, but emphasis over the next 20 years shifted to stream improvement and research to undo under management of the resource. Moore was upset when Republican fish biologists he employed were demoted, and fish farming turned into a "phase-out experimental program."[52] The governor's resource posture is best seen in his refusal to join Senator James Murray of Montana, who wanted to make almost all of Glacier National Park a "wilderness." Rosellini declared himself for multiple use and "historic policies." Fish, forests, and metals were made to be used.

The power conflict gave way to cooperation to meet compounding demand. The era of great dam building was ending as Rosellini's resolution against Idaho Power's three dams on the Snake died in committee in 1955. Washington and Oregon filed an amicus curiae with the National Hells Canyon Association against the FPC's approval of three low dams on the lower Snake, but the battle over placing a high one in Hells Canyon for flood control was over. The CVA was pronounced dead at the Western States Democratic Conference in Seattle in August 1962, where Girard "Jebbie" Davidson, President Truman's Western advocate, was general chair. Interest turned to the "new [atomic] process" and the power lobby's defeat of a reactor at Hanford.[53]

Competition with the federals over the Columbia turned to cooperation. New plants equal to a second Grand Coulee, a power intertie to send surpluses to California, and an agreement with Canada on upstream river storage were decided. Rosellini let the State Power Commission and the Northwest Governor's Power Policy Commission, which the PUD's saw as fronts for the privates, wither.[54] "For many years the greatest threat to our independent influence over the control of the Columbia has been the proposed Columbia Interstate Compact … one of the greatest menaces to the Public's well-being ever devised by special interest groups."[55] In the "Eisenhower" election of 1952, the GOP won control of both houses (25-21 and 58-41), but eight of the new Republican senators were from "PUD counties." They formed a coalition with 16 Democrats and locked up bills like HB 77, setting criteria for PUD condemnations, and SB 54, ending the use of eminent domain,[56] as Eisenhower's Federal Power Commission won a last round — three low dams on the Snake by the privates rather than the Hell's Canyon Dam.

But by 1959, 62 percent of Washington's power came from the 18 municipal plants, 21 coops, and 22 PUDs. Washington's ultimate hydroelectric potential of 23 million kilowatts (versus the TVA's 6.5 million) would be jointly developed and a peaceful use of the atom shared the load. Rosellini last met John F. Kennedy as he rededicated the world's largest nuclear plant at Hanford in 1963. Battelle took over management in 1964 when the governor's regulatory law on reprocessing was enacted and his Department of Commerce and Economics released its "Master Plan for the Development of … the State in the Nuclear and Space Age."[57]

## 1962: Fair Weather

The first eight months of 1962 were the governor's last pleasant ones. This was the last time there would be no even-year legislature. "Century 21," Seattle's cameo World's Fair came off as a tribute to local initiative, President Kennedy visited, and the Western States Democratic

Conference met in the Northwest's "Queen City."

Rosellini's contributions to social change were becoming visible. In 1941, Washington enacted equal pay for equal work. The 1947 legislature had set up the nation's first State Board Against Discrimination. In 1959, the governor got the Anti-alien Land Law prohibiting immigrants for owning homes repealed. Several blacks were appointed as managers and to commissions. In 1963, he established the nation's original Commission on the Status of Women by executive order and ordered his personnel director to promote regardless of sex.[58]

Civil rights unpleasantly came to the fore as he chaired the 1963 governors' conference in Miami. Republican presidential hopefuls Nelson Rockefeller, George Romney, and William Scranton represented states with large minority populations. They pressed for a two-thirds vote endorsing civil rights, to the disdain of George Wallace and Southern Democrats. Rosellini, who argued for a civil rights plank in the 1960 national platform, took a party-shielding stance on "Meet the Press." To have meaning, a nonbinding resolution must be unanimous. After fierce debate, the governors passed a "mild" one. He felt a civil rights act was overdue, "but we could not bind the other governors." Congress should adjudicate. [59]

## 1963: Bizarre Happenings, Bad Vibrations, and Blue Laws

Dan Evans's precocious 1957 cohort elected him House minority leader in 1961, and in two years, a new political era was gestating by another coalition. The wounds of Spokane Democrats who had lost the 1961 power fight (along with Washington Water Power) to Speaker John O'Brien's filibuster continued to fester. He was neutral as chair of the Democrats' 1962 Bellingham convention, but its left wing planks salted the wounds. January 14, 1963, O'Brien flushed in anger on the third roll call as the lead Republican, Dr. A. O. Adams, a physician, voted for Democrat Bill Day, a chiropractor. The legislature's best kept secret, a coalition of Evans's 48 Republicans and 8 Democrats was out. O'Brien was "absolutely wrathy" about the "unworkable" and "unholy" alliance. It was a "wrecking crew" the governor declaimed, "under right wing control. The real motive … was … to get me."[60]

The Rosellini agenda, his option for locally imposed gas tax surcharges in ten Puget Sound counties to relieve the state of ferry subsidies, a Puget Sound bridge, a Naches Pass Tunnel, carpooling, and liberalizing workmen's compensation were quickly frozen. A "constant tirade" by a pestiferous Legislative Council came back. Rosellini's startling post-session veto of appropriations for interim committees, unanimously upheld by the supreme court, jarred Republicans, but its intent was so obvious he was hurt more. The League of Women Voters knew Senate Majority Leader Bob Grieve killed the administration's public disclosure act after pulling its few teeth and had overridden their redistricting initiative. Grieve could no longer manipulate redistricting. Fearing a duel with Representative Slade Gorton, the coalition's floor leader in the House, Rosellini "quietly made sure" none passed, playing into Gorton's hands.[61]

The federal court threw out Grieve's alternative and made redrawing the first order of business for a 1964 special session. The bell began to toll. Untoward events cropped up. Adjutant General George Haskett fired six employees for trying to unionize the state guard's staff. The governor went on the King County Labor Council's "unfair" list, was picketed for six months, and then countermanded by his State Personnel Board, forcing an appeal to the supreme court. It found those in question were technically neither federal nor state employees, but the damage was done. After more "grief," national president George Meany told the council to take the governor off the "unfair" list, or he would pull their charter.

As a prosecutor, Rosellini had asked for the death penalty; while a defense lawyer, none of his clients had hung. As governor, he claimed he had "always ... a strong believer in capital punishment" as a deterrent and thought many so sentenced were unsafe and "useless to society." Several went to the gallows, several he commuted. Chester Self was on death row in Walla Walla for murdering an elderly Seattle widow in her laundry room. "This is a subject that cannot be disposed of quickly by simply saying, 'I'm for it,' or 'against it,'" the governor wrote Russ Barlow, listing three reasons for each view. Rosellini waited in his office for the warden's call at 11:30 pm, another a 11:55 pm (the warden did not believe in capital punishment), and finally for one at 12:05 am. He saw "no right to interfere unless there's ... mitigating circumstances."[62] Self was the last man executed in Washington until 1992.

The *Times* echoed Republicans' "smear tactics," implying the governor tolerated gambling, leading him to repeated denials. The legislature's new bill on the subject became law without his signature, but the issue would not die. When a referendum with 80,000 signatures disappeared over the weekend from the secretary of state's vault, "it kind of looked bad."[63] The Liquor Board was symptomatic of the incumbent's afflictions. Initiative 161 repealed the Washington Bone Dry Act in 1932, and in October 1933, Congress ended prohibition. The Steele Liquor Control Act of 1934 installed three commissioners as overseers; but vendors, franchises, and staffing stayed a staple of state politics for 35 years.

Hoteliers wrote themselves "Class H" licenses by Initiative 171 in 1948 to wipe out bar service in private clubs. It was written "tightly" to sell, and teetotaler Arthur Langlie's board got nine-year terms. Rosellini believed he should be able to name all boards and wanted to shorten its terms to six years. In 1957, after a bitter marathon debate before packed galleries, the Senate agreed.[64] Rosellini repeated he had no quarrel with the board and no wish to liberalize the law, but his ambivalence was evident. The scrupulous Don Abel became chair, but charges flew that Art Garton, the executive secretary and former Democratic state chair, ran the stores in a partisan and "liberal" way.

Rosellini wrote the board in 1959, insisting it was "autonomous" (with copies to the press), and that he wanted no new stores, a move so transparent it backfired. Republicans claimed his relatives and former business associates were franchised, bid records not kept, and of gross staff changes. In fact, Langlie's Evro Beckett had fired more, and nepotism and governor-endorsed special pleadings were few. The governor tried to lower his profile, yet refused an opinion on Sunday closing, only to see his silence "misinterpreted." If rumors of a "bad" appointment flared, the governor would name a surprise, like State Patrol Chief Roy Betlatch. His quick resignation, like Abel's, then Garland Sponburgh's, were "meaningless."[65]

A Republican senator, whose liquor store inspectors had been "harassed," gave the coalition the excuse to investigate. Rosellini's refusal to pay for the inquiry from his emergency fund "showed he had something to hide." Legislative Council Chair Bob Perry (D-Seattle) told a Goldwaterite: "Were not doing it to hurt you. We're doing it to 'get' the governor and embarrass the Democratic party."[66] Dan Evans predicted a major scandal: "There are affidavits," and inspectors were soliciting. Rosellini overreacted to the *Times,* charging it wanted to "control the governor's office to get a larger share of liquor advertising dollars." The probe was a "politically motivated conspiracy to turn the sale of liquor over to private hands." Consumption would rise without a state monopoly. Representative Perry backed away in May 1964, having achieved his objective. The governor protested too much.[67]

## 1964: "Saving the Republicans from Themselves"

Dan Evans had to be put in bed with Republican presidential nominee Barry Goldwater. Had he not voted against the 1961 memorial to Congress for Medicare and against repealing ratable reductions in public assistance grants to balance the budget and opposed burial despite color, creed, or race?"[68] Excoriating Evans and refuting allegations overshadowed holding the center. Evans, once outside his "blue-stocking" district, and no longer constrained as majority leader, rushed there. The governor left mixed messages as at the PTA convention: "reactionary forces" in the House would have prevailed had he not blocked "budgetary irresponsibility" instead of "preserving that absolute essential of good government — state solvency." Speaker Day and the Democratic renegades loudly disagreed.[69] Evans spoke extemporaneously; Rosellini was nervous on television and continued to drop his "g's", and used notes. ("Of course I have notes. It's the only way you can keep some people honest.") Anti-third-term sentiment and obsequiousness emerged: "Just call me Al … state employee." Experience was offered, and new blood sought.[70] Belatedly, the governor offered nine "specific proposals" to offset Evans' "Blueprint for Progress." Reducing "some taxes" to promote industry (like exempting new construction from the B&O tax), "stimulating" fees, guaranteeing school districts $7 a day per pupil, made easier by allowing *local* [emphasis added] special levies of up to 10 mils by majority vote for two years (instead of one) to avoid the need for any major surcharges.[71] A state "classification study" was underway as a base for "equal pay [for women] for equal work." The governor's Commission on the Status of Women (reporting on 4/7/64) recommended an "interdepartmental committee" examine practice. Reapportionment — in light of the defeat of the League of Women Voters', I-211, and the Supreme Court's edict on redistricting — was the first order of legislative business. An advisory council on Nuclear Energy and Radiation ("studies" had been underway since 1963) were belated bows to the future.

The generation gap opened wider as the professionally oriented Young Republicans of King County (virtually an Evans subsidiary), neared 1,000 members. Ensley Llewllyn, Director of Civil Defense and head of a Tacoma public relations agency running reelection campaigns since 1927, troubleshot and typified the governor's campaign staff. Grange executive George Prescott coordinated the campaign with the Governor's Office and headed the Political Speakers Bureau. Most of the congressional district leaders were departmental directors: General Haskett in the Third, Earl Coe in the Fourth, Agriculture Director Joe Dwyer for the Fifth, Charlie Hodde, and State Patrol Chief Roy Betlatch in Spokane. Senator Henry M. Jackson's vote was twice the governor's, the only statewide Democratic official to lose despite the Goldwater debacle. "I thought we should have a meeting of the cronies," he bitterly told the cabinet when they last met in November 1964. The man with the red rose in his lapel had survived three political generations.

## The Recovering Politician

Rosellini practiced law with Fred and James Dore. Having appointed a third of the state's judges, conflicts of interest arose in general practice. Instead, he represented national carriers, testifying before the ICC and FPC. Once Evans went "hog wild on expenditures" and created super agencies ("one of the biggest mistakes … ever"). The ex-governor began speaking and in 1968, when King County adopted home rule government, sought to be its first elected executive. Foiled by Evans's "machine" and a light March vote, he became "constantly critical." The failure of tax reform in 1971 was a "test of Evans' strength"; he should resign. "Spending reform" and attrition of some of the 30,000 new state staff since 1965 was a must.[72] Former Democratic chair Luke Graham advised it was too late to run for governor in 1972, as did old senate friends. State Senator Martin Durkan's chief of staff, Mike Lowry, had done so well a straw vote at the Young Democrats' convention went 200 for Durkan, 100 for State Senator Jim McDermott, and six for the ex-governor. After two months of temperature taking, Rosellini announced June 19.

A periodic tax revolt roiled the waters, and Durkan, the Senate Ways and Means chair, was made accomplice to Evans's profligacy. Devastating ads showed his "two faces." Rosellini outpolled both he and Evans in the primary. The Democrats' votes were nearly twice Evans',[73] whose bilious detractor on the right, State Senator Perry Woodall, endorsed the former governor. The *Times*' Ross Cunningham, a 50-year observer of gubernatorial donnybrooks, told Rosellini, "There's no way you can lose that election Al, unless you make some mistakes." Or, thought Rosellini, Evans "came up with some dirty tricks."[74] Evans, who had refused to debate him in 1964 and 1968, was now turned down. It was "understood" a student fair at North Seattle Community College was not to be a debate, but Evans began one, and with KOMO television's camera humming, Rosellini vented his spleen by calling him "Danny Boy" ("Something I should not have done.") "Was political revenge a motive?" the *Post-Intelligencer* asked. "I never thought of that."[75] Those affronted took a second look.

A week before the general election, the *P-I* and the *Times* front-paged Chief Deputy Attorney General Keith Dysart's accusation that Rosellini had called Honolulu's police on behalf of nightclub owner Frank Colacurcio, who was convicted a year before of importing gambling equipment. Rosellini's polls dropped 12 percent by the weekend. The Godfather was showing statewide: bumper stickers appeared saying, "Washington State does not need a Godfather." "If my name was Smith instead of Rosellini you wouldn't have a story," he angrily told the press. His credibility slipped again when his tax records for 1962, 1963, and 1964 were "missing." "Working papers" were promised; then his accountant issued a five-line summary. Next, Evans found Rosellini had sealed his papers in the State Archives for 20 years by executive order. Rosellini claimed he had not seen Colacurcio in the 30 years since defending him on a carnal knowledge charge. A younger brother had purchased a nightclub in Honolulu who was having trouble getting a license had made the "extremely devastating" request for help that "cost me the election." Evans survived by .07 percent.[76] The governor's calculating ways appeared to be a fatal obverse of Eagle Scout Evans.

## The Name of "The Rose"

The man with the rose in his lapel was a transitional figure as executive, an old-school partisan in politics, acculturated to be a "New Dealer," but philosophically closer to Eisenhower's America. At his best and worst he was as an administrator; he seated an able cabinet. He brought institutions and budgeting to the state of those arts. In the keenly felt arena of civil rights, Rosellini was a social precursor of the 1960s. He avoided a genuine civil service and tax reform but was overtaken by them. The governor urged much he had opposed as a partisan legislator, lest Langlie get credit. He was genuinely friendly, sharp of mind and memory, incredibly hardworking, and, after 16 years in the Senate, as knowledgeable as any peer. Rosellini was handicapped by a need for acceptance and consumed with being governor. Forty years after leaving the mansion, the nameplate on his desk, where he worked daily into his late '90s, said, "Governor Rosellini." The plates on his white Cadillac read "GOV."[77]

The other foot remained in the past: hangers-on, patronage, and a praised and delayed merit system. The administration was solid at the core, but ethically seeped at the seams. Payton Smith's sympathetic *Rosellini: Immigrant's Son and Progressive Governor* speaks of "moral neutrality" about questionable people. At 93, he delivered illegal checks to two Seattle City Council persons to press a parking rezone for a strip club owned by Frank Colacurcio and his son, who were his friends and convicted felons. Rosellini blew off "Strippergate" as "a lot of noise about nothing. Nothing occurred that's not part of the regular political system,"[78] or at least the one he had entered 40 years earlier. The compulsion to continue to be part of the action overrode discretion.

Risk aversion, especially to taxes, was the administration's chief limitation. In 1956, Rosellini knew the likely deficit for 1957-59 was $32 million but opposed an income tax or any new taxes for two years. The pretext was "analysis first" despite the 17 years of grappling with the system. He pressed the legislature for a balance, wiping out debt, and no taxes. Warren Bishop remembers it was "extremely painful" for the governor to tax. "He was willing to support the programs, but it was difficult for him to accept the consequences … responsibility for raising taxes." [79] "I think of the governors … during my lifetime," Rosellini confirmed. "I've probably been more fiscally conservative than anybody else."[80] The only governor to run for the office five times and lose three would have been the first to recover the office in the remarkable reprise of 1972 if, in Dan Evans' phrase, "the pendulum of politics" had not initiated a dynamic transition not seen since the New Deal.

Chapter 7

# Daniel J. Evans: Politics in the Blood

*(1965-77)*

## A Birthright Republican[1]

The Evans family was one of the few celebrating Washington's centennial in 1989 able to trace the westward movement, the frontier, and the urban west over five generations. Evans' great-grandfather D. B. Jackson left Maine in 1857, foundered in the California goldfields, and moved to Port Ludlow. By 1889, his Puget Sound and Alaska Steamship Company was prospering. His eldest daughter, Mae, wed Connecticut's George Evans, who arrived via Panama in 1878, as the Walla Walla convention was drafting a constitution. Their third son, Daniel L. Evans, born in Seattle in 1894 as its urban age began, retired in 1960 as King County engineer. Maternal grandfather Clarence was a state senator from Spokane in the Second and Third legislatures, managed U.S. Senator John L. Wilson's campaign in the legislature, and was a U.S. Marshall and collector of customs at Port Townsend. Daniel Jackson Evans' (1925- ) first memory of politics was his mother's shock at Hoover's loss to FDR in 1932. "I never thought about being anything else [but a Republican]. I would have been disowned."[2]

Dan grew up in Seattle's upscale Laurelhurst neighborhood and graduated from Roosevelt High School on a Friday in 1943. On Monday, he was at the University of Washington and in Navy officer training at 17. He was a radar officer on a carrier in the Pacific (1945-46) and on a destroyer in the Korean

War (1951-53), and near the Panmunjom peace table as an aide to Admiral Mendenhall. Evans got a Masters in civil engineering and went briefly into private practice as a structural engineer, becoming assistant manager of the Associated General Contractors, deepening his business contacts. He skied, hiked, went mountaineering, and joined the Jaycees. Asked by a neighbor if he wanted to be a delegate for conservative [U.S. Senator] Bob Taft for president at the county convention in 1948, Dan opted for still youthful former governor Harold Stassen, a moderate perennial.

Evans startled the county chairman by volunteering at headquarters in 1954. Two years later, he was chosen by the Forty-Third District Caucus to run for the seat of retiring House Speaker Mort Frayn, an Eisenhower Republican. Friends of 20 years uncovered in a reverse directory "doorbelled" Laurelhurst, Montlake, and the East side of the University District. Once nominated, he could not lose: the Forty Third had never elected a Democrat. Still, a journalist noted, his huge plurality pointed to "one of those extraordinary vote-getters who comes along occasionally."[3]

## Bridge Battles: Build It, and They Will Come

He and Rosellini immediately collided. Was the Second Lake Washington Bridge" to parallel the first Lacey Murrow span, or go down the "Montlake Cut" — the Lake Washington Ship Canal — dividing Evans' district? His first bill — on behalf of Montlakers, the Arboretum, and the City of Seattle — was backed by a consultant's report and "Eastside Commuters for a Parallel Span" (largely Mercer Island and Bellevue businessmen trying to co-opt Kirkland). Evans' argued paralleling would do less environmental damage, be easier to finance, and permit a third crossing from Sandpoint (a sop to Kirkland). Rosellini stood by his Highway Department engineers.

The House Highways Committee, chaired by the redoubtable Julia Butler Hansen, chose Evergreen Point to Montlake, with a fig leaf for Evans: if Mountlake proved impracticable, the Toll Bridge Authority would decide.[4] It appeared that 16,166 Eastsiders had prevailed over the Westside's 563,395 residents. Most people simply agreed with the *Seattle Argus*: it was "time to build a bridge." When the Seattle Chamber of Commerce refused to stand with him, Evans quietly gave up a role he had not played: "The time for appearing in the role of moderator has passed."[5] The price of the bridge doubled between 1953 and 1957 to $26 million, as Rosellini fumed, "I don't care where it's built." By 1959, federal highway money was flowing; the Evergreen passage was built, and paid its bonds in just 16 years.

## The "New Breed"

Next to his one-party district, Evans' good fortune was arriving in Olympia with the most talented class of legislators either party had elected.[6] Joel Pritchard (later state senator, First District congressman, and lieutenant governor), Charles Moriarity (later senate minority leader), James A. Anderson (later senate minority leader and chief justice), and Slade Gorton (house majority leader, attorney general, and U.S. senator), were roommates. In 1959, the GOP dropped to 33 (of 98) representatives, but in 1961 was back to 40, and elected Evans minority leader (21-15).

Legislative leaders adopt a second constituency, their caucus, which sometimes disagrees with their district.[7] Evans' conservative side was reinforced by his duty to reflect the GOP representatives. He endorsed a McCarthy-Age "loyalty oath" for state employees to protect against "Communist subversion." The Washington Education Association rated him eight times "right" and eleven "wrong," the major lapses being a graduated income tax and the supplemental (even year) budget. Democrats later made use of votes against administering medical care through the Social Security system, and holding relatives responsible for indigents.[8] But the first urban agenda was reaching critical mass and captured in legislation for METRO, merging King County's utility and bus systems, which he floor-managed. Evans voted for a landmark civil rights law, to remove the 40 percent turnout requirement for school levies, and OASI for teachers.[9]

The Democrats were fracturing over redistricting and a climactic fight between private and public power, and fell apart over the liberal platform adopted at their state convention in Bellingham in June 1962. The more conservative legislators walked out. Come January, there were 48 Republicans and 51 Democrats in the House. Speaker John O'Brien, who had presided at the convention, was to be elected to an unprecedented fifth term as speaker. Who the majority was in the Democratic Caucus remained in doubt. Dissidents had tied the "ironfisted speaker" on the first two ballots. His sequestering of a filibuster by amendment on the "Spokane Power Bill" meant to save private power by requiring a referendum on any condemnation by a PUD proved the last straw for Democratic "conservatives."[10] Representative Bob Perry (D-Seattle) approached Slade Gorton about a coalition, sealed at a remote house in the woods of the Cooper Point Peninsula. Republicans were to get half the committee chairmanships and sway over the Constitutions and Elections and Rules committees through which redistricting must pass. The best-kept legislative secret came out on the third ballot for speaker when Dr. A. A. Adams a Spokane physician, voted for Bill Day (D-Spokane) a chiropractor. In electing Day, eight Democrats took the GOP out of the minority for the first time in 10 years, and gave Evans visibility as the new majority leader. The "Evans cohort" had a forum.[11]

The conspicuous feature of the 1963 session was the coalition's cohesion. Setting the agenda, the essence of the Evans style surfaced. The freewheeling discussions with his roommates led to a seven-man "policy committee" integrating those beyond King County, embracing Speaker Don Eldridge of Mount Vernon (Speaker 1969-71), Speaker Pro Tem Tom Copeland of Walla Walla, and rancher Stu Bledsoe of Ellensburg (majority leader, 1969-71). Mary Ellen McCaffree from the east side of Seattle's University District filled out the inner circle as chair of the Revenue and Taxation Committee.

Their first offering was a Labor Bill of Rights with secret elections and public disclosure of outcomes "a great step forward in the growth of a sound Labor movement" — and something, Evans said, Republicans and the public agreed on. "Clear alternatives ... to stem the tide toward bigger, in favor of better, more stable government" were next.[12] "We have too long been the party of opposition," he told the media, offering an information kit. On the road, Evans' listeners were asked to "be a politician," to volunteer. "Give an investment in your future ... to your community, your country and your children." The more government answered personal problems, the larger and more impersonal it became. The GOP faithful liked to hear that "freedom," "conserve" and the idea one can only be effective through his party were "cornerstones" of his beliefs. "If this is what it means to be ... a conservative," said the man who would soon divide his party and be disparaged as a 'liberal,' "then I'm proud to be called a conservative."[13]

## Rushing Rosellini

The governor had been hearing footfalls since 1959. He ambiguously took $12.5 million from schools, advocated $500 salary boosts for teachers, restored kindergartens and submitted a 1963-65 budget $58 million out of balance. After he pled for unity in the House Democratic caucus, the *Bremerton Sun's* Adele Ferguson heard its "conservatives" saying, "Things are more Rosy than rosy. What went on in there would have brought tears to the eyes of the Sphinx."[14] Sixteen Democrats bolted to vote for Evans' resolution the governor specify new revenue, forcing him to endorse a "two-thirds of one cent" (from 3.3 to 4 percent) rise in the sales tax. Evans enjoyed the minority's privilege of having it both ways, saddling the need for revenue on a "majority" who lacked the votes to be one. He scorned "the most distasteful and unnecessary tax package ever heaped on the people," and denounced an income tax as "a thing of beauty, and a blight forever" and defeated it (53-45). His indignation rose at the Democratic senators' first move, having the Business and Occupations tax collected monthly to pick up $19 million (a one-time speed-up, or "shift" he later replicated). Otherwise he took shelter: "I don't believe the Minority can be specific in every area ... or it will antagonize everyone, only in major areas." The real question was "needs versus wants." Evans and the Democrats did agree on upping the minimum wage, and he was the pivot in sending half a cent of the gas tax to the cities, in the forefront of the environmental age with billboard controls, and for a State Arts Commission.[15] From March 1962 on, Evans was chairing campaign schools and the state GOP convention as it adopted the caucus' agenda. By the fall of 1963, he was "100 percent devoted to a campaign" for governor.

Only "three percent of the voters said they knew of him, but four percent said they would vote for him," Caucus Attorney Jim Dolliver recalled. "He figured with support like that he'd better go for it."[16] A poll in the spring of 1964 was more "heartening." Dick Christiansen, the Lutheran minister who had nearly defeated U.S. Senator Warren Magnuson two years earlier, drew 42 percent of the prospective primary vote, Joe Gandy, Seattle Ford dealer and president of the 1962 World's Fair 17, and Evans 12. Gandy and Evans agreed whoever was behind just before filing in July would drop out. In June, Gandy endorsed Evans. Fourteen months of continuous circulation, hundreds of "coffee hours," a network of legislative leaders across the state, and a superb campaign council beat Christiansen, the choice of the Right, three to two on primary day. Christiansen's "sincere young man here to throw the rascals out" approach, which had come close to toppling Magnuson in 1962, was neutralized by Evans' age, 39, and his directness. Criticism was carefully held to contrasting his lack of government experience with Evans. The minister's primary eve concession and endorsement confirmed the wisdom of assailing only Rosellini.

Except for 1952, President Dwight Eisenhower (1953-61) was unable to transfer his popularity to his party. In 1964, Washington was still 60 percent Democratic in statewide races. Evans needed all the Republicans (30 percent), 20 percent of the Democrats, and 10 percent of the "swing" voters to stop the first governor to try for three consecutive terms.[17] He could not be identified with Arizona's senator and conservative icon Barry Goldwater, whose bluntness and unsettling stands had been angering groups since his nomination for president by the regulars. They were on the platform together once and the Arizonan had been ignored. Half a million tabloids and brochures were mailed as fast as 13,000 individual contributors paid for them. From August on, Lee Jacoby, soon-to-be Evans' press secretary, churned out press releases scorching Rosellini. He had "multiplied taxes on top of taxes," more than doubled the state's bonded indebtedness, and put campaign public relations people on the state payroll. In addition, Liquor Control Board appointees and Fred Martin, Director of General Administration, were soliciting campaign funds in-house. Seattle Mayor Gordon Clinton, chair of the Citizens for Evans, countered a four-page Rosellini blast on Evans' votes on including workmen's compensation and civil rights by pointing to "bold-face lies" belied by the House journal.[18] Over 600,000 doorbells rang across the state for Evans.

Candidates have to dance to the right (or left) to gain the allegiance of the regulars who dominate primaries. Now the agenda of the "New Breed" could come to the foreground. "We had for too long been the party of opposition," Evans confessed again. "We waited to find out what the Democrats were going to be for before we decided what we were going to be against. Now we know the issues, we have alternative programs … to work positively to build a new Washington." He was behind until mid-October when a page a day was released from the "Blueprint for Progress," 35 specific ideas laid next the "overriding issue of moral integrity."[19] President Johnson got 62 percent of the vote and U.S. Senator Henry Jackson, 74 percent. Evans alone unseated a Democratic incumbent, by 100,000 votes. The key to the voter's "selectivity," the *Seattle Argus* enthused, was again the ten-man New Breed staff, including brother-in-law Bill Bell, Joel and Frank Pritchard, "Gummie" Johnson, Jim Dolliver, Slade Gorton, John Hayden, Bruce Baker, and Neal Jacoby. It could not have been done without legislative allies making conversions in their districts or the expertise gained as a legislator.[20] Evans kept the initiative for eight of his twelve years as governor — until the thrust of the classes of 1957 and 1959 was spent. It was they who evolved and implemented the "Blueprint." Rosellini was out-organized by a new generation.

## "The Greatest Speech Never Given"

The legislature's constitutional mandate to redistrict after decennial census had been honored since 1932. Eastern Washington was relatively smaller and did not want to lose seats, the majority Democrats resisted because their position would be hard to improve on in the large cities, and changing boundaries can mean political life or death for legislators. The Republicans now feared Democrats might agree on a bill to redistrict and Rosellini sign it before Evans was sworn in, keeping the GOP a minority indefinitely. The *Post-Intelligencer* reported a "secret … detailed 'map' about which enough is known to read what can be characterized as outright gerrymandering."[21] Passage of a Democratic bill seemed imminent.

GOP research showed the inaugural could be moved up to Tuesday midnight instead of midday Wednesday. Justice Richard Ott brought the Supreme Court's seal with him to the House chamber that evening. Beyond that, the New Breed could but call for "statesmanship, not partisan politics," knowing this was impossible and suggested, "Let's adjourn until shortly before noon." The Democrats could not agree on new lines, and the first "crisis" of the new administration passed before it entered office. "The Greatest Speech Never Given" (by Evans) hung on the wall of Justice Dolliver's private bath in the Temple of Justice for 15 years.[22]

## Pacing the Legislature

Calls for bipartisanship are a staple of inaugurations, but this one was more eloquent and forceful. "This administration is not ashamed of the word conservative and it is not afraid of the word liberal. I would rather cross the political aisle than cross the people," Evans said. There were "no Republican schools or Democratic highways, no liberal salmon or conservative parks." "We have come here to exercise leadership … we can never fail to reckon with the opportunities for responsible change." Heads turned with "We must face the fact that increased government services may require increased revenues. Let us begin anew." No one present, including the new governor, could imagine how far how far he would go in saying "We have to act, not react."

A broader "Blueprint" rolled out soon after. A Department of Transportation, one for Water Resources (soon Ecology), a call for a constitutional convention and a "comprehensive review" of operations preoccupied legislators for a decade. Evans' conservatism was in evidence too: "The greatest threat to basic freedom for individuals and basic integrity and independence for state and local programs … [is] the encroachment of federal activity in areas traditionally served by the state … which the state is perfectly capable of serving when its governmental machinery is in order." Here lay the ultimate conundrum for conservatives in post New Deal America; the only way the states could stop congressional programs was by co-opting them. Evans' motive could not have been more traditional: "If … Republicans are not willing to assume the burdens of leadership … at the state level … our only recourse is to prepare for an orderly transfer of our remaining responsibilities to the federal government."[23] Only activist governance to meet the "challenge of growth" could preempt the breakdown of Lincolnian government "closest to the people." In 12 years federal mandates and the need for 'matching' money to meet President Lyndon Johnson's "Great Society" initiatives and Evans' in Olympia created new realms for state government.

In 1965, Evans' staff pared and prioritized the governor's "executive requests" to what was "doable," if Democrats cooperated. Two-thirds of the "Blueprint," the model pollution control laws, and a Department of Community Affairs to channel direct aid to cities passed. An Optional Municipal Code permitted cities to modify and simplify operations. Counties might offer some urban services. Depending on one's view, the laws have encouraged every level of government to offer like services, confusing the public, or stifled duplication and made for seamless delivery. Boundary Review Boards, with appeals to the state level, have made decisions on growth more uniform. They also heralded the 1990's statute forcing cities to adjoin in urban zones, so police from now adjoining cities are where county sheriffs had inefficiently patrolled corridors. A new Department of Revenue joined the Tax Commission and the Urban Arterial Board. The Data Processing Authority failed to stem the rising chaos of conflicting systems, but a State Board for Community College Education put two dozen county-based institutions under the state's roof. Executive requests rose to a high of 76 in 1971, when the governor detected an inverse relationship between introductions and passes.

## The Four-Party System

As party leader, Evans faced the aftermath of 1964. In "two party politics" both are permanently divided to accommodate 180-degree span to the right or left of the center each, in theory, covers. The infusion of Goldwaterites decimated moderates in GOP organizations, left them deeply divided, and at a nadir. Lutheran minister Dick Christiansen's "Women on the Warpath" and the right-wing party chairs in charge of the two largest counties, King and Snohomish, soon became ongoing antagonists of the administration. The right wing was blind to the damage done by what the new GOP state chair C. Montgomery ("Gummie") Johnson called the "Birch bunch." They were inflamed by attacks on the preservers of the party's ideological purity fighting "the heresies of the Great Society, and those liberals who have infiltrated our ranks."[24] Evans reminded those who lost the presidency that parties can not become "ideological hobby horses." "I think responsible conservatism is perfectly legitimate, but merely to be negative, to complain, to have little faith in the future, little faith in new ideas, doesn't classify in my view as conservatism in any way, shape, or form." His "only real job … [was] getting the people on our side, and that requires the united support of the Republican party," one "big enough to include all the legitimate shades of opinion." If this were done, "doleful observations" about the GOP's future would prove wrong. "Republicans rather than … Democrats will be the party which will appeal to the young, urbanized, educated and intelligent majority."[25]

Contrary to most governors, who know they can only be hurt by taking sides, Evans "made a real effort to become part of the Republican party structure and exercise some leadership."[26] Knowing voters decide as much by knowing one's enemies as one's friends, he decided to make a virtue of his predicament by charging the Far Right. At the state convention at Port Angeles in January 1965, he read John Bircher's out of the GOP. This strategy was the handiwork of his pugnacious, proficient, and sometimes profane "Gummie" Johnson whose axiom was, "If there's a good fight going on, then they (the voters) know we're alive."[27] Each of the 39 counties had two seats on the Republican (and Democratic) State Central Committees regardless of population. Those east of the mountains, in part to keep the Westside from control, kept Evans tenuously in charge. The state party focused on candidate recruitment, technology, and even raised money. The shift in the state party's stance can be seen in "The Republican White Paper on Human Needs," a treatment of all groups from senior citizens, to social entitlements, and mental health.[28] The governor was "deeply disturbed by the constant questioning of purpose and motivation" and impressions "carefully nurtured" by "some in elective and political office in King County" of a "dictator" bent on "taking over" county organizations. This was the case by 1968. The "widening breach" had become an impassable chasm.

Johnson moved to "direct confrontation" with King County GOP chair Ken Rogstad. Evans was blunt. "King County … has never, in any way, done anything to aid or assist me. Quite to the contrary, they have … consistently tried to undermine and run down … the state administration and the State Republican organization …. The other … counties won … the great progress of our party."[29] Two "Precinct Projects" to replace conservatives with moderates and elect new chairs were doomed by the tenacity of true believers and the power of county chairs to fill vacancies.

The upside was a major infusion of new blood in the precincts and the legislature. Evans tried to ignore his tormentors, wistfully claiming the "influence of political parties has generally been unimportant in party nominations."[30] Using a national model, Johnson named a Republican Coordinating Committee, but the schism could not be healed. "Evans Republicans" on the sound were separated by a wall of wariness from the party, formed and funded their own campaigns and profited from stressing their independence. For the rest of the Evans years, it was to be the Olympians and outlanders against the urban county regulars on the Sound, the reverse of the usual posture of rural areas. The governor's only concession was after Ford-Reagan nomination melee in the 1976, when he was Ford's state general chairman. "Party unity is something more than an abstract slogan — it is a fact."[31] Evans' frustration was transparent in 1987, when he told the staid King County Republican Club that "short of holding public office" and getting people into it, "a political party becomes nothing more than a debating society." Parties have to embody "a wide variety of views."[32] Seattle, where most of the legislative seats had been held by moderate Republican professionals, has not had a GOP legislator since 1984, and is now the San Francisco of the north.

The GOP's second benefit in the 1960s was redistricting.[33] In 1964, the state supreme court ordered the legislature to redistrict before it did anything else, creating a 47-day gridlock. House Majority Leader Slade Gorton deliberately stalled negotiations to force the court to appoint a neutral "master" to redraw lines, correctly thinking this map would be fairer to the GOP than any compromise with the Democrat's Senator Bob Grieve, for whom the governor's veto was now an insuperable obstacle.[34] In 1966, with a leveler playing field and Evans' popularity, the House GOP took charge in its own right, rising to a high of 56 seats two years later. In 1983, Democrats were back in charge and overcame the chronic temptation to have the last lick. An amendment to the constitution put the legislature's most embarrassing imbroglio in the hands of a bipartisan commission, where a mutually chosen citizen is the tie-breaking vote.

## The Thrust to Regroup

The Evan's administration, more than any other, was a projection of its anchor figure. Jim Dolliver, Evans' chief of staff and a leavening influence for 11 years, worked in the background. Evans acknowledged his title, Administrative Assistant, should have been "Deputy Governor." Unflappable and authoritative without being intimidating, Dolliver's resonant baritone and sure political instincts could be heard in Evans' speeches. His reward was serving a "progressive" governor, "Where you can start with an idea and run it all the way through to execution, and wind up with a sense of accomplishment." The central staff, an extension of a robust personality, while not quite "gatekeepers, " became equals of the cabinet, converting ideas into a seemingly endless array of executive requests.

The executives' weakness had been the central theme of state government texts for 50 years. The nucleus of the problem, the "Governor's Task Force on Executive Reorganization" told him in 1968, was that "the governor is not boss." The founders had deliberately scattered executive powers among eight other statewide elected officials and now there 60 boards and commissions, only 18 of whom reported directly to the governor, along with 11 directors and 29 others.[35] It recommended reducing six human resource agencies to two, seven in transportation to two, three in pollution control to one, three in the governor's office to one, and a "line agency" with 17 staff at the governor's right hand. Over half of the recommendations became law in the next eight years melding the Central Budget Agency, awkwardly re-titled the Office of Program Planning and Fiscal Management (OPP and FM), adding Planning and Community Affairs as a funnel for federal funds, jettisoning the separate higher personnel board, and creating a Department of Social and Health Services (DSHS), as a "one stop shop" housing all institutions social operations. The Council of State Government's list varied only in urging a four-year term for the governor, already the case in Washington.[36] The "super agency" has been under continuous attack by advocates for groups who felt a loss of identity and that their legislator surrogates were "ungovernable." Periodic prison turmoil or abuses went public, feeding the fire. Caring for a million differently, and often multiply, challenged people was an unpredictable task. The next largest entities, Employment Security (unemployment compensation) and Labor and Industries (accident awards and safety) were still free standing, not a "Department of Manpower and Industries."

Dolliver, Walt Howe (the governor's original counsel and second budget director), and ex-House Minority Leader George Kinnear (then the unflappable chair of the Tax Commission) were the foundation. Garrett Heyns stayed on at the helm of Institutions for seven more years and the brilliant Charles Morris, Evans' last secretary of DSHS, were the other leaders in a solidly competent crew.[37] The full cabinet met just once, then it was divided into five sub-cabinets: transportation, education, human resources, natural resources and recreation, and general government, who met with the governor separately. Evans' liaisons from the central staff became the conduits and filters.[38] Dolliver oversaw the natural resources group sub cabinet, while Dick Hemstad (later a state senator) ran the one on external affairs and administration and was the governor's second legal counsel. Dave Peyton handled fiscal and economic matters and federal relations. Doug Toms steered the Highways Department (then presided over the National Highway Safety Board). Neil McReynolds superseded Lee Jacoby as press secretary. No one's ethics needed minding. The era of patronage, "job insurance," and in-house campaigning evaporated. It is easy for a cabinet to be sycophantic in the presence of a commanding personality. Those who believed that Evans was giving away the store were encouraged to give critiques, and did. But the governor, slide rule in hand, had to be confronted on his own level and on his own terms, something few were up to doing. Bill Jacobs of Labor and Industries, who was to be an Evans' chief of staff in the U.S. Senate, was given an "award" for being a duty devil's advocate.[39] In the cabinet views varied from Jennifer Belcher (later a Democratic Representative and Land Commissioner) to former Congressman Thor Tollefson at Fisheries, and the seemingly inscrutable former Wenatchee representative, Don Moos, at newly formed Ecology. If more care had been given to selecting key initial cabinet members, some substitutions might have been avoided. Charles Prahl left after siding too often with his Highway Commission bosses, whose macadam and concrete fixations ran crosswise to the governor's mass transit agenda. The recalcitrant Highway Commission fixated on roads. George Stasney, the first budget director, was beyond his depth. Sid Smith from Boeing, his peer at DSHS, was out of his element. Commerce was prosaically led. Bill Schneider at General Administration and John Biggs at Game were long in the tooth.[40]

The quality of the over 800 appointments the executive made each year, many of whom outlive a regime, were a wider gauge of a governor's taste. Evans' regulatory bearing was clear when another legislative contemporary, Don Brazier of Yakima, was given the chair of the Utilities and Transportation Commission. "My fundamental belief ... [is] either you regulate the industries of the industries will run the commission."[41] Judicial nominees buttressed Evans' reputation for probity. He was the first to name a minority (former UW law dean Charles Smith, a native of American Samoa) and place a woman (Carolyn Dimmick) on the supreme court. The governor preferred competent Republicans, but a third of his choices were Democrats. Judicial potential and electability were the next criteria. If more evidence of Evans' stubbornness is needed, two superior court judges were reappointed after being defeated. Dolliver was the one-hundredth and last judge named, to the supreme court. When the State Bar insisted it had prerogative of vetting the candidates and it was told, in effect, to go to hell.[42]

## The Fiscal Thicket

Dolliver said Evans was the only person he ever knew who liked budgets. The engineer and his slide rule drew dread into underprepared and daunted department heads. The "governor's budget" was his chief policy tool and greatest leverage over the legislature. The first edition comes together over 18 months and goes public on December 15 of odd-numbered years before the 105-day "long" session. All anticipated revenue is spent. The legislature, harried by pressure groups and divided by party, personality, house and constituency can insert its preferences only by offending groups who have been 'promised,' or augmenting. Lashed to spend more, it struggles to find votes for taxes in the face of critiques by the executive, who would arbitrate.

Al Rosellini's abiding fiscal conservatism and tendency to procrastinate had caught up with Evans. But raising taxes would ruin his prospects for a third term. He admitted his 1965-67 budget was $32 million out of balance. Evans called it a "fiscal sham." Presumed federal programs had not been drafted; the last Congress had rejected amendments to Social Security and distributing school monies to districts on a 12 month rather than 10 month basis was another one-time gain, of $42 million. The "real" deficit was $75 million on a total of $2.1 billion. Evans was on record as against raising the general sales tax, the main source of revenue, since it fell hardest on those with the lowest incomes. He wanted to extend it to largely professional services, halving "ratable reductions" in welfare and keeping dental and eye care offered to indigents and the elderly. "We can no longer tolerate a situation where some … live out their final years with dimmed vision, merely for want of a pair of glasses."[43]

The most acute pressure was always funding the public schools, 45 percent of state spending. Governor Langlie first tackled the endemic problem by trying to equalize property tax assessments that diverged wildly by county, from 19 percent of value to near the 50 percent required by the constitution. This would indirectly raise local school revenue in most counties, in theory helping to stabilize annually voted "special" levies by lowering them. The legislature partly answered Evans' renewed appeal: the 40 mill limit was changed to one percent, but capped at a rise six percent a year. An inclusive true value mandate finally came in 1973. In the interim, five-sevenths of the state's share of the property tax, which was equalized, was transferred to the districts.[44] "Special" levies quickly returned a quarter of school support, and "tax revolts" shook many districts. In 1976 the supreme court restated the constitution's twin dictate to "fully fund basic education" — without defining it — which fell back on the legislature, renewing the question of tax reform.

## Prime Time: The Second Term

Gregarious three-term Attorney General John O'Connell, chosen the "outstanding" one by his peers in 1961, was Evans' ill-starred rival in 1968. His cadences were Kennedyesque: "If you want things the way they were in 1920 … or 1930 … or even 1967 … don't vote for me." But he argued for no more than Evans had tried and was surprisingly unschooled. He "sensed" state employee morale was low, yet admitted he had not talked with them; he had little to say on schools, traffic, or parks. "This administration started with a candidate who had a long, established record of arch-conservatism," and had hoarded a "huge surplus." Evansites had to admit the accusation that spending was up 80 percent was "almost true." Alleging "cronyism" in the face of changes to civil service limiting "exempts" to a handful was no more plausible. The incumbent had ignored air and water pollution, and sold out to corporations in favoring a single-rate income tax. Evans was cold and machinelike, O'Connell moaned, and "A plan that is all head and no heart is worse than no plan at all."[45] The Incumbant's fear of federal domination and scouraging of the state's constitution was "woefully inadequate." His work on federal revenue sharing a "pipe dream."[46]

Evans broke the rule never to debate while leading and dared O'Connell to a series of contests. "We had a strong feeling he did not know state government in detail and … hour-long debates would … uncover this."[47] O'Connell's response to welfare was "'that it really wasn't that much of a problem.' I was amazed at how soon it actually occurred."[48] In September, he denied cashing a $10,000 check in Las Vegas in 1965 to cover a $900 card-playing debt. It was a "line of credit" at a casino, mistakenly mailed to his bank. Evans denied having advance notice; the attorney general called him a "liar."[49] Ahead by 10 percent in mid-October, Evans' positive profile was enhanced by the attractive "Action Team" of statewide candidates he had enticed. Slade Gorton became attorney general for 12 years, young Seattle City Councilman Lud Kramer was installed as secretary of state, and Art Fletcher, a black Pasco city counterpart came within an eyelash of being lieutenant governor. Evans' outcome was the best of any governor in 32 years.[50]

## Tax Reform: The Pearl of Great Price

The progressive Republican's tax reform rationale was for fairness, not increase. It was Evans' noblest effort and most disappointing defeat. During the desperation of the Great Depression, most states passed sales and income taxes to offset the property tax disaster, creating a "three legged stool" to for the state to sit on. The abominator of the income tax in 1964 underwent a final conversion when school levies began to crash in 1967. "In the long run, it is a more productive source of taxation and will provide us greater return as our populations and economy grows [sic] and … better stability and less necessity for … increases."[51] (See Appendix 6.) Given its half dozen defeats in the Supreme Court or by the voters since 1933, most legislators preferred the "chicken plucking" method of taxation ("A little here, a little there ...").

Evans insider Representative Mary Ellen McCaffree, a former president of the Seattle League of Women Voters and wife of a UW economics professor, chaired the House Revenue Committee, molding a comprehensive package with a "carrot and a stick." A 3.5 percent flat rate income tax for fairness and "elasticity," (a marginally greater gain in a growing economy) to compensate for the extra costs of urbanization and "stabilize" the system. The "carrots" for the public and business were reduction of the sales tax and a corporate income tax in place of the onerous "business and occupations" levy, which extracted dollars on gross whether they made money or not. Equity, constitutional lids on all three major taxes, revenue "neutrality" (no immediate gain), and six hour sittings with the governor, attorney general, and GOP caucus leaders, educated, cajoled, and eventually convinced all but 9 of the 56 House Republicans. Democrats wanted a graduated income tax. A compromise was struck by scheduling a second referendum in five years on conversion to one, if the flat tax passed.

The constitutional amendment needed a two-thirds vote, reached once a third of the Democrats came along. The Democrats, with their Senate majority, could not be seen blocking what they had long asked for, but delayed the vote until the fall of 1971 to distance and protect themselves from resentment in 1970, a presidential year when the Democratic vote peaked.[52] The reform (HJR 42), fell two to one.[52]

By fall of 1971, the "Boeing Bust" was on. The state's leading manufacturer's payroll fell from 105,000 to 30,000. Unemployment surged to 13.5 percent. A billboard on the I-5 freeway going south asked, "Will the last person to leave Seattle please turn out the lights?" The state's financial woes took second place for voters uncertain about their jobs. Evans was undaunted, thinking it "inconceivable" the legislature would not make a second try at tax reform. To him it was "what kind of tax policy is wise."[53] After the 1971 session he visited 70 cities in 30 days to find what was acceptable to the voters. A broadly composed "Committee for a New Tax Policy" of 82 individuals from every quarter was formed by executive order.[54] The legislators were led to courageously do what they otherwise would have shied away from. The House took the initiative again. The 1972 bill had technical refinements, a graduated income tax of up to 6.5 percent, the constitutional limits, and tied the sales and property taxes, making it doubly difficult to raise either. The governor crisscrossed the state once more.

This second attempt at tax reform in 1972 illustrated the power of the executive to initiate, lead, and legislate, even in the face of majority opinion. In November 1973, HJR 37 was defeated nearly three to one. For too many, tax reform meant tax increase. The doubling of the sales tax in the next decade did nothing to lessen the public's suspicion of the legislature. Washington's tax take was 27th in the nation in 1976, and the most "regressive" of the 50 states according to a University of Kentucky study. Presently, a family of four earning $20,000 a year pays twice as much in state and local taxes as one taking in $120,000. "Yes," say the skeptics, "but the federal income toll on income balances this." In truth, it negates about half the regressivity. The "third rail" of Washington politics has not been touched since. Washington remains one the five states without an income tax.

## Ecology

At his second inaugural in January of 1969, the governor put the critical question of our time: "Can we become urbanized and remain civilized at the same time?" In September, he had gathered his staff, the leaders of the Washington Environmental Council, and seven senior legislators at a cabin high in the Cascades. They agreed to bills on nuclear siting, oil spills, effluent standards, open space, surface mining, nuclear siting and coastline preservation. A deal was cut: there would be no changes and nothing else on the agenda. The Republicans were to deliver the House; the Washington Environmental Council the Democratically run Senate.[55]

The "environmental" First Special Session of 1970 showed how the legislature reflects strong public opinion. Having set the agenda and understanding the strength of this new wave among the public, Evans held three press conferences a week, dexterously explaining the bills. The bills were still in committee in March. "We have found in the last twelve months," he wrote a friend, "that environmental progress by the Legislature can take second place to economic concerns, when the unemployment ratio starts to rise. Saturday and Sunday environmentalists … push it all aside during the work week. I believe we have to work at both [citizens and legislators] on a seven-day-a-week basis …until we can accommodate both, we will make little progress."[56] The governor went on television. Hundreds of calls and letters and 5,000 telegrams flooded legislators' offices. Five of the six major bills passed, in 32 days. Washington leapt to the forefront of the environmental age, setting precedents used by other states. Evans correctly said, "Never has a legislature done so much of consequence."[57] The banner bill, coastline management, was enacted by an initiative in 1971.

In 1975, Evans' staff drafted an extension of the Olympic National

Park's "ocean strip" to the Makah Reservation and around Lake Ozette. Landowners and Congressman Don Bonker cooperated, and the bill passed in Congress in under six months. The governor's new agenda for 1977, growth management, was characteristically ahead of its time and ignored his lame duck status. "Wise and visionary stewardship" was preferable to over consumption of nonrenewable resources. "If you err," he avowed later, "I say err on the side of too much preservation."[58]

## The "Great Society:" A Federal Juggernaut Submerges the States a Second Time

The landmark Voting Rights Act of 1964 and resistance to the growing Vietnam War sparked pressure for expanding the social services, that prosperity and inflation was to make possible. In August 1967, Evans took a day to meet privately with minorities at the Madison YMCA, in the heart of Seattle's "Central Area." Six black teenagers burst into the room, one, a Black Panther, sat down in front of him, pointed a finger at the governor's forehead and said, "If I had a gun I'd shoot you." "What good would that do?" he asked. "One less honky white to deal with" was the answer. The conservative of the fifties came out of a ghetto in the sixties declaring, "Minorities just simply haven't had a fair shake in a century."[59] Invited to Olympia, the youngsters appeared in their best clothes and offered 20 ideas. An upshot was "Multiservice Centers" merging state social and health services under one roof. The invaders reappeared at the opening of the expanded office: "Governor, you did a good thing," and presented him with "the biggest, sharpest handmade machete in a leather sheath."[60] Evans followed up by naming the first African-Americans to the boards of the Seattle Community Colleges and the University of Washington.

The Game Department was run by a commission and Evans had no way to prevent its use of brutality to break up boats and shunt away Indians who assumed they had a right to fish for steelhead. Tepees were set up on the capitol lawn and sprinklers turned on in protest. The governor appointed an Advisory Council on Indian Affairs. Many Native Americans came to the first meeting in full regalia with "stony faces": the white man was again breaking the promises of the Medicine Creek Treaty of 1855 assuring Native Americans the right to fish in their "usual and accustomed places," confirmed by the Boldt Decision of 1974. Bill Jefferies, a Native American, was the first Special Assistant to the Governor for Indian Affairs. Eight years later, he wrote, "You have accomplished more with, and for, Indian Country than all of your predecessors put together." There was an "atmosphere of constructive change" in place of paternalism.[61]

The shooting of students at Kent State University and President Nixon's incursion into Cambodia to deny the Vietcong a safe sanctuary to attack Vietnam erupted while Evans was on a trade mission to Japan. Some 5,000 University of Washington students poured across the Freeway Bridge into downtown Seattle and broke a half dozen windows. The media featured the broken glass, not the generally orderly nature of the procession. KING television granted a half hour to Evans who urged the dissenters to go "beyond protest to better answers."[62] This did nothing to assuage writers of 600 letters, some vigilante in tone. He studiously avoided Vietnam though his sentiments, as of 1968, were clear: "I fully agree that the United States must continue fighting in South Vietnam to prevent a communist takeover in Southeast Asia." In 1975, when California Governor Jerry Brown said he did not want any Vietnamese in his state taking jobs, Evans invited them and greeted the first group of what became tens of thousands of expatriates.[63] President Ford revoked FDR's controversial executive order 8066 sending both Issei and Nisei to relocation camps during World War II, partly because Evans passed along a request for an apology from a Washington Nisei.[64]

The logical step beyond multi-service centers was a Department of Social and Health Services, embracing welfare, criminal and social institutions.[65] Its size (17,000 employees in 2005), the need to absorb and synchronize the deluge of unfamiliar responsibilities, juggle 300 state and federal financial streams, and the volatility and vulnerability of its clientele, from murderers to madmen and the easily victimized, has made the agency a magnet for controversy. The most disputed initiative, to cope with a rising tide of patients, was "deinstitutionalization," placing those eligible in their home communities. For example, the Cascadia Reception-Diagnostic Center for children at Tacoma had the heaviest intake ever in the first quarter of 1966 (370 children); 10.1 percent were given "diagnostic paroles," bypassing a residential institution. Inevitably, unfortunate episodes caused bitter reactions. The motives were both humanistic and fiscal, but the negative reactions from incidents on the street were just as real.[66]

Candidates for DSHS staff openings had fallen by two-thirds as salaries elsewhere raced ahead in response to the takeoff of inflation.[67] In the seven months after August 1971, no fewer than 604 new "high level" positions were created, only 16 to do the mergers.[68] "Layering" of managers, DSHS' eternal internal malady, flourished with more sub-specialized units. "The department created for itself a difficult image problem," budget director Wally Miller confidentially advised the governor, who halted reorganization. No more employees were added until a replacement was found for first Secretary Sid Smith.[69] The obstacles to righting DSHS endured: the double protections afforded by civil service and the State Employees Union (the WFSE), were the reverse of "fire at will" conditions existing before the New Deal. Only the most senior managers were exempt, making it harder to direct and discipline, and almost impossible to dispose of up to eight tiers of "subordinates." The other impediment, typified by DSHS, was unifying computer software of differing ages, uses and escalating complexity. The early technological angst of the Evans era is now under the aegis of the swelling Department of Communications.

## 1972: The Perils of Progressivism

Evans' second term showed the measure of the man; getting a third was a fortuity. On top of the accruing liabilities of incumbency, Evans did "four things ... any sensible governor, or politician would not have done."[70] When the wife of a black advisor was refused lunch at the Olympia Elks Club, he immediately issued an executive order barring any state meeting at a place which discriminated. Washington had the largest per capita population of Elks in the country. Second, in the spring before the election, two brutal murders were committed, one of a state patrolman by inmates on work release from the penitentiary. Evans stood by his view that because inmates were to reenter society, early release and reintroduction had to be made to work. Third and fourth, the governor argued for the income tax a second time in 1973, and against the death penalty.[71]

In the anti-government atmosphere of 1972, Martin Durkan, Senate Ways and Means chairman and gubernatorial aspirant, was in a double bind. He might complain that Evans had created "a monstrosity of a budget" but could not spend less or tax more and expect to replace him. "Liberal" by label, Durkan was a centrist in practice. To counter Rosellini, he planned a $100 million "spending reform" and tax cut to match the ex-governor.[72] Rosellini flayed him in the Democratic primary by tying him to a "profligate" incumbent.

Evans got 20 percent of all the primary votes, but a poll taken the next week showed him behind by just nine percent. He had denied Rosellini a third term, and was now asking for one. The "underlying issue" Evans insisted, was still integrity. He tried to mask his own vulnerability by dredging up a 1939 vote against property tax lids while Rosellini was a state senator and charging his predecessor with "excessive taxing, excessive spending and excessive deceit."[73] Rosellini had sealed his records in the State Archives for 20 years. Evans questioned, "Who is going to trust the future to a man who will not reveal his past?" Rosellini was "tricked" into a televised debate at North Seattle Community College

Candidate's Fair, where he patronized Evans as "Danny Boy" while a television camera whirred.[74] This momentum, exposure of legal advice given by Rosellini to the disreputable Frank Colacurcio at a time the Godfather was playing, and George McGovern's left-wing presidential candidacy let Evans survive by .07 percent.

## "Fiscal Excess" or "Deliberate Futurism"?

A billowing economy like that of the sixties is the best of all political worlds. Boeing sold record numbers of airplanes and trade with Asia escalated sharply, drawing surges of migrants from other states to new jobs. They needed schools and services. Expensive programs were added, such as the 1971 Education for All Bill to "mainstream" the challenged. Starting as a $5 million pilot program, it rose from two to eight percent of children, and to $200 million in two decades. It was impossible to define who was "challenged." Places had to be found in higher education for the children of postwar baby boomers. Evans led in making the county-based community colleges a system and obligation of the state. The Evergreen State College was built and students at the two state universities, most paying one-quarter of their cost, soon doubled.

Charlie Hodde quickly sensed the trend, and tucked his tongue in cheek. "An amazing fact ... with ... Dan Evans as Governor. He really is a spender. We all ... thought he was a conservative, and just trying to embarrass Governor Rosellini. It comes as somewhat of a shock to find that Dan is really serious about spending money. He is even willing to get it from an income tax if you prefer. I wonder if Dan has been reading history. He may have run across the old slogan — 'spend, spend, elect, elect.' I wonder if it still works?"[75] "General government" expenses rose 464 percent in Evans' first eight years as opposed to 14 percent under Rosellini. They accounted for $141.7 million of the 1971-73 budget of $4.41 billion, up 174 percent from 1961-63. Welfare surged 217 percent, all of education 154 percent, and state employees by half.[76] This was possible because taxes on property vaulted 266 percent, on alcohol and tobacco taxes by half, license fees by a third. "The challenge of growth" brought an unheard-of shower of money from President Johnson's Great Society, as income from Vietnam-driven inflation inclined inexorably from under 3.5 percent in 1965 to 14.3 percent in 1970-71. In the 1971 revenue sharing thrust to save federalism, the Nixon administration supplied $44 million of the state's $59.4 million surplus, and "conservatively" $64.6 million of the $150 million anticipated in 1973-75.[77] (See Appendices 5, 6 and 7.)

"Stagflation" set in after the Boeing Bust and revenue no longer raced ahead of population and escalating expectations. The administration resorted to controversial accounting to keep apace. The par excellence example was dragging anticipated income from the first month of the next biennium into the current one, a one-time gain of five percent. The *Times*' Ross Cunningham was not alone in feeling that state "government grows at an excessive rate unrelated to the functions it performs."[78] Evans' responded that society had changed, productivity had improved, and "demand" was unprecedented. "In 1964-65 ... there were 1,000 employees in Washington four year colleges and universities, and 40,556 students." In 1971, 15,616 and 67,967 respectively and in terms of "productivity," there were 3.9 students per employee as opposed to 4.4. The now six four year institutions of higher education went from 43,000 students in 1964-65 to 78,000 in 1975-76. In 1965, 8,468 DSHS staff served 142,387 clients; in 1971, it was 12,146 and 273,018. Here too the ratio of clients was up from 16.8 to 22.6 or 34 percent, obviating 4,000 new hires. In 1965, 1,000 children were on waiting lists for a state institution for the retarded; in 1971, none. Caseloads for Aid to Families with Dependent Children (AFDC) were 57,500 in 1965 and 146,000 in 1975-76. In 1971, there were 166,900 more students in the public schools than in 1965, yet Washington ranked forty-fifth in the teacher-student ratio. Parkinson's law was not in effect. Evans was arguing "work" did not have to "expand" with demand and that 278,000 more individuals were in institutions, being socially assisted, or in school. High-cost highway construction had forced the death rate per million miles driven to the lowest in the nation.[79] In the 12 years after 1965, the state's budget glided from $2.1 billion to $6.9 billion; state employees from 30,000 to 55,000.[80]

Evans' liberal image is deserved to the extent he spent unheard of amounts of new revenue — as did the legislature. This profile is inaccurate if one remembers that neither was the legislature able to leave anything on the table, lest they be accused of "underfunding" education, or face charges of raising unneeded dollars. Washington had the lowest tax growth of any state in the nation in 1977. The governor's State of the State address, first given to the Seattle Rotary, was the first annual report in a corporate format.[81] To the fated question, "Why can't you be like Governor Reagan?" he would defiantly retort, "Well, look what he did in California! He had the biggest tax increase in the history of the state ... and then found he raised too much money and started giving a portion of it back and made people feel good. In some respects I haven't spent enough." And telltale of an altered attitude: "Money spent in prompt and proper legislation is not a waste of the taxpayer's dollar; it is an investment in the taxpayer's future."[82] A powerful set of forces had coalesed; the demands of urbanization and affluence, inflation, federal enticements, and the adoption of environmentalism by the middle class, combined with a willful governor.

In the 1971 special session, Evans led off with six "Washington Futures" bonds worth of nearly half a billion dollars to soften the recession. Despite the tax revolt, five of the six passed, from water pollution control to recreation and community college facilities.[83] "This will give the basis or creating new quality in our communities ... [and] unquestionably, will make the next four years a lot more fun," the relieved governor wrote.[84]

## The Executive as Legislator

The care and feeding of legislators takes as much time as the public. Breakfasts at the governor's mansion gave the most junior Republican legislator a chance to feel important. Evans' weekly brown bag luncheons around the mahogany table in the governor's office with the lagging senate minority leaders were more a drill than a delight. He listened to floor debates on two "squawk boxes" while working in the morning. When they arrived for lunch, he knew what had been said, what it meant, and what he wanted next and pressed hard. The Democratic Senate leadership was seen going to and from Evans' second-floor office so often paranoid members of the now House GOP minority talked conspiracy.

Business had run from the environmentalist governor to the arms of business-as-usual Democrats. "Sawyercrats" (led by Speaker Leonard Sawyer), passed bills with an eye to reciprocal campaign contributions from lobbyists. In the Senate, August Mardesich replaced Bob Grieve as majority leader and he, with a minority of Democrats and 19 Republicans, gave business a "philosophical majority." Bills redistricting four senators, permitting a television tower to stay on a San Juan Island, and expanding card rooms and a lottery passed unmolested. Evans, with rhetorical overkill, saw his reforms "dismantled, ignored, or killed. We have seen a breakdown of the legislative process."[85]

In annualizing sessions through his power to call "special" ones he leveraged another threat — calling more. The one in September 1973 as the harvest began was a not just a hardship for a farmer politicians.[86] Evans asked the legislators to do "not what is easy, but what is right. I would rather cross the political aisle than cross the people. That must be our common pledge." Confident and savvy about the legislature, he testified before committees to the chagrin of those who saw their turf invaded. Few governors risk a grilling in this venue. This governor was willing to be snubbed: the Senate Transportation Committee ignored his personal request to appear and killed his Department of Transportation the same day.[87]

On May 7, 1975, when the 60-day regular session and 50 days of an extra one expired without passing a major bill, he turned to the least effective tool at hand, another tongue-lashing. It "would have to be classified as the worst session in a quarter of a century," one "dominated by special interests" and "ruled by the same old gang." He called a "Second Extra" in July. The legislative building was not air-conditioned and the "heat" was on. When a journalist asked the governor how he stood with Republican legislators, who complained about his "incessant meddling in legislative affairs," he retorted, "The governor always is involved deeply in legislative affairs. Part of the … process is … executive involvement," something rephrased by his successors. Mardesich's interpretation was that the governor had made himself a "super legislator."[88]

## "The Last Bounce": Legislating by Veto

A seasoned media man termed the last half of the 1975 session "a mindless reaction to a strong willed and sometimes stubborn governor."[89] When the Senate voted $65, not $100 million, to replace lost school levies, Evans rapped the legislators for "raising indifference and arrogance to new heights. "No new taxes' was the cry." "Deceit is a better name … . I could not in good conscience sign … and indicate … this was sufficient," he opined.[90] Seventy-five bills were on his desk: he signed 55, partially vetoed 14, and killed 6. "Whenever we try to do something," Senator Slim Rasmussen derisively complained, "a window opens, a cannon sticks its head out, and there is a puff of blue smoke."[91]

The veto was intended as a "check" on the errors and indulgences of the "third floor" and gives the governor continuous leverage over the legislature. Lawmakers go to the "second floor" to get the executive to agree to veto sections of a bill they do not want but are forced to adopt to pass bills, or to be assured one they want will not be excised. The veto forces trade-offs, disciplines legislators, and can be used for partisan advantage. The governor must sign or veto a bill within five days during a session, or it becomes law. Many were vetoed the day they reached his desk, including milk marketing, changes to public utility rules, and a presidential primary. Most major laws are negotiated and passed in the last week of the session; the governor has 10 days after adjournment to act. By that time, the legislators had dispersed statewide and were back to making a living when the axe fell. Asking two-thirds to call themselves into session and as many votes to override was nearly impossible. In Jim Dolliver's words, the governor almost always had "the last bounce."[92]

Evans stretched the Damocles' sword into a policy making instrument and articulated what became a default justification of his heirs: "As the only state elected official with legislative power who is responsible to all the people of the state," he was called upon "to act in what I believe to be the best interest of the people of the state." Abstruse rationales evolved to a high art. He vetoed a controversial small loans bill, while conceding lifting the interest cap of 12 percent when inflation was that high was necessary. He had "become increasingly concerned over the circumstances under which the bill was enacted," and at a stroke heeded the press and Labor, slapped down lobbyists, "probably alienated much of the business community," and overthrew the legislature. The veto can sink subterfuges. When antagonists passed his Department of Transportation without giving him the power to fire its director, it was red-penned for failing "to recognize the need for administrative accountability."[93]

The budget is the core of legislative-executive tension. Evans felt the boilerplate circumscribing his agencies was "too detailed." A section requiring staff reductions was "unclear," and giving "unanticipated [largely federal] receipts" to the Legislative Budget Committee to appropriate was "the latest ... take away from the executive functions ... and delegate them to legislative committees," violating "the fundamentals of good government." Could the power to appropriate be given to a committee? And could its acts be construed as representing the legislature? He ingeniously argued this would "transform the Legislative Budget Committee into a civil office and prevent any legislator from serving on it." The House and Senate Social and Health Services committees were both chaired by chiropractors, whose fondest hope was to get colleagues access to the health insurance plans doctors denied them. Evans vetoed HB 536, which was intended to do so, with the encomium that it was unwise to "mandate a substantial broadening of the scope of services offered."[94] One could visualize friend and physician's lobbyist Tom Owens standing at his shoulder. "We used to have an Italian named Al Rosellini," a Democratic representative quipped, "Now we have Danny Veto." (See Appendices 8A and 8B)

Evans' castigation made legislators more resolved to shear down the governor's most potent and versatile weapon. He was rid of what he did not want and could legislate, until he overstepped. In 1973, the Senate passed a 105-page Landlord Tenant Act after debating 103 amendments over three days. Evans systematically lined out items and sections, enlarging tenants' rights and remedies — and lost the item veto. In 1977, the supreme court found he had used the veto "in an affirmative way." The legislature submitted a constitutional amendment directly to the people, who restricted vetoes to an entire section. Dolliver, remorseful about the end of the executive's ability to stop "pork barrels and logrolling," mourned Evans' "greatest single loss."[95] (See Appendices 7B, 8A and 8B).

A postscript was apparently based on the rule that most states are required to balance their budgets, while Congress is not. Ronald Reagan, like five presidents before him, wanted power to veto individual appropriations. As U.S. Senator in 1987, Evans pressed a "modest," "modified line item veto" for the president, on a two-year "trial" basis. "A second opinion on congressional spending decisions may help us find a cure" to the growing deficit.[96] The item veto (of a section or paragraph), was to have been available only when Congress combined all spending in a single package, which it then did as often as possible to thwart the president by denying the maximum amount of voters their special delights. This caveat, as opposed to two or more sections, was a dilution of the 1984 edition, which had 24 signers, including Senators Kennedy and Proxmire, and failed to get traction during Republican control. Back in the majority, the Democrats knew where "huge trainloads of pork" would go and combined 13 bills into a $576 billion "continuing resolution" to preclude a veto.[97]

## The End Game: Turning Outward

Given the turgid atmosphere in Olympia, the third administration turned to and tried to engage the public to an unheard of degree. "People have become increasingly interested in public decision making." Washington was on "the threshold of a new opportunity" — if growth were managed for quality. Technology was slashing the time for decisions "to assure a favorable future." Alternatives for Washington (AFW) was underway in late 1972. Its mission was to mobilize "the great corps of volunteer citizens who wait silently in every community …to recapture, if not the violence of the American Revolution, at least its spirit." Over 40,000 citizens and 450 organizations responded to an open-ended "Delphi" questionnaire. In the last half of 1974, a working group of 150 held up to ten seminars a day across the state to prepare a report to the 1975 legislature. A new Office on Voluntarism was created by executive fiat within the governor's office and drew thousands of citizens to work with agencies. The reform era was fading into twilight and few of AFW's ideas got an immediate response, but most were enacted over the decade.[98]

The "legislative-executive" legacies trumpeted in Evans' 1977 State of the State address included less welfare cheating than any state since 1964, and the lowest percentage increase in state taxes per capita. More high school graduates were in college than all but one other state. The Evergreen State was first to offer special education for the handicapped, to have a Department of Ecology, and among the first five to pass a Solid Waste Disposal Act. Large tankers had been ruled off Puget Sound. The voice of the social liberal resounded for low-income public housing and a "judicial article" in the constitution for disciplining judges. Just eleven legislators who knew Evans as a freshman 20 years before were left to hear him.

## From WASP to Son of the Sixties

It is unlikely that Evans' legislative successes will be equaled. The Vietnam-tortured 1960s were a seedtime for government expansion unmatched since the two Roosevelts. He was the beneficiary and archetype of the era's expansive mind-set. The war stimulated economy, social turmoil, inflation, and federal dollars became allies of innovation. Then economic "stagflation," Watergate's numbing residue, disillusionment and detachment set in. By 1981, legislative staff tripled to 250 in session and professional lobbyists sextupled to 125, effectively adding two more "branches" to the three-part government. The process complicated and slowed, and interventionist courts regularly reinterpreted legislative intent. Since the 1990s, tax take away initiatives have pummeled legislators into a defensive position, as 400 new exemptions in the name of fostering clean industries or competing with other states have turned a distorted tax system into an indecipherable quagmire.[99]

The Evans regime's downsides include the belief that money would always be available or that more could be arranged, sometimes beyond fiscal wisdom. If a stable 40-year funding cycle for the five pension systems had been converted to a "five year rolling reserve" to free hundreds of millions of dollars, for lack of long-term investments, the cost of pensions would have doubled.[100] The "twenty-fifth month," crediting revenues from the first month of a new biennium to the last month of the old was a one-off expedient at the expense to the state's credit. "Light-bulb snatches," moving balances in smaller accounts to the General Fund subversions. Tailing a national trend to relax discipline in the prisons was dubious. Fortunately, the "Resident's Governance Council" did not take over the penitentiary. Work releases, sardonically maligned as the "Take a Lifer to Dinner program," quietly ended after the state troopers lost their lives. Collective bargaining, if added to tenure, would not have generated more money for higher education.

The sobriquet "Daniel Jackson Hardhead"[101] was earned. Legislative loyalists felt both admiration and irritation as executive requests were run out one more time. The admirable request for a constitutional convention was grounded by too many major interests with protections to defend. Public fears of what might happen were stronger than any embarrassment over a document longer than the Magna Carta or the U.S. Constitution. It was too much water for the legislature to carry: amending a paragraph at a time had to be settled for.[102] Further surgery on the executive branch went the way of Langlie's for the same reasons: partisanship, fear of an over strong executive, and resistance from statewide elected officials. The other great detriment to efficient service, a genuine state "merit" plan, was suffocated by the employee unions, who favor rigid seniority.

## Ability and Courage Meet at an Opportune Time

Evans' "fearlessness," and his willingness to invest his political capital are the statesman's gold standard. The two tries at tax reform, "the major unresolved issue,"[103] stand as the ultimate testament to his political fortitude. The challenge to the Right failed, but drew a new class of talent into the legislature and the precincts, compensating for Goldwaterism. Advocating the abortion referendum of 1970 piqued not a few of the churchly, but gave women the right to choose. The environmental laws speak to a sense of timing, careful preparation, and promotional ability. Conservationists enthused by the path breaking environmental laws were upset by Evans' endorsement of nuclear energy.

An aura of integrity was as evident as the controversies. His conscience preceded politics. The death penalty, which Evans came out against in 1972, was nevertheless restored two to one by the voters.[104] In the rebellious atmosphere of the 1970s, the *Tacoma News Tribune* noticed that Evans seemed to be campaigning more for the $465 million in "Washington Future" bond issues than himself, while Rosellini offered $100 million in cuts "as a minimum goal."[105] "I don't believe for one minute ... we should start shortchanging the people we are trying to serve by responding to political pressure," Evans responded. As early as 1964 he had joined citizens groups for "full disclosure" of campaign finances[106] and in 1971 the "openness" bar was raised by Initiative 271. Evans' mind retained incredible amounts of detail and translated it into cogent arguments in 1,262 press conferences. These were sandwiched between 1,495 intra-state trips and 160 more out-of-state ones on regional and national matters or to stimulate international trade.[107]

As early as January 1965, a journalist asked Evans if his "philosophy" had changed. "I'm really not aware that I've changed," he replied, "terminology" had.[108] How then did a "birthright Republican" mutate into the Progressive's Progressive, a Teddy Roosevelt in the social revolution of the 1960s, and the bête noire of his party's right? The answer is "politics in the blood." Evans was bathed in the Progressive WASP tradition of Northeast Seattle, home to civic mugwump-change-oriented Republicans who were city councilmen, mayors, and governors from the New Deal until the 1980s.[109] Two dispositions were ingrained.

His family's long public history was as party activists and pragmatic practitioners, not ideologues. Playing devil's advocate at the dinner table with two brothers may have sowed a Populist streak fleshed out by Jim Dolliver, a son of Kansas. Eagle scouting at Camp Parsons, where the sons of the bourgeoisie learned to "be prepared, clean, brave and reverent" instilled these virtues and later lent the valuable moniker "Straight Arrow." He acted as if politics was everyone's duty and on gaining a statewide constituency struck a "contrarian," independent course. Intent, penetrating, blunt, and diplomatic by turns, Evans was an anomaly, the serious man who did not take himself too seriously, "with a penchant for analysis and an appealing sense of purpose."[110]

Evans' prime asset was his capacity for growth; a mind that was both logical and imaginative. His ability, courage, and exceptional opportunities melded as the subdued fifties swung into the individualistic sixties. The "Blueprint for Progress" was classic conservatism — changing to preserve — metamorphosed into government-driven activism. "We are not now, and never will be again, the same nation, a fact history cannot deny … the future cannot prevent … the status quo cannot resolve," the governor reminded collegians in the 1970s. "I would like to see radical and unconventional ideas dazzle the conventional wisdom. For it is in innovation, and not convention, that the great solutions lie."[111] Rebuttals to critics that he was a true "conservative's conservative," fell on deaf ears. Evans believed, partly on sentiment and loyalty, he had not "changed." In a television special from the Evans School of Public Affairs at the University of Washington in January 2008, he insisted, "I would call myself a conservative … for limited government." The Republican Party had left him, not the reverse.

He was in fact one of few who became more liberal as they age. Arresting examples rose from his devotion to the university, and grew during three terms as a regent. In 2004, Evans and Booth Gardner campaigned for a one-cent, $1 billion a biennium increase in the sales tax to be devoted to public and higher education, the kind of "dedicated fund" he vociferously opposed as executive. In 2008, he lobbied the legislature for diversions from King County's food and beverage, car rental, motel-hotel taxes and a $20 million sales tax deferral on construction costs to enlarge and upgrade Husky Stadium. The liberal Speaker of the House rejected the idea, as the economy faltered in the face of loose mortgage practices. Had Evans grown too acccustomed to being on the side of the angels, even as the state's budget slumped into its worst pitfall in 70 years?[112]

Evans ability and courage met exceptional opportunities. Emboldened by the cornucopia of his times, "One of the 20 best governors in the 20th

Century" semi-consciously shifted to his left foot, edging toward being a "Progressive" in the New Deal sense while acknowledging only that he was a "Progressive" in the way of TR's New Nationalism. The state's second era of reform was four years past its apogee on March 24, 1976, when he set aside a fourth term with a celebration of TR's vigor: "It is not the critic who counts. The credit belongs to the man who is actually in the arena … who knows the great enthusiasms, the great devotions, and spends himself in a worthy cause, who, at the best, knows in the end the triumph of high achievement, and who at the worst if he fails, at least fails while daring greatly."[113] Evans was Washington's Wilson, Warren, La Follette, the hallmark of an era.

## Peer Leader: The National Stage

Republican governors have historically been more moderate than their peers in congress. Determination to enable the states to preempt Congress quickly put Evans in the front rank of governors, and subdue the blight of Goldwaterim. He chaired the Western Republican Governors Conference and the National Republican Governors Campaign Committee when its 17 members took the offense in 1965. "The Republican governors vigorously oppose any form of radicalism. We need to become inclusive, rather than exclusive. A great broad-based political party is more effective than any narrow, exclusive political clique can ever become." Senior governors tutored the newly elected, prefiguring the GOP's comeback two years later.[114]

The National Governors' Conference had been as much play as policy. Breaking away from the lugubrious Council of State Governments, the NGC's staff was beefed up and separately endowed a "think tank" to scrutinize emerging issues. The new approach took hold. On becoming president, Governor Jimmy Carter cleared all new federal regulations with the NGC before publishing them in the Federal Register. The NGC (now the National Governors Association) met in Seattle in 1973, with Evans presiding, 20 years after first appearing under Langlie's gavel. Many colleagues wanted to ignore Watergate: Evans pressed the states to take the lead in restoring confidence in government. Unlike Oregon's Tom McCall, he was opposed to asking the president to resign, if Nixon gave the House Judiciary Committee the records it asked. He and the Republican governors still believed Nixon's promise of "full disclosure" and claims of innocence, "But if full disclosure is damming, all I've said doesn't hold."[115]

"Many governors dream of being president, but in my time only five came close," Evans reminisced.[116] "If governors regularly voted on their selection of the ten best governors at any one time, neither Jimmy Carter nor Ronald Reagan would have made the list. Only Nelson Rockefeller was uniformly admired. He constantly yearned for the presidency but could never convince conservatives of his loyalty to the party."[117] This might be said of Evans' national interests.[118] The synchrony of the two is startling. Rockefeller viewed the relation of the states to the nation as the "cardinal question," "paid little attention to ideology," and vetoed between 35 percent in 1965 and 20 percent in 1971 of bills reaching his desk. (The reader should bear on mind that in New York bills pass at almost twice the rate of Washington, and many more deserve death).[119] Evans' backing of Rockefeller's last-minute lunge at Nixon for the nomination at Miami in 1968, like his over-rehearsed, secularly progressive, almost nonpartisan keynote, did not resonate with the regulars. "People are interested in action," he claimed, "not clichés, problem solving, not promise making; an active concern with the future, not a passive commitment to the past."

Evans divided his time with the youthful protesters outside the convention, trying to understand their animus. He concluded the GOP must align itself with America's impatient younger generation, who had "served notice that satisfaction cannot be measured alone by productivity, that there is a need for service and contribution beyond the attainment of material success."[120] The message went into the mist and Watergate wiped out the GOP's gains until 1980.[121] Evans, state general chairman for the Ford organization 1976, was left off the all-Reagan delegation, and never considered for an appointment when the Gipper won the presidency in 1980.

The first his three "Last Careers" was the presidency of the Evergreen State College (1977-83). Washington's riposte to Oregon's iconoclastic Reed College, with its interdisciplinary courses, evaluation portfolios instead of grades, and relatively homogenous student body stimulated Evans' expansive side. The "Geoducks" motto is "Let it all hang out," and the Evergreen's "Social Contract — A Guide for Civility and Freedom" leaves questions as to where the emphasis lies.

One task was never enough. He was on the Pacific Northwest Power Council in 1983 when Henry "Scoop" Jackson was felled by a heart attack after 30 years in the U.S. Senate. For ability and electability, Evans was the obvious choice for Governor John Spellman, and defeated Congressman Mike Lowry. He was in the majority (1983-86), supporting President Reagan 85 percent of the time in 1985.[122] Evans was assigned the Energy and Natural Resources, the Foreign Relations committee, and vice chair of the Select Committee on Indian Affairs. He co-sponsored S-1511, with mandatory child support and work training to replace AFDC, adopted by Governor Gardner as the "Family Independence Program,"[123] pursued sufficient funding to vitrify the nuclear waste at Hanford and won protection for the Columbia Gorge.

Evans left the senate five years later, at 63. Used to the driver's seat, he was in a back seat in a body renowned for its "deliberative" ways, and disappointed. The "duel of debate, the exchange of ideas," was not there. Often one spoke to an almost-empty room and committee meetings stalled for lack of a quorum. The Senate "had lost its focus and was in danger of losing its soul .... I have lived through five years of bickering and protracted paralysis .... I just can't face another six years of frustrating gridlock." His "unfinished agenda" encompassed gender pay equity, a bipartisan foreign policy, balanced two-year budgets, and a return of "the joy of debate."

The governor's image took on a patina over 30 years. He opened a boutique consulting firm overlooking Elliott Bay in downtown Seattle, joined the commentariat on KIRO television (1989-94), scribed for editorial pages, and sat on a half-dozen corporate boards.[124] In 1993, Governor Mike Lowry named him a regent of his alma mater. The booming voice with the probing questions rang out in the normally sedate sittings. Governor Locke renewed the term, and Evans was president of the board in 1996-97.[125]

The Evans era was enriched by an extraordinary partnership. Nancy Bell Evans' ancestors had held office too, and she was there for the "endurance contests" of the campaign trail despite three young sons. Dan Jr. and Mark were five and two when they moved into the mansion. Bruce arrived a year later. A Whitman graduate and former music teacher, the First Lady oversaw the restoration of the governor's mansion and created a Mansion Foundation with $250,000 to refurbish it with period furniture. She co-founded the Governor's Festival of the Arts, and three decades later was on the boards of the Seattle Symphony, educational television station KCTS, Whitman College, and fundraised for others. The Nancy Bell Evans Center on Nonprofits and Philanthropy is part of the Evans School of Public Affairs at the University of Washington. In 2003, they jointly accepted Seattle's First Citizen Award for "a lifelong definition of citizenship and community involvement."[126] A similar state title would have been just as deserved.

# *Pictorials, Section Two*

*Mon Wallgren looked like a governor.*

*Wallgren appointed former Montana Congressman Jerry O'Connell State Democratic Chair, to his regret.*

*State Representative William Pennock of the WOAPU broadcasting for welfare Initiative 176. He later came out as a Communist, and committed suicide.*

*"The New Order of Cincinnatus. From Left: (City Comptroller M.H. Strousse) councilmen Fred Hamley, Arthur Langlie, David Lockwood and their ally Mrs. F.F. Powell."*

*A "Trackless Trolley" that replaced the 'Street Railway' in Seattle in 1941. History Link*

*War supercedes the Depression: Governor Langlie meets New York Mayor Fiorello LaGuardia, the president's Director of Mobilization, at Seattle's King Street Station.*

*Senior military officers meet with the governor (at left head of table) in 1941 WSA*

**WARTIME CIVIL CONTROL ADMINISTRATION**

**Presidio of San Francisco, California**

**July 22, 1942**

# INSTRUCTIONS TO ALL PERSONS OF JAPANESE ANCESTRY

## Living in the Following Area:

**All that portion of the County of Fresno, State of California, within that boundary beginning at the point at which California State Highway No. 180 intersects the easterly limits of the City of Fresno; thence easterly along the southerly line of said State Highway No. 180 to the easterly bank of Kings River; thence southerly along the easterly bank of Kings River to its intersection with the Fresno-Tulare County Line; thence southwesterly along said County Line to the westerly line of U. S. Highway No. 99; thence northwesterly along the westerly line of said Highway No. 99 to the southerly limits of the City of Fresno; thence easterly and northerly along the limits of said City of Fresno to the point of beginning.**

Pursuant to the provisions of Civilian Exclusion Order No. 106, this Headquarters, dated July 22, 1942, all persons of Japanese ancestry, both alien and non-alien, will be evacuated from the above area by 12 o'clock noon, P. W. T., Tuesday, August 11, 1942.

No Japanese person will be permitted to move into, or out of, the above area after 5:00 A. M., P. W. T., Wednesday, July 22, 1942, without obtaining special permission from the representative of the Commanding General, Northern California Sector, at the Civil Control Station located at:

Sanger Union High School Gymnasium,
Sanger, California.

Such permits will only be granted for the purpose of uniting members of a family, or in cases of grave emergency.

The Civil Control Station is equipped to assist the Japanese population affected by this evacuation in the following ways:

1. Give advice and instructions on the evacuation.
2. Provide services with respect to the management, leasing, sale, storage or other disposition of most kinds of property, such as real estate, business and professional equipment, household goods, boats, automobiles and livestock.
3. Provide temporary residence elsewhere for all Japanese in family groups.
4. Transport persons and a limited amount of clothing and equipment to their new residence.

**The Following Instructions Must Be Observed:**

1. A responsible member of each family, preferably the head of the family, or the person in whose name most of the property is held, and each individual living alone, will report to the Civil Control Station to receive further instructions. This must be done between 8:00 A. M. and 5:00 P. M. on Monday, July 27, 1942, or between 8:00 A. M. and 5:00 P. M. on Tuesday, July 28, 1942.
2. Evacuees must carry with them on departure for the Relocation Project the following property:
   (a) Bedding and linens (no mattress) for each member of the family;
   (b) Toilet articles for each member of the family;
   (c) Extra clothing for each member of the family;
   (d) Essential personal effects for each member of the family, provided the total baggage does not exceed 150 pounds for each person over 11 years of age and 75 pounds for each child under 12 and over 5 years of age. Other personal effects can be shipped at the evacuees' expense, by parcel post or express to the Relocation Project.

   All items taken on the train or shipped must be packaged, tied and plainly marked with the name of the owner and numbered according to instructions obtained at the Civil Control Station where more detailed information can be obtained as to items likely to be needed.
3. No pets of any kind will be permitted.
4. The United States Government through its agencies will provide for the storage, at the sole risk of the owner, of the more substantial household items, such as iceboxes, washing machines, pianos and other heavy furniture. Cooking utensils and other small items will be accepted for storage if crated, packed and plainly marked with the name and address of the owner. Only one name and address will be used by a given family.
5. Each family, and individual living alone, will be furnished transportation to the Relocation Project. Private means of transportation will not be utilized. All instructions pertaining to the movement will be obtained at the Civil Control Station.

**Go to the Civil Control Station between the hours of 8:00 A. M. and 5:00 P. M., Monday, July 27, 1942, or between the hours of 8:00 A. M. and 5:00 P. M., Tuesday, July 28, 1942, to receive further instructions.**

J. L. DeWITT
Lieutenant General, U. S. Army
Commanding

SEE CIVILIAN EXCLUSION ORDER NO. 106

*Internment of Japanese-Americans in 1942, under Presidential Executive Order 1066. WSA*

Evelyn, Arthur and Carrie Ellen Langlie strike a campaign pose, 1944. WSA

*Ross Cunningham, Langlie's first Chief of Staff, and veteran Seattle Times Editorial Board Editor (in 1958). ST.*

*The McCarthy era: A hearing of the Canwell Committee at the University of Washington, 1949. PI/MHI*

*Reconstruction of the third (and present) capitol after the earthquake of 1949.*

*From left, Governors Langlie, Martin (then a member of the State House) and Wall-gren in 1949.*

*Langlie ran for the U.S. Senate in 1952, at President Eisenhower's behest.*

*Albert and Ethel Rosellini on their wedding day in 1937.*

*Dr. Garrett Heyns revived Institutions, then taught sociology at the University of Washington. WSL*

Elected to the State Senate in 1938, Rosellini ran for governor four times, losing the last race in 1972 by .07 perscent. In 1956, he campaigned with his daughters, from left, Lynn Janey and Sue Ann.
MHI

*Warren Bishop, left, served as both Chief of Staff and Director of the Budget. Former Speaker Charlie Hodde directed three departments as the administrations' trouble shooter.*

*Left to right: Mrs. Rosellini, the Governor, Pope Pius XII, Speaker of the Washington House John L. O'Brien. Rome 1958. He worried his Catholicism hurt politically.*

*U.S. Senator Henry M. Jackson, John F. Kennedy and Governor Rosellini campaign on Seattle's Fourth Avenue, Fall, 1960. "The hostile Seattle Times' Pacific Northwest section selected this photo for a feature story on Rosellini titled, "Success and Scandal: Champion of Progressives, friend of a felon, Al Rosellini embraces the paradox." PI/MHI*

*Ethel and Al, then a member of the State Transportation Commission, at the rededication of the Second Lake Washington Floating Bridge as "The Governor Albert D. Rosellini Bridge" in the 1980s. ST*

*Roommates, 1957. From left, Joel Pritchard, Dan Evans, Charles Moriarity, James Anderson and Slade Gorton. They held nine state, three federal and one judicial offices.*

*Dan Evans, aka 'Straight Arrow,' as an Eagle Scout in 1941.*

*Dan Evans, governor at 39.*

*Evans and Jim Dolliver, his Chief of Staff for 12 years, and later Chief Justice of the Supreme Court. WSA*

*Speaker John O'Brien glares down at Evans, as the coalition ousts O'Brien in 1963. AR*

*Governor Evans and his boys, late 1960s*

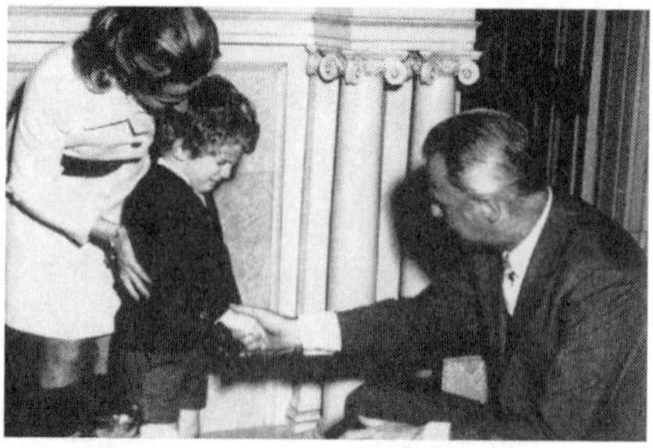

*Left to right: Definitely displeased: Nancy and Danny Evans, and Vice President Spiro Agnew. WSA*

*Evans was keynoter at the 1968 Republican National Convention. The speech was too substanial for the audience. Cover, Time 8/9/68.*

*Dan and Nancy Evans were named Seattle's "Citizens of the Year" in 2001.*

Chapter 8

# Dixy Lee Ray: Anti-Politics

*(1977-81)*

## The Year of the Outsider

Nineteen seventy-six was a year "ins" were ushered out. Voters sickened by Watergate, Georgia's earnest, idealistic governor, Jimmy Carter, was summoned to the nation's capitol. Washington State got more than it bargained for in its iconoclastic first woman executive. Dixy Lee Ray, 62, was a popular professor of marine biology at the University of Washington from 1945 to 1972, then in nine years, made the Pacific Science Center into a significant educational resource. She wore a red sweatshirt to work and toured Seattle in a Jaguar convertible with a hand-honked rubber horn. Ray was "the faculty club version of the bionic woman," assured, impressive, informal, lively, and a master raconteur.[1]

President Nixon, interviewing her for the Atomic Energy Commission (AEC) asked, "Are you a Republican or a Democrat?" "Neither," she replied. President Ford named her chair in 1973, but her relations with the White House became "somewhat distant." She complained of the controller's lack of competency to make technical judgments" and attempts to "involve himself in the programmatic activities of this agency." Asked by Secretary of the Interior Rogers C. B. Morton what the proper relation of agencies and the president's office should be, she "thanked" him. "It is the first time in my 18 months as chair my opinion on any issue of ... policy has been sought." Existing "staff-to-staff communications [only] serves as a means to circumvent top management and keep the bureaucracy in firm control."[2]

She concluded "People deserve better government than they're getting," and that the "real action" was at the state level. In July 1975, she was home and taking on speaking engagements. At the Science Center, she had become friends with Eddie Carlson, chair of Western International Hotels. A "go-to" public figure since the World's Fair, Carlson corralled his peers for breakfasts in places like the Grill of Seattle's classic Olympic Hotel.[3] Ray was back in her best milieu, in front of small, sympathetic, "teachable" audiences. Below the short gray hair, she wore her almost every day uniform — an open neck blouse and a polyester suit, hung on a wide frame over wedgies. Behind the transfixing stare, the bright eyes, and friendly face, charisma and practice on the national lecture circuit made for mesmerizing performances. There was no need to delve in detail on a welcome theme: how government could be more "businesslike." More credible endorsements emerged.

Lou Guzzo, former art critic and executive editor of the *Post-Intelligencer* and her administrative assistant at the AEC, introduced Ray downtown. "My name is Dixy Lee Ray and I'm running for governor," she would say, borrowing a Jimmy Carter line, and add another like, "The professional politicians who are my primary opponents should resign from office so others can step in."[4] The jabs hurt Wes Uhlman, her chief rival, who had been too close to his constituency as mayor of Seattle for nine years, more than State Senator Jim McDermott, a "citizen legislator."[5]

It is likely she ran as a Democrat thinking she could not beat John Spellman the low key highly visible King County executive in the GOP primary. The politically inept Guzzo, a Republican,[6] patched together a staff of three, ignored the Democratic Party and even considered dropping a party affiliation. Strategy sessions dealt with the size of bumper stickers. Political professionals were stunned as Ray's amateur campaign came on in a rush. The clumsiness ended when the staff director quit in a salary dispute and Blair Butterworth ex-aide to House Speaker Len Sawyer came to the fore. When 400 came to a fund-raiser costing $7,000 that cleared $23,000, Butterworth knew he was on to something. The remainders of Watergate, Vietnam, and incongruously the women's liberation movement were coalescing with a periodic voter rebellion. After the primary Ray mended fences with the Uhlmanites and U.S. Senator Henry Jackson duly endorsed her. She did not join the club; they joined her.[7]

John Spellman faced no serious opposition in two of his three elections. He got a slow start, was poorly informed on state issues, swallowed his words, and lost on his home turf. On November 2, "Hello Dolly" became "Hello Dixy." "All these people," she marveled at the victory party crowd of 500.[8] From there it was downhill, as amplified by the media. Spellman had been submerged by a tide of national publicity; Ray was sure she won despite the press. "We've shown that you the people are electing your representatives," she told the celebrants. "They are not being elected by the publishers and editors of the daily papers." The major papers were for Spellman. "So they backed the wrong horse. Do you think I'm going to forget that right away?"[9] Politicians get angry at the press but do not say so, and never try to get even. Ray's long memory was a millstone.

## Counselors from the Closet

Who would advise the first governor in 35 years to lack legislative experience? Ray ignored Uhlman and his social agenda and dismissed State Senator Martin Durkan, another primary opponent, after he told her an income tax was necessary. She distrusted the help proffered by Evans and his departmental directors.[10] During the summer, Guzzo had angrily distanced Ray from senior legislative Democrats. "The gangsters don't have any influence in this campaign," he told a reporter. "I threw [Senate Majority Leader August P.] Mardesich out of the office myself, but nobody will believe me."[11] She had virtually no middlemen wise to the ways of Olympia to pick politically astute managers. Except for outsider Orin Smith of Touche Ross who came to give advice on systems, the professionals were either ignored by or unknown to the amateur entourage who escorted her to the capitol.

She preferred irregulars like Taul Watanabe, a Burlington Northern vice president. Watanabe was fined $1,200 by the Public Disclosure Commission for over 100 admitted violations over four years. Crusty Merle Adlum, a maritime union head and port commissioner acted as point man in King County. Louis Pederson, Tacoma's George Meany, took the chair of the Liquor Control Board. None had been in Olympia for more than a day at a time.[12] Ray's staffing set the direction and capped the capacities of her administration. Evans had relied heavily on the central staff; she used agency heads. The ubiquitous Guzzo, her "alter ego" as "counselor to the governor," tapped friends and middle-aged party regulars. Old colleagues at the *P-I* blanched on hearing, "The spoils system has as much going for it as it does against it, but it is the best way I can see." Press Secretary Duane Treckker added "Being a loyal Democrat wasn't enough … Putting our people into place is a very scientific thing," but "when it boils down in the end you pick the one who was a Dixy supporter over the one who was not."[13] Ray turned a deaf ear to liberal Democrats' complaints about state employees being asked to resign. "I promised there would be change, and there will be," the governor persisted, "and with every pink slip we're going to send some Kleenex." The average age of the cabinet announced in late December was 56. There were six vacancies, including the crucial budget director. Ultimately, there was one woman (Diane Oberquell chair of the Board of Prison Terms and Paroles, a sub-cabinet rank, proved forceful) and one Hispanic. Five were conspicuously able and fully prepared. Ambidextrous, articulate, ex-Speaker Charlie Hodde reappeared as Director of Revenue. Former Senator Web Hallauer, an intelligent iconoclast, came out of his northeastern Washington orchards to take over Ecology, prescribing "benign neglect." Gordon Sandison gave up his senate seat for Fisheries. Colonel Bob Hollister left a business professorship to run Retirement Systems. Orin Smith stayed three years as an astute, if remote budget director, cryptically enforcing "competent management decisions where competency was lacking."[14] Ray's close friend Dr. Harlan McNutt, Health Director for Pierce County was far over his depth at DSHS and left in a year, finding it "more of an unmanageable morass than I had originally anticipated."[15]

Kasuo Watanabe at Commerce and Economic Development, Bob Mickelson at Agriculture, Lawrence Bradley the buffeted energy director, Ralph Larson of Game, Charles Odegaard the too eager egoist at Parks, Rosalind Woodhouse at Licensing, Betty McClelland at Emergency Services, State Patrol Chief Robert Landon, and DSHS veteran Jerry Thompson were competent if uninspired. Bill Bulley lingered at Transportation, and Senator Bob Bailey became chair of the regulatory Utilities and Transportation Commission (UTC). Passing over Joe Davis, who was nearing retirement as president of the United Labor Lobby for Department of Labor and Industries, denied Labor its traditional place at the head the department's tenured drones. The governor may have thought the bright, aggressive Labor warrior too demanding for her blood.

Others ranged from stodgy to stumbling. Vern Barnes, a truculent bureaucrat with 25 years' federal time took over General Administration and fired most of the agency's managers a week before taking over and left town. Barnes refused to be questioned by the powerful Legislative Budget Committee and took up battles as small as the legislator's reserved parking. Told it had always been thus, he announced, "I'm going to take it away from them." Asked four years later if he would join the early exodus of directors, he replied, "Hell no." The reaction of Eugene Weigman, an airy former president of the University of Puget who ran Employment Security until her 1980 defeat was, "I did not think at any time there was a possibility the governor would not win."[16]

Some were embarrassments. Bob Collins was given a full-time job as head of the Air National Guard, kept flying for an airline, drew both salaries and denied a time conflict. Retired Seattle police sergeant

Mike Rodosovitch was installed as the brigadier general in charge of the Army National Guard. Then it was discovered he had been fired as a policeman for unexcused absences. State Traffic Safety director Walt Friel, previously a Tacoma car dealer, soon admitted to DWIs. David Jenkins the attractive black designated "special assistant and spokesman," disappeared after escorting the governor at her ten inaugural balls. Lou Guzzo sparred with Blair Butterworth, now the governor's "Assistant for Human Problems and Urban Development," accusing him of taking kickbacks.[17] Butterworth threatened libel, got a written retraction, and left in the spring of 1977. Guzzo became the administration's resident eunuch, minding a "Cultural Affairs" portfolio from a corner of the first floor of the capitol.[18]

## Losing the Game in the First Half

No inexperienced outsider can expect success as governor. Ray underestimated her task and never caught up. So did Paul Bender a systematic retired army colonel she brought from the AEC as "my Jim Dolliver." He confirmed staff assignments on December 17, three weeks before the legislature convened, and left. "If any of you really needs me before January 9," he would "come back for a day or two."[19] Bender dwelt on organization and kept his door closed, often with the red light over it on. His "key purposes" were to "create a situation whereby the Governor can bring maximum possible executive authority to bear on … agencies in spite of existing organizational deficiencies," and avoid duplication of effort. Tasks were grouped by "similarity of purpose." Legal Counsel Jerry Hanna and assistants for Licensing and Public Safety, Resource Management, Energy, Environment, Natural Resources, Health, and Education, were to carry the entire professional load, 15 other staff the rest.[20] The governor's intent was to control the size of government, simplify regulation, secure more equitable taxation, "improve performance" in education, quality of life for seniors, and bring a "balance between economic growth and environment," with the latter subordinate.[21]

## Legislative Follies

"Welcome to controlled chaos," the new executive greeted a reporter in January 1977. Her inaugural speech began with the admission she did not "know all the answers" but wanted to "share my views and make some proposals." Most of the executive requests were secondary in importance and came from Evans' Productivity Council. In March, press spokesman Duane Treckker explained, "She has no legislative program as such. A governor can run and reform state government outside of a legislative program."[22] The media honeymoon lasted 10 days. Well-liked television newsman Joe Zaspel soon found being Legislative Liaison was firefighting. Ray sent a legislative intern to tell House Energy Committee Chairman Donn Charnley (D-Seattle) she was unhappy with changes to her executive request bills and expected to know beforehand "out of respect." Charnley snapped, "The Legislature will do as it wishes."[23] Engaging former senator Jerry Hanna, who came on as the governor's counsel and Zaspel's replacement in March, got agency heads to work through him and focused on "telling the [administration's] story." "You can't demand anything," he mused. "You have to understand [that] … the legislators … have their job to do, and respect that." The receptive conservative Democrats running the legislature were cheered.[24]

The first four of six "task groups," like "Economic Development and Employment," roughly aligned with the specialties of her professional assistants and were composed only of directors, were not convened until September. "Inasmuch as the entire process is to serve the needs of the Governor," Bender reiterated three times, "there is no plan to publish or distribute results."[25] The "full state funding" of public schools passed in 1977 (and implemented in 1979-80), was almost entirely shaped by Majority Leader Mardesich's seven senate committees, (nicknamed "Snow White and the Seven Dwarfs").

As inflationary money poured in, the legislature took away revenue, with Ray's endorsement, starting a 30-year trend of deletions, caps, and exemptions by killing the gift and inheritance taxes, extending six percent per year increase limit on property, and letting the surtaxes on sales and the B&O levies lapse. The task group on Social, Health, and Employment Services got the Human Rights Commission extended, immunization of school children and an inflationary adjustment to workmen's compensation, all but foregone conclusions in 1977, and power to adjudicate claims of the handicapped and criminal penalties for wrongly dispensing prescription drugs. Licensing of home health providers, criteria for a Housing Finance Commission, and developing "agricultural worker parks" fell, but were realized in the Gardner and Locke administrations. The three predictable acts excepted, there was nothing major, save the HFC's rules.

Ray decided not to call a special session in 1978 to keep the legislature out of the capitol, losing the momentum of most of 1977's initiatives. By 1979 she had lost her key sympathizers in both houses. Mardesich had been defrocked as majority leader in a scandal over loose handling of campaign funds. His heir, Gordon Walgren, and Co-Speaker John Bagnariol soon lost their posts to an FBI "sting." Over rushing urinals in the men's room in a Vancouver card room, they were recorded asking a cut of proceeds from expanding gambling.

"Nobody can imagine what this job is like until you're in it," the governor conceded.[26] She admitted her staff lacked the depth to translate her campaign pledges into law. "I will continue to use the task groups as a cornerstone of my administration," she said, on "reactivating" them in August 1979. Adequate meeting space, "some changes in membership to reflect a more mature administration … ample staff" from agencies and incorporating ideas from the private sector would improve yield.[27] A lesser set of suggestions, reflecting lack of staff imagination and her doubtful future came from the governor in June, too late for the session. There had been a proliferation of local ordinances since the 1971 environmental acts. The Task Force on Environmental Management offered one page on "Identification of Priority Issues" and no specifics, and asked only to "clarify and define the respective responsibilities of each unit [level] of government." "Review state laws and regulations affecting land use," echoed Hallauer's "benign neglect."[28] At the same time, Senate Republicans threw out their leadership and geared up for 1980. The Democrats were demoralized, Ray adrift.

## Flying Solo

The governor was "loathe to talk about" her management philosophy, saying, "I'm afraid I don't analyze myself very much." She thought of herself as a delegator — but intervened and found it hard to take advice. An agreement signed by Linda Broderick, her Appointments Secretary, is telltale. Mornings until ten were reserved for Bender and the staff. Ray filled the next two hours herself and no commitments were to be made after two P.M. No governmental official was to be scheduled without express permission. One director opined, "About the only way I can even get in to see her is to do something that makes her mad."

Ray's instrument of choice, a constitutional amendment to allow the executive to "reorganize" state government subject to veto by the legislature within 60 days, went the way of its predecessors. The goal of realigning state government into 20 divisions in three years was beyond reach.[29] Legislators thought government structure was their turf. Their axiom was, "The governor proposes, the legislature disposes." The governor's single voice was heard above the divided, clamorous, part-time bodies, but executive requests need sponsorship and active support by leaders. The governor must expect to see them altered, bargained over, and defeated. The Senate eviscerated the reorganization bill by exempting agencies, then by lowering the vote required to block any change. "It's not that I don't love Dixy Lee Ray," Senate Constitution and Elections Chair Gary Grant (D) explained. "It's just that I love our system of checks and balances better." The governor salted the wound. Senator C. W. "Red" Beck, a Ray loyalist, picked up his receiver to hear: "I just called to thank you for sabotaging my most important bill of the session. (Click)."[30]

## Retrograde Movements

The governor had promised to disassemble DSHS. "Super agencies" were not justified by size, but by "efficient and economical delivery of services." Its secretary, Dr. McNutt, set up three deputy secretaries and seven regions, extending Evans' approach. Ray sent orders to agencies without consulting their managers. When nursing home operators threatened to shut down if payments for state patients were not increased, she sent her own expert, which McNutt thought "unnecessary meddling." Sacked in May of 1978, he prophesied, "Dr. Ray is very much enamored of government by [financial] management, and if she continues it will be miserable for her."[31] Two of the governor's task forces convinced her DSHS should be left intact. A "good manager" could make it work, and Jerry Thompson, 36, advised by team of private sector experts, took over. This was the only thing she recalled changing her mind about.[32] All else failing, Ray and Bender decided they could at least clamp down on the "task groups, advisory bodies, boards, commissions, committees and councils spawned without explicit permission of the governor."[33]

Thompson complained in early December of 1979 of "serious overcrowding" in the prisons and that the parole board had stiffened its guidelines without informing him. A month later, driven by the governor and DSHS' preference for new wings at Monroe, his response to a House study urging adoption of the federal penitentiary on McNeil Island was that it was not available because it had not been declared surplus. In between Evan's solution, early release, was renamed "community programming." Over 500 inmates received them in a year, although at the outset Washington was second among the 13 western states in combined probations and paroles. Prison capacity in 1985 (apparently assuming Monroe's expansion) was to be 4,640, not the House's 4,231.[34]

Ray's anchor task force, chaired by General Administration's Barnes, was stocked from state agencies like Game, Fisheries, and Natural Resources and brimmed with their own ambitions. It opted for transforming McNeil Island to a park, wildlife refuge research platform, and "historic preservation" project, what fearful Steilacoom across the channel wanted, all at "no cost" to the state. Barnes' team implicitly acknowledged the prison would be available after October 1980, but the restoration cost of $14.3 million was forbidding. Ray told the superior court judges the "stigma" of overcrowding was an Evans legacy. She knew the public was turning "tough on crime" and that building new prisons took "three to four years." Even if crime rates stabilized, population growth meant more prisoners — then repeated Barnes' findings. The media had made McNeil "a major news story these past months ... for the wrong reasons." She was for taking it over — as "a multimillion dollar natural asset that cannot be replaced" and using it "for the planned use and enjoyment of the citizens ... protection of the wildlife and [the] natural environment of the island." The governor lived just east on Fox Island, and may have had the NIMBY syndrome[35] that stalled the opening of prisons everywhere.

The erosive effects of "deinstitutionalization," a child of the late 1960s, were well documented. The "tools of traditional prison control" — isolation and censorship, non-negotiable punishment, fear and freedom from public vision — had been taken away. B. J. Rhay, her state prison warden resisted the trend and then washed his hands of the "residents" new freedoms. Walla Walla bordered on Bedlam. "The ... custody staff lost control over life inside the walls." Conditions had continued to deteriorate in 1977, with two murders, inmate assaults, several escapes, and a lockdown uncovering a "large inventory" of weapons, drugs, escape paraphernalia, and other ... contraband. Acting Superintendent Douglas Vinzant was fired the next year. Inside prison industries were nearly bankrupt, and inmates got illegal leaves. Ray named James Spalding, "a career professional, intelligent, tough, conservative" to retrain and discipline the staff. The errant early release expedient ended.[36]

New laws and liberalizing court decisions impacted the other state institutions adding burdens and hastening patient turnover before communities were prepared. By 1976, large numbers of the developmentally disabled went to nursing homes, congregate care facilities, adult foster homes, and, in some cases, home. Northern State Hospital and the Spruce Canyon Youth Camp were closed; new construction tumbled. Ray changed managers to assure "a strong institutional base," reopened Northern State, built cottages in place of the archaic residential halls at the Rainier School and Lakeland village, added a 144-bed mental health operation at Monroe and laid out "long-range master plans." Her 1979 capital budget proposed "substantial renovation or replacement of all major facilities for adult corrections, mental health, and developmental disabilities over the next ten years." Director Thompson's extension of the umbrella [the multiservice center] approach, "promotion of regionalization, exempting of supervisors, moving managers with a "lack of skills and commitment," shrinking of overstaffed headquarters, restoration of order in the prisons, and drafting the capital plan, all with Ray's unstinting support, stand as her regime's sole significant achievements.[37]

## Finances: See No Evil

Faced with a $100 million gap for the upcoming biennium in January 1977, Ray imposed a hiring freeze, and belatedly put forward a spending plan $320 million below Evans'. Two small tax surcharges were retained and property tax collections speeded up, reminiscent of his "25th month" sales tax gimmick. At $10.2 billion, it had "nothing more than programs already being conducted," education, mental health, and prisons partially excepted, plus an inflationary factor of seven percent. To be "thoroughly prepared" for the 1978 session with a "quality" package, in September the panel on "Executive Management and Fiscal Affairs," was charged with "recommending ways to control the size and cost of state government without lowering the quality or quantity of services." The "inefficient" personnel system, "unsatisfactory" budget development and accounting, "unorganized" capital investments, "decentralized" purchasing, and the "difficulty" of appointing or removing senior executives were targets.[38] The state employee unions, the Democrats' largest clientele, blocked the second essential objective, performance evaluations. The two state employee unions resisted them as a preamble to merit pay and because of internal politics: rewarding the outstanding shrinks the money pool for the majority of the rank and file, and perhaps jobs. No traceable progress was made in the other arenas.

Ray's third prominent goal was "to place effective controls on major taxes, severely limit special levies … and impose a modest state income tax" as an offset. Charlie Hodde sold her his plan to get the same balance as HJR 37 of eight years earlier. It died in committee. "Don't get mad, Dixy," counseled Bob Cummings, dean of the capitol press corps, "you aren't the first."[39] In an inversion of the Evans years, Ray was left holding the line and riding ahead on the rising wave of inflationary income. "Management of state government is not to be measured solely on the basis of what it has done," she explained to the Spokane Club in the spring of 1978. "It is appropriate also to point to the benefits of some actions not taken. For example, for the first time in ten years a special session of the legislature will not be called 1978. I am more than ever convinced of our basic orientation here in Washington." The State Labor Council's Convention heard the answers were "developing a healthy economy to meet, the need for more jobs and … reducing the size and cost of government. The state had sloughed off 445 positions in 20 months. Boeing was hiring again; all was well. A year later at the Seattle Chamber of Commerce Ray described her proposed 1979-81 budget as "current level." "The economy of this state has grown, and I think it has grown in a responsible fashion. We can look forward … to a future that is very sound economically."[40]

## Reversing Field: Restraint Ends

In reality inflation and spending had driven the 1977-79 version up 36 percent, as inflation peaked at 13 percent a year. Her "conservative" chief molders of the senate, Majority Leader "Augie" Mardesich and Senator Hubert Donohue, chair of Ways and Means, counseled relying on the windfall to mitigate her political poverty. She shelved the Hodde Plan, insisting in some "small but significant ways" taxes could be made less regressive.[41] Tax reform gave way to the pleasant task of tax relief, guised as "spending reform." The elimination of special school levies was advanced a year. Shifting the state levy of $2 per $1,000 of assessed value on property could eliminate school levies altogether for those over 62 and a constitutional change provide low-income tax relief. Extending the six percent per year increase lid to all property taxes would please everyone. The counties and cities, who had "experienced [relative] declines in their respective rates of [revenue] growth," under legislative limits were to be empowered. City sales levies could double from 0.5 to one percent and cover gasoline; counties got a local option utilities tax, some of the state's sales tax, and ability to lift the 106 percent lid for "limited periods to fund specific projects."[42] The road to reform, an income tax, had been turned into avenues for local self-help by gubernatorial tepidity, legislative timidity, and the closeness of the 1980 election. "Good politics" is not always good policy.

Business went on as usual in the agencies despite Chief of Staff Bender's order to reduce administratively created task groups and advisory bodies by requiring "six elements" of justification. The "Governor's Breakfast Seminar Program" began to improve linkage with the cabinet and generate executive request bills. To get to "policy," Ray asked that they "drop discussion of organization of departments" and focus on specifics like prisons, the "place of lobbyists," and the economy. "This administration will be thoroughly prepared when the Forty-Seventh Legislature … meets in January 1981," she wrote the groups in August 1980.[43]

The governor had ignored anything with Evans' stamp and asked that 129 of his appointments sent to the Senate be returned. She submitted only 31 substitutes, leaving some college boards and commissions without quorums.[44] Parks Director Charles Odegaard refused to resign and was insulated by a board. Ray sought legislation to pack it, but spurned the invitation of senate parks chairman, Peter Von Reichbauer, to make her case before his committee. The Senate's enfant terribe' became an angry gadfly, puncturing the governor's offerings at every chance.

Her other appointments sustained her predecessors' push toward equality. As of January 1980, 300 women and 127 minorities were named, with 821 male Caucasians.[45] Unfortunately, their quality deteriorated inversely to rank: amateurs could fill local boards, but artifacts made poor regents. Another signal of change in the social climate came in 1977; the voters had defeated Referendum 40, establishing the Women's Council as a statute, countermanding the legislature. Ray, who had never been enthusiastic about it, reconsidered her pledge to restore it with emergency funds.[46]

## Nuclear Ecology

Environmental demonstrators who ringed the rotunda on inauguration day were disdained: "Radical environmentalists are people haters," the governor pronounced, "I reject the zero growth philosophies." Regulations are becoming restrictions and restrictions are becoming prohibitions." What initially were "very good" environmental laws, needed reexamination. "Today the biggest question in this state, and in all the states … is energy. The "problem" stems from a widespread lack of understanding … as to what energy is."[47] The anti-nuclear sentiment sweeping the state was "paranoia" due to "wax in the ears." The nuclear plant at Sedro-Woolley would go ahead despite its opponents, "all five of them." Nuclear power had to quickly supplant oil.

The GOP broke even in the House in 1978 and co-speakers John Bagnariol (D) and Duane Berentson (R) were soon running for governor. They raised the question of "low level" nuclear wastes at Hanford to embarrass Ray. To deflate them, she asked Senator Magnuson to have Congress put the waste sites under federal control and force each state to take its share, rather than Washington, South Carolina, and Nevada storing it all. The co-speakers were castigated for "an unwarranted intrusion into executive matters." Ray believed the governor's office was the "sole official organ of communication" with any government. "She doesn't understand that … we [the legislature] still are the policy-making branch of state government," Bagnariol retorted.[48] Ray's response was to temporarily shut down the Tri-Cities waste site.

Lawrence Bradley, the beset director of the Energy Office, retired at the end of 1978 for difficulties "more political then [sic] technical." Some legislators had become "instant energy experts," and without mentioning the governor, he advised his successor to limit executive request bills and have them introduced by other agencies.[49] What was needed in her area of expertise was missing: Ray saw no reason for a comprehensive energy plan. She was avidly pro-nuclear in an environmental state, one experiencing the biggest public default in the nation's history ($40 billion), with the collapse of the Washington Public Power Supply System (WPPSS, pronounced "Whoops"). The other premier ecological issue was oil spills in Puget Sound. Vetoing of an amendment by a conservative Republican senator to limit tankers in the Strait of Juan de Fuca to 100,000 deadweight tons set a collision course with U.S. Senator Warren Magnuson (D), who hung a replicate amendment on the federal Marine Mammals Protection Act.[50]

In April 1977, Ray had hosted the seven Northwest governors at the mansion. To strengthen her hand with the congressional delegation, she got their signatures for an oil super port at Cherry Point as the start of an "all American pipeline" for Alaska crude. The legislature opted for Port Angeles and the governor threatened a veto. Another Magnuson amendment killed Cherry Point. "I brought in some federal conceptions such as rigid separation of powers," Ray confessed. "Well, I'm learning."[51]

The governor's office is a place where stubborn legislators become supple. Junior legislators long to be in the aura of its 20-foot ceiling and 60-year-old tapestries and not a few come to covet the seat. Doing business there with Ray could be distracting. In June 1977, Mardesich, his deputy Dan Marsh of Vancouver and the author arrived at 8:30 a.m. to get her help on three pension bills saving the state $900 million, the largest single money bills in state's history. The votes of four Democratic senators were needed by 11:00 am, or they would be defeated, as had 25 bills over five years. Ray was by now traveling with up to half her cabinet to biweekly "town hall meetings" to rural and suburban areas east of the Cascades to balance the hammering she was taking in the Seattle media. She came in late, and as the legislators stood on one foot, coffee was again served. The governor went to her desk, bent over, and fumbled in a lower drawer. Jacques, the governor's poodle, used her office as a playpen. He had to be fed his biscuits on the bills before business could start. Another day, the elderly Japanese Ambassador Plenipotentiary arrived in pinstripes and tails to pay his respects and came to full attention ten feet before the governor's desk. Jacques disliked him, romped out, and urinated on his leg. An evening at the governor's mansion was no better. Representative Steve Tupper brought up McNeil Island. A constituent shared his feeling that the state should take it over, as a House study concluded. "Tell your constituent to go to hell," she replied. Ray's problem, explained Senator Ted Bottiger, the new Democratic senate majority leader, "was that you had to agree with her or you offended her."[52] "Another Year of Dixy," a cartoon calendar, was part of a new cottage industry.

The governor's veto pen was wielded in erratic, even startling ways. "Sunset" laws list agencies for extinction unless specifically renewed. In June 1977, the governor vetoed a sunset act as "totally lacking in executive participation," then signed an identical one when repassed.[53] The highly sensitive and oft reworked Juvenile Justice Act allowed the state to take control of runaways, enraging libertarian parents. Ray vetoed contracts for crises intervention services, together with another subsection. This did not violate the supreme court's finding in *Apartment House Association v. Evans*, she found, because the legislature had not defined a "section."[54] A bill letting the state take over an expiring federal gambling tax was axed, giving gambling and card room operators a $612,000 break. She had "grave concerns with a bill whose scope cannot be specifically determined." Ray let another fall because the Speaker had not signed it, rather than remind him to do so. Legislative oversight of exploding agency administrative rules created a "separation of powers problem." Permitting the Senate to reject gubernatorial appointments by inaction, she felt, was contrary to open government. It is also the quiet correct way to scuttle most rejections.[55]

## Pressed

Ray's media relations sealed her fate. "The governor really doesn't need a press secretary," Duane Treckker said as he quit in 1977. "She'd like to be liked by the press" but did not understand its role and took things personally.[56] The governor's press conferences ranged from schoolmarmly to scolding. She made no attempt to veil hostility and felt "unduly picked upon." Referring to reporters as "those odd humanoid types" got laughs at a Teamsters luncheon, but hostility bred enmity. Mike Layton and Shelby Scates of the *P-I*, known to her as "the morning paper," lamented she had learned to "make the medium the massage," and dealt out vengeance.[57] After a year, she wrote their publisher, Bob Thompson, "I would welcome an end, or if that is impossible, at least a truce in the constant harping on my 'feuding with the press.' … It is the press that continuously surfaces the problem. I have been making a sincere effort to be available, open, and responsive. It all seems to no avail."[58]

Newsmen dropped any pretense of neutrality, magnified her gaffes, set her up, and ate her up. Some came to doubt the need for more press conferences. But the *Bremerton Sun's* Adele Ferguson confessed, "It's too much fun the way it is now, with everybody clobbering Dixy every chance they get. When the hounds are in full cry, it's pretty difficult to persuade them to let the fox go and settle for a plate of table scraps."[59] A careful reading of her press conference transcripts convinced Ray that "not much of great interest" was covered, and she suspended them. "She kicked us out of school," Ferguson told her readers.

The governor decided to "use other ways to keep this government open ... and ... keep as much [correct] information flowing as possible." She turned to interviews with favored reporters, one-hour telecasts, and the "town hall meetings" in the hinterlands, where she felt most at ease. The press rubbed in salt by taking a poll of legislators in fall of 1977. Ray got 1.1 on a scale of 3, with a spread of just 0.3 between Republicans and Democrats. Her humor took on a twinge of the macabre. She butchered her Fox Island piglets named after the press corps and tossed the sausages to them at a press conference. "I never had a honeymoon period," she mused. "In fact, the press and I were never even engaged."[60]

A final bizarre episode exposed the foibles of both sides. Wayne Thompson of the *Oregonian*, one of her few friends in the media, got an exclusive interview after her defeat in the 1980 primary, which the governor blamed on a "deeply biased press." Thompson's recorder failed; there were inaccuracies. Suspended by his editors, the 26-year veteran wrote that he quoted "her mind not her words ... . I didn't hear them, or I didn't believe them." The *P-I's* Shelby Scates in getting the last word empathized, "You always hurt the one you love."[61]

## Lessons Learned?

"Two years ago I appeared before you with a maximum supply of political innocence and a minimum store of gubernatorial experience," Ray told the legislature in January 1979. "Attention to duty" had wrought "a few changes. So let's just say, this time we're starting out even."[62] No one learns the mechanics and personalities legislating in less than four years and Ray had been out of the office over half of her first 300 days, rafting rivers, steering tankers, and visiting Asia. "Welcome to an interesting, productive and short session," she greeted reporters. The 1978 legislative agenda could be done in 60 days, she thought if it worked six days a week and evenings and dropped "unnecessary" bills. Co-speaker John Bagnariol sarcastically observed it would be helpful if more than 20 of the governor's 37 executive requests were ready. He suspected she did not understand the political process.[63]

The House was divided at 49 seats for each party and at a disadvantage against the Senate's conservative coalition. The uneasy Democratic "majority" there, sensing a suddenly aggressive Republican minority, wrote a "no new taxes" budget. The houses stood each other off for a week until the end of the session. The governor vacillated over whether to call a special one or just let the legislators go home. "If I had the guts," Bagnariol exploded, "I'd just pass her budget … and let her live with it. I'm totally frustrated."[64] After Ray tongue-lashed leadership and demanded letters from all four caucuses limiting the special session to 20 days and specific issues, the dispirited Co-Speaker said, "This whole thing just blows my mind." On the way back from the governor's office, Berentson chortled, "I thought I was going to have hysterics. She was chewing Baggie's fanny and Baggie was more or less stonewalling it." Bagnariol sighed, "I guess she gets mad just looking at my face."[65] Angrily denounced by the co-speakers, the governor gave in to a new session on March 21: "Now it is time to let them decide on length." The supreme court had decided special sessions, once called, could only be shut down by the legislature. She was blind to legislative protocol.

Former senator Jack Rogers, lobbyist for the counties, doubted her request for fiscal home rule for local government would survive before a committee Bagnariol had begun; the governor's office had not worked with the interest groups and the idea was not well understood. The double-digit inflation allowed Ray to offer a 27 percent budget increase and $600 million in tax relief. "Full funding" of schools was advanced a year, despite the loss of $320 million when the sales tax was removed from food by initiative. Ray's call for ending the state inheritance tax set up a second initiative wiping it out, deleting $100 million more over four years. "If revenue forecasts hold up, that's great," Bagnariol observed presciently. "If there is a turndown we have serious problems."[66]

Ray worsened the situation by trying to capture issues from the co-speakers. She undercut Berentson by advocating a new Department of Energy. "It was the greatest speech, certainly by a non-politician, ever given," he snorted. In the end, the traditional delegation sent to inform her it was ready to adjourn sine die found a dark office on the second floor. It waited until the governor showed up in a T-shirt, slacks, and a jacket.

In the spring of 1980, Co-Speaker Bagnariol and Senate Majority Leader Gordon Walgren were indicted by a federal grand jury after the FBI's "Gamscam" sting operation. If Ray instigated the sting, as Walgren presumed, the likely target was Bagnariol. Walgren alleged the governor had promised him the next vacancy in the U.S. Senate for his legislative cooperation. "Gamscam" did not "kill" the administration by removing any perception of integrity. It was already dead.[67]

## 1980: The Unraveling

Ray was not romanced by the old guard who ran the State Democratic Central Committee. In 1977, she did not endorse state chair Neal Chaney until a week before the state convention, and then confessed there was no time to find a substitute. She settled on puckish labor leader Joe Murphy, who damned "100 percenters" and "sand castle politics" by the "one-issue people" of the party's left-wing. "Democrats seem prone to fight among themselves, but over the past eight years there has been a struggle that transcends the definition of a family affair." "I still say I'm a Democrat, always have been," the governor told interviewers.[68] Labor and the liberals in charge of the party in King County correctly decided she and Mardesich were closet Republicans; it was time for both to go. Ray knew they "would do anything to see me out of office." "Let me emphasize the word 'Democratic,'" the governor wrote unbelievers in April 1980, in a brochure that made no mention of her party.[69]

The Democrats' 1980 Aberdeen convention almost outdid their riotous classic there in 1936. Senator Magnuson hit his main point 40 minutes into a record recital: "I've walked through many a jungle and I never got excited by little monkeys throwing coconuts at me … . I've been called lots of names, visionary, socialist, a red. I've even been called a dictator." (An epithet Ray had tagged him with after his super tanker banning amendment). Washington would not be a dumping ground for nuclear waste; no Columbia River water was going to California. "And I wanna tell the governor, or any future governor, there ain't gonna be any vacancy in the U.S. Senate."[70] The crowd roared, as the band struck up "Happy Days Are Here Again." Ray perfunctorily shook hands with him and stalked out. Jim McDermott, again her opponent, stepped to the podium and asked "the seventy percent of you who support my campaign to stand up." A clear majority did.

Gummie Johnson, who once labeled Scoop Jackson "the most dangerous official in the United States," had been hired as the governor's "consultant-director" in October 1979, with "full control" at the munificent salary of $10,000 a month. It is likely Johnson came on board to prove he was still the "best" after five years of making a living passing school levies across the West. He was so intent on proving he could still raise the dead, he forgot the governor did not take advice. Johnson quickly found "many adjustments to habit patterns and attitudes are necessary," adding in June: "She demands a genuflecting loyalty to procedures and rewards spies and sycophants … rebuffs and punishes honest counsel. God how I have tried." The campaign could still be "fairly easily be turned around … when the governor chooses to do so" even if the executive committee of five was "dangerously short … of political experience and … there was a serious lack of volunteer bodies." Ray's advisory committee, gathered at the Seattle's Rainier Club, were told "success [was] still a matter of balancing her forceful and dominating personality. She is her own worst enemy, and in a game of tennis her opponent would be the net."

The minutes read, "No one completely trusts Gummie. He may be an SOB, but he's our SOB."[71] After Gummie spent an hour in the governor's waiting room, a state trooper appeared. "Mr. Johnson, I don't know how to say this, but the governor is outside hiding behind a rhododendron bush, and won't come in until you leave." He resigned with eight pungent pages that were an autopsy of a lost cause.[72]

Ray had antagonized every major lobby except business. Anticipating the fall of special levies in 1978, Superintendent of Public Instruction Frank Brouillet was joined by the eager-to-be-as-positive CEOs of the Business Roundtable in asking for a special session to be rid of levy lids, revise the Basic Education Act just enacted, and fatten the schools budget. Ray noted each had been "vigorously opposed by the organizations represented by Roundtable members" in the legislature. A good faith effort was in order.[73] Carol Coe, president of the WEA, claimed there had been "no cooperation" from "the anti-education" governor's office in four years. Former colleagues in higher education were jolted to hear Washington was "recognized around the country as a degree mill state," and that tenure was "not appropriate to … modern society." Ray questioned the right of public employees, specifically teachers to serve in the legislature, and had sought precedents in other states barring them.

With Mardesich defrocked and Bagnariol and Walgren en route to two years in the federal prison at Lompoc, California for racketeering,[74] Ray was now its backstop and "one of the best friends business has ever had," according to Boeing's Bud Coffey. But there would be no help "until the governor stops saying things that are embarrassing to us, or we can't answer or defend." Tutored by Blair Butterworth who had fled Ray's camp, Jim McDermott won the primary nearly two to one. John Spellman branded him a "liberal Seattle psychiatrist" and buoyed by the Democratic implosion and the rise of Ronald Reagan, won everywhere but Seattle.[75]

## The Accidental Incumbent

Dixy Lee Ray was intelligent, articulate, self-assured, and as charismatic as any governor. Her ability to attract attention was the envy of her peers. The political ingénue was made and undone by the media. She blamed "a deeply biased press that opposed me from the day I filed … and never let up." To her credit she was "unexpurgated" but did what no politician dares, serially take on all parties. The governor was proudest of expanding services and narrowing the tax base, something made possible by inflation, not the executive. She can be blamed for abetting inflation, but no executive in 80 years has left money on the table. "It is harder to withstand prosperity than poverty," she reminded electronics advanceman John Fluke.[76] Her Achilles' heel was the inability to take criticism, from a lifetime of doing it her way, when politics demanded compromise. The tendency to secrecy kept away "people who could be of assistance" as Walgren delicately put it. Ray, who claimed to be "right in the middle" in practice was a docent for New Dealers frozen in time and a lackluster "conservatism" well to the right of many of her Republican contemporaries. The marriage of convenience to the Democrats guaranteed a family feud.

Ray confirmed, "it takes a politician to deal with politicians." Politics is a profession. Politicians, not entrepreneurs, run the country's most complicated "businesses." They have no more than six years at a time to succeed, amidst criticism, competition, drifting opinion, and shifting alliances. Ray was a professor out of a classroom where she was the expert, a spinster who never split the blanket, a misplaced person temperamentally unsuited to a world whose essence is negotiated agreements. "It's pretty hard," she thought, "to ask people to accept a 65 year old maid newcomer who speaks her mind." At six o'clock in the evening of January 13, 1981, the governor had the State Patrol decoy newsmen and sped off in the fog to Fox Island, her Elba in the sound. Why did a maverick so isolated she could walk her dog around the legislative building without being stopped ask for another term? The "non-politician" had confounded the experts once and wanted to do so again.

Chapter 9

# John D. Spellman: The Uncertain Drummer

*(1981-85)*

### Present at the Creation

The Spellman's are one of the few families who have been in Seattle since 1889, the year of the great fire. John grew up on Hunts Point on the east side of Lake Washington and commuted to parochial school by ferry. He dropped out of Seattle Prep to join the Navy in World War II and was briefly at a Jesuit seminary before returning to Seattle University, where he was class valedictorian in 1949. At Georgetown Law School in the "other Washington," Spellman excelled in debate. He and Lois raised six children on View Ridge northeast of the university. This foundling ground for governors was also home to Mayor Gordon Clinton (the third of four consecutive GOP mayors from that quarter), who made the young lawyer chair of the Seattle Civil Service Commission.

### Early Legacies: The First King County Executive

In 1964, Spellman filed for mayor a half hour before closing and to no one's surprise lost for lack of preparation. Prosecutor Charles O. Carroll, orchestrator of the Republican courthouse old guard for whom he had worked urged a try for a county commissioner's seat in 1966, and omnipresent Evans ally Representative Joel Pritchard mentored him in. Spellman "made a rather complete break" in the Goldwater era fallout of Evansites and the King County GOP.[1] Keeping a low profile, he was to be the only major Republican figure not caught in the line of fire in the war of the wings. The P-I asserted the "upstart prince" had a "terrible apprehension" in the first months of being framed because he was not cooperating with Carroll. Spellman survived Watergate with his characteristic, if somewhat presumptive optimism. "There was no excuse for defeatism." The public was against "glib political opportunism." The "vast majority" shared Republican aspirations for constitutional government, a balanced budget, and a federal system. Republicans were on the side of the "people who take pride."[2]

Three years later he became the first King County Executive under the new home rule charter, the finale for the haggard, bailiwick-based, patronage-ridden commissioner system. They had been both policy makers and managers, and Spellman leapt at the chance to set a "radically" different tone. The new "high sheriff" brought in professional managers John Chambers and Joe McGavick as deputies. They wrote "very rigid" rules and executive orders, a string of ordinances and "put the new government in place before the legislative branch got organized."[3] He kept his lines open to Labor, ate brown-bag lunches with the councilmen, and was a bipartisan sharer of credit. In 1972, Spellman revamped the executive department to give more leeway to the now qualified department heads. "I'm proud of my style…strict adherence to propriety. People couldn't take gifts…trips on anybody else's money…no alcohol in the courthouse. That was a terrible shock. Alcohol was in all the desk drawers…. The tone was set…. This government is not for sale, even in a very small way."[4]

Civil rights marches were shaking sedate Seattle. "Neighborhood councils" budded as the suburbs flexed their newfound muscles. His "open hand" was "neither pro labor or pro management" but "pro getting the job done." The new executive brokered an accord between the unions building the new county administration building and picketers for a minority apprenticeship program. The unions agreed to merit pay. King County had the first CETA team in the country. It had run a deficit for seven years prior to 1969. A "productivity" program slashed administrative expenses 32 percent and the council adopted his proposal to telescope 21 departments into seven. Finances were tightened and a debt of $6.9 million was gone in 36 months.

On came the Boeing Bust of 1971. "I seemed to be around during the time of genuine emergencies," Spellman later mused. Even so, King County's bond rating rose to "AA," the highest of any local government in the state. His Employment Supplement Program (ESP), quickly adopted by Congress, funded the Economic Development Council

(EDC), drawing $20 million for temporary jobs. The Department of Rehabilitative Services was augmented by a "job line." King County sheriffs doubled to one per 1,000 citizens. One percent of the budget was set aside for culture.[5] Bonds for the Kingdome, Seattle's clam shell topped sporthaus won 62 percent approval, but lawsuits and inflation caused the contractor to walk off the job. Spellman rejigged the contract to make the stadium a $50 million a year "clean" industry. It was imploded after he threw out the first ball of the last Mariners game there 20 years later. His Environmental Development Council of 134 volunteers crafted innovative but ill-fated transportation and farm lands conservation proposals, the only significant defeats.[6]

The 1968 election ended another era in the county, as had the rise of the New Order of Cincinnatus in Seattle had three decades before. The downtown establishment, young professionals, and activists' fused agendas in the Municipal League for a "clean," calm, well-managed city operating within traditional bounds. The League reached a high of 5,000 members in 1950 and then began a secular slide. Its mission was renewed in the 1970's by Choose an Effective City Council (CHECC), the offspring of young Ivy League-educated lawyers, who needed just four years to turn out the tired city council by defeat or resignation.[7] CHECC was bipartisan, but respected GOP moderates like civic icon Jim Ellis and elected allies, typified by State Senator Pritchard (sent to Congress from the First District) and businessmen like his brother Frank were the drivers in Olympia as well, carrying Dan Evans to a third term at the same time. New GOP candidates emerged from the Young Republicans of King County, which drew 800 to its socials in the 1960s, many more than the Metropolitan Democratic Club. The firefight between Evansites and the King County Republican organization became a weekly event. Spellman promoted ecumenicism, freshened his ties with downtown, and broadened his base by chairing the county committee to re-elect the president.[8] Nixon crumbled in less than a year, a victim of his warped personality and Watergate, as a humbled nation withdrew from Vietnam. The GOP was eviscerated for another seven years.

In 1976, Governor Jimmy Carter's Georgia outliers ripped the regulars from the left, and California's Governor Ronald Reagan electrified the right, felling President Gerald Ford, who was burdened with Nixon's pardon. Spellman had a second false start, a stillborn gubernatorial campaign run by amateurs less schooled than Evans' acolytes, many of whom were exhausted after 12 years of intra-party combat. It never achieved a comparable synergy, even in Spellman's dependably Republican Forty-sixth District. He was himself: idealistic, "good grey

John."[9] Dixy Lee Ray tweaked her five opponents as part of a "permanent ruling class," and herself as an "instrument of catharsis." Spellman found the brash scientist an enigma. No one "could figure out how to run against her."[10] He promised what he could not deliver, "an exciting campaign" on her record, "which is terrible," and "the needs of the state, which are not being met." The public face of the collegiate debater, trial lawyer, Irish joke teller, and jazz aficionado coped with his shy side and an internal monitor of what was public or private. Leaning into the microphone to call Ray's regime "a cross between Saturday Night Live and The Gong Show" was out of character.

By January 1980, the Ray administration was disintegrating. A *Seattle Times* poll put her at 40.5 percent, Spellman at 51 percent. The question was "how to keep her alive so we could run against her in the general election." Primary crossovers nearly killed Spellman. Volunteers came back to headquarters saying, "We voted for [Jim] McDermott just to get rid of Dixy." In the draining $400,000, four-way primary, he just edged out conservative Co-Speaker Berentson, who railed for a "return to dignity" in Olympia. When the liberal State Senator Jim McDermott got the Democratic nomination, business opened its pockets. Spellman's donations rose to $1,205,285, making him the first "million-dollar governor." Both men had 95 percent name familiarity. But a poll found no one knew anything about McDermott other than beating Dixy Lee Ray.

Joel Pritchard was sitting in the back of the war room: "If they knew who he was they would never vote for him. This isn't the year for a liberal Seattle Psychiatrist to win." A strategy and slogan were born: "Spellman is the answer. McDermott is the question. Who is Jim McDermott?" "Attack campaigns," (mainly negative television spots), became vogue in 1980. Spellman pulled a waffle from his pocket on statewide TV to spotlight the other Irishman's ambiguity, which haunted him later when the press began to talk about "Waffle John."[11] After Ray, he argued, the public was desperate for a "manager." Aided by the strongest Republican state organization ever, legislative campaigns that delivered the GOP majorities in both houses of the legislature for the first time in 26 years and the Reagan landslide, Spellman was thrown into a crisis of different dimensions that foretold his fate as governor.[12]

## Olympia: The Horizon Widens

He guilelessly took electioneering and governing as two different things, not complimentary competencies of political animals. "I intentionally did not want to take my campaign staff and make them my office staff." The "thrill of the race, and the ecstasy of winning" had "nothing to do with getting the job done." He thought of patronage "hardly at all."[13]

Spellman had paid too little attention to Olympia. "It took four years to … get the training wheels off."[14] He was spared a debacle by the manager-politicians he intended to keep at a distance.[15] Two adroit political minds, versatile, voluble, young lawyer-campaigner Steve Excell, and previous House member Joe McGavick from Haskins and Sells managed the transition and selected most of the senior players. They were joined by Walt Howe, Evans' first budget director, on loan from Weyerhaeuser. The cabinet's ten men, included three minorities and three Democrats, and was equal to any previous one. The standout was Alan Gibbs, who the governor correctly praised as having "had a most positive impact in tougher times than anyone." Gibbs had previously been deputy commissioner of health for New York City, for human services for New Jersey, and an Under Secretary of the Army. The first secretary to get control of DSHS prioritized the agency's 300 accounts, allocated Reagan's shrunken "block grants" with sensitivity to clients and staff and an uncanny deftness with legislators.[16] Mild-mannered Karen Rahm streamlined Planning and Community Affairs, the amorphous pass-through vehicle for federal funds, then with grit and a searching intelligence, took over from Gibbs. The other conspicuous star was 65-year-old Amos Reed. Spellman believed "institutions were being terribly run wrong" in Evans' third term and worse in Ray's: "They all hoped everything was going to reform and they weren't reforming."[17] Reed, the dean of the American corrections, was drawn from North Carolina and soon had McNeil Island on line and the badly overcrowded prisons disciplined.

Three other dexterous Representatives were well suited. Congenial Rollie Schmitten went to Fisheries and Joe Taller was a vigorous and vocal, if at times a too self-assured budget director. Having lost the Fourth District congressional race, former House Majority Leader and rancher Stu Bledsoe settled into Agriculture. Bob Hollister, Ray's superb director of retirement systems, was one of two holdovers. Some strong Evans performers reenlisted: African-American Norwood Brooks at Employment Security, Keith Angier at General Administration, and the enigmatic Don Moos at Ecology. Labor's Sam Kinville was a natural at Unemployment Security. The cabinet never met except as sub-cabinets on items of common interest, or if across-the-board economies were called for.

Used to the unruffled pace of the county, needing time to think, and not wanting to be "schmoozed" by lobbyists, the new governor hired Dick Allison as chief of staff, a role he had played in scrubbing down the King County prosecutor's office when Christopher Bailey ousted Carroll. The austere Harvard history Ph.D., Nelson Rockefeller aide, and "good government" man spurned politics and failed to socialize or tap into the capitol grapevine. Department heads carped about a "palace guard," and in March of 1982 a coterie of business insiders who had paid dues to be the governor's sounding board berated Allison. Others said staff would leave if he did not. Spellman tardily decided his key aide was a "martinet" and abruptly told the stunned gatekeeper, "I think you and I should part company at the end of the summer."[18] Other letdowns were Hector Torres of Veterans' Affairs, who was "all steam and no rudder" and left after installing a wet bar in his office and aiding an initiative on state time. Licenses' John Gonzales never caught the curve of intricate computer conversions or bested the department's imbedded routineers. Loyal to a fault, Spellman knew his politically shrewd his 1976 manager Dick Shrock "brought a lot of controversy with him." The tactician exited after legislators compared notes and found him duplicitous. Oregon's highly touted John Anderson signed on at Commerce and Economic Development, and also left early. The governor nebulously thought him "a little too focused on a couple of counties.... I didn't think he was creative" or an "advocate."[19]

"I hate to think that you have to have a vast public relations staff that is creating puffery..." the governor later pondered. "I believe in getting the work done and then announcing the program." This was not a method for a man who had to first sell the legislature. Press Secretary Paul O'Connor, a Kennedy Democrat, "believed in me like nobody...I have to admire his extreme loyalty."[20] Spellman was not prepared to have his every word picked apart, and O'Connor never made the transition from PI reporter to governor's taster and foil, and became paranoid. The Bremerton Sun's Adele Ferguson a conservative who occasionally bared a knife to validate her independence, unglued him: "Where is that goddam bitch Adele Ferguson?" he asked, something duly repeated by Democratic staffers. She caught up with Steve Excell in the wings of the House: "Hell, he did not say it to one person. He said it to a couple of thousand!" O'Connor had a mental breakdown and called a press conference to blame the press and everyone else on his way out of town.[21]

This administration was as systematic as its forerunner was shambolic. In the first two years, there were 62 "Policy Memos for Agency Directors," ranging from appointments to procedures for requesting executive orders. Instructions were specific and tracked by agency activity reports. Seattle Lawyer Ken Grosse, a former counsel to the Senate Republican caucus (and soon made an appellate court judge), handled "policy letters." The thousands of other letters autotyped to constituents by departmental supervisors were prosaic in the extreme, saying little more than that the governor had signed or vetoed items of interest.[22]

Spellman was an independent thinker but wanted no surprises. His admirable judicial temperament was a handicap in the quicksand of the capitol. He mulled over incoming mail, and "every piece of paper he saw was initialed," Steve Excell recalled. "You couldn't just go in and brief him. He'd want a piece of paper with it all laid out." "He wanted to think on it for a few days and find what agency directors thought, and how it might fly with the courts." "My style was not so much top down as total responsibility.... I had to know what I was responsible for, and I didn't expect anything to be hidden from me. I tried...and I think successfully not to micro-manage" the governor said.[23] The staff's job and the department heads were to get me the [options] "...and let me make them [decisions]... so I could deal with problems as a whole. Yes, that's a very possessive form of government." Senior staff could be candid. Excell warned, "The voters did not elect you to be a judge. They did not elect you to manage state government. They elected you to be a leader."[24] Spellman delegated, but the eye of the needle approach worked better in the quiet corridors of the county than the rumbling halls of the legislative building.

The governor's first executive order (of 24 in 1981), was to buttress affirmative action. "Early on, I was desperately seeking minorities for the bench," he recalls. "In some counties...I just couldn't get a [suitable] nomination from the Bar... people in the hinterlands got a little upset with me. But there was a terrible imbalance on the bench." He interviewed only "legitimate" candidates. In 1982, a "Governor's Appointment Register System" (GARS) went online, smoothing the often hectic and always crucial task of filling 1,000 positions a year.

The ultimate appointment came in 1983, when "Scoop" Jackson died of a heart attack after 31 years in the U.S. Senate. Evans shared Spellman's international outlook, as did Joel Pritchard and former Assistant U.S. Attorney General Bill Ruckelshaus, who had defied Nixon. Both deferred to Evans to win the short race. "The numbers were overwhelming."[25]

## The Legislative Blues

"So you're my new legislator," the executive greeted Representative Marlin Appelwick of his Forty-sixth District, the soon-to-be Democratic minority leader. "And I doubt I had one more contact with him during the session," the flabbergasted freshman reflected. "Spellman was the one [governor] I had the least feel for," related caucus-mate Art Wang. "Not having a particularly good feel for the legislature, he did have some legislators in key positions."[26] Persuading primary opponent, 28-year veteran and former Co-Speaker Duane Berentson to be legislative liaison was a coup. Berentson had instant currency with Speaker Bill Polk, with whom the governor "fundamentally disagreed," and did much to keep their jousts from going public.[26]

Spellman fell off the high wire on tax policy. "John is against new taxes," a campaign ad cried in the summer of 1980. His inaugural address noticed the state's narrowed tax base: "We are one of only six [sic, seven] states that have no income tax." Revenue Director Glenn Pascall was the first cabinet officer to go, the victim of what might not have been an avoidable campaign promise. The brilliant idea man was incapable of focusing on his main task, under calculated the swelling deficit by $100 million, and was fired for telling the House Appropriations Committee an income tax "may be very useful."

The governor said he would not rule out an income tax if it helped. But when his Tax Advisory Council, with a unanimity rare among experts, duly advocated one in November of 1982, he turned sophist. Spellman would not endorse their proposal, but would help sell a "responsible" one. "I was looking for any solution when I appointed that committee. But I sure as heck wasn't looking for pie in the sky," he equivocated.[27] The state had carved out a tax-economic "niche," and "our tax system is not as unfair as people think it is." His specious definition of "real tax reform" was extending the sales tax to professional services. Advisors were chastised advisors for "leaking" downside economic data, and a hiring freeze announced.[27] The consequence of not wanting to be seen side stepping a "lost cause" was trying to rationalize the right answer away.

As titular party leader, Spellman turned to the less heated role of melding the Republican Party after the Evans years. The "radical moderate" was slightly to the right on economic issues, a "liberal Republican" on social ones, and consistently down played the cost conflict between the two stances.[28] He cooperated with Ken Eikenberry, a conservative legislator turned pragmatic, even-handed party chair in the GOP's 1980 sweep. If close ties had existed with the GOP legislative leaders, calls could have been made to clinch attractive candidates, or induce attractive individuals he had met to run, helping to dilute the hard core of Polk's antagonistic cadre. Any comparison to Evans' team tactics in recruiting is invidious.

The worst recession since the Great Depression had reached gale force by Election Day. It preoccupied the administration, bruised legislative relations, dictated a holding pattern, and predestined its fate. On hearing the new executive's upbeat inaugural and his rendering of "When Irish Eyes Are Smiling," and "The Sun'll Come Out Tomorrow" legislators welcomed a "fresh start."[29] A day later, the executive's budget was released, with what Joe Taller optimistically termed "decreases in reductions," the first of perhaps obligatory helpings of optimism in the face unknowns that eventually wore on credibility.

On January 16, 1981, at the first full gubernatorial press conference in two years, the governor's personality became a quandary. Spellman's shyness and underlying unease with the media emerged as ambivalence as the press probed his generalities for meaning. "Just as we should not make up our deficits from the pay envelopes of our employees, we must not be parties to balancing the budget on the shoulders of the poor," he stated at the inaugural. How was it to be done? Did he intend to veto an anti-busing bill? "I would, again, not predict. I have not spoken against school busing in the past… I think I would wait to see the outcome… [in the legislature] before telegraphing a message." The man who accused Jim McDermott of "waffling" soon became the cartoonists' 'Governor Waffleman.'"[30] Legislators found an "open door," a cautious listener and a nodding head behind billows of pipe smoke. The governor's often ambiguous dealings with journalists and legislators derived less from lack of courage than unfamiliarity with legislative protocols, the milieu, and mind sets. "Mr. Placid" was at sea before he got his sea legs. Absent a firm grasp of his options, and with a scanty politician's intuition in the increasingly unruly scene unfolding he was often the last voice heard.

## Bludgeoned by the Budget

The 1981 session was the first limited to 105 days.[31] Two more special or "extraordinary sessions" took place in 1981 and three in 1982 totaling over 300 days, a marathon struggle to keep the state afloat. The "fluid" style of the Grieve years, Evans' assertiveness, and Ray's financial summersault transmuted into Speaker Bill Polk's relentless, unrealistic focus on cutting as much as necessary. Spellman, who would be arbiter and negotiator, was little more a commentator and sometime proposer in a triangular melee between the House and Senate Republicans, with upper house Democrats holding the whip hand once three "conservative" dissenting GOP senators erased the GOP's short-lived one-vote "majority." For 20 months, and perhaps 70 hours, he sat at the head of the long oak table in the governor's conference room with the Speaker, Senate Majority Leader Jeannette Hayner, House Appropriations Committee Chair Rod Chandler, the author (as Senate Ways and Means chair), the senior Democrats, Senator Ted Bottiger and Representatives Wayne Ehlers and Denny Heck, and OFM chief Joe Taller, debating what became ten editions of the budget.

Spellman, titularly first among equals, was also luckless in being negatively compared to Polk and Hayner, two of the most forceful personalities to stalk the legislative halls in decades. His constructive alternatives were pushed back in his lap by the Speaker, who demanded two-thirds reductions and one-third new revenue, not the reverse. The newly displaced Democratic leaders told how few votes they could contribute to any approach, and themed the first supplemental budget of February 1981 a "budget of tears," having trimmed $236 million. It was not "the worst financial crisis in the state's history," but at that juncture no one put a calamity beyond possiblity.[32] The Senate minority offered restorative amendments for offended groups and commiserated with the press until the "majority" was bled white, then supplied the three votes in the Senate for needed taxes.

"I think I was cursed to always have a legislature of one party," Spellman tellingly brooded. "I would have loved to see somebody play off against somebody. I never did." Democrat Peter Von Reichbauer's party switch, what the Democrats called "the St. Valentine's Day Massacre" in March, 1981, giving the GOP a Senate majority, "was probably as bad as anything that ever happened."[33] "Is John Spellman a ninety-eight pound weakling?" an article asked, next to a cartoon featuring him in a beanie and short pants staring haplessly at legislative tough guys. Spellman's "style was to work with leaders individually, rather than to trot out [his] proposal and get into confrontations." It was accomplishment that counted, not rhetoric. "I believe profoundly that what you don't say is more important than what you say. If saying something would lessen my chance of getting an accord, I won't do it."[34] "The governor is part of the legislative process," he maintained. "There's lots of ways of exercising the governor's power. One of them is to send over your requests and wait and see what arrives on your desk." If the leaders would let him know what was in process, he would let them know how he felt. "I'm appalled by the suggestion of the legislature that, if they can't propose it, I can't propose it." Spellman was in fact reactive: the legislature was to propose, he would dispose.[35] He throve with the nine-person King County Council where modesty, firmness, fairness, and centrism sufficed. In this larger theater compromise came by combat, not consensus.

The deepening fiscal crisis kept him off balance. The second supplemental budget of 1981-83 passed on April 20, 1981, with another round of cuts. The governor found it "by and large a very acceptable compromise," something he had questioned two weeks earlier. The Senate had raised the House's social and health services figures by $30 million and education by $80 million. The executive was left "latitude" to bring the document into balance once the Congress decided on how to shrink federal grants.[36] The loss was still less than three percent, slashes the state could absorb without major hurt. Revenues fell another $655 million by September, turning the screw again. The governor ordered a 10.1 percent across-the-board cuts unless the legislature acted, as was required to rebalance the budget quarterly. Major interest groups were in extremis. President Gerberding of the University of Washington asked the regents to declare a "financial state of emergency" to deal with the "terrible crisis." The governor described the state as "hemorrhaging in a sea of red ink," and implied it was partly because the House had sliced too deeply, further damaging the economy.[37] His veto message set a pattern of objecting to restrictions on agency electives and travel, and easing their most severe pains. The proviso the Legislative Budget Committee had to approve all subsequent federal grants preempted "the Governor's statutory responsibility."[38] Forbidding the use of funds for deputy director positions at DSHS might slow restructuring. The attorney general regained his original sum. The auditor estimated reducing travel by 30 percent would bring a loss of $21 million, and got a reprieve.

Next, in the vortex of the recession the state's ferry workers struck, ratcheting up pressure on the legislative floor. The half million patrons on the sound and the Olympic Peninsula would be unforgiving if service was long interrupted. Spellman correctly thought Speaker Polk reacted with "a heavy hand" with a bill quashing the union. Some of Spellman's tendency to chest his cards until the last minute came from years of brokering labor negotiations as part of his law practice. He preferred arbitration and then vetoed it, and an impasse ensued between the two that front-end discussion might have avoided.[39]

Two other significant and disabling events confirmed the wisdom of stating a position no later than when the legislature's center of gravity becomes obvious. In January of 1982, in the name of creating jobs, the legislators voted to permit Chicago Bridge and Iron to construct oil derricks for Alaska at waterside south of Bellingham, an exception to the Shorelines Act. Environmentalists were overjoyed when the governor changed his mind and vetoed it. He claimed to have made "no commitment to the bill at all" and had demonstrated toughness. Instead of signaling his intentions to the irate Senate sponsors, he belatedly did the right thing at their expense.[40] The same inscrutability existed while leadership searched for alternate routes for a Northern Tier Pipeline to ship Alaska crude from Cherry Point or another coastal port to the Midwest. The governor was again right in saying it was "poor policy to exempt one company from established state law," but said so just ahead of a veto.[41] Evading confrontation elevated legislator's doubts about the governor's reliability.

The second special session came at the worst time, between the primary and general elections. On October 20, Spellman called a press conference to present his formula, a .08 percent sales tax hike and a 10 percent surcharge on the Business and Occupations tax generating over $400 million and takeaways of just $272 million, to the meet the new deficit of $685 million. A tense meeting with legislative leaders stalemated. The legislature, said House Majority Leader Gary Nelson, echoing Polk, wanted 75 percent cuts and 25 percent taxes. The Democrats sat back to watch. Senate Minority Leader Ted Bottiger knew his Democrats would not fund "anything over what Polk says we need," or "offer votes in exchange for anything." "There is every reason to be hopeful," the governor mystically told newsmen after the cast met again on Thanksgiving Eve. Two hours later the Senate defeated the option taken. "It was another indication, for the umpteenth time … that Spellman … was really out of touch with the Legislature," the state's best reporter wrote.[42] Not wanting to tax, Polk went past hope into the unreal. "Supply side" economist Arthur Laffer was hired and, as expected, assured the legislature that everything would be all right. Spellman called the report "embarrassing." The Speaker said the governor was just "shooting off his mouth."[43] Polk was as trapped as the governor, by his predisposition and the ideologues he had drafted. Hayner's more flexible reaction that Spellman's ratio of taxes to cuts was wrong reflected the predominant view in her caucus.

"Bill Polk's railroad" rolled on, sending the senate the death penalty and three-way "industrial insurance" (adding the alternative of private plans to the state's and those of large companies) and civil service reform, seemingly oblivious to the fact that the GOP senators had at best just 22 votes. It took weeks to break the gridlock by splitting the difference between the executive and the legislative majorities. He then vetoed 20 items, stripping off cramping boilerplate: "The funding formula was never intended as a spending plan, but rather a distribution model."[44] In 1981, of 2,119 bills, 356 passed, 7 were fully vetoed, and 25 partially vetoed and 93 of 114 gubernatorial appointments confirmed.

## The Flight of a Brick: 1982

Spellman's January 1982 speech opening the legislature was for hardy souls. Unemployment stood at 11 percent; the timber and construction industries were near a standstill. Prisons were bursting at the seams with a one-year gain of 1,000 inmates. The state's cash reserve was spent and in nine months a $400 million bank loan had to be paid. Moody's lowered the state's bond rating for the second time in six months.[45] Half a billion dollars had been removed from the original biennial budget of $12.8 billion; a new gap of "minimally" $309 million gaped. The governor set

4.2 percent cuts for April 1, calling them "unthinkable" and a "disaster." "I have made some mistakes in my first year as Governor," he acknowledged on statewide television. "I thought we going to have only a $600 million shortfall and that we could solve the problem totally by cuts and that we would not need to raise any new taxes during my term. I was wrong. I led the campaign to increase taxes" half-closing the hole, "but we are still in deep trouble." A "series of budgeting mistakes" over the prior decade, Evans' "25th month" piracy, Ray's contraction of the tax base and spending of the $400 million surplus in 1979 had deepened the cavity. Congress now pulled back as much.

DSHS had borne the brunt—$330 million—and could shrivel no more. Spellman: "I will prevent further cuts to fulfill my responsibilities. I will ask for $309 million in new revenue to cover [the new] $144 million shortfall, to pay…the $400 million loan, and establish a dual purpose fund" to buy back the '25th month' and meet another downturn." "Make-believe mathematics" had to end. Two-thirds of the money ($176 million) might be raised by extending the sales tax to gas.[46] A poll showed 72 percent of the voters, 75 percent of whom owned cars, were opposed. One of the last major funding avenues evaporated.

Things were surreal for Speaker Polk. The Republicans had anticipated and warned of the situation. It was hardest to act in hard times. Yet in the fall of 1981 he had passed a half-billion dollar .05 sales tax boost after two days of arm-twisting freshmen who had "vowed no new taxes." Now there had to be a no new tax solution. On January 26, the Speaker let loose a bombshell: a one percent across-the-board cuts, deferring $221 million in pension payments, a $34 million hiring freeze, a state lottery ($20 million), "productivity increases" ($15 million), and forcing state employees taking a day off without pay. This was as doomed as Spellman's mostly-taxes answer. Polk's fresh survey found 41 percent of Washingtonians were for cuts and 42 percent for trims and taxes, again without specifying either, a sure sign of resistance to both. Spellman scoffed at the poll "unscientific."

The Speaker stood pat: "I have beliefs that it can be solved without that [taxes]." He sardonically added, "but that may be too much hardball for Senate Republicans,"[47] again forgetting there was no majority in the Senate. The next evening three major tax bills on sales, income, and a package fell there in three hours. The highest number of "yeas" that could be mustered for bills doomed in the House was 13 of the 25 needed.[48] The merely awkward veered toward the absurd. Spellman branded the three Senate mavericks and Polk's right wing Troglodytes (cave men). They concocted an embarrassing and futile budget shrinking everything in sight, ending President Evan's controversial Evergreen State College and pushed Spellman for an exact reduction in state employees. "To have a fetish about body counts when we're facing 13 percent unemployment is sick," he snapped. This was a "dismal picture of…the state's reeling from hard economic times without [the legislature] having done what must be done for the good of all." He scoffed at the "childishness" of the Trogs and bristled when told "legislative leadership" doubted he understood the process. "That's baloney," he retorted. "The process isn't working. Maybe it should be changed." "Big deal!" the beset Hayner shot back. Two hours later, the legislature adjourned in frustration for the first weekend in three. The Senate had "obviously defaulted," the governor said.[49]

The default was not for lack of trying. It trudged on five nights and often seven days a week, sometimes after 9:00 pm. When the session's 60 days ran out, Spellman granted ten more days, then seven more on March 21, 1982. The economy continued to slump. To raise pressure, an executive order was released on the last day of the month imposing eight percent cuts to cover the deficit. A typical house Trog replied the governor would have to choose between that and what the legislature should do—trim two-thirds. Alan Gibbs, who had masterfully collaborated sighed, "I thought I was an old hand and didn't get upset, but I am upset now at the things that are going on in the House."[50]

On April 1, a "Gang of Twelve," a bipartisan budget conference committee, was still meeting eight hours a day as everyone else waited. The only thing they could agree on was that fissure was up from $304 million to $500 million (a net decrease of 7 percent of the administration's original budget). Progress was by inches, the pattern the same: the governor wanted mostly taxes, the House mostly cuts. The leaders of the Senate "majority" were caught in between and rendered impotent. He falsely suggested a "very small number" of legislators were "hamstringing the process."[51] Partisan politics kept all but a handful of Democrats at a distance until the "majority" was drained. Then they extracted a quid pro quo, a 13-week extension of jobless pay (signed by the governor on April 2). Democratic Representative Helen Sommers was then permitted by her House caucus to be the fifth and necessary signature (with four Republicans), on a conference committee report calling for $152 million in taxes.

As the Senate took up a patchwork of small tax bills at 10:00 pm, 20 House Trogs threatened to defect from the agreement: the cuts were too shallow. Polk had lost control of his right wing; the "railroad" was running into the roundhouse. He had driven the Democrats so hard that Minority Leader Wayne Ehlers could "count the number of 'yes' votes he could get to replace Trogs' "on two hands."[52] At 2:00 am, the legislature was at the end of the line, having passed $90 million in cuts and $114 million in new levies. (Some of the small tax bills were lost due to midnight lobbying.) The last $20 million, and a balance, was in a "painless" state lottery. It yielded twice that, leaving a $20 million surplus on June 30, 1983. The "Republican" Senate buttressed by the governor had done what most taxpayers seemed to want. They were repelled by two records: nine taxes and reductions for $750 million each, and media agonizing over the protracted messy struggle that is democracy. The second Republican majorities in 45 years survived 20 months; the last the GOP governor of the twentieth century, one term.[53]

## Shadowlands: 1983-85

Executives seize or lose the initiative in their first biennium. In the second one, they try to round out their record and advertise it. The fourth-year speech to the legislature opens the campaign season. The governor's 1983 opening day offeing was hyperbole; "I have seen the future and it is us," he rhapsodized. Washingtonians, the "culmination of the great American experiment in tolerance and cooperation" were to be "the turnstile to Asia." The new interceptor treaty with Canada to save salmon runs, foreign trade ("As chairman of the National Governors' Commission I've made lots of productive contacts ..."), discipline in the prisons, the "logic" of community-based corrections the State Patrol ("the best in history"), and a "pretty fair" tax system played until November 1984.[54] The economic sun had come out, and the Economic Revitalization Board was floating industrial revenue bonds.

One Senate seat shifted in November of 1982, turning the Senate majority back to the Democrats. Most of the House Trogs were unseated. The special handicap of Spellman's second two years was rival Jim McDermott, back as chair of Senate Ways and Means and hungry for a third try at the office. Spellman vacillated between advocacy and detachment from the Democrats, asking them "not to spend dollars we didn't have."[55] "I have had a record seven sessions in my first two years as governor," he told the New York City Community Forum. "We have looked at every possible solution and every possible cut and every possible priority many times over. We know the problems by heart. We know the answers by heart. The states, and the State of Washington in particular, are [now] in no danger of...having... an operation that isn't funded."[56]

Counting on the voters' brief attention span, the Democratic majorities passed a resolution saying they were at least as cost conscious as the governor, then made the first order of business passing a $1 billion, 1 cent sales tax hike to provide a "cushion." There was no backlash. This and economic takeoff floated the budget up 20 percent. By February 1984,

Olympia was awash in money. As the gubernatorial election neared, Spellman endorsed Initiative 465, the House Republicans' vehicle for halving the sales tax increase. Either through failure to organize or the new benevolence of a relieved public, the election-year club never made the ballot. The circle was closed in an October debate, when the governor warned he would "fight" any attempt at an income tax.[57]

## "Good Government in Bad Times"

Denied means for new programs, Spellman reverted to what he did best: administrative remodeling and consolidating systems in Information Services, community programs, and vocational education. An Energy Facility Site Evaluation Council became law. A 500-person medium-security prison, a Community Economic Revitalization Board, and area redevelopment financing are among his credits. A swath of the 20 boards and commissions he listed for extinction ended; four others scheduled for "sunset" review. (Termination if not reauthorized.) Drunk driver laws were tightened and higher energy conservation standards for buildings. A high proportion passed because they were timely, non-controversial, cost little, and had modest impact.[58]

In 1983, a State Finance Commission to guarantee low-income mortgages, and a public works inventory, reinforced by tax credits, recognized that small firms were the fastest-growing job sector. A Community Development Finance Corporation and its counterpart for technology, the Export Assistance Center, low-cost energy loans to business, work sharing, retraining, and youth employment pilot projects were underway.[59]

The economy in 1985 was the opposite of 1981. The "condition of the affairs of the state" was "good and getting better, but we cannot invent mirages of the future simply to satisfy the desires of today… I wish you well. I offer you my cooperation, an open door, and an open mind," the chastened governor told the legislators. "It would be nice if we could all get through the next 60 days as friends. But if we can't do that, we should at least be able to get through it as ladies and gentlemen." The Democrats spent the new bounty with "blinding speed."[60] If Speaker Polk's "railroad" was overloaded with more serious reforms than might be dealt within a decade, this one was heavily laden with reelection bills—325 streamed through both houses in 50 days. Controversies were left in the Rules Committees.[61] McDermott joined Eastern Washington senators in a $100 million bond issue for irrigation. Even State Democratic State Chairwoman Karen Marchioro could not derail a bill lowering the timber tax festooned with breaks for everyone from meat processors to silver buyers. A tuition freeze passed the Senate, though they were still below "comparison states." Democratic leadership reminded voters there were no new taxes or overtime. Spellman indulged in oratorical overkill on the other traditionally popular topic—welfare spending—calling the House's budget a "kind of cruel hoax" for giving $26 million more to recipients. The Democrats called a press conference to deny they were soft on welfare.[62]

## 1984: Mirror Images?

Legislatures break governors and peers seeking the office, to the advantage of outsiders. At the end of May, Steve Excell agreed to run the 1984 campaign, succeeding fund-raiser Brian McCauley, on the conditions he would be in charge, and that there was no "split" between the governor's office and the campaign. Spellman and McDermott saw their worst fears come true in 1984. A Republican poll at the June asking who was more likely to raise taxes, confirmed the confusion of the public and the effects of the recession: Spellman was at 35 percent, McDermott at 22.[63] Being conspicuously ahead in the categories of "caring" and "spending funds wisely" was small solace for the governor. McDermott received no quarter during the session and could not campaign until it ended. The Democratic leadership was all from Pierce County (Tacoma and environs) and endorsed Booth Gardner, its first county executive, for governor. He was in the same position Spellman had been four years before.

On the campaign trail, Gardner reiterated to Excell a conversation they had in the governor's office at the end of Spellman's third year: "I hope there's no hard feelings. I'm certainly not upset with you or John. You have to understand… the only reason I decided to run against John[,] who has doing everything I ever wanted… was my belief he couldn't get reelected. I … couldn't see having John go down to defeat and pass up an opportunity to run."[64] Spellman faced his reflection in Gardner, a somewhat shy, modest man with the voice of a munchkin. The adoptive son of corporate and community icon Norton Clapp (a former chair of Weyerhaeuser) had been associate dean of the Pacific Lutheran University's School of Business and talked in managerial jargon, convincing leading lights in business community he was one of their own. Gardner was also just across the centerline, but spurred by social sensitivities from his "dysfunctional" childhood. He would feel the stings of his party's liberals as Spellman was flogged by the right.[65] Gardner had not "spent a lot of time worrying about state government" since being a state senator (1971-73) and was eaten alive at Seattle Rotary by McDermott on issues. This proved the defining moment. He literally took a long walk on the beach and turned deliberate and decisive, realizing one "could be a nice guy and a tough campaigner."

Outspent by $100,000 in the primary, Gardner guaranteed $750,000 in loans from friends and associates for the general, and poured $1 million into advertising. His dignified demeanor appealed to Republicans, drawing crossovers that disastrously weakened Spellman.[66] A late September tracking poll found his "heard of/favorable" rating had risen to 66.8 percent, to Spellman's 41 percent. Worse, the incumbent's "strong ill-defined negatives" were at 37 percent, the challenger's "unfavorables" at 12.2 percent. Social service advocates and environmentalists reverted to the Democratic haven. Gardner was ahead by 18 percent, an apparently impossible situation.[67] Spellman was overshadowed by the recession and his equivocation, Speaker Polk, the death of Senator Henry M. Jackson and Dan Evans' seating in the fall of 1983, a Democratic legislature, and the Democratic primary. In contrast to his 1980 slogan, "McDermott is the question, Spellman is the answer," the governor was the question, with too few positive answers. Forced to be combative, he raised issues "in a zingy way to get into the media." The "real John Spellman," mild-mannered, good-natured and optimistic, the private man who ate brown-bag lunches in his office, and left public relations to others was again out of suit.

"I'm a good manager," the governor reiterated on election eve, adding with a shrug of the shoulders, "I guess maybe I'm not a very good salesman."[68] "We did the right things," he insisted. "Who could have done better?" He was proudest of "hanging in there in tremendously hard times." It was the voice of an instinctively moderate, intelligent, and often-hesitant captain whose thankless task was steering the ship of state in the stormiest seas in half a century. His staff selection process was strong, appointees' performances creditable to outstanding. Ending the "twenty-fifth month," controlling prison overcrowding, "restructuring" the Department of Agriculture, the Energy Office, and Fisheries were overdue. The firings of Glenn Pascall and Dick Allison were inept. He unfailingly divorced his policy positions from his religious ones, separating church and state. Spellman's Catholic faith and Jesuit exposures were deliberately subordinated to the lawyer's need to uphold the Supreme Court's decision on abortion. On affirmative action, he was unsurpassed. Amos Reed avoided the prison riots that plagued the nation. As an environmental steward, he toed the middle line, however awkwardly. Fairchild Camera came to Washington as did Hewlett Packard, and a "reverse investment" in overseas trade was underway.

Spellman thought himself a "party politician," meaning a loyal if non-ideological team player. "I had always prided myself in being able to get people to work together, across the aisle, but first with Speaker Polk hell-bent on his agenda, and the subsequent overturn in both houses, stalemate was as often the case."[69] Judicial by temperament and a functionary in style, Spellman was a fine administrator and a hesitant leader. The governor preferred to be brought solutions. The staff would engage in round table debates and then he would go off to decide, working late at the desk across from his bedroom in the mansion. "The plan is in the governor's head," Paul O'Connor explained. He "nods his head, puffs his pipe, goes away and does what he wants." He was an evaluator…not inclined to shape issues or put forward early proposals," who held his legislative options open too long. Legislative leaders are tough negotiators who know their positions and expect others to know theirs. He was at best an honest broker, not a catalyst.

"When Dan Evans spoke, people listened," Senate Minority Leader Ted Bottiger reminisced, adding, Spellman "refused to come out on anything controversial."[70] He did, but no one knew when or for how long. Spellman was, as House Minority Whip Dan Grimm put it, "like a horse trader dealing with someone who doesn't know horses." House Minority Leader Dennis Heck was blunter: "What the Legislature is about is counting votes." Speaker Polk, when asked about a caricature with him as engineer of a legislative railroad and Spellman scurrying to catch the caboose, replied, "I was able to deliver the votes [for taxes]. The governor has no votes." The absence of political intuition was greater than a failure of intentions. "In terms of the Legislature," Spellman confessed, "it was a lot worse than I thought it would be."[71]

All legislatures have freewheeling moments; 1981-83 was a chain of them. Those "leading" it were often at wits' end. Spellman, never a legislator, was hard-pressed to anticipate what if anything would happen next. A stage manager had been cast in the role of leading actor and handed a blurred script. He was the only statewide elected official of nine to lose.

Chapter 10

# Booth Gardner: Spread Eagle

*(1985-93)*

### "Public Policy Is Where I Hang Out"

Booth Gardner grew up on rural Vashon Island on Puget Sound, but Lakewood in South Tacoma became home. His parents divorced when he was four. Shuffled between them, he became a "dysfunctional young person." After his mother and sister were killed in a California plane crash when Booth was 13 and his alcoholic father fell off a balcony in Hawaii, he resolved to "narrow the range" of his emotions to avoid more pain. Booth coached minority kids on soccer at Seattle's Broadway field. Mike McManus, later a state senator, met him there in 1956: "He dressed poorly, looked shabby. He slept on a couch at our place and my wife and I fed him, clothed him. It wasn't until six years after we became friends that I found out he had money." Gardner was stepson of Norton Clapp, paterfamilias of Weyerhaeuser, one of the world's largest timber firms. An able if unexceptional student at the University of Washington and at Harvard, where he took an MBA, he turned to shopping center development and then was assistant dean of the School of Business Administration at the University of Puget Sound.

Despite Clapp's conspicuous Republican roles, Booth was still uncertain about his political gender. Given his family and business background, choosing a political party was a close run thing. He interviewed Gummie Johnson, "who never took his feet off the desk," and Bob Grieve, who testified for the Democrats in human terms. "The help I got for the poor people was from Democrats … That's how I happen to be a Democrat," the governor postscriptively told Grandview Rotarians. "The Republicans may have fancier rhetoric, but Democrats have better values. We care about people's lives and less about ideological purity."[1]

Seeking his métier, he successfully ran for state senator from Tacoma's blue-collar Twenty-sixth Legislative District in 1970, beating progressive one-term Republican Larry Faulk by 33,052 to 29,473 using Faulk's own playbook, which he had mistakenly printed. But Gardner was bored as one of only three freshmen sitting on the back row of an archaic body run for 16 years by Majority Leader Grieve, a master manipulator. He resigned in three years to run the Laird Norton Company, his family's building supply firm. No one expected to see him again in politics, but the disease took.[2]

Faulk was once more his foe in the 1981 race for Pierce County executive. Gardner spent twice as much and won by less than one percent. The county's departmental managers, part of an "old boy network," stonewalled him on their budgets. He called in downtown bankers who had contributed to them into his office for a second meeting, to suggest where cuts could be made. "They [the public officials] agreed, and I was over the hump." In three years, prosperity, updated property tax assessments, and retrenchments took the county from a $4.7 million debt to a $1 million surplus, while paying off a $1.5 million racketeering lawsuit. Tacoma had taken its first steps away from being "the Chicago of the West."[3]

## "Booth Who?"

Gardner insists he wanted to be governor from age 12, on seeing Al Rosellini's helicopter land on Vashon. A later admission rings truer: "I didn't get involved in government because of causes or issues. I just think the state can be run better, in a more businesslike manner." He simply wanted to be governor and knew it would be someone other than John Spellman.[4] Events colluded. His first and best move, in November 1983, was hiring Ron Dotzauer, Scoop Jackson's 1982 campaign manager, who came with much of the late senator's political estate. Dotzauer took calls from the candidate's driver and coaxed Gardner to get out of the backseat.[5] Appearances, mailings, and television ads costing $117,000 and raised his name recognition from virtually nothing outside Pierce County to 66 percent in two months. A computer purchased for $10,000 banking 2,000 Jackson volunteers and 250,000 telephone contacts were the winning edge. By April, Gardner had raised $420,000 to McDermott's $46,735, later adding his own $500,000 line of credit. The campaign shared a building with Brinks. A potential embarrassment became an asset: the campaign had run out of cash because of his unwillingness to ask solicit interest groups. He would be an "independent governor," in contrast to the lobbyist-afflicted chairman of Senate Ways and Means trapped in the 1984 session.

Gardner raised substantial amounts of "Republican" money, and had an extended network of friends who were "unbelievably loyal" to him. "He knew more people than anybody other than Al Rosellini that I've ever seen," said Dean Foster, a partisan operative for 30 years and chief clerk of the House and later Gardner's chief of staff. To ease any doubts of liberals, the candidate called for full funding of welfare for unemployed parents who had exhausted benefits. For Jacksonites, a goal of attracting 40,000 jobs, as many as Spellman netted in three years.[6] At the Democratic state convention in Tacoma in June, delegates spilled out of the Gardner reception as a Mariachi troupe played. A pianist entertained the few at McDermott's.

"Two John Spellmans, one a Republican, one a Democrat, is almost two much to contemplate," mocked a McDermott man. Most Democrats did not agree. This was the first time since 1964 they had a candidate they could relate to. Evans had run over them, Ray was out of reach; now they recharged.[7] There was tension between Booth's extended family and the Democratic establishment in Pierce County—and in the legislature. Gardner partisans House Speaker Wayne Ehlers, Senate Majority Leader Ted Bottiger, House Majority Leader Denny Heck were from the county, which helped to all but ensure McDermott's defeat in the state's second largest venue.

The legislators were invaluable in another way. In midsummer, McDermott and Gardner debated before 600 at the state's premier business forum, the Seattle Rotary. Gardner was under assertive and informed, caught by surprise, and overwhelmed. McDermott "just ate me for lunch. I didn't have to go after Jim, because he's his own worst enemy, but I had to be able to answer questions. I said it's time for me to take a long walk and decide if I really want this job or not." The second set-to went better.[8] Heck, playing McDermott, rehearsed him and Gardner came out punching. And McDermott, now on his third try for the governor's chair, was not wearing well. "I think people were looking for an excuse…not to vote for McDermott. Jim has a personality that grates on people, and when Booth beat him up a couple of times, it shocked him, but it … got him [Gardner] out of his shell too," Dean Foster observed.[9]

Spellman and Gardner were strikingly similar.[10] The general election was awkward: two individuals who liked each other sparring, contrary to their natures. Both began as legislators (one as a county commissioner, the other as a state senator) and were the first elected executives of the state's two largest counties, under new charters. Both were unlikely politicians, reserved, private, and minimally partisan, who wanted to separate policy and politics and preferred the former.[11] Each saw his strength as a "manager." Both administrations were limited by the governor's lack of force. Gardner's motif was, "Different times demand different styles of leadership;" Spellman's was, "I can bring jobs" theme of 1980. Gardner obscured his lack of combativeness by talking tough about Pierce County decisions and comparing a practical "cooperator" with a "conventional politician," whose "APPLE" agenda was "yesterday's pie."[12]

Spellman's handlers mistakenly thought McDermott would encore as the nominee, instead of going straight for groups he and Gardner both sought. "Booth Gardner will be the 'Charley Royer' [Seattle's mayor, defeated in the 1983 U.S. senatorial primary] of 1984, with even more disadvantages" manager Brian McCauley huffed after January 1984 polls. Spellman narrowly led McDermott, and Gardner's possible presence did not allow a delay in the campaign against him.[13] Gardner's elf-like openness appealed to voters where the incumbent's genial but often mask-like reticence could not. Spellman, battered by the economy, never caught up.

## MBWA: "Management by Walking About"

Transitions are crowded with campaign operatives who have nothing to do. The governor-elect's close friend Laird Harris did the initial organizing, as the folly of attempting to be completely prepared unfolded. A "tremendous power struggle" broke out between savvy politicos trying to vet their ideas for revamping state government, and volunteers seeking seats on the proliferating committees. Greg Barlow, Gardner's associate and intimate since Laird-Norton and personal agent for Norton Clapp, was given assignments of choice. This excited envy and controversy among the politicos, also take-charge people, but with a different style. Some thought he should be chief of staff, but others were put off by the idea. Gardner wisely made the decorated army officer the major general commanding the National Guard, retaining the counsel of a figure who preferred to work in the background. Barlow went on to run the Medina Foundation, the Clapp family charity.[14]

There was also amateurism. Papers were to be written on every agency under the governor's aegis. Orin Smith finally reminded the assembled that there was an inaugural to be prepared and a speech to be written. John Spellman, who may not have realized he was going to lose to the last minute and felt he was unfairly campaigned against, was not terribly cooperative. On the new administration's first day, almost all the files were empty. Computers had not been ordered. Contests over staff pay levels and the need to keep their prima facie numbers down were the reasons most were moved to OFM. Most of the later "head hunting" was contracted out to gain a national reach.

Gardner was first a businessman and a policy wonk; the ceremonial aspects of a job kept him from absorbing more data. To counteract his inclinations, as Pierce County executive he made it a practice to "get into the field." One morning he volunteered with a crew putting up signs until told "we could do it faster without you." He leaned against a truck, observing. Back in his office, he got a complaint that a member of the crew was just standing by, talking. Gardner asked, "Was he wearing a red flannel shirt?" The caller said, "Yes, that's the one. Do you know him?" "I know him well. I'll have a word with him."

The state was so much larger an operation that the personal touch was limited to touching down. He would drop in unannounced. At DSHS, the receptionist asked his name. "I said, 'Booth Gardner.' She looked at me and at the lady next to her and said, 'No you're not. I'm not falling for that.' "Even if I didn't get to somebody in those eight years," the Governor reminisced, "they heard about it, and it made them feel good about their work" — and the word traveled." Apart from what MWBA may have done for "efficiency," the governor's impromptu visits to state offices and schools for information gathering and "face time"...worked wonders for morale, leaving the feeling he grasped problems on the ground floor.[15]

Once the 1985 legislature left Olympia, Gardner turned "to do what I feel I do best...bring some good management to state government ... to bring some of the discipline which made us successful in the private sector to the public sector."[16] "What I do is run a business. It's a service business," he declared ten months into office, stressing the strategy of the successful corporation. The trick was to find the "fine line of balance between the people that need service" and those wanting more benefits. The 42-person Office of the Governor was amplified by an executive policy group of 24 in OFM—including several in public relations, but not listed as funded by the governor's office.[17] A fully computerized "Constituent Contact and Referral" (CAT) system gave complete control over "casework" on the 60,000 letters Gardner's personality drew in the first nine months of 1991.

"Most governors I know ... were afraid someone else was making decisions for them," Gardner reflected. He was not an intrusive manager and was not involved in hiring below the director level. The governor most often delegated: "You make the decision." The "Executive Cabinet" (the COS and his deputy, the directors of communications and OFM, and seniors in the executive office) met in the governor's large boardroom, on Monday mornings. Monthly cabinet meetings engaged all the directors, split into "large" and "small agencies," who came together for "brainstorming" retreats. "It's [the state's] not a very complex organization in the aggregate," he surmised, except for some "nuances." Top-heaviness and turf wars had to give way to service at the regional and street level. To speed the process, he announced, "We are reorganizing entirely the way we deal with agencies and how they deal with each other." To make the 35 agencies under his aegis more responsive, two "sub-cabinet management groups" were formed, with Management chaired by Institution's Chase Riveland, and Policy by Chief of Staff Dick Thompson. The governor came every third time to the latter and mostly listened. He shared information from his travels and, on occasion, "lectured" when goals were not met.[18] The "nuances" proved numerous. The policy makers poured over 30 topics in the first half of 1989.[19]

"Efficiency, accountability and performance," the administration's mantras, were to be the means of meeting social goals without new taxes. Beyond some strong urgings by minorities, the claim 22 months in was that "progressive public policies" had improved "teamwork." The employee suggestion program had "unleashed their creativity." The governor's ten (annual) Distinguished Leadership Awards, begun in 1985, honored mid managers "who have made a difference." Mission statements agreeing on "core values" and "business plans" drove expectations beyond the biennium. More concretely, the state's temporarily surplus "Rent a Cell" earned $28 million and institutions director Riveland's CAFE (Combined Action Food Economy) program reduced costs by a quarter while improving quality, earning him the National Governors Association's Distinguished Service Award in 1989. Junking 70 obsolete manuals and 3,000 forms were admirable "efficiencies" the governor sought. The State Patrol's productivity rose 22 percent. Claim simplification and a placement project in Employment Security conserved $9 million a year. The governor chaired the new Efficiency Commission,[20] which identified $100 million more in savings over four years. The transformation of Employment Security under Joe Dear was the pinnacle of these successes. Cost control and two legislative packages saved $41 million in 1986, which together with a brutal 18-percent rate boost, kept later ones low as medical claims soared. Dear turned the industrial accident fund from $225 million in the red to $88 million in the black by 1987.[21]

Governors also have to backstop cabinet officers set upon by large or militant groups such as recreational fisherman or farmers, who are powerful enough to paralyze an agency on an issue. Even Chiefs of Staff needed buttressing too. Commercial fishermen yelled and were "outright rude" to Denny Heck. Gardner gave them 40 minutes. "And for the first 20 they were very complimentary, and were so awed to be in the governor's office that they didn't attack. Finally, I said, 'Time out. You [have] used 20 of your 40 minutes, and what you may not know is that in two hours the farmers are coming in to tell me what they think about the level of the [Columbia] River.' That got them going, and they took some real good shots at me."[22] The Legislative Liaison was a principal gatekeeper for its leaders, scheduling three, four, or five "corners" meetings.[23] Then came committee chairs, individual legislators, lobbyists, community folk, and the governor's friends.

Children were Gardner's weakness. The office staff was coached to keep them silent on tours if there was an important meeting. If children's voices were heard, he might well get up and leave. "One time we [he and his State Patrol driver] were coming back from a mill in Shelton, and we passed an elementary school, and the driver didn't even ask. He just screeched to a halt and backed up. He only had to drive a mile, but he sped."[24] The Gardner administration brought women into their own as senior executives. His first appointment, Mary Faulk, wife of his Pierce County opponent, was stellar. She raised lottery proceeds by half ($30 million), then was sent to Ecology, General Administration, and Licenses as a troubleshooter, the second person to hold three cabinet posts. Christine Gregoire, who took Ecology (for Andrea Beatty, who left to manage Seattle-Tacoma Airport), was elected attorney general in 1992 and governor in 2004. Her singular service was negotiating a Tripartite Agreement with the federal government and contractors for a $52 billion, 30-year cleanup of nuclear waste at Hanford. Margaret Stanley put the nascent Health Care Authority underway. Paula O'Connor steered the Liquor Board and Sharon Nelson bore down hard on corporations as chair of the Utilities and Transportation Commission. Dr. Christine Gebbie, later President Clinton's AIDS chief, led the Department of Health. They were stalwarts in an administration with the second highest number of women executives in the country— 33 percent.[25]

The governor sought out minority managers and created the African-American Affairs Commission by executive order when the legislature failed to do so. When ferry system employees appealed to him about race relations in the old-line agency, he responded with a Task Force on Racial Equality and a "strong statement of expectations." Alan Momohara was drafted as executive director of the stumbling Human Rights Commission, with its 150 "lost or missing" cases. Inclusiveness was even more evident in Gardner's judicial appointments. He was "appalled, angered, and totally perplexed" by the bilious hearings over whether Clarence Thomas was to be a justice of the United States Supreme Court. In 1988, Charles Z. Smith, former Dean of the University of Washington Law School, became the first black justice of the state supreme court. Susan Agid went on the court of appeals. All finalists for the superior court got personal interviews, and a third of the appointments were women. By 1992, nearly 40 percent of the King County Superior Court's 46 judges were minority or female. A parallel "generational switch" swept in new university regents and trustees.

Inevitably, missteps emerged. Director of Licenses Theresa Aragon was not up to her task and was asked to step down. Oregon's John Anderson had a superstar image for attracting industry. Gardner also offered contradictory reasons why "his performance wasn't good…John was good at working with the locals, and put together seminars…[but] that doesn't work. Nobody's going to leave Seattle to go to Rochester or Chehalis." Boeing had a smaller share of the state's business when he left, but "we don't take credit for starting businesses…we take credit for helping them along the way."[26] The biggest upset was Isaiah Turner, who had done a "tremendous job" according to the governor in diversifying Employment Security until it was 27 percent minorities, 10 percent disabled persons, and 61 percent female. Turner resigned "with regret and remorse" after the *Times* discovered what he spent for "public relations" and entertainment, including two of every five nights at a hotel 20 miles from his home and $14,285 in personal telephone calls. Chief of Staff Denny Heck overreacted, sacking the department's number two man, the respected Ernie LaPalm, for saying "the amount of [Turner's] travel was necessary." Characteristically, the governor took time to go to a Seattle farewell party for the departed commissioner.

## DSHS: High Stress and a Fragmented Structure

The ever-vulnerable DSHS had four secretaries by the end of Gardner's first term, and only the last was confirmed—at the outset of the second term. Spellman's Karen Rahm had no interest in staying. Jule Sugarman, whose reputation rested on being at the "forefront of reform" as a founder of Congress' Head Start came to DSHS in June 1986. In the minds of Republican senators he spent too much time around the country sustaining his profile, dividing his loyalty. Charged with retooling welfare, he and Gardner were soon hotly defending the pioneering Family Independence Plan (FIP) as the first and "best program of its kind in the country." It would take a decade and an even stronger economy for the formula to be operational.

Timely implementation hung on federal waivers to transfer Medicaid, Food Stamp, and AFDC (welfare) dollars to FIP, with its new emphasis on work, education, and training.[27] FIP was to get underway by March 1988 and began in July. Then the federals refused to renew waivers for the experiment. Three months later, Sugarman advised the governor to "preserve your options." Nationally, Hillary Clinton's edition, a convoluted 1,300-page bill that even senior congressmen could not comprehend, was dead on arrival. Congress wrote its own, upstaging the state with a modified federal prototype lacking many of FIP's economic incentives. Sugarman was convinced it "will not result in the same reduction in welfare dependency," but lacked the "experience to compare accurately."[28]

Devising how to track 300 different federal and state funds and the agency's giant load of 700,000 clients with dozens of different maladies and meet the technical needs of 16,000 staff (one-third of state workers), became the crux and the emblem of the state's anguishes in the electronic age. Perfecting ACES the, Automated Client Eligibility [Tracking] System, embarrassed the Lowry administration as well. Gardner saw Unisys "was just in over their head," and DSHS managers were disoriented by the exotic technology and thus had no idea about outcomes. "There were too many moving pieces…you had to have all. We didn't understand the dynamic of getting people out of this cycle…putting them back to work and having their children fed well for breakfast. FIP was "probably an idea that was six years ahead of itself," Dean Foster reflected.[29] ACES was a black hole. "There is a risk that ACES' scope, cost, and technical complexity could all be much greater than the state desires," interim Secretary Paul Trause wrote.[30] Serious budget overruns rose as full implementation dragged on.

FIP's "phase down" in favor of JOBS (Job Opportunities and Basic Skills Training Program) began in October 1992, retaining the "positive aspects…respect for welfare clients, involving front-line staff in the decision process, and involving the community." Jerry Thompson worried that a second "Impact Report" on FIP lacked "statistical significance" but drew "broad conclusions" like, "It seems clear that FIP is not increasing either employment or earnings in the short run."[31] The "lessons learned" were to use proven technology, learn from the field, not to be driven by technocrats, do not quote costs, and get more varied oversight. The federals narrowed the state's "flexibility" to get more cost accountability, and new rules ran ahead of ability to police them. "I think today we could do it," Gardner mused in 2004. Despite DSHS's difficulties, JOBS was operating by October 1990 (except for FIP sites).

"What they [DSHS] did I think," the GOP's senate bugeteer Dan McDonald said, "was to mistake training for a job. And training was in their minds, and in the law, equivalent to jobs. So you had a tremendous amount of investment in training and people…[and] still not be out working. Whereas the Federal program, when it came out in '95, said, If we're going to do any training, it will be vocational…FIP, by every measure failed. There was a longitudinal study that went on for six years, and the unemployment amongst the recipients had actually increased." Gardner had given the impetus to welfare reform. "But I think [Jim] McDermott and Feather [Warren Featherstone Reid, his staff director] made it happen." "I don't think any one individual took the fall for the ACES delay," the governor mused as Sugarman took to the road. "Can anybody run the place?" the secretary was asked on his way out. "Yes," he responded, "if expectations were moderated."[32]

Gardner underestimated the headwind any administration faces in making structural changes. His desire to run the agency as a "service corporation" on a business basis and "make the system work," collided head on with DSHS employee's social service mentality.[33] Bud Shinpoch, who had left the Senate for Revenue, then General Administration, was sent to DSHS hatchet in hand. The rigid civil service system blocked dismissals, but six layers of management vanished as 1,300 supervisors were shifted to the "field." The average "span of control" for managers rose from 3.8 to 8.4 workers. Mike Ryherd, a veteran social service lobbyist felt Shinpoch "shook the hell out of the agencies." The administration had assumed that because the affected managers were not in the union, they would not "scream." But DSHS was the soul of state unionism and the next tier of employees, seeing their chances for promotion vaporizing, suspected job losses would soon engulf them. As a pacifier, six secretary's representatives were created to keep him in touch with local units.

Gardner's backing of Shinpoch fell as the backlash swelled. "Clearly Shinpoch was asked to refine some of his strong changes,"[34] Dean Foster admits. Soon it was plain the new secretary would not get confirmed by his former Democratic colleagues in the Senate, who were put upon by hundreds of agitated employees. Dan McDonald, for four years majority leader in the Senate, said Shinpoch "took his assignment as a mandate… And the governor lost his nerve. That was the defining moment for both of them. I don't think he [the governor's credibility] ever recovered from that."[35]

Fortunately, while running for Pierce County Executive Gardner met his most talented and versatile administrator, lawyer Dick Thompson, city manager of Puyallup. He came into the regime as Director of Community Development, moved to Chief of Staff, and headed DSHS, setting a record for staying power at the restless agency at 42 months. Thompson, "a frustrated CFO," finally took over OFM, and was in practice the "deputy governor" because the "policy shop" had been put there. He was the only person who has held each of state's "big three" executive positions.

## Ongoing Ambivalence

The underlying clash between Gardner's want of efficiency and his high social sympathies was omnipresent. Thompson knew it was the "heart of the heartache" long before preparing the 1989-91 budget. Higher education, health care, and pensions needed more money. Just reelected with 58 percent approval, the governor "had enormous political capital," part of which, Thompson argued as chief of staff, should go into a tax increase. The governor's fiscal moderate side urged him to live within his means. The senior staff divided down the middle. Gardener worried a week. Then Thompson said, "I want you to get up in the morning and visualize two headlines. One headline says, 'Booth Gardner can manage his way out of a paper bag; needs more money.' And the other headline says, 'Booth Gardner doesn't care about kids and poor people,' and tell me which of those headlines you hate most because they've both hit your core values." There was no tax proposal. There was "always, always" the dichotomy.[36]

The turmoil at DSHS gave an inkling of what was to come. The second substantial way to enhance performance was to renovate the boiler plated, constipated "merit" system. This chance was missed by a fatal, if understandable mistake, a promise made at the 1984 state Labor convention. One of the first laws he signed in 1985 repealed the pilot civil service reform the GOP passed in 1982, giving genuine merit equal standing with longevity and widening the possibilities for outside hires. Five years later, Chief of Staff Dick Davis (shifted from L&I) said, "The state's personnel system suffers from a clear lack of accountability at top management levels, too little responsiveness and effectiveness, and is encrusted with complex rules and regulations." Even the Department of Personnel's director was appointed by a board. "The governor needs the ability to manage using both hands."[37]

The governor was also a moderate on labor. For House Democrats, any reform was linked to getting unfettered collective bargaining. The governor's priorities were the reverse. A Task Force on Personnel in the executive cabinet devised legislation to enhance recruiting, training, and retention was known as the Workforce 2000 Initiative. Management's alternative to the WFSE's 1990 "wish list" was a trade-off. Gardner's price for collective bargaining was limiting issues, no bargaining on policy, and no strikes. This offended both Labor and the Senate Republicans, who killed the proposal in 1991.[38]

He ultimately sought "efficiency" by changing management modes rather than structural reform. This too was bucked by both the rank and file and mid- management — the "the unchanging face of state government."[39] The issue's tie to Democratic politics ensured the flawed core of monolithic non-merit system would not be cracked, as the upcoming Lowry team confirmed. Gardner confessed to State Personnel Director Dennis Karras that once he realized how "inflexible" the system was, signing the repeal of the GOP's 1982 reforms was "one of the biggest mistakes he ever made." "We all worked pretty hard on civil service reform but never managed to get at its entirety, the WMS reform notwithstanding," Denny Heck acceded.[40]

The other avenue to accountability was reorganization — placing major agencies under the executive or combining them — Evans redux. Turf protecting bureaus and allied interest groups hobbled Gardner, like all governors. His bills to have the executive, not the commissions on Game, Parks, and Transportation, name their directors all died in the Democratic House. The governor did meld the chronically troubled departments of Game and Fisheries as "Wildlife," unified a freestanding Department of [electronic] Information Services and hired the first Special Assistant for Transportation for multimodal transport.[41] More extensive use was made of loaned executives from the private sector, who deviseed the majority of the internal upgrades.

A stream of executive orders like the Governor's Alliance Against Drugs, and a "special reminder" on sexual harassment addressed other pressing issues. The Task Force on Day Care reported at the end of 1985. Gardner's "consensus…in place of confrontation" style helped settle the Seattle school strike (1985), tied the Seattle Mariners to the Kingdome, and resolved a billion dollar comparable worth suit. He and governors Cecil Andrus of Idaho and Neil Goldschmidt of Oregon wrote a drug interdiction accord and joined the states' congressmen for federal funding for the Hanford cleanup. Peers in Nevada and North Carolina helped Gardner have Congress to reallocate low-level radioactive waste. He was an early choice to preside over the Western Governors' Association (1987-88). In 1988, a Risk Management Advisory Committee chaired by Mary Faulk unsnarled unemployment compensation laws, a $28 million headache. Visible partner Jean Gardner co-chaired the state's 1989 celebration of the state centennial.

## The Economy: The Two States of Washington

Gardner's matchless gift through seven of his eight years was a vibrant economy. But long before the late 1980s, two Washingtons developed. On the wet side of the mountains Boeing, which survived on Cold War military contracts, now dominated commercial aviation, as Microsoft was doing in software. "Dot Coms" blossomed as venture capitalists sensed the future of biotech. The University of Washington drew $200 million dollars a year in federal research grants. Puget Sound ports funneled apples and wheat from the counties east of the Cascades to Asia, but lacking a critical mass in science, expertise or capital, their fate hinged on overseas prices. The affluent West Side prospered, the East Side stagnated.

The centerpiece of Gardner's January 1989 inaugural was economic diversification by "targeted recruitment of new industries for communities in need." "The Washington Plan ...without a doubt the most dramatic economic development effort ever undertaken by state government," was the child of John Anderson, head of the renamed Department of Trade and Commerce, whose budget had been boosted 80 percent. An Economic Development Cabinet and a Council of Economic Advisers was announced in March, as the governor left for Detroit to pitch for GM's new Saturn Plant. In April, he lobbied Congress, along with 20 other states, for the superconducting super collider, a huge tunnel for splitting the atom to be built on the Columbia Plateau.

"Team Washington" was to create private-public partnerships and sign agreements with development organizations in counties with 75 percent of the population. Community Revitalization Teams fanned out from Long Beach to Lake Crescent as "symbol[s] of this administration's commitment to helping communities ... hardest hit." A Small Business Improvement Council was entitled as a complement to big business' Washington Roundtable. In September, a Washington Economic Development Board was charged with fashioning a "game plan" for long-term growth and stability. In October, an Asian offensive launched. The governor held eight meetings with firms in Japan, three investment seminars for Japanese businessmen, a press conference there for Japanese travel writers, and visited China. Trade Advisory Council members joined several later Asian and European tours. He felt "the interest has been genuine."

Economic development has been accepted as a role of governors since Rosellini. It captivates business-oriented ones, promising both jobs and revenue, but is hard to coordinate. At the end of four years, the visible attainments were investments in five second-tier manufacturing plants, finding a buyer for a sixth, and direct aid to foster diversification in the nuclear-dependent Tri-Cities to ease the loss of its Fast Flux reactor, a casualty of the end of the Cold War. A Business Assistance Center, Agricultural Trade Centers in Spokane and Yakima, and the Early Winters Ski Resort in the Methow were underway.[42] A Public Works Trust

Fund and a five-year economic development agenda agreed on by state agencies was bruited. The vocational education system was reconfigured to put technical skills ahead of academic offerings in the struggling communities. A host of county and major city "Economic Development Councils" sprang up, often in competition with one another. With few exceptions, and without significant new tax incentives or "matching" money, they were anemic.

## Birds, Bombs, Bonneville, and Bureaucracy

Environmentalists shrewdly chose the 400 remaining pairs of the diminutive northern spotted owl, whose nests were in the shrinking stands of old growth timber on the Olympic Peninsula, as the beacon of what was wrong in forestry.[43] "The Spotted Owl," Gardner's aide Rich Nafziger agreed, "is our canary in the coal mine; it serves as an indicator of the health of the eco system." The heart of the matter was the ban on the export of raw logs from federal forests. Congress was cool to Gardner's initial ploy, putting them under regional control. Washington was after all, the only state in the Northwest without an export ban on state-owned trees. State forests supplied just 16 percent of the cut and half of it went Asia. He then favored a temporary bar on shipping state logs, but only after the U.S. Senate had done so. This closed a loophole allowing large private companies (particularly Weyerhaeuser) to export their timber, and substitute from federal lands for the domestic market.[44]

In confirming Christine Gregoire as Director of Ecology in 1988, Gardner said, "Chris and I share the philosophy that when environmental and economic interests conflict, the environment comes first."[45] Testifying to Congress again in 1990, he qualified, if not contradicted himself, stating environmental expense was the necessary price of economic growth. Any solution should be long-term, balanced, comprehensive, scientifically grounded, reductions in the cut from federal lands phased, ecological protection sustained, and state-federal cooperation assured, "within economic constraints." Short-sighted forestry practices, not loggers, were the villains in the impasse.[46] Seeking reelection, Gardner indulged in artful temporizing: it was not "environment versus jobs. A clean, healthful environment produces jobs."[47] He refused to accept the report by respected forester Jack Ward Thomas, complaining "the Federal Government's failure to provide the scientists … support and independence contributed to the serious problems we face today. Is there any way of calculating how likely it is that the conclusions about the current and future prospects of the spotted owl are correct?" he asked Oregon's Senator Mark Hatfield. Timber Team coordinator Rich Nafziger reiterated that Gardner did "not believe that export restrictions are the real solution to the state's timber supply problems." Ending over harvesting on private lands and import restrictions on finished products were.

The idea it was not jobs, or the owl, but "about the kind of world we choose to live in," was a thin arabesque, one the governor was highly motivated to prolong. In truth, all the available "science" pointed to the owl's peril and to exports driving excessive harvests. There was less federal forest to turn to, and it still took 40 years to grow a merchantable tree. An advisory board to the Olympic National Forest enabled by the Hatfield-Adams Amendment to the federal budget, presumably to find an excuse to raise the cut enough to ameliorate short-term pressures, was a placebo.

Rising prices for exports brought $100 million to the state treasury every two years. Somehow the ships had to continue to load from the 19 percent of the logs cut from federal forests. Gardner argued the Department of the Interior's "failure to follow the law" and remove the 25 percent restriction on the cut would doom the small mills on the coast.[48] In February 1989, he wrote Agriculture Secretary Clayton Yeutter asking that the restrictions on federal old growth forests be reconsidered to save 6,500 jobs. "A new way of thinking," leading to a negotiated settlement, set-asides of state-owned timber for local processing, speeding federal timber sales, and modernization of the industry were fathered by his inevitable task force. In the fall of 1989, a cumbersome combination of all stakeholders, the Olympic Discussion Group, ironically hosted by the Northwest Renewable Resources Center, took on overlooked long-term issues.

The governor's office, the land commissioner, and congressional delegation staff engaged in "creative policy option development" orchestrated by Gardner's Timber Team and the "Joint Executive Timber Council" coordinating the half dozen state agencies with stakes. In the spring of 1990, citizens, tribes, and "interested parties" were heard under the direction of the ubiquitous Bill Wilkerson and expert mediator Jim Waldo. Formulation dragged on into the summer, with the governor's men focusing on value-added products and technologies, looking to undervalued hardwoods (like alder), and identifying firms willing to diversify.[49] Despite the plenitude of panels, little progress was made apart from the economic revitalization thrusts already described; it was a no-win scene.

When Federal District Judge William Dwyer stayed federal harvesting in 1991 until science could do better, loggers lost the trees to export that were sustaining communities around the Olympic National Park. Gardner complained the judge had gone too far and put 9,000 jobs at risk.[50] As he left office, the governor's Timber Team was still searching for the impossible — a way for the axmen, exporters, and owls to win. Gardner's last two years saw "on-the-ground assistance" to firms in timber towns, another study to sustain medium-sized ones, and a commodity commission for the underused hardwoods for a "sustainable" future.[51] The bureaucratic symposia droned on, post-1970s tributes to the trade-offs between inclusiveness and incisiveness. Federal and state social subsidies and the community colleges helped the remote communities. But many citizens of Forks and Queets had left for the city.[52] The fact that the cut had to come down was never faced.

The end of the Cold War left Washington with the world's largest pool of nuclear waste. Dixy Lee Ray turned a blind eye as the voters' NIMBY (Not in My Backyard) Syndrome bloomed. They correctly suspected the 40 years of radioactive wastes at were not contained and were hostile to the U.S. DOE's intent to expand Hanford as a national depository. Gardner staked out a new position in 1987 when he got the National Governors Association to call for a halt to the search for a new permanent depository, abetted by Nevada and Texas who were also finalists and knew 85 percent of high level radioactive waste was generated in the East. The next year, having favored business' alternative initiative over a successful environmentalist option and seen it struck down, the governor was on point to find a way out.

His most vigorous environmental act was backing Ecology Director Christine Gregoire's negotiation of a Tripartite Agreement on nuclear waste with the U.S. Department of Ecology. The 30-year $52 billion pact seemed a dramatic stroke to undo saturation and dangers from four decades of plutonium production for bombs. Congress delivered only a fraction of the billions of dollars the president's administrators pledged. "We were pissed at the feds. They promised they'd do that in personal meetings," the governor growled. But "my take is a lot different than a lot of people's. The toxic waste at Hanford is crystallized and as long as it remains crystallized, it won't flow out into the Columbia or into the ground water. So as toxic as it is, it's probably not in a bad place, if it has to be there. I think Congress took the approach I took, which is to stabilize. They need the money more elsewhere right now."[53] This overlooked pools of waste in single-shell tanks, a few starting to leak, a few miles from the Columbia. In 1990, the U.S. DOE began the shutdown of the Fast Flux Test Facility, a loss of 400 jobs in the Tri-Cities. Gardner first sought international and commercial uses for it and then prevailed with Secretary James Watkins for a "new contracting strategy," giving workers the right of first refusal on retraining to an "environmental orientation."[54] Hanford grudgingly glimpsed a new age.

By 1954, Congress had completely dammed the Columbia's mainstream and most important tributaries. The coming of the

Eisenhower administration ended the 30-year struggle for a Columbia Valley Authority. President Kennedy's 1960 visit to the giant reservoirs can be conveniently taken as the end of the war between the private and public utilities. Nuclear power was to be the saving, if not graceful proxy for fully exploited hydropower. Demand forced producers and their distributor the Bonneville Power Administration to cooperate. The chance to set rules for the key dozen federal agencies in the Basin as well was lost. The 50 year struggle between the Northwest's governors and the federals was no longer over "states' rights," (although that lingering regionalism was always a political tool), or who should and could build dams, but a debate over ways to arbitrate, mitigate, or litigate a way out of environmental chaos.

Their failure to agree was a compelling argument for a Columbia Valley Authority. In May 1987, Dr. John Kitzhaber, then President of the Oregon Senate and soon to be governor, made comprehensive planning on the Columbia his prime cause. He labored mightily, uninformed by history. After four years of negotiations, Oregon and Washington, who had been locked in litigation, the United States, and five Indian nations signed a "Comprehensive Long-Term Management Plan for Fisheries" — terminating in 1998 — unless a "trigger event" ended it earlier.[55]

Half a century of drilling and damming, farm fertilizers and habitat erosion, Canadian interception of fish returning from Alaska, and chronic over fishing had long since gutted the Columbia salmon fishery. Gardner was at first skeptical of Idaho Governor Cecil Andrus's idea of drawing down dams on the Snake to increase flow and head off the extinction of three salmon runs. Scientists argued for it, and in December 1991, the Pacific Northwest Power Council adopted a "comprehensive recovery plan," including Olympia's ideas, to halt the decline of the Chinook salmon. The three states agreed at a Salmon Summit convened by Oregon's United States Senator Mark Hatfield in 1992 to charge the Northwest Public Power Association with "improving survival rates, and balancing fish, wildlife and energy needs." Predictably, little changed. The Columbia may yet be saved from Hanford's leaks, but it will never flow freely enough to restore a silver horde of salmon.

## 1988: A Year of Unease

Gardner was having second thoughts. "The visible focus" had been on programs, more than "management…I'm going to move to more leanness."[56] The stock market was volatile, consumer confidence down. When respected budget director Orin Smith quit in 1987, businessman Dick Davis was drafted as chief of staff to provide a stiff arm for the governor to lean on. "Dick is a bit of a contrast to me," Gardner told the press; he brought a "management cut." The cabinet heard a one percent reserve was not enough. "Prudent and good business practice" dictated plans for reductions of three percent by November 1 and an end to "development projects."[57] The protocol for the 1988 session was "to do effectively that which has already passed."

The 20 executive requests were "less comprehensive." Fifteen passed, including wetlands preservation and making the penalty for child rape equal to adults. Supplemental budget requests went to the legislature at $300 million and passed out at bare bones $95 million, including AIDS education and the governor's "Schools for the 21st Century." The landmark was the first workmen's comp rise in 17 years, and for many House Democrats the minimum wage bill was mandatory. The press probed the governor: would he sign any increase in the minimum wage? Gardner: "Well 'any' is too vague. I don't know." What do you think the minimum wage ought to be? Gardner: "Higher than it is." And, in the last two days, "Don't you think it's time since it's a priority for your party that you wade in or try to negotiate it?" The governor: "Something" ought to be done. "At what level?" Gardner: "Well, let's not set a level now." A reporter reminded him the legislation would be dead on the morrow. Gardner: "Well, then we've got 24 hours." The question, where was he on the sticking point, inclusion of farm workers? "I can't answer that now. I'm tired."[58]

He had just come from the Republican caucus, where senators from the agricultural areas east of the Cascades spoke loudest. The House's amending in of farm workers had been the kiss of death. "I think that anyone…making less than $3.25 an hour lost," the governor mused after sine die, "We'd accomplished as much as we could." Speaker Joe King knew the governor's "bottom line" for ending the session was rather state takeover of the overleveraged Washington Convention Center in Seattle to avoid a major embarrassment.[59] It had been built and added to with over $200 million in bonds in lieu of new taxes in the 1981-83 recession.

Political decisiveness and public applause are independent, and it can be argued, inverse variables. "Team Washington's" captain knew how to put the ball in play and position it up field, only to hesitate when the shin-kicking needed for goals began; a journalist tagged him "Prince Faintheart."[60] Yet in 1988 Gardner was in an enviable position. Revenues had rebounded and joblessness hit a 15-year low. The GOP passed over Norm Maleng, King County's effective but uninspiring prosecutor, for legislative gadfly Bob Williams, protracting a 16-year siege of self-immolation. The governor's factual, nonpartisan, unpretentious speeches and personal warmth led to a landslide in November. The opening of the new term was the best and perhaps the last time for major offensives. Made painfully aware of the limits of a light-handed style by staff infighting in his first term and pressured by close advisors, he anointed another alter ego, testy, tactile former House Majority Leader Dennis Heck to be Davis' deputy chief of staff and lead legislative strategist.[61]

## Tax Reform: An Abortive Reprise

A new attempt at tax reform was the defining issue. Gardner had to confront the reality that the governor was only one, absent a major crisis, with the clout for constitutional change. Asked about an income tax as an incipient candidate in 1983, he replied, "My position is not well formed." His "inclination" was to broaden the base. "But on the other hand," states with income taxes also had their financial woes, "so I think it comes down to how you manage the money you have more than the sources from which you generate the money." In the fall of 1987, he took it off the table. The media asked where he stood. "That's [an income tax is] a solution. But you can get there if you have a tremendously expanded base or some other form of taxation. If the legislature wants to look at prerogatives, that's their prerogative." Nineteen eighty-eight would be a gubernatorial election year. Would he advocate it then? "Data would probably not be available." Boosting the gas tax came up: "I do think there is a real streak of some aversion to taxes. I may not like the taste of taxes if they do it at all, but I'll take the program enhancements this time."[62] A pressman told Gardner some Democrats thought he was "flopping around."

In 1988, fiscal pressure mounted: the 1990s would put 100,000 more sons and daughters of baby boomers into grade school in four years, a third more people would reach age 75 in the next ten, impacting the health plan, and 30,000 more collegians were in the wings. Rate changes in recessions had pushed up the anchor sales tax to 6.2 percent (to the nation's second highest), and the Business and Occupations tax to eighth highest. "Sin" and "nuisance" levies like liquor and licenses were vulnerable as initiatives showed. Most tellingly, state collections between 1977 and 1987 were 11 percent below the growth in personal income. A "crossroads" had been reached: Gardner now "believed" in tax reform. "My attitude's real simple. It's been 16 years since we've sat down and said 'How do we wish to pay taxes in this state.' That's an awful long time." The absence of an income tax was a "scapegoat for making some hard decisions. So my belief is let's get it [an Income tax] out there."[63]

In January 1988, Revenue's Bill Wilkerson assembled a strategy committee. The governor was to proselytize the caucuses, Boeing, Weyerhaeuser, and key legislators; all other crucial constituencies were assigned. A poll revealed just 29 percent favored or "mildly favored" a trial package with a 3.9 percent income tax and lowering the sales tax to that level. Even if just 42 percent wanted this less visible tax reduced, the governor said, "My belief is that we will never see an income tax in this state until you see a substantial reduction in the sales tax." Finding 56 percent of the voters would be more likely to vote for a legislator who opted for a referendum was taken as an acceptable level political exposure. The "only real positive" was that 85 percent thought this the right approach.[64] In April, a wider Governor's Committee on Washington's Financial Future met. Seventy public meetings drew 3,500 citizens in 19 communities. All this to reconfirm what had been known 30 years: the best alternative was a near replicate of 1971's Referendum 42. What was different was taking another 75,000 of the smallest firms off the B&O rolls, rather than a corporate income tax in its place. Six years of inflationary adjustments and including parallel three percent per year boost in the gas tax anticipated the future.[65]

"I have not gone through this exercise for drill," the governor declared. Tax reform was his "top priority" for 1989. He was willing to see the session go over 105 days and wield the veto to get the package. But it was tentatively offered by asking opponents what they were "afraid of." The liberal House and the Senate Republicans by one vote, tried to ignore him. "We're going to be as committed as the governor is," one skeptical legislative leader said. The *P-I*'s Shelby Scates presumed to speak for the media: "Around the state house the governor is regarded as a major disappointment. Booth's warmth, decency and gentle humor is the political equivalent of a neutron bomb: It blows away the voters even as it leaves his old structural problems standing." Reactions in the governor's "town hall" meetings in Vancouver, Spokane, and Bothell were foreseeable. Pointing to the four sales tax raises since tax reform's last outing in 1973, he argued we should not wait for the next crisis. As the usual wild differences of opinion and loud nay-saying broke out, Gardner got more provisional. In visits with editors acted as if he was still testing the water. Was it to be "Ram Booth or Mr. Rogers?"[66]

Representative Art Wang's House Revenue Committee liberalized the bill, upping the income tax threshold from $30,000 to $40,000. A legislative "super majority" (60 percent) replaced the two-thirds vote to change major taxes, and the bill came out on March 31 on a party line vote. Seven Republicans were counted as ready to vote "yes" on the floor. The question was the Democratic majority. "I can't get anyone who's ready to go," one vote counter told Chief of Staff Heck. "I don't believe we ever came close…[to a two-thirds vote]," Wang reminisced.

"Gardner has been known for not following through…being reluctant to play the heavy." He remembered needing the vote of Tom Bristow, a moderate conservative from the woods of Stevens County in the northeast corner of the state on another tax bill. "Booth was coming up there [the Democratic Caucus] to close the deal. Tom came out of the room with Booth saying, 'He understood me. He understood why I can't vote for him.' So it just didn't work. That was not Booth's forte. He wasn't comfortable at it. He wasn't good at it. In some cases he probably did more harm than good. He wasn't really there a whole lot."[67] "History says he'll cave," said Democratic Senator Al Bauer.

The bill never saw the House floor. "He had people down to the Second Floor. And he sat 'em down and said, 'Look, this is what I want. How do we get there. He was very persuasive." But "I can't remember a time… when he did that [lobbied on the third floor]," Dan McDonald noticed.[68] Republican senators held out for separate referenda on tax limits to isolate the income tax, and for a "rainy day" fund. Gardner refused to solicit their votes one on one. The vehicle most voters wanted a chance to vote against died, and with it the future of the Children's Initiative. This was not to be the "watershed session," the font of new dollars for education the governor had hoped for. "We had the opportunity, we had the tools, but we lacked the will," he said.[69] How one sells tax reform in Washington is unanswered. Conviction and persistence will be components.

The compensating graces at other times were Ehlers, Heck, and Foster, former colleagues and friends of Speaker Joe King, who with him carried the governor's freight, but knew "we [often] didn't have the votes." Denny Heck pressed the governor to issue an "ultimatum" on "must" bills three days before the end of the regular session, "to clearly define… expectations." There would be a special session unless the legislature "gets its work done." The "musts" were a reserve of just $113 million ($40 million of which Gardner was free to use), expanded Medicaid eligibility for pregnant women and children under eight (8,500 and 16,300 persons respectively), and a floor of 25,000 in the Basic Health plan. From there the memo was vague: "Schools for the 21st Century" needed "sufficient funding to substantially increase the number of projects" and pay enhanced for teachers with master's degrees. There was a window of opportunity for higher education before the baby boom echo arrived; land for branch campuses had to be acquired.[70] House Democrats were seen with "Blame Gov. Heck" buttons. Speaker King insisted Gardner had learned that "politics is a contact sport." Jeannette Hayner said he had "not been a player."

When Gardner called a second special session, 27 of the 49 senators thumbed their noses by not showing up the first day. Those there noted he had not vetoed the transportation budget as promised for lack of a gas tax increase. Senate Democrats wanted a boost of no less than seven cents a gallon; Gardner came up to four, with two more phases to five cents. The Senate Republicans called his bluff in passing one at five cents. The session "should never have happened," King conceded. The House gave Gardner his first veto override on a bill to put burglars behind bars quicker and longer. "You just weep at the opportunities lost," Gardner said, signing the no-tax-increase transportation budget. The freeze broke on time in May's warmth and tedium. Mental health enhancements, partial pension reform, a six-year moratorium on offshore oil and gas leasing, the governor's "Washington Futures" to provide training for the unemployed, "Waste Not Washington," a massive solid waste recycling plan, and a presidential primary that had eluded the lawmakers for four years went to the second floor.

Gardner won a separate Department of Health, the Drug and Alcohol Treatment bill, prenatal care for low-income women, a portion of First Steps for preschoolers, branch campus land, expansion of the Housing Trust Fund (state mortgage guarantees for lower income families), and more medical care and mental health treatment for children. The Running Start and Learning by Choice alternatives programs allowed high schoolers to earn college credits, gave them more incentives to go on, and eighth graders the same with high school.

The ideas of Norm Maleng's Task Force on Community Protection were only half opened. The Community Protection Act did deal repeat offenders in longer terms. But Gardner's request for $30 million to help local government meet the new obligations was again ignored, as was new state prison capacity for the 6,500 more rapists, burglars and drug dealers expected in the next six years on top of the existing 15 percent overload. The governor thought asking for a "report card" at the end "seemed unusual, since the only similarities between the Legislature and school is that they're both very educational, and sometimes all of the assignments aren't done on time."[71] The jewels in the crown were purchased by prosperity. The diamond, tax reform, was lost by indecisiveness.

## The "Californication" of Washington

The urban analogy to the spotted owl controversy was how to compact the human flood of in-migrants driven to Puget Sound by flaccid rural economies and drawn by the burgeoning metropolitan one. The state's population gain of 20 percent in 10 years triggered a second environmental wave, less vigorous than the one 20 years before. Puget

Sound now had the highest number of vessel transits per capita on the West Coast. Sewerage was in the sound and on many summer days heavy smog hung over it. Seattle had gone from urban to metropolitan. There were gangs, drive-by shootings, and the nation's sixth worst traffic along the I-5 corridor.

When the legislature neglected a Washington Environment 2010 Plan begun in 1984, it was instituted by an executive order (1988) and funded by the EPA joining public and private sectors.[72] The Senate's 1985 refusal to vote $450 million in bonds to clean up the sound was a "profound disappointment" to the governor. He persisted until $20 million in Referendum 39 bonds passed, paid by an eight percent boost in the cigarette tax. In 1988, Gardner ended smoking in state offices, raised agency recycling a quarter in a year, and started a Senior Environmental Corps. In 1989, the legislature failed to designate wetlands. A last recourse, an executive order, once more did what the legislators should have done.[73]

The six pace-setting environmental laws of 1971 had spawned an enigma: county and city governments created a maze of subsidiary ordinances tailored to their "special" needs. Former Port of Seattle Executive Director Richard Ford, whom Gardner tapped to head a Growth Strategies Commission, fingered the puzzle: local government suffered "from too much bureaucracy and a failure to streamline and expedite permitting. Up and down the regulatory chain, decision making is in paralysis with very little benefit to the environment or growth management." Gardner was determined to simplify, but the attitudes of the '80s was made for rough sledding. In a "kind of ugly ending," in 1990, developers suffocated his growth management bill in the Senate. Environmentalists then overreached with I-547, which he labeled "ill-conceived" and had to help defeat. Smaller turns of the wheel included the $53 million granted to purchase wildlife, recreation, and conservation lands; and in 1991, Gardner's oil spill prevention, air pollution, energy strategy legislation was adopted. It was not the "most significant package of environmental bills passed in the state's history," but a respectable second to 1971.

Twenty years on, the contrast between the size of the human flood and the means to control it was transparent. The real instrument for attacking urban sprawl, an inclusive Growth Management Act (GMA), lay sequestered in the Senate State Government Committee. Speaker King had grabbed growth management as the fulcrum for his gubernatorial bid, using the traditional ultimate threat: he would hold the 1991-93 budget hostage. It was an idle threat because Senate Majority Leader Jeannette Hayner's unified Republican caucus and aggravating tactic: there was nothing she wanted enough to trade. King and the governor were forced to modify the bipartisan commission's bill. They compromised on growth management; she protected her caucus and their Eastern Washington constituents by leaving the 16 counties east of the Cascades free from Puget Sound values. It was the marvel of the session. The governor was the initiator, not the father of the reform. He did make sure the agencies concerned were adequately funded to enact the law and appointed strong people to the first boards. Some of the sclerosis was swept downstream, but Ecology did not have the staff to prune new rules. Gardner's assertion the state could "reap the benefits of growth while maintaining the quality of life" was aspirational.[74]

## Portents of the '90s

The 1991 session was a prototype for a decade of divided government. Democrats enjoyed a smaller 58 to 40 margin in the House; the GOP clung to the one-vote lead in the Senate it had enjoyed since 1987. The Senate Republican's advantage was their ability to adhere to the "Rule of 13." Contrary to 1981-83, whatever a majority of the majority decided was done, lending them extra leverage in competition with the House and governor. They set the tenor of the education debate, asking for merit pay for teachers, ending the mandatory master's degree, discretionary hiring of experienced professionals without certificates as teachers, and in demanding a uniform exam to graduate from high school. The WEA demurred, and the House's Democrats went the other way, toward freeing schools from state regulations (like the 180-day year and mandatory subjects and hours), but took the union's lead on forming a commission at arm's length from the legislators to devise tests. Reform bogged down over the master's and the GOP's refusal to lift the levy lid.

"These are not normal times," the governor had keynoted. "Thirty-nine percent of registered voters had voted in 1988, the lowest in history." It was "hard to understand. Cynicism can't solve our problems. If you want us to believe in and participate in governing," the public was saying, "show us…it's worth our while." The mandate was to "restore public confidence." The first Gulf War was unsettling. "Our mission [in Olympia] is to defend democracy with as much honor and courage as we demand from the young men and women we have sent overseas." It was a time for "soul searching to find the values that bind us together, for acting on the values in ways that rebuild the bonds of trust between us." How the budget was drafted would "affect whether people see us as agents of democracy or buffoonery."[75] This brief hortatory address, with no mention of his agenda, spoke to Gardner's bifurcated nature as much as any other act: his cautious side was up.

"We will not make the same mistakes that were made in the early 1980s" (meaning the inflation-driven spending by the Ray administration in 1979-81), Gardner had cautioned his directors in the fall of 1990 as the decennial recession began. "Prudent steps" had to be taken as revenue losses verged toward $700 million and taxes were out, the media was told in December when given his 1991-93 budget. "Program stability" and keeping the "rainy day" account intact were critical. The governor advertised his $15.4 billion budget as "austere" because there were no general [emphasis added] tax boosts or invasion of the $260 million reserve fund. It was up 15 percent and contained $300 million in new user fees. Most of the $1 billion new dollars went into teacher pay—up 8.2 percent (plus step raises for seniority). Stung by state employee criticism at being left out, he suggested legislators might look to skimming money from the bureaucrats' benefits! The 1985 assumption that the economy could be stimulated to narrow future revenue swings seemed strangely irrelevant. John Anderson's Department of Trade and Economic Development was the glaring loser, suffering $824 million in "reductions" from agency requests. He soon left. The medically indigent were hard hit, but FIP was "performing so well," based on "word of mouth" that it was untouched.[76]

Skilled senior staff like Dick Thompson at DSHS, Legislative Liaison (and former Speaker of the House) Wayne Ehlers, and ex-House Majority Leader and Chief of Staff Heck, all wise to the ways of the "third floor," carried the governor's freight. Gardner had his best session, passing 16 of 18 executive requests. Puget Sound Water Quality planning dollars doubled, as did those for managing air, oil spill, and wastewater pollution, for early childhood education, and a pilot project teaching four-year-olds. Wetlands protection was again snared. "Many were gains that came were from legislative leaders, not from the leadership of the governor," the *Seattle Times* saw, denying the executive credit.[77] The session was a déjà vu to the last Ray years. Tax rollbacks began. Senate Republicans voted to turn property tax assessments back to 1989 levels—with the telltale help of 11 Democrats. The House Democrats' quandary was, should they kill it in finance committee or let Gardner do it; they opted for the former. March 19, a united front, with some help from the governor's office, squelched the second try. And Gardnerian luck prevailed: the economy righted itself in four months. The March revenue estimate predicted $200 million more, cutting him slack. He "split the baby" four ways, principally to state employees and higher education.

## "All Kids Can Learn"

Gardner's 1987 State of the State address asked for half a billion new dollars for education: "We have not kept pace. I am going to talk about the issue of paying for excellence." In tough times, the best businesses did not "squirrel away money," it went into "product improvement."[78] This was to be education's year. SCORE, the State Committee to Revitalize Education, was baptized. His four-bill education package was new to the legislature, and Republicans liked the approach of Senator Cliff Bailey, ranking member of the Senate Education Committee. As of mid-April, the governor had not conversed with Bailey. "My basic personality is that I don't like to ask for help, and I don't necessarily give a lot of help… And I've yet to find a balance with which I'm comfortable in terms of being in the trading business," he admitted. Senate Republicans had enough Democratic votes to block the budget until five days before the end of the regular session. With Senator Bailey's alternative in hand they negotiated a package to within $200 million—without sealing it. April 27, Gardner called a special session, and on May 8, as it climaxed, was no more definite: "It's not for me to judge how much taxing it [the package] takes."[79] "They're going to pay for it with a prayer," he opined. "They pushed the problems ahead a couple of years." The upshot was $295 million new dollars for education funded by new revenue projections, a down payment on a "bow wave" of commitments and a growing credibility gap for the governor.

The executive gave the legislators four "A's"—for the "School Financial Improvement Act," lowering K-3 class sizes, partly by freeing special levies to rise to 20 percent of funds, expansion of an early childhood education pilot, Project Even Start to address adult illiteracy, and the Schools for the Future Act, which suspended regulations in districts to promote innovative curricula. Principal and teacher competency tests and master's degrees became mandatory. The "F's" were on environment (no hazardous waste fees), and improved support enforcement for welfare. Gardner insisted, "We set the agenda… [and] came out with some extremely good results." For those like Democratic Senate Majority Leader Larry Vognild, who claimed he had not done enough to break impasses, Gardner explained, "I'm not the flashy, bend arm type of governor. My style is my style. However, we had people everywhere. I think the results measure our effectiveness."[80] Intermediaries are just that.

The real actuator was "A Nation at Risk," the 1989 report of the president's Commission on Education,[81] which had engraved itself on the national psyche more than any in memory. It argued education must transform itself as much as the economy and the family had. President George H. W. Bush's summit on education led to a "shared vision" not seen since Sputnik. Freeing local boards from state rules was the new shibboleth. Gardner also tried to reverse a 30-year trend: to devolve control to let teachers, students, and communities set curricular goals. "Schools for the 21st Century" was "to answer what everybody complained about in the field"—handcuffing regulations — got a revaluation. "I said, 'OK, we're going to work to get rid of some of these.' They could not over the course of this thing name one thing that they couldn't have done anyway." He took the chair of the Education Commission of the States saying, "All kids can learn. I believe that if a child is failing, it is because we are failing the child."[82] "The public schools have to be the tool for teaching our national values," the fount of national unity.

The session had put the WEA on the defensive. The governor's relationship with the union was "up and down, because I could argue as good as they could." The WEA saw its task as getting "as much as they could in salary and benefits, and that wasn't good for the kids." "Do teachers get paid enough?" a reporter queried. Gardner: "We ought to pay teachers first, and all the best qualified people in the country ought to be teachers, and then everybody else ought to fight for what's left over." The WEA was unmoved, and near the end of the regular session in early April when he suggested a "cooling off period," it substituted a "burning up period." Thirty districts with half the state's students struck, and 20,000 teachers paraded for a week around the loop between the Temple of Justice and the capitol. "The signs were not complimentary to the then sitting governor."

Gardner, who had met with the WEA "more than my family" during April now heard, "Where is the governor in all this?" He angrily retorted, "The governor…you're looking at is the governor that has taken the only indexes that count in this issue," in raising per capita support from $2600 to $4,250 in four years, a real raise of 17 percent. "They've never had a governor that's made a greater contribution to education." His take on the superintendents of public instructions was, "they're irrelevant." They start off each session by presenting a budget… [that] is not realistic and so they've got nothing left to deal with. At times you would have to wonder if they weren't a surrogate of the WEA."[83]

His focus was getting the children back in school. When the regular session ends, it was protocol for the governor to have a news conference and say, "I'm calling them back tomorrow at noon." Gardner said, "I am going to call them back in June. There was dead silence." Speaker Joe King, whose caucus had left him under the pressure, came up. "'Governor, we're going to override you if you don't call them briefly.' I asked if he'd talked to [Minority Leader] Clyde Ballard. They looked at me like 'Oh my God.'" The Democrats were boxed. The teachers would be out of school by June and could not be remobilized. The other bombshell was an outside consultant's report of teacher salaries all parties had agreed to. It disputed WEA claims teacher salaries were twenty-third or worse nationally. It found pay and benefits were twelfth ($44,551), student-teacher ratio fortieth, soaking the association's believability.

At the expense of Social and Health Services, Dan McDonald had coaxed another 17-percent salary and benefit raise out of the Senate. He and Gary Locke, initiator of the House's budget and also a candidate for governor, could not say no to more. The legislature lifted the state debt limit from seven to eight percent of the prior biennium's revenue to permit a $1 billion capital budget to be paid over 30 years, the lion's share for schools, with higher education, environmental lands, and public housing, combining very popular causes. Gardner pronounced the obvious: the budget was "fully committed."[84] "Once the WEA realized they were…not in a position into push anymore, they came to us and said, 'You've got to give us something,' and we said, 'We've got just the thing for you.'" The sequel was "the Governor's Commission on Schools for the Twenty First Century," asked to come to the table with open minds, "think big" for fundamental change, and report a "focused, specific plan" in 18 months. "The chemistry and consensus on comprehensive action has not existed until now," Gardner contended. The WEA declined to send representatives, out of misgivings about change; SPI Judith Billings fought for her turf as strenuously as her forbears.

The panel's December 1991 interim report called for a "radically new vision" to "break this debilitating status quo." All students could learn at significantly higher levels — if dollars were targeted at "learning goals." How to achieve them "will be left largely to the community" and enforced by testing. Graduates of "outcome based learning" were to be granted a "Certificate of Mastery." Funding, projected at $100 million biannually for incentives to districts meeting goals, and a mentor program for first year teachers, was put off by the 1997 legislators. Competency testing of teachers, something WEA had long fought, was adopted by "grandfathering in," excluding the existing staff. The governor and his surrogates had been bold and enthusiastic. Boeing's CEO Frank Shrontz, in sore want of qualified technicians, led the converted.[85] But the competency testing was only for remediation. Could teaching standards and professional pride rise before inclusive goals were set? Or, as the WEA insisted, did more salary money and smaller classrooms come first? And if the simplified 1977 formula was set aside, would "rich" districts easily passing special levies capture most of the incentives? Testing would be arduous and expensive. And crucially, how could there be equality of in outcomes if 287 districts drew "unique" curricula?

It was again too late. By January 1993, the projected budget deficit was down $1.2 billion. As the WEA and the SPI carved on their dislikes, new programs fell by the wayside. Gardner, who began "G-Serve," and a decade long march for standards in what became the Washington Assessment of Student Learning (WASL), now developed doubts about it. He did not like the rating system pitting schools in different cities against each other or "publicizing the numbers," in a word, open competition. Would those who could not graduate from high school would be marred?[86] His worries were misplaced. By 2007, the WEA, parents frightened that their offspring would not be able to graduate from high school, and legislators made queasy by them, had eliminated first the physical education and music requirements, then those on social science, and delayed math and science five years, leaving a tenth-grade standard for reading and writing. This despite a spectacular improvement, an 85 percent passage rate.[87]

## 1992: Events Beyond His Control

"Every morning, all across the state, lawmakers are waking up, looking in the mirror, and seeing a U.S. Senator, a governor or a congressman," Senate Minority Leader Marc Gaspard observed. By early 1992, all the principals except Hayner, House Appropriations chair Gary Locke, Senate Ways and Means chief Dan McDonald, and Speaker Joe King were running for governor. Their ambitions made for a contorted session.[88] Speaker King confessed, "Dan McDonald and I have two things in common. One, we both want to be governor. And two, we know that if we are both in Olympia in May or June, neither of us are going to be governor"—a prediction that proved true. McDonald began the sparring at a pre-session press conference, reciting the 25 percent growth in state employees on Gardner's watch. Len McComb, now in charge of OFM, admitted to the new deficit—caused by population and service demands. The legislators were complicit: had they not added a quarter to programs for children and the mentally ill, to natural resources by 12 percent, to prison staffing by 10 percent? Gary Locke, the chief accomplice, quickly pointed out that only 7,000 of the 18,000 new jobs were funded by the state and held his own press conference to say he was shrinking the rest of state government to restore three percent pay raises for everyone.

There were to be 1,869 job losses and $40 million in petty fees. The convenient discovery of another $77 million in federal Medicaid money permitted Locke to put back Gardner's excisions from education block grants and disabilities, making the governor look tight. In an echo of 1982, the staff stripping was left to the executive once the legislature left town. Gardner was "livid," scolding both King and Locke. In stark contrast to his later stances as governor, Locke took almost all of the reserve (leaving a paltry $30 million) and even absorbed interest from dedicated funds. It was an "eat your cake and have it too" exercise, revenue director Len McComb fumed, and "fiscal chaos." Locke asked, "What is his obsession with the rainy day account?" The governor, who wanted to get the legislators out of town, swallowed his pride and proclaimed it a "go-home budget."

The bidding-positioning war turned earnest. McDonald asked his opposites to "put up or shut up"—to raise the $40 million and right the reserve—before he would agree to anything. The Senate GOP scratched twice the state jobs (3600), half from management, to keep the $260 million reserve—also leaving it to Gardner's men to choose who went. The GOP senators bowed deeply to teachers under the illusion that they, if not the WEA's militants, would consider McDonald a savior. Welfare and DSHS vendor increments were wiped out to give educators 17.5 percent raises over two years! Smarting from the loss of their majority in 1989, the GOP senators decided to play to their strengths, seeking to reduce class sizes and, in 1991, offering $8,500 per year more to classroom teachers and in higher education placing professional salaries in the seventy-fifth percentile nationally. Gardner damned this as "meaner and leaner" than his social formulas. Locke barked it was "heartless, unfair and unwise… and way out of balance." Behind the rhetoric, McDonald, Hayner, Locke, and King were meeting and threatening to take over if their conferees deadlocked.

Any semblance of rationality vanished on April 19, the ninety-fifth day of the 105-day session as the WEA got 21,000 (about 45 percent) of teachers to walk out and picket the capitol campus for a week. Their president emerged from a hastily called meeting with Gardner to say, "There's no solution in sight" and rule out a palliative new Blue Ribbon Education Commission he had announced. Speaker King bravely said, "The strike is well-intentioned but will have no effect on the legislature." It was bluff; his caucus had crumpled under the WEA's onslaught. Gardner's "sense of balance" found both parties "right." He bet on the next two quarterly revenue forecasts and, without talking to King, declared a "cooling off period," something both rejected weeks earlier. A new session could wait for the next estimate, June 15. "Only then will we have the possibility of a win for all concerned."[89] Legislative leaders knew only the desire to go home would keep enough pressure on the lawmakers. Gary Locke called the recess "crazy." Marc Gaspard groaned, "We feel like the rug has been cut out under us," and the Senate defiantly voted 48-0 to call itself back immediately. The WEA pressured House members to concur, and the governor was saved from overturn only because Republican leader Clyde

Ballard balked. The WEA's spokeswoman told the media, "In Texas, where I come from, it's called turnin' tail and runnin."

Gardner told the teachers to return to their classrooms to chants of "Get busy now." He knew in June school would be out and they would not return to Olympia, while the heat on the legislators would ratchet up: the fiscal biennium was to end June 30. "First the teachers went on strike and now the [budget] conferees have done pretty much the same … . What we are seeing is a lack of will." The GOP senators, intent on forcing the Democrats to choose between their social service and educator bases, were doubly deluded. The House Democratic Caucus would not be outbid.[90] Locke blared back, "I don't think we lack any will. A lot of things are going on that the governor isn't aware of…I think we are going to surprise Booth." Four days later, House Democrats compromised by taking $130 million (half) the "Rainy Day Fund," expecting it to be replenished by the June and September forecasts.

Reconvening was moved to June 10 — the Forecast Council had conveniently moved up its meeting till the next day. OFM head Len McComb tightened the screws on the state's chief economist Dr. Sohn, indicating he might vote against his prognosis (if it was not high enough) and take the two Democratic legislator members with him, denying approval. Dr. Sohn elevated his estimate of wage growth but resisted all else, offering up a modest $73 million. A week later, the governor's office "found" still more coming from the federal government for Medicare. The Democrats could now make ends meet without absorbing the reserve—and satisfy Dan McDonald. Coercing the Forecast Council, created in the 1960s as an independent voice to counteract roseate estimates by governors who preferred faith to fundraising in their budgets had compromised it, even as Gardner delivered his strongest show of resolve. In the end, the GOP got its half billion dollars for class size reductions and block grants, the Democrats a 6.5 percent welfare raise, and state employees and teachers 8.2 percent salary boosts, .08 below the governor's bid. The eternal law of democratic budgets that what comes in is what goes out prevailed.

Gardner's luck lapsed on the last lap. In September, the Forecast Council adjusted income down $26.5 million and in December by $700 million. He was forced to the crudest kind of budgeting, a 2.5 percent across-the-board reduction.[91] His tactic was identical: take away the more had been given. The 1993 salary and welfare raises, the block grants, 1,100 more state jobs, and the usual potpourri of lesser remedies. His defense was now the progressive's: there had been $40 million in new levies and $44 million in tuition increases. The WSFE is not impressed: Gardner was "the Grinch who stole Christmas."

## "Keep us at the Table:" A National Paradigm for Health Care?

In the unfinished business of democracy, governors want the legacy of a pacesetter. Gardner's prediction that no one in the nation would be without health care in 10 years was premature; devising a new delivery system between 1989 and 1991 was his signal of success.

There was no consensus on a national formula, regulating nonprofits, or contracting out. In the summer of 1989, the National Governors Association asked Congress to hold off mandating Medicaid. Rather than firing "a shot across the bow," the states should be in on the solution. Testifying before the U.S. Senate's Budget Committee in 1990, Gardner reminded them the Kaiser plan for construction workers at Grand Coulee was the country's first trial. He had been reworking a Basic Health Plan for 18 months: the criteria were universal access, cost control, care for the uninsured, coverage that did not penalize small business or the elderly, portability, and a role for the private sector.[92] His chairmanship of the NGA in 1991 was the forum for airing a state solution to a "national scandal."

His farewell message in 1992 dwelt on his "play or pay" plan. (Employers could adopt the state Basic Health Plan, or pay half, with their employees.) He went over the heads of the legislators on three television stations, as Evans had on the environment 20 years before. Why, critics asked, come forth with something so expensive in the face of the deficit? Here too, the credit belongs more to conviction than "legacy" seeking. The governor's liberal side was up: "The insatiable monster of health care inflation is eating up valuable dollars that could be going into schools," and the 550,000 uninsured had to be covered. "Washington State is not the kind of place where we're going to let people suffer because they can't afford to see a doctor." So was his preference for private sector "market incentives to do what's right." "Play or pay" was to be phased in over four years.

Selecting the "basic benefits" for the working poor and pricing them were the legislature's nightmares. The kernel of the debate was over a commission to set rates and benefit levels. Braddock's version had a panel of five do both. Fourteen Democrats sat tight, fearing a hammering for the "incalculable" outlays the GOP foretold. Chief of Staff Dean Foster later admitted, "We didn't know what we were talking about.... I think we were trying to make up the numbers." The House had assured defeat by dropping Gardner's taxes on business and employees; business knew the direction of the "cost-shifting," and the public was "lost in the middle."[93] Dennis Braddock, the House committee chair, mourned, "People had a chance to vote for reform, and they voted against it." A majority of the public agreed with the approach, but of course, was unwilling to pay

$700 million over five years for it. Distrust of any government-managed scheme figured in. Gardner lobbied for his last enterprise, but the public hadn't "coalesced," and he was uncomfortable with being a leader…if he was all by himself."[94]

The governor and GOP leadership met through the summer and fall. He considered a special session to force the issue, but by then was a lame duck. The impasse abruptly ended with Democratic takeover of both houses in Washington in 1993. Gardner's bequest became Mike Lowry's bouquet. President Clinton and Congress had their paradigm.

## What Manner of Man?

The cleavage between Booth Gardner the private, non-combative, even shy man, and the allures of public life he was infected with in the Senate was evident to close observers. To his lasting credit, he became a significant public servant without the natural buoyancy and ego compulsions politicians are presumed to have. Speaking to crowds, exhilarating to others and discomforting to him, took discipline. The temperament of the state's best-liked governor made for a tepid partisan, and Gardner drew the perfect opponent in 1984 in the equally mild John Spellman. If it got to "personalities," he would "rethink" his options. He did not endorse Michael Dukakis in the 1988 presidential primary; former Arizona governor Bruce Babbitt was a friend. He went to his precinct caucus, but not to the national convention. Gardner lived with divided government for six years. It took the vexations of Hayner's monolithic Senate Republicans to make him "reasonably active" in legislative campaigns in his second term. Booth kept to a gentleman's standard: "Rudeness, bad manners, and personal insults are not an acceptable substitute for debate, nor cynicism and apathy for overdue action."[95]

Vision was there, but large opportunities were lost.[96] Who is freer to arbitrate and advocate than an incumbent governor savoring prosperity, a businessman's Democrat able to seed his campaign?[97] The Gardner team asked the right questions, was long on origination, succeeded on worthwhile secondary issues, and fell short on major outcomes. Task forces tumbled after one another. Those who, unlike the "Timber Team," received unambiguous policy direction delivered. "Best business practices," his Efficiency Commission's insistence on training employees and talks on "teamwork," were no substitute for a shakedown of the manacled "merit" system. The "good broker" approach to environmental issues was not enough.[98] Progress in growth management belongs to Speaker King and Senator Hayner. A way of killing the campaign finance cancer, by then a bipartisan concern, might have had an impact equal to public disclosure. The GOP's I-134 mitigated the worst practices but is a striking example of how interest groups increasingly leverage advantages (in this case the GOP restricting union contributions) outside the legislature.[99]

Gardner deserves applause for seeding things soon realized. The Basic Health Plan became a national model. First Steps, Running Start, and allowing high schoolers to get community college credits, were genius and resisted by the entire educational establishment. ACES was up and running for his successor. Starting a "Capital [Budget] Forum" to plan ahead ten years was overdue. Persisting on welfare reform, accountability in education in the face of the WEA set the table for the next two executives. Proroguing the 1992 legislature without consulting leadership was a decisive move, but suggests a less-than-intimate relationship with it. Former Speaker Wayne Ehlers, Gardner's legislative liaison, said, "In [legislative] retrospect…he could have done more. He did not like the task. One-on-one horse trading was anathema."[100] "The mix and the mess" was "kind of fun," but in the clutch at session's end, the coach did not carry the ball: "contact sports" were for the playing field.

His premiere achievement was attracting first-rate managers like Mary (Faulk) Rivelin and her husband Chase, George Televick who was chief of the State Patrol for eight years, Chris Gregoire, Mary's replacement at Ecology, and Chuck Clark in Community Affairs (and later head of Utilities for Seattle) and chats at the table for minorities, exemplified by the Centennial Accord bringing the 26 recognized Indian tribes more status and respect. Carrying the WASL forward in the face of the WEA turned out to be pique as much as purpose. The failure of the Children's Initiative in 1989 slowed progress, but mental health programs steadily improved. In the divided government of his last six years, forceful Majority Leader Jeannette Hayner kept the Senate GOP united while House Democratic leaders' caucus was perennially fractured over the largest policy questions.

Booth Gardner dealt with two sets of ambiguities. His Republican-oriented upbringing, neo-conservative nature, and business background jousted with humanitarian instincts sharpened by his family's tragedies and a reserved personality averse to conflict in an environment often demanding aggressive advocacy. His need to force himself onto the offense against Spellman as well as legislators' suspicions as to how long and vigorously he would press tax reform grew from past hesitancies, illustrate both facets. Aborting tax reform revealed how tepid execution capped promise. Alter egos were stiffeners, not stand-ins.

The ongoing dichotomy between Gardner's predilection for "cost efficient ways to live within his means" and his social sensitivities were "always the heart of the heartache." Gardner "punted" when OFM director Dick Thompson recommended extension of the sales tax to professional services in 1987. Gardner's philosophy was to "run government within the funds that are available" and vary only in "dire need. Then I'd borrow to take care of them."[101] After the expected death of tax reform in 1989, he chose not to push another tax, delimiting his education agenda. He benefited as much as any executive, except Evans, from a prosperous economy. Asked if Gardner might have raised taxes in a downturn, Dick Thompson was at a loss.

Gardner was not reluctant to use the veto. His first was the only one overridden. Dan Evans congratulated him: "You haven't been governor until you've been overridden." They went from 8.9 to 13.6 percent in the first four years and up to 17.7 percent in 1989 on Heck's "get tough" urgings. "The Governor didn't have a strict constructionist approach. He believed that he was the final vote in the legislative process, and if there was a policy before him he didn't like he was entitled to vote no...and he did it a lot." The Constitution gives no guidelines. "It seems to imply... the governor is entitled to exercise his veto on any basis." He concedes Gardner rarely told legislators his preferences before they voted. Heck's argument that a bill is always subject to change and may not survive to the governors is less compelling than, "You take away your bargaining chips." Nor did the nature and frequency of Gardner's vetoes confirm Heck's claim he "exercised his veto authority most in our entire state's history," only that this was his chief of staff's typically firm interpretation.[102] Several latter day vetoes were dubious. Senator Bob McCaslin's expansion of the Spokane County Commission from three to five was killed, perhaps as a payback for holding the Growth Management Act in his committee. Victory was snatched from father's rights activists in gutting a bill reducing child support payments in 15 counties. Allowing judges to stiffen penalties for gang members was struck as potentially racist. Gardner found a porn tax unconstitutional but signed a bill barring the sale of "erotic" music to minors—and landed on the ACLU's list of "arts censors."[103]

"You've discovered you can't run state government like a business?" the Bremerton Sun's Adele Ferguson needled the governor in March 1987. "The state's not a business," he shot back it was a "service organization." There could be no quick moves to drop clientele to cover revenue losses, no way around civil service armor plate, or to avoid the "huge board of directors," the contentious legislators. "Everyone was for 'good management,'" he reminded the Spokane Rotary, but "it doesn't seem to inspire them to participate in it."[104] Asked what he would miss least, the citizen's politician replied draining "public situations" and "people who say, 'Why can't you just run government like a business?'" "And I say, one, you can make decisions quickly, and we can't. We could, but we wouldn't last very long in office. Second, the governor does all the things that nobody else wants to do. You take care of thieves and felons, children without homes...with cognitive disabilities."[105] Instituting the Capital Forum and passing it into a law mandating a ten-year projection on building needs, including social (e.g., low income housing) and environmental ones, and at a stroke changed the capital budget from something the senior members of the money panels did on a Saturday morning.[106]

By the fall of 1991, the governor was as dispirited as he had been as a legislator. "I never had any trouble making decisions, other than agonizing over personnel," he told the *P-I* 11 years later. "In 1992, I hit a wall. I was in depression. I stopped making decisions. I started delegating everything. I got tentative. I had seven great years, but the eighth year wasn't fun. I didn't know I had Parkinson's." Otherwise, "I probably would have gone for a third term."[107] His respites were taking private lessons on the grand piano in the ballroom of the mansion. The first recital was "me and twelve little kids." He also took up mountain climbing, cooking, and foreign languages to lower stress. Being governor was the "greatest public-service job imaginable"—but "an experience, not a career." Leaving was "excruciating. I felt like I'd lost an arm." "And 1994" he was asked? "That's a possibility, if you talk to me and not to my spouse." The erosion of his 30-year marriage to Jean, who opposed another term, was reason enough to quit.

Calling off a near certain reelection or not capturing Brock Adam's open U.S. Senate seat had an impact on the state comparable to Dan Evans' taking Henry Jackson's place. Mike Lowry opted to run for governor, facilitating Slade Gorton's return as a U.S. senator.[108] "I knew that there were 15 governors who were senator...who had been governors when I was. I went back to D.C. and met with every one of them. Fourteen out of 15 said 'The best job I've ever had was governor.'" Gardner told the 1993 legislature he had learned so much as governor he often thought he should have paid tuition. Alone among his peers, he did not dwell on his achievements.[109] There was no need to preen. Six boxes of personal replies to mail, some in his own hand, testify to a reaching out by and to Washingtonians. Speaker King recognized the "antithesis of a politician" that's why the public likes him so well.[110] The governor left Olympia with his political capital intact.

Chapter 11

# Mike Lowry: Liberal and Proud of It

*(1993-97)*

## The Odd Couple

Mike Lowry was born in 1939 in St. John and grew up in Endicott, a tiny wheat town in the Palouse where his family homesteaded beginning in 1882. His father celebrated the New Deal at the dinner table and raised a buoyant, good-natured, stubborn, moralistic, and sometimes temperamental son, his mother described as "a combination of Barry Goldwater and John the Baptist."[1] Mike graduated from Washington State University in 1962 and went west to Seattle, quickly becoming president of the State Young Democrats. He was chief of staff for the Senate Ways and Means Committee in Olympia (1969-73) and managed Chairman Martin Durkan's losing 1972 gubernatorial primary. They were an "odd couple." Lowry, an ebullient, hyperkinetic liberal teamed with the panel's gray-haired, oily, "last king," but the campaign stirred aspirations that shaped his destiny.

The last governor from east of the Cascades, Cheney wheat miller Clarence D. Martin (D), (1933-41), was a conservative constrainer of the New Deal. The population east had since shrunk relative to Puget Sound to quarter of the state, and no one had repeated the feat, much less that rare bird the "Eastern Washington liberal." Mike's 1992 "loyalty" vote was an asset and a compliment that was given despite the East's lessened influence. The progressive transformation of burgherly Seattle in the 1960s into a liberal, metropolitan, "San Francisco of the north," and an uninspired opponent who allowed him to co-opt businessmen made him governor.

Mary Lowry knew she had married a compulsive politician a year later when he challenged King County Executive John Spellman. "We had no jobs. He had no experience. I've always been nervous about these elections." Lowry later testified things had "one well" in King County under Spellman. If he won, "It will be the political upset of the decade." John was "a good guy" but beatable "because a majority of the people don't want the downtown business establishment running the courthouse." "Clear stands" on issues and a "more aggressive approach to human problems" could be paid for by a corporate tax of one percent on incomes over $10,000. The Vietnam War split Democrats, sealed his ties to the King County Democratic organization, who gave him an unusual preprimary endorsement over a "conservative" Democrat. "Had the Vietnam War not existed, and had the Central American and the Contras issues not existed I could not have got that special recognition."[2] Lowry got a surprising 42 percent of the vote in the general election.

## The Perfect Fit

Becoming Brock Adam's legislative liaison in the south end's Seventh Congressional District was smarter — his job was to go to every community meeting there was — a prelude to his election to the King County Council in 1975. In two years, Lowry was chairing the council and, in 1978, the Association of Counties. That November, he dispatched pin-striped conservative Congressman Republican Jack Cunningham, a fortuity of the incipient tax revolt in 1976 in the blue-collar-ethnic enclave that is the Duwamish Basin. His ten years in Congress (1979-89) was a serial protest against President Reagan's reverse priorities. Conditioned by Vietnam, he voted against the Nicaraguan incursion, tax cuts (as too deep), the Kemp-Roth higher education bill, and was nearly ritualistic in denouncing "excessive" military spending that should be shifted to social needs. Enhanced children's nutrition programs, for instance, were one of the few new "social bridges ... to keep us together."

The president's huge deficits could be offset by putting three, not ten percent of the budget into defense. Seventy percent of the jobs in the Seventh District came from Boeing.[3] Lowry's salvaging of the Export-Import Bank in the House Banking Committee justified as compensation for European subsidies to Airbus endeared him to the company and its lobbyist Bud Coffey, whose sympathy was crucial in his years as governor. He co-signed a letter asking the president to fire Interior Secretary James Watt and fought the navy's Everett home port on environmental grounds.[4] The values of a "jobs" New Dealer melded with those of an urban liberal.

A certified "Modern Democrat" was anchored in a sinecure heavy with dock workers and machinists. He was "right" on Labor's issues, but "wrong" on Indian fishing and gun laws, but "we figured Mike could hold up a liquor store and win in the Seventh," an aide said.[5] Gregarious and popular, Lowry won a seat on the House Budget Committee in his second term, arbited in conferences with the senate, headed its Task Force on Economic Policy, and chaired Subcommittee on the Panama Canal and the Outer Continental Shelf for the Merchant Marine and Fisheries Committee. Pervasive if not prominent, he peaked as chair of the 250-member Democratic Study Group while being the "maverick" in the traditionally "tight" Washington delegation.[6]

In the spring of 1983, Henry Jackson died of a heart attack after 30 years in the U.S. Senate. Lowry overwhelmed Seattle Mayor Charles Royer in the primary by keeping his south end base and splitting Seattle liberals, only to be trumped by the redoubtable Dan Evans, who had resigned as president of Olympia's Evergreen State College to take the appointment. Evans' broadsides that Lowry had tried to "reimpose the inflation penalty" and sponsored 32 bills in five years and passed none, was not rebuttable and hit hard. Lowry could not capitalize on his Eastside roots against Evans nor overwhelm him in Seattle. He took just six counties, doing best in the hard-hit Pacific timberlands while losing 55 to 45 percent.[7] A frustrated Evans abruptly exited in 1988, and Lowry launched a new campaign at a soup kitchen benefit for the homeless. Republican Slade Gorton, whom Brock Adams had upset in 1986, sought a comeback. Lowry's "liberalism" and Gorton's "arrogance" got them matched high "negatives" in the polls. The *Seattle Weekly* wondered if the election would go to the nominee "the voters decide they dislike least."

Lowry was too widely seen as an "ineffective arm-waiver" who was "too liberal." Asked by a journalist if he would be more politic, he replied, "I don't have to. I have no intention to."[8] Lowry mistakenly thought Gorton, who had voted for taxes and against social security boosts to cut recessionary deficits, would not reverse himself. Except for visibly toning down his criticism of defense, a staple in every corner of the state, his consciousness raising issues-oriented campaign extended his life as a congressional gadfly. He was competitive until two days after the primary, when he courageously voted against the omnibus drug bill on civil liberties grounds. Gorton shifted from a media emphasis in 1986 to put $400,000 in grassroots organizing, led by his talented manager Mike McGavick, later chair of Safeco Insurance, and a U.S. Senate candidate in 2006.[9] Reagan stormed to reelection. Democratic presidential nominee Michael Dukakis and Lowry went down face-first.

## 1992: Fate Intervenes

At 49, the young man on a treadmill had held two offices and suffered three defeats in thirteen years. But four years of teaching political science at Seattle University and co-chairing the Washington Wildlife and Recreation Coalition with Dan Evans did nothing to damp his ambition. The two senate races brought near universal name recognition, and he was still adored by Seattle's leading liberals. When U.S. Senator Brock Adams imploded for purportedly drugging a young staffer for sex in 1992 and Booth Gardner feinted toward then fell back from the Potomac, Lowry leapt into the gubernatorial race. Before retreating to Renton, Mary, a quiet non-practicing CPA who had lingered for four years at home mused, "I don't know if its [politics] is on relationships or it forces you … [to] work things out."[10]

The 42-city opening tour was disorganized. It was not the fault of campaign manager Sue Tupper, who refused to talk to the media. Lowry was "all over the place." At a spaghetti feed in a Seattle union hall, he pledged "to win this election on issues we've been right on all the time," education, health care, the environment, straight talk, and leadership. The state was headed into its fourth decennial recession: "It is best to have a governor…who cares about people programs. What you need in a tight budget is a liberal."[11] Back in Pullman in Whitman County's wheat lands he declared, "I definitely know more about Eastern Washington than just about anyone who ever runs for office." The Democratic primary was moot by July 26, when 1,500 came to Lowry's Annual Shrimp Feed at Kay Bullitt's Capitol Hill mansion in Seattle.[12] The Democratic base was on his side. The transparently sincere, rumpled Lowry, with eyes bulging, arms flailing, swamped them. The loudest hurrahs came when he touted the virtues of diverting defense contracts to domestic projects like mass transportation.

Seattle Mayor Norm Rice realized he was overrun and endorsed Lowry. A small plane towed a forlorn banner overhead: "Read the King Plan," 38 pages of prescriptions to lend gravitas to six-year House Speaker Joe King. The unabashed liberal was now a Clintonesque "can-do moderate," to the point of regretting the fate of a 1988 initiative for more state spending on children and endorsing the anti-crime Initiative 590, Three Strikes and You're Out. Revelations of campaigning by House staff and the diffidence of Democratic legislators hurt by his "macho" style as speaker kept him down five to one in the polls.[13]

Lowry's "strategy," being himself, upbeat, outspoken, and unrepentantly liberal was nonetheless risky. He was the first major candidate in 18 years to say an income tax was needed — if there was a vote of the people — and that the sales tax and those on small business needed reducing.

Public education could be "second to none." "Good environmental policy is good economic policy." So was Booth Gardner's health plan, even with minimum coverage, deductibles, and private participation. He had "earned the credibility to advocate the budget cuts and reforms that (Republican Attorney General) Eikenberry can only talk about," applauded the newly liberal *Seattle Times*. Lowry was also endorsed by the normally Republican-oriented Washington Medical Association, who found Eikenberry's free market postures and cooperatives unequal to spiraling health costs.[14] Lowry started the governor's race with $50,000 and limited contributions to $1,500.

Mainline GOP Bellevue State Senator Dan McDonald, the choice of Olympia's Association of Washington Business, marshaled a finance committee of 150 including George Weyerhaeuser, contractor-mogul Howard S. Wright, and ex-U.S. Attorney General Bill Ruckelshaus, but could not convince political cognoscenti of his appeal beyond his affluent suburb. Congressman Sid Morrison of Zillah raised $500,000, only to have Lowry cut into his east of the Cascades vote. Defeated, stung by Eikenberry's attack ads, and now asked to endorse him, he said, "I'll make that decision as a private citizen in the privacy of the voting booth."

A January poll gave him 27 percent of Seattle voters to Morrison's 4, and 19 percent east of the Cascades to Morrison's 25 percent.[15] The September 15 primary was Eikenberry's to lose. Six months of campaigning had drawn Lowry just 30 percent of the vote, few beyond his "core voters."[16] An end-of-October poll gave the attorney general a 45 to 33 percent lead He spent $600,000 in the primary, his opponents $2.7 million. But name familiarity and the unflinching support by conservative GOP county organizations for their former state chair put "liberal" King, Pierce, and Snohomish counties in Eikenberry's column in the low turnout primary. [17]

Eikenberry was raised poor on a small orchard outside Wenatchee, hawking 25 cent trees from a wagon in his youth. Ideological as a state representative (1971-77), even-handed as attorney general, and inclusive as the GOP's as a "big tent" state chair (1977-80), he revived the party's networks. In 1980, the GOP captured majorities in both houses of the legislature for the first time in 48 years, despite the millstone laid around his neck in June by the religious right. The GOP platform damned everything from homosexuals to the National Endowment for the Arts, declaimed on moral issues and even witchcraft.[18] The attorney general's intense and stolid and personality contrasted with Lowry's and concealed a quick sense of humor and a shyness that kept him from cementing social contacts in 18 years in Olympia. His "unfair" suits of business polluters were the reason of choice given by entrepreneurial defectors.

The attorney general's "sharp contrasts" with a "big-spending liberal" were unnecessary. Lowry ignored them; many swing voters could not. Creating a "free market" in health insurance, a "balance between socio-economic impacts" and environmental laws, "core values," deregulation, co-op schools, merit pay and skills testing for teachers were comparatively vague. He expected to be a one-term governor: "Sometimes that's the price you pay to do the right thing."[19] In their first statewide television debate on September 26, Lowry was "precise and realistic." Eikenberry skirted the projected deficit of $1.6 billion, beyond "reinventing government," getting rid of "old programs," and tapping an anticipated nine percent revenue gain. Dan Evans, now a commentator on KIRO TV, did not endorse him, and scolded Eikenberry for ignoring math: "Either he must be specific in how he will accomplish this miracle [of balancing the budget] or quit trying to mislead Washington voters."

The attorney general's inability to frame a positive identity was fatal. What of the 50,000 new public school students, the potential $500 million impact of the Gardner health plan, and runaway prison populations? Lowry's answers, erasing administrators and trying tax reform again were as unlikely to bring a balance, but sounded positive. When they met a third time in Tacoma's Temple Theater on October 22, even Lowry was more cautious, offering "difficult" budget cuts and a tax on professional services as a "last resort" aimed at "those who haven't been paying their fair share." Eikenberry was in near denial, telling one media questioner, "I don't know where you are getting your figures from..." when asked about a $1 billion deficit.[20] The psychological divide became transparent at Seattle's Downtown Rotary, where Lowry won applause for an apparently sincere stand on reducing business taxes. Eikenberry sounded like an angry Populist in reacting to UW Regent Sam Stroum's allegation that his staff had promised a regency position in return for a donation. Rotarian regents-in-waiting did not appreciate being dismissed as socialites mainly interested in trips on the Husky football plane. Lowry drew even in the dollar race with 11,500 contributors to his opponent's 4,500.[21]

## Capturing the Capitalists

Business ties to the GOP, eroding since the 1970s, were loosened further by multimillionaire Booth Gardner, who had no need to tax in a swelling economy. Its expediency grew apace, as highly paid political consultants were retained by all camps irrespective of, and partly to obscure partisan affiliations. Business strategy of backing the GOP in a defensive war against taxes and regulations was reduced to opportunism—funding Democratic candidates they "could work with" or who looked like a "winners." Eikenberry's performance at the Seattle Rotary and at the Washington Roundtable, a political education and pontification club for two dozen of the state's weightiest CEOs, opened doors for Lowry's chief political sorcerer, Democrat Bob Gogerty (Gogerty and Stark). Bob's Rolodex was paid for by "Republican" clients like Boeing and Weyerhaeuser, whom he now drew to a breakfast at the Norton Building's Harbor Club, a watering hole of the previously suspect "downtown elite." Lowry's turn-the-other-cheek approach, natural for a consensus-building legislator, fit Gogerty's "inclusiveness" mantra. The entrepreneurs sat quietly as Lowry with his engaging candor told them why they might have to pay more taxes. "It was the most remarkable thing I've ever seen," said Dan McDonald. "There was no new Mike Lowry, it was the same old one. He was…probably the most liberal governor we've ever had." And Eikenberry had annoyed a good portion of the business community. They wanted to believe that there was a new Mike Lowry. To Mike's credit, he never lied… he might let them live with their illusions, but he never lied."[22] Gogerty fashioned a coup on business' political naiveté and Eikenberry's inability to relate. The bill was six months off.

Lowry's November margin of 120,000 was the result of the Republican Party's antics, Morrison and Evans' defections, Eikenberry's lack of imagination, and an extraordinary quarter million new voters favoring Democrats. Lowry won the New Dealers over 65 and broke even with the wealthiest voters. Eikenberry carried most of those earning less than $20,000 a year. This partial inversion of a 60-year pattern was a harbinger of the GOP's loss of its grip on the suburbs, a tectonic trend culminating in 2006. Bill Clinton's moderation had smothered the lingering voices of the New Left from the 1970s, and the unheralded Patty Murray, "A mom in tennis shoes," catapulted from the State to the U.S. Senate. Democrats won seven of the nine congressional seats and both houses of the legislature. Secretary of State Ralph Munro, chief protagonist of the Motor Voter law, turned to Lt. Gov. Joel Pritchard, the other surviving Republican in state office, and said, "I'm a Marbled Murrelet and he's a spotted owl. You're looking at Washington's newest endangered species."[23]

Washington's "fertile crescent," the western slope suburbs, an arc from Blaine through Redmond to Camas, were now only tenuously Republican, a battleground Democrats were to win, leaving Republicans with no chance of regaining legislative majorities until they were retaken. At the opening of a decade of unheard of prosperity, these voters were as worried about services as taxes. The "old" Mike Lowry, inclined to spend his way out of the recession, was more palatable. He convinced a majority that "I can truly get things done. I've grown up." Two bow waves of prescriptive democracy also took effect: Initiative 134, the GOP's device to limit on campaign spending, particularly the unions', and Initiative 573's term limits. Like ones were passed by 21 million voters in 15 states.[24] The contradictions went unnoticed.

## Uncorked

The spontaneous style of the twentieth governor, the first Democrat to succeed another, surprised no one. Inaugural day began with Buddhist and Native American calls to worship and readings from the Old Testament. Gardner gave his valedictory, then stage whispered, "Michael, don't screw up." "Clear away the water pitchers, and push back your chairs," advised the new Speaker, Tacoma's Brian Ebersole, in describing Lowry as "a man who eats drinks and sleeps politics, who revels in the rough and tumble…a man who is passionate and vocal." Lowry abandoned his script for an aerobic, optimistic, humorous, conciliatory stump speech: the state was tired of polarization. He had to buy a new suit for the evening's ball, held in the rotunda under the capitol dome and in the State Reception Room. The massive oak desk and leather governor's chair sitting diagonally across the far corner of the executive's 40-foot-long suite reappeared as a modest one in front of a steel swivel seat in the left front corner. Executive orders holding the cabinet to high standards, banning sexual discrimination, affirming "a commitment to diversity" and zero-tolerance ethics" came first.[25] Lowry pledged to return $31,000 of his $121,000 salary to "lead by example." The era of the "vanilla" governors was over.

The 1993 session's Ethics Commission (SB5956) with citizens as 10 of the 17 members improved on the legislators' failure to self-police. Despite testimony implicating Speaker Brian Ebersole and peers for using staff for partisan purposes, they escaped punishment by signing statements indicting underlings. The caucuses paid modest fines of $100,000 each. In March, Lowry issued new strictures in an executive order. The public could not agree more, and doubled penalties with Initiative 134 in 1994.[26] The recurring ethical defaults are more institutional than individual. Each party's caucuses need partisan staff so that policy and strategy discussions are secure. When they are more than a few, the temptation grows to use "Communications Specialists" to write newsletters that are advertisements, or have leaders let it be known their jobs depend on doing campaign tasks on state time, even in the capitol, advantaging the Majority, which has the larger staff.

Hasty exercises in open government invite an excess of democracy and redundancy. The new governor overdid engagement, wearing himself down in 40 town meetings. Bob Gogerty, managing the transition, doubted the 61 person "kitchen cabinet," or the welter of 17 task forces could set policy. This was to be the most open of administrations Lowry insisted, they were "the widest statewide cross section possible ... everyone will be at the table." The critical Budget Task Force made "no formal recommendations, only suggestions."[27]

State capitols tend to be in towns like Olympia, not the easiest places to draw minorities to, and some Democrats were distancing themselves from affirmative action begun in the 1960s. Gardner's cabinet was largely white males wise to the ways of Olympia. A third of Lowry's task forces' 435 members were minorities. He raised the bar: it was time they were a significant segment of senior managers. His press secretary, chief lobbyist, and 11 of 28 in his cabinet were women; five were minorities. Asian American Evelyn Yenson kept the Lottery Commission. Bruce Miyahara, Director of the King County Department of Public Health took the role for the State. African-American John Franklin was a natural at General Administration. State Representative Art Wang ["Wong"], an able lawyer-legislator, was seated on the quasi-judicial of the Personnel Appeals Board. Of Lowry's 1,945 appointments to state boards and commissions, 749 were women.[28] Diversity seminars were made mandatory and a Sexual Minority Initiative was unfurled by DSHS. Lowry would not "tolerate intolerance" and backed the gay's "Hands Off Washington" Initiative.

The deep commitment to diversity led to some serious faux pas. Selecting African-American Harry Thomas, a former deputy King County executive (1982-87), then executive director of the Seattle Housing Authority as "staff director," not "chief of staff," so as not to give offense to American Indians, reeked of political correctness. Thomas, who proved "totally at sea" for lack of exposure to state government left after 20 months. Former House Majority Leader Lorraine Hine, a "legislator's legislator" (and initially the Legislative Liaison), took a surer grip.

Could the governor delegate? The sympathetic *Post-Intelligencer* thought Lowry a "notoriously indifferent administrator," a congressman who put campaigners in key staff positions and ignored staff infighting.[29] "He was his own person in that he determined what the agenda was going to be," Lorraine Hine recalls, "but he would work collectively." Mondays, the directors would gather and say, "Here are some opinions.... He listened. I have seen him change his positions. Mike had been in the legislative arena."[30] Firing the bulk of Gardner's policy staff and making his deputy campaign manager and longtime aide Don Wolgamot second in command left a vacuum. "Mike didn't need the policy shop as much as much because [he]... was full of ideas.... There were all kinds of things he wanted, he was in favor of everything...in marked contrast to the previous two governors...he didn't know when to hold back," Art Wang remembers. "He didn't really want to be Chief Executive, he wanted to be chief of staff," Dean Foster observed. "He wanted to be in the middle of every single meeting that every agency had. That might be an exaggeration, but only slightly."[31] Lowry was not all propeller and no rudder, but his forte was advocating, not managing.

An unusual number of Lowry's judicial appointments were upset. Blackfoot Indian Debora Juarez was sent to the superior court, and when defeated, made executive director of the State Office of Indian Affairs. Former counsel Ed Fleisher was also unseated, and 68-year-old Bernard Heavey, plucked from making sandwiches in Stevenson, resigned in just two months after 40 members of the bar in Skamania and Klickitat counties boycotted his court and a county prosecutor refused to bring cases before him. This called the governor's legal counsel's "thorough" staff work into question. Asked about the central staff's depth, Gardner's chief of staff, Denny Heck, said, "I don't think there is much of a message in these appointments. If some looked ugly taking off now that they're airborne you've got to admire them."[32]

Lowry preferred devotees of hands-on service delivery to hierarchical managers in the crucial agencies. Ruta Fanning, Jean Soliz, and Annette Sandberg became the first female heads of OFM, DSHS, and the State Patrol.[32] Fanning modeled for the talent that had come to the capitol in the 1970s and set an endurance record of four years.[33] Soliz, a "client oriented" lawyer, went from trying to "fix" DSHS from the outside as Gardner's policy assistant for human resources to running DSHS, one of the largest umbrella agencies in the country. Lowry wanted decentralizers, not visionaries. "Jean was very much, very much like Mike Lowry ...very passionate about people and about human services ... .One of the most anti-bureaucratic agency heads."[34] She knew "DSHS is so big, it is like an ocean liner ... and I need to turn it...faster than a mile." DSHS habitually hired expertise it did not need; "often the process has become the outcome." Told "to do more with less," she tried to "get back into community [sharing of responsibilities] somehow." Devolution was hard: local agencies lacked new dollars. She settled for closer collaboration and more accountability. Mid-management was shrunk a fifth, but they were only 10 percent of the agency's 16,335 employees. In the face of steady bracket creep, Lowry managed to get back to where Bud Shinpoch had left DSHS.

Soliz was soon snarled in the perennial struggle over parental control—whether case workers were overzealous in taking children from their families—and an uproar over sexual abuse at the OK Boys Ranch, a group home in Olympia. When the fourteenth secretary in 22 years quit after 23 months, the governor opted for another insider, Assistant Secretary Lyle Quasim, an African-American whom Soliz had rehired after he was fired five years earlier. "I've been chewed up and spit out before," Lyle mused, "and I'll be chewed up and spit out again. But along the way I plan to do a good job." Lowry wanted to be a "greater change agent," but without hurting clients or causing an uproar at the core of state union activism. "So it [the job] was one of moving on the margins; push as hard as you could, but not overplay your hand."[35]

Thirty-three year old Annette Sandberg was the first female State Patrol chief in the nation. It was top heavy—needed decentralizing, resignations, rank reductions, and a shift from reaction to outreach. She had been the agitating Troopers Unions' vice president and lawyer and was accused of being a turncoat after she thinned five majors at the headquarters at the governor's request. "It's hard for even an Irish politician to exaggerate the reaction to that," he sighed. Budget shortfalls, the union cried, were being used as a pretext for a "campaign to violate state labor laws." But the "Old Boys" network at the patrol was on notice. Remarkably, Sandberg lasted seven years. [36]

Agile and amenable Sid Morrison, the congressional colleague who lost the executive's chair, became director of transportation. "In Lowry's mind, DOT was 'just plain fat.' This [seven member Transportation] Commission can't handle the last half of the 20th Century, let alone the 21st." In light of Evans' 12 years of defeats in trying to get control, his bravado about gubernatorial control has to be seen as therapeutic. Morrison shared Lowry's enthusiasm for mass transit and did as much as anyone has to make the free-standing monolith multimodal. "In many ways was like being governor without the politics," he comforted himself.[37]

Labor had acquired the most heft since Mon Wallgren. State Employees Union lobbyist Mark Brown won Labor and Industries over former King County executive Randy Revelle for Labor's traditional seat, capitalizing on the exceptional performance of Gardner's Joe Dear. Three years in, Lowry held a press conference to ballyhoo the resuscitation of L&I. Claim frequency, medical inflation, and injuries were down, and the retro program (lower rates for reducing accidents), fee protocols, and business partnering with the department's Health and Safety Initiative were up. The $250 million deficit in the Accident Fund handed Gardner was now a $400 million surplus. There were no rate increases for the first time in five years.[38]

Two of the five Gardnerites who stayed were stars. Mary Riveland's stellar performance as a troubleshooter in her third department, Licenses, let Lowry shift her to Ecology to make it "business friendly." This meant taming a staff that had doubled to 1,700 in five years to meet new legislative mandates. "Common sense regulation," education before enforcement, and technical assistance lowered resentment. Her husband Chase worked magic in the overcrowded penal institutions. His agency was a national semifinalist in 1996 for the Innovations in American Government Award.[39]

"I ran for governor to make a difference," Lowry repeated. The legislature was where he made it. The premier achievement was making Washington a laboratory for President Clinton's proposed universal health care system, even as the bill failed in Congress. Claiming "if we had passed health care reform in 1981 we would not be facing a…deficit in 1993" was spurious, but trying economic incentives as levers to get clients off the rolls was potentially the most monumental social legislation since Social Security. Health costs were rising at three times inflation. Gardner's commission had proposed capping prices and letting private insurers and nonprofit groups spar for the uninsured 11 percent of the population, with universal coverage coming in 1998.[40] In mid-April 1993, several Democratic senators joined Republicans and the Democrats lost their one-vote negotiating edge with the GOP controlled House. "The forces of darkness [insurers and business] are coalescing outside the doors of the legislature," spear-carrier Senator Phil Talmadge intoned.

Lowry had the legislator's wisdom not to say, "Here's my plan," even if farm workers were "temporarily" left out, if there were two levels of benefits to lessen the impact on small business, and after a last-minute meeting with Boeing machinists, employers with over 7,000 workers were freed to self-insure. He was in the wings when with two Republicans joined the 30-16 vote for a "model for the nation." The Basic Health Plan covered 200,000 low income persons and Medicaid for 130,000 children. Five months into office, Lowry had reached his apogee. He was feted at the White House, where Hillary Clinton congratulated him on a national paradigm.[41]

By July 1997, businesses with more than 500 employees would have to pay half the cost of dependent's insurance as well. They never let up. "The business attack on … health care reform is incredible" the governor fumed. "The things they say are downright untrue, and we're going to have to work hard to make sure that they cannot roll back what … has accurately what would be best for their memberships. "Of course, that's crap," AWB president Don Brunell replied, responding with a 28-minute video on "How to Make Health Care Reform Work." They could agree only that "the process of Democracy is a wonderful thing to behold."[42]

As a commission began its implementation and applicants signed in, the AWB wrote an initiative to unburden its members, consumers pressed for more benefits, state employees scrambled to avoid sharing five percent of costs, and insurance companies strove to lift premium caps. A year later, Lowry signed repealers striking caps, tying premiums to inflation, and injecting managed care to save what he could. The reduced plan was nevertheless virtually identical to what the president had failed to get from Congress in 1994. "Flanked by beaming Republicans, subdued Democrats, ecstatic insurers and gleeful business lobbyists," the governor put on his best face. The revised law would "significantly improve" health care for the people of Washington State.[43]

## The Civil Service: The Waylaid Trade

Lowry's exclamation that "we Democrats have to decide if we're running state government or the unions are," was a bow to efficiency. Inclusive civil service arrived in 1961 by initiative when the State Employee Union's initiative overtook Governor Rosellini's procrastination. Lowry knew it had been "boiler plated" into "a very burdensome system." His reform criteria stunned the unions: broadening hiring options from five to seven persons, raising "exempts" from 187 to over 400, and reducing 78 bargaining units to 17, more management and diversity training. The governor was to negotiate salaries, while the legislature would take an up or down vote. Gary Moore, the WFSE's executive director, thundered, "This is the most anti-labor bill we have ever seen at the legislature. For this to come from a Democratic legislature is appalling."[44] It has in fact been to the union's advantage. If a liberal governor in a prosperous season agrees to unsustainable benefits, are the legislators likely to say reetract what has been "granted"? Since salaries are 70 percent of spending, the legislators have forfieted their most important decision, to keep the "heat"on the Second Floor.

"Only Nixon could go to China, and maybe only Mike Lowry can get this package through," Speaker Ebersole mused as the unions stomped. The House Labor Committee killed reform and Lowry went hat in hand to Appropriations, where Gary Locke was more amenable: "It is something not many people expected of the Democrats or of you. It is very bold." Lowry endorsed removing the right to strike, in trade for privatizations—if wages and benefits were the same — to entice Republicans. The Democratic House added more water and by the time ten Republican senators, seeing the handwriting on the wall but needing to be for "reform," joined in the upper house's edition, privatization was out, the right to strike restored, and fewer than 5,000 of the highest-level employees affected. In 2002, the Democrats were again in control of both houses, and by a two-and-one vote struck the legislature's right to concur, so a GOP legislature could not block any agreement.[45] The majorities had defaulted on their largest responsibility, the 70 percent of the budget that was wages, and let the executive take the heat.

In March 1993, just before the unions overpowered him, Lowry argued, "We need to show the public we're working to make this state government just as efficient as possible." His logic as to why the last-in-first-out "bumping" system straight-jacketing managers was "particularly onerous" was curious. It was not because seniority overrode ability, but because the victims were most often women and those of color. The Senate had given him the right to exempt just two percent of the managers and to hire the personnel director who could hire, fire, or reassign 1,000 others; 50,000 of the rank and file were untouched. Getting more "flexibility," in trade for collective bargaining was real "civil service reform," the governor crowed, and "significantly important." Gary Moore, who had abused him on the capitol steps as a "Judas," revealed more: "I'm not billing this as a win or lose."[46]

The union knew it needed a "credible response" to the media's coverage of "waste." "We must take the lead to reshape government," the executive board told their clients. "Who best knows how to improve delivery of services?" The WSFE's task was "to create an environment in each agency" for "cost-cutting suggestions" to the Productivity Board, a useful but peripheral panel since Evans' days. "Revitalization" was the union's response to "reinventing government." However, contracting out and privatization of "traditional" state supplied services had to be met with an "aggressive organizing campaign."[47] The governor had courageously taken on a system encrusted for over 30 years to stifle outside competition, one embedding seniority at the expense of "merit." Trading reform for collective bargaining was unavoidable, but it was hard to see how this "important management tool" placing the full brunt of negotiations on the executive left him "better off."

In 1994, Lowry assembled a gubernatorial task force to end "bumping up" of the incompetent or superfluous. In a new Washington Management Service, second-tier managers and above could get incentive bonuses of up to five percent for four years. Some 4,000 were already in WMS, as opposed to just 200 "exempts" before. "This gives management capability ... that was the main return," Lowry believed. Since all but a handful remained under civil service there was no risk, but rewards were given at a greater cost to the state.[48] Opening a closed system was too much for

Democrats threatened by their Labor base and too little for the GOP to embrace. Lowry's "real reform" was a self-delusion.

Calling another commission to "reinvent" government, as had Vice President Gore, caused several minor mergers the governor took pride in, but they were also largely mooted by the system. Combining Fisheries and Wildlife, and Commerce and Economic Development saved 22 percent or $7.5 million and 104 staff. Twenty-five department heads shrunk to 14, but almost all had reversion rights. Lowry's public-private ventures and sponsorship of conferences for the Minority and Women-Owned Business Program were admirable but hardly earthshaking. He deserved plaudits for expediting service in agencies like Mark Brown's delayering and regionalization in L&I and DSHS.[49]

## Caesar's Rendering

"The winds of change are blowing in Olympia this dark winter of the voters' discontent," the Associated Press' David Ammons observed in January 1993. Over a third of the legislature was new and wary. Gary Locke warned the Democratic majorities to unify their agendas: "We don't have the luxury of blaming the Republicans," and "the tax system is at saturation and the people don't want to pay any more." Nita Rinehart, the liberal chair of Senate Ways and Means, who also dreamed of being governor, obliquely offered three unsavory cut lists and intimated her version of the budget would need fewer dollars than the governor's. The temperate tone after the 1994 election can be seen in House Revenue chair Greg Fisher's request to SPI Judith Billings to prioritize her programs—with the "dogs" at the top of the list.[50] Leadership, nervous about a new ethics law covering conflicts, banned "Ulcer Gulch" the Third House's playground between the two houses to the basement. The free legislator shuttle service also died.

In Congress, Lowry was one of 435 and could say what he liked. In Olympia, in a February flash of spontaneity, he termed the tax system "stupid." The sales tax could go from 6.5 to 3 percent if the difference was made up by an income tax. "Lowy's Goal: State Income Tax" burbled the *Times* and its peers. He confessed that to too many voters this spelled tax increase. "I understand that fear ... Government's grown too much." And still more remorsefully, "those who thought I said the 'T" word too early are correct." His "last resort" now appeared to be the first, and he had crossed his Rubicon. "The truth is that governors don't have the luxury to think out loud," Denny Heck murmured.[51] A month later, the governor was blistering reporter's obsessions: "The media has become an unintentional subsidiary of the Republican Party." Headline writers, he acidly added, "love the word 'tax,' "because they can spell it correctly three out of four times."[52] "I will present a budget without IOUs, without gimmicks, without smoke and mirrors,"[53] and delivered. But by February bellwether Boeing had let go 19,000 employees. The ship of state could still be righted without damage he asserted, first by eliminating up to 2,000 *management* [emphasis supplied] jobs from Ecology and DSHS, then confessed this was "not anything close to the total number" needed. He fine-tuned Gardner's "Book II," "going deep ... for every efficiency possible," lopping off $634 million, finding $231 million in "alternative sources," (tuitions, fees, and "loopholes"), and extending the sales tax to the professional fees of those with "higher income." Including tax credits for new and high-tech businesses was shared by others began a debilitating drain.[54]

He ran head-on, as had Spellman and Gardner, into the ferocious trial lawyers, also the Democrats' partners. The "Citizens Opposed to a Sales Tax on Services" joined such natural enemies as realtors, architects, and newspaper publishers. Estate taxes were dropped after farmers protested. Fresh from the Senate, the governor misread the situation: "Did you see those hordes of lobbyists out there?" he asked with his usual jowl-shaking, shoulder-bobbing laugh. But Nita Rinehart conceded, "I don't have 25 votes."[55] The bill was interred in the Speaker's office at 3:00 am. Lowry fell back on what is least painful, another one cent, $1 billion boost in the sales tax.[56]

Come April, this too was dead, and corporate CEOs at last read their fate. Their warnings about a trade-off between taxes and jobs aside, Lowry defiantly backed bucking up the Business and Occupations tax. "Lawyers and certain elements of the business community ... after 115 days, beat my plan ... the attorneys came in and said, 'If you're going to raise the taxes on us, don't extend the sales tax to us, raise the B&O tax on us.' I am not a great fan of the B&O tax," Lowry said. Based on gross receipts, a percentage was paid by small businesses even if there was no profit. "What I'm doing down here is absolutely refusing to cut the things that really count for business ... higher education, the quality of our work force, our health and our transportation system." Boeing CEO "Frank Schrontz said he was for education reform," he went on. "Well, does he want us to pay for it or not? If they killed his transportation taxes would he be the first to complain congestion was killing the economy?" May 5, a smorgasbord of revenues clustering around the B&O Democrats had criticized as "regressive" passed. The 34 other fees and licenses raised from auto inspections to marriages hit virtually everyone, but business gave the most.[57]

Speaker Ebersole and Majority Leader Marc Gaspard met their

promise to make the governor a budget player. "I think it might be the fastest way to get things done," he agreed. The finished product was a "test of state government itself," one that "should win a prize for fairness." For the first time the legislature's budget was lower than the governor's (by $200 million) and dropped 800 state employees. But a new and unnerving trend was revealed: $511 million in fund shifts and a diversion of $95 million from the Highway Trust Fund was fiscal make-believe. "I told them I wanted a no gimmicks budget and that's what I got. This is a tight, tough budget," Lowry broadcast, and went off to Washington State University to deliver a commencement speech justifying higher tuitions.[58] The governor saw what he wanted to see.

Lowry had been a passionate, ubiquitous super-legislator, calling chairs, testifying before committees, arm-twisting opponents, eating with leaders, and pleading for public pressure. "Lowry is at the wheel, and overdriving his highlights in a flat-out race for results," David Ammons penned. "Robo gov" tread the legislative landscape "with an awesome in-your-face, ultra-involved performance not seen by a governor in decades." He had an "instant grasp of the folkways of the legislature."[59] Legislator appraisals of executive performance need to be discounted by the tension between the branches and parties. Still, six months in a poll of 30 Democrats and 13 Republicans (of King County's 48 legislators) rated Lowry to 2.48 (on a scale of 4). Some liberals complained management of state agencies was "sloppy." He exploded, "The stuff they fiddled around with for years we managed to pass in a couple of months." "They're not even close … I'm doing a hell of a job." Jim Ellis agreed Lowry had "done a helluva job — except he hasn't communicated that … If he does … he succeeds. If he doesn't, he fails."[60] Legislators usually huddle around the governor at bill signings. No one did. The House adjourned singing "Amazing Grace." They would need it.

The Democrats' schizophrenic message was a hard sell: "Outlays are down by $700 million, but we had to raise $1.2 billion to fund 55,000 new public school students, make space for 10,000 new collegians, soaring numbers of inmates, and cover health care. It is a good thing for the state." By March, 51 percent Washingtonians believed the state was "on the wrong track."[61] Trailing the public temper, the media began to wail about the "taxing session." The "bumbling Democrats," the *Times* complained, had made "the proverbial 'dance of legislation' look more like a gym full of awkward 14 year olds trying to master 'The Twist.'"[62] The editor of the *Pullman Herald* exploded, "Lowry and the legislators are lying. Period." In Seattle, KOMO TV's "You Paid for It" series featured the new Natural Resources building, the first constructed by the state in

17 years, and the fish tank in its lobby. Tales of DSHS's ACES software, whose price had soared from $8 to $14 million and the earlier COSMOS sand papered the public's raw nerves.[63] Keynoting the First Annual Governor's Conference on Economic Development and Environmental Enhancement before 450, Lowry acidly noted the people of the Olympia press "don't want to talk about anything but taxes. It … makes it so hard to get anything done." The liberal *Times* was quavering: the governor "had on his hands the makings of a full-scale citizen tax revolt" and had "yet to prove himself an artful leader" able to set priorities.

## Fall 1993: "Taxed to the Max"

(The slogan under the governor's face on Initiative 602 campaign buttons.)

Lowry was right in expecting "short-term fixes" for "the foreseeable future," and wrong in thinking the Washingtonian voters would "step up to the[se] tough decisions.... The voters [will] choose taxes and responsibility." In a "De-railing of Democracy,"[64] government by plebiscite struck. Twenty-one initiatives were filed in the three weeks after the legislators left for home. When signature gatherers for Initiative 601, which would repeal the new taxes and limit future ones to inflation and population growth, took in 300,000 signatures in the two weeks before the July 2 deadline, Democratic legislators ran for cover. Lowry was on the road, insisting, "We got the message...Democrats won't propose taxes...[in 1994]. It won't happen." At Seattle Center, he dwelt on "accomplishments and efficiencies," sounding facetious in proclaiming, "You've finally got a fiscal conservative in Olympia." To the irate, it seemed inconsistent to call the initiatives "simplistic and very dangerous...[and] preludes to "deep, devastating cuts. [That is] why the state needs more income. Most of the people aren't so much anti-tax as they [are for] reduced spending in those areas that need reducing." The most common inquiry was, "Why was I … about the only Democratic politician willing to be out front? One thing I can't stand the most and why I'm always in trouble," Lowry admitted, "I can't stand the politics of avoidance."[65] The Pied Piper of taxation profile prevailed over that of the cost-conscious manager. His "disapproval" rating hit 48 percent.

Lowry's rationale for business, namely that an educated workforce was essential to the economy, neutralized a few key CEOs. Big business' dragons, which had begun the counter offensive with "601," now went underground to protect their profiles. Boeing's Frank Shrontz was furious enough to consider backing "602," the more restrictive of two on the ballot, but stayed neutral, as did Weyerhaeuser, partly because of Lowry's and Dan Evans' impassioned talks to the Business Roundtable. Evans also led a too-late debate against the initiatives on behalf of the Committee for Washington's Future. The president of the Seattle Chamber of Commerce sought endorsement of both. Developer Jon Runstad, a Harbor Club attendee, was "too busy" to discuss Lowry's performance. October PDC filings told the truth: $1.5 million spent for and against the initiatives, in a face-off between business and public employees. The governor blamed the narrow passage of the less draconian I-601 on disgruntled lobbyists and the media, who had ignored his success in reigning in government growth and exaggerated his differences with business.[66] He heard half the message: more "efficiency." The public "wasn't saying hey, we don't care about health care ... 601 didn't say hey, we are looking at reductions... in education," and moved on to new "cost drivers." Six months later, he considered asking the voters for exemptions to "601."[67] Spending was justified if it was "efficient."

## The Mournings After

The Democrats now repeated the GOP's follies of two years earlier. State chair Charles Rolland preferred a "how do you elect Democrats" to a "how do you save the world" platform. He got one with 160 planks on everything from sex education in preschool to normalizing relations with Cuba, gay rights, alternatives to jailing criminals, and studies on the oppressiveness of drug laws. "Let's not hide from controversy anymore," shouted a Snohomish delegate. The GOP's Contract with Washington State mimicked its congressional one, starting with a photo of 100 candidates taking an austerity pledge on the capitol steps. Not one Republican legislator lost. Democrats lost 30 in the House and came within a vote of losing the Senate, in the largest reversal since 1946. Lowry was unmoved. It might have been federal refusal of a waiver to match dollars on health care. No "real analysis" was possible. "Are you going to scale back?" asked a dumbfounded reporter. "I believe the people...did not hire us to be on defense. The public is sending a strong message...[about rebuilding] the credibility of government...that is my top priority." "Would it be correct... to say...you're not changing your approach...one iota?" "That is true."[68]

The momentous shift of 1994 muted any intentions the governor had, yet the 1995 session was less than a reverse twist on its predecessor. The GOP had swept Eastern Washington, nearly offsetting liberal Seattle. But ideological lines had blurred in the fall, as Democratic legislators seeking election in closely contested suburban districts began sounding like Republicans. ("I have seen Democrats running to join Republicans," Lowry later opined, "I don't think it's right.") The "slow leak in liberalism," House Revenue chair Greg Fisher heard once they were back in Olympia, was tires running on their rims. The "transformation among House Democrats has happened quicker than the Berlin Wall fell down," the WSFE's Gary Moore moaned. A saving grace was the new Speaker, mannerly Clyde Ballard from Wenatchee, who was at the opposite end of the spectrum from Lowry, but able to "separate political from personal debate." The deeply religious man kept his caucus' moralists under tighter rein than Bill Polk, but could not avoid a vote on abortion, which Democrats tried to make the "defining" issue.[69]

The governor, essentially alone, was "even more optimistic" about the "State of State." He touted the biennial growth rate of the General Fund of 3.6 percent, the lowest in 20 years (as opposed to an average of 10.5 percent in the prior decade), and found another to make the most of his predicament. By lowering the reserve to $200 million, he pushed his supplemental budget $600 million *above* [emphasis added] what would have been the I-601 baseline for future spending to be set July 1. "Nobody says we have to live like this," he told the Associated Press. The economy had turned; he could offer tax credits for high-tech, high-wage jobs to cost $88 million in 1995-97, and was willing to repeal $231 million of previous year's taxes. The Democratic Senate, not to be outdone, sliced $200 million more imposed on 97,000 small business, and boosted the governor's budget by $260 million.[70]

All 25 Democratic senators rushed to repeal the employer mandate, and thus universal health coverage. Senator Kevin Quigley found "the [middle] ground gone below me" but held out for premium caps, for any revision would be "suicide to save [opponents] the burden of murder [by consumers]." Lowry, who had complained a year before that Congress had "caved in to business," (in refusing a waiver from ERISA to make business pay), knew segments of his insupportable dream could be spared only by adjusting to reality: "key elements ... remained .... We had to reconsider our options or face loss everything we had fought for. My responsibility is to work with the reality that exists. This legislation makes real progress on the status quo." "Some of it was survival, some of it was pragmatic politics," Speaker Ballard concurred.[71]

## "Hard Time for Armed Crime"

Fear was behind the other tidal wave of 1994, containing crime. Youth offenses were up 146 percent in a decade to 3,000 a year by 1991. Television fixated on domestic violence, drunk driving, and child abuse, rasping public irritation at government's apparent impotence. After gang violence hit Tacoma's Hilltop area in August 1993, Lowry added a ban on assault weapons to his nine-bill "Youth Agenda." The package also invested $83 million in job training and group homes, treatment for runaways, abused and neglected children, and extended hard crime sentences (generally, those with guns), and sex offenders. House Republican amendments, with Democratic complaisance, stiffened sentences and introduced "boot camps." To make prison room, the governor's "Tough on Crime-Smart on Sentencing" proposals reversed a decade old policy in granting judges' discretion on nonviolent offenders, sentencing alternatives to counties and shortening terms. It was opposed by the state's prosecuting attorneys and the Senate Law and Justice Committee chair pronounced the bill "dead on arrival." Once Lowry agreed to measurable standards, the legislature ratcheted up the penalties for drunk driving, pared the package from $26 to $15 million, and passed it. Much of the Youth Agenda, drafted after well-attended hearings across the state, had disappeared. When he threatened to veto the amendments, they were made into a referendum. The governor had been hijacked by a "tough on crime litmus test." House Minority Leader Marlin Appelwick, who backed the GOP's amendments reminded, "We always do this to governors. Lowry had done "very well at setting a tempo and … a tone." The GOP then swept the scene with a "Three Strikes and You're Out" initiative 593, completing the obliteration of the 12-year-old policy of judicial latitude, by locking any felon convicted of three offenses for life.[72]

## "Grog Shops?"

The denizens of the dome were ready for a drink. But the governor's move to get the state out of the retail liquor business was not the "no brainer" the *Times* thought.[73] The state's monopoly began with 1933's Steele Act repealing Prohibition. Lowry took on this oft-tried effort in the name of "efficiency" and probably as a nod to business. It was a big business, with 1,000 people running 180 stores and 158 agencies, turning a profit of $358 million on 8,778,000 gallons of liquor in 1991-93. Assured by a study that consumption would not rise and there would be no loss of revenue or jobs, the governor asked, "Why does it make sense for the State to be in the retail business" if there could be one-stop shopping and lower prices? The reality was like the lottery. Each yields the state so much revenue the legislature feared change. It was hard to find a Democratic sponsor: union allies were automatically in arms. Their spearman, Eugene St. John, spurned the bill as "Lowry's throw-away idea on downsizing state government." Churchmen saw relaxation of the state's historically strict supervision of alcohol. Potential vendors bickered, splitting the State Retail Association. The bill was "not high" on tea-totaling Speaker Ballard's list. He reasoned its guarantee that no employee would lose his job made for "mere transfers of payrolls rather than true privatization." The fight was not worth it to any other major interest.[74]

## Unfinished Business: Regulatory Reform, the Second Time Around

The legislative Democrats' rush to redefine themselves did nothing to repair the governor's shattered rapport with business. Resuming the offense, he was met head-on by the virulent Building Industry Association, which bought ads on 10 of the 19 radio stations broadcasting "Open Mike with Governor Lowry." He damned the 1994 legislature's regulatory reforms as "a lawyer's full employment act." The House GOP's amendments were "anti-government … don't confuse that with streamlining." Lowry had gutted it with partial vetoes, leaving more public involvement and control of any emergency rules in his hands. The legislators had just added to the paperwork morass, which the executive could block. Small business lobbyist Carolyn Logue was blunter: Now "It ain't worth spit." Speaker Pro Tem Ron Meyers, the bills' sponsor, quit the governor's Regulatory Reform Task Force, seeing no future in it.[75] Caught in a blast of criticism,[76] Lowry took pains to advertise five minor bills to cut red tape and signed an executive order urging voluntary compliance, fiscal notes on new regulations, technical assistance for business and no first-time penalties.[77]

Business' delayed gratification was international, not domestic. In November 1993, the governor appeared before Congress at President Clinton's urging for NAFTA, "quality job opportunities," intellectual property protection, and a stimulus for the state's environmental industries. Lowry could not convince the State Labor Council that Mexican wage laws would be enforced or tariffs lowered to two and one half times the United States' or of a "huge [Mexican] market" for 500 in-state firms making environmental equipment.[78] Boeing had the most at stake when the Asia-Pacific Economic Conference (APEC) met in Seattle. The gross product of the 16-member nations equaled 60 percent of the world's economy. Washington was third in exports to APEC nations, with a two-way trade worth $78 billion. President Clinton and the governor quickly reminded Washingtonians that one in five of their jobs depended on Asia, namely on aircraft, aluminum, apples, wheat, and microchips shipped to the Pacific Rim. Olympia's unrealistic goal was to turn 3,000 small and medium exporting companies into 40,000. The Labor Council was unimpressed and organized protesters. Lowry's free trade convictions "caused [more] consternation in the house of Labor."[79] In 1995, he asked the President to stop making human rights a condition for a most favored nation status for China, and Clinton did.

The reward was a 40-minute interview with Chinese President Jiang Zemin. They talked about Boeing, which expected to sell 800 airplanes worth $40 billion to China over the next 15 years. Lowry went on to Japan, South Korea, and South Vietnam. Business viewed his overseas trade offices there as ineffectual, as reflected in declining legislative support. Lowry reframed the discussion to parallel the president's business-government partnerships and raised overseas staff from five to twelve, giving Washington the second largest international trade presence of any state.[80] Looking to the Uruguay Round of GATT (General Agreement on Trade and Tariffs), he also persuaded Frank Schrontz and Bill Gates Sr. to co-chair a "Work Force Training Conference" to "discuss future high quality family wage jobs" and "new economy" skills. The legislature responded with a workforce coordinating panel, nearly drowned with rhetoric about "customer driven" approaches and "the public's right to accountability and awareness." It managed to integrate the offerings of the five technical staff to meet needs in job training.[81]

## "Upstreamers" and "Downwinders"

Times had changed and environmentalism, heralded by the State Environmental Policy Act (SEPA) of 1971, was strangling itself. The *Times* felt "there is broad consensus that the scales have tipped too heavily toward the rule-makers, that business and property owners have been unnecessarily constrained by bureaucracy." The question was not the environment versus jobs, or health or safety, but the environment and jobs. Boeing revealed it had spent $50 million and 18 months to open its Everett "777" facility.[82] A new Growth Management Act in 1991 failed to reconcile counties' and cities' largely superfluous rule making and Lowry's 1992 pledge to reign in the regulators had gone little beyond the 1993 and 1994 executive orders.

In 1995, 47 House Republicans signed a bill for a two-year moratorium on new environmental rules. The state gone too far, they claimed, and poorly managed its own holdings. The bill set out a firm, predictable timeline of 120 days for decisions, began one-stop permitting, shortened the appeal process, fenced in rule-making authorities (except for public safety), emphasized education over enforcement for first offenders, and gave small business right to recover up to $25,000 of attorney's fees if they prevailed. After a 89-10 vote, Democratic Minority Leader Ebersole praised House Bill 1010 as "a good outcome, a workable bill." A single Democrat's vote pulled the bottled-up bill from a Senate committee, and five others, including Majority Leader Marc Gaspard and Caucus

Chairman Sid Snyder, broke ranks to join the 24 Republicans for the House's unstoppable amendments. The bill passed as a referendum in order to preclude a veto.

Lowry lamented it "puts public health and safety at risk," but his hands were tied. He was doubly incensed by passage of "takings" Initiative 164, sponsored by the builders, mandating government to pay for any loss of value caused by land-use regulations, and honored Earth Day by writing a $1,000 personal check to repeal it."[83] He gutted HB 1010,[84] requiring justifications for rules, removing fines for minor violations, and making it easier for citizens to sue regulators. Education was the answer: "Enforcement is simply punishing people and having to stay on top of them." "To some extent," he fretted, "the legislation attempts to fix a broken process by adding more process. The greatest need is for a change in attitude."[85]

Population growth, clear-cutting, deterioration of water quality, and nullification of the Pacific Salmon Treaty by Alaska's "built in veto" were all damaging the $1 billion a year North Pacific fisheries industry. The usually sympathetic *Times* said Lowry had "accomplished the improbable—three swings, three misses" in offering three unsuitable nominees to Senator Murray for the North Pacific Fisheries Management Commission.[86] Sport fishing was closed in Washington in 1994 to preserve weak runs of Coho salmon, while thousands from the state were caught by Canadians west of Vancouver Island. Canada's offer to catch 600,000 fewer Coho (versus 1.8 million the previous year), if Washington took 300,000 less Sockeye was not compelling when so few of the latter were running. Lowry saw the imperative for a long-term solution, offered an even trade and appealed to the president and Vice President Gore to no avail.[87]

Upstream salmon were afflicted by a record low spring run-off. Lowry pled with the federals to raise water velocity on the Columbia by a "flush from storage dams." The commerce department declared a" fishery resource disaster" — and released twice as much as needed, imperiling power sales.[88] Lowry and Governor John Kitzhaber of Oregon asked Congress for "flexible" debt repayments in low water years to sustain investments in salmon recovery. "We need a reassessment of the way Bonneville does business in the region," by the Northwest Power Planning Council (steeped with their appointees). Any hope for an "equitable distribution of costs and benefits" was shattered when the Department of Energy contracted with the direct service industries (essentially the aluminum companies) for 80 percent of power consumed, to keep Bonneville afloat pending restructuring, at a loss of $475 million a year.[89] One standing dispute did get settled in late 1994. Congress voted to remove two old dams on the Elwha River in the Olympic National Park to the benefit of tribal fishermen and the economy of forested Clallam County. Lowry's request for the $32 million needed counted for less than Senator Slade Gorton's change of mind.[90]

The governors were as frustrated by the federals as their predecessors. Shadowing Governor Langlie's states' rights tactics, they connived to take over water management on the lower Columbia. Lowry felt regional fish and wildlife agencies, the states, federals and the tribes were "co-equal managers" of a river needing to be "addressed in a comprehensive way." The 60-year-old quagmire taught the two governors history lessons: the ability of the federal bureaus to stonewall and outlast administrations, and the futility of "coordination" short of a Columbia Valley Authority. In one of Lowry's last meetings as governor, he and Kitzhaber watched staff redraw proposals, with deregulation thrown in. "This [the fish crisis] is our one chance," the heavily invested Kitzhaber intoned. "Unless we can speak with one voice … I don't think Washington [D.C.] or anyone else is going to listen to us."[91] Lowry's plea to Interior Secretary Bruce Babbit to designate the 50-mile Hanford Reach, the last free-flowing stretch of the Columbia and a natural spawning grounds for up to 300,000 wild fish a federal refuge failed.

More hung on "leveraging" federal dollars to bring off Gardner's 1989 agreements with the federal departments of Energy and Environmental Protection to seal 60 million gallons of nuclear and mixed wastes in single-shell tanks. Congress has yet to commit but a fraction of the $57 billion needed to glassify the residue of 50 years of weapons production in into logs. Leaking tanks a few miles from the river remain Washington's greatest environmental disaster in the making. Secretary of Energy Hazel O'Leary met with Lowry in Olympia in March 1993. She was "intending to follow the dictates for this serious business," but would not rule out delays. Two days later the general accounting office asked Congress to shelve the project due to poor design, mismanagement, cost overruns, and stifling appropriations. Incentives were given to Westinghouse and deadlines extended, with no perceptible acceleration. The governor's threat to refuse more out-of-state plutonium pending a "real commitment" rung hollow in view of the recession in the Tri-Cities caused by the shutdown of the reactors.[92] His last-month try to restart Hanford's Fast Flux Facility to make medical isotopes rather than tritium was as fruitless as the congressional delegation's attempt to make the FFF a national cancer research center.

Protecting the entire ecosystems of forests became federal policy in the 1970s. All remaining "old growth" forests in Washington were federally owned but under the "piecemeal … frustrating and counterproductive" management of the Forest Service, not known as nature friendly.[93] The timber crisis became a matter of survival for coastal communities once federal Judge William Dwyer's 1991 injunction stopped logging in them to force the feds to confront the old growth question with a scientifically defensible plan to preserve endangered species. Lowry struck a moderate stance on the spotted owl controversy, instructing the State Forest Practices Board to act on science, "coincident with the maintenance of a viable forest industry," and to "understand the social and economic costs of any regulations" but, like Gardner, opposed stopping log exports.[94] He felt "Option Nine" (long under consideration) the best compromise "because … all sides are mad at it." "Nine" allowed for annual cuts of 1.2 billion board feet on federal land in the Northwest, a fourth of what was cut under President Reagan. Doubting Congress would act, leaving the "worst of all situations," continued uncertainty, the governor he asked the president to decide.[95] The loss of 9,500 jobs was partially offset by a $1.2 billion community assistance package to the Northwest. Lowry's "closer to the ground" argument for co-managing the "flexible" funds to retrain loggers got as far as his on the Columbia. In 1995, the U.S. Senate seemed about to expedite timber sales by shortening environmental reviews, which Lowry immediately recognized as an economic benefit at the expense of the environment. He was delighted with Clinton's veto of the portion of a "recession" bill stipulating "sufficiency" as compliance in salvage logging. "This might have become a standard way of avoiding citizens' right of review and appeal,[which] is a sham."[96]

## Education: "Local Control" Versus "Accountability"

Since the Education for All Act of 1970, superintendents of public instruction had unilaterally redefined special education students up from 2 to 11.6 percent, raising cost from $5 million to $400 million. The fall of local levies during the property tax revolts of 1976 and the supreme court's dictate to "define" what was "adequate" support for the public schools also dramatically raised the legislature's commitments and ended all but symbolic "local control." The state's share of funding was already the lion's share; now special levies were capped to minimize disparities between districts. Gardner's belated Governor's Council on Education reforms poured tens of millions more dollars into equalization and reducing class sizes. A Commission on Student Learning went into law to design "outcome based education" and refine "core competencies" for high school graduation.[97]

Lowry sustained what became a 20-year joust for standards with conservative home-schooler parents and the turf-protecting SPI and WEA. His "Council on School to Work" fostered apprenticeships, tech-prep, cooperative education, career academies, and transitional "work pilot projects" to close the widening gap between the high-income and the low-skilled. The governor's persistent pressure for both delayed measures in the face of resistance by these Democratic bastions ranks second to his successes in health reform.[98]

The secular fall in state dollars for higher education of 30 percent over two decades while students grew by 50,000 was not his doing. The questions asked by his Higher Education Task Force about "accountability" and possible "savings" were set aside by its academic majority in favor of divining "a new funding system" to counteract I-601. Appointed in July 1995, it reported a year later, to no effect. Lowry also fought elimination of the Direct Student Loan program. It had "introduced competition into the student loan business."[99]

## "The End of Welfare as We Know it," or "Scapegoating the Poor"?

Chastened by the collapse of his universal health plan, polls on the public mood, and the onrush of the congressional GOP's Contract with America, President Clinton was reborn to fiscal restraint. His 1993 Five-Year Plan shaved $505 billion in projected outlays. Congress' eclectic adoption of welfare reforms from several states (notably Wisconsin) left liberals grieving at the "last gasp of the traditional Democratic way." "If … Congress wants to pass other responsibilities down to the state," both the "strings" and the matching requirement would have to be loosened (to 12 percent), Lowry told National Public Radio. He got one, but not the other.[100] The governor argued for keeping welfare almost the same and especially against a "family cap" that was "punishing" children. "For the life of me [I] cannot understand why after two years, we can say to a five year old 'Go out and get a job. You went on the grant when you were three years old, you've now been on for 24 months, why don't you go out a get a job you little ne'er do-well?'" Penalizing children to get their parents off welfare was the evil and "mocking them, denying them aid, keeping their children from receiving medical care or going to school neither helps them nor helps society. Providing them tools…helps us all." The focus should have been on at-risk teens, attacking fraud with electronics, supporting collection, getting DSHS to partner with businesses and education, attacking fraud with electronic chases, tax incentives, and mandatory participation in training.[101]

The morality-tinged House version in Olympia, stopping benefits after two years, was mean-spirited, punitive, "just don't make sense," and intruded into recipients' private lives, evoked Lowry's first veto threat. Democratic Minority Leader Marc Gaspard reflected the changed stance of his caucus with two bills to crack down on fraud and end "stealing from the poor and from the taxpayers." The legislators followed Congress' lead and the governor conceded after getting double his $20 million ask for child care, tax breaks, and retraining. Replacing Gardner's innovative, but more expensive. FIP with incentives and without punishments was progress. Rolls fell 40 percent in five years.[102]

In 1996, Lowry asked Congress for $220 million more to "mitigate the impact on seniors, children, and the disabled and assailed Clinton's approach as mean … discriminatory … un-American and politically frightening." At the Democratic National Convention in Chicago, he followed Housing and Human Services Secretary Donna Shalala into an elevator. "She wasn't pleased one bit" when he told her he disagreed with her. "Well, I'm not pleased with your position on welfare either." "Forget about modifying it," she retorted. "Give us a Democratic congress and we'll take care of it." "Mike certainly wants to leave his mark," said Speaker Ballard, "but the truth is, in eight weeks, Mike is unemployed."[103]

## Policy Making with the Red Pen

Lowry met several times with Gaspard and Ballard, but "nothing was resolved" until the difference was split, scaling back cuts to $503 million. "Two years ago, the Governor really dominated the legislature," Clyde Ballard consoled himself, "This time, it was a new dynamic." Soon he was seeing red. Lowry, in questionable faith, vetoed exemptions for equipment ($148 million), the one-time property tax reduction ($54 million), and 17 others, leaving just $275 million in reductions, as "absolutely necessary to protect our state's financial stability." Ballard, who was "really amazed at the constant commitment to raise taxes," vainly vowed to bring the legislature back in the summer to override the governor. Lowry conceded the property tax cut had been a small "down payment" on overall tax reform. The Senate's version, a fair measure of legislative sentiment, also cut taxes 500 million, had passed 36-11. In July, two-thirds of the House backed a petition calling itself back into session, but it fell 8 votes short in the Senate where 17 Democrats who voted for the relief said they no longer supported it because of the new buoyant economic forecast.[104]

Lacking a Senate leadership willing to consistently block and tackle for him, Lowry's was the first administration where the veto was the only defense; it was also a precursor to Governor Locke's tenure, where it became an offensive tool as well. "I do not think you should legislate with the veto," he said, "but rather 'participate' in the legislative process. The most important lobbyist in the legislature should be the governor. If you fail to do that and…use the veto to legislate, I do not agree with that. The governor proposes legislation…you compromise and work it out, you approve and sign."[105] This sentiment had not kept him from becoming the master of the partial veto. The panoply of justifications for them became more exotic. The legislature's version of the Regulatory Fairness Act had been reworked so often it had to be re-engrossed twice. Lowry vetoed numerous sections and then issued an executive order restating some of the same elements to make it conform to his wishes. "Like beauty," he wrote, "regulatory reform is really in the eye of the beholder."

The Youth Violence Act of in 1995 had "technical problems," such as the definitions of who was "at risk." Lining out "over broad implications" and federal requirements on grants to community networks, reflected DSHS's reservations.[106] Substitute House Bill 1123 (1995) "enhancing international trade" was vetoed because it "could be interpreted to establish a new agency." He believed that the Trade Representative should act as an "arm" of the governor's office, in collaboration with DTED.[107] Three sections of a Long Term Care Delivery (ESSHB 1908) came back "without my approval." The "single point entry system," the findings of a 1991 commission, did "not receive full public scrutiny" and "need more debate."[108] Having the Department of Transportation look at privatizing the ferry system would violate collective bargaining agreements (Labor was opposed). The counties, cities, and Locke, now chair of House Appropriations, vainly urged Lowry to sign the "modest" $146 million property tax relief bill, fearing a Californiaesque "Prop 9." The governor wanted the dollars.[109] When the Public Disclosure Commission wanted to stop listing employers who contributed $100, the veto was cloaked under "privacy protection."[110]

In the wide view, the veto could protect civil rights. In a politically expensive move, Lowry blasted an anti-pornography bill as censorship. Trying to keep sexually explicit material out of the hands of minors by a rating system, was vague and "endangers some of our most important freedoms." Out went the provision giving schools access to police records as a safety measure. Clyde Ballard was galled: "Suddenly, we have an overseer of morality…" he steamed. "Why spend all this time on task forces and legislation when you have a governor who says I'm going to have it my way?"[111]

Halving again business tax repeals to $250 million marked the largest impact of a veto to date, possibly excluding Evans' reversing the intent of the Landlord-Tennant Act. A new revenue projection that showed the wiping out of a half billion dollar surplus was a convenient rationale; Lowry claimed he was protecting the state's credit and building a reserve. Later events suggested his motive was to keep the budget as close to I-601's limit as possible. July 1 was the revenue base date. Lifting it later would need the approval of two-thirds of the legislators or a majority of the public, leaving the GOP in control.[112] The unilateral lifting of the lid by a quarter billion dollars carried forward into subsequent biennia.

Lowry was impartial where his personal interests conflicted. U.S. West tried to put off other companies competing in the long distance market. Its CEO, George Walker, who had gathered business backing for Lowry in 1992, hired Bob Gogerty to change the governor's mind. When he did not, Bob explained, "The good news and the bad news about Mike is that he doesn't make these decisions…on friendship." The decision was properly the Public Utilities Commission's, not the legislature's in the first place.[113] Despite bitter criticism and five attempts at overturn by the House Republicans, all 45 vetoes stood.[114]

Overall, there was restraint. In 1995, just 11 bills were totally vetoed and 34 partially, out of 454 to reach his desk, and just 33 and 110 of the 1,333 passed in Lowry's first three years. The targets of the vetoes meant more than the volume. Increasingly, the threats, alterations, or obliterations were philosophical not technical disagreements. Vetoes were made at a turn of a pen, often on the advice of few, and overrides were properly difficult. There had been just two in 19 years and four governors (Gardner and Lowry had one each, Ray and Spellman none). Yet the veto was widening from an exceptional corrective device to one where the executive negated a majority of 147 legislators. Who was to set policy, who was to implement it? The constitution and practice were at odds.

## The Albright Darkness

Vetoes gave Lowry and the Democrats in marginal control of the Senate a bigger stick than the GOP House. In 1995, the power and the future of a man who often spoke of personal integrity, voluntarily limited his campaign contributions, and cut his salary evaporated at a boil. Suzzanne Albright, his communications director resigned, accusing him of sexual harassment. She left the office in tears when asked if other women had complained and asked the governor seek treatment for alcohol as a condition for a non-financial settlement. This was the second charge in a year. A female State Patrol technician's complaint in March could not be substantiated. His office foolishly tried to keep her name secret, claiming fear of exposure might keep others from coming forward.[115] Sue Tupper, who headed his 1992 campaign, was "shocked." "It just cuts completely against the grain of what people think when they think of Mike Lowry."

In September, he thanked Attorney General Chris Gregoire after the first harassment training seminar of two for state employees. "Many of us came away more than a little awed by some of the obvious and not-so-obvious dangers and the subtle situations where one can hurt or be hurt by words or actions," he wrote.[116] The Albright incident became public on November 18, after anonymous tips alerted reporters. At least four other women now made accusations, including two who had been in Lowry's congressional office, and hired an attorney in 1992 to go "on the record." Lowry denied any wrong doing and announced for reelection on "the character issue." Asking Mary Alice Theiler, a former president of the King County Bar Association, to be his investigator was flawed, not for lack of sterling credentials, but because she had contributed $100 to Lowry's campaign.

In February 1996, Jenny Durkan, the governor's legal and political counsel and perhaps de facto chief of staff who had argued for an external investigator, resigned. "Events" had "rendered it virtually impossible to do the job."[117] Durkan's insistence that she had a "deep personal affection" for the governor was less than a ringing endorsement. Mary sat beside him a week later as he said on television he had "never, ever done anything that was ever meant to make anybody feel uncomfortable." The next day Anne Fennessey, Albright's successor quit, saying she had never seen harassment but could not take the stress, and not because she was the supervisor of an accuser, but "because she could not effectively speak for or defend the governor." The media, now in full frenzy, found a St. Patrick's Day incident on the police blotter where Lowry was spotted behind Olympia's Westside Tavern in a car with an OFM policy analyst.[118] He claimed she was a longtime friend and that there was nothing improper. A sworn statement by an Olympia police sergeant was at odds with the governor's version.

Collateral damage rained down. A *Seattle Weekly* story titled "Governor Goner" quoted top campaign aides warning him that rumors about how his drinking could be fatal to the 1992 campaign. On February 14, Lowry denied he had ever had a drinking problem. Then Don Wolgamot, Lowry's senior aide in Congress, said he had one in the early 1980s. When staff rang the alarm during the 1988 campaign, Lowry "cleaned up his act," only to be confronted again in 1992. Two key staffers allegedly quit. Lowry termed these overreactions but admitted there had been a "showdown." Now he put the episodes off as a "ridiculous question. What is this, a joke?" Then on television, he candidly conceded ruminating in the 1980s: "Hey, Mike, I wonder if you're drinking too much" and had reigned himself in. Both Wolgamot and Nate Ford, another key aide, characterized their boss's intake as "normal" for Congress.

The pattern of denial and apology hurt, and defenders did little to redress a schismatic profile. Bob Gogerty had known Lowry two decades, and "I've never heard anything like this. Drinking? Yes. Arguing? Yes. But sexual harassment? Never. Not once." His congressional confidant

Jan Shinpoch asserted the stories were "exaggerated by people who just can't believe he would treat them that way when he was sober. Yelling [at] people is no real gauge of whether Mike has been drinking." A more detached Walt Crowley, the governor's sometime political advisor and speech writer, caught the dynamic: "The passion is there in private and in public. It translates into unwavering beliefs and a sense of what's right [and]...into impatience, stubbornness and anger that can make him a difficult person." When the Machinists Union backed a primary opponent, "he felt we were very disloyal. He was, to say the least, very angry. He wears his emotions on his sleeve," remarked Linda Lanham, the union's political director.[119]

Two dozen interviews by two seasoned reporters led them to draw a split personality: one kind, gregarious, and respectful of women; the other short-tempered, even abusive, "with a fondness for drink and a tendency toward making what today might be considered unwanted advances." Lowry insisted that no previous governor had faced such personal scrutiny. "There is innuendo, non-specifics, rumors, anonymous phone calls, et cetera, et cetera, et cetera. The press has really gone over the edge," Bob Gogerty complained. "People are writing stories solely to avoid having white space when another paper has a story."[120]

The Theiler Report splashed across television March 23. She walked a legal tightrope, finding the governor's behavior "offensive" or perhaps socially awkward, but not harassment.[121] Asked on television if he had sexually harassed an employee, Lowry responded, "No … I have not, did not in any way.…I do sometimes lose my temper." Mary seconded, "Mike, you have done absolutely nothing wrong." She was sure his warmth had attracted Albright and that others "misread the way he is." Theiler reacted, "This report does not clear Mike Lowry. [It] puts responsibility squarely on his shoulders, for conduct that distressed and offended a valuable employee."[122] Reality was held at bay during the settlement press conference on July 14 revealing an Alford agreement. "In consideration" for $97,500, Albright assented, "Neither this agreement, nor the payment … shall … be construed as an admission or an acknowledgment by the settling parties that any of them has acted wrongfully or improperly with respect to the other."

The governor had paid to avoid further distraction, to get Albright's charge behind him and to restore his credibility. None was possible. Headlines and editorials like "The Governor Can't or Won't Face the Truth" said, "the governor either clearly, clearly doesn't get it, or clearly, clearly does and is trying to bedazzle us with guile. It is a tossup as to which is worse" and, "Mike Lowry still doesn't understand the Albright episode is about his behavior, not about the perceptions of others," were death knells.[123] The man elevated by candor, who refused to run negative ads, acted against discrimination, and mandated awareness training, was revealed as volatile and vulnerable. The resilience, energy, and desire to be in office of the man who "ate and slept politics" kept him from seeing that his public life was over.

From the onset of the 1995 session, the burned Senate Democrats had backed away from the governor, especially budget chair Nita Rinehart. Despite her failure to shake a "Lowry Lite" label by the end of the session, 10 of 24 Democratic senators had endorsed her for governor. Eight were up for reelection. It was "respect for Nita … not disrespect of the Governor," Marc Gaspard insisted. "When the governor says we're only looking at an election year, that's bullshit," fumed his Harvard-educated critic Senator Kevin Quigley. "Our knuckle headed governor. It's like he's totally alone." State Democratic chair Paul Berendt said the same thing another way: party people would be were "genuinely happy" to see Rinehart in. The silence of the Democratic hierarchy marked Lowry as damaged goods. The 900 who showed up at his annual shrimp feed still loved Mike, but Jean Gardner, Kay Bullitt, and Patsy Collins endorsed Rinehart, and Labor was looking elsewhere.[124]

Once the legislators left the capitol, Lowry took to the road, holding 34 "town meetings" to tell the "untold story of jobs and environment" and "to refocus media and public attention." He was featured on three statewide radio broadcasts in the first week of August alone. "He wants to give everyone ample reason to believe that he's still a player," a Democratic consultant cynically remarked.[125] Asked at the end of a year if he would run for reelection with two-to-one negative ratings, Lowry replied, "Yes! Of course." He was baffled: "I have never done anything inappropriate." Borrowing the Seattle Mariners "Refuse to Lose" theme, he started the 1996 race in September before 500 delegates to the state labor convention. The Republican Congress' tightening of Social Security and animus of the "intolerant right" in the statehouse would swing the pendulum back to the Democrats. A better barometer of the governor's predicament was that seven GOP hopefuls, four exceptionally qualified, were strutting their stuff for the Mainstream Republicans' Cascade Conference, 17 months before the election.[126] Flooded with talent, the GOP once more fell on its sword. State Senator Ellen Craswell, the lone "conservative," wailing against "liberal, socialist government," was the benefactor.[127]

## Mariners Stadium: The Sports Lobby Flexes

The summer's most specious sight, part of a national pattern, had both U.S. senators, the governor, and the legislature kneeling before the massive sports lobby. The chronically anemic Seattle Mariners baseball team, which had lost $60 million between 1992-95 in the Kingdome, rebranded themselves as an economic gift to the community, not a business. Threatening to pull up stakes if the state did not put up $265 million for a new stadium, they offered to put up a quarter of the cost. East of the Cascades opponents viewed it as a "Seattle thing" and the subsidizing of privileged athletes. Paul Isaki, later director of the Department of Economic Development, swung the governor's support. Calling an October session to "save major league baseball for Seattle," committed him to raising an initial $40 million in 30 days. Leadership's reactions were "mostly positive," he reported. "Geez, the Mariners are doing so well I can't wait to vote," enthused Senate Majority Leader Mark Gaspard, sporting a new "M's" cap.

The timing was perfect. The Democrats, smarting from their 1994 fate and having trounced business, were eager to make a gesture. GOP naysayers, worried about being set up as "the party that killed baseball," were lassoed by Senator Slade Gorton. Up for reelection in 2000, and in town to help, he obliquely reminded them, "This is an emotional and cultural question." Retired Boeing lobbyist Bud Coffey volunteered to lean on legislators — along with nine business lobbyists. Two-thirds of the public agreed that the stadium was a good idea, but 53 percent predictably opposed using state money and 77 percent of those did not go to games. King County voters turned down a referendum on their share — albeit by a narrow margin — only to see the King County Council obligate them and the legislature pass the package.[128] The impetus was the economy and fear of outraged fans. "Lowry, legislature save the Mariners," blared the governor's news release. The Mariner's stadium opened in 2001, became a symbol of "Why government can't be trusted" to those who would vote for a new string of tax rollback initiatives.

## 1996: The Last Liberal?

Lowry adapted well, as he had on health reform. His 1996 supplemental budget had grown by the smallest increment since 1982. It resorted DSHS, pressed out another 270 positions, and asked for only $78 million in new taxes to ensure spending just under the I-601 expenditure limit of $17.9 billion. "The most pressing needs"— children's health and safety, the environment, access to higher education, and incentives and tax deferrals for timber communities and high-tech were there. He also endorsed a 40 percent increase in the minimum wage.[129] Staring at the fall election, the first day of the session the Democratic Senate again rolled back property and business taxes. Caucus chair Val Loveland admitted, "We're not necessarily trying to get out in front of the governor, but we wanted to get out in front of the House Republicans." Lowry waved a veto pen and begged them wait a year, pointing to the likely loss of $4 billion federal dollars over the next seven years. "It is a vision of Election Day 1996," he fumed, "and not one day beyond." The level [of deductions] is not affordable." Senator Kevin Quigley rebutted that this was the "defining moment for the party...[a] passing of the torch. Mike represents the old guard." The House then overwhelmingly overrode Lowry's veto, restoring the $132 million in relief for business.[130]

The legislature collapsed in a heap in April, but Lowry who wanted to advertise his successes, seek vindication, and espouse liberal values, was unwilling to see it leave. After a 90-minute meeting where leadership refused a special session, the governor said he would take 10 days to mull one over, even if his agenda was not emergent.[131] Ballard and company feared that the wait would reopen welfare reform, overture the property tax rollback and the ban on same-sex marriages, and challenge juvenile justice laws. Senator Sid Snyder spoke for the Democrats: "Most members do not want to come back now." House Minority Leader Marlin Appelwick (D) was piqued: "For all we know, the governor will wait until the summer when the campaigns are more complicated, or he'll wait until the biggest fund-raiser ... Why not? He has nothing to lose." Blair Butterworth was merciless "Maybe he has figured out that he is now irrelevant. When he vetoed or signed his last bills, he could just as well have tossed the keys to [Lt. Gov.] Joel Pritchard."[132]

Making good on his promise to stay engaged, the governor spent his last 11 months belt tightening, promoting trade, combating youth violence, and trying to get tax incentives to create "family-wage" jobs. On his November "budget road show," Lowry told editorial boards and business leaders in the major cities, "Something has got to give.... It is simply not possible to maintain the current level of services," in pleading for revisions to 601.[133] The greatest economic surge in human history was underway. Economists were saying, "The [state's] fiscal outlook is more promising now than at any point in the last two decades," and the "cost-saving measures ... [by] Governor Lowry had the Legislature have held [budget] growth to the slowest in more than a decade." By *assuming* [emphasis added] changes to I-601, he drafted a "responsible" proposal—still leaving two-thirds of the $677 million surplus anticipated on July 1, 1999. "This liberal congressman was a tremendously conservative fiscal person." By 1997, the tax increases of 1993 had been erased by the rollbacks of 1994,1995, and 1996.[134]

Lowry scolded GOP candidates for making "fiscally irresponsible ... handcuffing ... promises," and pointed to gubernatorial candidate Ellen

Craswell's absurd intent to make a 30 percent budget cut. "People were choosing carefully," he nodded when she went down with 41 percent of the vote. They were saying, "I want balance," and "Meet us in the Middle." Bill Clinton won the electoral college by a landslide after failing to get 50 percent of the popular vote. Three GOP congressmen were thrown out, Democrats retook the congressional delegation by 5-4, and all but one of the nine state offices. But the GOP held the state House and recovered the Senate by one vote. It was "unfortunate all the legislators were not Democrats, but…the outcome will mean a moderate legislature that will work together with an excellent governor," the outgoing governor mused. The 1992 and 1994 "mandates" of the Lowry era were gone, superseded by perennially divided government. Democrats could thank the almost nine million Americans who registered to vote by renewing their drivers' licenses under the new Motor Voter laws. Six in ten of them turned out in Washington and a phenomenal 75 percent of all voters in the general election, as compared to a national turnout of 48.8 percent, the lowest since 1924.[135]

## The Contrarian

In parting, the last scion of the New Deal declared, "One path divides us, denies us the common good and closes the door of prosperity to all but a few. The other…unites us, seeks the common good and opens the door of opportunity to everyone." There was the path "of least resistance," or "the path of … political courage. Government is not the enemy." These words and his 1997-99 budget — with $500 million more for children, the poor and the elderly—summed his philosophy. There was stingy applause — then a shower of praise caught best by Clyde Ballard. They "got along surprisingly well…if we didn't agree, we did it with class…if he told you something, I didn't have to worry about it. He…pursued…his beliefs throughout his career. He never … wavered. Consistency was his strong point." "He was a man…out of step with his times … but I thought he did a good job," Dan McDonald echoed. Marlin Appelwick's judgment was, "He's a straight-shooter who loved the process, worked hard, who spoke clearly and would have been a two-term governor except for the challenges of sexual harassment."[136]

The Lowry administration was as managerially uneven; he was a legislator and idea man, not a recruiter or delegator. Sending Mary Riveland to reshape Licenses, "a poster child for inefficiency," was neutralized by naming directors who agreed with him. Harry Thomas was "totally ineffective" in this setting and Jean Soliz without managerial credentials. The leader of Gardner's OFM "policy shop" was replaced with an inferior.[137]

The refusals to admit defeat were often disingenuous. Declaring the civil service changes a success was part of a pattern of treating "changing attitudes" as structural reform. Signing repeal of universal health coverage was a "step forward."[138] "The Theiler Report" he said, "clearly clears me." Sincere attempts at operational "efficiencies" were transmuted into fiscal conservatism. "You're looking at one of the most frugal men," Lowry told Seattle's City Club a month before leaving office, "one shrinking state expenses the old-fashioned way, a line item at a time."[139] He was complying with necessity not overriding his congenital liberalism, as pressing outlays as near to the I-601 lid remind us. The voters' messages to "back off" were taken to mean "maintain speed with less fuel."[140] In reality, idealism and impatience set Lowry's "governor" at one speed: "full throttle.[141] Strategy was for others. "If I were dictator for a day ... I'd eliminate all pollsters and political strategists," Lowry joked. "He met often with the leaders and members of all four caucuses," Lorraine Hine remembers.[142] Then "Robo gov" rushed the parapets, gathering troops as he went, excited by the power to make changes ("It's me. I'm governor and I have to do this," he told Bob Gogerty.) "Of all the governors I've served under," Dan McDonald thought "he probably [was] the hardest working and the one that was most effective in his first two years. His personal problems caught up with him. He was the best governor that I served under, because he knew the power of the office and he 'made it happen.'"[143]

If Arthur Langlie was a "Republican Governor in a Democratic Age," Mike Lowry inherited a time that clashed with his temperament. "He was a "powerful civic conscience ... a populist in the 1990s when one was not wanted. The result was not pretty."[144]

Chapter 12

# Gary Locke: Legacies of Two Lands

*(1997-2005)*

## Upward Bound

Gary Locke spent his first six years in Yesler Terrace, a World War II housing project on the hillside ten blocks above downtown Seattle. He helped his dad, a survivor of Normandy, who worked seven days a week at his Pike Place Market grocery. The second of five children began public school not knowing how to speak English and feeling "somewhat alienated." "The world turned upside down" when he got his wrists slapped as a third grader for having rice, porridge, fish, and vegetables, not the traditional American breakfast. "But it was important to all of us ... to become American as fast as we could, and as thoroughly as we could," even if in one sense it meant "rejecting the culture of our parents."[1] The Eagle Scout graduated from Franklin High School in 1968 and attended Yale with part time jobs, financial aid, and scholarships. The "nonconformity" of the 1960s convinced him of the wisdom of "old traditions and timeless values," and that history could be improved on given "the power of education to move ... civilization forward." The legal process was the way to do it: he received a law degree from Boston University in 1975.[2]

The young assistant prosecutor for King County "doorbelled" for others, and as a bill analyst for the State Senate in 1981 found himself asking, "Why not me?" He was elected to the state house from central Seattle's Thirty-seventh District in 1982.[3] Mirroring its liberalism, he introduced a gay rights bill and an income tax (three times), but voted against a 1989 anti-drug package because it expanded wiretapping. He joined the GOP in 1985 in drafting legislation requiring crime victims be notified of key trial dates so their statements could be filed with the court. Locke's traditional side put him behind halving the blood alcohol level definition for drunk driving. He "led the charge" in Gardner's only override, restoring increased penalties for burglary.

By 1991, he was the House's chief budgeter, labeled "a tax-and-create-a-program liberal," a "policy wonk" and a workaholic with a "passion for process." "He didn't have a girlfriend," a lady senator explained. "He had the budget."[4] Dean Foster, a versatile Democratic administrator for 30 years and chief of staff to Gardner, thought him a consummate numbers cruncher, who unfortunately took the same approach as county executive and governor. "He forgot to delegate … and became so specifically involved with understanding numbers that he lost his ability to be creative in leadership."[5] Borrowing private sector techniques, he hacked $900 million from Gardner's budget to restore three percent salary increases for teachers and state employees. Half the 1,869 jobs that vaporized were early retirements amortized into future pension costs. The others were managers, assistant directors, public information officers, special policy and government-relations assistants. The rank and file was impressed by his "creativity, compassion and fairness. Booth missed it by a mile," the WFSE's Mark Brown marveled. "Gary's [budget] is damn near a bull's eye." Welfare grants were restored "on the condition that you are engaged in rehabilitation" or community service. Higher education got "fiscal home rule," the right raise their own tuitions to offset 4.3 percent cuts, pleasing the University of Washington's president.[6] Not all those sharing the limelight were charmed. He and Nita Rinehart, the Senate's stern-faced negotiator, also bitten by the gubernatorial bug, were closeted in "Gridlocke" for two weeks as her aggressive opposite insisted on "management efficiencies."[7] The Senate's $600 million in adds forced him, as is customary, to split the difference, driving record-breaking taxes on business leading to the 1994 Democratic debacle at the polls.

Locke quit his job at U.S. Bank in 1992 to run for governor. He and Lowry met over an April weekend and agreed, "If I ran he would not, and would endorse me. If I didn't, he would." Lowry was to decide by Monday; instead, he announced. With too little time to put together an organization to equal Lowry's name familiarity, Locke was preempted. "I felt betrayed," said Locke, "he told me three times … he would defer [and] … indicated a willingness to endorse me. We differ a bit politically. On some issues I'm liberal, and on some I'm conservative. I'm a kind of Scoop Jackson Democrat."[8] The disappointment was Locke's first large dose of a phenomenal run of good luck. Boyish, good-natured, unassertive King County Executive Tim Hill had narrowly won a second term in the suburbs. In 1993, Locke needed only to widen his base there as Seattle drifted to lopsidedly liberal. Perceptions of Hill's vulnerability and Locke's power as Appropriations chair got 30 corporations (including Boeing, which had jousted with him) to pay for a buffet with 5,000 invited.

Campaigning with customary intensity, he collected 34 percent of the vote in a six-way primary, more than three other name Democratic candidates together. A Republican consultant called it "an absolute juggernaut ... the most remarkable campaign I can remember."[9] Olympia had prepared Locke for the assertive Republicans who took control of the expanded 13-member King County Council. The county's merger with Metro, the deaths of construction workers at the Kingdome, and aggressive sports team owners were not unexpected. But sparring with Ken Behring, owner of the Seahawks and everyone's ogre as he tried to threaten the county into a second stadium proved the most visible and popular thing the county executive could do.

Doing away with two of an initial triumvirate of deputies to end a power struggle was instructive about his delegation and tempered Locke's tendency to micromanage. He cinched in the budget, expanded transit, rewarded departments for saving money, and put his predecessor's growth management plan in place. Locke was well suited to manage "a steady, intelligent transition from insular county to regional powerhouse," the *Times* concluded.[10] But trouble was in the offing. The Kingdome was a drudge until it was imploded and the county's tax base was shrinking. Mike Lowry's self-demolition conveniently offered a timely way for Locke to extricate himself.

## Onward Christian Soldiers: The 1996 Gubernatorial Race

Locke's third spate of good fortune began in Yakima in June 1996 as organization Republicans began their quadrennial rite of falling on their swords. Planks like ending federal civil service did more damage than the Democrats' desire to substitute life in prison for capital punishment. "You get your choice of a relentlessly liberal world view or the Christian right's morality play ... with the vast middle where nearly every election is won ... left behind," frowned the AP's Dave Ammons. "Platforms can do only harm."[11] The regulars compounded their folly by felling more gubernatorial timber than grew between 1984 and 2004. Norm Maleng, the admired longtime King County prosecuting attorney had been high-profiled in the press by garish murder cases. Harvard-educated Dale Forman was the House majority leader from Wenatchee. Jim Waldo, a skilled natural resources mediator-lawyer and former Evans campaign manager spent the primary explaining why State Senator Ellen Craswell's "radical" idea of shrinking state government by 30 percent according to "God's plan" made her unelectable. The "Gentle, genuine, and gracious," and reality-challenged Craswell, the idyll of the Christian right as Mike Lowry was to compulsives of the left, won the nomination with just 15 percent of the primary vote.

Locke's chief Democratic competitor and philosophic look-alike, Seattle Mayor Norm Rice, failed to ignite the regular Democrats. The legislative "star" and anointed front-runner was free to court moderates from the outset.[12] His goals were predictable: to "streamline government and reduce top-level management, institute a savings incentive program, and use more private sector executives." Craswell was swamped in Lockean sea of "annoying brilliance" and fiscal detail. By October her profile was 38 percent negative, his 48 percent positive. In November, there was "a Democratic landslide of biblical proportions … an absolute rout" retracting the GOP's seven of nine seats congressional wins two years before."[13]

## Chinese New Year

The Chinese-American community, welcomed as railroad laborers then persecuted as competitors, had reason to be skeptical of government. In 1886, only Governor Watson Squire's federal troops kept "coolies" from being run out of Seattle by the Knights of Labor. In Tacoma, 300 Chinese escaped, leaving their belongings behind. Locke's grandfather was working as a "house boy" a mile from the capitol in exchange for English lessons, when the sheriff, merchants, and civic leaders held off a mob bent on burning down Olympia's Chinese section. Sixty years later, the Cold War movie "The Manchurian Candidate" portrayed a repatriated, indoctrinated Korean War veteran running for president, uncovered only at the last moment. Gary Locke's elevation to be the first mainland-born Chinese-American governor was the first time Asian ethnicity was a political advantage at the state level. The governor-elect said it affirmed his family's faith "in the essential goodness of mainstream America." Chinese Americans took pride.

Locke had two meetings with the Chinese ambassador before the primary and Asian language newspapers on both coasts reported stories about them. Master Lu of Redmond's Eastside Buddhist Temple spoke for the 5.3 percent of Washingtonians of Asian origin: "Obviously, history is in the making here."[14]

The inaugural was emotional, the sequel heady. "It has taken my family over 100 years to travel one mile. But what a journey it has been … a journey of hope hard work, and faith." Four thousand turned out for the ball in the Capitol, featuring Korean and Chinese lion dancers, a mariachi band, and the Royal Regiment of Wales choir. It was "hard to imagine, hard to believe." Republican leaders presented a cradle for his baby due in March. President Clinton closed his State of the Union Address by pointing to Locke, in Hillary Clinton's VIP perch in the congressional gallery, as a symbol of the strength of the nation's ethnic diversity. "He represents the future we can all achieve."[15]

Locke's fall 1997 trade mission to China was also a personal odyssey to the village where his father and forefathers had been born and to the house in Shanghai where wife Mona's father spent his adolescence. "The most glaring contrast of all was how much America had changed in 50 years." A son of the celestial kingdom now watched from high station as his adopted country struggled to renew its "moral fabric." The Chinese were right to cling to the "values of family unity, mutual support, and hard work."[16] The new reality was that Washington's largest trading partners were now Asian and 55 percent of all exports to China passed through the state's ports. Hosting the National Governors' Conference in Seattle in June 1999 and standing behind President Clinton's call to make China a member of the World Trade Organization to create a prosperous and open China constrained by "global norms," Locke played to his strength. The WTO's disorganized gathering at the hotel featuring three days of anti-globalization riots did not stop Congress from normalizing of trade relations. Chairing the Democratic Governors Conference assured Locke a national profile.[17]

## 1997: New Blood

*"Party politics in terms of [appointing] Cabinet members really makes no difference to me. The election results are in some ways are a rejection of extremist views and a statement by the people … they want consensus building."*

Gary Locke, November, 1996[18]

Locke believed "we really do need a change. We're going to be putting in our own team. Most important is reaching out of the immediate Olympia environment. " "We are going to try to get out of the box," Tom Fitzsimmons, administrator for Thurston County for ten years, director of the transition, Ecology and soon to be chief of staff repeated. State senior management was now a specialty of those in charge of 500 to 15,000 people, to which few in the private sector could be lured for half their salaries. The governor needed to absorb six briefing books totaling 1,800 pages and get 35 cabinet and sub-cabinet officers, 70 mid-managers, personal and confidential staff in 60 days, and a budget by December 15.[19] He had the good fortune of being a recent "insider," an asset his three predecessors lacked.

The crucial choices were the best. Dick Thompson, Gardner's chief of staff, was sent to OFM. When Joe Dear took the first role, the governor got a mental extension of himself. Boyish, intense, all business and common sense, Dear tried to be "invisible." His "overwhelming reasonableness" had its limits: there was a bowl on the conference table for the fines of those late to daily staff meetings. Backgrounders for the governor's briefing book were obligatory; assignments were pictogrammed on the wall. Locke was a stickler for clarity: "Tell it to me in a way that I can explain it to my grandmother." There could be no higher allocade than Speaker Frank Chopp's, "When I talked to Joe Dear I felt like I was talking to the Governor." "He gave me a lot of authority and I used as much of it as I could," Dear said of their "non-ideological centrist" partnership.[20] Compared to Mike Lowry, "Gary Locke was very much a pragmatist and not a hands-on kind of person. People were nervous because they saw him as a micro-manager from having been House Appropriations Chair. We owe [it] to Joe Dear ... who made sure Gary stayed more gubernatorial." Not a few of those who knew best dissented. Speaker Wayne Ehlers, later Locke's legislative liaison, asked about his power to delegate responded, "I don't think he has ever done that."[21]

The drawing of Asians to Olympia was as dramatic as Chinese trade at the ports of Seattle and Tacoma: five were in the cabinet, when fourth chief of staff Fred Kiga relieved Paul Isaki. Lyle Quasim was reinstalled at DSHS in 1995 when Jean Souriz, who had sacked him left after incidents at the OK Boys Ranch, where 26 youth who were sexually molested, were ousted. The eighteenth and longest serving secretary quit in April of 2000, having spent most of his last year overly defending DSHS's role in the Linda David wife abuse episode and earning praise for directness, credibility, and staying in power. "It's a very, very tough job ... emotionally draining [and] ... a huge management responsibility. Lyle has done an incredible job all through the years," the governor applauded. The few tragic episodes of challenged clients being put upon were in fact a credit to the agency's diligence given its exposure, 20,000 of the most vulnerable. Some legislators believed tort liability payouts had reached "crisis status" when the state settled three cases in as many months for $34 million in the summer of 2000.

The ACES tracking system was finally up, this time ahead of schedule and under budget.[22] Locke needed someone who could keep apace of the technology chase and appointed Dennis Braddock, the acerbic former chair of the House Social and Health Services Committee, a person of "considerable vision." His "goal was to have zero bad events." "In the real world that doesn't happen," Braddock knew. Two months later, he was characterizing the "sporadic events" as system failures, not ones of oversight. Both were true.[23] Locke felt DSHS was "manageable," though some more "consolidations or pulling pieces out," like early education, childcare, "health eligibility functions," and a "processing center" for a "variety of agencies" would be better. The drop in welfare claims was a national phenomenon due largely to the prosperity of the 1990s, but more pronounced than in only several other states.

Duels with the union and the old guard at the patrol had drained Annette Sandberg. The governor's bringing in of the first out-of-state chief, Ron Serpas of New Orleans, raised eyebrows. Yet by 2003, the patrol was recognized as the foremost law enforcement agency in America by the Association of Sheriffs and Police Chiefs.[24] Fred Kiga brought in Washington Mutual Savings Bank and Anderson Consulting to Revenue. Appeals fell and business tax filings began. Technology made it possible for John Charles' Retirement Systems to eliminate waits of up to five months for teachers shifting to pensions. Ecology speeded the issuance of 90 percent of water quality permits to 90 days. Local licensing was now simultaneous. The "one-stop" permitting of the Evans era had been improved upon.[25] The "devolution" Locke had called for, managing from "the bottom up as well as the top down" awaits a true merit-based civil service.

The chronic rough spots defied smoothing. Jeff Koenigs, a key figure in resolving the Alaska-U.S.-Canadian salmon disputes, was battered as director of Fish and Wildlife by the endless battles between sportsmen and commercial fishers, low agency morale and resources, habitat loss and over harvesting. In 1999, the governor decided the Department of Trade and Economic Development's six-year experiment as a "kitchen sink" had failed.[26] Seattle City Councilwoman Martha Choe came in as director, and former Bellingham vice mayor Tim Douglas, but the Democratic Senate resisted splitting the Community Affairs side out as "too hasty." Beyond the lightning rod agencies, a palpable evenness set in and turnovers slowed. When just one new woman appeared among 24 cabinet appointees in the first six months (the three others were inherited), the governor pointed to 10 of 23 in the sub-cabinet and exhorted, "We can do better." He was unimpressed by quotas, "I don't believe in saying, 'That's a woman's slot or a man's slot.' I don't count," he responded when asked again in 1999. Moderate Democrats were now equal to liberals, and the pragmatists prevailed.

Judicial nominees sent the same signals. Chief Justice Barbara Durham resigned from the Supreme Court in 1999. There was a need for a healer to meld a volatile and factious bench. Bobbe Bridge, a daughter of the Seattle Democratic business dynasty, was the listener Locke wanted. Three of his first four choices to the King County Superior Court were female, with an emphasis on practicality, "These are well rounded people with legal skills, demeanor and real-life experience." Dan Evans was renamed to the UW's Board of Regents. The next three were Magnuson protégé Gerry Grinstein, chairman of Delta Airlines, Jeff Brotman, cofounder of Costco, and Ark Chin a retired architect. All had business skills. Rafael Stone and Spokane businesswoman Elizabeth Cowles went to WSU, another preference for experience over experiment.

## New Beginnings, Old Resentments

While campaigning, the first Democratic governor to face a Republican legislature since 1919 said, "Good public policy … isn't the property of either political party." Lawmaking was "all based on trust." He had to prove up. Locke's sometimes sharp-tongued partisanship as a representative left a residue. Speaker Clyde Ballard remembered "demeaning" comments, and moves that could be considered duplicitous, "Gary consistently played games," he said, and at one point called the Appropriations chair a "liar," an unexpected word from the Christian gentleman. But this was not 1993, and the governor's "more taxes, more spending, more government intrusion" path was passé. "We're setting the debate now." The House quickly voted (62-32 with 8 Democrats joining in) to make a four percent drop in the state's share of the property tax permanent.[27] The governor had pulled Ballard aside with an equivocation as the House was about to vote: "I do not want homeowners' property taxes to go up in February, so I do support continuing the current property tax cut that is set to expire … but I don't think we should make it permanent." His veto bore what soon became an expectable finesse: he preferred something "that focuses on middle-class homeowners." Locke backed away from his campaign pledge to end the rest of the 1993 business tariffs. For two years the state had granted business $1 billion in tax relief, "virtually none of it to the hard-working families of Washington State." We should not be doing this on a first come, first served basis. He was not breaking a campaign promise: "I have never mentioned an effective date." By the end of the 1997 session, his warnings about tax relief profligacy proved correct: bills on his desk lowered taxes by another $414 million over four years, assuming voters passed the property tax referendum, done to avoid his veto.[28]

## The GOP's Social Agenda, Welfare Reform, and the Question of "Trust"

The governor profited from the abiding schism between the GOP's moralists and moderates. Clyde Ballard knew why he lost the majority in 1996 and strained to keep his caucus on "mainstream" issues and avoid identifying it with the "social agenda" the Pro-Family Coalition was pressing. Bans on same-sex marriages, third-trimester abortions, parental notice, and a "parents' rights" bill were stillborn in a storm of vetoes. "Our overarching principle should be to promote civility, mutual respect and unity. This legislation fails to meet that test," Locke wrote in vetoing an anti-gay bill. "What's disturbing to me about this issue is it tries to raise imaginary devils or bogeymen to attack. It stigmatizes gays and lesbians who are contributing members of society." Locke worried aloud that a second referendum the GOP was concocting to avoid him might bring "about violence and a mean-spirited campaign" and the outpouring of right-wing voters Democratic leaders warned of. The lack of courage shown in lopsided votes in both houses on these issues told of the times; the lawmakers had seen the 60-40 defeat of a gay-employment rights initiative at the polls in November 1996.[29]

The defensive-assertive governor-legislator launched unrestricted veto warfare, torpedoing 125 of the 519 bills reaching his desk (half partially), in the veto's final transition into an inclusive instrument of policy. How this torqued the legislative process is seen in welfare reform. The timing of President Clinton's pledge to "end welfare as we have known it" was also fortuitous. In his last year, Lowry had secured a waiver from the Clinton reforms to avoid changes to the system. Locke saw a "once in a lifetime chance to redesign our social safety net" and partner the state with business to put recipients to work. It "enabled us to make a huge corporate culture change within DSHS." Caseworkers went "from determining eligibility to ... being job counselors. They [the clients] need to understand that the taxpayers are not willing to pay their bills or stock their refrigerators," he noted. "Trying is no longer optional," even if the work found was on "the bottom rung."

The House GOP's bill mimicked the federal law, requiring work or job training to collect, imposed a five-year limit, and suspended the business and driver's licenses of deadbeat parents. Locke's Work First program also lifted 20,000 more into subsidized child care and took in illegal immigrants, but was not "radically different." The GOP Senate amended the bill in his direction and to control the $60 million cost limited payments to two years. "We had a lot of meetings and conferences on it," Locke acknowledged, then struck down the "enhanced" version and "negotiated" coverage for legal immigrants, telling the legislators he "was prepared to veto all the work done on a bipartisan basis." The difference was split and he again vetoed several sections, one charging low-income mothers higher co-payments for child care than he wanted. Removing clauses gave him "greater discretion than what the legislature ever contemplated." Caseloads dropped 45 percent by 2003 and Locke put the savings into increased subsidies for child care. Sixty percent of parents stayed off the rolls, leaving 2.3 percent of Washingtonians on welfare, the fewest in 30 years.[30] Senator Alex Deccio, who made the concessions on behalf of the GOP, said the governor had broken faith and stormed out of the bill signing news conference.

The governor had represented Seattle's Thirty-Seventh Legislative District, then the only one in the state where minorities were the majority. Latte Land's liberal media who bemoaned his deliberate ways as governor might have anticipated a more traditional approach once he had a statewide constituency. Locke heralded what "may very well be the best welfare package in the United States" with its "single-minded focus on work … its fairness to all people," restored "the American dream for the poorest of the poor."[31] He told shaken United Fund Drive volunteers 60 years of entitlements to create "a kind society" had proven "a clumsy and expensive substitute for the old-fashioned safety net of relatives, neighbors, friends, religious groups and nonprofit[s]. Making the government the first resort for people in need had actually made us less kind. Now we're making government the last resort again."[32] Implementation, improved on by investing in child care, community college training for working parents and a bubbling economy, was superb. A Welfare to Work "Leadership Breakfast" held in June for CEOs of selected small businesses with the governor presiding, was followed by a forum at the Seattle chamber for large ones, a realization that long-term success hinged on the private sector.[33]

The administration's regulatory reforms were more "permanent" than any change in DSHS's culture. The 20,000 pages of agency rules had become longer than statutes they were meant to enact. The governor stole the march with his first executive order. "Real progress" was shrinking them "not by the line, but by the pound," he said in March, dramatically tossing 591 pages of rules into a recycle bin. The House GOP's bill requiring Labor and Industries, Ecology, DOE, and the Insurance Commissioner to get the legislature's approval for new ones was thus "unnecessary." "I promised to bring some common sense to government regulations.

This fulfills that promise." In 18 months, 2,000 rules were quashed and hundreds of others put "in plain English." But the ongoing scrubbing, overseen by a sub-cabinet, applied only to agencies under his control, and did little to slow the stream of new strictures, even if overdue oversight kept the legislators off his turf.[34] Gubernatorial exhortations impacted the lifestyles of state managers insulated by both civil service and union contracts less. "Leadership is simply patriotism in action," he told them. Now that the external threats of the twentieth century were gone, people "want our country to be strong for a moral purpose," a recalibration to "era of where the 'big citizen' succeeded where the era of big government fell short." "Dumb media stories" and "our own shortcomings" had left the voters doubting that the bureaus "spend their tax dollars wisely. Too many public managers have embraced the comforts of bureaucracy and regulation." "Every state agency should be led both from the bottom up and the top down." Devolution of authority and a "clear definition of success" were checks on a "culture of fear" where decisions were bumped up the line. "Governing," he told Democratic businessmen, "is a lot like conducting an orchestra. Unless you have a large group of willing musicians, it's a useless exercise in waving your arms." Few wanted to change their tune.[35]

## Budgeting: The Burden of Plenty

Campaigning, Locke often advocated amending I-601 to base public school funding on growth in the number of students, not the state population. Finding the legislature's Republican and Democratic support scarce, he agreed to "live with the cap and try to make government more efficient." The watchwords were "stability and investment," an end to the "roller coaster" budgets of 1981-83 and 1991-93, building a reserve "for the inevitable rainy day" and avoiding across-the-board tax cuts.[36] His budget was $300 million below the lid and the promise to "invest as much as possible in education" kept; it got 72 percent of new revenue. Other agencies tendered 5 percent cuts, with the incentive of keeping half of what they saved.[37]

The GOP fell into the trap of sending its version to his desk too early in the 1997 session. To reorient it to his priorities, the governor vetoed 36 sections on education, "critical services for working families," abused and neglected children, the environment and the economy, financial aid for property-poor school districts, and increases in "sponsorship" and premiums for the Basic Health Plan, acting "in a restrained and constructive" fashion. "I think he's been less than forthright and less than timely in his dealings with us," Senate Majority Leader Dan McDonald groused. To the governor it was just checks and balances: "I respect their right to pass legislation that might not meet with my approval, and I would hope that they would respect my right to veto the legislation. If they don't like what I do they can override my vetoes," he retorted, knowing the votes for overturn were not there. The final edition was just under I-601, which must have been Locke's original intent. Then he turned to administrative palliatives. DSHS, for instance, was told to be more lenient in enforcing higher co-payments for child care for the low income. The GOP went to court, arguing he had to veto money as well as restrictions. The Supreme Court overturned the governor and chastised the legislators for putting long-term policy in spending bills! [38]

On balance, Republicans were pleasantly surprised at the governor's fiscal restraint, Democrats disappointed. "We felt he had a huge amount of political capital and was reluctant to spend it," complained House Democratic Leader Marlin Appelwick. "We are setting the stage for major policy initiatives," Locke promised. He added, "Many of us ve worried that the political center in this country has been pulled further haand further to the right, and that we are becoming meaner, more selfish and more economically divided. We can create a new center with a practical common-sense agenda" reflecting "our best values, not the usual ideological divisions."[39]

## The Seahawks Soar: Vox Populi or Circus Maximus?

A better yardstick of the governor's political agility was the delicate dance underway in February 1997. The question, in the face of a massive professional sports lobby demanding subsidies, was how to get citizens statewide to pay for building a new $402 million football stadium after King County had voters said "no," to meeting Paul Allen's conditions for purchasing the Seattle Seahawks. He hired 18 lobbyists for up to $7,500 a month. A phone bank assailed the legislators; television commercials roused sports fans. The governor thought his Citizens Task Force's ideas of taxing logos, raising car rentals, and expanding the lottery were "very creative." When the votes were not there, he shifted the burden, first to a five percent wholesale levy on merchandise and memorabilia, and then to a 2.5 percent retail sales levy. "Those who pay for the stadium must be those who benefit from it." Retailers fought back, getting 60 members of the House to sign a letter in opposition. The reclusive Allen then personally lobbied and put up $50 million for start-up costs. Painful avoidance was perfected in mid-April by extending the hotel-motel tax used to pay off the Kingdome, with the new portion not taking effect until 2016. Clyde Ballard was cornered. His caucus could not be tagged as football's killers. Seattle's second stadium was erected with the votes of reluctant Eastern Washington Republicans, after a conscience-salving protective referendum was added. Opponents soon found Paul Allen had never voted.[40] And those who had opposed the stadium in the first place now had a monument and another reason to distrust government.

## 1998: Starting Down the Primrose Path?

"Times are pretty good. That's not a time to do radical reconstructions. I think Gary is reading that," Howard Dean, chair of the Democratic Governors was quoted.[41] "Economically, we're in a state of euphoria,"[42] Locke exulted at year's end. Unemployment was the lowest in 22 years, but he was still committed to "fiscal prudence." "I do not want to leave even the slightest chance of creating a situation forcing … us to choose between cutting funding to … schools and colleges or raising taxes." Two-thirds of the new money again went to the public schools. Higher education was pacified by giving regents tuition-setting power (immediately used), to absorb 10,000 new students. Low-income families got tax relief and more went into the Basic Health Plan. The Business and Occupation tax was ended for 17,000 smallest businesses, narrowing the tax base (something Locke had refused to do a year before).

It was questionable how "prudent" this was. Attorney General Christine Gregoire's counsel not to use any of the $325 million first installment from the national tobacco settlement was ignored. It was "securitized," at 50 percent of value by the Senate, setting a precedent for augmenting the General Fund with discounted dollars originally designated for health prevention.[43] Defining "sustainability" in good times and bad as a "strong reserve" (to $583 million from $416 million), or less than five percent of the budget has to be seen as the governor's political, not his preferred reality. Hints that the economy was wobbling came in July. The always cautious Locke asked agencies for tentative seven percent reductions or $541 million, two-thirds of which would come from DSHS.[44] Locke's original budget had the lowest spending increases in 16 years. But his mid-session mollifications revealed a man under pressure and contradicted the first edition's premises. Urging the legislators to spend more of the reserve was interpreted as claiming credit both ways. On the other hand, the new version still fell short of meeting the federal "Goals 2000" educational standards. Locke left out pay raises for teachers and state employees and lamented three percent in two years was not enough. Faculty salaries and help for the unemployed were "low," and premium increases in the Basic Health Plan would force out many enrollees. There was enough revenue to be spent in the March projections, without breaching I-601. The legislature's edition came back stripped of 47 sections with over half of all new expenditures in education and colleges. Locke had signed into law only what he approved of, leaving the legislators to plead their wants.[45]

## Unrequited Love: Education

*"What matters ... is that the year after next [1999] our results must improve ... . The whole point is to raise academic standards."*[46]

Gary Locke, 1997

Lyle Quasim saw "there was a sea-change in money that left human services and went to education." The savings in welfare were reinvested in human services.[47] Locke's generosity toward education did nothing to diminish the decade-old struggle to build up accountability. His managerial instincts clashed with the 75,000 member WEA, voice of the status quo and the cosmetic alternatives it authored to the WASL. Teachers it contested, should not be held to a higher standard with the same resources. Any advances in quality hung on Locke's persistence, as the union struggled to soften the Education Reform Act of 1993 and keep the superintendent of public instruction and senate Democrats in tow. Teacher testing, part of his accountability commission's agenda, brought forth a Professional Educator Standards Board to advise the State Board of Education on implementation. The bill was "eight feet under" in March of 2000 until the governor personally brokered compromises. The union objected to four advisory board members being named by the legislature as creating a "political playground." The House GOP's four nominees strengthened its argument: one was for free-market remedies, one a member of WEA's nemesis the Evergreen Freedom Foundation, one for wider school choices, and the last a charter schools advocate. The governor pacified antagonists by negotiating the caucuses' pick of six of the nine board members.[48] In 2001, his attempt to refashion the *Common School Manual* a two-inch compendium of rules, into something of use. It gave preference to merit over seniority. It offered merit pay in the form of up to 15 percent raises for national certification and drew on the expertise of retired professionals even if they did not have teaching certificates, all ran against the union's grain. The WEA split the Senate Democrats, the governor's usual allies, delaying accountability by putting off intervention in failing districts until 2006.

Sensing the tests might be embarrassing to everyone may have prompted Locke to favor narrowing it to the "basics": math, reading, writing, and science. Despite a December 2002 poll showing 60 percent of the public backed the WASL he edged back, asking the legislators to "tweak" it to permit retaking exams and put off science till 2010. The testing was too complex, but the larger question was could a "leg" of the hard-fought benchmarks be sawed off without toppling the stool.[49]

Locke's only real defeat in 1997, by a combination of liberals and conservatives, was on the cutting issue of charter schools. One feared draining the public schools, the other thought the proposal too "weak" and state-regulated. The governor was impressed with the success of those who had failed in the public schools, many of whom were minorities. Despite the WEA, he opted to charter 50 schools as an "experiment in flexibility." Proponents fought off crippling amendments to protect certified staff and keep the state's hand in contracting private schools. They could not agree on his financial hardship stipulations and the five percent limit on student participation. Renamed "opportunity" schools in 1998, chartering passed the House for the fifth time, only to again fall to the educational establishment in the Senate.[50]

No one was surprised that despite hours of lobbying on the governor's part the 2003 session was unable to jell accountability, "refine" the WASL, pass charter schools, or agree on how to aid struggling students. He fretted, "There was no reason [the bills] could not have been brought up much sooner" — except for the pervasive pressure of the union.[51] "The priorities of the state are always left until the very end." Locke consistently put schools ahead of the rest of state government, kept accountability at the forefront, and enjoyed mixed success in innovation in spite of the WEA. It had given $2 million since the summer of 2002 to Democrats and massed 20,000 teachers at the capitol the first day of the 2003 session to "keep the commitment" to its pay initiatives, and imagined it had lost. The union gratuitously insulted the governor, announcing it would not support him for a third term even before he decided.[52]

Washington's public universities were not under unified control (as in California), and competed as much as cooperated with each other, under boards who are advocates more than overseers. "Locke can make his mark," the *Times* persisted, by "retooling the state's higher education system." He dutifully appointed a "2020 Commission" headed by a former Weyerhaeuser CEO and a Costco senior vice president. Its 15 point blueprint advised accelerating course work for the capable and a "Certificate of Mastery" for community collegians, aimed at qualifying people for family-wage jobs after 14 years of education. Beyond this, the "2020 Commission" suffered the disabilities of its predecessors: the Higher Education Coordinating Council (HECC) and private sector partisans of higher education seconded the biases of the institutional representatives honed on money. The governor chose to widen access (by three percent or 6,310 students), faculty pay, and "stabilizing" tuitions by taking $116 million from other agencies. To neutralize a 4.3 percent tuition bump, $31 million more was poured into financial aid and scholarships. Tuition was raised another 16 percent at his request in 2002 and 2003 to just under comparable institutions in other states, as preferable to taxing. Performance goals like improved graduation rates were attached, an "accountability index" introduced and $17 million committed to "proficiency." "This is a new form of contract with our institutions," the governor exclaimed. "We are giving them flexibility, but we are also expecting accountability and efficiency." The results, while more visible than the efforts since the 1970s to get metrics, were at the margins. Rhetoric sufficed for relating offerings to the market. Booth Gardner and Dan Evans' answer as to how to meet the "baby echo boom" in students, a $1.5 billion bond issue, fell flat at the polls.[53]

Overall, the 1998 session was "a truly forgettable outing," apart from a modest highways referendum, the governor's salmon protection plan ($25 million), and his reading volunteers in schools ("The Washington Reading Corps," for $8 million).[54] The "radically moderate"[55] Locke, realizing his fate now hung on having a Democratic legislature, reacted as one provoked. Bowing to the necessities of partisan politics, he skewered the GOP as "borrow and spend conservatives," soft on crime, beholden to fat-cat businessmen, and "callous to man in the street." Republicans were "against" everything worth doing and only for "phonics," too little in a knowledge-based economy. New majorities were perquisite to an "agenda of hope, opportunity and equality" to meet needs, not "blind adherence to ideology." In the fall, he doorbelled in Federal Way, Everett, and Snohomish and Whatcom counties where the balance would be tipped.[56] "If the Senate goes Democratic, I think we can credit Gary Locke," the normally nonplussed Democratic state chair said. The 1994 "Republican revolution" ended in November. Conservatives who continued to flog their social agenda were the conspicuous losers. A change of one seat gave Democrats the Senate majority, but lack of 111 votes statewide created a 49-49 tie in the House, the second in 20 years. Washington was high-centered.[57]

## 1999: Saving Graces

The governor was no longer the last line of defense. "I hope we won't have to use the veto pen as much" he quipped, "We're not ordering as many red pens." But now either party could force a tie in the House, and Democratic leaders were even more sensitive to the public's exasperation and volatility. "There is no talk of tax increases," assured Sid Snyder, the new Senate majority leader. Seattle liberal Frank Chopp the new co-Speaker nodded. "We will be pushing moderate mainstream issues." "All I want is a governor to be truthful with me," a chastised Clyde Ballard groaned. "All I want is some honesty."[58] Most importantly, two new torpedoes had hit the ship of state. Locke was right in opposing the WEA's initiative, I-708, but the voters passed the two percent automatic salary increases, with no revenue source. The blow fell once more on DSHS' clients.

In March, the quarterly revenue forecast projecting a $159 million bonus offered a way out. "Personally, I would like to see this ... go to education but because of 601 ... it will have to go into our savings account instead," the governor placated. His "prudent" side kept the revised numbers $60 million below the I-601 lid, and $500 million in reserve. His compliant side doled out $253 million more than the state expected to take in.[59] Then $170 million in delayed federal payments surfaced. A month long impasse broke when two House Republicans, seduced by items added for them by the Senate Democrats broke ranks. The governor played verbal dodge ball, "I indicated [to one of the defectors] I would be able to sign the bill if they passed it down to me." Senator Don Carlson got money for autistic children. Representative Tom Campbell's chiropractors got into the state medical assistance program, and Locke signed SB 5742, a "legislative atrocity" halting a land fill at Graham in Pierce County. "I made no quid pro quo," he insisted.[60] Ballard went to the hospital with chest pains.

## Natural Resources: Fish, Fission, Fallers, Futility

Environmentalists were defensive. Coping with growth, stanching the ongoing decline of salmon fisheries, meeting power shortages, and containing nuclear waste took the forefront. The Northwest's governors refought the half-century-old struggle to make their states the arbiters on the Columbia, only to be again turfed out by a myriad of federal agencies. Meeting at Boise in April 1998, the four formed a legislative task force on river governance, looking to "joint action." All they mustered were papers on hatcheries, hydropower, habitat, and harvest. Oregon's Governor John Kitzhaber idealistically pressed his "three Sovereigns" approach (states, tribes, and federal agencies), hoping for the "collaborative decision making process" eluding the states. He wanted the PNWPPC (Pacific Northwest Public Power Council) to run the river even if "it has not proved particularly effective to date." Locke's declination was fatal. This was "distracting from other issues," notably negotiation of new contracts with the BPA. So was breaching four dams on Snake. "Breaching dams is not guaranteed to bring back salmon. Why trade known benefits for something that's very iffy?"[61] The "states' rights," mentality, analogous to "local control of schools," lived on in a vacuum.

When the federals listed several Puget Sound Chinook runs as "endangered," Locke feared a takeover and promoted a salmon restoration strategy relying on local government to improve habitat. Once the King, Snohomish, and Pierce county executives were in harness, he proclaimed, "Washington State is in control of its destiny not Washington D.C."[62] The 2000 "State of Salmon" report by his Salmon Recovery Office, a footnote to five decades, dwelt more on strategies than impacts. Pointing to an independent scientific review's scathing critique of the states' efforts as disjointed and ineffectual, Curt Smitch, now the governor's special assistant for natural resources, challenged BPA's scheme for saving salmon as fatally slow, but confessed "nothing would be done were it not for federal law: the [in-state] political will is not there."[63]

Locke took a typically protective stance in June 1999, when two boys playing with a lighter ignited a creek-born flood of 277,000 gallons of gasoline leaking from a pipeline near Bellingham. He passed a state Office of Pipeline Safety, transferred it from the UTC to the DOE (SB 6441), and had the NGA adopt parallel guidelines. The governor's Fuel Accident Prevention and Response Team's "Final Report" fended off the federals.[64]

Depressingly repetitious letters went to the president and the federal Department of Energy pleading they live up to the 1989 "Tripartite Agreement" on cleaning up Hanford. It had been amended 287 times and Congress failed to commit enough cash. Radioactivity had reached groundwater 200 feet down and would inevitably make it into the Columbia. In April 1998, Locke termed the situation an "underground Chernobyl waiting to happen," and sued to make the federal courts monitors. Congress stepped up funding but ignored the clear and present danger.[65] Locke and Department of Energy Secretary Bill Richardson signed a "statement of principles" in September 1999. Eighteen months of negotiations for a "guaranteed progress of vitrification" for Hanford's tank effluents in return for Washington's taking more low and mixed-level wastes was rejected by the secretary's staff. Five months later, DOE designated Hanford as one of two sites for "low" and "medium" level wastes, with the caveat none would be sent if a new contract for tank waste was not signed by January 15, 2001. There was to be a "sharp increase" in funds.[66]

The state's energy policy in the 1990s, conservation and alternate sources, failed. Demand rose to 24 percent, capacity 4 percent.[67] Still, in the summer of 2000, the Northwest helped California avoid blackouts by lessening water flows in the Columbia intended for salmon restoration.

A week after the election, the regulators, big business and the Western governors meeting in Olympia confronted wholesale energy prices that were up 1,000 percent in the year. Locke fingered Southwestern and California suppliers as "obscene, manipulative and extortionist" and joined his peers in calling for price caps, a futile deterrent in the face of static supply caused by the California environmental wars.[68] The BPA's CEO admitted, "This past week we had the first test of a previously untried regional effort to look and act ahead to prevent power emergencies."[69]

Locke led the governors in fashioning a diversification-oriented bipartisan energy conservation package to absorb 10 percent of needs and offered a feeble $5 million in incentive tax credits to utilities to give low-income rates, for grants to spur power generation, alternative equipment, antipollution gear for natural gas plants, and to get large users to build their own power units. Here, as in Fisheries, there were no immediate answers. Were it not for Washington's first call on the energy pool and these admirable, after-the-fact, and inadequate ways of offsetting environmentalism gone awry, Locke might have suffered the fate of California's Gray Davis, who lost his job.[70]

Environmental law had been constantly refined for 30 years. Now the critical question was strict enforcement or monitoring and voluntary compliance; Locke took the second path, part of a national deregulatory trend. When a Representative complained that just 10 percent of Puget Sound's polluters were fined, he replied that 97 percent of cities and industries were in compliance. "Issuing penalties is often not the most effective way to achieve compliance. More often … an administrative order … a compliance schedule, providing technical assistance … a warning letter, or even just talking to a discharger is sufficient."[71] A March 1999 memorandum of agreement on oil spill risks that excluded regulating transport of oil in state waters was a half measure. The governor lost in the U.S. Supreme Court in *United States v. Locke re Puget Sound*, which placed primary responsibility for prevention of oil spills on the Coast Guard. He asked the president for an executive order to effect collaboration, then appealed to the Guard's parent agency the U.S. DOT, and was sidestepped.[72]

The administration's major contribution was revamping the Growth Management Act of 1990 to disentangle the players at every level of government and better address suburban development. The GMA was, as the *Times* intimated, a case of "good intentions gone bad." The governor's three mediators simplified rules for everything from houses to docks and industrial development and made it more difficult for three appeals boards to sustain the quagmire of differing local approaches. Uniformity was a "balanced approach that preserves the state's commitment to long-term planning for growth," Locke reasoned. The AWB's Don Brunell applauded as a "truly landmark agreement between parties who rarely agree."[73] The underlying enigmas, confused criteria and complexity caused by superimposing local ordinances on the state framework proved as hard to enclose as suburban sprawl.

The arrival of 400,000 migrants in the last four years of the millennium made water shortages the ascendant ecological issue on both sides of the state, widened the East-West divide and worsened partisanship. Democrats owned Seattle, Republicans the Eastside, and after two consecutive ties in the House, everything hung on winning in the western suburbs.[74] Locke knew the state's water laws were "a century behind." Ecology implemented the 23 suggestions of his 1998 study commission. His five bill package on how to divide water between farms and fish begged the question: use state-of-the-art technology, clearly define state versus local authority, and speed permit changes got lackluster responses. In 2001, he offered an "Action Agenda," featuring $8 million in DOE projects, enhanced by up to $60 million federal dollars. Borrowing $1 billion at low interest rates to ensure water adequacy and purity echoed Evans' "Washington Futures."[75]

## 2000: Of Crime and Punishment

The governor's attitudes on law enforcement reflected his traditional values and sensitivity on civil liberties. As a prosecutor, in two cases Locke fended off vigorous attacks on the constitutionality of the state's death penalty. Privately he felt, not without mixed feelings, that both defendants should have been hanged after the King County trials he was part of. In 1990, representing his liberal district, he wrote a letter to the parole board claiming he would have opted out at the penalty phases. He still believed the death penalty "is appropriate for the most heinous murders." He understood the racial "unfairness" issue, but noted safeguards like automatic Supreme Court review. The governor denied an appeal from Seattle's Catholic archbishop to stay the execution of James Alledge, the third of four convicts executed in 20 years, who wanted to die. Nor did Locke follow Illinois Governor George Ryan's lead in temporarily halting all executions on the basis of unqualified defenses.

He voted for the "three strikes" bill as a new legislator, but opposed it in 1993 as "over broad." "I think robbery is a very frightening experience. My father was almost killed in a grocery-store robbery." Vetoing bills that added nonviolent drug crimes to the list of "strikes" and making methadone one, countered large majorities from both parties, because life imprisonment should apply only to "very serious and violent crimes."[76] Mandatory minimums and the "legislative penchant" for longer terms had reached the limits of their usefulness. John Carlson's capture of the GOP gubernatorial nomination in 2000 betokened the times. The father of three initiatives argued he had accomplished more from outside government than Locke had inside. Never in office, the articulate commentator and "here-to help" outsider-Populist underestimated the power of the office in prosperous times. Senior businessmen bet three times as much on the incumbent. The governor's office put out 120 news releases, twice its average. Seattle TV stations featured the governor and his camera-savvy wife, Mona, in education PSAs as the *Times* extolled the virtues of Locke's reading program. The governor toured the state speaking on children's health care, school safety and prescription drugs, issues playing well with suburban "soccer moms." Washingtonians were "pleased with the progress … I've been able to achieve," he proclaimed on election eve as he won by ten percent.[77]

## 2001: The Best of Times Burst

In 2001, there were new pinnacles of prosperity, spending, and tax relief and the reserve still grew, convincing many taxpayers the state was taking in too much. Then in May, the stock market broke, "dot coms" collapsed, venture capital for biotechnology dried up, Boeing's orders fell precipitously, and Puget Sound's newly "diversified" economy stalled. This tipping point converted the Locke administration from the dispenser of plenty to the taskmaster of take backs. The trajectory at the outset of all but one of five earlier decades recurred, in doubled dollars. At first, Locke used his budget wizardry to give as little ground as possible. He spent half of the prodigious $1.2 billion reserve (lowering exposure to new anti-tax initiatives) and sluiced $1 billion over six years to school districts to cut class sizes.[78] "Creative financing" reached its apogee by effacing what was left of "601," not by raising the lid, but by shrinking the retained reserve. It never equaled five percent of the budget, after which any excess had to go to school construction. The governor also wanted to split any surplus with the taxpayers via a "prosperity dividend" and tax credits to local government. Millions were added to outlay without technically exceeding the cap, while the base for next biennium's lid was driven up. "If [this approach] is good enough for … stadiums and convention centers, then it is good enough for our children," he declared.[79] Betting on the outcome and a boiling economy over the next five years, kept the price from being paid. The crunch came in 2005 when he was out of office; in order to hire 8,000 new teachers, school districts needed to raise property taxes.

If the GOP was put on the defense by this legerdemain, the Senate's liberal Democratic Senate finance chair Lisa Brown was underwhelmed. Her idea was to sustain outlays that outran revenues by $1.4 billion by "securitizing" the last $525 million of the state's "Tobacco money" and by wiping out the reserve. Colleagues saw an "easy out," rationalizing that inflation would decimate the value of payments, or the tobacco companies might go broke.[80]

The House's more judicious Helen Sommers acknowledged the majorities were "well aware … that we are not fixing the bigger structural problems" or facing reality. Republicans jeered with their rendering of a Nat King Cole tune: "Unsustainable, that's what you are."[81] A rush was on for more tax relief in April, to quell surging tax revolt fever. The House GOP balked at repealing $200 million Senate Democrats said was "non-negotiable." To break the month long standoff, Locke invited leadership down and, as a special new session began the Monday after Easter, laid down a "common ground" compromise: "I'm demanding, I'm insisting, they give an up or down vote on this." The senators folded once their House counterparts agreed to reinsert a symbolic $26 property tax reduction (on a $150,000 House). The GOP settled for $1.5 billion in highway bonds, paid for by committing interest earnings on reserves. Given the close partisan cleavage, a disgruntled and disengaged public and looming referenda, these anemic outcomes may have been the best in sight. Locke mitigated the damage by courageously vetoing a 25-cent-an-hour raises for home care workers, then neutered the across-the-board property tax cuts of four percent. The apogee of executive power was near: for the second time Locke had significantly rewritten the legislature's budget.

## Running on Empty

*"You have sat too long here for any good you have been doing.*
*Be gone, I say, and let us have done with you. In the name of God, go!"*

Britain's seventeenth-century Lord Protector
Oliver Cromwell to the Long Parliament.

Defeating an appointee, Democrats retook the House 50-48. But timidity on taxes and the 60 percent plurality needed for bonds tilted power back to the GOP's one-vote Senate majority. The governor reverted to "a transportation system that works, an education system that enriches every child, enough water and energy … the basics," and made anticipatory veto threats. "What we are going to try to do differently is to make it very clear earlier on what is acceptable or unacceptable." The voters' 1999 refusal to pay for transportation infrastructure characterized the era. Traffic was up 85 percent since 1980. The gas tax was boosted five cents 1990, and the voters who passed Referendum 49 for $2.4 billion in infrastructure in 1998, now took it away with Tim Eyman's I-695. The governor rationalized, "Putting off transportation projects ... is better than consigning our kids to a lifetime of poverty for lack of education." When he suggested opening up HOV lanes and privatizing some rest stops as money substitutes, the *Times* sighed, "This is about politics, not traffic flow."[80] Intimidation by initiative was also surging. Locke and the overawed legislators rushed the initiative's $30 car tabs into law, only to have the supreme court strike I-695 down in March 1999.

Counsel Everett Billingsley assured jaundiced journalists that the reelected governor was now "definitely willing to spend a lot of his political capital to get some things done."[81] This was different, traffic tangles threatened the sagging economy. Locke stayed on the stump, doing up to seven radio shows in two days for a new $9.6 billion, 6-year building package, but refused to specify a revenue source, reigniting the charge he held his head down on tough issues. Staring at "some of the worst traffic congestion in the nation," in May 2001, he belatedly moved to fund it with a seven cent boost of the gas tax, two more cents per dollar on car sales and a surcharge on weight fees on trucks. Puget Sounders were offered a referendum for $17 billion in regional improvements. "We need a fix, a comprehensive fix." What preceded was insufficient; this was overkill. Fearing the public's reaction, Locke reversed himself to oppose making the package a referendum. Business agreed and both descended on the hapless legislators. Speaker Frank Chopp was unwilling to put Democrats at risk without the cover of a public vote and nearly sealed the scheme's fate in demanding private companies be eliminated as partners in erecting Tacoma's Second Narrows Bridge.[82]

The governor was "very disappointed. Frank was encouraging people to vote no [unless there was a referendum]. "It's not leadership encouraging your members to vote no." Clyde Ballard agreed it was the voters' call, did not "give a rip about Boeing," and demanded "efficiencies." The governor acquiesced, "This alternative is better than no bridge and is better than continued delay." "A crucial reform that will speed up ... projects, yet maintain environmental protections" was worth it. There was too much nervousness, too many variables. As a third extra session opened July 16, Locke's approval rating fell below 50 percent for the first time as his rhetoric rose: "While we fiddle and procrastinate, the transportation arteries ... our economic lifeblood, slowly clog." Business' pressure on the House GOP wrought an agreement on an $8.8 billion package, paid for by a nine cent rise on the 23 cent state gas tax, a quarter going to mass transit, offered as Referendum 51. As the legislature wrangled, Locke looked brave by comparison.[83] The voters demurred, and in 2002 the House passed a double referendum, one to allowing Puget Sound to tax itself for transportation.

Locke gave business lobbyists a month to round up enough Republicans for a bill without a referral. "We are going to have a referendum," Frank Chopp defiantly told him, divulging only 30 of his Democrats could be counted on in any event, and had his way.[84]

The governor recruited Slade Gorton as campaign co-chair to keep Eastern Washington at bay, hoping jammed Puget Sound could carry the measure. "What kind of a state do you want?" Gorton asked as he and the governor met with two dozen organizers. "Easterners" were unmoved. The *Walla Walla Union-Bulletin's* editorial, "Governor of Two States" spoke for them: "We're the Rodney Dangerfield of the Pacific Northwest – we get no respect." Neither did Locke after 136 stops there pleading, "Will we invest in the future or lose jobs?" In King County, where Sound Transit's shortfalls fueled more skepticism, he pep-talked executives of the three counties in a closed-door "Governor's Regional Transportation Summit." The "traffic will only get worse and more expensive to fix."[85] The $3 million spent on in radio and television advertising was for naught. The crashing November defeat was a refusal to pay, in an election with no presidential, U.S. senatorial or gubernatorial race, where objectors were an even larger fraction of a low turnout. The dogged governor reasoned the rebuff of $54 a car a year tax was a desire for accountability. "We've already begun conversations with legislative leaders." No one held much hope.[86] In a third try in 2003, Locke lifted the freeze on $400 million of state construction and refloated his plan as "the responsibility of the Legislature." In a made-for-television event, negotiations in his office went on till 3:00 am on April 2, with the governor handing out pajamas. "Of course, we have plenty of food, so there's no excuse that we need a food break or whatever.[87] There's no reason in my mind that the House and Senate can't agree."

There were several: the damming of direct democracy, the East-West divide, and close partisan divisions which had turned "Transportation … into one of the most ideological of issues … like abortion and same sex marriage," according to the chair of House Transportation Committee. Locke scurried between the chambers to make deals so the legislature could close on time for the first time in four years and to save his new majorities. It was "hardball," recalcitrants did not "deserve projects in their districts." Legislators who had voted "aye" a year before had little to lose and in November, the voters, sobered by the recession, decided they had. The victory under duress, if not decisive, was overdue.[88]

## Bringing Down the House

*"We are putting some dreams on hold."*

Governor Locke, Summer 2001

Locke's last three years were adroit exercises in damage control and conspicuous thrusts to round out his legacy. The February 28, 2001, Nisqually earthquake that drove him out of the Legislative Building for his last two years was the least of his worries. Washington's economy had soared above the rest of the country's for 18 years; now it fell faster, to the worst unemployment rate in the nation.[89] Boeing, virtually synonymous with Seattle, moved its headquarters to Chicago. After September 11, the stock of Amazon, king of the "dot coms," fell two-thirds. Venture capital for Seattle's nascent biotech industry vanished. In August 2002, Locke instigated a "Northwest Energy Technology Collaborative." Washington was "already a leader in software, aerospace and the biotech industries" here was a chance for a "revolution" in clean energy.[90]

How was he to sustain state spending, up to 66 percent between 1991 and 2001, in the face of a $2 billion, or 11 percent revenue shortage? He was out of fiscal finesses. Mr. Micawber's prediction "something will turn up" at last proved empty. OFM Director Marty Brown conceded that in August 2002, before the transportation debacle, Locke's advisors would have settled for the standard "50-50 solution" (half taxes, half cuts).[91] The governor thought otherwise. The die was cast in September at the AWB's "Policy Summit." Put to the wall, he was decisive. This was not a crisis. There would be no general tax increase. It was a chance to "reshape and, if necessary, reorganize state government," by answering the question "Is it necessary?"[92] He aligned with the GOP's Senate majority to block the House Democrats, whose budget meant significant tax increases. "This is a governor who has hoarded his capital, and is now doing the right thing. His friends should be careful not to kick him in the teeth," advised Senate Majority Leader Jim West. His GOP caucus sensed they were on the winning side if they stayed unified.[93] The Minneapolis-based Public Strategies Group was hired. "Results Teams" of directors and businessmen framed "purchasing plans" to "reinvent" the state's 1,400 "activities." The Priorities of Government (POG) process created the state's most comprehensible spending plan.

Suspending the three popular initiatives boosting spending for health care and education costing $450 million was a quarter of the cure. The reserve was halved again (to $222 million). Locke knew chopping $215 million in social services "deemed less than necessary to immediate health and safety needs" did "narrow the state's role as a social service provider," but still protected "the most vulnerable children and adults." Some 2,000 state jobs ended, and 1,200 "low risk" prisoners released early. To cushion the "deep and painful cuts," Locke proposed putting 13,000 to work building everything from prisons to schoolhouses by a bond-fed $2.5 billion construction budget.[94] In a stunning turnabout, the governor, whose leadership style had been persistently faulted in the liberal media, was now sanctioned. The hurting *Times* agreed the private sector was "in no shape to pay." The *P-I* praised a "'Reality budget [that] shows leadership.'"[95]

Conservatives who had never seen Locke spend his political "capital" blinked at the newfound assertiveness. For the first time the governor appeared before both houses' money committees as his own advocate. He was grilled, politely but relentlessly, by fellow Democrats. Speaker Chopp shrugged. "We just disagree with him on some key points." Helen Sommers was hopeful, "In past years he had not been all that active. Given the crisis … I think there will closer communication." Traditional Democratic allies, the unions, teachers, and service providers were furious. Phil Talmadge, ready to announce for the Democratic nomination whether Locke ran or not, told the party's Winter meeting in Olympia, "A progressive governor would engage the legislature and the public about how to head off draconian cuts," and got a standing ovation. "The rank and file … are incensed. It doesn't bode well for the Governor." Locke's "common sense and compassionate" response? "The reality is we only have so much money."[96]

And a star was born. Mediagenic Senate Ways and Means chair Dino Rossi got ahead of the curve by asking for immediate reductions to lessen later pain, with the blessing of Marty Brown. Rossi's "marginally less ugly" edition was captioned, "Following the Governor's Lead." The disarmed House Democrats were "all over the board" and dismayed at the media beating. Their weakness was evident on April 16, when a symbolic alternative with just $59 million in taxes survived House Appropriations 14-13, after Speaker Chopp arm-twisted an uneasy alliance of Seattle liberals and hesitant newly elected moderates from the suburbs.[97] The WEA made their lives miserable, running ads and threatening to cut them off. The Service Employees International Union which had unionized home care workers, jammed committee rooms with their disabled clients.

To buck the pressure, Locke extended his agenda: a prescription drug program for seniors, changes to student testing, charter schools, an antiterrorism bill, protections for gays and lesbians, and new taxing authority for local governments. He salvaged Medicaid for 40,000 children and restored $200 million in social service cuts. Rossi and the GOP senate got "90 percent of what we were looking for," while protecting "the most vulnerable among us, within a conservative framework of not raising taxes." "The striking thing about the budget … is how similar it is to the … plan Governor Locke offered six months ago."

The governor complimented the Republicans for heeding his "Priorities of Government" [POG]. Together they won a singular exception to a 70-year pattern of split-the-difference outcomes. More media plaudits showered down.[98] The Democrats' 2002 grant of collective bargaining (in addition to civil service) to the state unions in return for limited outsourcing and minor inroads on the seniority system, which the governor arbited, was indeed "probably the most sweeping change in the internal operation of state government in decades." As 70 percent of the budget went to salaries and benefits, negotiation of the package by the governor for an up or down vote of the legislature was an unprecedented accretion in gubernatorial power at the expense of the legislature. Could Democrats retreat from a contract ready to be signed, even if it absorbed all the money available? Would Republicans stand in the way knowing that defeat was all but certain? One person was substituted for a majority of 147. The WSFE had those who paid only their union, but not political dues, cut off from raises. Union membership grew 20 percent in 24 months.[99]

## Whatever it Takes: the Sky-High Stakes for Boeing

*"We're ready to compete for Boeing, but we wish we didn't have to."*

Congressmen Norm Dicks[100]

Business' complaint was unequal footing. In 2001, Locke formed a "Competitiveness Council" on regulatory reform whose suggestions ranged from merged permitting to an ombudsman. A year later, he claimed 34 of its 99 ideas had been acted on. In two years, each of the "big five," a no-tax-increase budget, enhancing education and highways, and making DOE "user friendly" were attained. But a thunderous 2003 clash over draft ergonomics rules that left the onus on employers to find ways to prevent repetitive motion injuries reopened business' wounds. First the governor said he would veto any attempt to adjust them, then under fire delayed enactment a session to give lawmakers their say. The

AWB's consultant pegged first year costs at $725 million, ten times Labor and Industries' estimate, and volunteered companies for a pilot project.[101] Locke then composed a review board to assay costs to small business, formed an Ergonomics Task Force to write a compliance guide, and finally offered $5,000 grants to aid businesses in implementing the rules. Despite vociferous pro-union rhetoric ("I will veto any bill that repeals the ergonomics rule," "I believe in unions", and "You fight to maintain strong labor standards, increased workplace safety, and you are the voice for the working poor"). He once more opted for the middle way.[102] Ergonomics became a referendum and was narrowly defeated by the voters in 2003, after a heated battle between business and Labor.

All this was overshadowed in May 2003 when Boeing revealed bids from 13 other states to build its new 7E7 (the "777") Dreamliner. Fear of losing of Boeing forced serious regulatory reform the way that dead-end finances changed budgeting methods. Advantaged by port access to Asia and a skilled staff in a highly educated state, Boeing was tangled in regulation and two costly overheads: injured workmen's and unemployment insurance premiums. The latter was the second highest in the country. Boeing's "UC" at $722 per employee annually was the most costly of the 27 states the company did business in. Boeing was also a "deep pocket" carrying more than its share. Locke and two-thirds of the lawmakers agreed in 2002 to hedge on actuarial reality, but the high-risk contractor industry persuaded voters to annul it.[103]

The fright tilted the political equation in business's favor for the first time since the New Deal. The Machinist's eagerness to cooperate on UC to keep the company from moving put Democratic leaders and Labor on the defense. Anxiety gripped Speaker Chopp, who "committed" to every one of the company's seven requests and set up a "Strike Force" to quell criticism his caucus had not done enough. The governor, told by the Boeing that the state was not in the running, hastily formed an advisory group to tailor a response. On June 6, a day before the end of the 30-day special session, he stood in front of the 35-person "dream team" of business, labor, and civic leaders to pitch yet another five cent gas referendum and advertise fast-tracking of the environmental review of a pier Boeing sought in Everett. "We want to continue being home to the world's best commercial airplanes. We want those jobs. We expect to win."[104]

The price of the bid was dazzling: $16 million in state credit[105] and a reduction in premiums and taxes by $2.4 billion over 20 years. "I don't think we're trying to be the low[est]-cost state, but we need to be pretty close," Chief of Staff Fred Kiga confirmed.[106] The $4.1 billion transportation package excepted, business' victories came at Labor's expense. Boeing, which had plead for sensible changes and gotten token ones for years got more than it expected. UC benefits for seasonal workers went down, were limited to 26 rather than 30 weeks, and the maximum benefit capped, saving $100 million a year. "It's extortion by the Big B," Labor's lobbyist howled. When WSFL President Rick Bender charged the governor was siding with business, Speaker Chopp groused, "The governor's been good at that."

Locke was undeterred, "The legislative leadership realizes this is about the future of the state of Washington." The legislators were back to the wall and could not afford to lose. For Locke it was, "Don't be the governor who lost Boeing." His legacy and future were at stake. For six weeks he called news conferences, issued releases, and staged events to shape public opinion. "We will do whatever it takes to win."[107] U.S. Senator Henry Jackson was known as "the Senator from Boeing." Locke now became "the governor from Boeing," a new flight path for one used to flying under the radar. On December 16, Boeing announced it would build the 7E7 in Everett. Locke rejoiced, "Washington is open for business." This year will be remembered as one in which the future of Washington was at stake, and we refused to let it slip away."[108] "He [had] utterly dominated the scene," the *AP's* David Ammons wrote. "Starting with that chill December day when he stunned Olympia [with] … a no new taxes budget, vexing his former allies. He got nearly the entire agenda in the all-out bid for Boeing and risked his career … triangulating with legislative Republicans and often rolling over the Democrats."[109] "The "Boeing House" across the street from the legislative building was dubbed "The Owner's Box." Whether the price was right and broadly benefited the state, or will lead to still more single-interest relief was yet to be seen.

## The Power of One: A Veto Creates One Party General Elections

Gary Locke, even more than Dan Evans, never gave up being a legislator. At first, most significant vetoes were matters of principle, later to reset "policy." Locke not only vetoed more than any governor, he made it an intensely personal device. The governor's need to assert himself in 1997 and blunt the GOP's tax rollbacks, deregulation, and its eagerness to satisfy its Eastern Washington constituents' demands for water and relief from Ecology's rules brought vetoes down on a record quarter of the bills reaching his desk. [See Appendix 8A.] What Dan McDonald termed "selective amnesia" allowed him to treat verbal agreements as works in progress, frustrating legislators of both parties.[110]

Rationales ranged from policy to politics, needed correctives to purely personal preferences, the ingenious to the contorted. Fiscal motives kept the 4.7 percent reduction in the state property tax from being permanent; it cost the state $158 million in the biennium. Locke cleverly noted only 58 percent of prior relief went to families and the rest to business, taking "away dollars for substantial relief for homeowners." The 1998 revisions to health insurance drew 20 "stabilization" vetoes, to sustain "previous commitments." The political risk in killing inflationary adjustments low-income seniors would have to keep qualified for property tax exemptions was deflected by pointing to the deductions some had for health insurance and veterans' disabilities.[111]

Protecting bureaucratic turf took precedence when the legislature reasserted its right to allocate agencies' fines. The governor said no "comprehensive assessment" had been done. Philosophical differences explain the death of the GOP's attempt to end uncompensated "takings" of private property for public use. Locke said this was "redundant" of the attorney general's guidelines. On water allocation, he wanted more left for fish and felt his Natural Resources cabinet could do better.[112] The crucial transportation bill of 1998 (ESSB 6456) attracted 25 deserved partial vetoes, illustrating how error and replication could be snuffed out.

Personal predilections and politics lurked in the loss of five sections of a bill letting school districts partially waive rules, dismissed as a two-year "experiment." The real objection was a perceived threat to "special populations" (the disabled, bilinguals, and to sexual equality), and to probationary periods for employees, a disgust of the WEA. In 2003, a section of HB 2079 denying *illegal* [emphasis added] immigrants resident tuitions at public colleges was excised because "a college education is part of the American Dream." Chesting his intents sometimes hurt, as it had Spellman. The sponsor of a 1997 bill to create farm worker housing by relaxing building codes was never able to determine Locke's position as it moved through the legislature. Down it went, under fire from both farmers and Latinos. A "commendable effort" had been made, but "our state can do better."[113] Civil rights surfaced repeatedly. The "strong supporter" of capital punishment nullified SB 5093 because it did away with the supreme court's "proportionality review" relating punishment of minorities to like offenders. The governor unapologetically tried to breach the supreme court's ruling that no less than a full section could be struck, allowed in 1974 after Evans' Landlord-Tenant rampage. Locke claimed he and the sponsors had agreed on what to take out. After two similar vetoes in 2002, the legislators drew a line and he lost in the supreme court a second time.

Abuse of the veto climaxed in 2004. The political parties, arguing the "cross-over" voters denied them the right to choose their nominees, overturned the 69-year-old "blanket" primary in court. "Washingtonians are proud of their independence." "I'll fight for that tooth and nail," Locke reacted.[114] The legislature knew the voters' wanted what they had and despite pressure from their parties sent him the nearest thing, Louisiana's "Cajun" primary, where the "top two" vote-getters go to the final. To get enough votes they had to affix a backup, Montana's, where electors must choose one party's ballot in the *primary*, and then *between* [emphases added] the finalists and minor party candidates in the general election. Aware the dual approach was likely to get enough votes for a "solution in the legislature" the governor artfully warned, but never flatly said, before passage that a veto was certain. A clear majority of both legislators and voters were overridden and the length to which the governor would go to have his preferences prevail was defined.

The defiant veto of "Cajun" primary was the one monumental blunder of Locke's tenure. Negative reactions evoked a suspicious and unusual defensiveness from him (stopping just short of saying the legislators had deliberately tailored the bill to make him take the onus of ending cross-over voting), lacked logic, and smacked of partisanship. The reasons given, "security,"(not recording the choice of a party in the primary), was not even a question. Given the prevalence of one-party districts and the power of incumbency, most "final" decisions are made in the primary. If the infirmity was having two persons of the same party to select from in the final, the district was likely to be so lopsided as to make two-party contests a charade. Widening "choice" in the general election was equally dubious: no third party since the Progressives of 1912 had gotten more than 10 percent of the vote, so why deny minor parties visibility in the primary? The "urgency" of settling on a new system to avoid "endless litigation" was moot. As expected, there was an immediate suit to kill Montana's approach, and the Grange, the original sponsor of the blanket primary, easily gathered enough signatures for a referendum, staying Locke's veto. The specter of party caucuses selecting nominees favoring those farther to the right or left, raised its head.

There was now no fallback position, no primary, and a "jungle general" in November. Forced to one party's slate then, the prevailing Democratic pattern would be reinforced, as the 2004 general election confirmed. If the governor was "extremely disappointed" with the parties, he fell prey to his own. The partisan primary, overturned by the U.S. Supreme Court on March 18, 2008, was an unfortunate upset for a person and an administration of integrity.[115]

## The End of the Age of Expectation

"I think most people … would be happy to know we are living within our means," the governor said, touring the state after the 2003 session. "I think people understand these are really tough times." He had $420,000 banked for reelection, nine times what State Senator cum Justice Phil Talmadge had. "If money speaks louder than words, Locke is running for a third term," the *Olympian's* reporter deduced. "It was hard to criticize the governor during the session when he was doing everything Republicans wanted him to do," GOP Chair Chris Vance admitted, still lacking a viable challenger. The angst was among nominal allies. In 1996, Locke told Labor he would veto anything they disliked. It tipped the legislature to the Democrats after 1998, only to "take it on the chin" in 2003. State President Rick Bender pronounced the governor in "serious trouble." The WEA "unendorsed" him. At the same time, 68 percent of the voters approved of the Locke's performance. Three years later, it was 33 percent; just 11 percent were "certain" to vote for him again.[116] His parabola tracked Arthur Langlie's 60 years before: a boom, then a smothering web of obligations and shrinking options. Like Dan Evans in 1972, he was paying the price for decisiveness.

Emily and Dylan, the Locke children, scampered across the mansion lawn as the governor gazed down at Olympia's Lake Fair fireworks and began to call close friends, "In the end we were trying to decide what's really best for the family." The answer? "A normal life. He put his family first," Mona Lee Locke rejoiced. "What more can you ask for?" Locke lessened his authority in 2004 by declining another term in July 2003, for other good reasons. He knew Langlie's and Evans' third term paled before their first two, about the historic bias of a bloc of voters against a third term, the odds for stymied ideas if replayed, and how hard it would be to keep directors in the final two years.[117] The decision to go made, the economy turned up, and the battle for Boeing won. Then for the first time in 20 years the GOP found a competitive candidate. Would State Senator Dino Rossi sweep in as the "new broom," and ally of the conservatives that Locke had to consort with?

Locke's governorship was a protracted reversion of his true self, a reverse "pendulum swing" to Dan Evans'. The "liberal" sponsor of an income tax in 1983, pointed to welfare reform, a no-new-taxes budget, and retaining Boeing as his prime achievements. Welfare reform was a steamroller that only needed steering, setting the "Priorities of Government" the greatest attainment. Reinforcing the budget reserve was unusual, sincere, and tactical; a small cushion was available when the legislators next overcommitted. While a reelection run was pending in the winter of 2003, the governor was forced to choose between damage control and disaster in closing the $2 billion gap. He trimmed, but also lowered the reserve to $200 million (to 1.2 percent), then proposed spending of just $193 million in 2004, in the face of a projected deficit of $750 million in 2005-07. This evinced a will-weakening preoccupation with a "legacy,"[118] common to end games. Endorsement of the $1 billion initiative by educators to be paid for by a one cent sales tax increase was also with an eye to history, and a blind one toward a potentially huge dedicated fund beyond the reach of the executive or legislature.

Locke managed a "tight ship," demanding plans for "quality improvement," and expecting agency steering committees to write "charters" (contracts) to tie his "visions" to "deliverables" and buttress the "personal commitment" of directors. Combining Printing and General Administration and the Personnel and Retirement Systems were advances, but hardly compare with creating DSHS or Ecology. The assertion that "our state is a national leader in innovative management functions, including digital government, regulatory and quality improvement, personal privacy protection, and financial management" held water. His Structural Reform Council reassessed over 100 agencies. The reshaped Shorelines Act that Locke negotiated was common sense; renovating the Growth Management Act "settled a lot of wars simmering over water."[119] If he and Chris Gregoire "got the federal government's attention" by suing over Hanford, no one could keep it. His environmentalism was mainly reactive. The criticism that Boeing was unleashed only after Locke's hand was forced is valid. The delayed Boeing offensive, like late-blooming executive requests tell of an offense often as unpredictable as implementation was thorough. Under union pressure the legislative Democrats insured inequities at the core of unemployment insurance and workmen's compensation were never touched.

Gary Locke, like Al Rosellini and Booth Gardner, was a centrist in a liberal's party, one with "simple values" from his Chinese heritage, cautious instincts, and a lawyerly testiness. "Prudent yet bold" agendas translated to "middle of the road." Childhood circumstances evoked education as "the great equalizer," attention to civil rights, immigrants, and the social safety net. "Is Gary a Democrat?" a liberal Democratic senator reported people asking. "It depends on the day you ask." Blair Butterworth rejoined: "Gary is not of those politicians who say they will cure the world. He doesn't over promise. That's a virtue."

For six years the governor was often justifiably accused of "hoarding political capital" or "ducking unpopular decisions to preserve popularity." "I have already met the lawyer in me," he told reporters at his first press conference. There was sophistry in others, as he avoided taking positions even "in essence," on major questions. "You just don't try to speculate unless you know exactly what the language says." Not knowing the final form of bills is the abiding predicament of legislators and executives alike. Democratic Minority Leader Marlin Appelwick felt the governor's concern with his credibility was "at times ... very counterproductive and comes off as being evasive, or cute."[120] Locke did take sides on controversial issues, most often where he was definitely aligned with majority opinion. The 30th anniversary of the *Roe v. Wade* decision on abortion drew the usual counter marches. He said, "We are a strongly pro-choice state .... I am proud of the way our state has led the way in reproductive rights for women."

## The Stop and Go State

The first Chinese-American state executive was one of Washington's most conspicuously prepared, suited, able, meticulous, energetic, and intelligent governors. His professionalism and that of his staff and appointees was consistently excellent. Criticisms converge on three areas. Where Mike Lowry "wanted to talk about visions," remembers senior lobbyist Mike Ryherd, "Gary wanted to talk about nuts and bolts. Gary ... did not have the patience that comes from being ... an overall leader, to sit and listen. He wanted to jump to certain conclusions."[121] Another was not "indecision," but a too close political calculus that left others to be bloodied first and last. He committed late, as on how to fund highways, diminishing his impact. Third, legislators who indicted him for duplicity saw a man who could be too clever by half, a casuist always reaching for extra leverage after deals were struck. "Gary has two flaws," Dan McDonald asserted, "buyer's remorse and amnesia. He would work it [a deal] around in his mind that he really didn't say that, when in fact he really did. And it probably works for him, but it sure doesn't work for the people that negotiate with him."[122] Last, a few perceived back-flips deepened distrust in key quarters. Allowing the Public Employee Benefits Board to enroll gay couples after telling the GOP leadership he would remain neutral was the final stroke for Speaker Ballard. There was "no misunderstanding. He said he was for the benefits but opposed to it because of cost. I feel it was a major betrayal."[123]

All three contingencies belong in the context of Locke's time. The erosion of their power left lawmakers tender. Their pay, raised to $7,600 in 1977, came when sessions lengthened to five months, and lagged till 1983, when a board was assigned the task of adjustments. Disclosure drove lawyers out. The independence of members bloomed and leadership lost critical mass on key votes and the ability to direct, much less coerce.

In the eighties lobbyist money reached flood tide, enhancing the Third House's power to protect incumbents, fracture the caucuses, and chill change, which slowed. Given close partisan divisions, the parties were less bold, each shielding its thin margin. In these circumstances, despite his caution, the governor often came off as more decisive than the legislators.

Second, another early-in-the-decade recession, followed by the unprecedented prosperity and spending of the late nineties exacerbated the ratchet effect. Deeper cuts and more taxes were needed, automatically lifting revenue and outlay in the up cycles and hurt on the way down. Come a new recession in 2001, the voter initiative takeaways and a cascade of tax exemptions in the name of boosting the economy compounded the malaise. After 2008, ongoing special sessions and and multi billion deficits led to excision of a quarter of the budget.

Finally, the unsettled, skeptical, cross-threaded voters fell victim to a new phenomenon, the professional initiative peddler, personified by Tim Eyman, who captured those in a mood to "just say no." Those who felt the governor should "face him down" did not volunteer to do so. Locke was caught in government by plebiscite, a current as strong as reformism in the 1960s and environmentalism in the early 1970s. Democracy was "derailed;"[124] decisions conditioned on initiatives and referenda. Legislators and the governor patched more than progressed.

Graying journalists reliving the "great expectations" thinking of the 1960s seemed oblivious to these ironies of affluence and the vises of volatility. The *Times*' Editorial Page Editor Jim Vessey modeled for them. "Our governor is such a competent and decent man that sometimes you just want to shake him," he wrote on hearing Locke's precise recital of betterments in the business climate. It was "a perfect litany," but he had "missed the chance to ignite this crowd and define this moment." There was a "sense of lost opportunity. People are no longer looking for perfection, they are looking for 'the power of one' for the exuberance of a happy warrior or the passion of the truly and deeply caffeinated." Locke was "one of the most puzzling politicians this state has ever produced." The relentlessly liberal *P-I* adjudged his two terms as "mixed, maybe decidedly so." He "started strong, but despite an impressive daily performance in the middle years … [ then] persistently missed opportunities," and failed to evolve from manager to leader. "He's cautious, passionless and devoid of grand dreams," Lowry's speech writer Walt Crowley lamented, "He's spent all his time in the engine room, it seems." "The people know … that I have gotten results," the governor growled at the shadows trailing overhead.[125] Alas, Camelot lost, reality faced. Gary Locke was only the last to suffer the eternal chasm between those called to govern, and onlookers who pen what might have been.[126]

# Pictorials, Section Three

*Two of the governor's legislative nemeses, Senate Majority Leader Gordon Wallgren, left, and co-Speaker of the House John Bagnariol, both democrats.*

*The governor at her desk with Jacque. WSA*

*When Ray's relations with the press deteriorated she stopped holding press conferences and relied on town hall meetings, like this one at Forks, as a means of communicating with citizens. WSA*

*Spellman singing, "The Sun Will Come Out Tomorrow" at his inaugural.*
*His fate was set by the recession of 1981-83*

*The governor takes his lumps; The firing of Glen Pascall." PI*

*The Norrthern Tier equivocation. Brian Basset ST*

*John and Lois Spellman and their six children. WSA*

*Not Quite a Legacy: The Implosion of the Kingdome. PI*

*John Spellmen puffed his pipe as he contemplated. King County Executive. WSA*

*Governor Booth Gardner at his desk. ST.*

*Lyle Quasim returned to direct DSHS, the state's toughest job.*

*Jean and Booth Gardner at his valedictory, 1999. WSA*

*The second term: 10,000 teachers "strike" at the capitol for a week.*

*Sparring for Governor, 1992. From left, Attorney General Ken Eikenberry, Congressman Sid Morrison, Congressman Mike Lowry, State Senator Dan McDonald and Speaker of the State House Joe King. ST*

*Making good on diversity. University of Washington Regents Ann Daley (left) and Shelly Yap.*

*Governor Mike Lowry delivering his State of the State address. Speaker Brian Ebersole, D-Tacoma, is at left. The Olympian*

*The Grey Eminence: Political Consultant Bob Gogerty.*

*Lowry the Pooh and the Revenue Tree. Brian Bassett ST*

*Mary and Mike Lowry in a television defense against his sexual offense charges in 1995. ST*

*The WWII projects housing on Seattle's First Hill where Locke grew up. The Harborview (King County) Hospital is at the center in the background.*

*The capitol cost $7 million to build in 1923-28. Renewing it after the 2001 quake cost $105 million.*

*Keeping Boeing (2002): From left, Governor Gary Locke, Fred Jarrett, director of revenue, King County Executive Ron Simms, Snohomish County Executive Bob Drewell (at the podium) Seattle Mayor Greg Nickels, and at right front Director of Commerce Martha Choe. ST*

*The govenor, left, House Minority Leader Clyde Ballard and Speaker Frank Chopp put their heads together at the end of the 2003 session. ST*

*The art of the veto: Doubts about the 'Montana Primary.' Devericks cartoon, ST.*

*The Lockes kiss at their first inauguration, January 1997.*

*The Locke family.*

*Locke returns to his ancestors: Chenghu, China, 1997*

*A political collage of the '80s and '90s. From left; Gary Locke, President Carter, Governor Booth Gardner, Governor Dixy Lee Ray, Presidents Clinton and Reagan, Governor Spellman (with pipe), U.S. Senator Slade Gorton (with computer), and U.S. House Speaker Newt Gingrich, lower right. David Horsey PI.*

*Left to right: Governors Mike Lowry, Christine Gregoire, Booth Gardner, Dan Evans, and Gary Locke celebrate Governor Al Rosellini's 96th birthday at Seattle's Olympic Four Seasons Hotel in 2007. ST*

# Preconditions for Progress: A New Voter Mind Set

***I. Recognizing politicians are not a separate and inferior "class."*** Contrary to what the detached or disingenuous want to believe or do not want to admit, the glory of democracy is that elected officials *do* reflect their constituencies. It cannot rise far above their interest level.

***II. Putting an inexperienced "outsider" in the governor's chair is no longer an option.*** Frustration is no excuse for a botched administration. The "conversion rate" of the newly elected governor must move at warp speed. Anyone lacking a current understanding of the state's government and the "whys" of a multibillion dollar budget, cannot sort or set policy in the 40 days between the general election and December 15, when a budget must go public. Administrations are made or marked down in the first two years. Three governors in the 1970s had been legislators. Of the 50 in office nationally in 1988, 31 had been lawmakers and nine in leadership. Only state or significant local office or large scale managerial experience will suffice. Who sits in the leather chair with the Great Seal on the back is the best single measure of the state's political maturity.

***III. Setting aside the term limits folly.*** The remedies for inept officeholders is going to a coffee hour or "town meeting," joining a campaign and voting. Dispatching good and bad alike discourages superior candidates from running, limits the useful life of the best practitioners, removing able survivor-leaders, and raises the power of lobbyists, who can convince journeymen more easily.

***IV. Government, no matter how efficient, will cost more as society urbanizes.*** When roads are not just scraped twice a year by a grader, but need stoplights every second block, it costs more. This need not lead to compounding biennial double-figure advances in budgets. Initiative 601, the vaunted "cap" of the 1990s, was eviscerated by exceptions in ten years. A reasonable constitutional limit, subject to a 60 percent override in both houses, adjusted for inflation and population with a "compaction factor" based on the census is a better way to link urbanization to outlay.

***V. Initiatives and referenda*** begun a century ago as vehicles for the people to correct oversights and undo special interest legislation are replacing representative with plebiscitary government. The sponsors and benefactors tend to be powerful interests who can pay signature gatherers to get what the legislature denied them, or single-interest networks of the disgruntled, who in the e-mail age can be marshaled and put their frustrations on the ballot with relative ease. The repeal of automobile license tabs graduated on value (Initiative 695) is a prime example. The owner of a worn antique or a luxury car now pays the same amount. The governor and the legislature were so intimidated that a repeal passed before the supreme court decided its legality. Raising the initiative signature from 8 to 10 percent of voters in the last gubernatorial election and from four to six percent for referenda is insurance against the commercialization, and democracy by ballyhoo. Governors and legislators who know the power of media publicity and money politics and are willing to open themselves to charges of "foiling the will of the people" are to be encouraged, not cast out.

***VI. Limits on candidate spending*** based on constituency size and adjusted for inflation can force "retail politics" back toward "grass roots" organizing and canvassing, rather than negative advertising. The two most expensive *state* senate race in 2010 spent over a million dollars. When governors and legislators can raise only a fraction of the dollars needed to campaign from constituents, whose pressure do they feel the most? What kind of legal logic limits individual contributions, but allows "corporations" to spend without let through allied committees? "Freedom of expression" in the media age means placing interests backing incumbents in front of citizens.

***VII. The fourth and fifth elements of what is now "five-part government" must be constrained.*** Full-time legislative lobbyists in Olympia have grown from 20 to 200 over 35 years; over 1,000 register. Legislative staff rose from 40 full time to 250, and over 700 in session. Excess hands have slowed and diffused the legislative process, shifting power from part-time legislators swamped by the swirl of legislation and amendments concocted and massaged, and to incumbents with under used "district offices" and advantages like professionally written, glossy, and usually self-promoting newsletters. Setting a ratio of 1.3 staff to the 147 citizen-legislators upwardly adjusted for population would stifle congressionalization. Limiting any entity in the "Third House" to the full-time equivalent of two full time lobbyists per organization would go far to level the playing field.

***VIII. Foremost, individuals must act on their obligations to renew and sustain a civil society.*** The "Third Sector" (next to private enterprise and government) is "the arena where citizens come together to advance the interests we hold in common." Voting has dramatically declined for 50 years despite more education and information. State legislative candidates are sometimes nominated in primaries by fewer than 15 percent of the adults. Affluence has brought distractions, entertainments, financial security and early retirement. Leisure and self-amusement are not excuses for letting government, the matrix by which America succeeds or fails, again fall victim to organized interests. If individuals do not engage, where are competent legislators and governors to come from?

# Reclaiming the Real Washington: Challenges and Measures of Success for Early Twenty-First Century Governors

Washington's tattered "progressive" tradition is badly in need of *voter* sanity and major surgery. If Captain George Vancouver's vision of the Northwestern most state is not to be clouded by urban pollution and governmental impotence these critical issues have to be faced:

***I. Setting Priorities.*** The pronounced trend of two decades is a diffusion of resources. New social services, loans for middle-class collegians, subsidies to local hospitals, and funding for historic organizations previously the roles of counties and cities, have been shouldered by the state. It has entered private enterprise, lowered mortgage rates by lending credit, offered a maze of selective tax breaks for businesses "to compete with other states," and half a billion dollar "private-public partnerships for sports stadiums "to stimulate economic growth." Each has diluted the state's ability to perform its historic missions: public and higher education, transportation, law enforcement, institutions, and support of the neediest. Government at all levels offering similar services creates confusion, obscures responsibility, and encourages pressure from new clienteles. Those seeking special or enhanced help, together with those already dependent on government, may now be the margin in most elections, defeating candidates who refuse them. A Scandinavian style one-party state, chosen by those who can be counted on to vote "yes," a benign dictatorship without a dictator, is possible. Will governors first concentrate on ordering Washington's priorities, or will we imitate the amorphous events on the Potomac, doing ever more things less well?

***II. Restructuring Washington's Constitution.*** It is longer than the Magna Carta, and the federal Constitution, has been amended 100 times and spreads over 212 pages of the *Legislative Manual*. The nineteenth-century creation designed to limit the governor by dispersing power to eight other state officials whose profiles are now too low and tasks too technical for the voters to assess needs consolidation and coherence. If three least visible, the commissioners of Public Lands, Insurance and the Superintendent of Public Instruction were non-partisan appointees of the executive the bedlam of "bed sheet ballots" also crowded with initiatives and referenda would be reduced. Eliminating the Secretary of State, as two Western states have already done, and transferring his duties to the Lieutenant Governor would create a full time station attractive as an understudy to would-be CEOs. (No lieutenant governor has succeeded a sitting governor other than by death or disability). Free standing major operations like the nearly invisible Transportation Commission, which spends amounts equal to a tenth of the operating budget also need to be under the state's most visible officer, who is held responsible for, but controls less than half of state operations.[9] The century old framework defeats strong leadership, a key to why Washington's vaunted "progressivism" is now anemic.

***III. Tax reform.*** The wall has been hit. The sales tax, the source of half the state's revenue, is the second highest in the nation and if pushed near 10 percent is likely to be successfully referended. "Sin" taxes (e.g., on liquor and gaming) are at their practical limits, the lottery fully exploited. Washington has had recessions in the first part of each decade for 50 years. Raising the Business and Occupations tax during one compounds the blow on the small businesses which are most vulnerable and generate the most jobs. A corporate income tax on profits, not one on gross even if no profit is made, is a must. Six balanced, learned commissions over a half century have come to nearly identical conclusions. Fairness alone demands an income tax so that the sales tax can be lowered as much. Constitutional limits on the major taxes can keep the configuration in balance. The state has the nation's most regressive revenue system, a potpouri of 45 levies, which when combined with local taxes take twice as much from a family of four living on $20,000 a year as one earning over $120,000 (in 2007 dollars). Those for whom voting "no" has become a badge of honor need to think about fairness.

***IV. A Constitutionally Mandated Reserve Fund of at least five percent of the state operating budget.*** Budgets spend all income. The lesson of recessions is that at least half the deficit is made up by new taxes. This ratchets up the spending when prosperity returns, deepening the next down cycle. If the "downside" is cushioned, the "ratchet effect" will be less. An adequate reserve fund has been hindered by citizens who think one means too much money is available, rather than a stabilizer.

***V. Electoral Discipline.*** The Motor Voter law of the 1980s permits those with driver's licenses to vote. Who checks to see if they are citizens? More recently, voters who do not know their precinct can "conditionally" vote. Minimal citizenship needs to demand more from the is being voted on? The 2004 gubernatorial race was settled by 126 votes.

***VI. Quadrennially Convening the Equivalent of the Federal "Base Closing Commission"*** (such as Congress appointed when it could not close military bases), to review and recommend elimination of superfluous boards, commissions, and regulations created by agencies to implement and often "improve" on laws. The result would go, as does labor negoiations now carried out by the governor, to an up or down vote by the legislature. Governors and part-time legislators do not have the time for this, and turf protectors and special interests make it a political quagmire. Regulations are now longer than the statutes.

***VII. Reconstituting an Uncivil Service.*** Since it was secured by initiative in 1961, the law has been boiler-plated to protect insiders until nothing short of a major moral failure or repeated malfeasance justifies firing. Automatic pay raises reward the mediocre and discourage the meritorious. We need not return to the fire-at-will and patronage practices prior to 1935. We do need a means of ousting non-performers, bringing in new talent, and rewarding superior service. In 2006, just nine of 40,000 state employees were fired, five demoted, and five temporarily suspended without pay after second-level appeals.

***VIII. Restoring a Genuine Blanket Primary.*** Fewer than two-thirds of voters claim a party, yet all are now forced to align with one in primary elections. Only half as many people vote in primaries, which most often determine elections, as most legislative districts are "one party," or incumbent dominated. Partisan activists, a disproportionate share of the primary vote, skew nominations to those on the left or right. Centrist and "swing" voters, are often left with unpalatable choices. The Ninth Circuit Court's ruling that under the open primary the parties are denied control of their nominees reflected uninformed lawyers', not working politicians' understanding of voting mechanics. The upshot is that party regulars unrepresentative of the state as a whole distort the results, often killing their party's chances.

***IX. Ridding the state of the presidential primary***. This too over weights the partisan vote, advantaging candidates at the ends of the spectrum. Rushing these elections by a year favors candidates who can raise large amounts of money quickly and leaves the last states to hold elections bystanders. Continually moving dates back, protracting the length of campaigns, adds to candidate banality, and voter boredom.

***X. A constitutional amendment that sponsors of initiatives include a revenue source which must pass as a two part package.***

***XI. Civics.*** Most citizens do not know the structure of the two major parties, the requirements for and limitations of initiatives or referenda, or the respective (and overlapping) activities of three tiers of government. No wonder only three-quarters register to vote, just half of those vote in the primaries, and half of those voting for a president in the general election "fall off" before getting to state representative. This means nominations, and thus most legislative seats , can be won with the support of less than 15 percent of the adults. One semester of civics should be mandatory in the eleventh grade (since eighteen-year-olds vote).

# Appendices

## IMMIGRATION ROUTES AND EARLY SETTLEMENTS 1820-60

***Appendix 1:*** *From Philip L. Jackson and A. Jon Kimmerling, eds., Atlas of the Pacific Northwest. Corvallis, OSU Press, 1993. page 16*

darken

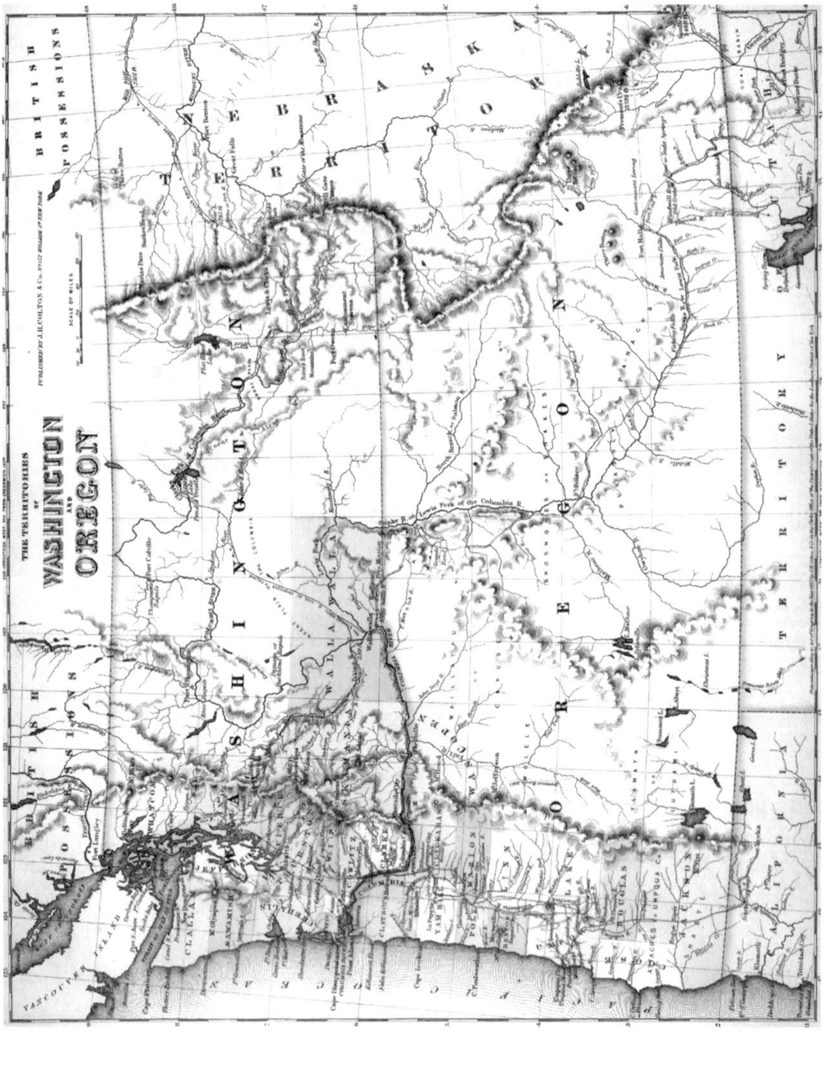

## STATE GOVERNMENT UNDER THE REORGANIZATION ACT OF 1921

*Appendix 2*

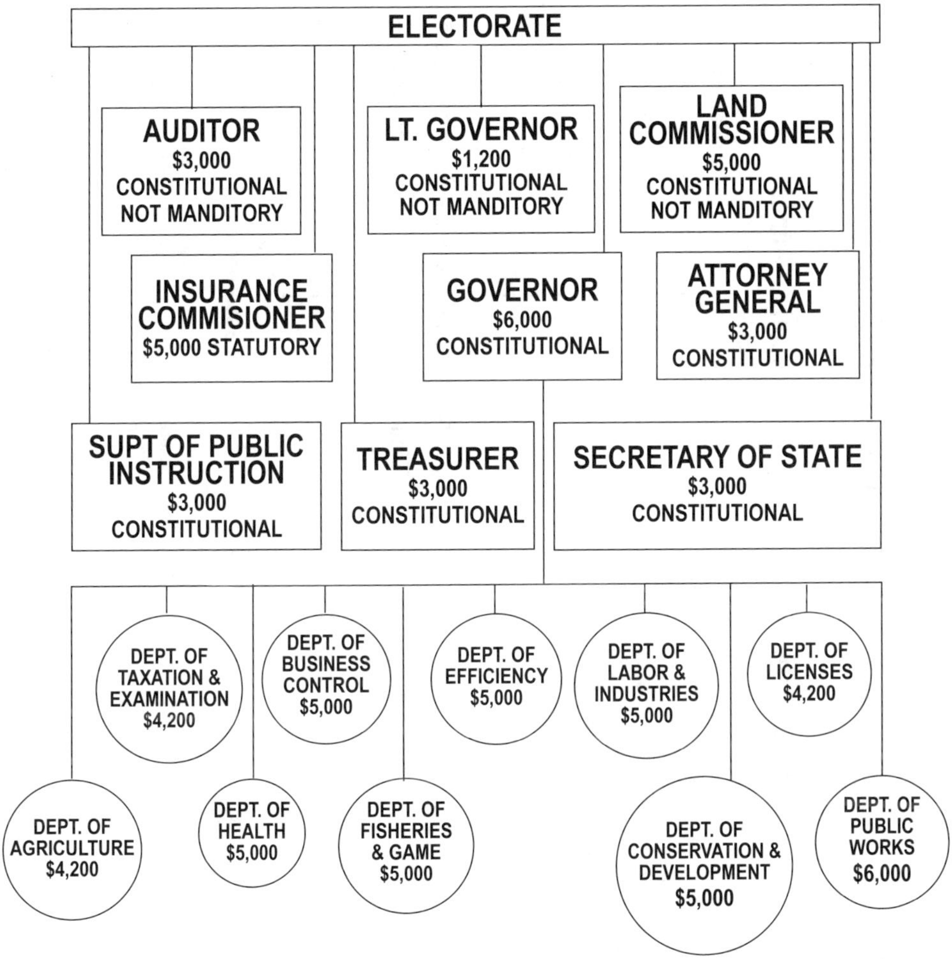

# 2009-2011 WASHINGTON STATE GOVERNMENT ORGANIZATION CHART

***Appendix 3:*** *Prepared by the Office of Financial Management, October 2009.*

## Legislative Branch

### Senate

- Joint Legislative Audit and Review Committee
- Joint Legislative Systems Committee
- Joint Transportation Committee
- Legislative Ethics Board

### House of Representatives

- Legislative Evaluation and Accountability Program Committee
- Office of the State Actuary
- Redistricting Commission (activated dicennially)
- Statute Law Committee (Code Reviser)

## Executive Branch

## Judicial Branch

### Supreme Court

- Administrative Office of the Courts
- Office of Civil Legal Aid
- Court of Appeals
- Commission on Judicial Conduct
- District Courts
- Law Library
- Municipal Courts
- Office of Public Defense
- Superior Courts
- Supreme Court

## Agencies Managed by Statewide Elected Officials

### Commissioner of Public Lands

- Department of Natural Resources
- Forest Practices Board

### Insurance Commissioner

### Treasurer

- Public Deposit Protection Commission
- State Finance Committee

### Lieutenant Governor

### Governor

#### Office of the Governor

- Office of the Education Ombudsman
- Governor's Office of Indian Affairs
- Office of the Family and Children's Ombudsman

### Attorney General

- Executive Ethics Board

### Superintendent of Public Instruction

- Board of Education
- Professional Educator Standards Board

### Auditor

### Secretary of State

- Productivity Board
- State Library

**Environment and Natural Resources** | **General Government** | **Transportation** | **Health and Human Services** | **Education** | **Community and Economic Development**

## Agencies Led by Governor-Appointed Executives

Dept. of Agriculture (commodity commissions)
Dept. of Ecology
Pollution Liability Insurance Program
Puget Sound Partnership
Recreation and Conservation Office

Board of Accountancy
Office of Administrative Hearing
Dept. of Archeaology and Historic Preservation
Consolidated Technology Services
Dept. of Enterprise Services
-Building Code Council
Dept. of Financial Institutions
Office of Financial Management
-Personal Resources Board
-Sentencing Guidelines
- Technology Services Board
Lottery Commission
Military Department
Dept. of Retirement Systems
Dept. of Revenue

Dept. of Licensing (occupational regulatory boards)
State Patrol
Traffic Safety Commission
Dept. of Transportation

Dept. of Corrections
-Indeterminate Sentence Review Board
Dept. of Employment Security
Dept. of Health (occupational regulatory boards)
Health Care Authority
-Public Employees Benefits Board
Dept. of Labor and Industries
Council for Children and Families
Dept. of Services for the Blind
Dept. of Social and Health Services
Dept. of Veterans Affairs

Center for Childhood Deafness and Hearing Loss
-Board of Trustees
Dept of Early Learning
School for the Blind
Workforce Training and Education Coordinating Board

Commission on African-American Affairs
Arts Comission
Commission on Asian Pacific American Affairs
Dept. of Commerce
- Economic Development Commsion
- Energy Facility Site Evaluation Council
-Public Works Board
Commission on Hispanic Affairs
Office of Minority and Women's Business Enterprises

## Agencies Under Authority of a Board

Columbia River Gorge Commission
Conservation Commission
Environmental and Land Use Hearings Office
-Growth Management Hearings Board
-Shorelines Hearing Board
Fish and Wildlife Commission
Board of Natural Resources
Parks and Recreation Commission
Washington Materials Management and Financing Authority

Caseload Forecast Council
Citizen's Commission on Salaries for Elected Officials
Economic and Revenue Forecast Council
Gamling Commission
Horse Racing Commission
Investment Board
Law Enforcement Officers' and Fire Fighters' Plan 2 Retirement System Board
Liquor Control Board
Pension Funding Council
Public Disclosure Commission
Public Employment Relations Commission
-Marine Employees' Commission
Board of Tax Appeals
Utilities and Transportation Commission
Board for Volunteer Firefighters and Reserve Officers

County Road Administration Board
Freight Mobility Strategic Investment Board
Board of Pilotage Commissioners
Transportation Improvement Board
Transportation Commission

Criminal Justice Training Commission
Board of Health
Health Care Facilities Authority
Human Rights Commission
Board of Industrial Insurance Appeals
Tobacco Settlement Authority

State Board for Community and Technical Colleges
Eastern Washington State Historical Society
Governing Boards of Four-Year Instititions of Higher Education
-University of Washington
-Washington State University
-Central Washington University
-Eastern Washington University
-Western Washington University
-The Evergreen State College
Higher Education Coordinating Board
Higher Education Facilities Authority
Spokane Intercollegiate Research and Technology Institute
Board of Trustees
-Community Colleges
-Technical Colleges
Washington State Historical Society

Convention and Trade Center
Economic Development Finance Authority
Housing Finance Commission
Life Sciences Discovery Fund Authority

# WASHINGTON STATE OPERATING BUDGET EXPENDITURES[1], POPULATION[2] AND U.S. IMPLICIT PRICE DEFLATOR

***Appendix 4:** Dollars in Thousands, LEAP Office*

| BIENNIUM | TOTAL BUDGETED FUNDS[1] | % CHANGE | GENERAL FUND STATE[1] | % CHANGE | ALL STATE FUNDS[1] | % CHANGE | ALL FEDERAL FUNDS[1] | % CHANGE | AVERAGE ANNUAL POPULATION[2] | % CHANGE | AVERAGE ANNUAL IPD[3] | % CHANGE |
|---|---|---|---|---|---|---|---|---|---|---|---|---|
| 2001-03 | 45,054,081 | 11.3 | 22,548,787 | 7.1 | 28,227,604 | 9.6 | 10,042,193 | 16.4 | 6,070,005 | 2.3 | 1.00000 | 3.7 |
| 1999-01 | 40,468,590 | 13.3 | 21,046,741 | 9.9 | 25,755,494 | 10.8 | 8,629,279 | 19.5 | 5,934,516 | 2.5 | 0.96462 | 4.1 |
| 1997-99 | 35,733,782 | 10.5 | 19,158,885 | 8.1 | 23,242,418 | 8.8 | 7,224,089 | 12.3 | 5,790,400 | 3.1 | 0.92691 | 2.8 |
| 1995-97 | 32,350,256 | 10.8 | 17,729,007 | 9.4 | 21,365,510 | 11.7 | 6,432,237 | 7.6 | 5,615,800 | 3.7 | 0.90129 | 4.3 |
| 1993-95 | 29,202,345 | 11.8 | 16,199,695 | 8.1 | 19,132,604 | 8.5 | 5,979,560 | 16.6 | 5,417,200 | 4.1 | 0.86503 | 4.6 |
| 1991-93 | 26,116,451 | 22.6 | 14,980,357 | 16.7 | 17,629,591 | 17.7 | 5,128,432 | 38.3 | 5,203,450 | 5.2 | 0.82731 | 6.7 |
| 1989-91 | 21,299,935 | 24.5 | 12,841,714 | 23.5 | 14,980,298 | 23.8 | 3,707,226 | 30.9 | 4,944,000 | 5.8 | 0.77531 | 8.8 |
| 1987-89 | 17,106,217 | 14.4 | 10,401,336 | 13.3 | 12,101,569 | 14.7 | 2,831,568 | 17.8 | 4,672,500 | 4.0 | 0.71248 | 7.5 |
| 1985-87 | 14,955,445 | 15.7 | 9,178,682 | 15.4 | 10,547,318 | 12.6 | 2,403,019 | 20.6 | 4,494,650 | 2.5 | 0.66279 | 6.1 |
| 1983-85 | 12,931,376 | 21.7 | 7,956,256 | 21.7 | 9,369,945 | 19.6 | 1,992,495 | 21.1 | 4,384,950 | 2.2 | 0.62494 | 8.4 |
| 1981-83 | 10,623,503 | 14.5 | 6,538,895 | 13.2 | 7,836,646 | 13.4 | 1,645,279 | -1.7 | 4,291,850 | 2.7 | 0.57667 | 14.9 |
| 1979-81 | 9,278,272 | 35.8 | 5,775,901 | 32.3 | 6,908,581 | 37.3 | 1,673,845 | 10.4 | 4,180,750 | 7.0 | 0.50209 | 20.1 |
| 1977-79 | 6,833,592 | 24.8 | 4,364,504 | 24.9 | 5,031,491 | 23.1 | 1,516,307 | 23.0 | 3,907,700 | 6.3 | 0.41817 | 13.9 |
| 1975-77 | 5,476,865 | 24.2 | 3,495,522 | 30.0 | 4,087,693 | 27.6 | 1,232,990 | 22.6 | 3,675,150 | 3.9 | 0.36710 | 15.0 |
| 1973-75 | 4,409,127 | 20.0 | 2,689,703 | 17.0 | 3,202,441 | 15.9 | 1,006,074 | 45.5 | 3,538,300 | 2.9 | 0.31928 | 15.7 |
| 1971-73 | 3,675,183 | 16.9 | 2,299,557 | 7.5 | 2,763,966 | 10.2 | 691,559 | 43.5 | 3,437,300 | 0.4 | 0.27587 | 8.1 |
| 1969-71 | 3,142,648 | 48.2 | 2,139,579 | 28.0 | 2,507,740 | | 481,968 | | 3,424,750 | | 0.25511 | |
| 1967-69 | 2,120,768 | 35.0 | 1,671,000 | 34.2 | | | | | | | | |
| 1965-67 | 1,570,830 | 17.5 | 1,244,900 | 16.2 | | | | | | | | |
| 1963-65 | 1,336,984 | 12.3 | 1,071,100 | | | | | | | | | |
| 1961-63 | 1,190,210 | 21.9 | | | | | | | | | | |
| 1959-61 | 976,583 | 1.8 | | | | | | | | | | |
| 1957-59 | 959,680 | | | | | | | | | | | |

[1]Expenditure data for 1957-59 through 1967-69 from Governor's biennial budget documents or LEAP archives; data for 1969-71 through 2001-03 from LEAP database
[2]Unofficial fiscal year population estimates based on quarterly interpolation of OFM April 1 population estimate provided by Economic and Revenue Forecast Council.
[3]U.S. IPD converted to biennial basis (2001-03 =1.0); source data from Economic and Revenue Forecast Council March 2005 forecast

## TOTAL EXPENDITURES BY FUNCTIONAL AREA ALL FUNDS

***Appendix 5:*** *Total Expenditures by Functional Area, 1981-2006 OFM, Data Book, 2007, page 37*

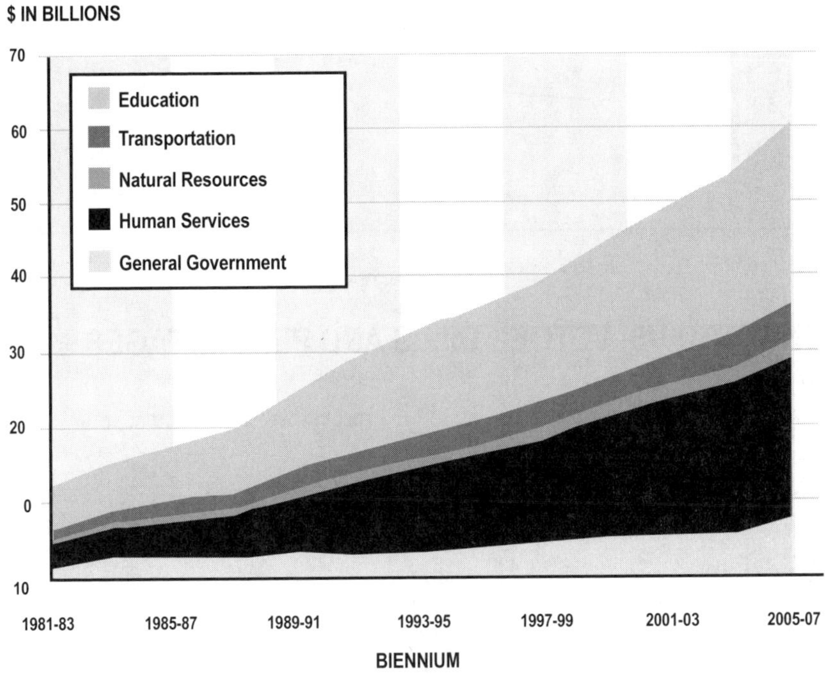


## EXPENDITURES AS A PERCENT OF PERSONAL INCOME

***Appendix 6:*** *1983-2007 OFM, Data Book, 2009 page 31*

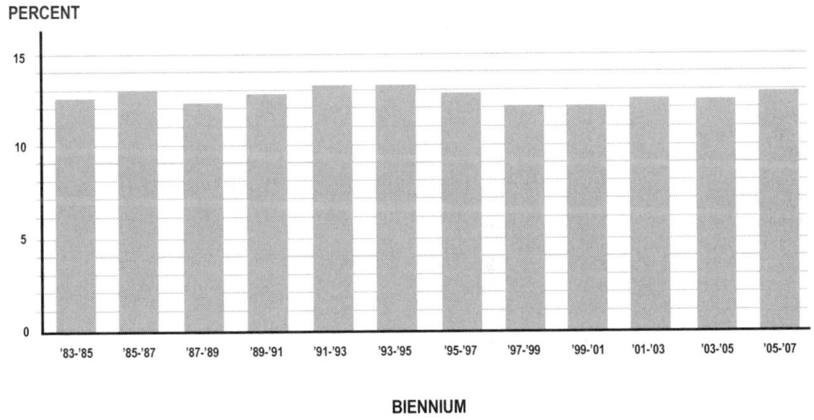

# FULL-TIME EMPLOYEES PER 1,000 POPULATION

*Appendix 7: 1975-2006 OFM, Data Book, 2007, page 42*

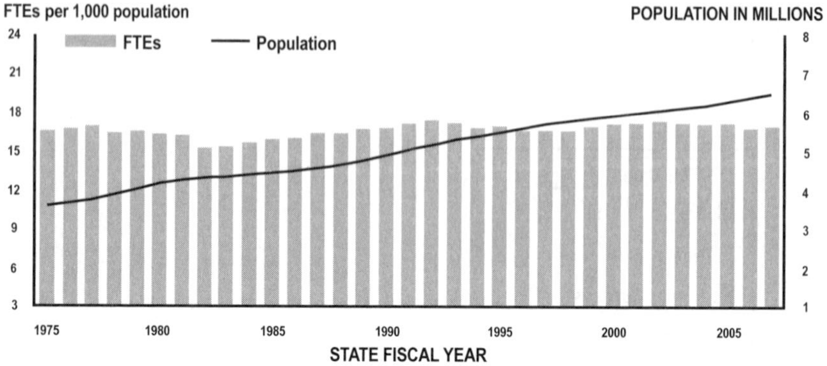


# ENACTED VS. VETOED BILLS AND PERCENTAGES

*Appendix 8A: 1965-2008*

| YEAR | GOVERNOR | ENACTED | PASSED | % | FULL VETOS | % | PARTIAL VETOS | % |
|---|---|---|---|---|---|---|---|---|
| 1965 | Evans | 332 | 317 | 95.48 | 15 | 4.52 | 24 | 7.23 |
| 1967 | Evans | 391 | 391 | 100.00 | 0 | 0 | 28 | 7.16 |
| 1969 | Evans | 426 | 425 | 99.77 | 1 | 0.23 | 42 | 9.86 |
| 1970 | Evans | 104 | 103 | 99.04 | 1 | 0.96 | 14 | 13.46 |
| 1971 | Evans | 391 | 384 | 98.21 | 7 | 1.79 | 40 | 10.23 |
| 1972 | Evans | 157 | 156 | 99.38 | 1 | 0.64 | 14 | 8.92 |
| 1973 | Evans | 416 | 402 | 98.83 | 14 | 3.37 | 35 | 8.41 |
| 1974 | Evans | 198 | 190 | 95.96 | 8 | 4.04 | 31 | 15.66 |
| 1975 | Evans | 361 | 341 | 94.46 | 20 | 5.54 | 34 | 9.42 |
| 1976 | Evans | 132 | 130 | 98.48 | 2 | 1.52 | 8 | 6.06 |
| 1977 | Ray | 454 | 443 | 97.58 | 11 | 2.42 | 18 | 3.96 |
| 1979 | Ray | 424 | 419 | 98.82 | 5 | 1.18 | 20 | 4.72 |
| 1980 | Ray | 185 | 179 | 96.76 | 6 | 3.24 | 10 | 5.41 |
| 1981 | Spellman | 382 | 354 | 97.79 | 8 | 2.21 | 27 | 7.46 |
| 1982 | Spellman | 302 | 299 | 99.01 | 3 | 0.99 | 18 | 5.96 |
| 1983 | Spellman | 395 | 381 | 96.46 | 14 | 3.54 | 22 | 5.57 |
| 1984 | Spellman | 289 | 281 | 97.23 | 8 | 2.77 | 25 | 8.05 |
| 1985 | Gardner | 477 | 470 | 98.53 | 7 | 1.47 | 52 | 10.90 |
| 1986 | Gardner | 325 | 324 | 99.69 | 1 | 0.31 | 46 | 14.15 |
| 1987 | Gardner | 544 | 535 | 98.35 | 9 | 1.65 | 85 | 11.95 |
| 1988 | Gardner | 291 | 288 | 98.97 | 3 | 1.03 | 27 | 9.28 |
| 1989 | Gardner | 450 | 432 | 96.00 | 18 | 4.00 | 85 | 14.44 |
| 1990 | Gardner | 334 | 326 | 97.60 | 8 | 2.40 | 37 | 11.08 |
| 1991 | Gardner | 397 | 388 | 97.73 | 9 | 2.27 | 45 | 11.34 |
| 1992 | Gardner | 240 | 233 | 97.08 | 7 | 2.92 | 26 | 10.83 |
| 1993 | Lowry | 553 | 545 | 98.55 | 8 | 1.45 | 35 | 6.33 |
| 1994 | Lowry | 317 | 310 | 97.79 | 7 | 2.21 | 27 | 8.52 |
| 1995 | Lowry | 439 | 422 | 96.13 | 17 | 3.87 | 41 | 9.34 |
| 1996 | Lowry | 325 | 303 | 93.23 | 22 | 6.77 | 27 | 8.31 |
| 1997 | Lowry | 457 | 394 | 86.21 | 63 | 13.79 | 63 | 13.79 |
| 1998 | Lowry | 348 | 320 | 91.95 | 28 | 8.05 | 41 | 11.78 |
| 1999 | Locke | 412 | 406 | 98.54 | 6 | 1.46 | 23 | 5.58 |
| 2000 | Locke | 282 | 259 | 98.85 | 3 | 1.15 | 14 | 5.34 |
| 2001 | Locke | 370 | 381 | 97.57 | 9 | 2.43 | 27 | 7.30 |
| 2002 | Locke | 368 | 363 | 98.64 | 5 | 1.36 | 26 | 7.07 |
| 2003 | Locke | 444 | 436 | 98.20 | 8 | 1.80 | 32 | 7.21 |
| 2004 | Locke | 277 | 273 | 98.64 | 4 | 1.44 | 18 | 6.50 |
| 2005 | Gregoire | 516 | 509 | 98.64 | 7 | 1.36 | 32 | 6.20 |
| 2006 | Gregoire | 370 | 384 | 98.38 | 6 | 1.62 | 17 | 4.59 |
| 2007 | Gregoire | 524 | 524 | 100.00 | 0 | 0.00 | 37 | 7.06 |
| 2008 | Gregoire | 328 | 325 | 99.09 | 3 | 0.91 | 25 | 7.62 |

## WASHINGTON STATE LEGISLATURE ENACTED BILLS AND VETOES 1965-2005

***Appendix 8B:*** *Gubernatorial Vetoes Compared, 1965-2005. Sources: WSS, Committee Services and LEAP (Legislative Evaluation and Appraisal Program.*

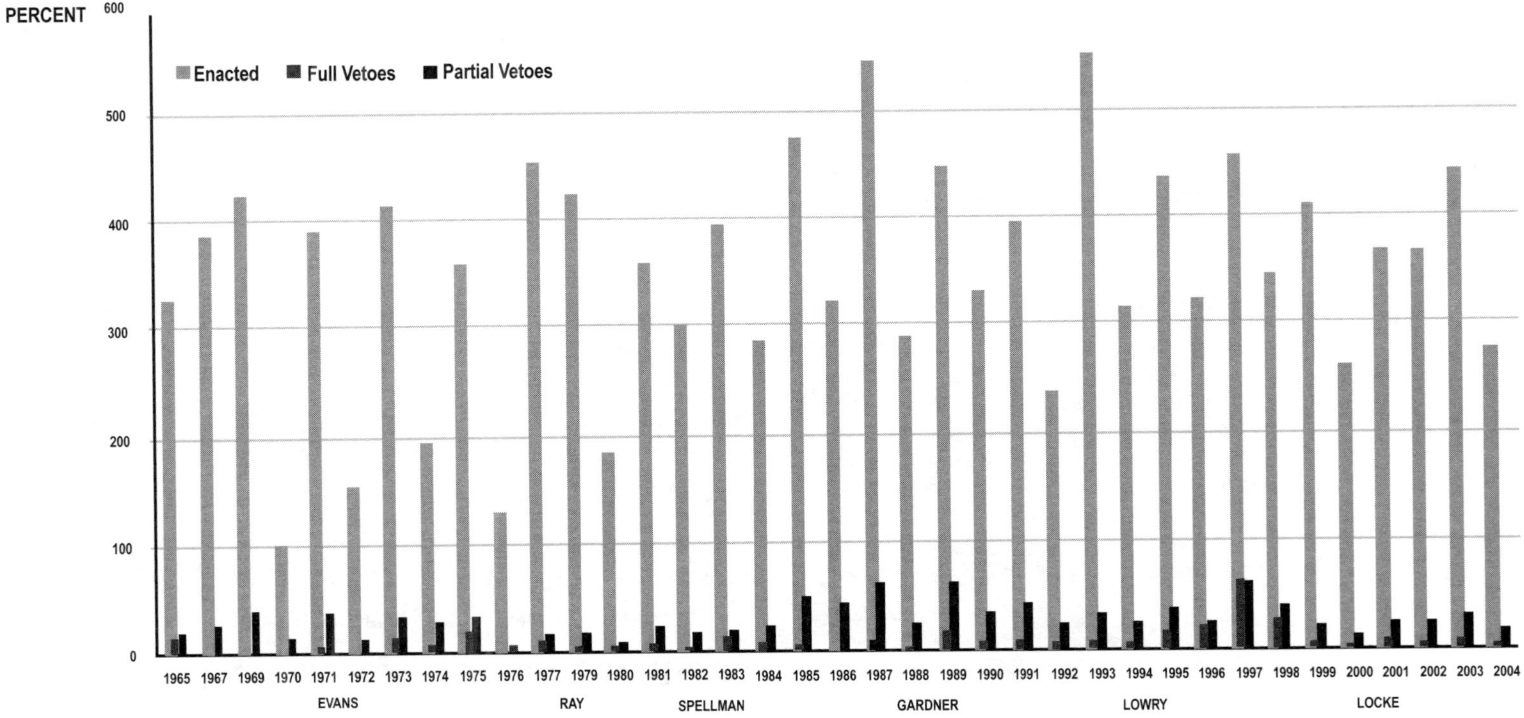

*Appendix 9:*

## PERSONAL AND PROFESSIONAL BIOGRAPHIES OF THE GOVERNORS, 1889-2005

| Governor | Term(s) | Party | Year born | Birthplace | Education | Profession(s) | Home |
|---|---|---|---|---|---|---|---|
| Elisha P. Ferry[1] | 1889-93 | R | 1825 | MI | " Common School," Read Law | Lawyer, Mayor (Waukegan, IL), Bank Commissioner (IL) Surveyor General (WA) | Seattle |
| John McGraw | 1893-97 | R | 1850 | ME | Elementary School | General Store Clerk, Owner American House, gold miner, police-man, Seattle City Marshall, Police Chief, King County Sheriff, lawyer, [President Sea-First Bank] | Seattle |
| John R. Rogers | 1897-1901 | P; D | 1838 | ME | "Common School" | Pharmacist, Drugstore owner, Farmer, Editor, Grocer, State Representative | Puyallup |
| Henry McBrde | 1901-05 | R | 1856 | UTT | Trinity College, CT, Read Law | School Teacher (Oak Harbor),Telegraph Office, Lawyer, Skagit County Prosecutor, Superior Court Judge, Lieutenant Governor | Oak Harbor |
| Albert E. Mead | 1905-09 | R | 1856 | KA | Public School, Southern University Law School | Mayor of Blaine, State Representative, Whatcom County Prosecutor | Blaine, Bellingham |
| Samuel Cos-grove | 1909 (d. 3/28/1909) | R | 1847 | OH | BA, Wesleyan University | Lawyer, Mayor of Pomeroy | Pomeroy |
| Marion E. Hay | 1909-13 | R | 1865 | WT | Business College | Store Clerk (MI) General Store (Davenport), Mercantile (Wilbur) Big Bend Land Company (Spokane), Lieutenant Governor | Davenport, Wilbur, Spokane |
| Ernest Lister | 1913-19 | D | 1870 | Halifax, England | Business College | Iron Molder, Chair Tacoma City Council, State Board of Control | Tacoma |
| Louis F. Hart | 1919-25 | R | 1862 | MO | "Public School"; Read Law | Teacher, Lawyer, Grand Secretary, International Order of Odd Fellows, Lieutenant Governor | Snohomish |
| Roland H. Hartley | 1925-32 | R | 1864 | New Brunswick, Canada | "Public School," Minneapolis Academy | Secretary to the Mayor, Brainerd, MN, lumber business, Secretary to the Governor (MN), Everett City Council, State Representative | Everett |
| Clarence D. Martin[2] | 1933-41 | D | 1886 | Cheney | Cheney Normal School | Mayor of Cheney, Flour Miller, Chair Democratic State Central Committee, State Representative | Cheney |

| Governor | Term(s) | Party | Year born | Birthplace | Education | Profession(s) | Home |
|---|---|---|---|---|---|---|---|
| Arthur B. Langlie[3] | 1941-45, 1949-57 | R | 1900 | Lanesboro, MN | BA, LLB, UWA | Lawyer, City Councilman, Naval Officer [President, McCall's Corporation] | Bremerton, Seattle |
| Monrad C. Wallgren | 1945-49 | D | 1891 | Des Moines, IA | "Public School, " business and Optometric School | Jewelry store/ Optometry clinic, Congressman, U.S. Senator | Everett |
| Albert D. Rossellini | 1957-65 | D | 1910 | Tacoma | BA, LLB, UWA | Lawyer, Assistant King County Prosecutor, State Senator, [WA. State Transportation Commissioner] | Tacoma, Seattle |
| Daniel J. Evans[3] | 1965-77 | R | 1925 | Seattle | BS, MS, UWA | Naval officer, Civil Engineer, State Representative, [President ,The Evergreen State College, U.S. Senator, Consultant, UWA regent] | Seattle |
| Dixy Lee Ray | 1977-81 | D | 1914 | Tacoma | BS Mills College, PhD, Stanford | Associate Professor Marine Biology, UWA, Director, Pacific Science Center, Chair, Atomic Energy Commission | Seattle |
| John Spellman | 1981-85 | R | 1926 | Seattle | BA, Seattle University LLB Georgetown U. | Lawyer, King County Commissioners, King County Executive | Seattle |
| Booth Gardner | 1985-93 | D | 1936 | Tacoma | BA UWA, MBA Harvard | Associate Dean, School of Business UPS, State Senator, President, Laird Norton Co, Pierce County Executive [U.S. Ambassador to GATT] | Tacoma |
| Mike Lowry | 1993-97 | D | 1939 | St. John, WA | BA, WSU | Chief of Staff, Senate Ways and Means Committee, King County Councilman, Congressman [non-profit executive] | Renton |
| Gary Locke | 1997-2005 | D | 1950 | Seattle | BA, Yale LLB, Boston University | Lawyer, Asst. King County Prosecutor, Counsel to State Senate Democratic Caucus, State Representative, King County Executive, [U.S. Secretary of Commerce, Ambassador to China] | Seattle |

Source WSA, State Governors

[1]Ferry was appointed the first Governor of Washington Territory by President Grant (1872)

[2]Clarence Martin was the first governor born in Washington and the last resident of Eastern Washington

[3]Arthur Langlie and Daniel Evans are the state's only three-term governors.

Abbreviations and notes:

"Common School": is assumed to be six years," Public School" six or eight years, and "normal School two years of college.

Birth places: WT = Washington Territory; UTT = Utah Territory.

Party designations: R = Republican, D = Democrat, P = Populist

Bracketed items at the end of the professional roles indicate tasks after being governor.

# ASSESSING THE GOVERNORS

***Appendix 10:***

The State Constitution says only: "The supreme executive power of this state shall be vested in the Governor, who shall hold his office for a term of four years," (Article III, Sec 2), and that he shall "enforce the laws." The "understood" tasks have become very clear. For continuity, the chapter on each governor in the last 65 years has these key threads for appraising him/her as:

**I. Politician and Party Leader.** Governors are now less ideological and partisan and more pragmatic.4 But they are still the titular leaders of their party, and politics is a team sport. How deeply the governor can be involved in other races without alienating the opposition is a delicate balance. What did he/ (or she) do to gain or sustain majorities in both houses of the legislature, or if part of the Minority, work with opposites to achieve what was possible by negotiation and compromise? Did he (or she) attract and help and tutor prospects for other state offices and the legislature, and campaign for them? An assertive executive exerts effectively chooses the state party chair, and thus which wing of each has the upper or blocking hand. And critically, can he fully exploit his unique forum, one which can be equal to 147 legislators?5 Is he lucid with the media? Does he attract their attention or animus? This is an art form, as the media are prone to focus on conflict and exaggerate disputes. How many of the over 500 yearly invitations to speak to the public are accepted, and are the messages effectively delivered?

**II. Executive/Administrator.** Does he have credibility and network to attract a skilled transition team and 40 cabinet and "small agency" directors in 60 days? Are his judicial appointments, and the 1,000 a year to 275 boards and commissions of consistently high quality? Is he quick to understand and shape a $43 billion biennial budget (2007-09), and relate to the 50 central staff and those in the Office of Financial Management who convert the executives intents into policy?6 Does he have cordial relations with the state's congressmen regardless of party, and a grasp of the host of major federal agencies which control distribution of funds? Has he played a significant roles with peers in the National Governor's Association, and contributed to its collective influence on the Potomac? The "new federalism" demands it. How much power the governor has in expanding the state's economic potential internationally remains in doubt, but overseas "missions" have now a part of his/her mantra.

**III. As Legislator.** The capacities of legislatures have risen dramatically, even as decline in civic ethics has drained them of leadership caliber talent. In 1960 only 18 state legislatures met annually. By 1980 most did, and there were 18,000 full-time legislative staff in the 50 states. Gubernatorial jousts with lawmakers rose in tandem. Governors claim to be the only one who can speak for the state as a whole, rather than parochial interests, and with a long-range view. Yet the more assertive an executive is, the greater legislative resistance. Divided partisan control, favored by many voters, has been often as not the case in Washington. Contrarily, large partisan majorities invite splintering. Is the governor a melder in his party, and between the parties, or often a source of contention? Does the governor highlight, if not set the agenda with substantive "executive request" bills? Are they prioritized, and limited in number? What is his success rate? Is he proactive, or lets bills come to him? What is his comprehension of the issues being debated, and those to be anticipated? Does he/she keeping an open door, listen, lobby, and play the "honest broker" with lawmakers? What is his reputation among skilled professional lobbyists?

**IV. Wielder of the Veto.** This Damocles' sword, swung with increasing frequency, is now a chief legislative instrument of gubernatorial power.7 Is it used discreetly on sound advice, to erase errors, duplication, or what is constitutionally questionable? Or is it overdone as a partisan weapon or a means to force personal preferences? Governor Evans was overruled by the Supreme Court after he effectively reversed the intent of the Landlord-Tennant Act in 1977. Governor Lowry, a "strict constructionist," proved the most adept practitioner of the partial veto. Gary Locke vetoed a quarter of the initial offerings of the GOP 1995 legislature because he philosophically disagreed. All this underlines a visible shift to using this power as circumstances dictate. "The governor is part of the legislative process," but to what degree should he alter its results post facto? Does he give early warnings and signal clear alternatives, or axe crucial bills after the legislature has gone home? How often does is he persuaded by his directors? And do they have viable reasons for objecting, or are they simply protecting prerogatives?

**V. As a Profile, in Ethics.** At term's end, a retiring governor should leave no reasonable informed person, as opposed to predictable partisans, disappointed office seekers or cranks with reason to challenge to his essential integrity. Has he set a positive example of public service, kept citizens informed, given them opportunities to participate? Are the number of firings or defaults by appointees minimal? What do credible observers think of their quality? Do judicial appointments reflect a philosophical balance of the state, how many are rejected at the polls, and what has been his interaction with the High Court?

All of this to underline the matrix of capabilities needed and the magnitude of the governors' tasks. Executive leadership is hard to isolate, and harder to predict. At the end of the day it is the ingenuity element, the governor's personal chemistry, ability and agility in using his power that spells default or dignifies him in the eyes of those best able to judge.

The ultimate criterion is: does he/she spend political capital, or simply raise it, and reserve it for the next election? All major reforms worthy of the name attract hordes of enemies, are politically risky and erosive. Is the incumbent willing to make the investments needed to meet the toughest challenges?

## AN APPRAISAL OF WASHINGTON'S GOVERNORS 1941-2005

*BASED ON THE FIVE SIGNIFICANT CRITERIA APPEARING IN EACH CHAPTER. SCALE 1-5*

| Governor | Leader | Administator[1] | Party Head/ Politician[2] | Ethics/ Profile[3] | Legislator[4] | Totals |
|---|---|---|---|---|---|---|
| Langlie | 3 | 3 | 3 | 3.5 | 4.5 | 17 |
| Wallgren | 1 | 1 | 2 | 2 | 2 | 8 |
| Rosellini | 3 | 3 | 3 | 3 | 2.5 | 14.5 |
| Evans | 5 | 4 | 5 | 5 | 4.5 | 23.5 |
| Ray | 2.5 | 2 | 1.5 | 2 | 2.5 | 8.5 |
| Spellman | 2.5 | 2 | 2.5 | 2 | 3 | 12 |
| Gardner | 4 | 3 | 3.5 | 3 | 4 | 17 |
| Lowry | 2.5 | 2.5 | 3 | 2 | 4 | 14 |
| Locke | 4 | 4 | 3.5 | 3.5 | 4 | 18.5 |
| **Averages** | **2.6** | **2.9** | **2.8** | **3.1** | **2.8** | **14.33** |

*[1] As a leader, force of personality*

*[2] Administrative ability and effort, talent of cabinet, improvements in progress.*

*[3] Effectiveness as a campaigner, in recruiting and supporting elected officials of his/her party, as its titular head.*

*[4] Demonstarble ethical allegations against the executive or his cabinet, consistency or lapses in personal ethics. Did he/she leave the office better in the public eye it was found?*

*[5] Number, import and passage rate executive requests; the governors relations with the legislature and the United States congressmen, and facility in promoting his/her interests.*

# WASHINGTON STATE GOVERNOR GENERAL ELECTION RESULTS 1892-2004

*Appendix 11:*

| 2004 CANDIDATES | PARTY | VOTES | PERCENTAGE |
|---|---|---|---|
| Christine Gregoire | D | 1,373,361 | 48.87% |
| Dino Rossi | R | 1,373,232 | 48.87% |
| Ruth Bennett | L | 63,465 | 2.26% |

| 2000 CANDIDATES | PARTY | VOTES | PERCENTAGE |
|---|---|---|---|
| Gary Locke | D | 1,441,973 | 58.38% |
| John Carlson | R | 980,060 | 39.68% |
| Steve W. LePage | L | 47,819 | 1.94% |

| 1996 CANDIDATES | PARTY | VOTES | PERCENTAGE |
|---|---|---|---|
| Gary Locke | D | 1,296,492 | 57.96% |
| Ellen Craswell | R | 940538 | 42.04% |

| 1992 CANDIDATES | PARTY | VOTES | PERCENTAGE |
|---|---|---|---|
| Mike Lowry | D | 1,184,315 | 52.16% |
| Ken Eikenberry | R | 1,086,216 | 47.84% |

| 1988 CANDIDATES | PARTY | VOTES | PERCENTAGE |
|---|---|---|---|
| Bob Williams | R | 708,481 | 37.79% |
| Booth Gardner | D | 1,166,448 | 62.21% |

| 1984 CANDIDATES | PARTY | VOTES | PERCENTAGE |
|---|---|---|---|
| John Spellman | R | 881,994 | 46.69% |
| Booth Gardner | D | 1,006,993 | 53.31% |

| 1980 CANDIDATES | PARTY | VOTES | PERCENTAGE |
|---|---|---|---|
| John Spellman | R | 981,083 | 56.68% |
| Jim McDermott | D | 749,813 | 43.32% |

| 1976 CANDIDATES | PARTY | VOTES | PERCENTAGE |
|---|---|---|---|
| John D. Spellman | R | 687039 | 44.43% |
| Dixy Lee Ray | D | 821797 | 53.14% |
| Henry Killman | SL | 4137 | 0.27% |
| Art Manning | AI | 12406 | 0.80% |
| Evelyn Olafson | USL | 1364 | 0.09% |
| Red Kelly | OWL | 12400 | 0.80% |
| Patricia A. Bethard | SW | 3106 | 0.20% |
| Maurice W. Willey | L | 4133 | 0.27% |

| 1972 CANDIDATES | PARTY | VOTES | PERCENTAGE |
|---|---|---|---|
| Albert D. Rosellini | D | 630613 | 42.82% |
| Daniel J. Evans | R | 747825 | 50.78% |
| Vick Gould | TAX | 86843 | 5.90% |
| Henry Killman | SL | 2709 | 0.18% |
| Robin David | SW | 4552 | 0.31% |

| 1968 CANDIDATES | PARTY | VOTES | PERCENTAGE |
|---|---|---|---|
| John J. O'Connell | D | 560262 | 44.28% |
| Daniel J. Evans | R | 692378 | 54.72% |
| Ken Chriswell | Constitutional | 11602 | 0.92% |
| Henry Killman | SW | 1113 | 0.09% |

| 1964 CANDIDATES | PARTY | VOTES | PERCENTAGE |
|---|---|---|---|
| Daniel J. Evans | R | 697256 | 55.77% |
| Albert D. Rosellini | D | 548692 | 43.89% |
| Henry Killman | SL | 4326 | 0.35% |

| 1960 CANDIDATES | PARTY | VOTES | PERCENTAGE |
|---|---|---|---|
| Lloyd Andrews | R | 594122 | 48.87% |
| Albert D. Rosellini | D | 611987 | 50.34% |
| Henry Killman | SL | 8647 | 0.71% |
| Jack W. Wright | SW | 992 | 0.08% |

| 1956 CANDIDATES | PARTY | VOTES | PERCENTAGE |
|---|---|---|---|
| Emmett T. Anderson | R | 508041 | 45.00% |
| Albert D. Rosellini | D | 616773 | 54.63% |
| Henry Killman | SL | 4163 | 0.37% |

| 1952 CANDIDATES | PARTY | VOTES | PERCENTAGE |
|---|---|---|---|
| Hugh B. Mitchell | D | 510675 | 47.35% |
| Arthur B. Langlie | R | 567822 | 52.65% |

| 1948 CANDIDATES | PARTY | VOTES | PERCENTAGE |
|---|---|---|---|
| Mon C. Wallgren | D | 417035 | 47.22% |
| Arthur B. Langlie | R | 445958 | 50.50% |
| Russell H. Fluent | P | 19224 | 2.18% |
| Henry Killman | SL | 780 | 0.09% |
| Daniel Roberts | SW | 144 | 0.02% |

| 1944 CANDIDATES | PARTY | VOTES | PERCENTAGE |
|---|---|---|---|
| Mon C. Wallgren | D | 428,834 | 51.51% |
| Arthur B. Langlie | R | 400,604 | 48.12% |
| Henry E.O. Gusey | SL | 1,369 | 0.16% |
| Allen Emerson | PR | 1,676 | 0.20% |

| 1940 CANDIDATES | PARTY | VOTES | PERCENTAGE |
|---|---|---|---|
| C.C. Dill | D | 386,706 | 49.49% |
| Arthur B. Langlie | D | 392,522 | 50.24% |
| P.J. Ater | SL | 426 | 0.05% |
| John Brockway | C | 1,674 | 0.21% |

| 1936 CANDIDATES | PARTY | VOTES | PERCENTAGE |
|---|---|---|---|
| Clarence D. Martin | D | 466,550 | 69.36% |
| Roland H. Hartley | R | 189,141 | 28.12% |
| John F. McKay | S | 4,221 | 0.63% |
| Eugene Solie | SL | 466 | 0.07% |
| O.M. Nelson | U | 6,349 | 0.94% |
| Harold P. Brockway | C | 1,939 | 0.29% |
| William M. Bouck | FLC | 1,994 | 0.30% |
| Malcolm M. Moore | CH | 1,947 | 0.29% |

| 1932 CANDIDATES | PARTY | VOTES | PERCENTAGE |
|---|---|---|---|
| John A. Gellatly | R | 207,497 | 33.75% |
| Clarence D. Martin | D | 352,215 | 57.29% |
| John F. McKay | S | 9,987 | 1.62% |
| Maslen Meade | IC | 378 | 0.06% |
| Edward Kriz | SL | 449 | 0.07% |
| L.C. Hicks | LB | 41,710 | 6.78% |
| Fred E. Walker | C | 2,532 | 0.41% |

| 1928 CANDIDATES | PARTY | VOTES | PERCENTAGE |
|---|---|---|---|
| Roland H. Hartley | R | 281991 | 56.21% |
| Scott Bullitt | D | 214334 | 42.73% |
| James F. Stark | SL | 3343 | 0.67% |
| Walter Price | S | 1262 | 0.25% |
| Aaron Fyslerman | WC | 698 | 0.14% |

| 1924 CANDIDATES | PARTY | VOTES | PERCENTAGE |
|---|---|---|---|
| Roland H. Hartley | R | 220162 | 56.41% |
| Ben F. Hill | D | 126447 | 32.40% |
| J.R. Oman | FL | 40073 | 10.27% |
| David Burgess | SL | 770 | 0.20% |
| Emil Hermann | S | 898 | 0.23% |
| William A. Gilmore | STA | 1954 | 0.50% |

| 1920 CANDIDATES | PARTY | VOTES | PERCENTAGE |
|---|---|---|---|
| Louis F. Hart | R | 210662 | 52.74% |
| W.W. Black | D | 66079 | 16.54% |
| David Burgess | SL | 1296 | 0.32% |
| Robert Bridges | FL | 121371 | 30.39% |

| 1916 CANDIDATES | PARTY | VOTES | PERCENTAGE |
|---|---|---|---|
| Henry McBride | R | 167809 | 44.43% |
| Ernest Lister | D | 181645 | 48.09% |
| James E. Bradford | P | 2894 | 0.77% |
| A.B.L. Gellerman | PR | 3514 | 0.93% |
| L.E. Katterfield | S | 21117 | 5.59% |
| James E. Riordan | SL | 623 | 0.16% |

| 1912 CANDIDATES | PARTY | VOTES | PERCENTAGE |
|---|---|---|---|
| M.E. Hay | R | 96629 | 30.36% |
| Ernest Lister | D | 97251 | 30.55% |
| Anna A. Maley | S | 37155 | 11.67% |
| Abraham L. Brearcliff | SL | 1369 | 0.43% |
| Geo. F. Stivers | PR | 8163 | 2.56% |
| Robert T. Hodge | P | 77792 | 24.44% |

| 1908 CANDIDATES | PARTY | VOTES | PERCENTAGE |
|---|---|---|---|
| Samuel G. Cosgrove | R | 110190 | 62.56% |
| John Pattison | D | 58126 | 33.00% |
| Geo. E. Boomer | S | 4311 | 2.45% |
| A.S. Caton | PR | 3514 | 1.99% |

| 1904 CANDIDATES | PARTY | VOTES | PERCENTAGE |
|---|---|---|---|
| Albert E. Mead | R | 74278 | 51.34% |
| George Turner | D | 59119 | 40.86% |
| Wm. McCormick | SL | 1070 | 0.74% |
| D. Burgess | S | 7420 | 5.13% |
| Ambrose H. Sherwood | PR | 2782 | 1.92% |

| 1900 CANDIDATES | PARTY | VOTES | PERCENTAGE |
|---|---|---|---|
| J.M. Frink | R | 49860 | 46.81% |
| John R. Rogers | D | 52048 | 48.86% |
| R.E. Dunlap | PR | 2103 | 1.97% |
| Wm. McCormick | SL | 843 | 0.79% |
| W.C.B. Randolph | SD | 1670 | 1.57% |

| 1896 CANDIDATES | PARTY | VOTES | PERCENTAGE |
|---|---|---|---|
| J.R. Rogers | | 50,840 | |
| P.C. Sullivan | | 38,151 | |
| R.E. Dunlap | | 2,542 | |

| 1892 CANDIDATES | PARTY | VOTES | PERCENTAGE |
|---|---|---|---|
| John H. McGraw | R | 33,281 | |
| Henry J. Snively | D | 28960 | |
| C.W. Young, | Peo | 23,750 | |
| Roger S. Greene | Pro | 3,937 | |

# *Endnotes*

## Chapter 1: The Territorials

1 See Paul L. Beckett, From Wilderness to Enabling Act: The Evolution of the State of Washington. Pullman: WSUP, 1968.

2 Max Ferrand, Legislation of the Congress for the Organized Territories of the United States, 1789-1895. Newark: Michael T. Simmons, "The Transition of the Washington Executive from Territory to Statehood." PNQ 55 (4/64): 76.

3 Earl S. Pomeroy, "The Territories and the United States: Studies in the Control of Dependencies." MA, UW, 1940, 237-60; Congressional Globe, 32nd Congress, Second Sess., 1020, 1853; Organic Act, Sec. 1.

4 Wilfred J. Airey, "A History of the Constitution and Government of Washington Territory." Ph.D., UW, 1945, 23-24. See "Washington's Secretaries of State — Past and Present." Olympia: OSOS, 2001, and the author's "The Elastic Executive: A Brief History of the Office of Secretary of State." Unpublished MS, 1998, AP. Illustrative individuals are in John Macceachem, "Elwood Evans, Lawyer-Historian." PNQ 52 (1/61): 15-23; H. K. Hines, D.D., An Illustrated History of the State of Washington. Chicago: The Lewis Publishing Company, 1893, (on O.W. Holmes); and, As Told by the Pioneers: Reminiscences of Pioneer Life in Washington. V. 3. Olympia: The State Printer, 1938 (On Dr. Ernest Hutchinson).

5 Mason was acting governor in 1854, 1855, and 1858-60. His praiseworthy service ended at age 29 for the reason above. Mason Estate, WSA acc. 87-8-481, 1, "First Election Returns, 1854"; Pioneer and Democrat (Olympia), 7/9/1859; Henry McGill filled the chief executive's post for so long the word "acting" was dropped from his title in popular usage. He saved the capitol at Olympia from the predatory designs of Vancouver by spending $3,000 to start work, ignoring orders from "Washington [D.C.] City." See Robert E. Ficken, Territorial Washington. Pullman: WSUP, 2002, 2-53.

6 "Washington's Secretaries of State," Appendix 2, of The Secretary of State: The Office and Duties. Lexington: The National Association of Secretaries of State, 1991. In Oregon, which became a state in 1859, the secretary accrued power for a century. He, the governor, and the treasurer were a Board of Control, and "ran the state." The secretary prepared the budget until 1921 and was on the Board of Equalization and the Tax Commission. At the office's peak in 1951, he had a branch office in Portland and 22 field offices employing 647 people. Washington's secretary has never supervised more than 200. Oregon State Constitution, Article V, Section 8a, and Article VIII, Section f. In Oregon, the office now supervises the Archives, Audits (partially performing the roles played by the State Auditor in other states), Business Services, Corporations and Elections, is on the Board of Accountancy, and the Tax Examiners. In Washington, it has the first and third functions, the State Library, and a several tertiary tasks. The office is now an

artifact. Governor Dan Evans (1965-77), and Secretary of State Bruce Chapman (1975-81), tried to eliminate it, as Alaska and Hawaii have. See PI 5/22/80. Supervision of elections might go to the Lieutenant Governor, filling out a part-time job, the Archives to the State Historical Association, now a quasi-state agency, and licensing of non-profits to the Department of Licenses, shortening the ballot, and opening a needed "annex" for the governor's office.

7 In the Jacksonian period, the executive's work in the older states was done by legislative committees, and legislators controlled governors. Only when this became impracticable did a true executive and the distribution of power to other statewide elected officials emerge. Michael T. Simmons in "The Transition of the Washington Executive from Territory to Statehood." PNQ 55 (4/64): 76 terms the system "dual-plural," with the executive branch reporting to both the president and state lawmakers.

8 His evidence was strong enough to convince Secretary of the Interior Jefferson Davis, the future confederate president, who favored a southern route. Kent Richards, Isaac Stevens: Young Man in a Hurry. Provo: Brigham Young University Press, 1979: 103,127-51.

9 Charles M. Gates, ed., Messages of the Governors of the Territory of Washington to the Legislative Assembly, 1854-1889: 3-6.

10 Washington Council Journal, 1st sess., (1854), 215. Stevens also deserves credit for starting a territorial library and selecting its original stock. The appropriation was $5,000, identical to the capitol. DO 2/29/1904.

11 The governor was allowed to appoint two lieutenant generals to his personal staff. The need of five generals for a militia of under 1,000 can be laid to the aspirations of lawmakers for epaulets. The units elected all other officers.

12 Organic Act, United States Statutes at Large, 10 (172-79), secs. 1-8.

13 Elwood Evans, who became secretary in 1857, captured the prevailing view in his History of the Northwest: "civilization" and "barbarism" could not co-exist: "American settlement cannot be made except by occupancy of American territory by Americans. [It was] 'survival of the fittest.'" See Laws of Washington, 1st Sess., 1854: 43-45, and Edgar I. Snowden, History of Washington: The Rise and Progress of an American State. V. 3. New York: Century, 1909: 257-309, re the treaties. The 1850 census gave Washington's population as 3,965 whites, and four times as many Indians.

14 James G. Swan, The Northwest Coast. Seattle: UWAP, 1972, 333-48; Robert Ficken, Washington Territory. Pullman: WSUP, 2002: 43-52 passim; Brad Asher, in Beyond the Reservation: Indians, Settlers, and the Law in Washington Territory, 1853-1899. Norman: UOKP, 1999:36-37, deals with the clash of cultures, and terms Stevens "highhanded."

15 Hubert Howe Bancroft asserts Stevens had "with him the ultra anti-Indian element." History of Idaho, Washington, and Montana, 1845-1889. San Francisco: The History Company, 1890:202. The even more patriotic Edmond Meany concedes, "It is altogether probable that the treaties contributed to the causes of the wars," as did the "punishments for murder." History of Washington: 168-178. The 10,000 whites (and 15,000 Indians) in the territory at the end nine years had cost Congress $1.1 million a year, or $90 a head. Airey, 60-61. The only justification of martial law was the breakdown of civil order, which had not happened. See Samuel F. Cohn, "Marshall Law in Washington Territory." PNQ 27 (7/36): 203-04, 211; Friends paid the fine, but President Pierce disliked him enough to appoint Oregon's Joseph Lane to succeed Stevens. The Senate took no

action. Stevens paints his relations with tribes East of the Cascades in a better light in Stevens to George Manypenney, U.S. Commissioner of Indian Affairs 5/31/56. W.T. Government Reports, W.T. Papers 1853-56, 74, UWASC. See Alexandra Harmon, ed., The Power of Promises: Rethinking Indian Treaties of the Pacific Northwest. Seattle, UWAP, 2008.

16 The judiciary won, although Stevens tried to pardon himself.

17 Richards, ch. 7, "The Governor,": 151-62; Olympia's legislators, seeing a main chance, futilely petitioned Congress to have all federal appointees and the supreme and district courts elected.

18 Stevens was as a "Breckinridge" Democrat opposed to secession. See Robert W. Johannsen, The Frontier, the Union, and Stephen A. Douglas. Urbana: University of Illinois Press, 1969: 37-51; Keith A. Murray, "A Governor's Place in History." PNQ 44 (4/53)L 58-60; WS 12/27/1862. Southern sentiment was very visible in the Territory until 1861, but the struggle over slavery was distant for most. David K. Hansen, "Public Response to the Civil War in Washington Territory and Oregon, 1861-1865," MA, UW, 1965. The 1861-62 legislature did pay the $7,755 war levy, and a regiment was raised that relieved regular army members in the North. House Journal, 9th Sess., (1861-62): 181-82; Robert Johannsen, "National Issues and Local Politics in Washington Territory, 1857-1861." PNQ 42 (1/51): 3-31; Frank A. Kittredge and E.O. Easterbrook, "Washington Territory and the War Between the States." WHQ 2 (10/17): 33-39. The idea of creating a "Pacific Republic," to avoid choosing between the Union and the South held considerable interest early in the war, but was condemned in later legislative resolutions; Joseph Ellison, "Design For a Pacific Republic." OHQ 31(12/30): 319-342. 1/4/1861; WS, 5/18/1861, 12/27/1862.

19 See Airey, ch. 3, "The Increase of the Power of the Governor,": 134 ff. The veto was advocated by Republicans to check the Democratic tendencies of the legislature. The decline in both public as well as commercial morals is transparent in Leonard D. White's, The Republican Era: A Study in Administrative History. New York: The Free Press, 1957, which traces the three decade struggle to pass the Pendleton [Civil Service] Act in 1883, and the need to defend it until 1901. See pp. 278-316. Identical conclusions are put in a broader context in Robert W. Johannsen ed., Democracy on Trial, 1845-1877. New York: McGraw Hill, 1964.

20 See Airey, "Quality of Legislation," 208-21; The prime plum was state printer. The secretary got the right to appoint him in 1874, to the most profitable of state contracts. See W. A. Katz, "Public Printers of Washington Territory, 1853-1863." PNQ 3 (7/60): 103-107; Arthur S. Beardsley, "Early Efforts to Locate the Capitol of Washington Territory: a Bibliographic Essay." PNQ 76 (4/85): 42-51; WSA, Index to the Laws, Memorials and Resolutions Passed by the Washington Territorial Legislature 1853-1887. Olympia: OSOS, 1993.

21 Arthur S. Beardsley, "Members of the Legislature of the Territory of Washington and Other Territorial Officers, 1854-1857." Typewritten ms, Seattle, 1951. UWASC; In Washington Territory, Robert E. Ficken appraises Stevens as an "atypically [emphasis added] strong governor in an inherently weak and insignificant political system … rather than a representative figure or model for subsequent behavior … . Stevens excepted, occupants of the office had more prestige than genuine stature … ." 25, 26. A contrary view is in Jack E. Eblen, "Status, Mobility, and Empire: The Territorial Governors, 1869-90." PNQ 60 (7/69): 145-53. He concludes "That the average territorial governor was at least as 'good' as the average contemporary state governor, and quite possibly better." 153. Supporting data is on 148-49. This "second empire" of (expansion from 1848 to

1890), is detailed in his, The First and Second United States Empires: Governors and Territorial Government, 1774-1861, op cit. Pittsburg: University of Pittsburg Press, 1968; Airey, 32; Mercedes Sprague Gleason, "The Territorial Governors of the State of Washington, 1853-1889." ML, UW, 1953.

22 Bancroft, Washington, Idaho, and Montana, 11.

23 (U.S.) Secretary of State Lewis Cass to McMullin, 7/29/1857. W.T. Executive Papers, UWASC; McMullin to Cass, 11/3/1857, 1/21/1858. W.T. Papers, State Department.

24 Gholson to Cass, 11/1/1859. W.T. Papers, State Department.

25 Gholson to Cass, 1/27/1860, 6/4/1860. W.T. Papers, State Department.

26 The Secretary of State was the Acting Governor, as was frequently the case.

27 Merle W. Wells, "The Creation of the Territory of Idaho," PNQ 40 (4/49): 106-22; Annie Laurie Bird, "Portrait of a Frontier Politician: William Henson Wallace," Idaho Yesterdays I, (Spring-Fall, 1957):12-23. For his activities in W.T., see Bird, "William Henson Wallace, Pioneer Politician," PNQ 48 (4/58): 61-76.

28 Wallace to "S. S." (Secretary of State Seward), 4/10/1861. W.T. Papers, State Department.

29 Turney to Seward, 4/11/1862. W.T. Papers, State Department.

30 Smith to Chase, 10/5/1861, in A.H. McNeely (ed.), "Lincoln-Time Letters," WHQ 15 (10/25): 268-69.

31 Lincoln to Seward, 2/16/1864, in Roy Basler (ed.), Collected Works of Lincoln. New Brunswick, N.J.: Rutgers University Press, 1953-55: VII, 188.

32 Pickering to Fred A. Wilson, 12/19/1863. Pickering Papers, UWASC; Evans to (U.S.) Comptroller, 3/30/1863. W.T. Secretary's Letter Book 1863-1867, UWASC.

33 Wells, "Idaho Territory … ."

34 J. Wolf to President Grant, 12/24/1869. E. S. Salomon Appointment File, State Department.

35 WSA, Territorial Governors, 1853-1889. Olympia: OSOS, 1984: 43.

36 Garfielde to Saloman, 9/8/1870. W.T. Papers, State Department; H. H. Bancroft, Washington, Idaho and Montana, 279-82; Johannsen, Frontier Politics: 87, 133, 215-16.

37 R. H. T. Leipold to Secretary of the Treasury Boutwell, 7/24/1871. W.T. Papers, State Department; Secretary of State Fish to Salomon, 9/18/1871. W.T. Papers, E. Salomon files, State Department.

38 (U.S.) Secretary of State Fish to Salomon, 9/18/1871. W.T. Papers, E. Salomon files, State Department.

39 Keith A. Murray, "The Movement toward Statehood in Washington." MA, UW, 1940: 73-74.

40 Ferry to E. B. Washburne, 3/16/1869. E. P. Ferry Appointment File, State Department; Kenneth N. Owens, "Frontier Governors: A Study of Territorial Executives in the History of Washington, Idaho, Montana, Wyoming and Dakota Territories." Ph.D., UMN, 1959:173.

41 Snowden called him "The greatest of all the Territorial governors," Stevens possibly excepted. IV, 257-66.

42 James B. Hedges, Villard and the Railroads of the Northwest. New Haven: Yale

University Press, 1930: 62-66, 80-82.

43 Laws of Washington Territory, 1883: 125-28; Frank Doran, et. al., to Newell, 3/25/1882. Territorial Governors Papers.

44 Alan Hynding, The Public Life of Eugene Semple: Promoter and Politician of the Pacific Northwest. Seattle: UWAP, 1973. "Scrambling for Governor," 50-72, and "The Frustrations of Territorial Administration," 130-33.

45 Squire, "Biennial Message to the Legislative Assembly Session of 1985-86." Olympia: Thomas A. Cavanaugh, State Printer. 1895. Squire Papers, 1/29; See Airey, "Causes of Martial Law in the Chinese Riots," 361-78, and, "An Evaluation of Martial Law," 379-86. Squire covered himself by suggesting to the 1885 legislature they ask Congress to amend the Chinese Restriction Act, and modify the treaty with China, "to protect American working men from extended competition with cheap Chinese labor." Gates, 261-62. When King County Sheriff (and later Governor) John McGraw lost control of the crowds in July, 1886, Squire was "fearful of violence," but delayed asking President Cleveland for federal troops thinking it "very humiliating — a typical expression of Western independence." Squire to King County Sheriff Lewis Byrd, 10/15/1885. Squire Papers. Records of the Governor, 2/1, Chinese Riots.

46 Jules A Karlin, "The Anti-Chinese Outbreaks in Washington." WHQ 20, (4/48): 105-09.

47 Reports to the Secretary of the Interior, 49th Cong., 2nd Sess., Ser. 2468, 885.

48 Owens, 270-71, 341-42.

49 W. H. White to Semple, 10/3/1885. Semple Papers, UWASC.

50 When Squire got President Cleveland to declare an emergency and suspend habeas corpus, Semple cried "tyranny," and sanctimoniously aligned the Democratic Party with justice. His earlier denunciations of the "Mongolian menace, the heathen horde" were tied to his sympathy for Labor and hostility to the railroads' undercutting of wages by hiring Chinese; the Suffrage Act proved futile, as the new supreme court ruled the constitution of 1889, which ignored the question, superseded.

51 Semple to U.S. Senator J. F. King, 3/11/1886, Semple Papers, UWASC.

52 Hynding, 113-31.

53 Telegram, [Kittitas County] Sheriff Packwood to Semple, 8/27/1888. Semple Papers, UWASC.

54 Semple had the last word, passing a law against "private armies." The governor was put in charge of the militia in 1888.

55 Semple's subsequent service was on the then important and now obscure State Harbor Line Commission, where he fought private interests eager to take over tide lands.

56 See Robert E. Albright, "Politics and Public Opinion in the Western Statehood Movement of the 1880's." PHR 3 (9/34): 296-306, and Frederick Paxon, "Admission of the Omnibus States, 1889-90." Wisconsin Historical Society Proceedings for 1911. Madison: 1912: 77-96.

57 Miles Moore the transitional governor in 1889, was a Walla Walla merchant and banker, probably seated so another internecine fight for governor, along with the contest of heavier weights for the U.S. Senate would not swamp the GOP. Elisha Ferry narrowly succeeded against the Democrats led by Semple, and Watson Squire went to the Senate. N. H. Owings to Ferry, 7/31889, 8/11/1889. Nicholas

Owings Letters, UWASC.

58 See Ronald R. Marsh, "The Republican Party in Washington Territory," on the Democrats' "economic conservatism." MA, UW, 1966, passim.

59 Turner argued that the difference between American and European civilization was that settlers who had to adjust to the geography had fewer social controls and less culture as they moved westward, "Americanizing" them. See "The Significance of the Section in American History," in Frontier and Section: Selected Essays of Frederick Jackson Turner. Englewood Cliffs: Prentice-Hall, 1961: 115-35, and Ray A. Billington, The American Frontier Thesis: Attack and Defense. Richmond: The American Historical Association, 1961: 3-8, and John M. Findlay, "Closing the Frontier in Washington: Edmond S. Meany and Frederick Jackson Turner." PNQ 82 (4/81): 59-60. Gerald R. Nash, an eminent Western historian, has declared the Turner Thesis "not very applicable" after 1898. Richard White a leading "new" Western historian is reflects their views in Its Your Misfortune and None of My Own: A History of the American West. Norman: UOKP, 1991. Devotees of "place" will want to peruse White and Findlay's Power and Place in the North American West. Seattle: The Center for the Study of Pacific Northwest History and the UWAP, 1999.

60 See the author's "Scandinavians in Washington's Politics." The Swedish-American Historical Quarterly, 16, (10/05): 230-67.

61 In 1890, Seattle, the largest city was 5,000. Land values from 1890 to 1910 are hard to track because many assessor's reports have been lost, and values were inflated or deflated according to the needs of county government, which could be done without changing the millage. It is safe to say that much productive farmland in the Skagit Valley, and on the benches of the Columbia and its tributaries could be had for prices lower than the homesteads migrants left. For baselines see, e.g., Township 3N 3E (Mount Vernon), and 17N, or 18E (near Ellensburg), both 1872, and 2n 1E, (Vancouver), 1861.

**Chapter 2: The Populists and Progressives**

1 *Walla Walla Union*, 4/13/1878, 4/20/1878; *Walla Walla Statesman*, 3/2/1878. The same view is in WS, 1/1/1886; The estimated population of 51,883 of 1878 was too small, but rose to 175,000 by 1886.

2 Paul L. Beckett and Walfred H. Peterson, "The Constitutional Framework," in Thor Swanson, William F. Mullen, John C. Pierce, and Charles Sheldon, eds., *Political Life in Washington: Governing the Evergreen State*. Pullman: WSU, 1985. Over half the delegates in 1878 were lawyers. Ibid., 439-40. The 1889 convention was more representative, with 43 Republicans, 28 Democrats, 2 independents, and 2 Labor delegates, but less erudite. Justice James Dolliver, "The Mind of the Founders," Appendix C, of James M. Dolliver, *An Oral History*. Olympia: Washington State, OSOS, Oral History Program, 1999.

3 *Washington State Constitution*, Article III; See Wilfred Airey, "A History of the Constitution and of Washington Territory." Ph.D., UW, 1945: "The Executive," 459-63.

4 A Mining Bureau and the office of State Geologist were added. See Vernon Frost, "The Political Adolescence of Washington State." MA, UW, 1949: ch. 6; The Legislature, *Washington State Public Documents, 1890-1891*: 5, 27-31, 47-49, 56-57.

5 Article VIII, Secs. 5, 7, and Article 12, Sec. 9 appear inviolate; Article VIII (Sec. 1) was amended in 1999 to raise the original modest $400,000 debt limit to no more

than 9 percent of the average of the last three year's general fund receipts. (Article XVI, Sec. I).

6 Articles XV and XVII.

7 Knapp, Lebbeus J., "The Origin of the Constitution of the State of Washington." PNQ 4 (10/13): 228-44, 265-70.

8 *2005-2006 Legislative Manual*. Olympia: The Legislature, 2005: 64-276.

9 See, "A Curious Constitution," in the author's *A Majority of One: Legislative Life*. 3rd ed., Seattle: Civitas Press, 2012: 318-25.

10 Ferry defeated former Governor Semple 33,711 to 24,732 on personal popularity, and the state's Republican lean.

11 Ferry, "Admission Day Address," 11/11/1889. Ferry Papers, UWASC, 1.

12 Michael Malone and Richard Etulain imply a "fragmented" executive function with eight other statewide officers is a dubious improvement.

13 Ferry, "Governors Address to the State Legislature," 1/18/1889. Ferry Papers, UWASC, 2/8.

14 Bancroft, 317.

15 Rayner, 117-77.

16 Ferry, "Retiring Message to the Legislature," 1/11/1893. Ferry Papers UWASC, 2-10.

17 Ferry to John McGraw, 10/1/1892, 11/1892. Ferry Papers, UWASC, 1, letterpress book: 388. The state tax of 3 mills in 1892 was lowered to 2.5, likely in anticipation of the election.

18 See Appendix 4 for the value of the dollar, and Matthew Josephson's classic *The Robber Barons*. New York: Harcourt, Brace, 1934, and especially, "[J. P.] Morgan and the Railways," 290-314, for an undressing of the business practices of railroad building. For the battle for civil service in the last half of the 19th century read Leonard D. White, *The Republican Era: A Study in Administrative History, 1869-1901*. New York: The Free Press, 1958: 21-44, 278-302, 365-85, for the 40 year struggle for civil service.

19 Ferry to Henry Landes, 2/18/1892, 4/12/1892. Ferry Papers, UWASC, 2/3, letter press book: 172.

20 See "Reluctant McGraw Elected Governor." PI 5/23/1968: 21. His address to the legislature and policies are in the WS 1/13/1895; Herbert Hunt and F. C. Kaylor offer of synopsis in *Washington West of the Cascades*. Chicago: S. J. Clarke, 1917: 25-28; "Leading Citizens of the City of Seattle … " in *Memoirs of Arthur A. Denny*. Chicago: Lewis Publishing Co., 1903: 225-28

21 McGraw to Erastus Brainerd, 2/13/1896, 1/5/1901, 1/28/1902, 3/1/1905. Brainerd Papers, UWASC.

22 The Populists were most favored in the poorer agricultural areas east of the Cascades, who viewed the cities with "alarm and suspicion." See David Griffiths, "Populism in the Far West, 1890-1900." Ph.D., UW, 1967. Important on the endless reinterpretation of the movement are in: John D. Hicks,' *The Populist Revolt*, Minneapolis: UMI Press, 1931, the original standard. Walter T. K. Nugent, *The Tolerant Populists: Populism and Nativism*. Chicago: University of Chicago Press, 1963, Richard Hofstadter, *Age of Reform: From Bryan to FDR*. New York: Vintage Books, 1955, Lawrence Goodwyn, *Democratic Promise: The Populist Movement in America*. New York: Oxford University Press, 1978, and Norman

Pollock, *The Just Polity: Populism, Law and Human Welfare*. Urbana: UILP, 1991, and O. Gene Clanton, *A Common Humanity: Kansas Populism and the Battle for Justice and Equality*. Manhattan, KA: Sunflower University Press, 2004, is best on the seminal state. He concludes the Populist's real contribution was to be a "positive educational experience." Populist farmers worked for themselves, and were unaccustomed to "institutional discipline," Norman F. Tjaden, wrote in "Populists and Progressives of Washington, A Comparative Study," MA, UW, 1960: 68-78. Stephen Peters, "The Populists and the Washington Legislature, 1893-1900," MA, UW, 1967, defines the chaos there. The shift to urban life was mirrored in the legislature. Sixty-five percent of the Populists were either farmers (44 percent) or editors (21 percent). Just 5 percent were "other professionals," 7 percent businessmen, and 9 percent lawyers. Among the Progressives it was 0, 7, 3, 33; Tjaden, table 1.

23 Warren M. Blankenship, "The Political Thought of John R. Rogers." PNQ 37, (1/46): 1-3, 13; Thomas W. Riddle, *The Old Radicalism: John R. Rogers and the Populist Movement In Washington*. New York: Garland Publishers, 1991, is the other closest appraisal.

24 Karel D. Bicha, "Peculiar Populist: An Assessment of John R. Rogers." PNQ 65 (7/74): 110.

25 Rogers to Dr. J. Eugene Jordan, 2/8/1898, and to U.S. Senator George Turner, 2/16/1898. Rogers papers, WSA.

26 Rogers to J. C. Van Patten, 3/2/1898. WSA, 2C-2-22, corr. out, 3/1898. Ibid., 2/5/1898.

27 Riddle, 240-41.

28 Karel D. Bicha, "Peculiar Populists: An Assessment of John R. Rogers." op cit.

29 McBride was a Roosevelt bolter at the Aberdeen convention of 1912, but never joined the Progressive Party. He was denied his party's nomination in 1904, only to be given it in 1916, when the GOP needed a "name." His tepidity, like the Republican platforms of 1912 and 1916, testified to a party rent down the middle, its thrust spent. Roland Hill Hartley was the runner-up. Robert Saltvig, "The Progressive Movement in Washington." Ph.D., UW, 1966, 389; ST, 4/7/1918.

30 Gerald Nash, *The American West in the Twentieth Century: A Short History of An Urban Oasis*. Albuquerque: University of New Mexico Press, 1977: 2, 3. In *The American West: A Twentieth Century History*, Michael Malone emphasizes the 1890's were a transition "not a precipitous break with precedent." Lincoln: University of Nebraska Press, 1989: 5.

31 Mead to Richard A. Ballinger, 12/10/1907. Brainerd Papers, UWASC, 4/2. For the battle for civil service in the last half of the 19th Century, read Leonard D. White, *The Republican Era: A Study in Administrative History 1869-1901*. New York: The Free Press, 1958: 21-44, 278-302, 365-85.

32 Mead to Brainerd, 2/9/1907. Ballinger Papers, UWASC, 1/54.

33 This was the the Second capitol, now the Office of the SPI at Sylvester Park in downtown Olympia.

34 Mead to Brainerd, 1/10/1906, Brainerd Papers, UWASC, 4/2. This may have been the reason T.R. decided not to have a cabinet member back him over U.S. Senator George Turner, who was of a different stripe. W. E. Clark to Brainerd, 11/1/1906. Brainerd Papers, UWASC, 2/5.

35 See "Theodore Roosevelt and the American Paradox," in David W. Noble, *The Progressive Mind, 1890-1917*. Chicago: Rand McNally, 1971: 152-64.

36 Samuel Cosgrove, disowned by his father and driven by ambition, was a lawyer. He was in the 1889 constitutional convention and mayor of Pomeroy for five years.

37 "The first week of my campaign was spent in convincing my friends I had a chance." Hay to J. R. Conrad, 11/15/1912. 2H-1-1, corr., 1912; Hay to W. P. Brown, 1/13/1910. Hay 2G-2-26, politics 1909-10. WSA, *Guide to the Governors Papers*, Vol. 3: 27-28.

38 See Hermas J. Bergman, "Progressive on the Right: Marion E. Hay, Governor of Washington, 1909-1913." Ph.D., WSU, 1969: 25, 83-84. The leadership of the Progressive Party in Washington, as elsewhere, was half lawyers, former "gold" Democrats, and Protestant, non-corporate Republicans in the state an average of 19 years; David B. Griffiths, in "Populism in the Far West, 1890-1900." Ph.D., UW, 1967: 43-67, confirms the findings of George E. Mowry's *The Era of Theodore Roosevelt*. New York: Harper and Brothers, 1958, and Richard Hofstadter's *The Progressive Movement 1900-1915*. Englewood Cliffs, N.J.: Prentice Hall, 1963.

39 Hay to W. B. Hibschman, 4/14/1909. Hay Collection, EWSHS.

40 Hay to Charles Dougherty, 6/10/1912. Hay 2G2/17, Industrial Insurance Commission.

41 Chief (U.S.) Forester Gifford Pinchot's new set-asides were "impractical," and trampled on states' rights. Hay to R. A. Ballinger, 9/26/1910. Hay, EWHS. For context, see Bergman, "The Conservation Struggle," 193-209; See Lawrence Rakestraw, "The West, States' Rights, and Conservation: A Study of Public Land Conferences." PNQ 48 (1957): 91-94, and Elmo Richardson, *The Politics of Conservation: Crusades and Controversies*. Berkeley: UCAPB, 1962.

42 Hay to George Long, 9/26/1910. Hay Papers, EWSHS; H. J. Bergman, "The Reluctant Dissenter: Governor Hay of Washington and the Conservation Problem." PNQ 62, (1/71): 27-33.

43 SR 10/11/1911; Hay to W. H. Cowles 8/25/1910. Hay Papers, EWSHS.

44 e.g., "Report of the Investigating Committee to His Excellency the Governor of the State of Washington, 1910." Olympia: Washington State Legislature, 1910.

45 Vernon R. Frost, "The Political Adolescence of Washington State." MA, UW, 1949: 40. See also, "Theodore Roosevelt and the American Paradox," in David Noble, op. cit.

46 Hay to Fred W. Crone, 11/22/1909. WSA, 2G-2-26, politics. Hay claimed to favor a presidential primary, but balked at the cost of a special session to create one. For the GOP's unraveling after 1910, see Saltvig, 248-74: *Third Message of Governor M.E. Hay* [to the legislature], in *Washington Public Documents, 1911-12*: 1-43. Olympia: State Printer, 1912.

47 At the raucous Aberdeen convention, TR's men had 196 votes, Taft's 133, and Phillip Lafollette's 7, but the Progressives were outmaneuvered. Two sets of delegates went to Chicago.

48 Keith A. Murray, "The Aberdeen Convention of 1912." PNQ 38 (4/47): 99-108.

49 Hay to Phillip LaFollette, 7/7/1912. Hay Papers, EWSHS. Saltvig, 264, and Keith A. Murray, "The Aberdeen Convention of 1912." PNQ 38 (4/47): 99-108. In the split the GOP lost the governorship, 2 congressional seats and 63 legislative places.

50 See "Theodore Roosevelt and the American Paradox," in David W. Noble, op. cit., 152-74.

51 Hay to Brainerd, 9/22/1908. Hay Papers, EWSHS, 3/12.

52 Until Monrad C. Wallgren (1945-49) and Mike Lowry, (1993-97).

53 PI 10/11 10/13, 10/19/12.

54 *Washington Public Documents, Abstract of Votes Polled in the State of Washington at the General Election Held November 12, 1912.* Olympia: OSOS, 180-83. The GOP's McBride was hardly a "bold and unscrupulous demagogue," but rather fatally 'neutral' in 1912. In 1916, he was a conspicuously weak head of the ticket. In the *P-I*'s view, "Any other entry ... would have picked Henry McBride. Editorial, 11/9/1916. The paper had opposed Lister in 1912.

55 *Message of the Governor of Washington*, 1/15/1913: 28-29, 40, 59. Olympia: OSOS, 1913.

56 PI, 10/11, 10/13, 10/19, 1912; Lister's legislative accomplishments are in Herman Sliezer, "Governor Ernest Lister: Chapters of a Political Career." MA, UW, 1941:1-7, 17-20.

57 *Journal of the House*, 1913: 560; Sliezer, 37. Lister persuaded employers to accept a moderate "first aid" bill for Labor in later sessions, and in 1917, and disingenuously dispatched a syndicalism bill for lack of "sufficient force" to cope with "false doctrines." More likely, his worry was free speech. *Journal of the Senate*, 1/19/1917: 14-15; The governor "sadly misuses executive power," the *P-I* concluded. 3/22/1917.

58 See Arthur S. Link's timeless *Woodrow Wilson and the Progressive Era, 1910-1917*. New York: Harper and Row, 1954: 1-24, 223-251; An interview with the President helped. SS 10/28/1916, 5/22/1917, SR 10/24/1916.

59 *Senate Journal*, 1915: 79; *Session Laws, 1915*, ch. 54: 186-97, ch. 55: 197-206, and ch. 181: 645-46.

60 Saltvig, 402, 486-93. See "Nationalizing the New Freedom," in Arthur S. Schlesinger Jr., *The Crisis of the Old Order, 1919-1933*. Boston: Houghton Mifflin, 1964: 32-36.

61 Lister to J. A. Cross, 4/12/1918. Lister papers, 2H-2-117, legislature, 1918. Given the "stunning" number of accidents in the lumber industry it had been in the interest of employers to collaborate with the Washington State Federation of Labor and the Grange to finance workmen's compensation. Another reason was minimizing class antagonism. The supreme court aided, in refusing to make a "fetish" of due process , and upheld labor legislation as expressions of "police power." See "Labor Legislation and Acute Social Stress 1914-1919," in Joseph F. Tripp, "Progressive Labor Law in Washington State (1900-1920), Ph.D., UW, 1973: 110-73.

62 Lister appointed a State Council of Defense at the President's suggestion, chaired by Henry Suzzallo, President of the UW. He had seconded Lister's futile letter for an eight hour day. *Washington State Bureau of Labor Biennial Report, 1917-1918*. Olympia: 1918. In March, 1917, a gunman "shamming insanity" took over the Executive Office for 20 minutes. Lister thought "The amazing part" was that the Olympia police had trailed the zany from downtown, and allowed him in, [despite] "knowing he had a gun ... and ... feeling that he was either insane or vicious." Lister to the Secretary of the Governor of Michigan, 3/19/1917, and to Alex Polson, 3/22/1917. 2H-2-117, assassination attempt.

63 "All that I need," he assured a friend in June, 1918, "is a real rest. This I can get by keeping away from the office. In a short time I shall be in my usual good health." Lister to Henry M. White, 6/11/1918. Lister 2C-2-12, personal. WSA.

**Chapter 3: Between the Wars**

1 The other "general strike" was by the San Francisco-West Coast Longshoremen in 1934; See George Soule, *Prosperity Decade: From War to Depression, 1917–1929*. New York: Harper, 1947, 81–106; Nearly 750,000 acres of wheat land was taken out of production in Eastern Washington in 1924; John Fahey's *The Inland Empire: Unfolding Years, 1879–1929*, Seattle: UW Press, 1986, spells out the impact of declining wheat prices east of the Columbia.

2 See James N. Tattersall, "The Economic Development of the Northwest to 1920." Ph.D., (economics), UW, 1960, and particularly, "The Great Expansion 1880-1920: A Summary," 86–136.

3 Hart's decision to run in 1920 was likely prompted by fear the reactionary Roland Hill Hartley would undo the Progressive Period. In a field of 11, they got 28.4 and 24.7 percent of the primary vote.

4 Douglas R. Pullen, "The Administration of Washington State Governor Louis Hart, 1919–1925." Ph.D., UW, 1974, 80–127.

5 Hart's claim that "no serious opposition had developed" was belied by the report of a "Special Committee" to investigate it. Hart to F. J. Tooze, 3/12/22. WSA, Hart, 1, administrative board; In the 1919–21 budget of $36,422,000, the largest raises were the executive office ($48,500 to $72,000) and highways $7, 017,000, to $11,109,000. The governor's salary was $6,000, as it was in 1941. He had an "assistant," six "secretaries," four accountants, and three stenographers. "Estimated Revenues of the State of Washington" [for the biennium beginning April 1, 1919], WSA, Hart, 12, 1919–21; *Fourth message of Governor Hart to the Legislature, Seventeenth Session, 1921*. Olympia. The State Printer, 1921.

6 Ch. 20, Laws of 1890; The departments are set out in Ch. 7, laws of 1921. The key department, Efficiency, the governor's first "control agency," enabling him to make a [fiscal] "survey" of all but the Legislature and the Supreme Court. In 1925, it facilitated the first inclusive state budget. The others were Public Works, Health, and Conservation and Development, Agriculture, Fisheries and Game, Labor and Industries, Business Control, Taxation and Examination, Public Works and Licenses. Taxation and Examination's duties were transferred to a governor-named three-person tax commission in 1925. (Ch. 19, Laws of 1925 and *Journal of the Senate*, 1925, 48). Highways was added to the "Code" departments in 1929 (Ch. 15, Laws of 1929). The governor presided over an administrative board of agency heads, which soon became an endorser of what he and his confidants had done. See Ernest G. Miller, "The Management of Washington State Government: The problem of Central Staff Organization." MA, UW, 1953, 3–9; Walter S. David, "The New Administrative Code in Washington." APSR, 15, (11/21), 568–76.

7 Hart to Polson, 11/7/21. WSA, Hart, 55, tax investigation committee; Hart, *Address to the Legislature*, 1923, 5-6; "The Governor's Conference on Retrenchment." Hart, 55, taxation investigation.

8 Hart, *Address to the Legislature*, 1923, 7, 23.

9 Opinion, Attorney General George H. Thompson to Hart, 8/2/21. Hart, 12, equalization board; Pressure on county assessors to undervalue property led to appraisals of less than half the 50 percent of value mandated by the State Constitution and wide fluctuations between the counties, causing large variations in the resources of local governments and school. This was not remedied until the 1970s.

10 "Report to the Governor for the State Equalization Committee," 9/5/22. WSA, Hart, 12, equalization board.

11 Hart, *Third Message to the Legislature* (1923). WSA, Hart, 35, 7; In 1921, the legislature imposed what was misinterpreted to mean a "poll tax" on those who paid no taxes to fund the soldier's bonus. On this basis, it proved unpopular, and with the governor and legislative Republicans back peddling was repealed by initiative three to one in 1922.

12 Hart to J. C. Keesling, 11/20/23. Hart, 24, gas tax.

13 *Third Message*, 7, 15.

14 Hart to Lieutenant Governor W. J. Coyle and Majority Leader Speaker Mark Reed, 3/5/23. Hart, 35, legislature, house bills.

15 Hart's vetos were fewer overall than his peers.

16 Hart to Jones, 7/19/13, Jones, 4/23. "Conciliation" of the right-wing was the answer Jones, who was sliding in that direction, wrote 15 HB 190; Hart to House, 3/8/21. Hart, 34, legislature, '21-'23; John Blum, "Nativism, Anti-Radicalism, and the Foreign Scare, 1917-1920." *Midwest Journal*, (1950-51), 44-53; John Beffel, "The Line Up in Washington State." *The Nation*, 119, (11/5/1924), 492.

17 Hart to Ruth Rhodes, 12/12/23. Hart, 24, forestry.

18 "House [Investigative] Report," 2/9/23, ibid.

19 Albert F. Gunns, "Roland Hill Hartley and the Politics of Washington State." MA; UW, 1963, 5.

20 *SA* 9/6/24.

21 Democrats failed to capture the urban centers and ignored farmers. Labor was split between James Duncan's Seattle Central Labor Council and the conservative WSFL led by William Short; The Democrats were divided between Jeffersonians and "bourbons," the first led by their two most important officeholders, U.S. Senator C. C. Dill, and Fifth District Congressman Sam Hill. They fell to third party status in 1924. See Robert L. Cole, "The Democratic party in Washington State, 1919-1933: A Barometer of Social Change." Ph.D., UW, 1972; Secretary of State, *Abstract of Votes*, 9/9/24; *Tacoma Ledger*, 2/11/24, ST 1/18/25

22 There were but two nays in the Senate and six in the House to adjourning. *Journal of the Senate*, 1925, 58, 78, *House Journal*, 1925, 118; *ST*, 1/14/25; PI, 1/15/25. In 1926, he vetoed the supplemental budget, sent him ten days before the omnibus bill, "as a protest against the high-handed, double dealing methods it was put through the House." WSA, RHH mss, 41, *Message to the Legislature*, 1/4/26, '26 Legislature.

23 *House Journal*, 1925, 118, *ST*, 2/4/25; No department was to spend its funds until the probe was complete. See Joseph F. Tripp, "Governor Roland Hill Hartley and Labor Legislation [1925–1927]," PhD, UW, 1973, 277–301.

24 "Memorandum on the Timber Situation in the State of Washington Submitted to Vice-President Charles G. Dawes by Governor Roland H. Hartley." n.d., WSA, RHH, 39, speeches; untitled Hartley speech, 10/20/25, ibid.

25 *Journal of the Senate, First Extra Session*, [1925], 16–17.

26 RHH to the 1926 Legislature, WSA, RHH, 41, speeches; RHH to Schuyler Wallace, 7/27/26, ibid.

27 P.O. 7/15/25.

28 P.O. 5/6/20, 7/15/25.

29 RHH, "Speech to the 1926 Legislature," WSA, RHH, 41,speeches; The regents' meeting with the governor found the university and the Department of

Efficiency's accounting differed. The latter arrived at $3,505,400 overall, $86,124 under 1927–1929. Ibid.

30 Gunns, 111; *Journal of the Senate, First Extra Session,* [1925], 189.

31 "Report of the Tax Investigation Commission . . . 1930." WSA, RHH, 40, tax investigation commission; Veto Message on SB 62, 3/12/31, RHH, 33, legislature, Senate '31; "Federated Industries of Washington, list of vetoes as of 3/16/31." Ibid, '31 legislative messages; Virginia Price's paper, "Governor Roland Hill Hartley, 1925–1933," skillfully amplifies on these issues and personality clashes. Charles M. Gates Papers, UW, 23–12.

32 Tripp, 278; Hartley "Address to the 1933 Legislature," 3–10, 13–14. *Washington Public Documents, 1931–1932.* Olympia: State Printer, 1933. Hartley blindly and unsuccessfully ran for GOP nomination again in 1936 when it was worthless.

33 Martin was born in Cheney in 1886, the first native son to hold the office. He had chaired the State Democratic Central committee from 1924 to 1930; His "Pledge of Faith," n.d., [1932], with its downplaying of factional and "dictatorial" behavior could have been written by his successor. CDM Papers, WSUSC, 16,19; The animating conditions are best described in "The Politics of Hard Times," in William E. Leuchtenberg, *Franklin Roosevelt and the New Deal: 1932-1940.* New York: Harper and Row, 1963, 1-17. One State Representative was elected while in the King County jail charged with statutory rape. PI, 2/14/32.

34 In 1935, the GOP was reduced to seven Representatives and three senators, all of whom the governor needed.

35 Among 25 other points were, equalization of valuations between corporations and individuals, curbing corporate lobbyists, higher minimum wages for women, "protection" of old age and pension systems, an end to log-rolling in highway building, and a Constitutional Revision Commission. "Martin: The Man for Governor." [1932]. WSU, CDM Papers, 50; *TNT* 1/11/33.

36. Secretary of State, *Abstract of Votes ... Primary Election September 13, 1932,* 24; In 1936, Martin overwhelmed hapless Lieutenant. Governor John Gallatly 352,215 to 207,419, a plurality larger than FDR's.

37 In 1935, the W.E.R.A. was superseded by the Department of Public Welfare, signaling the change from emergency support to continuing public assistance. It became Public Assistance in 1953. Miller, 11, 12; Other additions were the Athletic, Horse Racing, and Columbia Basin Commissions. Fisheries and Game were divided. (Chps. 184, 55, 81, and 3, Laws of 1933).

38 ST 1/18,20,26/33; Judge Pemberton became Supervisor of Inheritance Taxes, and E.K. Murray, ex-Tacoma Corporation Counsel, went to Public Works. Lacey Murrow proved to be an outstanding Director of Highways, and Ernest Brabrook the second Director of the Department of Efficiency and Budget survived from the late 20's to the 50's. In 1938, the governor appointed Representative Belle Reeves as the first female Secretary of State; "Wish you were here to see the thousands of applications ... " CDM wrote Lewis Schwellenbach," it is almost impossible to separate them." (12/6/32). WSA, CDM, 1-4; SR 4/19/33.

39 The "Governor's Budget" is due December 15, before the "First Wednesday after the first Monday" in January, the convening date of the legislature in odd-numbered years.

40 Charles N. Randolph, "Crisis and Change: Washington State's Reaction to the Depression, 1932-1933." MA, WSU, 1970, 78-124, 90, 125; PI, 6/23,8-22/34; In 1935, Public Works became Public Service, and Efficiency, tellingly, Business

Control, then Finance, Budget and Business. It retained a "schizophrenic character" as a manager, and operator of the divisions of Public Institutions, Banking, Savings and Loan, and Purchasing. A larger consolidation was Welfare's renaming as Social Security in 1937, aggregating Emergency Relief, Child Welfare, Old Age Assistance, Employment Compensation, aid to the blind, and employment service programs (Ch. 176, Laws of 1935, and Ch. 111, Laws of 1937).

41 See *Washington State Constitution*, Article VII, Sec.1, and Article XI.

42 CDM, *First Inaugural Address*, and, *Special Message to the Legislature*, 1933. *Washington Public Documents, 1931-1932*, Vol. 1; A mill is 1/1,000th of value; the Columbia Basin Commission was allotted $35,000 to lobby Congress, and succeeded in getting $63 million for a "low" dam in six months. E.F. Banker, Chair, to the legislature, 9/14/33. WSA, CDM, 24, CBC; Responding to CDM's letter that "power interests" were trying to squelch the Grand Coulee, FDR reminded him that irrigation projects had to be offset by taking land out of production. FDR to CDM, 10/1/33. WSA, CDM, '33, president; *PI* 9/21/32; 3/1,7, 22, 25/33, 3/4/34.

43 PI 6/16, 8/15/33.

44 King County's relief roll was already at 43,000; *PI*, 3/1/34; Martin expected the last $1 million of the bond to be used by March, 1934. After that, "the funds must be made available by the federal government." CDM to U.S.S. C.C. Dill, 12/13/34. WSA, CDM, 72-64.

45 NYT, 3/7/34; "Proceedings of the Washington State Federation of Labor Convention," 7/9-12/34.

46 PI, 10/18/34; Fayette Krause, "Democratic Party Politics in Washington during the New Deal." Ph.D., UW, 1971, 107; PI, 12/15/34; The Left suffered from a different kind of hesitation, as a 94-2 vote on a bill denying the Communist Party a place on the state ballot, and another of 72-2 to retain the syndicalism law of the Red Scare of 1919-20 demonstrated.

47 CDM had "strengthened the position of the administration, and corrected mistakes," *The* Wenatchee World asserted (3/23/33); There were "Twenty-odd members of the House and quite a few in the Senate who would like to pull some spectacular thing," the governor expected, "but I cannot believe the legislature will permit same"; Speaker George Yantis was reelected for the 1934 Special Session 37-24, assuring the regular Democrats control. CDM to U.S.S. C.C. Dill, WSUSC, CDM, 12-64; CDM to the House of Representatives, 3/21/33. WSUSC, CDM, 12-60; TNT, 12/4/33.

48 Given his desperate need for leverage, CDM's use of the veto was restrained. It took an act like SHB 29 (1933), intended by him to end abuses in mortgage foreclosures, and amended to preclude any recoveries, and thus threatening credit, or SB 381 (1933), "seemingly ... intended to prevent payment of excessive salaries in higher education," after regents had "signified willingness to accept and carry out the spirit of the legislature." CDM to the House, 3/23/33, and to the Senate, 3/21/33. WSA, CDM, 51, vetoes, regular session, '33; *PI*, 2/28, 3/1, 3/1,8/35; See James T. Patterson, *Congressional Conservatism and the New Deal: The Growth of the Conservative Coalition in Congress, 1933-1936*. Westport, CT: Greenwood Press, 1981, especially chapter 9, "The Zenith of the Coalition, 1939," (288-324); CDM wrote Ellsworth French [President of WSC], "I certainly am pleased at the way the Republicans are handling themselves." CDM, WSUSC, 2-12, 12/1/33.

49 The federal National Recovery Administration had expired. *PI*, 2/12/35; In the

midst of the 1934 turmoil Clarence Dill 'retired' from his U.S. Senate seat, and FDR sent clear signals favoring Lewis Schwellenbach, virtually precluding the governor from going to Congress if he had wished. Krause, 107.

50 Both succeeded the more radical Unemployed Citizen's League (1931-33), and the Commonwealth Builders, Inc., in what became I-119, (1934), the Production for Use initiative modeled on Upton Sinclair's EPIC (End Poverty in California). The nature of all three organizations and Martin's confrontations with them are in Albert A. Acena, "The Washington Commonwealth Federation: Reform Politics and the Popular Front." Ph.D., UW, 1973, 55-71.

51 DO, 9/2/36; With the Steele Act of 1933, the State became the sole wholesaler of liquor, capturing both the mark-up and taxes; The stability of the state budget, from $105,251,288 in 1931 to $101,594,636 in 1933, was due to federal benefactions. Salaries and "educational institutions" were the largest losers at nearly $8 million. "Comparative Statement of Appropriations by Functions." WSA, CDM, 29, efficiency department, '33; "The Record of Governor Martin." WSUSC, CDM, 16-100.

52 Congressman Marion Zioncheck, the WCF's choice, had jumped from a fourth story window in Seattle's Arctic Building. *PI*, 7/26,27/36. Stevenson, it was discovered, was wanted for fraud in another state. *ST*, 9/5, 9/36; Hartley's tirades that the governor was a factotum of the "[Teamster President] Dave Beck — [Seattle Mayor] John Dore gangster machine" reinforced burgher disgust at the city's "circus politics," and prefigured Langlie's tactics into the 50's. *ST*, 10/20, 22/36; Daniel M. Ogden, "The Blanket Primary and Party Regularity in Washington State." *PNQ*, 39, (1/48), 33-38. Other Democratic candidates averaged 62 percent of the vote. In the gubernatorial primary they garnered 80 percent. Martin got 166,313, Stevenson 129,888, and Otto Case 86,753. The voters returned to the center, rejecting state distribution of power, Stevenson's pension plan (I-115), and the WCF's (I-119), (which Martin opposed), by the spectacular margin of 370,140 to 97,399.

53 Addressing the Washington Newspaper Institute, Martin concluded the recession was not all that bad: "People had been going too fast since the last depression." PI, 1/10,11,12/37; Of the $88 million the state spent in $73 million came from real estate taxes, which the 40 mil limit had reduced by $25 million. License and liquor profits were stable for the decade. The difference was made up by the sales tax, and 15 excise taxes, from insurance premiums to admissions. Cash balances in 1940 were $16,343,000, on projected net revenue for 1941-43 of $103,100,000. "State Investments and General Obligation Bonded Debt, 10/1/40." WSUSC, CDM, 18-139.

54 FDR to CDM, 2/8/37, and, CDM to FDR, 3/8/37. WSA, CDM, 33, president.

55 In 1936, the WCF jettisoned production for use in favor of joining the Comintern's "Popular Front Against Fascism." At least five of the 15 members of the Executive Board in 1937 and Executive Director Howard Costigan were Communists. Acena, 146-47, 203-04; A similar situation obtained in Oregon after 1935. See Gary Murrell, *Iron Pants: Oregon's Anti-New Deal Governor, Charles Henry Martin*. Pullman: WSU Press, 2000, Ch. 10; James T. Patterson wrote in *The New Deal and the States, Federalism in Transition*. Princeton: Princeton University Press, 1969: "The Governors of Oregon and Washington most thoroughly disgusted liberals." Both were "hostile to the New Deal." 129; Oregon reverted to Republican Charles Sprague in 1938. In Idaho, "neo-Populist" C. Ben Ross and New Dealers moved in "opposite directions," sundering the coalition in four years. Republican C.A. Bottelfson was elected in 1938. See Michael P. Malone, "The New Deal in Idaho."

PHR, 38 (8/69), 293-310; In California, the GOP was usually in control of the Assembly and the governorship, the liberal regime of Cuthbert Olson (1935-39) excepted. The Progressive strain begun by George Pardee (1903-07), and brought to full bloom by Hiram Johnson was abetted by moderate's cross-filing, reinforcing the majority party as long as it was centrist — through Governor Earl Warren, (1944-53). Factionalism and Barry Goldwater's presidential candidacy ended GOP dominance in 1964. See Robert E. Burke, *Olsen's New Deal for California*. Berkeley: The University of California Press, 1953, and, H. Brett Melendy and Benjamin F. Gilbert, *The Governors of California: Peter H. Burnett to Edmund G. Brown*. Georgetown, CA: Talisman Press, 1965, 260-442.

56 FDR to CDM, 2/8/37, and, CDM to FDR, 12/21/39. WSA, CDM, 33, president.

57 SB 242, 1937; As late as April, 1935, the governor addressed Seattle Teamster chief Dave Beck as "My Dear Friend." Sixteen months later he wrote Representative George Gannon, "They are trying to trap me in the Seattle PI situation .... There has been no justification for force and there has been no desire for arbitration. This episode ... is only indicative of the industrial unrest being caused by agitators and communistic influences ... . Something drastic will be necessary one of these days ... ." CDM to Beck, 4/24/35. WSUSC, CDM, 4-20; to Gannon 8/3/36, ibid, 6-30; "Confidential Report Supplementing the Hearings Held at McCleary and Aberdeen Pertaining to Labor Disturbances." n.a., WSA, CDM, 49, labor, McCleary strike, 1935; "Pacific Coast [Maritime] Activities." n.a., 10/31/36, [file "Communists or strike" in CDM's handwriting]. WSA, CDM, 48, labor strikes, '36-'37; Curiously, John Boettiger, the President's son-in-law and the PI's publisher backed Martin's Department of Social Security and his fiscal conservatism. E.g., PI 2/3, 18/37.

58 Krause, 182-83; PI, 7/28/38.

59 Charles Ernst Papers, UWASC, 2-1, reports.

60 *NYT*, 4/21/38; PI, 4/16, 22, 24, 26/38.

61 Martin's allies disdained Dill's "opportunism" (i.e., detachment from the Democratic Party ), dating from the 20's. E.g., Dill to CDM, 10/9/36, WSA, CDM, 5/31, and Edith Dolan Riley to Dill, 5/1/28, Riley Papers, UWA, 1-27; "Governor Martin for Stability and Progress." Flyer (1940), and, "Forward, Washington," radio address by CDM, 8/19/40. Naomi Benson Papers, UWA, 32-18; The dynamics of the 1940 campaign are in Kerry E. English, *Clarence C. Dill: The Life of a Western Politician*. Pullman: WSU Press, 2000, 135-54, and in George W. Scott, "Arthur B. Langlie: Republican Governor in a Democratic Age." Ph.D., UW, 1971; "The Governor is responsible for making Langley [sic] as strong as he is ... and now seems terribly surprised that Langlie is thinking of running," State Senator Mary Farquharson wrote Speaker George Gannon, Something she encouraged to deny Martin his Republican votes in the primary. 6/29/40 MWF 391-1, 1-4, '40, governor; When Martin ran for governor a fourth time in 1948, saying "All is not well in Olympia," Dill backed the Democratic incumbent, New Dealer Monrad C. Wallgren. The PI adjudged CDM as "Either a Republican or a man without a party." (8/31/48).

62 CDM to Frank Martin, 9/16/40. WSU, CDM, 15-96. Of FDR's opponent Wendell Willkie, he said, "He is a fine fellow, but I am afraid he will not score in many of our western states." CDM to Clarence "Dan" Martin, 9/23/40. WSU, CDM, 49-9.

63 James T. Patterson, "The New Deal in the Northwest." PHR 38 (8/69): 317-20.

64 Bruce D. Blumell, "The Development of Public Assistance in the State of Washington during the Great Depression." Ph.D., UW, 1973, 468. The per capita cost of relief in

Washington in 1937 was $10.53, or 8th nationally, compared to an average of $7.64 for all the states. The shift of burden to the state was dramatic: $41,473,018 was paid in 1937-39, versus $6,467,399 by the counties. "State of Washington Comparison of National Income and Per Capita Cost of Relief." CDM, 65, social security department, '39; his critics include Krause, 120-21, 166-68, and Earl Pomeroy in *The Pacific Slope*. New York: Alfred D. Knopf, 1965, 242-46.

**Chapter 4: Arthur B. Langlie**

1 For a full biography, see the author's Ph.D. dissertation by the same title, (UW, 1971), and his "Scandinavians in Washington's Politics." *The Swedish-American Historical Quarterly* LVI (10/2005): 230-66.

2 George W. Scott, "The New Order of Cincinnatus: Municipal Reform in the Seattle in the 1930's." PNQ 64: 4 (10/73): 137-46.

3 SLN cited in Ralph B. Potts, *Seattle Heritage*. Seattle: The Superior Publishing Company, 1955: 116.

4 ST 3/5/35.

5 "Minutes of the General Meeting," 1/7/1936: Hamley Diary, Albert King Diary, 1/1-7/1936, passim. Both UWA.

6 John F. Dore, "Opening Speech in Campaign for Mayor," in Seattle Lighting Department MS, speeches and writings, 4. UWA.

7 ST, 2/26/36.

8 Interview of Arthur B. Langlie by Richard C. Berner and Prof. R. E. Burke, 8/11/196l. (On the 1936 mayoralty and the 1944 gubernatorial races.) ABL Papers.

9 ST 3/8/1938; "Beck and the Teamsters stayed [with Dore] to the bitter end, and are swearing undying hostility to Meyers," Earl Milliken told WGM, 8/22/1938. WGM 3181-2, 46-26. "It would seem ... that the people are getting somewhat fed up with the constant fighting and bickering," WGM wrote Henry Broderick, 2/22/1938. WGM, 3181-2, 46-5; ST, 5/29/1938; PI, 7/13/1938.

10 Hamley to ABL, 9/7/1938, 12/31/1939. Hamley-Langlie Correspondence; Hamley Yearbook, 4/22/1939. Hamley Papers; Hamley OH, WSA; Fire Chief William Fitzgerald OH. Charles W. Bender, *A Report on Politics in Seattle* , Vol. II. Cambridge, Massachusetts: Edward C. Benfield Joint Center for Urban Studies of the Massachusetts Institute of Technology and Harvard University, 1961: 55 ff. Langlie appointed William F. Devin and Cincinnatan James Hodgson police court judges. Devin was mayor from 1942-52. He and Gordon S. Clinton (1959-66) struck the "young citizen in government" pose of their predecessor. Magnuson's intelligence operative in Seattle detected "a decided conservative trend." Howard McGowan to WGM 3/23/1940. WGM 3182-2: 48-58.

11 Martin was reelected in 1936 by GOP cross-overs in the first "open" primary. CDM's friends worked for ABL in the general election. Baker OH.

12 Burke-Berner interview of ABL. The strategy was to "hammer away" at "liberal Democrats," aim to get Martin men, and set up a separate precinct organization to get Republicans despite a "non-partisan" stance. FGH to ABL, 6/30/1940. Hamley, 17/1; Fred Baker OH, WSA. No other Republican running for statewide office came closer than 8,000; Dill's vociferous "regular" Democratic enemies included Edith Dolan Riley, long a power in Democratic ranks in Spokane County. EDR to Nellie Taylor Ross, 2/19/1934. Riley Papers, 10-5; Krause: 14-37, 262-77. This was the closest statewide election between Governor Ernest Lister's

in 1918, and Governor Christine Gregoire's in 2004.

13 Langlie was 38. Minnesota's Harold Stassen was the youngest, elected in 1938, at 31.

14 "The Governors Inaugural Address and Message to the Legislature," 1/15/1941, L, 26; ST 1/16/1941. Dill's manager Clarence Coleman now state Democratic chair and the legislative Left had the Democratic caucuses hear charges of election fraud for four and a half hours before inaugurating Langlie. Senator Rosellini's resolution to investigate was put down 97 to 45 Daniel J. Chasan, *Speaker of the House: The Political Career and Times of John L. O'Brien*. Seattle: UWAP, 1990: 22-29; Howard McGowan to WGM, n.d., (1/41). WGM 3181-2, 49-18.

15 Hamley's "Department Reorganization" "adopting modern business methods, fixing responsibility and "checks" on spending typified internal moves. FGH, "Memorandum to All Employees of the Department of Public Service." (1941). ABL 2M-1-17, public service; Langlie, a tea-totaler, was especially sensitive to the WSLBC with its ever vulnerable to "breakage," (unaccounted for bottles), and political favoritism in licensing. Becket became President of the National Alcoholic Beverage Control Association in 1944. Their premises are in the latter's presidential address. WSA, ABL, 162, NABCA, 1944.

16 Assistant to the Governor Merritt Benson said, "It is the policy of the administration to give consideration to experience as contrasted to academic education wherever possible." To Gordon Tongue, Chair, State Personnel Board, 6/22/1944. WSA, ABL 2M-7-65, personnel board 1943-44; "Minutes of [the] Standards Committee," 4/8/1949. ABL 49, personnel; SR, 6/27/1941. About 1,000 Democrats were replaced of 6,000 state employees.

17 All three Langlie administrations had several Democrats as directors and judges, beginning with Judges Hodson and Hamley.

18 "Historical and Statutory Background of the Washington State Personnel Board." ABL 2M-1-5, personnel board. In 1942, specifics followed. "Draft of a State Personnel Act." 9/42. Ibid.; ABL to "All Department Heads," "Authorized Rules Governing Certain Employment Practices." 3/1/1944. ibid.

19 SR 5/3/1941, 5/15/1941; SC 5/8/1941; ST 4/3/1941.

20 Telegram, LaGuardia to ABL, 6/17, 12/7,1941. ABL 2M-1-4, defense council, 1941; DeWitt to ABL 12/17/1941, 7/17/1941. ARG 12-4. The Governor dispatched 4,000 guardsmen to tunnels and bridges from the Columbia to Deception Pass on the morning of December 8, 1941. Only 3,000 had rifles. The Washington State Attorney General advised the governor that martial law and the suspension of civil liberties was beyond his constitutional authority, which was limited to calling out the militia. Whether this was under serious consideration or an option being checked is open to question. General DeWitt found it "desirable in the national interest" to revise restrictions on Japanese on furlough to move freely in 1943, in Public Order #17; "The policies of the War Relocation Authority are only now being developed," Tacoma attorney Milton S. Eisenhower its Director wrote ABL. Ibid, 3/30/1942.

21 ABL, "Testimony Before the House Committee on Defense Migration," 2/28/1942, WSA, ARG 12-7. On another racial matter, Hamley later argued the federal allowance of segregation of busses on the Tri-Cities nuclear reservation might be "equal," but was not "reasonable," as the law required, and got reconsideration. FGH to ABL, Hamley Papers, 1944; See [Governor] Earl Warren, "War Time Martial Rule in California." *Journal of the State Bar Association of California* 27 (1942): 185-204. Congressman Magnuson resisted repatriation in 1943, "For the safety of the Japanese themselves, as well as the best interests of our citizenry."

WGM to Dorothy R. Fisk, 11/13/1943. WGM 3141-2, 6-52.

22 e.g., David A. Takami's *History Link*, (Seattle) article on "Japanese American Incarceration-World War II," which claims this "was the "worst violation of constitutional rights in American History," overlooking the plight of African-Americans in slavery.

23 The legislature enacted ABL's Washington State Defense Council, (HB 596), in two days on 3/21/1941. National coverage of defense plants was left to nine Army regiments (about 7,200 men). ABL to LaGuardia, 8/12/1941; ABL to U.S. Senator Homer T. Bone, 3/2/1942. ABL 2M-1-4, defense council, 1941.

24 ABL submitted nine other bills in 1943, from a restrictive Bank Loan Act, to the War Housing Act; ABL to Frank S. Gaines, Office of Civilian Defense, 1/18/1944 loc. cit., defense council, 1943-44.

25 ABL, radio address, 10/28/1942. L, 19-5.

26 Dolbeare, 82, 83, 86, 89.

27 "Constitution of Washington State World Commerce Commission," (1944), ARG, 12-3. WSA.

28 State and congressional district commissioners, agency liaisons and county were ready in August. "Missionary" work was still necessary in 1944. "Roster and Directory Emergency Commissioners for National Defense," 8/15/1941. ABL 2M-1-4, defense council 1941.

29 Washington State Planning Commission, "Ten Years of Progress," 12/1944. WSA, ARG: 12-14; WSPC, "Report Month of November" [1941] WSA, ABL 2M-1-1, SPC 2/1941. The Council was initiated by CDM in 1934.

30 The income tax was be on incomes over $1,000, netting $80-100 million a biennium. The Supreme Court would have to reverse its prior ruling that an income tax was a levy on property subject to the 40 mill limit. In 1954, the attorney general told Langlie it would be "Absolutely impossible to draft any act imposing a flat income tax which would be constitutional. " AAG Ralph Davis to Roger Freeman, 12/1/1954. AG 90-8-1053, 32, governor 1954-56.

31 Defining assets and other forms of income was the nub of Attorney General Smith Troy's argument to the Department of Social Security, 9/23/1941. WSA, ABL 2-M1-19, social security department 1941-44"; "Memo on Washington Old Age Assistance Program," (1942), ABL, UWSC, 19-4; PI 10/22/1942; ABL to Richard Neustadt, Regional Director; Federal Social Security Board, to ABL, 3/20/1941. WSA, ABL 2M-1-19, social security department 1941-44;

32 Thomas E. Dewey to ABL, 1/8/1945, L, "M"; Inez Lewis (the governor's secretary), to FGH, 10/27/1944. Hamley Papers, 17/4/1931; ABL to Dewey, 1/5/1949, L, "L"; State level Democratic activist and legislator Tom Smith said at the end of 1943 that they did not have "a real candidate yet. Most of the big shots are scared to death of Langlie." 11/29/1943. Smith papers, 1/8.

33 MCW speeches, 9/25/1944, 10/25/1944. L, 56-10.

34 Dewey in 1944 and 1948, and George H. W. Bush in 2000 and 2004.

35 MCW, speeches, 9/25/1944, 10/25/1944, L, 56-10.

36 Reeves to WGM, 8/14/1944. WGM 3181-2, 55; WGM to John Boettiger, 10/18/1942. WGM 3181-2.

37 ABL got 197,817 votes in the primary. The total GOP vote for governor was 254,361, Wallgren got 98,162 of the Democratic total of 98,228. Secretary of State, "Report of

the Vote in the Primary Election, July 11, 1944." Olympia: OSOS, 1944. Turnout was the critical element. In the primary 46.4 percent of the registered voters did; in the general, 84.5 percent, a record disparity. The latter dropped 14.1 percent in 1948 or ABL would have been defeated again. See POQ 8 (Summer, 1944): 278; PI 10/30/1944. ABL's first term accomplishments are laid out in his 31 page "Message to the Twenty-Ninth Legislature," 1/9/1945, in *Washington Public Documents 1943-1944*. Olympia: State Printer, 1945. State Senator Lady Willie Forbus did ABL considerable damage east of the Columbia with "drys" with her claims that the Liquor Board's buying of the stock of the Waterfill and Frasier distillery to sustain sales had inured to ABL's personal benefit. Baker OH. "In 1944, Roosevelt was the only Democrat capable of winning the presidential election," Robert Ficken concludes in "Roosevelt or Ruin." Langlie knew "It was my open and constant support of Tom Dewey … that cost me the election … " PI 10/30/1944; ABL's first term accomplishments are in his "Message to the Twenty-Ninth Legislature," 1/9/1945, in *Washington Public Documents 1944-1945*. Olympia: State printer, 1945.

38 SR 7/15/1948.

39 Baker OH.

40 Kenneth Dolbeare, *The Evolution of the Public Sector in Washington State*, Vol. 2. Olympia: The Evergreen State College, 1988: 89-90.

41 ABL, "Special Message to the Thirty-First Legislature," 2/21/1949. Olympia: State Printer, 1949. "Information on State Government, Legislative and Administrative Matters, for Assistance to Legislators," by the administration. 4/20/1949. ABL 35, 33.

42 ABL, radio speech, 10/24/1948. L, 26,1948 speeches. MCW tried to blunt "spender" accusations before the election, cutting his departments' requests for 1949-51 from $834,088 to $627,451 million (excluding the estimated $55 million needed to fulfill I-172), ignored new obligations in pensions, highway construction, and wiped out capital construction for all institutions. Net revenue was anticipated to be $414,076,408, still leaving a 30 percent gap. After the election ABL privately asked experts for tax alternatives. They offered ones on soft drinks, bar syrups, and insurance premiums that raised a mere $16.5 million. Tightening "enforcement" (presumably property tax assessments) might gain another $95 million. In light of the constitutional limit on property (at 40 mils) and the prohibition on an income tax, the sales tax was the only real option. WBGR, "An Analysis of the Governor's Budget Submitted by Governor Mon C. Wallgren to the Thirty-First Legislature," (November, 1948), and, Lew Selvedge, James K. Hill, and Donald Webster to ABL, 12/21/1948. Both WSA, ABL, 2P-1-59, taxes 1949.

43 Roderic Olzendam to ABL, 9/20/1949. WSA, ARG, 42; ADW, 12/7/1949; "I'm personally frank in saying that in the 1948 election I didn't come out against 172. I was against it but didn't make it a campaign issue. As a practical politician I realized I would be defeated if I announced my negative stand on it," ABL later told interviewers. Yarnell, "Pensions …"154.

44 "Ratables" were across-the-board percentage cuts in welfare payments, legalized in 1951.

45 Director of the Budget, "Analysis of the 1951-1953 Budget," L, 35-22.

46 The carry-forward deficit was doubled to $93 million. The state had been in the hole six years, and "in a relatively short time" the banks would refuse state warrants. ABL to the House 3/20/1951. WSA, ABL 2P-1-29, 1951, House corr.; A Democratic view of this period is in Daniel J. Chasan's *Speaker of the House: The*

*Political Career and Times of John L. O'Brien.* Seattle: UWAP, 1990: 57-86. The property tax was ruled out. In 1949 it reached an all-time high average of 51 mils. This would have not been so if county assessors had kept appraisals as low as 19 percent of true value current. Overall, ABL was restrained. In 1943 for instance, the Legislature passed 292 bills. Eight were vetoed, three partially vetoed, and nothing of consequence.

47 The WOAPU's I-157 had been defeated nearly two to one in 1944, and Referendum 25 allowing the PUDs acquire their private counterparts three to two. All gas taxes were dedicated to highways by two to one, and the 40 mil limit affirmed by the same margin; Allen Yarnell, "Pensions and Politics in Washington State, 1948." PNQ 61 (7/70): 147-55.

48 Under constituent pressure, county assessors ignored the constitutional mandate to be at of 50 percent of actual value, "Some taxpayers are permitted to get away with fraud, while the honest taxpayer is penalized because of his honesty." ABL, "Revenue Problems of the State of Washington," Address the Fourteenth Annual Institute of Government, BGRS, UW, 1949; Hodde Papers, WSA, 10, "revenue problems, 1949, op cit." "Comparison of 1949-1951 Budget with 1947-1949 Budget," n.d., (1949). ABL 59, taxes.

49 Speaker R. Mort Frayn OH, 7/15/1985. Later Speaker Don Eldridge (1967-71), then a freshman, found the GOP caucus' leadership weak. Frayn and Floor Leader Newman Clark had as "Their reason in life ... to harp on anything Langlie wanted to do." Eldridge OH, OSOS, 168, and, OH by the author, 3/22/2005.

50 The prime stumbling block to the FPA was Land Commissioner Jack Taylor. Senator Lady Willie Forbus, "The Legislative Up-To-Date," (1943 session), LWF Papers, 2-1 speeches. The exasperated governor had pled for his "executive requests," a permanent (Highway) Safety Council, a Toll Bridge Authority, a corporate franchise tax to raise $35 million a biennium for the state, enabling counties to enact a business tax, and cities to raise fees and saw them all stalled with 15 days left in the session. Vetoing the redistricting written by the Democrats, a patent gerrymander, exacerbated the situation. The Senate's conservatism was in part due to failure to redistrict, blocked after the 1930 and 1940 censuses by members from relatively smaller districts east of the mountains determined to keep their leverage. The average size of congressional districts should have been 339,831. The first district (Seattle and North) was 18.6 percent above that in the bill sent the governor, and the Sixth District (Tacoma and South) 19.2 percent below, another gerrymander. ABL's veto of a bill allowing counties to license pinball machines was plainly a personal attitude. ABL to House 3/1/1951; Vetoes of HBs 425, 227, and 434, and S.B. 85, 1951 Regular Session. ABL 2P-1-29, 1951, House corr. In 1952, five of the state's seven congressional districts were held by Republicans, a number not exceeded since the 1920s. Newspaper man Don Magnuson, running at large and profiting by name identification with Senator Warren Magnuson was the only statewide Democratic winner.

51 Realized as the Seattle World's Fair of 1962 by the Rosellini administration.

52 See Carsten Lein, *Olympic Battleground.* San Francisco: Sierra Club Books, 1995, for the environmentalist view.

53 USFS, "Olympic National Forest-Fiftieth Anniversary Report" (1905-55). ABL, 2P-1-49, Olympic National Park, 55-57; ABL to HST, 12/2/1952, ibid.; Marckworth to ABL, 3/3/1953; Minutes of the Review Committee, 5/28/1953; Marckworth to ABL 2/5/1954. All ABL, 2P-1-49, 1-8. See Gerald W. Williams, *The U.S. Forest Service in the Pacific Northwest: A History.* Corvallis: OSUP, 2009.

54 In 1954, Charles E. Andrew, Chief Consulting Engineer, TBA, claimed the "System

is in the best financial condition since its inception." To W. A. Bugge, 9/1/1954. TBA 2R-161, highways; William J. Gore and Evelyn Shipman, *Commuters vs. the Black Ball Line: Washington Purchases the Puget Sound Ferries*, found "The terminals and floating equipment were in a serious state of deterioration," forcing the state had to take out a second lien at higher interest rates until new boats increased earning power." The Inter-University Case Program of the University of Alabama State Press, University of Alabama, 1959: 4; "Analysis of Operations of Washington State Ferries," Olympia: DOH, 1/1/1956. ABL 63, TBA, ferries 1955. For ABL's and MCW's roles in acquiring a system neither wanted, see the author's "The politics of Transportation." C (Spring, 1995): 13-19.

55 APR was on the Transportation Commission 30 years later, when it was renamed the "Governor A. D. Rosellini Evergreen Point Bridge"; W. A. Bugge to ABL, 3/9/1955, ABL, UWASC, 17-18.

56 ABL to Representative Al Leland, 8/28/1952. ABL 2P-161, Second Lake Washington Bridge, 1953, WSA; To Norton Clapp, 10/1/1953. ABL 2R-1-16, TBA 1953; PI 7/20/1954; ST 4/21/1954; Clinton OH; Governor-elect Al Rosellini was present at ABL's invitation, and the bridge opened seven years into his terms

57 i.e., the Fallon Bill, HR 8836.

58 See Professor Melvin Rader, *False Witness*. Seattle: UWAP, 1979.

59 "Report of the Joint Fact Finding Committee on Un-American Activities," (1/49), ARG, 10, WSA. Preface, and section 32, of *Washington Public Documents 1947-1949*. Olympia: SPI, 1949; House of Representatives, "Report of the Special Committee" 2/21/1955. ABL 2P-1-48.

60 "Memorandum to the Governor by the State Department of Civil Defense," 7/6/1954. ABL 2D-8, 61, civil defense, 1954.

61 "A Word From the Governor," 10/5/1953. ABL 2-9; ON, 7/18/1951.

62 Mitchell was U.S. Senator Mon Wallgren's chief aide, whom he appointed successor in 1944.

63 Hugh B. Mitchell OH, WSA; "Langlie Rally Norway Hall," 1952 Speeches, (10/1/1952), ABL, UWAWC, 28; ST 3/2/1998; Radio speech by HBM, 10/1/1952. Naomi Benson papers, UWASC.

64 Telegram, Guy Gabrielson [Chair, RNC] to ABL, 7/5/1952. ABL 3-2; Telegram, Henry Cabot Lodge to ABL, 7/2/1952, ibid; ABL, "Fair Play Amendment," ABL 2-28; Adams to ABL, 7/ 25/1952. L 3-2. It was written on TR's 1912 model by Herbert Brownell and Governor Christian Herter, soon to be attorney general, and secretary of state; Paul T. David, Malcolm Moos, and Ralph M. Goldman, eds., *Presidential Nominating Politics in 1952: The West*. Baltimore: The Johns Hopkins University Press, 1954: 160-84.

65 See Richard N. Smith, *Thomas E. Dewey and His Times*. N.Y.: Simon and Schuster, 1982: 579-90.

66 Seven institutional heads were retained, and six replaced; "Report to the 1943 Legislature by the State Charitable, Penal and Reformatory Interim Investigating Committee." ABL 2M-1-13, institutions investigation 1942-43; McGee to ABL, 4/24/1944. ABL 90-7-873, govs. offc., 1943-44; Budget Director David E. Lockwood to ABL, "Accomplishments of the Department of Finance, Budget and Business under the Present Administration." ibid., department of business, 1941-43; "Lack of finances has been a great handicap … particularly in … personnel. The first paycheck comes in and they [the guards] … have to give up." Warden John Cranor to H. D. Van Eaton, Director of Institutions, ABL 102A-

55-10, penitentiary 1949-50.

67 Director of Institutions Harold Van Eaton was convinced ABL had done "a terrific job of selling," but could not overcome the legislature. Van Eaton, OH, 11/17/1970; "The maintenance of "practically all … State institutions was substandard, in fact, genuinely deplorable," but was being rectified. H. D. Van Eaton to ABL, 1/29/1953. ABL 2P-I-24, institutions 1952-53; Van Eaton OH. 8; Harris to ABL, 1/21/1955. ABL, 03A116, 35, governor's office 1954-55.

68 Dr. Karl Menninger to ABL, 7/9/1956, ARG, 26.

69 A "CVA" was first attempted by Congressman Knute Hill in 1941 (HR 6076), as a "Columbia Power Authority"; F. A. LeSourd, the assistant secretary of the Northwest Public Power Association testifying on the CVA, 9/29/1941. ABL 2M-1-03, construction and development, Columbia Basin, 1941-43.

70 Telegram, Hugh B. Mitchell to ABL, 2/2/1949. ABL 1-9.

71 Horan to Kirby Billingsley, 4/11/1945: "Friendly Analysis of the Columbia Basin Bill." Radio address, Horan Papers, 131. Olympia: the SPC (Office of the Governor), 12/31/1954. ABL 2P-1-51, SPC.

72 "Statement of Governor Arthur B. Langlie before the [House] Committee on Public Works." ABL 1-32. See Wells Wyatt, "Public Power in the Eisenhower Administration." *Journal of Policy History* 20:2 (4/08): 227-62.

73 Holland Houston, "A Program for the Washington State Power Commission," typescript, (1951) ARG 38. The convincing Houston was a "terrific influence." Baker OH. Jack V. Rogers, his Director of Conservation and Development (an ambivalent title), and arch-antagonists Auditor Cliff Yelle and Commissioner of Public Lands Jack Taylor were the others. "Minutes of the Committee to Administer Chapter 175, Laws of 1933 [as amended]," 7/21/1949. ABL 2P-1-11, conservation and development. "The Commission is expressly denied the right to engage in the distribution business," Attorney General Don Eastvold warned, and projects would have to be financed by revenue bonds. Eastvold to James N. Canning, 7/13/1954. ABL 2P-1-51, power commission, 85; PI 5/22/1952; ST 9/17, 11/7/1952. Senate Majority Leader Albert Rosellini insisted the SPC was ABL's "means of trying to work with the private power people." ADR OH, 11/27/1970, LOHP 1.

74 Devin and Fred Baker urged a "Bonneville-like middleman" to ward off the twin threats of the PUDs and the "Grant [County-] like privates." Houston Memorandum, 1/24/1949. ABL SPC, ibid., 1951. The convincing Houston was a "terrific influence." Baker OH; "Minutes of the Committee to Administer Chapter 175, Laws of 1933 [as amended]," 7/21/1949. ABL 2P-1-11, conservation and development.

75 Minutes, PNWGPC, 12/7/1953. AG, 90-8-1053, 132, governor, 1952; "Statement by Paul J. Raver, [Director of the] Bonneville Power Administration before Subcommittee of [U.S.] Senate Committee of Public Lands and Surveys"; Democratic Speaker of the House Charles A. Hodde, "Radio Address," 3/1/1951. Hodde Papers 5, sps; WSPC, "Interim Report" 12/31/1954. ABL 2P-1-11, construction and development, SPC 1953-55; Hodde OH, 9/17/1989, tape 2.

76 Memo, Houston to ABL, 3/4/1955. ABL 6-22; J. F. Ward to F.P.C., 9/9/1955. ABL 9-22.

77 ST 4/12/1954; SR 10/10/1954.

78 LMT 1/22/1954.

79 "A Program for Power in the Northwest," 2/23/1955, typescript. ABL 6-22; Dr. J.

Paul Raver wrote in 1951 that Houston's "The Place of Generating Stations in the Orderly Program of Electric Development in the Pacific Northwest " contained some good information … a number of statements that are questionable, and others that are contrary to fact." The latter were enough to substantially destroy the conclusions. Raver to ABL, 9/7/1951. Mitchell 17-9.

80 Governor Douglas McKay to ABL, 10/12/1953. ABL 9-14; SR 11/14/1953.

81 ABL, "In Regard to the Proposed Dams on the Cowlitz River." Radio and television speech, 8/11/1955. ABL 8-36; TNT 4/3/1956.

82 "A Report on the Administration of Pollution Abatement in the State of Washington." ABL 2M-1-15, Pollution Commission, 1942-43; Chapter 216, Laws of 1945; *Makah Indian Tribe v. E. F. McCauly, et. al.*, A. G. No. 263, 83, (1941). Director of the Budget, "The General Fund Receipts and Expenditures, by Months," (1919-55).

83 ABL 2P-1-36, budgets. In the 14 years between 1927 and 1941, General Fund expenditures exceeded revenue by only $5 million. During World War II a $76 million surplus accrued. In fiscal years 1945-46 and 1946-47 outgo jumped from $75 to 122 million. Initiative 172 was passed in November 1948 and by March 1949 outgo was $28 million above income for the year. When taxes could not be agreed upon, the 1949-51 budget was left out of balance $93 million. The governor excised $17 million. Ibid. "Your Dollars' Worth of State Government" (1952), ibid: 1, 3. Total revenue for 1949-51 was $320,132,605, the deficit $22,788,091, or 7 percent, which next occurred in 1981-83. Forty-three percent of the General Fund went to the Department of Social Security. Ninety-eight of every 1,000 adults were receiving welfare in 1940 and just 51 in 1949. In the two subsequent biennia, the deficiencies were 21 and 19.5 percent, leaving a total shortfall for 6 years of $130,009,609, despite the 1953-55 Legislature's transfer of 27 cash accounts with $30 million to the General Fund. Director of the Budget to ABL, 11/29/1955. ABL 2P-1-36, budgets; AAG Ralph Davis reported to ABL, 12/1/1954. "You can safely say that it is impossible to impose any effective flat income tax under our present constitutional provisions." AG 90-8-153, 32, governor, 1954-56.

84 Speaker "Don Eldridge: An Oral History." Olympia: WSOHP (OSOS), 2005: 103; Eldridge OH by the author, 3/22/2005; Governor Rosellini rated ABL "no worse than average." ADR, OH, 11/27/1970.

85 Ernest C. Miller, "The Management of Washington State Government: The Problem of Central Staff organization." MA, UW, 1953: 79.

86 Dolbeare, 94; Freeman OH.

87 ABL, "Stronger states in the Federal Union: Why and How." In *Address to the Eighth American Assembly* 10/15/1955. ABL 53, governor; ABL, "States' Rights, and States' Duties," VSD, (XXL), no. 21, 8/15/1955, and ABL, "Easy Money From Washington Can Weaken the States," USNWR, 9/9/1955.

88 Kinnear OH by DDEL, 4/24/1972. 6-9/12, in WSA as OH 3941; Frayn OH 3/22/2005, WSA.

89 Norm Schut (President of the WSFE), OH 12/17/1989. LOHP 1. Congressman Thor Tollefson, OH by DDEL, 4/24/1972, copied in WSA as OH 338, 67; SC 9/7/1956. "Eastvold helped me," Governor Rosellini told the author. OH 11/27/1970. LOHP I.

90 T 5/3/1956.

91 ABL turned the president down in December 1955, but "his conscience got to him." Baker OH.

92 T 5/3/1956.

93 NYT 3/29/1956.

94 Magnuson's HR 6100 died in committee. This statement was later denied. SR 10/26/1956; The UP's Leroy Hittle, ABL's first choice as campaign manager, felt the high-principle-personal attack approach "backfired." Leroy Hittle OH, 12/17/1989. LOHP 1.

95 "The Myth that is Magnuson," brochure, 1956, ABL "L."

96 "High Office Demands High Principle." ABL 53, governor; D. D. Eisenhower to ABL, 8/29/1956. ABL "L."

97 ABL, "Message to the 35th Legislature," 1/14/1957. L 43; OH, Arthur S. Langlie, 11/15/1970, WSA; Norton Simon the Los Angeles financier who owned McCall's Magazine, then the world's second largest, made ABL CEO. Madison Avenue was skeptical, but by 1962, he was cast as "a seasoned politician … an able lawyer, and a clear thinking administrator." Angina pectoris advanced after a "slight coronary" in April, 1961. ABL retired to Seattle for his 65th birthday in 1965 and died a year later.

**Chapter 5: Mon Wallgren**

1 "Remarks on Mount Olympus National Park," by Representative Mon C. Wallgren, 6/9/1937. MCW 12; Henry M. Jackson Foundation, Interview of [Senator] August P. Mardesich (on Democratic Politics in Snohomish County in the 1930's). UWASC; MCW's approach is captured in "Washington State and the New Deal," *Record of the 74th Congress, 2nd Session*, Vol. 80, part 10, 10304-05.

2 The Martin-appointed Washington State Planning Council noted that with the reservation of 360,000 acres for the Olympic, one quarter of the state would be a federal preserve. "Further large extensions" were "entirely unnecessary." Left in the hands of the Forest Service for sustained yield, the excluded land would kept from "the mercy of private exploitation." "The Proposed Mount Olympus National Park: A Land Use Study of Public Lands On the Olympic Peninsula." Olympia: The Council, 1936; MCW's original bill of 1936 captured 728,360 acres (HR 10024). The law of 1938 enclosed almost 900,000 acres, nearly three times the Council's suggestion. A complete outline of events from 1909 is in Forester Fred W. Cleater's "The Olympic National Park Controversy: A Review" (1953). WSL, Olympic National Park Review Committee, MST 32, file 3. In 1946, Wallgren prepared to testify to Congress against logging in the park, then agreed with Senators Mitchell and Magnuson on selective cutting of 20 million board feet of Douglas fir to relieve the housing crisis. Truman responded to post-war industry pressure by extending the park along the coast to its present boundaries. Carsten Lien, *Olympic Battleground*. San Francisco: Sierra Club Books, 1991: chaps. 9-12.

3 PI 1/23/1945. He was appointed December 18, to fill out the term of Lewis B. Schwellenbach, who became a federal judge, then Truman's Secretary of Labor. This to gain seniority over the class of 1940, in the same way that Langlie did for Magnuson four years later. Democrats won six of the seven U.S House seats, and WGM in Seattle's First with 62 percent. FDR took 58 percent statewide, MCW 54 percent.

4 Leroy Hittle and Jack Gorrie; MCW is one of few in national history to give up a Senate seat for a governor's chair. In 1948, 28 ex-governors served as senators; ABL's perceived strength in 1943 was such that no Democrat was preparing a challenge, with FDR's availability in 1944 uncertain. "Everyone is casting about for a definite candidate for governor" State Treasurer Tom Martin wrote WGM, 10/23/1943. WGM 3181-2, 51-2; MCW, "Speech at Masonic Hall," 9/25/1944.

ABL 50-10.

5 Records show that Wallgren spent over 100 days of his administration in California.

6 "MCW Speech at Everett Central Labor Council," 10/4/1944. L 56-10; MCW "Broadcast from Spokane," 10/25/1944. L 56-11; The Democratic State Committee's goal was to move from 830,000 registered voters (of 1,003,000 possible) to 925,000 was met. J. R. Binyon Finance Director to Pearl Wanamaker, 10/11/1944. Wanamaker Papers, UWASC, 16-19.

7 NYT 10/29/1944; WGM to Andrew Winberg, 8/24/1944. WGM 3181-2, 55/8.

8 The *P-I* had put MCW in the Senate, WGM wrote confidant Howard McGowan. "He was one of those who didn't "realize what a campaign is … who still think there is a Democratic party to pull them through." 3/27/1944. WGM 3181-2. 51-49. 10.

9 MCW to "Dear Friend," 9/3/1944. HMJ 3560-2, 45/22. Saul Haas to Lt. Charles J. Kamm, 9/30/1944. Haas 2213-23, 23/1.

10 Secretary of State Belle Reeves and Superintendent of Elections Ken Gilbert to WGM, 8/14/1944. WGM 3181-2, 55/1. State Senator Lady Willie Forbus, who did ABL considerable damage east of the mountains over the Waterfill and Frazier liquor deal, observed at the end of September, "The [Democratic] National Committee and the State Committee have not started a very vigorous campaign as yet." LWF to Carl Mobler, 9/29/1944. LWF 259-2, 1, demo organizations.

11 Senior Senator Homer T. Bone's leg had been contracting since he broke his hip in 1939 and he had no taste for another campaign; John Salter to Ed Hennessey, 2/22/1945. HMJ 3560-2, 6/85. SR, 1/17/44; (Congressional Staffer) to Salter, 12/6/44. HMJ 3560-2, 6-23.

12 SR 11/17/1944.

13 ST 3/22/1949.

14 WGM to Bone, 12/21/1944. WGM 3181, 51/32; *Seventh Annual Report, 1946-1947*. Olympia: The Board, 1948.

15 Salter to Hennessey, 5/2/1945. WGM 3560-2, 6/24; MCW to ABL, 12/20/44. L 56-10, 6/4.

16 Tom Smith to Rep. Arthur S. Cory, 2/22/1946. Smith Papers, 6/8.

17 Jack Ballew, Director of Institutions to MCW, 11/30/1948. MCW, 10, institutions.

18 Salter to Hennessey, 5/2/1945. HMJ 3560-2, 6/24; Speaker George Yantis to Ed Fussell, 5/14/1945. Yantis Papers, 1, corr. out; Representative and future Democratic Speaker Charlie Hodde rated Gorrie as "very competent," and "ran" the governor's office. Art Garton was "strong." But MCW "could have picked some of the department heads at random and done as well." Hodde OH, LOHP I.

19 Representative A. B. Comfort to ADR, 11/26/1958. Comfort 1/23; PI 1/29/1945; Hugh DeLacey to Senator Tom Rabbitt 1/8/1945. Rabbitt papers, 1, gen. corr., 1944-46.

20 Langlie sent Seattle Fire Chief Bill Fitzgerald to Wallgren to wish him well and to ask to confer on the transition. The new governor refused, saying he would not go in the office until the incumbent was gone. Fitzgerald, interview with the author, 4/19/1970; BH 1/21/1945; PI 4/4/1945; *Kirkland Sentinel* 8/10/1945. Re Labor, see P.A.E.N. 10/21/1948.

21 "Analysis of Appropriations by 1945 Legislature and Comparison with Appropriations for the 1943-45 Biennium," MCW, budget; ST 3/20/1045. It was reported

that 12 "executive requests had passed." Since none were spelled out in the inaugural address and none are present in MCW's files, it is assumed that they were items he advocated and the legislature enacted.

22 "Minutes of the [State] Development Board," 11/26/1945. MCW 5.

23 ST, n.d., in Hansen MS, Scrapbook, 1501-4; "Report of the Advisory Committee on Teachers' Retirement," 11/9/1945. MCW 14, teachers' retirement, 1947; Marie Rosenberg, "Women in Politics: A Comparative Study of Congresswomen Edith Green and Julia Butler Hansen." Ph.D., UW, 1973: 16.

24 ST 8/3/1945; DO 9/16/1946; The Study committee produced the "Strayer Report" a useful blueprint that shaped public education for two decades. ST 7/2/1945.

25 MCW, *Inaugural Message*, 1/10/1945, in *Washington Public Documents, 1943-1944*. Olympia: State Printer, 1945; HMJ to Attorney General Smith Troy, 2/22/1945. HMJ 3560-2, 6/85.

26 Earle N. Anderson to Jack Gorrie, 10/20/1945. MCW 1, L&I. In 1947, Anderson told the Senate Appropriations Committee he would spend as he saw fit, regardless of their figure; Ballew to MCW, 11/30/1948. MCW 2N-1-10, institutions department, 1948. It had requested $19 million from the 1947 legislature, and gotten $8 million. D. E. Sergeant to MCW 9/2/1947. Institutions, 90-7-873, 8, govs. offc., 1947.

27 PI 8/7/1945; SR 8/7/1945.

28 "Remarks by the Governor to the Democratic State Convention," Olympia, 1946.

29 ST 1/15/1947; Defeating WCF Communists Tom Rabbitt and William Pennock, for instance, transferred strife in the legislature to the Democratic Party organizations, especially in King County. Representative Charles Savage unsuccessfully ran against Coe of State Chair, and against the administration. SS 12/7/1946.

30 In 1953, Senate Majority Co-Leader Tom Hall feigned ignorance: "No legislator I know of is running for office in 1948." In fact, Co-leader Victor Zednick and Speaker Herb Hamblen were considering state office; WGM to HBM, 1/27/1947. HBM MS, 927, 1/15.

31 Daniel Goldy to C. Girard Davidson, 12/8/1947. HBM 927 15/1/; HBM to MCW, 3/7/1947; to Earl Coe, 3/17/1947. HBM 927, 14/40.

32 A total of 40 (of l44) were on public payrolls.

33 Fred K. Ross to ABL, "Report on Wallgren," ABL 56-17; e.g., "Report of Talk by Governor Wallgren before Democratic Rally at Bellingham," 10/18/1948. L 56/17.

34 *Victoria Times* 9/8/1945; SR 8/8/1948.

35 PI 3/26/1948; John Boettiger to WGM, 7/22/1942. WGM 3181-2, 49/56.

36 "Report of the Washington State Senate Committee Appointed to Investigate the Licensing ... of Clubs." 11/15/1948. MCW 11, Liquor Control Board.

37 Charles Andrew (Chief Construction Engineer, TBA) to C. B. Shain, 6/21/1946. MCW 14, TBA; MCW to Jim McGovern, 6/14/1946. MCW 15, TBA.

38 Rogan Jones to Shain, 2/20/1947. MCW 14, TBA.

39 W. G. Pebbles, "Prospective Sale of Tacoma Narrows Bridge Revenue Bonds," 2/9/1948. MCW 14, TBA.

40 Harry Girvan and George Farnsworth to ABL, 1/23/1949. MCW 14, TBA.

41 Revelle, "Statement of Facts in Ferry Rate Case," n.d., MCW 15, transportation.

42 Attorney General Smith Troy to MCW, 3/8/1948. MCW 14, TBA.

43 PI 4/25/1948. In 1948, Langlie promised only an "honest solution" to the ferry quagmire.

44 "Governor Wallgren's Ferry Address," 9/7/1948. MCW 14, TBA.

45 ADW 6/18/1948; Member Ruth Peeler noted the Parks Commission "has functioned as a majority and minority group," and Martin had resigned "owing to friction ... over the expending of funds." Of the $999,850 set aside for parks by the 1957 legislature $629,615 went to Dry Falls/Sun Lakes. "Biennial Report" of the Commission for 1947-49. WSDA, ABL 2N-9-50, parks, 1947-51.

46 EDR 8/16/1948.

47 Harry J. Martin to HMJ, 6/11/1947. HMJ 3560-2, 5/18; Harry Henson to HMJ, 3/27/1948. HMJ 3560-2, 3/80. The animus with State Treasurer Fluent, Chairman of the Progressive Party, was such its "principal objective" in nominating him for governor was to beat Wallgren. He would not file if the more conservative Martin won. ADW 8/13/1948.

48 SR 7/15/1948.

49 Gorrie OH.

50 Memo by HBM, 8/26/1948. HBM 927, 2/59. After polling politicians and commentators *Newsweek* named him the most likely vice presidential candidate before the national convention. PI, 8/8/1975.

51 Beck to WGM, 11/2/1946. WGM 3181-2, 47/27; Norm Schut OH. MCW, press release, 10/13/1948. HBM 927, 2/59; SR 8/31/1948.

52 Hittle OH, Rosellini OH, 11/27/1970. LOHP I.

53 ST 4/14/1976; PI 9/28/1961, 8/8/1975; Waldron in the PI 7/7/1948; Cunningham in the ST 9/20/1961; Hodde and Gorrie OH's.

**Chapter 6: Albert D. Rosellini**

1 CSM l/14/1957.

2 Senator "Saltwater" Ed Henry of Seattle, not to be confused with Representative "Freshwater" Ed Henry of Spokane. Both were Democratic "conservatives."

3 O'Brien became Speaker of the House and was the nation's longest serving legislator when defeated in 1992. See Daniel Jack Chasan, *Speaker of the House: The Political Career and Times of John L. O'Brien.* Seattle: UWAP, 1990.

4 Between 1941 and 1943, he and Senator Lloyd Shorett partnered in the Smith Tower. Referrals from the prosecutor and the attorney general paid the rent.

5 Hodde OH, 1/12/1970.

6 Billington, Davis OH's. His style was reflected in his self-attached understudy Bob Grieve, Majority Leader (1958-75). Rosellini was "surprised" Grieve won, preferring gifted Snohomish County lawyer Bill Gissberg, whom Grieve outworked in the manner of his mentor and defeated by one vote.

7 As early as 1937, George Ryan, Chair of the King County Democratic Club, and a State Committeeman, wrote Magnuson, "Things in Olympia are moving very slowly. There quite a clash between the liberals in the House and the conservative leadership in control of the Senate." 2/12/1937. WGM 3181-2, 41-51; Interviews of ADR by former Senator Jack Rogers, 11/1987: 116, 118. L.O.H.P.; "The Baffling

Riddle Named Rosellini." SM, (9/64), 28; ADR: "Our American Society has become truly democratic only in social mobility from one class to another has been provided by open to all through our [public] education system," and, "Few other states can compare with our fiscal soundness" and "business-like methods, began his 1965 farewell to the legislature. "Governor [ADR] Message to the Thirty-Ninth Legislature," 1/12/1965. WSL, MS Collection 007.

8 ADR to WGM, 3/25/1943. WGM 3181-2, 51/44; Scott, "Arthur B. Langlie … " 268.

9 Rogers, 87.

10 Rogers, 135-37.

11 Rogers, 111.

12 ADR, OH, 11/27/1970; CSM 1/14/1957; Liquor-by-the-drink was legalized by initiative in 1949 and Cousin Victor Rosellini's "Rosellini's 410," ("The Algonquin of the Northwest") (1950) and the "610" (1956), became watering holes for downtown Republican influentials. Victor was the first president of the Washington Restaurant Association (1966-67), its national counterpart (1977-78), and was prominent on major civic boards. ADR's brother, respected surgeon Leo Rosellini, was also a complimentary profile.

13 Rogers, 126, 132.

14 Rogers, 135. 15. e.g., ADR to State Representative Pat Comfort, 11/20/1958. Comfort MS, 1/23;

15 "Inaugural Message of Governor Albert D. Rosellini to the Thirty-Eighth Legislature," 1/16/1957. ADR 23.

16 Rogers, 137-38; "Eastvold helped me," ADR confirmed. OH, 11/27/1970.

17 The attorney general advised ADR he could not withdraw all the previous governor's appointments not confirmed by the Senate, or make nominations while the legislature was not in session. John J. O'Connell to ADR 3/1/1957. WSA, AG 90-8-1053, 132, governor 1957-59. The state bar, which wanted judges to come from its list was told, no "enemies." In 1963, when it criticized Howard J. Thompson of the King County Superior Court as an exception to its vetting, the governor reminded them publicly it was his right.

18 Heyns, "The Dramatic New Role of Washington Institutions." ADR, 03A-116, 39, Heyns.

19 In March 1957, the three mental hospitals needed 89 physicians to meet national standards. They had 44, and 14 were leaving. G. Lee Sandritter, M.D., Acting Director, to ADR, 3/28/1957. ADR 6B-4-116, 35, institutions 1957. The expansions were in special recruitments to acquire the 400 professional and technical persons necessary to gain accreditation. Institutions and the Board of Prisons, Terms, and Paroles, which had been removed from merit, were reinstated, 6/11/1959, when the hiring process was complete. WSPB, "Report on the [1957-59] Biennium." The Board, 12/12/1959. ADR 98A-4769, SPB, 1959-60.

20 Director's comments in the Institutions section of *Washington Public Documents, 1961-62*, Vol. 2. Olympia: State Printer, 1963.

21 In three years the patient census dropped by 500, or 9 percent, more having been discharged leaving a total of 6,594 as of December 1959. ABL memorandum, re: "State Mental Hospital Progress." ABL 03A-116, 39, Heyns corr., 1960. Heyns stayed until 1966.

22 "One of the serious shortcomings of Governor Langlie's administration," ADR said in his inaugural address, was that "He never gave the legislature an adequate

revenue program." ADR, memorandum to "All Directors," 7/29/1958. ADR 52, governor's board of directors meetings, 15. He chose ABL's route, tightening collections.

23 Bugge OH, re: the Hood Canal Bridge; ST 2/21/1960.

24 Henry Schmitz, (Chair, Governor's Cross Sound Transportation Study Committee), to ADR, 1/30/1961. ADR, 232, TBA; ADR to E.R. Babcock, 7/9/1957. ADR, 232, TBA. The Evergreen Point Bridge opened In 1963, after 14 years. ADR proposed "A toll-free Hood Canal Bridge and Second Lake Washington Bridge and … the Naches Tunnel [through the Cascades] might be done by placing the 11 most congested counties on Puget Sound in a "benefit district,"(i.e., the option of imposing a one cent a gallon mark-up on themselves), something defeated in 2006; ST 2/8/1963.

25 ULL, "Partial Proceeding of the First Annual Convention," 7/14/1958, 7/17/1958. Weston, 3/25; Davis, LOHP 1, 4; (typescript), "Telephone Call from Governor Rosellini re: Joe Davis," 11/20/1957. WSFL 450-3, 4. Mon Wallgren's bruises from being too cooperative with the Teamsters may have influenced ADR to keep his distance. ADR, LOHP (1), 11/27/1970.

26 Dave Beck asked for commutation of his racketeering sentence. After some "anguish" over the political fallout, Rosellini granted it, and was a pall bearer at Beck's 1993 funeral. Bishop, Davis and Schut interviews.

27 Workmen's compensation, bringing 16,000 public employees under OASI, and teacher salaries improvements in 1957. This was considered to be primarily the legislature's doing.

28 The patronage estimate is from Chasan, *O'Brien*, 97; Charles W. Bender's "A Report on Politics in Seattle," says ADR had the "strongest personal organization. It is based on extensive patronage." Cambridge: Joint Center for Urban Studies of the Massachusetts Institute of Technology and Harvard University, 1961: II, 78; Norm Schut to ADR, 7/26/1957. ADR 8, employees, state. DiJulio also represented Jim Beam before the Liquor Board; Hittle OH.

29 Ibid., 8/1/1957; Sam Long to ADR and Warren Bishop, 12/17/1957. ADR 8, employment security department.

30 Schut to Ed Weston, 11/22/1957. WSFL, 450-3, 4/8.

31 It was not unusual for directors to be "Organization leaders and Liaison persons" in campaigns, only that over half of the 20 were. Hodde 3, "Report of Rosellini Campaign Meeting," 3/8/1960; All state employees got a letter on the governor's stationary reminding them of the coming of OASI, "realistic" per diem, and merit to Institutions and the Parole Board, which he had sponsored as a senator, and twice asked the legislature for. "Naturally, I am strongly supporting Initiative 207." Memo [1960]. Hodde, 1, corr. 1960.

32 "Memorandum to all Directors," 7/29/1958. op. cit. In 1962 Hodde reported, "We are happy to report registration for voting in the Tax Commission is 99+ percent," excepting one employee, "whose car broke down." Legislative Council, "Recommendation No. 5," 8/29/1958. ADR 98A-426, 8, merit system info; Central Personnel, "Suggested Code of Ethics," (1959), ibid, central personnel; ADR, "Directive to all Directors" 2/24/1958. WSP, 52, governor's directors meetings [re: prohibitions]; A 1960 memo to directors asking for lists of their employees was retracted. Hodde, 1, ADR to department heads, corr. 1960; Tax Commission, Interoffice Correspondence from Hodde, 8/8/1964; Re: registration, Hodde to ADR, 10/8/1964. Hodde, 3, corr. 1962-64; Re: [reinforcing the prohibitions]. Hodde, 3, corr. 1963-64; Re: "Did not respond." Hodde to Ernest Jonson, [1964].

Hodde, 4, ADR gubernatorial campaign 1964; "All District Managers or our Tax Commission offices of the 5th Congressional District have been asked to handle posting of signs to reelect judge [sic, Justice] Orrin J. Hamilton to the Supreme Court. Judge Hamilton has been a good Democrat." Hodde to Carl J. Walden [Stevens County Democratic Chair], 7/24/1962. Hodde, 3, corr. 1962-64.

33 "Judges and Attorneys Rap Patronage." ST 6/10/1959.

34 ST 4/15/1960.

35 Two firings for bribery and three resignations resulted.

36 Hodde, "From Wanderlust to Politics." LOHP 9/16/1983: 117-21.

37 *Message of Governor Rosellini to the Thirty-Sixth Legislature*, 1/13/1959. Olympia: State Printer, 1959. A six year capital plan for 1961-67 was also adopted, under the guidance of the new Central Budget Agency. Memorandum, ADR to All Agencies, 3/18/1960, in "Budget and Accounting Manual [1961-63]," 6/6/1960. ADR, 98A-426, 9, CBA memos, 1959.

38 Langliesque memos against authorized accrued funds continued to flow, but the "nut" of departments working every channel available had been cracked. e.g., Directors memorandum 61-4, 5/10/1961. ADR 03A-116, 3, Heyns corr. 1961-64.

39 Rogers, 229; ST 6/l4/1959.

40 "Memorandum, ADR to All Agencies," 3/18/1960, in "Budget and Accounting Manual [1961-63]," 6/6/1960. ADR 98A-426, 9, CBA memos, 1959.

41 Herb Legg [State Democratic Chair], Memo "Regarding Organization to Re-Elect Governor Rosellini," 3/8/1960. Hodde 3, "D party state, org, '60" "Minutes of the [ADR] Strategy Committee … " 9/10/1959. Graham, 1, Rosellini campaign; "Campaign Strategy," [1960], ADR 145, Democratic campaign, 1960; "Report of the State Chairman, January 1959-January 1961," Graham, 1, State Committee. A more detailed look at the administration's achievements is in "Remarks Made by Chas W. Hodde to Democratic Women [at the] State Democratic Convention" 6/26/1964. Hodde, 4, speeches, 1964; SR 10/29/1963; ADR in ST, 4/15/1960; See also, Warren A. Bishop to Central Budget Agency Employees, (1959). ADR, 138, Bishop file.

42 SA 11/4/1960; Washington State, Secretary of State, *Official Abstract of Votes, State General Election 11/8/1960*. Olympia: State Printer, 1961.

43 ST 4/14/1960.

44 Robert Long, Statement to the author, 11/14/1993. See PI 6/2/1964.

45 ADR to directors, 2/19/1960, 5/3/1960. ADR, 146, memo to directors, [1960], ibid.

46 Andrew's "Positive Program for Governor," is in the DO 10/28/1960. ADR's role in the Democratic National Convention was limited to avoiding being identified with the factions; TNT 7/17/1960.

47 Rosellini took 50.34 percent of the 1, 206,109 votes cast.

48 VC 1/16/1963; ADR to Esther Baker, 2/20/1961. ADR, 219, education.

49 ADR, *Message of Albert D. Rosellini to the Thirty-Sixth Legislature*. Olympia: State Printer, 1/13/1959; Rogers, 154. "We are going to adopt the soundest tax program possible within the limits of the existing tax structure and the constitutional framework," the governor told the PI, 2/11/1959.

50 Scott OH, LOPH 1, 35, 36.

51 Rogers, 230.

52 Milo Moore to Luke Graham, 2/31/1965. Graham 7.

53 ADR, "Progress Thorough Low Cost Power." Speech to American Power Association Annual Convention, 5/27/1959; "Report of the Committee on Natural Resources, Western States Democratic Conference, Seattle." 8/5/1962-8/7/1962, C. Girard Davidson, General Chair." Coe, 6/7.

54 Gus Norwood, (Executive Secretary, Pacific Northwest Public Power Association), to John Richardson (Director of Finance, State of Oregon), 4/24/1957. ADR, 21, power, general.

55 "A Policy Statement by [the] Governor [ADR] About the Columbia Interstate Compact." WSL, Johnson papers, 2, natural resources.

56 See Billington, (the PUD's lobbyist), "1951-1956: Face-Offs, Fights and Failures," 75-95.

57 Rogers, 285.

58 Men owned all of executive and judicial ones, 88.5 percent of school boards, and 265 of 267 mayoralties. In 1960, 344,478 women in the state worked, or 31 percent of the labor force, of whom just 3 percent were nonwhite. "Professional and technical work" occupied 46,775, "managerial and office occupations" 14,523, and clerical work 105,207. In government, men held 90 percent of legislative offices. There were but 66 women city council persons. Washington (State) *Governor's Commission on the Status of Women*, n.p., 1963.

59 SM 5/64, 30.

60 Comfort OH, Rogers OH, 274.

61 "The disorganization in the House is disturbing" Charlie Hodde wrote an inquirer, "but not as it would be in a session where we had a positive program to push. The administration is pretty much 'hold the line' this time, and in some respects disorganization assists this position." To LWV, 2/1/1963. Hodde, 3, corr., 1962-1969. Rogers, 280.

62 e.g., ADR to Phil Liston, 3/20/1964. ADR 318, capital punishment; Rogers OH, 290, 291.

63 Rogers, 297.

64 PI 2/27/1957.

65 Abel, who was DSCC chair (1953-55), managed ADR's 1956 campaign and was first named to the Public Service (now the Utilities and Transportation) Commission. He had been hooked on politics since being Lewis County Prosecuting Attorney in 1922, and was vigorously opposed to any relaxation of liquor enforcement. ADR, Scott OH, LOPH 1; PI 2/27/1957. ADR denied he had asked for the legislation, but Don Abel doubted the fight would have been undertaken without at least tacit approval of the governor's office. ST 2/15/1961.

66 "Liquor Investigations," ADR 9, Liquor Board.

67 ST 5/22/1964. As a legislator, he had been for slot machines in private clubs and a state lottery, but was against gambling "in principle"; Sponburgh acknowledged two of three persons charged with bribes had been allowed to resign. ADR damned those who tried "to create a scandal" where no scandal existed. LDN 6/3/1964. One of the self-sustaining rumors was that Italians were being hired en bloc by the Liquor Board. Its total employment as of 3/1/1959 was 663; 37 were of Italian ancestry or 5.5 percent, 16 of whom were hired by the Langlie administration. Abel

to the SA, 6/2/1959. 72-10-94, 169, personnel, 1960-69. Nor was there anything unusual about the number of licenses issued, from 709 to 802, between 1957 and 1959. Net profit had increased by $2,233 per employee since the end of ABL's administration. During Evro Becket's first two years 482 out of 658 employees were released (76.6 percent). Under Abel, it was 372 of 673, or 56 percent. Abel to ADR, 8/3/1959. WSA, ADR, 72-10-9, 165, liquor control board. On the other hand, there are strong indications the governor intervened on behalf of friends in a limited number of instances, advising Abel to "take another look." e.g., ADR to Abel re Nick Supino, 4/25/1960. ADR 72-10-904, 105, liquor board.

68 Memo, [Democratic State Chair] Frank Keller to DSC, et al., 8/14/1964. HMJ, 3560-2, 3/17.

69 Speech by Speaker William S. Day to Washington State Junior Chamber of Commerce. ADR 318, campaign 1964.

70 PI 9/5/1964; ADR's platform is in "Keep Him Working for Washington." HMJ 3560-2, 26/35/1961.

71 "A Statement by [ADR] Concerning a Six Point Program on Taxes and Government Finances," 10/23/1964. WSA, Hodde, 4/26.

72 He advised Booth Gardner in 1987, that "conservatively … at least 5,000 jobs could be eliminated." ADR to BG, 2/23/1987. BG, Office of the Governor, 4, Barlow.

73 The combined anti-Evans vote was 581,000, ADR's 225,000.

74 Rogers, 345.

75 Rogers, 346-47; PI 6/23/1972.

76 Rogers, 348. Rosellini considered running again in 1976, losing interest when Evans retired. He backed Dixie Lee Ray, and served two terms on the Transportation Commission. Evans' Campaign Manager Jay Gilmour acknowledged hiring private detective Jerry Poth who had taken assignments from the attorney general's office, to look into "rumors." Slade Gorton fired Keith Dysart, who joined the National Governors' Conference. James Dore was appointed to the King County Superior Court. Fred Dore, Gorton's opponent, later became chief justice of the State Supreme Court. Son John Rosellini served in the House and ran for attorney general in 1980.

77 Smith, Payton, *Rosellini: Immigrants Son and Progressive Governor*. Seattle: UWAP, 1997; ST 11/15/2003, 1/21/2005, 7/13/2005; See, "Al The Rose," T 1/28/1957; CSM 1/14/1957, and "Rosellini — After a Quarter Of A Century." SA 8/30/1963. Contrarily, Republican House Majority Leader George Kinnear, a man not given to exaggeration, told the author in 1970 that ADR's strength was not in his party, "but on straight dishonesty, and then feeding favoritism." Kinnear OH, 1118/70. (LOHP 2). ADR was President of the Council of State Governments in 1962-63, where he fought states' rights southerners. ST 12/4/1963; ADR was still in his office nearly every day at 97, in 2007. See PI 1/23/2007.

78 Bishop OH.

79 OH, ADR, LOHP I, 11/27/1970.

80 Rosellini OH, LOPH 2.

**Chapter 7: Daniel J. Evans**

1 Dolliver OH, LOHP.

2 DJE, "Chapters from an Unwritten Book." Speech to the "Diet," (Seattle),

2/11/1997, 1-2. Author's possession; James Warren, "The Pioneer Roots of Daniel Jackson Evans," *Portage* X (Spring, 1989): 9-12, 31.

3 CHT 11/9/1956, 2/19/1957, 2/28/57.

4 The chair of the Transportation Committee (and later Congresswoman) Julia Butler Hansen insisted Evans be placed on the Highways Interim Committee, a plum assignment for a freshman. He was patient," "extremely courteous" and did "splendid work."

5 ST 2/19/1957, 2/28/57; A 3/9/1957; DJE, "Memo on Telephone Conversation with W. A. Bugge, Director of Highways. DJE, Scrapbook I, in DJE's possession.

6 A 1/18/1963.

7 PI 7/6/1972; Author interview with Lieutenant Governor Joel Pritchard, 4/20/1994.

8 WEA, the *Washington State Teacher*, 9/1957; to wit: SHBs 719, HB 200, and HJM 16 (1957), HB 668 and SSB 400 (1959).

9 A critique of Evans as representative is in WSDCC, "The Voting and Quoting Record of Dan Evans." WSL, "Governors, State," DJE file.

10 *Journal of the House*, 1963: 3-29.

11 Bill Day, Bill McCormick, and Margaret Hurley of Spokane, Dick Kink of Bellingham, Chet King of Pacific County, and Perry of Seattle met separately in the Speaker's office, with Evans as the go-between; Comfort, LOHP; See Daniel J. Chasan, *O'Brien*. Seattle: UWAP, 1990: 106-139; See John C. Hughes, *Slade Gorton: A Half Century in Politics*. Olympia: Secretary of State, Legacy Project, 2011: 49-95.

12 Author interview with Lieutenant Governor Joel Pritchard, 4/20/1994.

13 DJE, "Lincoln Day Message to Whatcom County Republicans." DJE, Scrapbook 3. AP.

14 BS 1/11/1965.

15 WSDCC, "The Voting and Quoting Record of Dan Evans." "Governors, State, Evans, Dan, f. WSL

16 Dolliver LOHP; Central Surveys, Inc., Shenandoah, IA, "An Opinion Survey of Washington Voters." 6/6/1963-6/19/1963.

17 Governor Ferry had been appointed twice and elected once, and Langlie to three non-consecutive terms.

18 Memorandum, "Thoughts About the Final Campaign." n.a., (9/1964). DJE 260-3-3-4, 1964 clippings.

19 "Blueprint for Progress." DJE 25-2-174, senate R memos; Evans Committee press releases, 8/12, 20, 9/3, 5, 7, 8, 11, 24, 29/ 1964. DJE 25-2-174, senate R memos.

20 The ongoing interplay with legislative leaders can be seen in Slade Gorton to Dan Evans Committee, 9/18/1964. Gorton legislative papers, SG's possession; The GOP was reduced to 17 governors nationally and from six of the seven U.S. House seats to two. Jack Westland (2), Thor Tollefson (6), and Walt Horan (5) joined Rosellini and Lt. Governor Vic Meyers in defeat. All had been in office 20 to 30 years.

21 SA 11/6/1964.

22 Slade Gorton, "Memo to Republican legislators," 5/7/1963. DJE, scrapbook 4; See a "History of Redistricting and Reapportionment in Washington State," in

*Members of the Legislature.* Olympia: The Legislature, 1987. "Gerrymandering" spreads excess votes from the secure districts of the party in control to adjacent ones to make them winnable. This could be done while conforming to the mandate they be the same size, and moving oppositeion voters into as few districts as possible.

23 DJE, Inaugural Address," 1/13/1965. WSL, "misc. collections," passim; DJE LOHP 9/24/1991. "Redistricting Calls for DJE," in draft "Book Outline" 11/1988, part 1: 9-10. AP.

24 DJE to Stuart Oles, 12/7/1967. WSA, DJE, 25-1-14; Ashley Holden to Bob Timm (Republican National Committeeman), 6/28/1967, "Minutes, Republican Coordinating Committee" 9/15/1967. RSC f. All WSA, DJE, 25-1-48.

25 PI 10/28/1978; YHR 11/4/1976.

26 DJE on a KCTS special from the Evans School of Government, University of Washington, 1/9/2008; See Sarah Morehouse, *The Governor as Party Leader: Campaigning and Governing.* Ann Arbor: University of Michigan Press, 1998. She admits parties have been in decline since the rise of telecommunications in the 1920's, but argues "party organization matters," in a fragile pleading for "responsible [parliamentary type] government" in a 'presidential' system. 1-8, 272-78

27 "The Winter of Our Discontent." Speech by DJE to the RSCC, 9/10/1965, Appendix A, to "James M. Dolliver, An Oral History," by Norman Clark. WSA, 1999; NTM 2/7/1977.

28 DJE, O3A116, 29, institutions, 1965-68

29 DJE, LOHP, 9/24/1991; Norm Schut, LOHP, 2/4/1989, 2/5/1989; DJE to Victor Denny, 4/24/1970. WSA, DJE, 260-3-2-5, corer, 1970.

30 This is not so. Except for John Spellman, the GOP ran aground with Christian conservatives, culminating in 1998, when Ellen Creswell was the nominee for Governor and Linda Smith for U.S. Senator. Evans endorsed Dino Rossi in 2004, who said little on social issues. Evans may have been more interested in having a business-oriented Republican in the post-9/11 economic doldrums. ST 12/9/2004.

31 DJE to "Fellow Republicans," 9/20/1976. WSA, DJE, 260-3-2-10, Ford presidential campaign. Of the legislative candidates he helped up to 1974, all were moderates. Nine won and four lost. DJE 260-3-2-7, corr. pers., 1974. After that nothing stemmed the loss of seats in the traditionally Republican north end Seattle districts. DJE to Representative John Rabel, 6/1/1974. WSA, DJE, 260-3-2-7, corr. pers., 1974.

32 DJE, "King County Republican Club Lincoln Day Speech," 2/11/1987. WSA, DJE-5, 260-1-1-36, speeches and statements, 1986-88.

33 Mandated by the State Constitution to be done after each decennial census, but ignored since the 1930s. The Democrats could hardly improve their position, and Eastern Washington legislators saw a loss of seats to faster growing Puget Sound.

34 DJE to JW Phillips, 3/6/1965. DJE, 25-2-67, redistricting. Gorton, "Memo to Republican Legislators," 5/7/1963. DJE, scrapbook 4.

35 "Report of the governor's Task Force on Executive Reorganization," 11/17/1968. Olympia: The Task Force, 1968. WSA, DJE 25-2-337, "feo," 2. A comparison should be made here to DLR's. DJE's task force was mostly outsiders, with Warren Bishop and Harold Shefelman were the grey eminences. Dean Brink of the UW School of Social Work and Brewster Denny of its Graduate School of

Public Affairs (chair), Boeing's T. A. Wilson, and Weyerhaeuser's Walt Howe, Representative Bob Charette (D), and Senator Frank Atwood filled it out.

36 *State Executive Reorganization, 1967-1969.* Lexington: The Council of State Governments, [1969?]. This was the follow-on from the "Little Hoover Commissions" 1950s; DJE to "State Department Heads" [ca 1969]. DDE 5, 260-3-1-5, personnel appointments, 1969.

37 Dolliver OH, LOHP.

38 Glenn Pascall, soon to be Director of Revenue under Governor Spellman was Legislative Liaison, Jo Garceau Coordinator of Correspondence and appointments, and Esther Seering oversaw the secretarial staff. See Raymond W. Cox III, "The Management Role of Governors," in Eric Herzik and Brent W. Brown, *Gubernatorial Leadership and State Policy.* N.Y.: Greenwood Press, 1991: 55-67.

39 Dolliver, LOHP; Author interview with Bill Jacobs 7/11/2006.

40 See DJE to Schneider, 5/1/1970. DJE 260-3-2-5 corr. pers., 1970. Both shortly retired.

41 DJE to Arthur Siegal, 2/14/1973. DJE 260-3-2-6, corr. pers., 1973, appts., regulation.

42 DJE to J. Murray Kleist (President, Washington State Trial Lawyers Association), 2/9/1976. DJE, 260-3-2-10, appointments, Dolliver.

43 DJE, *1965 Inaugural Speech.* Olympia: State Printer, 1965: 32-36.

44 Between 1962 and 1972, the state's share of the property tax rose from $3.6 million to $15.5 million a 200 percent increase in constant dollars; "Fiscal Message of Governor Daniel J. Evans Before Joint Session of Washington State Legislature," 2/1/1965. DJE 03A116, 3, govs. offc., 1965-66.

45 SR 5/20/1968; WR 8/1/1968.

46 Evans campaign, "O'Connell in Brief," fall, 1968. State Senator Martin Durkan (D), took the more conservative approach. DJE 260-3-1-4. O'Connell, 1968; BH 5/23/1968; SDC 7/15/1968.

47 DJE to Bill and Harriet Douglas, 10/23/1968. DJE, 260-3-2-5, corr. pers., 1968.

48 Former Tacoma Mayor Harold Tollefson told DJE on 7/30/1968, that "something was strange" about O'Connell's finances. Other Evans operatives may have followed up. DJE, "Book Outline," (ca 1990), prt. I: 25. AP.

49 Dolliver LOHP; re: 1966, DJE "Book Outline," prt. I: 14. .

50 DJE, *Lessons in Leadership.* Seattle: The Agora Foundation, private printing, 1999; "Governor Dan Evans on Tax Reform." Statewide television, 1/23/1969. DJE 25-2-418, tax reform; DJE to Randolph Cunningham, 10/1/1970. DJE 260-3-2-5, corr. pers., 1970; In the decade between 1966 and 1976, manufacturing values were predicted to rise from $3.3 billion to $6.2 billion and per capita income to $3,800, up from $1,000. "The Republican White Paper on Business and Industrial Growth." Olympia: RSSC, 1970[?]. DJE, 260-3-1-7 RGW, 1966. "The beverage tax, on car rentals, and on motel taxes, and defer $20 million states sales tax on construction costs to repair and enhance Husky Stadium." PI 2/6/2008. It fell flat, as a recession was in the offing, and the state was projected to be $5.4 billion in the hole for the 2009-11 budget. Evans has been engaged in over two dozen other organizations since coming home, most recently with Bill Gates (III) and former U.S. Attorney General William Ruckelshaus in initiating the Seattle Initiative for Global Development, an alliance of business and civic leaders striving to make an

end to poverty central to the nation's foreign policy.

51 Senate Democrats killed Evan's annual elections bill in 1970, to make the Republican's again run on what was suspected to be an unpopular proposition. DJE, "Book Outline," prt. 1.

52 HJR 42.

53 DJE, news conf., 10/18/1971. SF 6, govs. news confs.

54 DJE, news conf., 10/8/71. SF 6, govs pr. confs; The dissenters included Weyerhaeuser chairman Norton Clapp. Clapp to DJE, 4/20/1972. WSA, DJE-5, 260-3-2-12.

55 Dolliver LOHP; Evans OH, LOHP.

56 At 33 days, the environmental session holds the 20th century record for brevity and productivity.

57 DJE, news conf., 1/23/1970, 2/9, 1970.

58 DJE, *"American Priorities"* in *The Linfield Papers,"* Seattle: Private printing 1969.

59 PI 3/28/1976.

60 Evans OH.

61 William Jeffries to DJE, 12/29/1976. DJE 260-3-3-13, Indians, 1976.

62 DJE, Outline of "Chapters," 9.

63 Mary Hanneman and Minh-Anh Thi Hodge, "Making a New Home: Vietnamese Refuges Arrive in Washington, 1975." C 15 (Spring, 2001): 17-22.

64 DJE to Donald C. Morris, 12/15/1968. WSA, DJE 25-2-83, Vietnam. The revocation plea came from a local Nisei to Evans, who sent it on to Ford.

65 Dr. Garrett Heyns to DJE, 5/17/1966. DJE 0319116, 39, Heyns, 1963-65. Dr. William R. Conte continued the same approach after August, 1966, "terminating the past practice of each institution an island in itself," separately approaching the legislature. The rationale is in Dolliver to William Conte, 10/2/69. DJE 03A116, 35, govs. offc., 1969; "Statement by the Governor," 1/19/1968. DJE 03A, 116, 35, govs. offic., 1968, Institutions. For a synopsis of human services in the state, see "A History of Human Services. DSHS in Detail," 3/13/2004. WWW, 1.dshs.wa.gov/in detail/3 history.html.

66 Miller to DJE, 4/27/1972 WSA, DJE-5, 260-3-2-3; Memorandum, DJE to Sid Smith, 12/15/1972. DJE 5, 260-3-2-12. "Deinstitutionalization" was an "acceptable and relevant" approach according to former Director of Institutions Richard A. McGee, now a consultant. "Recommendations and comments Concerning the Organization, Administration and Progress of the Department of Adult Corrections and Probation and Parole of the Department of Institutions of the State of Washington." 3/70, DJE 2S-2-493, institutions.

67 Memo, DJE to Sid Smith [Director, DSHS], 12/15/1972. DJE 5, 260- 32-12.

68 Wallace Miller [Director, OPP&FM], to DJE 2/13/1973. DJE 5, 260-3-2-3.

69 Miller to DJE, 4/27/1972, ibid.

70 Joe Davis, LOHP.

71 See ST 11/1/1977; "The Perils of Political Virtue." A 10/20/1972; WDW 12/1/1975; TNT 1/15/1976.

72 DJE to Senator Martin J. Durkan, 1/20/1966. DJE 25-123. Transcript of Durkan on KOMO's "Issues '71," 10/28/1971, sf 6, govs press confs. Background on

the Evans-Durkan-Rosellini clash is in the ST 1/9/1972 and 2/13/1972; EVH 10/24/1972.

73 See "The Evans Years," and "The Rosellini Years," ST 10/29/1972.

74 ADR, LOHP, 11/21/1991.

75 Hodde, speech outline, n.d., WSA, Hodde, 4, speeches, 1964. The quote is from Harold Ickes, FDR's Secretary of the Interior.

76 ST 3/27/1972.

77 DJE, "Book Outline," prt. 2: 11.

78 ST 3/27/1972.

79 DJE to Cunningham 3/31/1972. DJE, 260-3-2-6, corr. pers., 1972.

80 For a counter view of the budgets, see WDW 3/2/9/1976, and, "Book Outline," prt. 2.

81 DJE, *Twelve Years: A Report to the Citizens of Washington on the Administration of Governor Daniel J. Evans, 1965-1977*. Olympia: State Printer, 1977.

82 DJE, *Address to the Legislature*, 1/12/1970, sf 3, news cols, HR 12/26/76.

83 DJE to Charles Bartlett, 11/25/1972. DJE 260-3-2-6, corr. pers., 1972.

84 PI 10/11/1974, 1/28/1982.

85 ADW 3/25/1975.

86 Special sessions in even numbered years are now limited to 45 days by constitutional amendment — subject to a call by the governor, or two thirds of the legislature.

87 DJE, press conf., 2/19/1969, sf 2, press confs.

88 Memo, Senate Majority Leader Gordon Walgren and Senator Daniel Marsh to Majority Caucus Counsel Max Nicolai, 11/2/1973, instructing him to look for means "to successfully control the Governor's veto power." Woody, 3. The entire Senate calendar of 6/7 and 17 was proposed overrides. Two of the three minor ones passed by the House were concurred in. When that of SHB 2119 was not overturned, the revolt was over.

89 TNT 8/10/1975.

90 SR 1/16/1975; DJE to House, 7/2/1975. bsf, s-z, vetoes. Evan's inclusive view of the veto is in the ST 5/28/1977 and 5/19/1985, and as a budget balancing device in DJE pr. conf., transcript, 12/13/1971. Most legislators lost patience when he vetoed $65 million in school levy relief as too little, necessitating an extra session in 1976. This was a clear case of personal preference. NTM 6/19/1976; The fact is, the governor has the power. The question is, is it appropriately used. "In Washington, as in other states, the item veto is recognized as a legislative function The governor of Washington, of all the states [sic] governors, appears to possess the most powerful and versatile veto." The Supreme Court had ruled "section" meant "a provision, clause, sentence, sub-division or an entire act," and the veto must be negative, not affirmative. Washington State Legislative Council, "The Item Veto in the State of Washington." Olympia: The Council, 1962: 1-3. DJE, 2-5-2-83, veto power.

91 Senator Slim Rasmussen quoted in NTM, 5/29/1975; Dolliver, LOHP.

92 Dolliver, LOHP.

93 DJE, "Book Outline" prt. 3: 13.

94 Transcript, governor's pr. conf., 7/1/1975 and DJE to Senate, 7/2/1975 re SB 2341;

bsf, s-z, vetoes.

95 The epithet came in 1970 after Evans vetoed a veteran's bonus bill. Governor's veto messages 1970, sf 2; Speaker Leonard Sawyer to DJE, 2/13/1974. DJE 30 Rosellini set a precedent in 1957 when, for confessedly "political" reasons, he vetoed his own salary increase — and later successfully lobbied an override. ADR, LOHP, 11/21/1991. He was stymied by the Supreme Court, and the veto was limited from section, to a line. Legislative intent could be reversed by vetoing a "not," in "shall not." e.g., Evans partially vetoed a 16 page 1971 gambling bill 43 times; See Washington State Constitution, Art. III, (12), (2); "*Washington State Association of Apartment Associations Inc., et al, v. Daniel J. Evans,* " (re ESSB 2226, C. 207, Laws of 1973). Evans admitted that when he got through the bill "looked like a letter from a war zone." If the legislators had not interlocked their points to make it "veto proof," he would have vetoed the individual sections. DJE, LOHP, 10/29/1991; Dolliver, LOHP.

96 S402 was made into an amendment to the debt ceiling legislation. DJE to the Senate, 7/28/1987. *Congressional Record*, 2/28/1987, re S1256.

97 DJE to Majority Leader Howard Baker, 9/25/1984. DJE 260-1-2-3, corr., line item veto, 1984-88.

98 OPP&FM, "Alternatives for Washington: The Cost-Trade-Off Survey Findings," 10/11/1976, bsf 14; AFW, "An Agenda for the Future." bsf, a-e. The five bond bills created 11,000 jobs when matched with federal funds; DJE to Speaker and House, 1/20/1971, contains the governor's other executive requests for 1976. sf 6; "American Priorities," in *The Linfield Papers*, Seattle: private printing, 1969: 8-12.

99 A synopsis of the regime is in *Twelve Years: A Report to the Citizens of Washington State on the Administration of Governor Daniel J. Evans, 1965-1977*. Olympia: State Printer, 1977.

100 Memorandum, Donald Sorte to John W. McCurry [Director, OPP&FM], 10/17/1972 and Miller to DJE, 11/15/1972. Both DJE 5, 260-3-2-3. Evans wanted combine the five systems. Two, the Law Officers' and Fire Fighters' (LEOFF), and the Judge's, were so unique this was impossible. He did back legislative reformers, who after a bloody five year struggle in 1977 reduced LEOFF benefits from 92 to 36 percent of salary, and created three new systems. DJE to Lee Buffington (Director, OPP and FM), 12/24/1974. DJE 5, 260-3-2-12, exos 1974.

101 An infliction of the Bremerton Sun's Adele Ferguson.

102 Known as the "gateway Amendment;" e.g., the amendment giving the gas tax to "highways," narrowly defined, and the one percent lid on property taxes.

103 In 1969, Evans proposed three sites for nuclear reactors: Roosevelt Beach in Grays Harbor County, Kalama in Cowlitz County, and Kiket Island.

104 DJE to Rev. Dale Turner, 5/6/1968. DJE 260 3-2-5 corr. pers. 1968. DJE facetiously suggested the legislators decide who lived or died.

105 DO 1/12/1977.

106 Comfort, LOHP; See Scott, "Politics in the Blood: The Rise of Daniel Jackson Evans." C (Spring, 1998): 40-44. Disclosure passed as Initiative 276 in 1973; DJE to Anson Moody, 7/16/1973. DJE 2603-12, 6, corr. pers. 1973.

107 DJE, "Book Outline," prts. 1-3, final pages.

108 Evans' gubernatorial career is captured in the PI 3/28/1976 and In the ST 12/14/1977.

109 e.g., Mayors Devin, Langlie, Clinton and Braman, and all three GOP governors

since 1940.

110 SM 1/1965: 20-25.

111 DJE, "American Priorities," in *The Linfield Papers*. Seattle: private printing, 1969, 8, 12. On January 5, 1977 in his last major talk. "I leave office satisfied and gratified." ST 1/11/1977.

112 The stadium was refurbished within six years by fan donations, sale of overhead salons, and greater anticipated ticket sales.

113 Quoted in the DO 3/25/1976.

114 RGC, "Proposals by the Republican Governors Association. Toward a Party that Wins Elections and Serves America." DJE, 25-2-30, RGC; "Schedule for Republican Governor's Campaign Conference, 5/27/1966-5/28/66, (Denver). DJE 260-3-1-7, RGA; The national level appraisal of DJE is in George Weeks, "A Statehood Hall of Fame." A Paper delivered to the Annual Meeting of the Southern Political Science Association, 1981, republished in SG 55:3 (1982): 67-73.

115 T 8/9/1968; Neal Pierce, "Evans Helped Create New U.S.-States Ties." WSJ 12/13/1973.

116 Michael Dukakis (MA) was the Democratic nominee in 1988, Spiro Agnew (MD) was Nixon's Vice President, as was Nelson Rockefeller (NY) to Ford.

117 Robert H. Connery, *Rockefeller of New York: Executive Power in the Statehouse*. Ithaca: Cornell University Press, 1979: 82-84, 98-107, 418-34.

118 Evans was on the "short list" for Ford's vice president in 1973, to the point of having security placed on his hotel suite. His actions as Ford's chair for the state, and as a "delegate hunter" at the convention assured that he would be ignored by Reagan. The only other federal office he would have accepted, both because it was executive and important to the Northwest, was Secretary of the Interior, but it was not offered. Jacobs interview, 10/31/2006.

119 Richard Norton Smith, *Thomas E. Dewey and His Times*. New York: Simon and Schuster, 1982: 361-64.

120 Evans was introduced by New York's Mayor John Lindsay. "Keynote Address," Republican National Convention (Miami Beach FL, 8/5/1968); Nixon centered between Rockefeller and Reagan, feinted to the left and picked Maryland's morally challenged Spiro Agnew to be his spear-carrier for the Right and to take votes from Alabama's Governor George Wallace. T 8/9/1968: 17-18; Evans, who had worked closely with the president on revenue sharing, felt Nixon was a "a flawed man … [who] exhibited extraordinary skill and strength in foreign policy." DJE, "Chapters," "J": 14, 15.

121 DJE, "Keynote Speech to the 1968 Republican National Conventton."

122 Bill Jacobs, DJE's Director of Labor and Industries in Olympia, and Chief of Staff while in the Senate, confirmed Evans was driving to Olympia to meet with Governor Spellman when he decided to take the Senate seat, if offered. Being there had its rewards, but being in the Northwest was preferable and staying another term might have circumscribed his usefulness at home. Jacobs interview, 10/31/2006; "Why I'm Quitting the Senate"; NYTM 4/17/1988: 48, 90; DJE, "Notes for Speech on Senate Floor," 3/3/1988. DJE 260-1-1-36, speeches; DJE LOHP; Majority Leader Bob Dole was first among Republicans, backing the President 93 percent of the time. Alaska's Ted Stevens was at 82 percent, Gorton at 80, down to Connecticut's Lowell Weicker at 44 percent.

123 *Congressional Record* 9/20/1987, S12826, (and, Ch. 74.21 RCW); DJE, "American Priorities," in *The Linfield Papers*, op cit.: 8, 12. His Senate accomplishments are in the ST 10/20/1987; e.g., "Washington State: Where Do We Go From Here?" PI 11/11/1992.

124 "The Goal is to Govern — Revival: A Manifesto for the GOP — Cut loose the Fringes and Hold on Tight to Party's Old Values." ST 5/16/1993.

125 I-884, 2004. The legislature was facing a $2.4 billion operating shortfall, and "dedicated funds" take away its ability to prioritize and may preempt its ability to raise taxes for the General Fund. It was soundly defeated.

126 DO 10/6/1974; SBJ 12/20/2002-12/26/02; James Warren, "The Pioneer Roots of Daniel Jackson Evans." P, X, (1), (spring, 1985); DJE, "On Leadership." ST 10/13/2002; "Dan and Nancy Evans: A Legacy of Leadership and Service," and Carol Tice, "First Citizen[s] Dan and Nancy Evans: Service with a Passion." PSBJ 5/16/2003, A-4, and ST 6/16/2004. If the Evans presentation seems overdrawn, there are 810 archived boxes from his administration in the WSA alone. No other governor has more than 375. DJE 6-25-08.

**Chapter 8: Dixy Lee Ray**

1 WDW 1/10/1977; Despite being on the Executive Committee of Friday Harbor Laboratories (1945-60), her facility as a teacher, publication of *Marine Boring and Fouling Mechanisms* (1959), and professional articles, she never became a full professor. PI 8/11/1972, 8/15/1976.

2 See Don Duncan, Jim Matassa, and Jim Simon, "Dixie Lee Ray: Unpolitical, Unique, Uncompromising," ST 1/3/1994; Public Law 93-126 created the Bureau of Oceans and International Environmental and Scientific Affairs (OES), to provide foreign policy guidance and coordination. DLR was Assistant Secretary, as well as chair of the A.E.C. She had been a Special Consultant for Biological Oceanography to the NSF (1960-62), Chief Scientist and Visiting Professor of the Stanford Research Vessel Te Vega on the International Indian Ocean Expedition (1964), and on the Presidential Task Force on Oceanography (1969). John Abbadeson to Ray, 9/6/1974, DLR to Rogers Morton, 8/19/1974, and to President Ford, 9/9/1974. HISU, 39, White House corr.; ST 8/15/1976.

3 DLR to Carlson, 7/23/1975. HISU, DLR 9, Carlson, E., 1967-86. Norm Schut, a close observer in state government for 40 years, stated that it was Carlson who advised her to run as a Democrat. It was "smart," and business could have it both ways. Schut, LOHP (1), 12/17/1989

4 A 10/15/1976.

5 John Salter, Senator Jackson's alter ego, introduced her around Snohomish County; DLR to HMJ, 2/18/1977. HMJ 3560-5/9.

6 At the Women's Republican Club of Bellevue in 1995, Guzzo said "We face an economic calamity, courtesy of the Democratic Party … culminating in Bill Clinton's bowing to the welfare state, [and] a takeover by environmental extremists. America has been sliding dangerously closer to Socialism and the welfare state. The so-called Democratic Party … the Gimme Party … is actually Socialism in sheep's clothing … . I can tell you from firsthand experience." "Women are the Hope of the Future." 3/17/2005, author's possession. His message in a "Memo to Evans" after the 1972 election had the same tone: "Taxes absolutely must be reduced substantially." PI 11/11/1972.

7 YHR 11/4/1976.

8 Wkly 12/26/1976.

9 PI 10/28/1978; ST 3/14/1977.

10 YHR 11/4/1976.

11 Two years later DLR wrote Esther Kohler that she held "Senator Mardesich in high regard," 7/13/1979. DLR 36, Mardesich apt; "Ernie Conrad [Vice President for Finance at the UW] tells me … Democratic officials … are furious at me for catching them off base. Sorry about that, but guys like Mardesich I don't want to buddy up to," DLR to Carlson, op. cit.; ST 1/10/1977, 10/21/1979. LOHP, Hodde (1), 1985. See obit, ST 6/29/1999.

12 SR 4/16/1978.

13 EVH 1/6/1977.

14 ST 4/16/1978, 10/21/1978,

15 PI 1/ 21/1977.

16 JA 6/8/1977.

17 Bender to Ray, 12/17/1976, and memo, Bender to staff, "Organization of Immediate Office of Governor Ray," 2/15/1977. Ray 34, Organization of Governor's Office; Ray to House State Government Committee, 2/21/1977. "Comments on House Joint Resolution 27 and House Bill 570 Regarding Reorganization of State Government." DLR, 34, Organization of Governor's Office; Ray, "Report to the People: The First Sixty Days," 3/15/1977. Ray, 26, First 60 Days; EVH 1/22/1977.

18 Reference to Jenkins is in Ray 44, misc. corr, and DO, 3/22/1977, 10/1/1977; JA 6/8/1977.

19 "Key purposes of the Organization," and, "Organization of the Office of the Governor." Memos, Bender, n.d., [12/1976]. HISU, DLR 144, govs. offc.; DO 2/23/1977.

20 Memo, Ray to directors, 11/29/1978; memo, Ray to agency directors, 8/6/1980. Ray 47, department head memos, 1980.

21 Evans' 1965 request to retract 67 of former Governor Rosellini's appointees were "adequate precedence" according to Senate Majority Leader Gordon Walgren. WSS, tape, 1/21/1977. In the 23 community colleges, nearly half the trustees had to be replaced due to the effectuation of the Public Disclosure Law. ST 4/l/1977, 4/5/1977, 5/16/1980. TNT 6/4/1978, ST 6/28/1978; NTM 4/19/1977.

22 DLR, "Report to the People: The First 60 Days," 3/15/1977. DLR 26, First 60 days. DO 2/23/1977.

23 Norm Schut, the canny past president of the WFSE who had studied five governors, thought it was Ray's "lack of knowledge of state government" that was her undoing. Schut, LOHP (1), 12/17/1989; DO 2/23/1977.

24 ST 1/10/1979.

25 "General Description and Operating Procedures for the Governor's Task Groups" n.d., [19/77]. DLR 159, tf's, and grps.

26 DLR to [revised] Task Groups, 8/27/1979. DLR 81-41-1214, 39, governor's cabinet and sub-cabinet meetings.

27 Bender, Directions to the "Social to the Health and Employment Services Task Group, [1978]; "The Governor's Task Force on Environmental Management,' DLR 159, tfs and grps, and 93A165, 1, govs task force on env. mgmt.

28 ST 1/20/1977; Robert Hollister, Chair, "Proposed Recommendations on the Issue

of the Consolidation of State Government." HISU, Ray, 159, task forces and grps.

29 TNT 6/4/1978; ST 6/28/1978; DLR 45, daily schedules.

30 SR 4/16/1978; EVH 4/19/1981.

31 TNT 6/7/1978; DLR, "Report on My First Year in Office," DLR, 27; DLR. *Report of My Second Year in Office*. Olympia: The Office of the Governor, 1979. ST 4/5/1977, 5/16/1980.

32 PI 1/29/1978; Gerald Thompson to Paul Bender, [DSHS' contribution to the governor's report], 12/15/1978. DLR 86-5-478, 4, DSHS, govs. Offc.; "Secretary's Administrative Policy Statement." [12/1978]. HISU, DLR 144, office procedure guidelines.

33 Bender to all Agency Directors, 6/1/1978. DLR 93.

34 DSHS, "An Analysis of Alternate Correctional uses of McNeil Island: A Report to the Washington State Houses of Representatives," (1/28/1980). HISU, DLR, 145, prisons, McNeil Island, general; Thompson to Paul Bender 12/3/1979, ibid., 168, WS agencies, prisons terms and Paroles, board; DGA, "McNeil Island-State Plan for Utilization, and, DGA, "The Truth about McNeil Island," [1980]. Both HISU, DLR, 144, prisons, McNeil Island.

35 "Governor's Speech to Superior Court Judges." 3/27/1980; Ibid.; i.e., "Not In My Backyard."

36 Thompson, "Adult Corrections: History 1969-79 and Current Status," 11/14/1978. HISU, DLR 144, prisons, general; Since DSHS administrators periodically suffer from human failures in handling their unruly or vulnerable charges, there is little reason to believe these criticisms are exaggerated; "Highlights of Governor Ray's Accomplishments, 1977-78," 12/18/1978.WSA, Ray, 27.

37 DSHS, [Thompson,] "Status of Institutions in Washington State," 4/23/1979. HISU, DLR, 168, WS agencies, soc and hs dept; "Chart for DSHS management team." HISU, DLR, 168, WS agencies, DSHS; gov's pr. off.

38 TNT 5/1/1977; The inclusion of Bob Benson, a rock hard conservative who would direct the House Ways and Means Committee under Republicans in 1981-83, was indicative of intent; Ray, "Veto Message to the Senate," 6/3/1977 and 6/21/1977; to House 6/25/1979 and 6/ 29/1979, re HB 516 (the budget), Ray 3; TNT 5/1/1979; ST 4/7/1980.

39 The Hodde Plan was "designed to place effective controls on major taxes, severely limit special levies …and impose a modest state income tax" to replace them, its two percent to five percent spread beginning at $10,000 and peaking at $32,000. "Materials Explaining Governor's Income Tax Proposal," 3/21/1977, near DLR; "I am seeking tax reform — not new taxes," Ray said in January of 1978; *Washington State Research Council, Monthly Repor*t, 11/1/1979. bsf, e-h, Governor Dixie Lee Ray, 1978-79. "My philosophy is to focus on those things which government should or must, and leave the rest to the private and non-profit sectors," Ray said in a 1979 rephrase of Lincoln, " to focus on those things which government should or must and leave the rest." DO 2/23/1977; BH 2/1/1977; TNT 1/13/1977.

40 "Speech to the Spokane Club," 4/13/1978; DLR to the Washington State Labor Council Convention, 1978. DLR 152, WSFE 8/31/1978; "Comments by the Honorable Dixy Lee Ray Governor of the State of Washington to the Seattle Chamber of Commerce," 2/9/7199. Both DLR 154, Seattle Chamber of Commerce; According to Joe Davis, the director of the Department of Labor and Industries "was as miserable as we've [Labor], ever had." He renounced Ray as a "closet Republican;" Davis, LOPH (1), 10/14/1989.

41 TNT 6/6/1977.

42 "The Washington State Local Government Fiscal Capacity Study," and "Report to the Governor of the Task Group on Reforming the State Tax Structure." 12/1980. DLR 159, task forces and grps, (3).

43 "Governor's Breakfast Seminar Program," nld, Ray 33, Executive Task Groups; State of Washington Governor's Office, Executive Order 79-08, 1979; Memo, Bender to agency directors, 6/1/1978. Ray 47, department head memos, 1980. "Status of issues Under Study by the Growth Management and Environment Task Group," 6/1980. acc. # 86-7-777, 28, gov's task grps; ST 6/26/1977. In fact, as of June l980, only one of the six tasks set out by the Task Group was more than 30 percent complete. The impression left is that the groups either could not generate ideas, or after the first 24 months saw the futility of doing so.

44 BS 3/6/1979.

45 TNT 6/4/1978; The Governor reestablished the Governor's Office on Indian Affairs by EO 80-02. HISU, DLR 120, appointments; Remarkably, 240,000 voted "yes," and 600,000 "No."

46 Mormons, "small government" devotees, those who thought there was no problem and confusion over nine other initiatives referenda and resolutions contributed. Janine Perry, "n.d., in evidence over the last 100 years," Ray told the Seattle Rotary 8/14/1991.

47 See her *Trashing the Planet: Global Warming, Ozone Depletion, and Other Myths.* New York: Harper Perennial, 1992.

48 YHR 9/21/1978. DO 4/4/1979; DLR to Magnuson, 8/14/1979; Bagnariol to DLR, 9/26/1979. HISU, DLR, 14, Bagnariol; Ray's views are in, "Nuclear Power Should Not be Accepted Because There is a Crisis ... It should be Accepted Only on the Merits of Being A Safe and Reliable Energy Source ... Nuclear Power in Search of an Ombudsman." HISU, DLR, 12.

49 Larry Bradley to the American Society of Heating, Refrigerating, and Air Conditioning Engineers, 12/13/1978. HISU, DLR 165, energy.

50 ST 10/25/1977.

51 ANJ 3/18/1979; PI 11/16/1980. The same logic was applied when the Steelhead Trout Club protested her opposition to designating a section of the Skagit River "wild and scenic." "Federal designation would lock up the Skagit ...and does not give the state the opportunity to manage this resource." Director of Ecology Web Hallauer to Pat Patterson, 10/20/1977. acc. 8-5-524, 46, DOL.

52 ST 1/10/1979.

53 TNT 3/6/1979; PI, 2/13/1980.

54 DLR to Senate, 3/29/79. WSA, DLR, 86-5-478, 4, govs. offc.

55 "Vetoes, 1977." DLR acct. 1024, 3.

56 DLR to Senate, 3/29/1979. DLR 86-5-478, 4, govs. offc.

57 BS 1/10/1979; PI 1/17/1980, 4/18/1979; ST 11/20/1978; Referring to attacks on her appointees, the governor said, "I believe the Post-Intelligencer to be the most dishonest, the most irresponsible newspaper I have ever known. The only trouble is that it ought to be printed on yellow paper." DLR, pr. conf., 4/28/1980. acc. # 86-7-777, 28, pr. rels.

58 DLR to Robert Thompson, 12/8/1977. HISU, DLR, 126, pers. f; Bob Hollister, her Director of Retirement Systems insists the governor was "not aware of how much

it [the press] was hurting her." She "would read transcripts of press conferences at cabinet meetings," pointing out where she had been 'misinterpreted.' Hollister, LOPH (1), 10/14/1989.

59 TNT 3/6/79.

60 T 3/8/1979; ST 1/10/1979, 9/27/1977, 3/6/1979; OR 9/21/80.

61 OR 9/19/1980; Guzzo advised "demanding page one space in the P-I and all the newspapers that ran the charges, and file a multi-million dollar lawsuit [against Hearst and Scates] ... to put a stop to additional insinuations." Guzzo to Ray, 5/6/1980. HISU, DLR, 117.

62 DLR, "Address to the Joint Session of the Legislature, 5/16/1979" in The Doorway to the Eighties. Olympia: State Printer, 1979.

63 TCH 5/16/1977; PI 2/9/1980, EVH 4/19/1981.

64 ST 9/18/1978. KCLS 10/1976; T. S. Galbraith (Special Assistant for Education), to Paul O'Neill, 7/18/1979. WSA, Ray, 33, h ed; Ray to W.T. Deal, 2/26/1979, ibid.; ChHE, 4/17/1978.

65 ST 1/30/2977; TNT 4/3/1979; SR 1/25/1977. A year earlier Bagnariol admitted Ray was off to a "shaky start," but expected her to become "outstanding," and would not consider running against her. "She ran as a politician and continued to act as a non-politician .... I told her ... once you're elected you become a politician, and she had accepted the fact." TCH 5/16/1977.

66 PI 2/2/1980; BS 6/16/1980; Ray to state senators and representatives, and, Bagnariol to Ray, 9/6/1977. Ray, pr. conf., 2/21/1980, pr. confs, 3/19/1980, 4/28/1980, Ray, 3; Questioned about her lack of legislative experience by the media, she retorted "If anything I'd say it's an advantage".

67 Ray to Chaney, HISU DLR 41, SDCC.

68 5/4/1979.

69 BS 6/16/1980.

70 T 9/29/1980; Minutes of the King County Dixy Lee Ray Advisory Committee 8/14, 18/80. HISU, DLR 117, advisory committee. It began in 1978 as the "Hubert Humphrey Club." Merle Adlum was chair, Eddie Carlson, Martin Durkan, former King County Commissioner Ed Munro, Restaurateur David Cohn, ADR, Andy Smith, CEO of Pacific Northwest Bell, and attorney Gordon Culp were present.

71 "The investigation was in no way ever politically motivated," she told the press. "The State Patrol does not even have any device with which to bug." DLR, pr. conf., 4/25/1980. 86-7-777, 28, pr. confs. The FBI told the author the related tapes and papers had been destroyed. Those sent to WSA by the attorney general are under lock for forty years (as of 1980), per its rule that no one living is to be hurt by false implication.

72 Via Senator Richard Hemsted, 2/12/1996; TNT 6/7/1978.

73 DLR, press release 12/15/1977. DLR 113, govs. offc. corr. 1977; Col 10/1/1980.

74 See, "*United States of America vs. John Bagnariol, Gordon Walgren, and Patrick Gallagher*." Western District Court of Washington, no. CR 80-126, V, IX, 2246-2651 (1980). Walgren claimed the governor had instigated the "sting," and promised him the next open senate seat for his cooperation. Ray: "I learned that Walgren's support would depend on some quid pro quo ... . I did what had to be done." Later she admitted, "I had no intention of appointing him." Ray 3, pr. confs. 4/28/1980; Bagnariol admitted, "I'm not sure how much the governor

was directly involved," other than being aware of the investigation. Interview, C. Lenza and S. Hudson with John and Edna Bagnariol, 12/15/1980." Ray 24, n-rs.

75 ST 11/21/1978; Between 1/1/1980 and 8/12/80 she had raised $218,000, and spent $270,000. But total accrued cash was $535,000, most of it raised in the prior two years from business. There were four county and nine statewide paid staff. HISU, Ray 117, fund raising; the "liberal psychiatrist" strategy was the handiwork of Steve Excell and Congressman Joel Pritchard. Excell, LOHP (1), 15; For other judgments see the SR 1/14/1978, DO 2/22/1980, WDW 10/13/1977.

76 OR 9/21/1980; Ray to John Fluke, 2/9/1979. Ray 14, director's replies.

**Chapter 9: John D. Spellman**

1 JDS interview, "Inside Olympia," KTW TV, 5/11/2000; JDS OH, 12/12/1991. JDS 91-31. He practiced law or 13 years, and was president of the Puget Sound Council of Governments, and the King County Economic Development Board. DJE had urged him to run, needing a counterweight to conservative party control and to deny Al Rosellini a comeback; JDS saw an "erosion" the relationship of executive and council since, with the Council has directed departments and commissions to report to it. JDS OH, 1-13.

2 KCA, RG04.601, 3, JDS sps 1969-86, [1972].

3 PI 2/4/1980; DO 2/12/1980; ST 6/21/1981.

4 JDS OH, 15.

5 JDS to Council Chair Ruby Chow, 1/1/1979. KCA, Stern Papers, 1936-7, 5.

6 "John Spellman's Record of Accomplishments." McGavick, 97A-172, 3; Excell OH, 6; JDS, "The State of the County. [5/17/1976]. KCA, JDS RG 4-001, 3, sps, 1969-e.

7 See the author's "The New Order of Cincinnatus: Municipal Politics in Seattle During the 1930's." PNQ 64 (10/73): 137-146, and Peter LeSourd, "The Transformation of Seattle: CHECC's Role." 2008. Online at History Link.

8 JDS was a delegate to the 1962, 1964, and 1968 county conventions, and president of the Young Men's Republican Club of King County.

9 Rahm OH; The county was winning awards, Excell supposed in part, because it was an "invisible government," and not interfered with. OH, 9; JDS, "State of the County." [1976]. KCA, Stern, 8, sps. 1970-79.

10 KTW TV, "Inside Olympia," op cit.

11 EVH 4/19/1981; Ferguson reported a new menu item on Washington State Ferries, "The John Spellman breakfast. You get your choice between waffles and milk toast." TCH 6/3/1981.

12 PI 4/10/1983.

13 JDS OH, 19-20.

14 PI 4/26/1981; BS 4/21/1981; State of Washington, Office of the Governor, "The Anatomy of a Fiscal Crisis." Olympia, 1981, 11 ff. UWASC, GWS Papers, sf e-h, JDS.

15 EVH 9/19/1981.

16 NTM 10/20/1982.

17 ST 4/19/1981; KING-TV, "Transcript of Interview with Governor John Spellman," 9/20/1981, GWS, bsf eh, Governor Spellman; ST 12/6/1981.

18 JA 3/2/1983; BS 2/2/1982; ST 10/8/1981.

19 JDS, "Address to the Forty-Seventh Washington State Legislature, 1982 Regular Session," 1/11/1982. Olympia: Office of the Governor, 1982.

20 In 1979, when the economy peaked, the Republicans tried to set aside a "rainy day fund" equal to 3 percent of the General Fund, but failed.

21 JA 3/30/1982.

22 ST 2/25/1982; Governor's Office, 1/1982, UWASC, GWS Papers, f 21; JDS to department directors, 4/5/1982. JDS, 37; David H. Jackson concludes in *The Administrative Reorganization Experience in the State of Washington*. Seattle: Institute of Governmental Research, UW, 1971, "One cannot determine the importance of any particular recommendation as an input to the Legislature." In the last opportunity, there were 25 executive request bills as of 1/13/82. UWASC, GWS, sf e-h, JDS.

23 Excell OH.

24 Ibid.

25 Appelwick and Wang OH's.

26 O 4/1/1982. "Proclamation by the Governor ... Extending the 1982 First Extraordinary Session." GWS bsf l-m, 1982, legislature. UWASC.

27 PI 3/10/1983; ST 3/10/1982.

28 ST 3/19/1982.

29 Governor's press conference transcripts, 3/9/1982, 3/21/1982. JDS 38. j439

30 BS 3/18/1982; O 3/27/1982.

31 Governor's press conference transcript, 3/11/1982. JDS, 38.

32 JDS to "Agency Directors, and Executives of Boards and Commissions, 3/31/1982. JDS, department heads, memos, 1982.

33 ST 1/9/1983.

34 PI 2/25/1982.

35 When the report came out, the governor told a reporter he had said to the Senate Republican Caucus, "If they had time to study this, [they] may think it's the greatest thing that's been along in years." pr. conf. transcript, [1982]; ST 11/23/1982, 1/9/1983. JDS, 38; TNT 12/28/1982; JDS to Annette C. Mary, 11/18/1982. JDS 20.

36 JDS OH.

37 Excell OH.

38 PI 4/8/1982; press conference transcript, 2/16/1984. JDS 47.

39 The Speaker's bill was SB 3354, removing ferry wages and some benefits from bargaining, and imposing a $2500 a day fine on the unions while striking; PI 2/5/1984.

40 ST 3/31/1984; O 3/6/1984.

41 There was "no compelling need." JDS to Senate, regarding partial veto of SB 3250, 2/22/1983. WSA, JDS 35; PI 2/28/1983, 4/ 5/1984.

42 Richard Larsen in ST 10/8/1981.

43 ST 3/4/1984, 3/9/1984.

44 TNT 1/20/1984.

45 ST 10/25/1984, 1/9/1983; Wkly, 11/14/1984-11/20/1984.

46 Excell OH.

47 JDS, "A Report to the People." 1/7/1982. JDS 86-5-590, 26, govs. offc., and, JDS *The Condition of the Affairs of the State: Address to the Forty-Seventh Washington State Legislature,* 1982 Regular Session, 1/11/1982, ibid.

48 JA 3/10/1982; Asked in March of 1982 what was holding up the bill to extend unemployment compensation payments the governor said, "I really don't know." Everyone on the Third Floor knew it was Polk's trading chip with the Senate Democrats. TNT 12/28/1982, 1/2/1983. These were also the last "title only" bills in Senate Ways and Means to which new bills could be amended; "Proclamation by the Governor … Extending the 1982 Extraordinary Session." GWS bsf, i-m, '82 legislature, UWASC; O 1/13/1981.

49 JDS OH.

50 The Britannica edition of *Funk and Wagnall's Standard Dictionary* (1963), defines a "Tro-lo-dyte" as a 1) cave man, or, 2) Figuratively, "a hermit, anyone with primitive or degenerative habits."

51 O 4/1/1982. JDS, "Third Year Highlights." JDS 3; See Thad L. Boyle, "The Governor as Chief Legislator," SG (Winter 1978): 2-10.

52 PI 3/10/1983.

53 BS 3/18/1982.

54 O 3/27/1982.

55 Governor's pr. conf. transcripts 3/9/1982, 3/21/1982. JDS 38.

56 Governor's pr. confs. 3/9/1982, 3/11/1982, 3/21/1982. JDS 38.

57 The Governor continued to avoid tax reform as not a "compelling need."

58 ST 1/9/1983.

59 "John Spellman Media Recap," 9/4/1984-9/10/1984, news rel. 10/25/1984. Paragon Papers 5; TNT 2/20/1981; Memo, Jim Waldo to JDS, 9/5/1983. JDS 40, 1983.

60 TNT 1/20/1984.

61 JDS to the Municipal Forum, NY, NY, 3/31/1983. JDS 86-556, 35, govs. pr. rels.

62 Excell OH, 42-43.

63 JDS, "Executive Requests, 1982, and 1983. JDS 2-U-102; ST 3/31/1984; O 3/6/1984; The House Democratic caucus' counterpoint was "Recovery Strategies for Washington." It mainly used state credit and pension funds to create a Community Development Finance Corporation, public works, and "Youth Employment Pilot Projects." 1/19/1983. ST 4/4/1984, 4/9/1984. "John Spellman Media Recap," 9/4/1984-9/10/1984, news rel. 10/25/1984; Paragon Papers, 5. TNT 1/20/1984; "Washington/Brushfire Poll," 9/6/1984. Paragon Papers, 3.

64 Excell OH, 77.

65 Both were reserved. JDS countered his shyness with "bravado," while BG came out as being "coy," according to long-time respected lobbyist Mike Ryherd. Ryherd OH, tape 2; "John was hesitant to engage," adds House Minority Leader Marlin Applewick, "He was almost invisible to us." Applewick OH.

66 PI 9/19/1984.

67 Excell OH.

68 ST 11/11/1984.

69 JDS OH.

70 Wkly, 10/24/1984-10/30/1984.

71 ST 1/9/1983.

**Chapter 10: Booth Gardner**

1 For a sensitive introduction to Gardner's contorted youth see John C. Hughes, Booth Who? Olympia: OSOS Legacy Project, 2010: 13-62. "The Governor Who Loves to be Loved," the ST 7/26/1987, is eloquent on the losses he suffered; "I didn't know if I was a Democrat or a Republican. My family [were Republicans], but I didn't necessarily like all my family." BG OH, 4/13/2004: 1-3; BG to "Clinton Rally," 2/26/1992. BG 8, press; TCH 4/5/1984; BG, conversation with the author, 7/8/2003; Gardner's social philosophy is in "Speech to Central Area Economic Development Council," 4/2/1992. BG 8, govs. offc., press.

2 Re his tenure in the Senate and as chair of the Education Committee, Gardner declared his achievement to be "None. I love the administrative aspect of government. I tolerated the legislative aspect of government." Hughes, 84; BG OH, 4/13/2004: 5-6; SR 2/14/1984.

3 Joe Davis OH, 12/10/1989; Grieve OH, 5.

4 PI 2/10/1984, 3/29/1984; "Democratic Campaign Strategy," n.a., Merle Adlum MS, 3, "BG for Gov '84," UWASC.

5 BG quoted in PI 9/10/1983; Dotzauer in TNT 5/10/1984; Re BG's loan to himself, see TNT 8/7/1984; See John Hughes Oral Historian, The Paradox of Booth Gardner. Olympia: OSOS, The Legacy Project, 2010: 135 ff.

6 Foster OH, 4/9/2004: 11-12; Heck OH, 1.

7 Foster OH, 4/09/2004: 13-15; Contrary to his predecessors, who involved themselves in choosing state party chairs for both offensive and defensive reasons, BG engaged in that "not at all" Heck reported, "Even if Karen Marchario, a McDermott fan, held it." He did campaign for Democrats who were friends, but "He wasn't a party politician … before, he wasn't while he was governor, and he isn't now." Heck OH, 27.

8 BG OH, 4/13/2004: 16.

9 Foster OH.

10 McDonald OH, 3/6/2004: 4.

11 Foster OH, 4/9/2004: 13-15.

12 Ryherd described Spellman's shyness as occasionally mock "bravado," and Gardner's as "coyness." "He felt much more comfortable at times with children." Spellman initiated things by talking 'man to man,' and then 'let's get on with serious things.'" These modes transferred into how they did business, with Spellman wanting to talk things out, and Gardner starting with a "let's be friends" approach asking about family, and backing into the questions at hand. "He was much more staff oriented. " Ryherd OH (1), 3/25/2004: 4.

13 McCauley performed much better as a fund raiser than as a strategist or public face.

14 Greg Barlow, BG's friend for all seasons and grey eminence, did the "creative

personnel work," roles later played by COS's Dick Davis, Dean Foster, and Denny Heck. See PI 11/12/1984; There were significant scandals in Pierce County in 1980, prompting the move from the county commissioner system to a county executive and council. He went on to run the Medina Foundation, Gardner-Clapp family charity; Gardner was "squeaky clean," and instituted professional management. The humbled carry-over members of the Council were compliant, but thereafter some of the old ways crept back. Lyle Quasim, senior administrator to the Pierce County Executive in 2006, may have exaggerated for effect in saying that when he came he found "a criminal enterprise equal to any of the old gang bosses in New York." Quasim OH, 3/23/2004: 1-4; Art Wang OH, 3/4/2004: 3; Foster OH, 4/9/2004: 22-23.

15 In his oral history and in exception to his modest ways, Gardner credits himself with "superb people skills" and "outstanding instincts." His chief weakness was attention deficit disorder: "I can't sit down for very long," or for briefings of more than 30 minutes. BG OH , 4/13/2004, 7; Ehlers OH, 2/17/2004: 5.

16 BG, "Inaugural Address," 1/13/1985; Memo, Anderson to Gardner, 9/27/1988. BG 4, govs. offc., staff files, Thompson, WSA.

17 Gardner OH, 4/21/2004: 6-7; He tried "to study all of state government in a month and a half."

18 Foster OH, 4/9/2004: 13-15; Heck OH, 9.

19 Gardner to Sub-Cabinet Management Group, 5/9/1988. BG A9210-385, 23, gov; C. Riveland to same, 7/17/1989. 99A159, 3, govs. offc., DSHS, secretary.

20 Foster OH, 4/9/2004: 22-23; Formerly the Productivity Board; pr. rel., to "Interested Parties," (re: reorganization), 11/18/1985, BG 9; Pr. confs. 11/26/1985, both WSA; Mary Faulk to Dick Davis, "Highlights of [the] 1985-1987 Efficiency and Service Improvement Initiatives," 7/28/1987. BG 4, govs. offc., staff files, (Thompson), WSA. There were lapses. The Commission imagined $30 million in savings at the State Motor Pool, "but they couldn't put their finger on it." Dan McDonald found half to be real, and added it to revenue. Then, "What the governor did was just veto the savings." Two years later the same numbers were in the governor's budget. Senate Ways and Means set up a "Government Efficiency Account," and gave it no budget. "And do you know what" he rhetorically asked, "They made it all up. I think there was a lot more form than substance" [as to efficiency]. McDonald OH, 3/6/2004.

21 BG OH, 4/21/2004: 6-7

22 Ibid, 10-17.

23 "Three Corners" is the governor and both party's senior leader in each house; "Four Corners" means the four senior leaders of both parties meeting without the executive, and "Five Corners" he and all leaders. Then the order of preference was committee chairs, individual legislators, "community folks," lobbyists, and the governor's friends. Thompson, 11-12.

24 BG OH, 4/21/2004: 8-9.

25 e.g., Chief of Staff Dick Davis to Dean Shacklett, 1/31/1989. BG 32, govs. offc., suppt. srvcs. comm., WSA; Wkly, 8/27/1984; Memo, Alan Momohara, Executive Director, Human Rights Commission to Chief of Staff Heck, 2/21/1990. BG 1, govs. offc., commissions, and on comparable worth, see pr. rel. 12/31/1985; BG OH, 4/21/2004: 10.

26 BG OH, 4/21/2004: 10.

27 DSHS, Division of Income Assistance, Memo on "Welfare Reform-Work

Programs," 2/11/1992. 99A163, 3, FIP.

28 On FIP and the federals, see Louis Sullivan, Secretary, HHS, to Speaker Thomas S. Foley, 4/18/1990. BG 2, govs. offc., dtry. of legis. and fed. rels, corr. See also, "Sugarman Takes Look Back at Term in Social Agency," O 1/15/1989. BG to U.S. Senator Patrick Leahy 10/7/1987 [re P.L. 100-485, 1988.] 260-1-2-3-21, FIP memo; Sugarman to Gardner 12/9/1988. 92-10-385, 23-92, gov.

29 Foster OH 4/9/2004: 19.

30 DSHS did "not have expertise" to write and test the enormously complex bid proposal. Department of Information, Services, Planning, and Policy Division, "ISB Review of ACES" 4/10/1991 and Paul Trause Secretary, DSHS, from James A. Peterson Assistant Secretary, Medical Assistance Administration, 9/18/1092. 92-9-512-52, 4, ACES.

31 Lyle Quasim, inured to the latter approach, claims the results were uneven, but "Overall … easily a passing score." He admits to ten layers, but Shinpoch's "delayering" "never occurred," and was "more apparent than real." Quasim, OH; "He didn't get very far," Dean Foster affirmed. "The union found out about it, and put pressure on legislative Democrats. Clearly, Shinpoch was asked at the least to refine some of his strong changes." Foster, LOHP; "He didn't have a chance," Dennis Karras, the long-time head of the Personnel Department. Karras OH.

32 Ryherd OH, (1), 15; McDonald OH, 3/6/2004: 9-10; BG OH, 4/21/2004: 2-4; Lyle Quasim, who returned to DSHS as Governor Lowry's Director, claims FIP "Suffered from poor design and poor execution." It needed high transitional resources and got a "highly publicized and failed computer system." Quasim OH, 3/23/2004: 11.

33 Quasim OH, 3/23/2004: 13-14.

34 Foster OH, 4/9/2004: 18.

35 McDonald OH, 3/6/2004: 9, 36.

36 Thompson OH.

37 BG, pr. conf., 6/8/1987. BG 9.

38 e.g., McDonald OH, 3/6/2004: 8.

39 BG, Testimony on ESHB 1557, collective bargaining, and "OFM Labor Relations Action Plan," 1988. BG 1, govs. offc., cos; Appelwick OH.

40 Karras OH, 2 /27/2004: 6; Heck OH, 2/9/2004: 29-30.

41 BG to Jack Fay, 5/9/1985; BG, 1-F, govs. offc., pers. corr.; D. Heck, notes, (re collective bargaining), 9/18/1990, and. BG 1, govs. offc., DOP governance. Both WSA.

42 "Governor Booth Gardner's Accomplishments 1985-1991." BG 29, govs. offc., central f, and, BG to Agency Directors, 11/13/1987. BG 27, dept. hd. memos, govs. suppt. svcs., central f.

43 Timothy Egan, The Good Rain: Across Time and Terrain in the Pacific Northwest. New York: Knopf, 1990 and Carsten Lein, Olympic Battleground: The Power Politics of Timber Preservation. San Francisco: Sierra Club Books, 1991.

44 "Booth recognized this, [is the nub of the problem], but ducked it." Ryherd OH, (1), 15; McDonald OH 3/6/2004: 9-10; Gardner OH, 4/21/2004: 2-4.

45 Pr. conf., 7/21/1991, BG 9.

46 BG, Testimony to the U.S. House of Representatives, "Hearing on Forest Service

Old Growth/Timber Supply Issue," 8/31/1990. BG 8, govs. offc., pr. rels.

47 Pr. rel., 3/8/1988. BG 11, govs. offc., press. Gardner's environmental views are stated best in "Environment 2010 Speech." BG 8, govs. offc., pr. rels.; Land Commissioner Brian Boyle's views, often at odds with BG's, are in Boyle to (Counselor to the President) Clayton Yuetter, 3/10/1992. BG 43, govs. offc., suppt. staff, "Spotted Owl Protection Plan." Studies were initiated by the WSLC's SB 5911 of 1989. "Background" on the Olympic Discussion Groups, n.a., [1989]. 94A57, 4, exec. timber team; Rich Nafziger to Ray Ryan (Deputy Director, OFM), "Information for the Executive Timber Team," 9/11/1989. BG 1, timber/owl..

48 BG, pr. rel., 5/25/1985. BG 9; BG to Barbara Franklin (U.S. Secretary of Commerce), 4/17/1992. BG 43, govs. offc. suppt. svcs., log exports f. This also impacted the public schools, recipients of the timber tax. During the early 1990s it fell from 14 percent of the cost of building them to 7 percent.

49 A full treatment is in American Forests (9/10/1990): 21-24.

50 BG to Judge William L. Dwyer, 6/11/1992. BG 43, govs. offc., suppt. srvcs., old growth forests and jobs, f.

51 The State of the State: Transcript of Address by Governor Booth Gardner, 1/13/1987. BG 9, re, the "Report of the Federal Interagency Scientific Committee on the Northern Spotted Owl;" BG to Hatfield, 5/21/1990 and Nafziger, "Testimony Before the Subcommittee on National Parks and Public Lands, Committee on Interior and Insular Affairs, U.S House," 5/20/1990. 94A51, 1, exec timber team; "Governor's Forest Resource Programs," (1/16/1990) and BG to USS Mark Hatfield, 6/13/1990.

52 The Timber Team "bought a lot of time, and came up with some solutions" Dean Foster affirms. "I am not sure what could have been done." People "bought into the Spotted Owl because most were not affected." Foster OH, 4/9/2004: 2.

53 BG OH, 4/21/2004: 11.

54 Secretary of the Department of Energy James Watkins to BG, 4/13/1992. BG 5, govs. offc., Hanford; "Letter of Agreement Between the Governor of Washington and the Secretary of Energy," 10/15/1990. BG 27, DOE/gov model f; BG 4/21/2004: 11.

55 BG, pr. cone, 5/8/1987; Kitzhaber to Gardner, 5/15/1987; and memo, Jack S. Wayland (Director, Dept. of Wildlife) to BG 10/28/1987; Interstate Compact, (2nd SHB 426). BG 42, cent. staff files, offc. of fed. srvcs.

56 BG, pr. conf. 2/12/1988. BG 9.

57 Ibid.

58 Dick Larson in the ST 2/3/1991.

59 BG, pr. conf., 6/30/1987. BG 9; On the leadership question, see Wkly 1/11/1989 and, "The Voters' Booth," ST 10/23/1988.

60 Wlky 5/18/1983.

61 BG, pr. conf. 9/20/1987, BG, 9.

62 BG, pr. conf. 4/19/1988, BG 9.

63 "Basic Speech." BG 99A159, 3, govs. offc.; TNT 4/9/1989; Don Borrows, "A Progressive State with Regressive Taxes," in George W. Scott, ed., Turning Points in Washington's Public Life. Seattle: Civitas Press, 2011.

64 See, "Tax changes in Washington Since 1935." WSL, Calvin Johnson MS, 2, Tax Commission; The AWB wanted to replace the B and O will a corporate income

tax of 16 percent.; The majorities may have resisted, apart from not having the votes, because piece meal reforms took pressure off for overall overhaul.

65 Notes on "Strategy Conference," (by Heck), 1/14/1989. BG 3, govs. offc., strategy group; Dennis Okamoto questionnaire later asked Heck, "Did you choose public service deliberately?" Why?" His responses: "Yes"; "Congenital defect." BG, govs. offc.; TCH 5/21/1989; When Gardner came into office much of the windfall of 1983-85, meant to take the new Democratic majorities out of the recessionary holes the GOP had been in, was spent. In 1983, McDermott had gotten the Senate Democrats to pass a one cent raise in the sales tax, raising a billion dollars in the biennium. "They did it right of the bat. We [the House GOP], were caught totally off guard .... We had an all-night debate that ended at 9 o'clock the next morning. But there was no way you could stop it." McDonald OH, 3/6/2004: 5.

66 "Preparing for Washington's Second Century," in Budget in Brief Update, 1989-91 Biennium, Final. Olympia: State Printer, [1991]: 69; BG to Senate Majority Leader Jeannette Hayner, 4/20/1989. 95A159, 3, gov; Davis OH, 3/4/2004: 3-4.

67 BG to "Dear Friend," 7/1989. 99A159, 7, govs. offc. Introducing Wilkerson's replacement Dennis Okamoto a U.S. West vice president in February of 1990, the governor admitted the new director was "not up to speed" on tax reform. What role would he play?" the press asked. The governor: "Well, if we pursue it, and to the extent to which we intend to pursue it, the chair of the Department of Revenue will have a lead on that." Queried again, he said he didn't mean to say "if"; Wang OH, 4-6.

68 McDonald OH, 3/6/2004.

69 BG OH 4/21/2004: 5-6.

70 "Remarks by the Governor to the Senate Capital Facilities Committee," 2/26/1991. BG 8, govs. offc., press, and, "Remarks by the Governor to the Senate Education Committee," 2/14/1991, ibid.

71 McDonald OH, 3/21/2004: 7.

72 BG, pr. rel., 5/25/1985.

73 Richard D. Ford to BG, 9/13/1992. BG 2, govs. offc., suppt. srvcs., central f, agencies; Ryherd OH, tape 1: 23-24.

74 In Olympia, Gardner ordered agencies in his purview to lead his Washington State Environment Advisory Committee. A steering committee was formed to monitor and document the executive branch's policy of "actively supporting environmental education ...within existing resources." Natural resource agencies formed a parallel "Governor's Council on Environmental Education" to establish goals in air quality, reducing single occupancy rides, waste reduction, and prepared a biennial "State of the Environment Report." Admirable as these efforts were, they ended with the administration. "Toward 2010: An Environmental Action Agenda." Washington Environment 2010 Advisory Committee," 7/18/1990. Per EO 88-09. BG 33, environment; See BG "Executive Report." 5/1990.

75 BG, State of the State Address, 1/12/1988. Olympia: State Printer, 1988.

76 BG pr. conf, 4/19/1988.

77 ST 4/2/1990.

78 Gardner's response was an Advisory Commission on Investment in Human Capital, leading to the changes in technical education and Work Force Training and the administration. The proposed biannual budget was up 12.2 percent, the

smallest increment in 12 years.

79 BG pr. conf. 1/15/1991, BG 9; or, see BG to Washington State Labor Council, 8/26/19. BG 8, govs. offc., pr. or, BG, "Remarks to Democratic Party State Convention," 6/5/1992. Ibid.

80 BG, pr. conf., 6/8/1987.

81 Gardner's state response was an Advisory Commission on Investment in Human Capital, which led to the changes in technical education and Work Force Training and its administration.

82 "Remarks by Governor Booth Gardner [to] Boeing Management Association," 11/25/1991. BG 8, govs. offc., pr.; BG OH, 4/21/2004: 13.

83 Wkly 4/27/1992; Billings was kept at arm's length. The SPI's budgets were historically "unrealistic," and therefore "irrelevant." At times you've got to wonder if they aren't a surrogate for the WEA," which resisted everything "unless they invented it," he concluded. BG OH, 5/20/2004: 2; Foster, OH, 4/9/2004: 8-9.

84 BG OH, 4/21/2004: 12-16 and 5/30/2004: 3; McDonald OH, 3/6/2004: 12-15.

85 BG felt the SPI's budget were historically "unrealistic," and therefore "irrelevant. At times you've got to wonder if they aren't a surrogate for the WEA," which resisted everything "unless they invented it," he concluded; BG OH, 5/20/2004: 2.

86 BG OH 4/21/2004: 15-16.

87 See WWUB 1/25/2008, EVH 1/27/2008, C 1/22/2008, and O 1/30/2008 for the span of views on the WASL.

88 In 1988, two state senate candidates had just spent $200,000 each for a $20,000 a year job. Unions had sent involuntary "taxes" to Democrats. Checks of over $100 were easier for businessmen to write the GOP. I-134 lidded personal contributions at $500 per (because the GOP had more of them). Democrats had wanted lids of $1,000 for legislators, and $5000 for statewide candidates, because they had large organizations like WEA and WFSE behind them. The Republicans prevailed because banning large gifts from labor unions PACs and corporations was compelling — even if there was no overall spending limit — which the courts had said was legal only if there was public funding, which the voters opposed.

89 BG pr. conf., 4/19/1998.

90 Wayne Ehlers to House Minority Leader to Speaker Clyde Ballard, 7/17/1991. BG 6, govs. offc.; e-mail, Ehlers to BG, 6/16/2003.

91 Ed Seeberger, "Switches: A History of the 1981-1982 Sessions," 211, 212, 217. AP; Foster LOHP; Brunell, OH.

92 Washington's Health Care Authority was first appointed in 1990; ST 2/19/1992. The price was $138 per month per employee. See BG in TCH 10/22/1991. He felt the Canadian 'single-payer' system aroused "unwarranted political passions." His move anticipated the Bush Administration's Social Security Advisory Council; Col 12/20/1991; Senator McDonald asserts the plan originated with Warren Featherstone Reid, a long-time Magnuson staffer, and himself. Reid was back with the legislature after the senator's death. McDonald, Reid OH.

93 Foster OH, 4/9/2004: 19.

94 Davis OH, 9-10.

95 Pr. conf., 1/15/1991. BG, 9; or see BG to Washington State Labor Council, 8/26/1992. BG 8, govs. offc., pr, or, BG, "Remarks to Democratic Party State Convention," 6/5/1992. Ibid.

96 Memo, Richard Thompson to BG, 5/18/1989. WSA 99A160, 4, tax ref; Denny Heck testifies BG was "not a strict constructionist, but believed he was the final vote in the legislative process, and would veto it if he did not agree with his policy. Heck OH, 23-24.

97 BG's personal estate, in a blind trust since 1973, was estimated at $30 million in 1989.

98 Gardner ordered agencies in his purview to lead his Washington State Environment Advisory Committee. A steering committee was formed to monitor and document the executive branch policy of "actively support environmental education," "within existing resources." Natural resource agencies formed a parallel "Governor's Council on Environmental Education" to establish goals in air quality, reducing single occupancy rides, waste reduction, and prepared a biennial "State of the Environment Report." Admirable as these efforts were, the ended with the administration; "Toward 2010: An Environmental Action Agenda." Washington Environment 2010 Advisory Committee," 7/18/1990. Per EO 88-09. BG, 33, environment; See BG, "Executive Report," 5/1990.

99 In 1988, two state senate candidates had just spent $200,000 each for a $20,000 a year job. Unions had sent involuntary "taxes" to Democrats. Checks of over $100 were easier for businessmen to write the GOP. I-134 lidded personal contributions at $500 per (because the GOP had more of them). Democrats had wanted lids of $1,000 for legislators and $500 for statewide candidates (because they had large organizations like WEA and WFSE behind them). The Republican's prevailed because banning large gifts from labor unions, PACs, and corporations was compelling — even if there was no overall spending limit — which the courts had said was legal only if there was public funding — the which the voters opposed.

100 Ehlers OH, 2/17/2004: 4; John Hughes' The Paradox of Booth Gardner. Olympia: OSOS Legacy Project, 2010, dwells on the "reluctant dragon" theme, especially from pps. 63 to 82.

101 Thompson LOHP, 6-9. He was the only cabinet member to hold the "big three," the OFM, COS, and DSHS directorships; Marty Brown, the longest-serving director of OFM, feels Gardner "did not have an overwhelming desire to have more money in the coffers." Brown OH; BG OH, 4/13/2004: 22; Marty Brown, the longest-serving director of OFM, feels Gardner "did not have an overwhelming desire to have more money in the coffers." Brown OH, 4/22/2004: 1-3.

102 Heck OH, 23-25.

103 Memo, Richard Thompson to BG, 5/18/1989. 99A160, 4, tax ref; Denny Heck testified BG was "not a strict constructionist, but believed he was the final vote in the legislative process, and would veto if he did not agree with his policy. Heck, LOPH.

104 "Remarks by Governor Gardner to Spokane Rotary," 2/28/1991. BG 8, govs. offc, press; TCH 10/24/1991; "Our political system is nearing meltdown … . The nineties just have to be a back to the drawing board decade." The country needed "A cold war political culture that draws people in rather than one than shuts people out. All of us have to pay more dues." He engaged with the Parkinson's Foundation, teamed with Dan Evans to try to pass a one cent, $1 billion sales tax initiative dedicated to public and higher education 2003, and was presidential candidate Howard Dean's state chair.

105 BG OH, 4/13/2004: 4; BG to Western Treasurers Conference, 7/26/1992. BG 8, govs. offc, pr. The best exposition of Gardner's approach to public service is in his "Washington State University Convocation Speech," 10/10/1989, ibid.

106 Ryherd OH, tape 1: 21-24.

107 Parkinson's is a progressive disease of the central nervous system inducing a loss of stamina, memory, and balance, and creating tension and depression in 1.5 million Americans. "Parkinson's is what I have, not what I am," BG said. "I border on compulsive to make sure I'm contributing. It [continuing to work] was a bad idea."

108 Memo, Bill Wegleben to Denny Heck, April 3, 1990. BG 1, govs. offc., chief of staff; PI 6/10/2003; Gardner came out against the other monumental question of 1992, correctly predicting the term limits the initiative "will be the worst thing that could happen. It's a cop-out." Wkly 4/27/1992; U.S. House Speaker the U.S. House Tom Foley of Spokane may have lost in 1994 by attacking the initiative.

109 "Remarks by Governor Booth Gardner to Foley/Labor Rally," Spokane, 10/24/1990. WSA, BG 8, govs. offc, press. Gardner unsuccessfully sought to be Secretary of HHS, and ambassador to Japan, but was appointed U.S. Ambassador to the World Trade Organization, 1994-97, then became an "independent policy consultant" at Ron Dotzauer's Northwest Strategies. Overall assessments are in the PI 1/8/1993, and ST 1/13/1993.

110 Foster OH.

**Chapter 11: Mike Lowry**

1 ST 1/15/1993.

2 ML OH (1); Jim Moore, who made a credible try at Superintendent of Public Instruction in 1972. PI 5/15/1973; The PI, ST, and Teamsters endorsed JDS. ST 10/4/1973, 10/7/1973;

3 The Boeing-Coffee-Lowry relationship was an important take-away from the congressional years. Representative Art Wang reported that Lowry had promised to "consult" with Coffee over appointments to the Pollution Board, and he was "black balled."

4 On defense, see HR 1681, CR 4/10/1981 and his Report (to the Seventh District), 1/1981, and "robo" ltr 1707r, 4/30/1981, ML 152, 3, UWASC. He credited the president with missile reductions in Europe, START, and lessening the chance of war by miscalculation and backed the Trident sub base, while resisting other military increases. On crime see "robo" ltr, 1317k, 4/24/1986. ML 43; on campaign finance reform the tack was to cut PAC, and raise individual limits. ltr 1572r, 10/6/1986, ibid.

5 See CR 4/10/1971, House, 1681 on his expertise in energy and urban affairs; ST 1/12/1997, 10/21/1983; Lowry's 1982 rating by the ADA was 95 percent, by the ACLU 100 percent, and by Labor's COPE 81 percent.

6 See "Lowry Mania." Wkly 11/2/1983-11/8/1983.

7 Tabloid, "Dan Evans for U.S. Senator," 1983. ML 1, 1, and, "Mike Lowry knows Washington State too." ML 2, cpn. lit., Evans cpn; For endorsements, see PI, 9/30/1983. Twelve bills were "private"; only two were considered in any committee. His one floor amendment was rejected 93/245 on 11/13/1980.

8 Wkly 9/26/1988; ST 11/9/1989. Thirty seven percent of Gorton voters praised his "good performance," 26 percent thought Lowry "too liberal," and 22 percent did not "like" him. Conversely, 34 percent were for Lowry because of his "stands on issues," and 20 percent because they did not like Gorton. ML, 2, Memo PP, positions 1983.

9 Critique of the "Lack of a Recognizable Campaign Structure" that helped sink Gorton in 1986 by his own staff helped him dramatically improve his approach. Bruce and Sara Kendall, Deborah Storey, and Scott Celley to Gorton, 1/11/1988. DJE 260-1-5-3, Gorton; See TNT 11/29/1987. Only six U.S. Senators since 1945 had recovered lost seats. WP 8/7/1988.

10 PI 1/15/1992.

11 PI 5/15/1973.

12 Doyen of the KING Broadcasting Company, environmentalist and philanthropist.

13 PI 7/27/1992; OR 9/3/1992; ST 5/30/1992, 8/24/1992; DO, 6/21/1992.

14 ST 8/25/1992, 10/25/1992; PH 5/29/1992.

15 Morrison ultimately came aboard as a "team player," but Evans' failure to endorse the nominee was not lost on centrists. ST 8/23/1992; EW 5/25/1992; PI 9/23/1992, 10/15/1992.

16 Memorandum, Dresner, Sykes, Jordan and Townsend to Eikenberry, 1/14/1992. ML 1, 1; PI 9/30/1992.

17 PI 9/30/1992.

18 See Chapter 3 of the author's A Majority of One: Legislative Life. 3nd printing, Seattle: Civitas Press, 2012. Political nativists almost blocked Eikenberry's reelection to a third term as state chair after the GOP tide in 1994. DO, 12/31/1994.

19 Brochure, "Eikenberry for Governor," ML 1, 1.

20 TNT 10/23/1992.

21 "Lowry Wins Praise from Republican Rotarians." JA 8/16/1988.

22 McDonald OH, 3/6/2004, 16; Evans stalwart and civic icon Jim Ellis helped draw them in. ML, LOHP (1), Foster, LOHP (1); Re: Boeing, Brunell LOHP.

23 Registrations had doubled since 1988 due to the new "motor-voter" law, where a driver's license was the only credential needed to register. ST 10/22/1992, 10/26/1992, 10/29/1992, 11/4/1992.

24 See "Population Politics." Washington D.C.: U.S. Bureau of the Census, 1990. For the first time a majority of the voters were suburbanites. BH 8/14/1992; ST 10/11/1992, 10/26/1992, 11/4/1992, 12/6/1992; Wkly 11/18/1992; HJR 4203 and SB 5095 did not pass in 1993. Lowry was non-committal. ML to M/M Dennis Kane, 11/9/1993. ML 94A62, my vote cards. The rise of woman power in statewide offices became palpable with election of AG Christine Gregoire, and Commissioner of Public Lands Jennifer Belcher, who joined the SPI. WDW 1/4/1993; ADW 1/7/1993.

25 ML to Senate Government Operations and House State Government committees, 1/5/1994; "Draft Recommendations of the Commission of Ethics in Government and Campaign Practices," 12/1/1993, and, EO 93-02 9, "implementing" ch. 42.18 RCW, the Executive Conflict of Interest Act. "While we have many laws … relating to ethics, they have little meaning without education and application."

26 Ibid.

27 Paul Skinner, a Seattle business anchor and active Democrat who had needed no winning over conceded, "So far there's more style than substance. Will his style change? He's going to have to." PI 12/23/1979, 2/14/1993. Dan McDonald's impression was that ML's energy made the governor's office "a bit chaotic" with touches of "abrasiveness." McDonald OH, 3/6/2004: 15; Executive Order 93-07, "Affirming [a] Commitment to Diversity; VDN 1/13/1993.

28 Memorandum, "Citizen Cabinet Enhancements" [12/92]. ML 94A161, citizen cabinet. ST 2/2/1993, WSA; "Voices of Washington." [The] Citizen Task Forces' Report to the Governor-Elect, 1/12/1993. ML, 1, 3, WSA; Hine OH, 3.

29 Washington had 11.8 percent minorities in 1990. The capitol lagged. See "Diversity in State's Top Management." ST 8/10/1993. The "Minority Initiative" was seen as necessary advocacy. Edward Rodriquez, Director, Diversity Initiatives, to Shirley Brundage, 4/13/1995. ML 33, sexual minorities; DSHS, Program Status Report, n.p., [Olympia], 2/1995, "Hands Off Washington." ML, Press Conference, 1/12/1994; Not everyone was pleased, e.g., Minority Leader Clyde Ballard to ML, 5/5/1994. ML 97-A-31, 3, reps. and sens. Lowry wrote Congressman Randy Tate protesting that his "Same Sex Marriage Act" was "profoundly unfair." ML, 95A-65-2, congress; re women, see Hine OH, 18.

30 ST 6/10/1993; Hine served as a mayor, President of the King County Council of Governments, as Democratic Caucus Chair in the House and after 1992 as Majority Leader. She insists "several" of Gardner's "Policy Staff" were kept. "We got better as time went on." Anne Daly, briefly OFM Director, and Ruta Fanning, her successor, "were outstanding." Hine OH 8; "Totally at sea," and "hold back," Wang OH, 8-9; Foster OH, 4/9/2004: 34-35.

31 Heck, OH; TNT 5/18/1995. Bernard Heavey Jr. to ML, 5/16/1995. ML 97 A 31-5, judicial appointments, WSA. Heavey, a former King County Democratic chair, was likely seated at the request his son, the chair of the Judiciary Committee in the Senate, and his brother Ed, a former legislator already on superior court bench; Lowry "agreed in principle" to reduce size of the supreme court from 9 to 7, to change selection of the "Chief" (from auto-rotation), and to and work on "judicial reform"; Justices Barbara Durham and Robert Utter to ML, 12/15/1994. ML 33, supreme court. WSA; PI 11/10/1995; TNT 5/18/1995; Shelley Yapp, Director of the Pike Place Market, was named to "reinvigorate" UW regents, and was joined in 1995 by former Budget Director and then Assistant State Treasurer Ann Daley. They replaced businessmen Paul Skinner and Andrew Smith. Frank Blethen publisher of the Seattle Times was typical of those asked for different "regent possibilities." Blethen to ML, 1/25/1995. ML 97A316, regents, WSA; Lowry tried to rebalance the Utilities and Transportation Commission by making former Representative and lobbyist Don Brazier the 'Republican' member. The UTC was so consumer oriented the president of Puget Sound Power and Light held a novel press conference to damn a rate decision. ST 6/28/1995.

32 Thomas to Professor Jon M. Peha, 6/8/1993, and to "Management Team," 1/14/1993. ML 97A-48. st. dtrs, corr., 1993; Heck in PI 2/14/1993. Not everyone was pleased. See Minority Leader Clyde Ballad to ML, 5/5/1994. L 97-A-31, 3, reps. and sens.

33 Daley left the "high burnout" job after a month; re Sandberg, see ML OH, 5/18/2004: 3-5; The wizardly, enigmatic Len McComb went from OFM to Revenue. TNT 2/8/1996; Gary Moore, 19 years with the WSFSE who personified Labor, was ML's first Director of Legislative Relations, then Deputy Staff Director. Curt Smitch, a lightning rod in the endless wars between commercial and sports fishermen, resigned from Wildlife in December 1993.

34 "It was always a strange appointment: Dan McDonald thought. "Jean had always been sort of in the background … he reached down … I think she was always a bit uncomfortable with it … . She never had a real command of the complexity of [DSHS]. McDonald OH 3/6/2004: 17; Soliz to Phyllis Campbell (Chair, AWB), 2/16/1995. ML 97A31, DSHS, 3; PI 12/22/1992; Dennis Karras, the State Personnel Director, termed her "A policy 'wonk' who understood the legislature

but whose executive experience was 'next to none'"; Quasim OH, 3/23/2004: 17.

35 Quasim, a strenuous defender of DSHS, began as a night shift counselor at Western State Hospital and was promoted until fired as head of the Division of Mental Health in 1987, either because he was "not leading," or, "refused to lie to the legislature" about his budget, as Lowry believed. In 1991, he was awarded $240,000. "He minced no words," the Governor said, a quality he admired, despite Quasim's controversies. See Lowry OH, 5/18/2004: 1-2. ST 12/5/1995, 4/27/2000; "He was always very positive, able guy," Dan McDonald felt. OH 3/6/2004: 17; Re the "OK Boy's Ranch," see JA 12/12/1995; Quasim OH, 3/23/2004: 25.

36 The union preferred "partnership," (i.e., co-management). Eugene St. John to ML, ML 97A654, Labor; Sandberg had been a finalist the previous year. Roger Bruett, a short term chief, had been churned out amidst union turmoil.

37 Morrison angered Republicans by also advising Senator Patty Murray on her transition. PI 12/22/1992; ST 6/6/1993, 6/23/1993; LMT 11/30/1992; TCH 11/29/1992; The Governor made Teamster Lawrence Weldon as first black member of the Transportation Commission.

38 Dear was praised by the AWB's President as "The best ... I can remember." ADW 1/20/1993; PI 2/7/1993. Dear's hard-nosed forbear Dick Davis also deserves credit; "Labor and Industries Press Conference," ML 97 A 18, 6, L & I, WSA. Larry Kinney was rescued from an uphill fight for reelection to as president of the State Labor Council with a seat on the State Board of Tax Appeals. Sending Ron Judd to Ecology was a short-lived faux pas. The biases of the former Business Agent for the Electrical Workers Union were all too evident when he helped the Washington Environmental Council defeat the Early Winters Ski Resort in the Methow Valley. Agriculture Director Peter Goldmark went back to his Okanogan family after six months, and State Senator Jim Jessernig took over.

39 ML to Mary Riveland, 5/15/1996. ML 95A-65, 6, cabinet; C. Riveland to ML, 3/29/1994. ML 97A654, Labor; TCH 1/29/1993.

40 The cost of SB 5304 was projected at $229 million in 1993-95, rising to over $1 billion in 1997-99, when all 500,000 uninsured were to be covered. BG had asserted the Health Care Commission's recommendations would save the State $4 billion by 2001; ML said $7 billion by 2005. DO 1/12/1993; TCH 3/11/1993. "Summary of the Recommendations of the Health Care Commission," 11/30/1992. ML 99A163, 2, gov; govs, pr. conf., 1/21/1993. ML 97A18, 5, health corr.

41 SB 5304 passed the Senate 30-16, with all but two Republicans voting no, and 56 to 42 in the House; Washington Health Care Authority, "The Basic Health Plan." Olympia: The Authority, 10/1993; ML to Craig B. Kirby, 9/8/1994. ML, 2, health care reform, WSA; "Statement [re passage of] Health Care Reform," 4/23/1993. All ML 94 A161-1, governor.

42 TNT 3/15/1993.

43 PI 5/9/1995. See "Senate Votes to Repeal most of Health Care Reform." ST 4/15/1995. The vote was vote 39-9 in the Senate.

44 O 3/16/1993. Business' backing price was blocking "unnecessary boosts" in unemployment insurance taxes.

45 ST 6/22/1993; Col 4/4/2000; "WMS ... was a move forward, but not a great leap forward," was Lyle Quasim's appraisal. OH, 3/23/2004: 23.

46 Transcript, govs. pr. conf., 1/25/1993; DO 4/22/1993. "Moore got a sharp dressing down in private." PI 4/20/1973; ST 4/23/1993.

47 Howard Jorgenson and Gary Moore to Council 28 Executive Board (WSFSE),

7/15/1993. ML 4, civil service.

48 See Scott, A Majority of One, ch. 12, "The Uncivil Service"; "In a way we feel jammed to do this," Mark Brown complained to ML, 1/4/1994. ML 197A31, 2, civil service reform; ML to Senator George Sellar and Representative Clyde Ballard, 3/9/1994, (re HB 2810 and SB 6479). ML 97A31, 3, reps; ST 3/8/1994; ML OH, 5/18/2004: 10; "We came very close" to passing both WMS, collective bargaining and some contracting out" according to Lorraine Hine, "But we just could not get the [full reform past the] Senate." Hine OH, 12.

49 See HBs 1992 and 2129, SB 5940, and Department of Trade and Economic Development, "Transition 1992." Olympia: The Department, 1992. Labor's wins included upping the amount a worker could collect for permanent partial disability 32 percent (HBs 248 and 1249), permitting law officers to retire at 55 (instead of 58), (HB 1294), and raising the minimum wage from $4.25 by $4.90. PI 5/13/1993; "Merger Plan DCTED," 11/15/1993. ML 99A161, 3, DCTED, and "Governor's briefing on Merger Plans," 11/21/1993. ML 94A61, 3, fish and wildlife merger. The Office of Marine Safety was consolidated into Ecology. ML to Mary Riveland, Director of Ecology, 7/24/1995. ML 97A31, 7, ecol; Jack DeYounge, Exec. Policy Asst. to Phyllis Arnold at Fish and Wildlife, 4/7/1994. He claimed a saving of $1 million over 18 months. ML 95A128, 51, fish and wildlife merger; Ruta Fanning, Acting Director, OFM to ML 10/15/1993. ML 97-A-18, 2, 1993 budget; He "tried to take them on through merging units … thinking that ought take out [employees]. It just added. They had more people just sitting there … through retirement." Ryherd OH, 16.

50 O 3/12/1993; PI 2/21/1993.

51 ML, pr. conf., 1/25/1993. ML 5, House; ST 2/5/1993, O 2/5/1993. See "Mixed Message," PI 2/5/1993. The AP's statewide story that Lowry "will launch a drive for a state income tax," was retailed by the Seattle television stations; See TNT 2/6/1993; HR 2/14/1993.

52 O 3/23/1993. In Spokane in the Summer of 1994, Lowry defined "tax reform" as a "three legged stool," with constitutional amendments lowering the sales and B&O taxes, freezing property levies, and a new income tax as the "only way I would ever go." (i.e., a close variation of HJR 42 of 1971).

53 ML, Inaugural Address, 1/13/1993. ML 5.

54 The rates on professional services (lawyers to public relations), went from 1.5 to 2.5 percent, raising $164 million. Adding the 6.5 percent state and local sales taxes to consumer services, and a like surtax placed on wholesaling and manufacturing produced $102 million, one on hotel and motel laundries and even escort services $124 million, on financial services 1.7 percent, for $18.3 million, and raising other businesses to 2 percent, $149 million. College tuitions were lifted by $98 million. Taxes on less defended personal services (e.g., landscapers), paid for new unemployment benefits, making it the nation's highest. The capital budget, dubbed "Pork Lite," (SB 5717), focused on college buildings, low income housing, prisons and natural resources.

55 ST 4/16/1993; re (Seattle) JOC 4/16/1993; ST 3/31/1993; DO 4/13/1993.

56 ST 4/25/1993; DO 4/18/1993; JA 4/1/1993. ML to Representative Kim Perry, 2/8/1995. ML 97 A13, Perry Buck, 4/28/1995, a-b; ADW 4/11/1993, 5/9/1993.

57 The 61-member "kitchen cabinet," headed by Frank Blethen of the Seattle Times, included Weyerhaeuser's Jack Creighton, Washington Mutual's Kerry Killinger, the Seattle Mariner's Howard Lincoln, and the Bon Marche's Bill Fix was Bob Gogerty's tip of the hat to "big" business. ML 93-4, "Kitchen Cabinet"; Budget

Address, 3/24/1993. ML 97A18, 5, budget; See "Ax and Tax," ADW 5/6/1993.

58 BJA 4/14/1993. See TNT 4/20/1993; SR 1/7/1997; ST 5/9/1993; Transcript of Kirkland Town Hall Meeting, 7/1/1993," ML 97A13, rev, a-b.

59 See "Lowry's Tax Reform Loses … " ST 5/6/1993. BJA 4/14/9193. See TNT 4/20/1993; SR 1/7/1997; ST 5/9/1993; PI 4/13/1993; SR 4/7/1993; TNT 4/18/1993.

60 PI 1/9/1994; Ellis in EW 5/26/1993.

61 ST 3/28/1993.

62 ST 3/14/1994, PI 8/5/1994; An example of positive coverage is in the TNT 3/16/1994.

63 PH 5/8/1993. Others disagreed, e.g., the TNT 5/9/1993. ML to Edythe Yokem, 7/20/1993. ML 94A66, ethics.

64 See David Broder, Democracy Derailed: Initiative Campaigns and the Power of Money. New York: Harcourt, 2000.

65 OFM, "Initiative Measures 601 and 602: [An] Overview of Provisions and Financial Impacts." Olympia: OFM, 1; Transcripts, Seattle, Town Hall Meeting 6/21/1993, passim, and the Kirkland Town Meeting, 7/1/1993. The transcripts from the Kirkland, Bellingham and Moses Lake run 50 pages, a three-hour marathon at Aberdeen 98; ML to J.D. Alexander (Executive Editor, the PI). All ML 94A161-1, editors/responses; ST 5/29/1993, 9/7/1993. ML 97A18, 5 and 93-164, 3.

66 Frank Schrontz, chair, Business Roundtable to ML, 7/21/93, and Walter C. Howe president, BR, to ML, 9/17/1993. ML 94A161, 3; Senate Majority Leader Marc Gaspard and Speaker Ebersole to Luke Helms, CEO, SeaFirst Bank, et al., 6/29/1993. ML 94A161,3; ML, Address to the Seattle Rotary Club, 10/13/1993; I-602's narrow loss was hardly "decisive," and "601" won by less than 2 percent. "Governor's Remarks," press interview 8/21/1993. ML 93A, 5, lobbies and business; ML to Wendy Roedell, 3/6/1995. ML 20, r-s.

67 The deeper damage was in the onset of an era of government by plebiscite. Personal optimism was rising as faith in government declined, with those expressing little or no confidence going from 27 percent in 1976 to 65 percent in 1994. The Republican's clever I-34 limited the size of contributions — especially those of groups like the WEA — had been thunderously endorsed in 1992 as ML was elected. Then came term limits (I-573), "Three strikes you're out" (I-593), and life terms for persons convicted of three violent felonies. See ST 1/18/1994. The first victim of term limits was the Speaker of the U.S. House of Representatives, Tom Foley of Spokane, who successfully opposed it in court, then lost his 30-year seat in Congress. ST 2/13/1994; See "Initiative Measures 601 and 602: Overview of Provisions and Fiscal Impacts." Olympia, OFM 9/20/1993.

68 ML, "Post-Election Media Availability," 11/9/1994; Brian Ebersole in ST 11/14/1994.

69 ST 11/14/1994, 2/8/1995; HB 1519 was modeled on a Pennsylvania law, and would have imposed a 24 hour waiting period; HB 1518 required parental consent for girls under 18.

70 ML-David Ammons interview 1/5/1994. ML 97A18, Ammons int; ML to Representatives Ebersole and Ballard, Senators Gaspard and Sellar, 9/22/1994. ML 97A31, 4, 1995 sess. Between 1984 and 1993 state staff increased an average of 2,500 FTEs a year. In 1993-95 it was 4.5 percent, or half that, and the "actuals" were even lower, ending with 554 fewer employees, for the first time since 1982. This despite the hiring of 400 new prison guards. I-601 limits were effective June

30, 1995, and required a referendum on any tax increase passed. ML to Donald Anderson 2/20/1995. ML 50, revenue, a-b.

71 See ML "Special" to ST 5/9/1995. The BJA (quoted in TNT 5/14/1995), stirred the ashes: "Governor Pollyanna ... invited the tone of the coverage when he tried to portray a political defeat as a victory."

72 In 1993, ML told a House committee he did "not see any real protection for the public" in locking up first time offenders, including drug addicts and burglars, because they would be released soon. LMT 2/24/1993. Moves to reduce costs and "comforts" in state's 13 prisons were bipartisan. HB 2010 also saved $40 million in overtime and revised purchasing practices, things Chase Riveland, Lowry's Secretary of Corrections viewed as "flat-out micro-management done for rhetorical and symbolic reasons." SR 2/28/1995. Lowry signed ESSHB 2319; Kent Caputo, Legal Counsel to ML, [11/94?]. ML 94A161, sentencing reform standards, WSA. Congress enacted with the monumental "Violent Crime Control and Law Enforcement Act of 1994," hiring 100,000 new police, and spending $18.4 billion on prevention, justice agencies and the courts.

73 ST 1/20/1994, "State liquor Monopoly is Not Good Business," 7/28/1994 and the editorial of 8/12/1994.

74 Lowry had appointed Joe McGavick, a former Evansite state representative later with Touche Ross, Chair of the Liquor Board. McGavick to Lois Howard, 1/17/1995, to Anthony Paz, 1/20/1995, to Kim Beauty, 3/14/1995. ML 48, LB, McGavick; St. John in TNT 12/13/1994; ST 1/9/1995. Former Speaker Ehlers speculates that Lowry "decided to show business that here was a good privatization issue ... that he was on their side." Ehlers OH, 3/26/2004: 4. "Republicans had managed to have a pretty good sound bite that we needed to privatize things and this was the one thing that maybe could privatized [by the Democrats]," adds Dean Foster. "The math of it just never worked for anybody." OH 4/9/2004: 38.

75 "Washington State Governor's Task Force on Regulatory Reform, Final Report." Olympia: the Task Force, 1994; ML, handwritten ltr. for general circulation, [11/93]. ML 94A161-1, governor; TNT 1/11/1995; HB 2510; Lyle Quasim: "Governor Lowry's look at regulatory reform was not particularly significant. It was not structured in a way that you'd get to regulatory changes." OH 3/23/2004: 29; WWUB 4/6/1994; ST 4/18/1994.

76 As affirmed by his Press Secretary, Suzzanne Albright. ML 7; TNT 10/3/1993; TNT 2/5/1994.

77 CFLW, "Washington at the Crossroads: Deregulation of Reform?" ML 95A128, 3, reg. ref. In 11/1995, by EO 95-05. The governor terminated the Task Force and his prior executive order. ML 97A72, 1, EOs.

78 ML to U.S. senators and congressmen, 11/10/1993. ML 97A 161, 3, NAFTA; "Governors Remarks [on the] North American Free Trade Agreement ... "8/17/1993. ML 97A161, 5.

79 Two-way trade with China rose 38 percent between 1991 and 1994; Washington was home to 60,000 Vietnamese-Americans.

80 ML to Clinton, 5/4/1994. ML 97A18, 5, Clinton; "City Club Speech," 12/9/1993. ML 97A18, 6; PSBJ 12/17/1993-12/23/1993.

81 "Work Force Training Press Conference." ML 9/22/1994-A, higher ed.

82 See T.M. Sell, Wings of Power: Boeing and the Politics of Growth in the Northwest. Seattle: UWAP, 2001: chs. 3-5.

83 PI 4/19/1984, 4/22/1984; ST 5/10/1995. EO 93-06, to agencies in the same arena,

was effected by temporary coordinating committees and model policies improved communication and education.

84 DOE's Terry Hussman added market-based alternatives and decentralization, all of which apparently pointed toward a comprehensive as opposed to a site specific approach.

85 ML OH, 5/18/2004: 12. In 1990, a similar HB1547 had been denounced as "extremist," and went down three to one, but prompted the GMA. See EW 5/3/1995.

86 ST 6/23/1994.

87 ML to U.S. Secretary of State Warren Christopher, 2/1/1994. ML 94A66, 5, Clinton administration; ML to Clinton, 6/21/1994, to Vice President Gore, 7/1/1994. ML 95A128-28, 5, fish wars, Al Gore; Chris Drivdahl (DFWL) to Jerry Dierker, 5/5/1994. ML, ibid., fisheries, salmon summit.

88 Washington and Oregon consume 90 percent of the power from the Columbia's dams, the salmon's chief enemy. Roger Heitman of Idaho Power and Light to ML, 1/21/1994. 95A128, 28, fisheries drawdowns; U.S. Secretary of Commerce Ron Brown to ML, ML 97A31, 1, commerce.

89 ML, LOPH, (2). Governors Lowry and John Kitzhaber to U.S. Senator Bob Packwood (OR), 9/15/1995, and Secretary of Energy Hazel O'Leary to ML, 11/7/1995. ML 91A31, 1, DOE. Lowry and the state congressional delegation also fought the Clinton Administration's alternative, a "BTU" tax on the DSLs, to "protect jobs," despite the nation's lowest power rates. ML to Susan Bakker, 7/14/1993. ML 94A66, 44, power.

90 ML to Secretary of the Interior Bruce Babbitt, 12/21/1994. ML 95A128, 52, Elwha/fish. Pointing to DOE studies, the same day Lowry refused to sign a certification for a gas-fired power, saying it would add to pollution in the Chehalis River though it was to use reclaimed waste water anticipating needs equal to a city half the size of Seattle. TNT 11/7/1996.

91 See Scott, "Governor Arthur B. Langlie, the Columbia Valley Authority and Eisenhower's 'Partnership.' JOW (winter 2005): 27-37; ML to Northwest senators, 9/7/1995. ML 97A31, 1, congress. ML to DOE Secretary Hazel O'Leary, 3/15/1995. ML 97A31,1, DOE. The Snake River Salmon "recovery plan" fell under the aegis of the Northwest Power Planning Council. ML to Donald Bevan, 12/10/1993. ML 94A161, 6, executive policy, fisheries. Lowry chaired the National Governor's Conference's Committee on Natural Resources in 1995-96, sounding the predictable "common goal of creating jobs and protecting the environment." ML 95A128, 3, NGA, pr. rel.

92 ML to J. L. Watts, 8/24/1994. ML 97A128, 26, hazardous waste; ML OH, 5/18/2004: 16.

93 "A Primer for Policy Makers." Olympia: Washington State Governor's Timber Team, 10/1992. See also, Carsten Lein, Olympic Battleground. San Francisco: Sierra Club Books, 1991.

94 ML to Howard L. Armstrong, 4/25/1994. ML 65, timber team issues; ML OH, 5/18/2004: 17.

95 ML to Clinton [1993], and Clinton to ML, 6/26/1993. ML 94A161-1, Clinton visit, 2/23/1993; Dan Evans agreed the president had to be ready to go it alone. PI 6/29/1993. See "Old Growth Forests and Timber Towns: Thinking About Tomorrow." Seattle: IPPM, UW, 1994.

96 The House and Senate insisted on the timber rider, leaving the agencies

discretion. The Department of Ecology was not a victim of "loose management," but doubledf its size and responsibilities in four years, and needed "integration" among a dozen major components. Lowry's "Environmental Kitchen Cabinet had a "powerful hold on him." He wanted to be more "up-front" with developers, county commissioners, and boards of initial jurisdiction." Riveland OH, 3/25/2004: notes, 1. ML to Clinton, 3/23/1995 and Clinton to ML, 6/22/1995. ML 97A31-1, Clinton, 2.

97 HB 1209.

98 See "The Three 'R's," Richard S. Page to The Diet, (Seattle), 2/8/1984. ML 20, ed. The alternative education laws paralleled Congress' "School to Work Opportunities Act" of 1993.

99 ML, "Executive Order Establishing the Governor's Higher Education Task Force," 7/24/1995. ML 97A72, 1, executive orders; ML to U.S. Senator Slade Gordon [sic] 10/20/1995. ML 96 A 31, 3.

100 Congress sent block grants, with the states required to match 80 percent.

101 TNT 1/11/1995, 10/24/1994. WSA, ML 97A27, 30; DSHS, Economic Services Division "Briefing on Welfare Reform Initiatives for Governor Lowry," 10/24/1994. ML 92A27, 30, welfare reform briefing.

102 Lowry's package was in HB1202, the legislatures' in HB 1481 and SB 5198. The state's statistics showed that 85 percent of two-parent welfare families and 75 percent of single-parent families left the system within two years. DSHS appealed to HHS to gradually reduce benefits for those who had been clients for four years, and to continue support for families where one parent had a part time job. By 1994 Colorado, Florida, Vermont, and Wisconsin had gotten waivers for demonstration projects; ML OH, 5/18/2004: 8-9: In 1994 House Appropriations chair Helen Sommers pushed welfare reform "when it was not at all popular, and a 'phasing out over time.'" Lowry was "not totally comfortable with that, and vetoed the 'teeth.'" Sommers OH, 12. Both GOP caucuses had welfare reform as a priority, with Senator Alex Deccio in the lead. The social concern was tying childcare to the ability to pay, to avoid the "runaway entitlements" Oregon experienced. Language was put in the budget in response to Lowry's veto, and lost in the supreme court; McDonald OH, 3/21/2004: 1-2.

103 ML to Clinton, 3/8/1994, 6/13/1994; Clinton to ML, 6/8/1994, 8/21/1995. The President's course was decided a year before, after 32 states had begun experimenting with waivers. ML 5, Clinton; Jean Soliz, Director, DSHS to ML, 7/11/1994. ML 5, congress; To U.S. Senator Patty Murray, 3/17/1995. ML 97A37, 3, Murray; Carol Felton, Director, Division of Employment and Social Services, DSHS to Lisa Gordon. ML 52, DSHS, b. The 75 federal programs in Aid to Families with Dependent Children (AFDC), served 13.5 million people at a cost of $22 billion in 1992. Medicaid cost $120 billion, and participation was up 40 percent in 10 years. The states split the burden on both. LMT 8/26/1996.

104 ST 5/28/1995, 7/2/1995; "He really learned a lot of what he believed … at the federal level where they just print money … . The idea of a balanced budget … is extremely difficult for him because of the things he wanted to do. He seized on … merging agencies as a way of trying to save his budget capacity … kick government in the ass a little bit to get it moving." Ryherd OH, 17.

105 ML OH, (2), Ryherd OH; ML to House, 4/6/1994. ML 94A157, 4, house veto messages, First Extra Session. In his first two years ML vetoed all or part of 107 bills, the most having to do with civil liberties; ML OH, 5/18/2004: 18-19.

106 Senate Bill Report (on Amended bill), 3/30/1995. ML 95 A 216, 1, ESHB 1010;

ML veto mess, 5/16/1995, ibid.

107 ML 95A 216, 1, reg. sess.

108 ML to House, 6/15/95, ibid.

109 ML Message to the House, 6/15/1995. ML 95A216, 5, veto messages, First Special; Stan Finkelstein and Gary Lowe, (AWC), to ML, 6/14/95. ML 95A216, 5, 2 Second Special.

110 i.e., I-276 as amended; HBs 2604 and 2790 were struck in 1996 for lack of a "comprehensive and consistent policy."

111 SB 5684, 1995; ML to Legislature, 4/6/1994, re: HB 2319. ML 94A157, 4, house veto messages. ST 4/7/1994; TNT 4/6/1994.

112 Initiatives to the legislature cannot be amended by it in the first two years. The mechanics of I-601 meant limits would get progressively tighter in the face of mounting demands ML told to Donald Anderson, 2/20/1995. ML 95A216, 50, revenue (a-b); Office of the Governor, "Enrolled Bills Delivered to the Governor for Action," (54th Legislature, Regular, First and Second Special Sessions), ibid., 1, house log; Office of the Governor, "Enrolled Bills Analysis Report" (re: SSB 5231). ML 95A276,13; ML to Students Maplewood Cooperative Elementary, 7/7/1995. ML 95A216, 20, education. By 2002, pressure groups had effectively neutralized I-601 with exemptions.

113 In SB 5156; TNT 4/19/1995; PI 4/22/1995, 5/25/1995. US West's ESSB5156 passed the Senate 41-7, and the House 87-10; GL to ML, 7/14/1995. ML 95A216, 5, Second Special.

114 This was the milder Senate-GOP edition, rather than the House's alterations to the Governor's Task Force on Regulatory Affairs, which had been concurred in 62-32. Representative Tom Campbell (D) a disillusioned member of the Task Force, voted "aye," and soon joined the GOP. ST 5/19/1995.

115 TNT 2/7/1995; SR 2/8/1995; ST 2/7/1995.

116 Defined by the U.S. District Court of Appeals in 1991, as what a "reasonable woman" would consider pervasive or severe enough to create a hostile working environment." Theiler had tried sexual harassment cases, and been Counsel for the State Judicial Conduct Commission.

117 ML to AG Christine Gregoire, 9/22/1994. ML 95A128, govs. offc.

118 ST 2/13/1995, 2/14/1995. She was the daughter of Lowry's mentor State Senator Martin Durkan, and had been attorney for Kari Tupper, whose sexual allegations had led to U.S. Senator Brock Adams's the resignation.

119 ST 2/16/1995-2/19/1995, 2/26/1995; TCH 2/7/1995.

120 Wkly 2/15/1995; ST 2/21/1995; TNT 2/22/1995. In fact, some outlets were skeptical. See "Lowry Stories Invade Dubious Territory," TNT 2/22/1995; "Probe Clears Lowry," ST 3/24/1995; "Report: No harassment, Lowry's Acts Defensive," and "Lowry, Accuser both on the Spot." TNT, 2/7/1995, 3/24/1995.

121 "Albright Report," and, "Settlement Agreement and Release," 7/14/1995. ML 24, Theiler.

122 Memo, Mary Alice Theiler to Staff Director Lorraine Hine, 3/22/1995. Albright complained of touching "as well as suggestive comments. ML insisted it was "neutral or harmless touching." See "Conclusions from Investigative Report," PI 3/24/1995 and "Lowry Not Vindicated," ibid., 3/28/1995.

123 TNT 4/2/1995; ADN 3/26/1993; ST 4/2/1995.

124 WDW 1/4/1996; PI 12/2/1995; VDN 4/2/1995. A September survey of district leaders showed 50 of 88 wanted Lowry; polls indicated 60 percent of women were adverse. DO 9/26/1995; ST 1/29/1995. Backers included 59 percent of the Democrats, 28 percent of the independents, and 13 percent of the Republicans. DO 1/8/1995; TNT 9/23/1995.

125 PI 8/5/1995.

126 Harvard educated Majority Leader Dale Forman, a "man of the middle," was from Wenatchee. Veteran King County Prosecutor Norm Maleng was a skilled negotiator and dismal campaigner. Dan McDonald was a Bellevue civil engineer, Senate Majority, and Minority Leader. Versatile attorney Jim Waldo, who had managed Evan's and Gorton's campaigns, lacked magnetism.

127 BA 6/4/1995; TNT 1/9/1995.

128 ST 10/4/1995, 10/8/1995. The county's share of $208 million came from an added .05 percent added sales tax on restaurants, on rental cars, and a 10 percent surcharge on the admissions tax. Any shortfalls would be picked up by the state's General Fund; Gary Locke, then chair of House Appropriations, notes it was doubly difficult to oppose the Mariners after their winningest season. He justified the subsidy on new tax dollars generated — on the same basis as convention centers. GL OH, 6/30/2004: 17-19. In 1996, the Seahawks Football Team asked Governor Locke for $150 million to improve the Kingdom, lest they move.

129 TNT 1/10/1996; Dean Foster correctly credits Lowry with leading the "realistic charge not to lose all kinds of health care programs," in falling back in the 1995 session. OH, 4/29/2004: 29.

130 The Senate's vote was 41-7, the House's 76-21. ST 1/25/1996.

131 On July 1, the Fish and Wildlife Commission gained the right to name its own director.

132 "Special Session? Surely Lowry Jests," YHR 4/24/1996, "Legislature Cool … " TNT 4/20/1996 and, "Lowry Leaves Lawmakers Befuddled," O 5/9/1996.

133 TNT 11/7/1996; Col 11/26/1996. Lowry wanted to alter Section 5, (2), of I-601 to include "costs of a federal or local government [pass-through] program … transferred from the state downwards, when they had a direct effect on the state. [Emphasis added].

134 Hine OH, 4; "Washington's Financial Outlook and Key Budget considerations," [12/96]. ML 87 A72, 1, bud, admin, and, govs. offc. orders, 1992-96. The boom kept the "601" level from being reached. "I don't think he really tried to get around 601," Mike Ryherd said of ML. "He found ways of doing provisos in the budget … Dan McDonald and Gary Locke worked very closely with Mike. When you don't have any money you give flexibility to how state employees use their sick leave and allow them to stack that …. He put in things that didn't cost money, family leave and other things." Ryherd OH, 2, (sides 3-4, 8-9); "Population and inflation were anticipated to be 4.5 percent, outlays up 4 percent; Ruta Fanning to ML 1/13/1997. ML 97A65, 3, 1997 bud. Fanning served dexterously as Director the first 14 months, resigning to become vice president for Finance and Administration at The Evergreen State College. Fanning to Lowry, 3/11/1996, ibid.; ML, State of the State Address, 1/9/1996. ML 97A652, sp; OFM, [1996] Executive Request Legislation, and, Capital Plan, 1997-2007. ML 97A65, 3, 1997 budget. HBs 2260, 2397, 2413, 2505, 2624, 2745, 2763 2764, 2797, and 2898.

135 Congressmen Randy Tate and Linda Smith lost, and Jack Metcalf survived by 1,000 votes. GOP Moderate Rick White comfortably took the First despite a $2

million onslaught by Labor and the Greens. Ken Eikenberry reprised as state GOP chair to build "a new kid of coalition" of contributors, activists and officeholders. A cry of "over taxation" started the 1994 campaign. PAN 11/30/93. He resigned after four years of dueling the right. PI 10/22/96; ST 11/6,8,11/96. USA Today 10/15/96; Office of the Secretary of State, Official General Election Abstract, November 5, 1996; SGN, 12/96, 38.

136 Ballard, McDonald, (2), Appelwick OH's. McDonald adds: "Of all [three] governors [he worked with, ML] was probably the hardest working and the one that was most effective — in his first two years." "He was a known quantity," added Dick Davis in his OH; DO 1/9/1997, 1/15/1997; TNT 1/14/1997.

137 Re Thomas: Wang OH; re Soliz: Karras, OH; ST 1/12/1997.

138 ST 4/25/1996, 4/27/1996.

139 Brown, LOHP. e.g., see ST 3/26/93, 4/30/1993, PI 6/23/1993.

140 Ryherd OH; In the mid-1980s Lowry was one of the few congressmen to urge their pension system be put under Social Security. When it happened, he withdrew. His three years on the state Senate staff, four years county councilman, and governor had vetted him at PERS — had he bought back the time. ST 12/15/1996.

141 A significant possible exception was atypical equivocation over the death penalty for the notorious murderer Charles Campbell. Was he opposed to the death penalty the media asked? Yes, on an "individual basis" The media's phrase that he was "morally opposed" was not "relevant," rather he doubted if its "unrestricted" use was wise policy. Lowry set up a "clemency process" to get a prompt review, then let the sentence stand. ML, news conf., 3/21/1994. ML 97A 18, 6. His Director of Institutions said flatly that ML opposed the death penalty and was so conscience stricken he flew to Walla Walla the night before the execution to talk with Campbell. C. Riveland, Lowry OHs; NPR interview, 1/5/1995; PI 2/5/1997.

142 Hine OH, 9; McDonald OH, 3/6/2004: 14-15; ST 3/26/1993, 11/27/1996.

143 In 1997, the governor told the Post-Intelligencer he could have won if he had run again. "My family asked me not to … based on how bad they'd been hurt." He ran for State Land Commissioner In 2000, saying, "I've been involved In these (environmental) issues before." The unquenchable need to be in public life led to pure illusion. State Senator Georgia Gardner had already been campaigning two months. The scandal caused the State Women's Political caucus to endorse her, as had the National Abortion and Reproductive Rights League (NARAL), leaving environmentalists and party regulars. Moderate Republican Doug Sutherland, the Pierce County Executive, won. SR 1/16/2000; ST 7/25/2000. See, incumbent Jennifer Belcher, "Managing the Public Trust," in TNT 7/23/2000; ST 4/23/2003. In 2003, ML joined the living governors in opposing an expansion of gambling to offset a new recession: "It is the most regressive tax of all."

144 Ross Anderson in ST 1/12/1997.

**Chapter 12: Gary Locke**

1 GL to the Yakima Rotary Club, 2/12/1998. GL 1, sps. 2/1998; Locke believed in affirmative action "because I am a product of … [it]." His SAT scores would not have gotten him into Yale — but an A. A. program for minorities from the West Coast did.

2 GL to Boston University Commencement, 5/17/1998. GL 1, sps, 5/1998.

3 ADR's turf 44 years earlier, from 1938 to 1957. It included the Rainier Valley, and is the most diverse in the state, with large Jewish, East European, Black, Hispanic,

and Asian blocs and wide variations in income.

4 J. A. Wilson in the Wkly 10/23/1996; ST 11/1/2000. Locke's early short marriage had ended. Wkly 2/5/1992; HB2983; O 1/2/1992, 2/2/1993. HB1509 of 1993; O 3/2/1993.

5 Foster OH.

6 Raising tuition didn't "really matter," as long as financial aid rose in tandem. GL OH, 5/18/2004: 23-24.

7 O 3/2/1993.

8 WDW 4/12/1992.

9 ST 12/24/1993; PI 9/16/1993.

10 ST 9/5/1996.

11 PI 7/6/1992.

12 ST 7/14/1996.

13 Wkly 10/23/1996, quoting County Councilman Chris Vance, who lost his Ninth Congressional District race and became state GOP chair; ST 11/5/1992. The WEA was placated by saying I-601 would have to be "adjusted" to absorb school enrollments, and farmers by "modifying" the Growth Management Act. Locke had opposed the property rights (the "taking") Referendum 48 in 1992 "because it went too far." Ecologists were also pleased by his backing of I-188 to improve salmon habitats.

14 Temple-related contributions grew to $13,500 and 15 percent of Locke's war chest of $116,000 by October was from Asians and a significant portion from several big-city fundraisers. ST 8/11/1998 and "80-20," ST 5/26/2000. The statute "to Protect Free White Labor Against competition with Chinese Coolie Labor and to Discourage the Immigration of Chinese" virtually excluded Chinese for the first 20 years of the 20th century. Those here were forbidden citizenship until 1924. The Chinese Exclusion act of 1882 was not repealed until 1943. On 11/8/1960 the voters refused to repeal the "Alien Land Law" in the State Constitution. It was not removed until 1966.

15 ST 2/2/1997.

16 ST 2/2/1997; GL to naturalization ceremony July 4, 1997. GL 1. sps. 7/1997.

17 Martha Choe, Dtr., DTED, to L 5/8/2000. WSA, 01A250, 6, trade missions; Clinton to Locke 10/19/2000, ibid., box 7. H.R. 4444 was signed by the president 10/10/2000. The mission to China was the first of eight to Asia and one to Mexico.

18 ST 11/7/1996.

19 ST 10/4/1998; 11/14/2000. Apart from the mandatory one of Labor leader Rick Bender, the 13 appointees to his team were professionals and downtowners. Locke's first 19 staff and directorships had 193 years of state and 50 years of local government experience. Adjoining offices went to the Governor's Counsel Everett Billingsley, a close friend and Seattle corporate lawyer (the only "outsider"), lobbyist Marty Brown, Press Secretary Marylou Flynn, and DeLee Shoemaker who handled external affairs. Gary Moore, who shifted from Employment Security to Labor and Industries, had been Executive Secretary of the WFSE for 10 years. Former Dean of the UW Law School, Wallace Loh, was briefly Policy Director. His aide-de-camp Sue Crystal and Mona Locke ("You can't help but get a reality check from your spouse") comprised the "kitchen cabinet." O 1/14/1996; DSHS Transition Binder, GL O1A241, 24.

20 Dear brought a dowry: a 2.3 percent reduction in Workmen's Compensation

premiums gained by his improved safety record as Gardner's Director of Employment Security, and huge investment returns. He became Public Affairs Director for Tacoma's Frank Russell Company, then Director of the State Investment Board in 2002. Ronal Serpas took over as Chief of the WSP in August 2001, adding two women and a black man to his six person inner circle.

21 Lyle Quasim, OH, 3/23/2004, 31; Ehlers OH, 3/26/2004, 11; Paul Isaki, a Seattle Mariners vice president and versatile government veteran took his place. Tom Fitzimmons, the fourth COS, notes that the statutes creating agencies pitted one against another, so sub-cabinets like Domestic Security were created to offer ferment to the bi-weekly full cabinet meetings. There were monthly reports to the COS on Performance Agreements," and the governor read the weekly "alerts." Fitzsimmons OH, 2/27/2004: 5-6.

22 GL to Quasim, 6/7/1999. GL 00A121, 5, DSHS. Locke formed an "Action Group" to "review all high risk care giver situations," develop proposals by October, enhance training and accelerate automated information gathering. He claimed "many significant improvements" had been made in protection for vulnerable adults since 1995 in training and neglect reporting, and introduced SB 6401 (in 2000), creating an abuse registry for employers and contractors and a Long-Term Care Ombudsman to guide volunteers; July 1, the USDA publicly notified the governor Washington had the nation's highest error rate for food stamps (14.8 percent, of which 2.8 percent were underpayments), a loss of $35 million for the year. As quality control inspectors got better data, the rate dropped to 6.55 percent (versus the national average of 10 percent) in six months, but the Secretary's news release stung. The necessity of having effective computer tracking was seen in July 1998. GL directed DSHS to clean up its Food Stamp act. In the prior six months 90,000 cases had been reviewed by ACES, catching $846,000 in errors and $11 million on benefits, a drop of 50 percent in October-December 1997. The overall error rate fell from 17.9 percent in first half of 1998 to 8.2 percent. Quasim to GL, 1/31/1998, 12/16/1998. GL A020, 4, DSHS, govs. offc. VIP corr. Quasim to GL 6/29/1998. 98A183, 6; DSHS' Performance Agreement, 6/1998. 99A183, 6, DSHS, mgmt.

23 GL to Co-Speakers Chopp and Ballard, Senators Snyder and West, 3/29/2000. O1A250, 7, exec. requests; DSHS' exposure was horrific. e.g., 6000 children in licensed adoptive homes and 4,000 in non-licensed ones. DSHS, Children's Administration, "Report to the Legislature: Recruitment of Adoptive and Foster Homes.", A020, 4, govs. offc., VIP corr. 1998, DSHS. The number of claims had in fact decreased as the size of judgments rose. Representative Gary Alexander to GL, Gregoire, and DSHS Secretary Dennis Braddock 7/25/2000; GL to Alexander 8/30/2000. O1A250, 2.

24 Locke OH, 7/9/2004: 31.

25 Ibid., 34-36.

26 ST 11/24/1999. Put together in 1993, DTED had two incompatible missions: economic development and, housing, community services, and local government. TNT 12/21/1997. Locke had appointed former Representative Busse Nutley to take the second half, and got his way a year later.

27 To protect their position, House Democrats had endorsed a $205 cut a week before.

28 PI 1/18/1997, 1/23/1997. The compromise was a one-year reduction in SB5212; PI 2/13/1997. Locke found other reasons for vetoing a "Christmas-treed" beer bill ($9.3 million), one for warehouse and grain operators ($6.6 million), and for Centralia's coal-fired power plant ($5 million). ST 5/2/1997.

29 Thirty-eight other states had a "Defense of Marriage Act," most passed during the 1990s, denying some 360 benefits and burdens of marriage, despite a 1974 State Court of Appeals decision affirming a right applying equally to men and women; TNT 2/22/1997; The Senate passed SB5400 on March 6, 41-8.

30 "Governor Gary Locke's Inaugural Address," 1/15/1997. GL 1, sps. 1/97; "President Clinton: Moving People from Welfare to Work," 8/4/1998. Locke announced elimination of a last vestige of old system, and HHS revised its regulations to allow state to provide Medicaid to two-parent working families meeting the state's income guidelines. A820, 4, 1998 go's. offc. VIP corr.

31 Washington welfare recipients received an average of $800 a month in cash and food stamps, compared with $773 in Oregon, and $630 in Idaho. PI 2/26/1997.

32 GL to U.S. Secretary of Labor Alexis Herman, 3/25/1998. 99A183, 6, social/session. The greatest inhibitors were HHS's rules, which in effect turned block grants into a matching requirement. GL to HHS Secretary Donna Shalala, 2/16/1998. 99A183, 6, welfare, and to U.S. Senator Slade Gorton, 4/21/1997. 98-408, 24, Gorton; SR 7/11/2001. Locke relaxed the five year limit on assistance to 3,200 families failing to cooperate in 2001, "Their children should not suffer." Under the law, he might have done so for up to 20 percent. PI 11/13/2001; Remarks by GL to the "Welfare to Work" Partnership, 6/12/1998. GL 1, sps 1998. Outlays went from $477 million in 1998 to $282 million in 2002. Advocates insisted caseload reductions were deceiving. Half who left the rolls earned less than the federal poverty level ($1,219 a month for a family of three). ST 9/3/2002; OFM, "Work First Performance Report 2000, #9." 1A250, 8, govs. offc., VIP corr. 2000-01, log 360075.

33 Ballard OH 6/19/2004: 21-22, McD OH. House Minority Leader Marlin Appelwick's take was, "I think there are times he would have a conversation and he would express no disagreement. He would express sympathy and say 'yes.' It could be that he simply forgot. I grew to believe that he … wasn't prepared at those early stages to make commitments that he felt were binding … .I do think that he, like others … wanted commitments and would walk away thinking they had commitments, but weren't careful that he knew they were looking for a commitment. That certainly handicapped him in dealing with Speaker Ballard." Appelwick OH, 3/19/2004: 6; Dean Foster feels a reason the legislature handed the governor his sole override in 1997 was that leadership thought that they had a commitment to a veto, only to find the governor had signed a bill. A wariness set in, harming relations. Foster, OH, 4/9/2004: 43-44.

34 GL pr. conf. on quality/reg-ref initiatives, 12/9/1997. GL 6, sps 12/97, reg/ref; Deputy Chief of Staff Fred Stephens to agency heads, 6/23/1997, re EO 97-02, ibid. The platform was the Regulatory Reform Act of 1995, (ESHB 1010); Gary Smith, Executive Director of the Independent Business Association, commended the governor. Smith to GL, 12/30/1997. 99A183, 6, reg/ref.

35 GL to Washington Management Service [managers], 4/30/1997; GL to Democratic Business Luncheon, 6/16/1997. GL 1, sps, 6/97.

36 "The Governor never promised to drop a bill' on 601," said his spokesman. BH 1/3/1997; GL to AWB, 9/25/1977. GL 1, 1, sps 9/97.

37 GL to Everett Area Chamber of Commerce, [7/97]; and, "Introduction of the State of Education Report," 9/4/1997. GL 1, sps 7/97.

38 For violating the constitution's "one subject" dictum. (Article II, Sec. 19). Justice Barbara Madsen's concurring opinion threatened repetitions that "will … ensure this court's future and an open-ended intervention in the legislative process."

See WSJ 11/3/1999. The session ended on time for the first time in 40 years. See "Rousing Success of Legislature." BH 4/28/1997; "A Legislative Session to Write Home About" ST 4/29/1997 and, "An Action-Packed, Productive Session," TNT 4/28/1997.

39 GL to Democratic Business Luncheon, 6/16/1997. GL 1, sps. 6/97. GL to Washington State Association of Counties, 6/25/1997. GL 1, sps. 6/97. "The Era of Big Government is Over." GL sp. to Spokane Visitors and Convention Bureau. GL 1, sps. 9/97; GL to Democratic Party Dinner, n.p., 12/7/1997. GL 1, sps. 12/97.

40 After grinding six hour caucuses, the stadium passed the House 56-41, with 28 Democrats and 28 Republicans voting "aye." The governor's baseline criterion as to whether this type of public-private partnership was worth it was the return in new tax dollars. GL OH, 6/30, 04/19.

41 HST 1/11/1998.

42 GL to McClatchy Board Dinner, 1/21/1997. GL 1, sps. 9/97.

43 The tobacco suit netted $4 billion over 25 years, with $323 million anticipated in 1999-01; GL, "Budget '98 announcement," 12/15/1997. GL sps. 12/97; Locke "reluctantly" agreed with securitizing. "Once we did it, we said we would not do it again." If so, there was to be a $325 million "bow wave" for that much in the next biennium. The actual reserve was then $258 million or just over two percent. The total deficit in 2004 proved to be $1 billion, and the reserve was lowered to $200 million, "because we were not going to raise taxes." GL OH, 7/09/04, 40-41; GL to Gary Yazwa, 12/29/1998. GL A020, 11, go's. offc. VIP corr. See NGA, "Media Backgrounder" 2/10/1998. 99A163, NGA.

44 GL to Senate, 4/3/1998, re ESSB 6108 (Chap. 346, Laws of 1998). 98A301, 6, bill file; Offce of the Governor, "Revised Supplemental Budget Plan," 2/19/1998. ibid., budget.

45 In 1998, 13 of the 33 excisions were for the first time "confidentially" labeled "policy vetoes." Half of these were requests by agencies unwilling to shift funds to cover minor unfunded mandates, which in turn voided 12 other provisos. The level of detail was either admirable or exasperating; "1998 Supplemental Budget Update." 98A301, 2nd ESSB 6108; SR 11/5/1998; WSRC, Fiscal Report. "Key Budget Actions: The Supplemental Budget," 6/17/1998.

46 "Remarks by Governor Locke, Centennial Elementary School, Olympia, School District Meeting on 1209 Assessments," 3/26/1997. WSA, ABL 1, sps 3/97, standards.

47 Quasim OH, 3/23/2004: 33.

48 The WEA objected to testing until the schools were "adequately" funded.

49 SSB 5748 (1999); CC 7/30/1999; TNT 9/9/1999; ST 9/14/1999.

50 Senator Steve Johnson, Representatives Dave Quall and Gigi Talcott to GL, 2/19/1998. U.S. House HR 2616 forbid federal funds where the number of charters had been capped. Connie Aiken to GL, 3/25/1998. 98A408, 15, charter schools.

51 The key figure was Rosemary McAuliffe, chair of the Senate Education Committee, who agreed with the WEA, and kept the bill in her file.

52 See "The State Teachers' Union Needs a Remedial Lesson in Public," BH 8/8/2003; PI 6/17/2003. In October 2003, he intervened in the state's longest teacher strike in Marysville, meeting the parties separately, then appointed former Chief Justice Robert Utter and Denny Heck to clarify the issues. The district won an injunction, collapsing the strike; charter schooling finally passed in 2004, amidst

growing fear about the passage rates of the WASL, mandatory for graduation after 2008. The legislators agreed with the governor, eliminating social studies, arts, and physical education, and authorizing up to three retests.

53 "2020 Commission Announcement," 2/4/1998. GL 1, sps. 2/98; O 2/28/1997; PI 2/28/1997; ST 4/7/1998, 11/15/1998.

54 ST 3/15/1998.

55 ST 11/6/1998.

56 "Remarks by Gary Locke at Democratic Party Crab Feed," 2/16/1998. GL l, sps. 2/98; O 3/14/1998; "If the senate goes Democratic, I think we can credit Gary Locke with that," the Democratic state chair said. ST 11/5/1998; TNT 11/8/1998.

57 ST 11/5/1998, 11/10/1998; TNT 11/8/1998.

58 O 11/8/1998.

59 i.e., above the current quarterly projection.

60 Campbell was from South Pierce County's Second District, Carlson from the southeast corner's Forty-Ninth District.

61 Kitzhaber to GL 99A183, salmon/Columbia, 4/98.

62 TNT 1/29/1998; Ruckelshaus was formerly U.S. Attorney General, and head of the EPA; GL co-signed the letter.

63 The Capitol Press (Olympia), noted an independent scientific review's scathing critique of the states' efforts as disjointed and ineffectual. 12/29/2000, 1/12/2001. Smitch in TCH, 3/28/2000.

64 James L. Witt, Director, Federal Emergency Management Agency to GL, 5/3/2000. L, A250, 4; TNT 1/29/1998; PI 2/15/2000; U.S. Senator Patty Murray introduced S2004, "The Pipeline Safety Act of 2000" with Locke's encouragement. GL to Murray 1/16/2000. 1A250, 6, pipeline. "Testimony of Governor Gary Locke, State of Washington, before Congress," 5/11/2000. A0200, 3, govs. offc., VIP corr.; WSJ 9/27/2000.

65 Attorney General Gregoire to U.S. Secretary of Energy Frederico Pena 1/3/1998, 2/1/1998, 6/8/1998; GL to Clinton, 4/30/1998; Tom Fitzsimmons (Dtr., WA DOE) and Chuck Clarke (Regional Administrator U.S. E.P.A.), to Jim Owendorff (Acting Assistant Secretary, U.S. DO.E.), 5/14/1998 and to Assistant Attorney General Lois J. Schiffer, 9/24/1998. All GL 98A183, 6, Nuclear/Hanford. On 8/25/1998, Secretary of Energy Bill Richardson reiterated the pledges, and indicated a shift to privatizing recovery efforts. A026, 3, govs. offic., VIP corr., Hanford.

66 GL to Richardson, 1/18/00, 2/7/00. Richardson to GL, 9/20/2000. 01A250, 5, Hanford. DOE the estimated a clean-up cost from 2000 to 2070 for the 586 square mile reservation to be $151 to $195 billion. In a preemptive letter President Clinton noted a Spanish company (ENRESA) had all the necessary federal licenses, and that low-level waste regulation was the state's responsibility. The president and Secretary of the Interior Bruce Babbitt's motion to make the Hanford Reach a national monument are in Clinton to GL, 7/13/200-, 8/11/2000. L01A250, 5, Hanford.

67 WSJ 9/27/2000.

68 In January, the state filed a brief urging the FERC to enforce "just and reasonable" rates. Kitzhaber joined Locke, but the other Western governors, meeting at an "Energy Summit" in Denver, refused offering a "Five Step Plan." ST 12/22/2000; TNT 12/15/2000; EJ 2/3/2001; WGA pr. rel., 2/2/2001. The privates resisted. The

Public Power Council agreed — if its conditions were met.

69 The "Winter 2000-01 Energy Emergency Plan" was still in draft. GL to Davis, 12/11/2000; Davis to GL, 12/14/00; L to FERC Chair James Hoecker 12/13/00, Hoecker to GL, 1/18/2000; Stephen Wright (BPA CEO) to GL, 12/15/2000. Governors Davis, Kitzhaber, and Locke, wrote Congressmen Hebert, Massey, and Breathitt, 3/9/2001 for relief. GL 1A250, 4, log 4059505.

70 ST 1/24/2001. By April 2000, wholesale cost to utilities went from $16 to $380 a megawatt hour, and the eight aluminum companies in the region shut down. SR 4/11/2001.

71 Hans Dunshee to GL, 7/7/1998; GL to Dunshee, 8/12/1998. L1A250, 4.

72 Attorney General Christine Gregoire to Congressman Norm Dicks, 6/15/2000; Clinton to GL, 7/13/2000; GL and Gregoire to U.S. Secretary of Transportation Rodney Slater, 6/5/2000. L 01A250, 5, oil spills.

73 ST 1/31/2001. The GOP member's positions are in a letter to DOE Director Tom Fitzsimmons, 8/7/2000. GL 01A250, 5, shorelines; Col 12/21/2002. When GL challenged two decisions over urban growth boundaries in Snohomish County in September 2003, the Republicans on the Snohomish County Council cried foul: he was "mandating growth decisions on the duly elected representatives." PI 9/11/2003.

74 See "State Districts Become Competition-free Zones." In 2000, 26 of the 98 seats went by default, and 8 of 24 in the senate. YHR 2/9/2001. DOE's 7100 water permit application backlog was the prime pain for the GOP's farmers.

75 TNT 10/24/2001; GL to Representatives Linville and Chandler, and Senators Morton and Fraser, 3/2000. 1A250, 7, govs. offc., VIP corr.; See SB 6525; Speaker Ehlers felt "Gary has never been a strong environmentalist like Mike Lowry." OH 3/25/2004, tape 3: 8. The permitting process was amended to create two "lines." Those wanted to shift their water rights are first served, then those seeking new ones.

76 In 1998, the police and prosecutors came to same position against making every felony in that a "strike." GL to Superior Court Spring Conference, 4/24/1998. GL 1, sps. 4/98; ST 3/29/2000, 9/2/2000. Since 1981, when aggravated, premeditated first-degree murder was made the only offense eligible for death penalty, three had been executed. Fourteen were death row in 2000; O 2/4/2000.

77 See "Locke and Carlson on Business." Washington CEO 10/00; ST 11/9/2000. The subdued race was overshadowed by Maria Cantwell's hairbreadth win over U.S. Senator Slade Gorton.

78 TNT 4/2/2000. Wkly 1/18/2001.

79 SR 2/4/2000; WSJ 12/22/1999, 1/19/2000, 2/9/2000; HB3077; Senator McDonald conceded I-601 was essentially killed with the help of the House. ["It was] one of the few times I really, really, really disagreed with Clyde Ballard." McDonald OH, 27; Ballard concurred that all four caucuses and the governors all contributed to "gouging" I-601.

80 ST 3/7/2002; "Democrats danced for weeks between the political pitfalls of steeper cuts and higher taxes." Then they "copped out" with a raid on tobacco and pension funds, said the ST 3/10/2002.

81 ST 1/11/2001; CC 1/6/2001; "Who's the New Guy?" Col 2/10/2001.

82 Even though Bechtel had been contracted. The Speaker claimed $400 million in savings if the state's credit was used. TNT 6/14/2001; "That was the strangest thing I've ever seen," Dan McDonald said. "Frank Chopp … pirouetted. He was

the one who essentially kept us from passing a gas tax increase." OH 3/21/2004, 7; The differences between the Speaker and Governor were both philosophical and personal: "Someone once said that Frank Chopp is a lot more about [working class] Bremerton, where he grew up, than he is about Fremont [in Seattle], where he resides." Ibid., 37; "The reason that he did it," Mike Ryherd believes, "was that he knew that [Tim] Eyman would be able to get the signatures to force it," and if it looked like they [the legislators] were trying to bypass Eyman it would make people even madder." 3/25/2004, (3), 5-6; ST 4/3/2003.

83 O 7/26/2001. "Give the Great Wary One Credit" wrote the TNT's Peter Callaghan; PI 6/17/2001; PSBJ 7/13-19/2001; PI 7/20/2001.

84 PI 1/31/2002, 2/16/2002; TNT 1/4/2002. Locke's most enthusiastic partner was Senator Dan McDonald of Bellevue. At one point the Speaker gave the governor an angry look and stormed past him red-faced out of his caucus and into his office. PI 3/2/2002 3/15/02; PI 3/23/2002.

85 PI 7/15/2002.

86 See "Statewide Transportation Plan Short Changes Mass Transit." ST 6/5/2002.

87 ST 4/3/2003.

88 "Chopp was a Populist on almost every issue ... every issue should be on the ballot for the people to decide." Second, if the legislature voted for it with a tax increase, they would be less likely to vote another for social services," former Speaker Ehlers believed., Ehlers OH, 3/26/04, 20; "Speaker Chopp is a far more political type leader" than the governor, Helen Sommers observed. Sommers OH, 7. A referendum, if supported equally by both caucuses, gave his members "cover."

89 See "The Unfinished Recession," The Economist, 9/28/2002: 2.

90 PSBJ 8/30/2002-9/5/2002.

91 Brown OH; "50/50," meaning cut half, tax half.

92 See ST 9/27/2002. Apart from initiatives and the economy, the core of the fiscal meltdown was Medicaid and tax repeals. Medicaid, jointly financed with the federals, rose from 23 to 41 percent of the budget in a decade, led by drug costs. Locke's attempt to control premiums, co-payments and enrollment caps were stymied by the congressional delegation. Medicaid cost the state $5.4 billion for 900,000 people in 2001-03. See O 5/30/2002. The 100 tax breaks granted since 1994 outstripped $6.3 billion in new revenue. They ranged from professional services including doctor and lawyer fees, and intangible assets ($3.8 billion), to high-tech building, and infrastructure ($108 million, 1.4 billion in 1994), manufacturing machinery and equipment 338 million in 1995-96), and B and O credit for high tech and biotech firms ($48 million in 2001-03).

93 "The governor built the box. I don't think it was the POG that drove no new taxes. I think it was the atmosphere, the philosophy ... that swept in earlier, which drove his position." Sommers OH: 3, 6; McDonald OH: 19; O 1/19/2003; TNT 4/6/2003. Rossi had salary boosts for beginning teachers and poorly paid school workers, and restoration of half of I-732's smaller class sizes came from prenatal care for illegal immigrants, less Medicaid funding, by lowering eligibility from 250 to 175 percent of the poverty level, leaving a new total of 40,000 children uninsured, and cutting Basic Health Plan enrollees by 42,000.

94 Chopp on TVW 10/22/2003; EJ 12/22/2002; O 2/2/2003.

95 e.g., PI 6/2/2003, 12/18/2003; SR 5/01/2003; PSBJ 6/13/2003-6/19/2003; See "Gary Locke, Poster Boy for State-Budget Reform," and, "Hard-Times Budget Without Compromise," ST 4/14/2003 and 4/25/2003. The Times' change of heart

may have had something to do with its decline due to an ill-timed strike, and an extended suit to drive the P-I out of business in a shrinking market.

96 "Locke and Senate Set the Right Priorities." WWUB 4/22/2003; McDonald OH 3/25/2004, tape 2, 22.

97 The three plans are compared in ST 4/18/2003, 4/24/2003. See "Legislature: a Tale of Two Leaders," O 4/27/2003; "Democrats Unveil Tax Plan" reported the Times. ST 4/16/2003; "Tax Boost Emerges from the House" echoed the P-I. PI 4/17/2003; O 5/18/2003, 4/28/2003.

98 ST 6/8/2003; SR 5/1/2003; PSBJ 6/13/2003-6/19/2003.

99 Dues to operate the union are mandatory; to fund its political operations there is an optional "check-off."

100 PSBJ 5/23/2003-5/29/2003; ST 4/20/2003.

101 See "Whatever it Takes: Bidding for Boeing — and Beyond." ST 4/20/2003. The proposed rule was WAC 296-62-051. Congress had repealed those Clinton had handed down; Don Brunell, President, AWB, to Gary Moore, Director, L&I, 2/24/2000. 1A250, 8, govs. offc., VIP corr. 2000-01.

102 O 3/01/2003.

103 Referendum 53; In 2003, faced with not just losing 7500 7E7 jobs, but 20,000 of their own, the builders got aboard.

104 O 5/22/2003; EVH 5/25/2003; PI 4/30/2003, 5/21/2003.

105 Acknowledged as perhaps unconstitutional. See Washington State Constitution, Article VIII, Sec 5.

106 ST 6/6/2003; TNT 6/10/2003.

107 ST 6/24/2003, 6/26/2003; O 6/15/2003. Locke and DTED Director Martha Choe personally delivered the packet to Renton. "We think we have submitted a tremendous winning proposal … . It will be cheaper for them to build the 7E7 here than any other state." O 6/21/2003; PI 6/12/2003; ST 12/26/2003. Promised Boeing," ibid., 1/21/2004, and, "How Washington Won the Battle for the 7E7." ST 12/21/2003.

108 PI 6/12/2003; Notes by the author from the governor's City Club presentation 2/19/2004; See "Boeing Tax Breaks Show What we Must do to be Competitive." TNT 12/24/2003; Locke justified the price in a ST editorial 12/26/2003. In 2004, the governor's Competitiveness Council, formed in 2001 after Boeing announced its intent to move its headquarters out of state, pronounced the business climate decidedly improved. PSBJ 5/7/2004-5/13/2004.

109 GL to NARABA, 11/23/1997. GL 1, sps. 11/1997.

110 Ehlers OH, 3/26/2004, 21; McDonald OH, 3/6/2004: 24, 30; Mike Ryherd: "What trips Gary up … sometimes, as well as the people who are dealing with him, is that they will make a general statement and the implementation of that statement will not have been nailed down;" See "Labor in Retreat." O 6/18/2003, 8/17/2003; Attorney General Chris Gregoire, who announced for governor the next day, was convinced he could have been reelected. SR 7/22/2003.

111 EVH 7/22/2003; "I've never given any thought to a life in politics in Washington, D.C." he insisted on TVW, 1/16/2003.

112 GL to House, 1/22/1997, (re HB1037) and 5/20/1997. 98A17, 1, house veto messages; GL 98, Office of the Governor, "Enrolled Bill Analysis Report" (1977 Regular session), ibid., House veto messages; GL to Senate re SB 6533, 4/3/1998.

98A301, 6, bills. SHB 2724 on fines was a response to his 1997 veto of SB 6039. The House had voted 98-0, the Senate 39-6; GL to Senate re ESSB 6497, 4/2/1998. 98A301, 6, bill file; O 10/7/2003. See "Locke's Vetoes Run Counter to the Constitution." YHR 10/8/2003. Evansesque "super-editing" is seen in transferring $40,000 in the Highway Trust Fund to another use; "Confidential" staff memorandum" [4/1998], on "Policy Vetoes" n.d., and GL to Senate, 4/3/1998. 98A301, 6, re ESSB 6108; GL to Marty Brown, 3/31/2000. GL 07A250; See Appendix 7, re his vetoes.

113 Insulation, electricity, refrigeration and the like were not included, and the bill did "not have the support … of the people it was intended to help." He signed a more extensive one two years later. See "Farm Worker Housing. Talking Points," 5/20/1997. 97A181, sps.

114 This was an administration "priority." GL to Mel Carter, 5/3/2000: 114. O 10/07/2003; YHR 10/08/2003. To his credit, Locke instigated a ten year plan for developing permanent housing for seasonal farm workers in 1999. See ST 7/01/2004; Executive Order 97-03, 4/30/1997.

115 Preston, Gates and Ellis' David McDonald advised the governor, "The Montana primary is not consistent with the [Washington State] Democratic Party's rules, and it would challenge the veto in court. ltr, 3/16/2004. Most journalists took Locke to task, e.g., WDW 3/15/2004, TCH4/2/2004, LDN 4/2/2004, BH 4/2/2004, O 4/11/2004, YHR 4/5/2004, ST 4/26/2004. Those in a favor included the TNT 4/2/2004, and the WWUB 5/5/2004. The Governor defends in the TCH 4/2/2004, ST 4/2/2004; seven of the state's nine congressmen backed the Montana approach, likely on incumbent calculus and for partisan reasons; Locke established the single year record for vetoes in 1997 at 63, and did more in total than Evans in three terms. "None of these vetoes were taken lightly," he declaimed; Typical reactions on the overturn are in the TNT 3/20/2008 and TCH 3/19/2008.

116 "Governor Locke's Major Accomplishments 1997-2003," Washington State Home Page, Office of the Governor, 10/28/2003, listed over 250.

117 TNT 2/19/2003; ST 2/18/1998; "I have never given any thought to a life in politics in Washington, D.C." Locke said on TVW's "Inside Olympia," on 1/16/2003; TCH 7/22/2003. Having practiced international law with Davis Wright Tremaine, Seattle, on May 1, 2009 Locke was sworn in as President Obama's Secretary of Commerce. He was the third Asian to join the cabinet.

118 Clyde Ballard warned Locke in 1999 that I-695 would pass if he did not move the price down on car tabs. "I think that was a turning point for the initiative process." ST 7/22/2003; "Bolder Action by Governors and Legislatures More Responsive to the People will Dissipate Energy Spent on Initiative Drives," the P-I insisted. See ST 11/4/2003, 5/6/2000, 9/13/2000, 11/8/2000; PI 4/1/2000 4/13/2000. See David Broder, The Derailing of Democracy. New York: Harcourt, 2000.

119 TCH 7/22/2003.

120 Appelwick OH, 8.

121 Ryherd OH.

122 McDonald OH.

123 EJ 5/14/2000. Other indications are in the TNT 5/6/2000, PI 5/24/2000, and O 4/9/2001.

124 Broder, op cit.

125 ST 5/6/2000, 9/13/2000, 11/08/2000; PI 4/13/2000.

126 GL was unanimously confirmed as Ambassador to China. ST 5/24/2011; Miami Herald, 5/26/2011.

## *Bibliography*

Given this volume's reach of 151 years, 32 administrations, and all issues of import at the state level, these entries are selective. Only collections, the major histories and interpretations, and periodical literature essential to understanding the executives, their eras, the legislature, the courts and the Third House are included. Sometime references appear only in the endnotes.

The sequence in each sub-segment is books, journal articles, manuscripts/collections, secondary government and miscellaneous publications, newspapers, dissertations and theses and oral histories. All but the miscellany and newspapers appear under the period/ administration in which they are most relevant. Citations to journals published after 1900 are abbreviated, e.g., (7/43). The papers of actors in multiple administrations are listed under the one in which they first appeared, and those important to subsequent regimes asterisked. Locations are given only for those collections not from the University of Washington Special Collections Division. Elected or appointive positions follow the entries. Consult the acronyms.

### A. References

Barone, Michael, and Grant Uyifasa. The Almanac of American Politics 1984: The Senators, the Representatives and the Governors: Their Records and Election Results, Their States. Boston: Gambit, 1972.

Berner, Richard C. Washington Territorial Government Papers 1853-1878, at the UW Libraries. Seattle: The Libraries, 1963.

Congressional Quarterly Inc. Gubernatorial Elections, 1787-1997. Washington D.C.: CQP, 1998.

Brewster, David, and David M. Buerge eds. Washingtonians: A Biographical Portrait of the State. Seattle: Sasquatch Books, 1988.

Paul, Karen D., comp. Guide to Research Collections of Former United States Senators, 1789-1995. Washington, D.C.: U.S. Government Printing Office, 1995.

Quatennens, Joanne, comp. Senators of the United States: A Historical Bibliography. Washington, D.C.: U.S. Government Printing Office, 1995.

Northwest Digital Archives. "The 50 major newspapers in the Northwest." Olympia: State Printer, 1985, ff.

Nicandri, David. "Washington State: A Bibliography." PNQ 74 (7/83): 114-15

Washington State Legislature. Final Legislative Report. 1967, ff.

Washington State, and OFM. Washington State Data Book. Olympia: OFM, 1970 ff, annual.

Washington State Research Council, Olympia. Research Council's Handbook on State and Local Government in Washington. (1961-1962. Annual. Concludes 1973).

Washington State Library. Washington State Government and Politics, 1845-1971: A Bibliography. Olympia: Tumwater: WSL, 1971.

Washington State Secretary of State. Abstract of Votes: Primary and General Elections. 1908, ff.

Beyle, Thad. "Gubernatorial Elections, 1977-1990." CSP 12 (2): 18-21.

Deutsch, Herman J. "A Prospectus of the Study of the Governments of the Pacific Northwest States in Their Regional Setting." PNQ 42, (10/51): 277-301.

**B. Understanding the Public Place in Washington.**

Billington, Ray A. and Martin Ridge. *Westward Expansion: A History of the American Frontier*. 6th ed. Albuquerque: UNMP, 2001.

Clark, Norman. *Washington: A Bicentennial History*. New York: W.W. Norton, 1976.

Dolbeare, Kenneth. *The Evolution of the Public Sector in Washington State*. Olympia: TESC, 1988.

Clark, John G., ed. *The Frontier Challenge: Responses to the Trans-Mississippi West*. Lawrence: UKAP, 1971.

Frank, Robert G., and Richard E. Ross. *Regionalism in the Pacific Northwest*. Corvallis: OSUP, 1983.

Meinig, Donald W. *The Great Columbia Plain*. Seattle: UWAP, 1995.

Nash, Gerald D. *The American West in the Twentieth Century: A Short History of An Urban Crisis*. Englewood Cliffs, N.J.: Prentice-Hall, 1973.

____. *The American West Transformed: The Impact of the Second World War*. Bloomington: INUP, 1985.

Hine, Robert V., and John M. Farrager. *The American West: A New Interpretive History. New Haven:* Yale University Press, 2000.

Kauffman, Robert. *Henry M. Jackson: A Life in Politics*. Seattle: UWAP, 2000.

Meany, Edmund. *History of the State of Washington*. New York: Macmillan, 1910.

______. *Governors of Washington: Territorial and State*. Seattle: UWA Printing Plant, 1915.

Putnam, Robert D. *Bowling Alone: The Collapse and Revival of American Community*. New York: Simon and Schuster, 2000.

Robbins, William G. *Colony and Empire: The Capitalist Transformation of the American West*. Lawrence: UKAP, 1994.

Scates, Shelby. *Warren G. Magnuson and the Shaping of Twentieth Century America.* Seattle: UWAP, 1997.

Schwantes, Carlos A., and G. Thomas Edwards. *Experiences in a Promised Land: Essays in Pacific Northwest History*. Seattle: UWAP, 1986.

Snowden, Clinton A. *History of Washington: The Rise and Progress of an American State*. Vol. 4. New York: Century History Company, 1909

Scott, George, ed. *Turning Points in Washington's Public Life.* Seattle: Civitas Press, 2011.

Stewart, Edgar I. *Washington, Northwest Frontier*. 4 vols. New York: Lewis Historical Publishing Company, 1957.

Swanson, Thor, William F. Mullen, John C. Pierce, and Charles H. Sheldon. *Political Life in Washington: Governing the Evergreen State.* Pullman: WSUP, 1985.

White, Richard. *It's Your Misfortune and None of My Own: A History of the American West*. Lawrence: UKAP, 1991.

White, Richard. *It's Your Misfortune and None of My Own: A History of the American West*. Lawrence: UKAP, 1991.

Frykman, George A. "Regionalism, Nationalism, Localism: The Pacific Northwest in American History." PNQ 43 (10/52): 251-61.

Jewell, M.E. "Voting Turnout in State Gubernatorial Primaries." WPQ 30 (6/77): 236-54.

McNitt, A.D. "Comparison of Explanations of Completion for Gubernatorial and Senatorial Nomination: 1954-1974." WPQ 35 (6/82): 245-57

Morehouse, Sarah McC. "The State Political Party and the Policy-Making Process." APSR 67 (1/1973): 55-72.

Murray, Keith A. "Issues and Personalities in Pacific Northwest Politics, 1889-1950." PNQ 41 (7/1950): 213-33.

Ogden, Daniel M. "The Blanket Primary and Party Regularity in Washington." PNQ 39, (1/48): 33-38.

Pierson, K.L., et al., "Sources of Candidate Success in Gubernatorial Elections, 1910-1970." JOP 39 (11/77): 939-58.

Pollard, Lancaster. *The Pacific Northwest: A Regional Study*. OHQ 52 (12/51): 211-34.

Simmons, Michael T. "The Transition of the Washington Executive from Territory to Statehood." PNQ 55 (4/64): 76-86.

Thorson, Winston B. "Washington State Nominating Conventions." PNQ 4 (1944): 99-120.

### C. Governors and Governing

#### 1. Administration

Anschell, Susie, ed. Public Policy Making, Washington Style. Seattle: IGR, 1968.

Behn, Robert D. ed. Governors on Governing. Lanham, M.D.: University Press of America, 1991.

Beyle, Thad, and L.R. Muchmore, Being Governor: The View From the Office.

Durham, N.C.: Duke University Press, 1981.

Beyle, Thad ed. Governors and Hard Times. Washington D.C.: CQP, 1992.

______, and L.R. Muchmore. Being Governor: The View From the Office. Durham, N.C.: Duke University Press, 1981.

Brooks, Glenn T. When Governors Convene: The Governor's Conference and National Politics. Baltimore: The Johns Hopkins University Press, 1961.

Bowman, Ann O'M, and Richard C. Kearney. The Resurgence of the States. Englewood Cliffs, N.J.: Prentice-Hall 1986.

Cook, Virginia L. The Governor: The Office and Its Powers. Lexington: CSG, 1972.

CSG. Gubernatorial Transition in the States. Chicago: Lexington: CSG, 1968.

____. Issues in Gubernatorial Succession. Lexington: CSQ, 1969.

____. "The Governors Powers." SG 55 (Summer 82): 74-105.

Eblen, Jack E. The First and Second United States Empires; Governors and Territorial Governors, 1784-1912. Pittsburg: University of Pittsburgh Press, 1968.

Elazar, Daniel J. American Federalism: A View from the States. 3rd ed. New York: Harper and Row, 1984.

Herbert, F. Ted. "Gubernatorial Influence and State Bureaucracy." APQ 11 (2): 243-64.

Herzik, Erik B., and Brent W. Brown eds. Gubernatorial Leadership and State Policy. New York: Greenwood Press, 1991.

Jackson, David H. The Administrative Reorganization Experience in the State of Washington. Seattle: Institute for Governmental Research, University of Washington, 1971.

Kallenbach, Joseph E. The American Chief Executive: The Presidency and the Governorship. New York: Harper and Row, 1966.

Manning, Gail B. comp. The Lieutenant Governor: The Office and Its Powers. Lexington: CSG, 1987.

Marcelli, Ralph J. "State Administrative Officials: Methods of Selection." SG 51 (2): 88-94.

Martin, James W. Staffing the Office of Governor. Lexington: CSG, 1971.

Meany, Edmond. Governors of Washington: Territorial and State. Seattle: Department of Printing, University of Washington, 1915.

Schlesinger, Joseph D. How They Became Governor: A Study of Comparative State Politics 1870-1950. East Lansing: Michigan State University Press, 1957.

Ransone, Colman. The American Governorship. Westport, CT., Greenwood Press, 1982

Sharkansky, Ira. The Maligned States: Policy Accomplishments, Problems and Opportunities. New York: McGraw-Hill, 1978.

Sprengel, Donald P. Gubernatorial Staffs: Function and Profiles. Iowa City: The Institute for Public Affairs, University of Iowa, 1969.

Van Assendelft, Laura. Governors, Agenda Setting, and Divided Government. Lanham, M.D.: University Press of America, 1997.

Brooks, Glenn T. "The Governors and National Politics." Ph.D., The Johns Hopkins University, 1960.

Kingston, M. Jean. "Explaining Gubernatorial Outcomes: 1950-1985." Ph.D.,

University of Georgia, 1989.

Schlesinger, Joseph A. "The Emergence of Political leadership: A Case Study of American Governors." Ph.D., Yale, 1955.

Ahlberg, Clark D, and Daniel P. Moynihan. "Changing Governors and Policies." PAR 20 (Autumn 1960): 195-205.

Bazzini, Craig S. "The Executive Budget Process," In James Nolan, ed. Inside State Government. Urbana: University of Illinois Press, 1982.

Berkman, Michael, and Charles Barrine. "Do Governors Matter? Budgeting, Rules and the Politics of State Policy Making." Political Research Quarterly 56 (12/2003): 409-17.

Beyle, Thad L. "The Governor's Formal Powers: A View from the Governor's Chair." PAR 28 (11-12/68): 540-45.

_____. "The Governor as Innovator in the Federal System." Publius 18 (3): 131-52.

Blair, Diane K. "The Gubernatorial Appointment Power: Too Much of a Good Thing?" SG (June 1982): 88-92.

Charles, William S. "The Gatekeeper Function of the Governor's Staff." WPQ 33 (1/80): 67-93.

Glendening, Paris N. "The Public's Perception of State Government and Governors." SG (Summer 1980): 115-24.

Katz, Robert. "Skills of Effective Administrators." HBR 33 (1): 33-42.

Kincaid, John. "The American Governor in International Affairs." Publius 14 (4): 95-114.

Mueller, Keith J. "Explaining Change and Variation in Gubernatorial Powers, 1960-1982." WPQ, 38 (3), 1985, 424-31.

Ransone, Colman. "Political Leadership in the Governor's Office." JOP 26 (2/64): 197-220.

Schlesinger, Joseph A. "The Politics of the Executive." In Herbert Jacob and Kenneth N. Vines, eds. Politics in the American States: A Comparative Analysis. Boston: Little Brown, 1971, 210-37.

Sigelman, Lee, and Nelson Dometrius. "Governors as Chief Administrators: The Linkage between Formal Powers and Informal Influence." APQ 16 (1/58), 157-70.

Thompson, Mark E. "The Electoral Fortunes of Gubernatorial Incumbents." JOP 46 (5/84): 520-43.

Thorson, Winston B. "Washington State Nominating Conventions." PNQ 35 (4/44): 99-119.

CSG. "The Governor's Powers." SG 55 (Summer 1982): 74-105.

Wyner, Alan J. "Staffing the Governor's Office." PAR 30 (1), 1970, 17-24.

Connelly, James K. "Administrative Reorganization of Washington State, 1889-1951." MA, WSU, 1951.

**2. Gubernatorial Politics**

Casey, Thomas M. Campaign Dynamics: The Race for Governor. Ann Arbor: University of Michigan Press, 2000.

Fiorina, Morris. Divided Government. 2nd ed. Boston: Allyn and Bacon, 1996.

Gray, Virginia, and Herbert Jacob. Politics in the American States: A Comparative Analysis. Washington, D.C.: CQP, 1996.

Jewell, Malcolm E. Parties and Primaries: Nominating State Governors. New York: Praeger, 1984.

Jonas, Frank H., ed. Western Politics. Salt Lake City: The University of Utah Press, 1961.

Leaford, John. The Rise of the States: Evaluation of American State Government. Baltimore: The Johns Hopkins University Press, 2002.

Moorehouse, Sarah McC. The Governor as Party Leader: Campaigning and Governing. Ann Arbor, Michigan: University of Michigan Press, 1998.

Alexander, Herbert E. "Financing Gubernatorial Elections Campaigns." SG 53 (Summer, 1980): 140-143.

________. "Politicians and Professionals: The Influence of State Agency Heads in Budgetary Success." Political Quarterly, 63 (3/92): 153-68.

Morehouse, Sarah, McC. "The Governor and His Legislative Party." APSR 60 (4): 923-42.

__________. "The Politics of Gubernatorial Nominations." SG 53 (3):125-28.

Muchmore, Lynn and Beyle, Thad L., "The Governor as Party Leader." SG 53 (3): 121-24.

Ogden, Daniel. "The Blanket Primary and Party Regularity in Washington." PNQ 39 (1/48): 33-38.

Ransone, Colman. "Political Leadership in the Governor's Office." JOP 26 (2/64), 197-220.

Sabato, Larry. "Gubernatorial Politics and the New Campaign Technology." SG 53 (1980): 48-52.

Schlesinger, J. H. "The Politics of the Executive." In H. Jacob and K. N. Vines, eds. Politics in the American States: A Comparative Analysis. 2nd ed., Boston: Little Brown, 1968. 210-37.

Simmons, Robert H. "The Washington State Plural Executive: An Initial Effort in Inter- Action Analysis." WPQ 28 (6/65): 363-81.

**3. The Veto**

Cameron, Charles M. Veto Bargaining: Presidents and the Politics of Negative Power. Cambridge, UK: Cambridge University Press, 2000.

Herzik, Eric B., and Brent W. Brown. Gubernatorial Leadership and State Policy. New York: Greenwood Press, 1991.

Abney, Glenn, and Thomas E. Lauth. "The Line-Item Veto in the States: An Instrument for Fiscal Restraint." PAR 45 (6/80): 372-77.

______________________________. "The Governor as Chief Administrator." PAR 48 (1-2/83): 40-49.

Backman, Ada E. "The Item Veto Power of the Executive." Temple Law Quarterly 31 (Fall 1957): 27-34.

Benjamin, Gerald. "The Diffusion of the Governor's Veto Power." SG (Summer 1982): 99-105.

Bernick, E.L., and C.W. Wiggins. "Executive-Legislative Power Relations: Perspectives of State Lawmakers." APQ 9 (4): 467-76.

Brough, Regina K., "The Powers of the Gubernatorial CEO: Variations Among the States." SG 59 (2): 58-63.

Burke, Timothy P. "The Partial Veto Power: Legislation by the Governor." UWALR (2/74): 603-16.

Gove, Samuel F. "Why Strong Governors?" NCR 53 (March, 1964): 131-36.

Herzig, Eric, and C. Wiggens. "Governors Versus Legislatures: Vetoes, Overrides, and Policy Making in the American States." OAS 17 (9/89): 641-62.

Sherman, Sharon. "Powersplit: When Legislatures and Governors are of Opposing Parties." SL X, # 5 (5-6/84), 9-12.

Walker, Alexander J. "The Governor's Veto Power." University of Virginia Newsletter 55 (12/77): 3-16.

Washington State, House of Representatives. "Report on the Partial Veto Power and the 1986 Partial Vetoes." Olympia: The House, 1986.

#### 4. Legislatures

Clynch, Edward J., and Thomas J. Lauth. *Governors, Legislatures, and Budgets: Diversity Across the American States*. New York: Greenwood Press, 1991.

Rosenthal, Alan. *The Decline of Representative Democracy: Process, Participation and the Power in State Legislatures.* Washington, D.C., CQP, 1998.

________. *Governors and Legislatures: Contending Powers*. Washington, D.C.: CQP, 1990.

Scott, George W. *A Majority of One: Legislative Life*. 3rd ed., Seattle: Civitas Press. 2011.

Seeberger, Ed. *Sine Die: A Guide to the Washington State Legislative Process*. Seattle: UWAP, 1997.

Abney, Glenn, and Thomas Lauth. "Perceptions of the Impact of Governors and Legislatures in the State Appropriations Process." WPQ 40 (6/87): 342-55. ( 9 /96): 359-81.

Sharkansky, Ira. "Agency Requests, Gubernatorial Support, and Budget Success in State Legislatures." APSR 62 (12/68): 1220-31.

*5. Regionalism, and Federal-State Relations*

Elazar, Daniel Jr. *American Federalism: A View from the States*. 3rd ed., New York: Harper and Row, 1984.

Malone, Michael P., and Richard W. Etulain. *The American West*. 2nd ed., Lincoln: UNEP, 1984.

Nash, Gerald. *The American West in the Twentieth Century: A Short History of an Urban Oasis (1898-1960)*. Englewood Cliffs: Prentice-Hall, 1973.

Sharkansky, Ira. *Regionalism in American Politics*. Indianapolis: Bobs-Merrill, 1970.

Stratton, David. *Washington State Comes of Age: The State in the National Experience*. Pullman: WSUP. 1992.

"The New Regionalism in America, 1970-198," in William G. Robbins, Robert J. Frank, and Richard Ross eds. *Regionalism and the Pacific Northwest*. Corvallis: OSUP, 1983. 37-96.

### D. The Governors and Their Eras

#### I. The Territorials

Asher, Brad, Beyond the Reservation: Indians, Settlers, and the Law in Washington

Territory. Lawrence: UKAP, 1999.

Bancroft, Hubert H. History of Idaho, Washington, and Montana, 1845-1889. San Francisco: The History Company, 1890.

Baird, Dennis, Diane Mullickan, and W. R. Swagerty, eds. The Nez Perce Nation Divided: First Hand Accounts Leading to the 1863 Treaty. Moscow: UIDP, 2002.

Beckett, Paul L. From Wilderness to Enabling Act: The Evolution of the State of Washington. Pullman: WSUP, 1968.

Billington, Ray A. The Far-Western Frontier: 1836-1860. New York: Harper, 1956.

Bogue, Allan G. Frederick Jackson Turner: Strange Roads Going Down. Norman: UOKP, 1999.

Denny, Arthur A. Pioneer Days on Puget Sound. Olympia: C. B. Bagley, State Printer, 1889.

Farrand, Max. Legislation of Congress for the Government of the Organized Territories of the United States, 1789-1895. Newark, .NJ: W.A. Baker, 1896.

Ficken, Robert E. Territorial Washington. Pullman: WSUP, 2003.

______. Washington State: The Inaugural Decade, 1885-1889. Pullman: WSUP, 2007.

Galbraith, John S. The Hudson's Bay Company as an Imperial Factor, 1821-1869. Berkeley: UCAPB, 1957.

Gates, Charles M. ed., The Messages of the Governors of the Territory of Washington to the Legislative Assembly, 1884-1889. Seattle: UWAP, 1940.

Hynding, Alan. The Public Life of Eugene Semple; Promoter and Political of the Pacific Northwest. Seattle: UWAP, 1973.

Jacobs, Orange. Memoirs of Orange Jacobs. Seattle: Lowman and Hanford, 1908.

Johannsen, Robert W., ed. Democracy on Trial, 1845-1877. New York: McGraw-Hill, 1966.

Lang, William L. Confederacy of Ambition: William Winlock Miller and the Making of Washington Territory. Seattle: UWAP, 1999.

Lavender, David. Land of Giants: The Drive to the Pacific Northwest, 1750-1950. Garden City, NY: Doubleday, 1958.

McClelland, John M. Jr. Cowlitz Corridor: Historical River Highway of the Pacific Northwest. Longview, WA: Longview Publishing Company, 1953.

McConaghy, Lorraine. New Land, North of the Columbia. Seattle: Sasquatch Press, 2011.

Morgan, H. Wayne ed. The Gilded Age: A Reappraisal. Syracuse: Syracuse University Press, 1963. 111-39.

Morrison, Dorothy N. Outpost: John McLaughlin and the Far Northwest. Portland: OHSP, 2004.

Pfeffer, E. Louise. The Closing of the Public Domain: Disposal and Reservation Policies, 1900-1950. Palo Alto: Stanford University Press, 1951.

Pomeroy, Earl. The Territories of the United States, 1861-1890: Studies in Colonial Administration. Philadelphia: UPAP, 1947.

Richards, Kent. Isaac Stevens: Young Man in a Hurry. Provo, Utah: BYUP, 1979.

Rogers, John R. The Inalienable Rights of Man. Olympia: Private Printing, c. 1900.

Turner, Frederick Jackson. The Frontier in American History. New York: Henry Holt,

1920.

Blankenship, Russell. "The Political Thought of John Rogers." PNQ 37 (1/1946): 3-14.

Brown, Arthur. "Promotion of Emigration to Washington." PNQ 36 (1/45): 3-18.

Bunting, Robert M. "Work and the Settler Culture in the Western Pacific Northwest, 1853-1899." PNQ 96 (Fall 2005): 198-204.

Cohn, Samuel F. "Martial Law in Washington Territory." PNQ 27 (7/86): 195-218.

Condon, John N. "Documents: Washington's First Constitution, 1878." PNQ 10 (1/19): 57-68, and (4/1919), 110-41.

Delorme, Roland L. "Crime and Punishment in the Pacific Northwest Territories: A Bibliographic Essay." PNQ 76 (4/85): 42-51.

_______. "Westward the Bureaucrats: Government Officials on the Washington and Arizona Frontier." Arizona and the West 22 (Autumn 1980): 238-86.

Eblen, Jack. "Status, Mobility and Empire: The Territorial Governors, 1869-90." PNQ 60 (7/69):145-53.

Ellis, David W. "The Forfeiture of Railroad land Grants, 1867-1894." MVHR 33 (6/1946): 27-60.

Findlay, John M. "Closing the Frontier in Washington: Edmond S. Meany and Frederick Jackson Turner." PNQ 82 (4/91): 59-69.

Gates, Charles M. "Historical Sketch of the Pacific Northwest." In the Charles Gates Collection, UWSC, 5-18.

Gates, Paul W. "The Homestead Act in a Spurious Incongruous Land System." AHR 61 (7/36): 652-61.

Hollander, Russell. "Mental Health Policy in Washington Territory, 1853-1875." PNQ 71 (10/80): 152-61.

Karlin, Jules R. "The Anti-Chinese Outbreaks in Seattle, 1885-1886." PNQ 39 (4/48), 103-20.

Johansen, Dorothy O. "A Tentative Appraisal of Territorial Government in Oregon." Northwest Review 18 (11/49): 485-99.

_______. "Spectators to Disunion: the Pacific Northwest and the Civil War." PNQ 44 (7/53): 106-14.

Johannsen, Robert W. "National Issues and Local Politics in Washington Territory, 1857-1861." PNQ 42 (3/51): 3-31.

Johannsen, Robert W. "The Kansas-Nebraska Act and the Pacific Northwest Frontier." PHR 22 (5/53):129-41.

Lokken, Roy. "The Martial Law Controversy in Washington Territory, 1856." PNQ 43 **(4/52):**

Long, John W. Jr. "The Origin and Development of the San Juan Island Water Boundary Controversy." PNQ 43 (7/52): 187-213.

Murray, Keith A. "A Governor's Place in History." PNQ 44 (4/53), 50-60:

Meany, Edmond S. "Richard Dickerson Gholson." WHQ 8 (7/17), 180-82.

______. "The Political Beginnings of Washington Territory." OHQ 6 (6/05):147-58.

______. "The Cowlitz Convention: Inception of Washington Territory." WHQ 13 (1/22): 3-19.

______. "Newspapers in Washington Territory." PNQ 13 (7/27): 181-95 and 14: 21-29,

100-107,180-200, 269-90.

______. "The Cowlitz Convention: Inception of Washington Territory." PNQ 13 (1/22): 3-19.

Merk, Frederick. "Genesis of the Oregon Question." MVHR 36 (3/1950): 583-612.

Nash, Gerald D. "The Census of 1890 and the Closing of the Frontier." PNQ 71 (7/80): 98-100.

Paxson, Frederic F. "The Admission of 'Omnibus' States, 1889-1890." Wisconsin Historical Society Proceedings (1911): 77-96.

Pickering, William. "Washington's First War Governor." WHQ 8 (4/1917): 91-93.

Pohl, Thomas W. "Seattle, 1851-1861: A Frontier Community." Ph.D., UWA, 1970.

Prosch, Thomas. "The Indian War in Washington Territory." OHQ 16 (3/15): 1-24.

Simmons, Michael T. "The Transition of the Washington Executive from Territory to Statehood." PNQ 55 (4/1964): 76-86.

Tegeder, Vincent G. "Lincoln and the Territorial Patronage: The Ascendancy of the Radicals in the West." MVHR 35(6/1948): 77-90.

"Washington's First Constitution, 1878." WHQ 9 (1918) and 10, (1919): 51-68.

Berner, Richard, Project Director, and Kari Inglis and Ruth Johnson Preparers. "Washington Territorial Government Papers, 1853-1875." UWAL, 1975.

Hicks, John D. "The Constitutions of the Northwest States." University Studies, (Nebraska), (1-4/1923): 5-154.

Rosenow, Beverly P., ed. The Journal of the Washington State Constitutional Convention, 1889. Seattle: Book Publishing Company, 1962.

Shapiro, Scott E. Watson C. Squire: Senator from Washington, 1889-97. Seattle: Book Publishing Co., 1962.

Squire, Governor Watson. Biennial Message to the Legislative Assembly Session of 1885-86. Olympia: Thomas Cavanaugh, Public Printer, 1895.

State of Washington, Governor. Report to the Secretary of the Interior. Olympia: State Printer, 1879, 1884-89.

Messages of the Governors of the Governors of Washington Territory to the Legislative Assembly. Olympia: Bagley and Harned, 1873, ff.

U.S. Department of the Interior. Territorial Papers, Washington, 1854-1902. Microfilm, UWAL.

Washington State Senate. "The Constitutions of the State of Washington. The Original Version[,] Adopted in 1889 with Amendments Thereto, Including the 48th Amendment Approved November 8, 1966." Olympia: The Senate, 1967.

Washington Territory, Auditor's Office. Washington Territory, Auditor's Office Records, 1858-1861.

Waugh, Kathleen, comp. "Tenth Biennial Report of the State Board of Control." Olympia: The Board, 1902.

Yoder, Fred R. The Farmer's Alliance in Washington — Prelude to Populism. Pullman: Studies of the State of Washington, 16 (9/48): 123-78.

Airey, Wilfred J. "A History of the Constitution and Government of Washington Territory." Ph.D., UWA, 1945.

Driscoll, John J. "Washington Territorial Institutions." MA, UWA, 1940.

Fitts, James L. "The Washington Constitutional Convention of 1889." MA, UWA, 1951.

Frost, Vernon R. "The Political Adolescence of Washington State." MA, UWA, 1949.

Gleason, Mercedes S. "The Territorial Governors of the State of Washington, 1853-1889." MA, UWA, 1958.

Hansen, David K. "Public Response to the Civil War in Washington Territory and Oregon, 1861-1865." MA, UWA, 1965.

Johannsen, Robert W. "Washington Territory and the National Political Parties, 1854-1861." MA, UWA, 1949.

Lamm, Charles P. "An Analysis of the Arguments Presented at the Walla Walla Treaty Council of 1855." MA, WSU, 1970.

Marsh, Ronald R. "The Republican Party In Washington Territory, 1867-1872." MA, UWA, 1967.

Meneely, Alex H. "The Anti-Chinese Movement in the Northwest." MA, UWA, 1922.

Murray, Keith A. "The Movement toward Statehood in Washington." MA, UWA, 1940.

Owens, Kenneth N. "Frontier Governors: A Study of the Territorial Executives in the History of Washington, Idaho, Montana, Wyoming and Dakota Territories." Ph.D., UMN, 1959.

Beardsley, Arthur, WSA.

Burke, Thomas. UWASC.

Carstensen, Vernon. UWASC.

Denny, Arthur, SR.

Ferry, Elisha P. Papers. UWASC, WSA; SR, G.

Gates, Charles M., Collection. UWASC.

Mason, Charles, Correspondence. WASL; WSA.

Moore, Marshall. WSA; G.

Newell, William A. WSA; G.

Pickering, William. WSA; G.

Rogers, John R. WSA, (Scrapbooks); SR, Gov.

Salomon, Edward S. WSA; G.

Semple, Eugene F. UWASC, WSA; G.

Squire, Watson. WSA; Bancroft Library, UWASC, UCAB; G, USS.

Stevens, Hazard. WSA.

Stevens, Isaac, papers. UWASC; EWSHS; G.

Swan, James G. (microform). UWASC.

Washington Territorial Papers. WSA.

### II. The Populists and Progressives

Argersinger, Lawrence. The Limits of Agrarian Radicalism: Western Populism and American Politics. Lawrence: UKAP, 1995.

Clanton, Gene O. Populism: The Humane Preference in America, 1890-1900. Boston: Twayne Publishers, 1991.

Clark, Norman H. Mill Town: A Social History of Everett, Washington from its Earliest

Beginnings on Puget Sound to the Event Known as the Everett Massacre. Seattle: UWAP, 1970.

Cooper, John M. Jr. The Warrior and the Priest: Woodrow Wilson and Theodore Roosevelt. Cambridge: Belknap Press, 1983.

Crawford, Harriet A. The Washington State Grange, 1889-1924: A Romance of Democracy. Portland: Binfords and Mort, 1940.

Goodwyn, Lawrence. Democratic Promise: The Populist Movement in America. New York: OUP, 1976.

Hayes, Samuel. The Response to Industrialism, 1885-1914. Chicago: UCP, 1957.

Hicks, John D. The Populist Revolt: A History of the Farmer's Alliance and the People's Party. Westport, CT: Greenwood Press, 1981.

Hofstadter, Richard. The Age of Reform: From Bryan to FDR. New York: Knopf, 1955.

Kennedy, David M. Over Here: The First World War and American Society. New York: OUP, 1980.

Mowry, George. Theodore Roosevelt and the Progressive Movement. Madison: UWIP, 1946.

Noble, David W. The Progressive Mind, 1890-1917. Chicago: Rand McNally, 1970.

Richardson, Elmo R. The Politics of Conservation: Crusades and Controversies, 1897-1913. Berkeley: UCAPB, 1976.

Riddle, Thomas W. Old Radicalism in America: John R. Rogers and the Populist Movement in Washington, 1891-1900. New York: Garland Publishers, 1991.

Robertson, James O. No Third Choice: Progressives in Republican Politics, 1916-1921. New York: Garland Publishers, 1983.

Sanders, Elizabeth. Roots of Reform: Farmers, Workers, and the American State, 1877-1917. Berkeley: UCAPB, 1999.

Schiesl, Martin. The Politics of Efficiency: Municipal Administration and Reform in America, 1800-1920. Berkeley: UCAPB, 1977.

Schwantes, Carlos A. Radical Heritage: Labor, Socialism and Reform in Washington and British Columbia, 1885-1917. Seattle: UWAP. 1979

Ellis, Daid M. "The Forfeiture of Railroad Land Grants, 1864-1894." MVHR 33 (6/46): 24-60.

Jones, Wesley. "Washington's Political Development." PNQ 19 (1908): 398-401.

Stiles, Theodore L. "The Constitution of the State of Washington and its Effects on Public Interests." PNQ 4 (1913): 281-87.

Woody, Carroll H. "Populism in Washington: A Study of the Legislature of 1897." PNQ 21 (4/30): 103-19.

Boone, Michael D. "The Washington State Legislature of 1897: A Study in Populism." MA, UWA, 1966.

Gunns, Albert L. "Civil Liberties and Crisis: The State of Civil Liberties in the Pacific Northwest, 1917-1940." Ph.D., UWA, 1971.

Peters, Stephen H., "The Populists in the Washington State Legislature, 1883-1900." MA, UWA, 1967.

Nesbit, Robert C. "Judge Thomas Burke: Satrap to the Empire Builder: A Biography." Ph.D., UWA, 1957.

Pullen, Douglas. "The Administration of Washington State Governor Louis Hart, 1919-1925." Ph.D., UWA, 1974.

Ferry, Elisha. "Retiring Message to the Legislature [1/11/93]. Ferry papers. UWASC, 2/10.

Shimmons, Earl W., "Revolt in the Far Northwest." N 135 (11/9/32): 452-453.

AFL-CIO King County Central Labor Council, Papers, 1890-1969.

*Jones, Wesley, USS.

Lister, Ernest. WSA; (scrapbooks), UWASC; CC. G.

Bridges, Robert. CC.

*McGraw, John, WSA; G.

Ernst, Charles, DD.

Martin, Clarence. WASUSC; CC, G, SR.

Geraghty, James M. DD, SSC.

Poindexter, Miles, USS

Johnson, Lon. WSUSC. LtG.

Washington State Federation of Labor.

**II. Between the Wars: The Twenties and Thirties**

Braeman, John, Robert H. Bremner, and Everett Walters, eds. *Change and Continuity in Twentieth Century America: The Twenties.* Columbus: Ohio State University Press, 1968.

________, and David Brady, eds. *The New Deal.* Vol. 2. Columbus: Ohio State University Press, 1975.

Burke, Robert E., and Richard Lowitt, comps. The *New Era and the New Deal, 1920-1940.* Arlington Heights, IL: Harlan Davidson, 1981.

________. *Olson's New Deal for California.* Berkeley: UCAPB, 1953.

Burner, David. *The Politics of Provincialism: The Democratic Party in Transition, 1918-1932.* New York: Knopf, 1968.

Clark, Norman. *The Dry Years: Prohibition and Social Change.* Seattle: UWAP, rev. ed., 1988.

Ficken Robert E. *Lumber and Politics: The Career of Mark E. Reed.* Seattle: UWAP, 1979.

Friedheim, Robert. *The Seattle General Strike.* Seattle: UWAP, 1964.

Frisch, Martin J., and Martin Diamond, eds., *The Thirties: A Reconsideration in the Light of American Political Tradition.* DeKalb: Northern Illinois University Press, 1968.

Graham, Otis L. Jr. *An Encore for Reform: The Old Progressives and the New Deal. New York*: Oxford University Press, 1967.

Hansen, Ole. *Americanism Versus Bolshevism.* New York: Doubleday, 1920.

Hillman, Arthur. *The Unemployed Citizen's League of Seattle.* Seattle: UWAP, 1934.

Leuchtenberg. William E. *Franklin D. Roosevelt and the New Deal, 1932-1940.* New York: Harper and Row, 1963.

Lowitt, Richard. *The New Deal and the West.* Bloomington: Indiana University Press, 1984.

Murrell, Gary. *Iron Pants: Oregon's Anti-New Deal Governor, Charles Henry Martin.* Pullman: WSUP, 2000.

Neuberger, Richard L. *Our Promised Land.* New York: McMillan, 1938.

Kempner, Paul. "Politics Without Parties." In Gerald D. Nash and Richard Italian eds.

*The Twentieth Century West: Historical Interpretations.* Albuquerque: UNMP, 1989.

Lowest, Richard. *The New Deal and the West.* Bloomington: INUP, 1984.

Malone, Michael P. *C. Ben Ross and the New Deal in Idaho.* Seattle: UWAP, 1970.

McKay, Floyd J. *An Editor for Oregon: Charles A. Sprague and the Politics of Change.* Corvallis: OSUP, 1998.

Patterson, James T. *Congressional Conservatism and the New Deal: The Growth of the Conservative Coalition in Congress, 1933-1936.* Westport, CT: Greenwood Press, 1981

Pomeroy, Earl. *The Pacific Slope: A History of California, Oregon, Washington, Utah, and Nevada.* New York: Knopf, 1951.

Preston, William Jr. *Aliens and Dissenters: Federal Suppression of Radicals, 1903-1933.* Cambridge: HUP, 1963.

Schriftgiesser, Karl. *This Was Normalcy, An Account of Party Politics During Twelve Republican Years: 1920-1932.* Boston: Little, Brown, 1948.

Preston. *The Great Crusade and After*, *1914-1928.* New York: McMillan, 1930.

Stewart, Edgar I. *Washington, Northwest Frontier.* New York: Lewis Historical Publishing Company, 1957.

Arrington, Leonard. "The New Deal and the West: A Preliminary Statistical Inquiry." PHR 38 (9/69): 311-27.

________. "The Sagebrush Resurrection: New Deal Expenditures in the Western States, 1933-1939." PHR 52 (2/82): 1-16.

Blum, John. "Nativism, Anti-Radicalism, and the Foreign Scare, 1917-1920." *Midwest Journal* 3 (1950-1951): 46-53.

Friedel, Frank. "Franklin D. Roosevelt in the Northwest: Informal Glimpses." PNQ 76 (10/85): 122-31.

Link, Arthur S. "What Happened to the Progressive Movement in the 1920's?" AHR 64 (7/59), 833-54.

McKay, Floyd J. "Charles Sprague's Internal Wars: Civil Liberties Challenges of An Editor and a Governor." OHQ 96 (4/96): 326-61.

Patterson, James T. "The New Deal in the Northwest." PHR 38 (8/69): 317-320.

Acena, Albert A. "The Washington Commonwealth Federation: Reform Politics and the Popular Front." Ph.D., UWA, 1975.

Blumell, Bruce D. "The Development of Public Assistance in the State of Washington During the Great Depression." Ph.D., UWA, 1973.

Chaskel, Ruth J. "The Administration of the Work Projects Administration in the State of Washington," MA, UWA, 1942.

Cole, Robert L. "The Democratic Party in Washington State 1919-1933: Barometer of Social Change." Ph.D., UWA, 1972.

Gunns, Albert. "Roland Hill Hartley and the Politics of Washington State." MA, UWA, 1963.

Hall, Margaret A. "Henry Suzzallo and the Washington State Council of Defense." MA, UWA, 1975.

Krause, Fayette. "Democratic Party Politics in the State of Washington During the New Deal." Ph.D., UWA, 1971.

Lyons, Roy D. "A History of Political Campaigns in the State of Washington During the New Deal, 1932-1936." MA, UPS, 1956.

Miller, Margaret A. "The Left's Turn: Labor, Welfare, Politics, and Social Movements in Washington State, 1937-1973." Ph.D., UWA, 2000. Randolph, Charles N. "Crisis and Change: Washington State's Reaction to the Depression, 1932-1933." MA, WSU, 1970.

Scott, George W. "The New Order of Cincinnatus." MA, UWA, 1966.

Vjres, Brian Q. "Roland Hill Hartley and the Election of 1928." MA, WASU, 1973.

State of Washington, Department of Social Security, [Ernst, Charles]. "The Social Security Program in the State of Washington." Olympia: The Department, 1937.

"The Republican Convention [of 1920]." In Griffiths MS, 19-14.

Washington State Planning Council. *Ten Years of Progress, 1934-1944*. Olympia: State Printer, 1943.

Bone, Homer T., PLUSC; USS.

*Burke, Robert E., Collector. Washington State. Old Age Pension Union.

Chadwick, Stephen F.

Fink, John B.; DD.

*Farquharson, Mary, SS.

*Hansen, Julia B. SR, USR.

*Hartley, Roland H. (newspaper clippings).

Hill, Knute. WASUSP; SR, USR.

*Houghton, Cluck, Coughlin and Schabat

*Jackson, Henry M. PA, USR, USS.

Kinnear, Roy. SR.

Kizer, Ben.

*Magnuson, Warren G. SR, USR, USS.

*Martin, Clarence D. WSA, WSUSC; CC, G, SR.

Myers, Guy.

* O'Brien, John L. WSA, UWSC; SR (Spkr).

Reed, Mark E. (corr); SR, ML.

*Reeves, Belle C. WSA.

Riley, Edith Dolan.

Smith, Thomas. SR, DD.

*Speer, Lillian. PUDB.

*Wanamaker, Pearl A. WSA; SS, SPI.

*Washington PUD Association.

*Weston, Evan M. UWASC.

Yantis, George. SR (Spkr).

*Zednick, Victor. (scrapbooks); SS.

Zioncheck, Marion. USR.

### IV. Arthur B. Langlie

Ambrose, Stephen E., ed. Eisenhower: A Centenary Assessment. Baton Rouge: Louisiana State University Press, 1995.

Blanchard, Leslie. The Street Railway Era in Seattle: A Chronicle of Six Decades. Forty Fort, PA: Harold E. Cox, 1968.

Berner, Richard C. Seattle 1921-1940: From Boom to Bust. Seattle: Charles Street Press, 1992.

_______. Seattle Transformed: World War II to the Cold War. Seattle: Charles Press, 1999.

Blum, John. "World War II." In C. Vann Woodward, ed., The Comparative Approach to American History. New York: Basic Books, 1968, 315-27.

Brinkley, Alan. The End of Reform: New Deal Liberalism in Recession and War. New York: Knopf, 1995.

Brooks, Karl B. Public Power, Private Dams. Seattle. Seattle: UWAP, 2006.

Hanford Cornelius. Seattle and Environs, 1852-1924. Seattle: Pioneer Publishing Company, 1924.

Ferhind, Kevin J., ed. The Cold War in the American West, 1945-1989. Albuquerque: UNMP, 1998.

Findlay, John M., and Bruce Hevly, eds. The Atomic West. Seattle, Washington: Center for the Study of the Pacific Northwest in Association with the UWAP, 1998.

Irish, Kerry E. Clarence C. Dill: The Life of a Western Politician. Pullman: WSUP, 2000.

Lowitt, Richard, ed. Politics in the Postwar American West. Norman: UOKP, 1995.

McKinley, Charles. Uncle Sam in the Pacific Northwest: Federal management of Natural Resources on the Columbia. Berkeley: UCAPB, 1952.

Mansfield, Harold. Vision: The Story of Boeing. A Saga of the Sky and New Horizons in Space. New York: Duell, Sloan, and Pearce, 1966.

Miles C.L. History of Seattle Police Department. Tacoma: Washington State Historical Society, 1940.

Nash, Gerald. The American West Transformed: The Impact of the Second World War. Lincoln: UNEP, 1960.

____. World War II and the West: Reshaping the Economy. Lincoln: UNEP, 1990.

Polenberg, Richard. America at War: The Home Front, 1941-1945. Englewood Cliffs, N.J., Prentice-Hall, 1968.

Reichard, Gary. The Reaffirmation of Republicanism: Eisenhower and the Eighty-Third Congress. Knoxville: University of Tennessee Press, 1975.

Sale, Roger. Seattle Past and Present. Seattle: UWAP, 1976.

Scates, Shelby, Warren G. Magnuson and the Shaping of Twentieth Century America. Seattle UWP, 1997.

Schmid, Calvin F. Social Trends in Seattle. Seattle: UWAP, 1944.

Smith, C. Mark, Raising Cain: The Life and Politics of Senator Harry P. Cain. Bothell, WA: PCCE Publishers Network, 2011.

Smith, Richard N. Thomas E. Dewey and His Times. New York: Simon and Schuster, 1982.

Ball, Donald, Pam Cameron, and Peggy Watson, "Senators Magnuson and Jackson Analysis" [of Vote, 1944-1962], Political Science 451 Research Paper, University of Washington [1965], in "politics, candidates general file," N 979.7, UWA.

Ogden, Daniel M. Jr. "The 1952 Elections in Washington." WPQ 6 (3/53): 132-33.

Paddock, Joel. "Beyond the New Deal: Ideological Differences Between Eleven State Democratic Parties, 1956-1984." POQ 43 (3/90): 181-90.

Scott, George W. "The Politics of Transportation." C (spring, 1995), 13-19.

Voeltz, Herman G. Genesis and Development of a Regional Power Agency in the Pacific Northwest, 1933-1943." PNQ 53 (4/62): 65-76.

Wells, Wyatt. "Public Power in the Eisenhower Administration." JPH 20 (1/2008): 227-62.

Yarnell, Allen. "Pensions and Politics in Washington State, 1948." PNQ 61 (7/70): 147-55.

Puget Sound Regional Planning Commission. "Post-War Development: A Report of the Washington State Planning Council in Cooperation with the National

Resources Planning Board." Olympia: State Printer, 1943.

Ficken, Robert E. "The Democratic Party and Domestic Politics During World War II." Ph.D., UWA, 1973.

Scott, George W. "Arthur B. Langlie: Republican Governor in a Democratic Age." Ph.D., UWA. 1971.

____. "The New Order of Cincinnatus." MA, UWA, 1966.

"Boeing's Role in the War." Pacific Northwest Industry 43 (12/44): 39-43.

National Resources Planning Board. Development of Resources and Economic Opportunity in the Pacific Northwest. Washington, D.C., U.S. Government Printing Office, 1942.

Pacific Coast Board for Intergovernmental Relations. "Economic Outlook for the Pacific Coast, 1950-1960." v. 2. San Francisco: The Board, 1950.

Engle, N.H. "1946 Business Outlook of Western Washington Pacific Northwest Industry." (12/45): 46-51.

Richardson, Elmo. "Olympic National Park: Twenty Years of Controversy." Forest History 12 (4/68): 7-12.

Showell, Morris. "Political Consciousness and Attitudes in the State of Washington." POQ 17 (Fall 1953): 394-400.

Washington State Planning Council. Six Year Public Improvement Program. Olympia: The Council, 1943.

Lindsay, Arthur G. "The Washington Old Age Pension Union, A Political Pressure Group." MA, UWA, 1940.

Miller, Ernest G. "The Management of Washington State Government: The Problem of Central Staff Organization." MA, UWA, 1953.

Clinton, Gordon. M.

Comfort, Arthur. SR.
Coe, Earl. WSA, UWSC; SS, SOS.

Devin, William. M.

Forbus, Lady Willie. SS.

Freeman, Miller.

Freeman, Roger.

Hamley, Charles. (Scrapbook).

Hinkle, Van R. WSA; DD.

Kizer, Ben. WSA.

Langlie, Arthur B. WSA, UWASC; CC, G.

______. DDEPL. Williams, Walter (Sr.). DDEPL. DD.

Lockwood, David. (Scrapbooks); CC,

*Meyers, Guy. Milliken, William E.; M.

*Mitchell, Hugh B.; USS, USR.

*Moore, Milo; DD.

Municipal League of Seattle.

Norwood, Gus.

*Pelly, Thomas. USR.

Potts, Ralph.

Powell, Mildred; CC.

*Rabbitt, Thomas. SR.

Shannon, William D.; SS.

Tollefson, Thor. C.

Van Eaton, Harold; DD.

Wall, Senator Harry. WSA; SS.

Wanamaker, Pearl. UWASC, WSA; SR, SS, SPI.

Washington State Pollution Control Commission.

Westland, Jack. USR.

Westberg, Alfred; SR.

Wolfstone,Micheal.

Woods, Rufus.

**V. Monrad C. Wallgren**

Hamby, Alonzo L. Beyond the New Deal: Harry S. Truman and American Liberalism. New York: OUP, 1995.

Lein, Carsten. Olympic Battleground. San Francisco: Sierra Club Books, 1991.

Gunns, Albert F., "The First Tacoma Narrows Bridge: A Brief History of Galloping Gertie." PNQ 72 (10/81), 162-69.

Fiset, Louis. "Redress for Nisei Public Employees in Washington After World War II." PNQ 88 (1/94): 21-32.

Prina, L. Edgar., "The Harry Cain Mutiny." Colliers 136 (9/2/1955): 32-34, 36.

Roloff, Clifford A., "The Mount Olympus National Monument." PNQ 25 (7/34): 214-29.

Seattle Transportation Commission. Seattle Municipal Street Railway Annual Report (1932-1938). Seattle: Department of Public Works, Division of Railways, 1938.

SMRL. "Reports and Miscellaneous Material on Rehabilitation Program. Seattle: Municipal Street Railway, 1930-1939." 1942.

_____. Seattle Elections Clipping File: "Seattle Municipal and Port Elections 1933-1934."

League of Women Voters of Seattle. Seattle City Government. Seattle: The League, 1959.

Municipal League of Seattle and King County. Annual Reports. (Various) Seattle, 1951, ff.

Washington State, Secretary of State. "War Production in Washington." Olympia: OSOS, 1944.

U.S. Department of Commerce [Stanbery, V.B.]. Growth and Trends of Manufacturing in the Pacific Northwest, 1939-1947. n.p., USDC, 1950.

Wallace, Henry A., "Report from the Northwest." NR 116 (6/16/47): 12-16

*Benson, Naomi. PUDC.

Gorrie, Jack. GCOS; UWASC.

Hill, Knute USR. WSUSC.

Hodde, Charles R; Spkr; DD; WSA.

Horan, Walter. USR. WSUSC.

Houghton, Cluck Coughlin and Schubat.

Jones, Rogan, WWUA; DD.

Washington Old Age Pension Union.

Mack, Russell. USR.

Pennock, William, SR.

Pettus, Terry.

Rabbitt, Thomas. SR.

*Smith, Tom, Cty C, DD.

Truman, Harry S. Truman Committe Records. HSTPL.

Wallgren, Monrad C. WSA, HSTPL; USR, USS.

Wanamaker, Pearl. SR, SS, SOS.

Washington Old Age Pension Union.

**VI. Albert D. Rosellini.**

Chasan, Daniel J. Speaker of the House: The Political Career and Times of John L. O'Brien. Seattle: UWAP, 1990.

Smith, Payton. Rosellini: Immigrant's Son and Progressive Governor. Seattle: UWAP, 1997.

Sorte, Gerald L. "Budgetary Reform in Washington State." MA, University of Montana, 1964.

Brewster, David. "The Remarkable Rosellinis." A (10/6/72).

Bishop, Warren. WSA; DD, COS.

Brouillet, Frank. WSA; SR, SOS.

Democratic State Central Committee
Northwest Public Power Association.
of Washington.

Norwood, Gus.

Durkan, Martin J. WSA; SS.

Gluck, Joe.

Grant, Gary. WSA; SR, SS, PC.

Grieve, Robert. WSA; SS, CtyCl.

Hodde, Charles. WSA; SR (Spkr); DD.

Hurley, Margaret. SR, SS.

Johnson, Calvin. WSL.

KTWTV, (Olympia). Inside Olympia. Taped Interview with Albert D. Rosellini. Aired Spring, 2000.

Moore, Milo. WSA; DD.

Myers, Guy.

Northwest Public Power Association.

O'Brien, John. WSA; SR (Spkr).

Rasmussen, Albert ("Slim"). WSA; SR, SS, M.

Rosellini, Albert D. WSA; SS, G.

Smith, Sam. SR, CC.

Winberg, Andrew. CC, SR.

**VII. Daniel J. Evans**

Braddock, David A. "National Deinstitutionalization Study." SG (Autumn 1970): 220-226.

Conte, Dr. William A. WSA; DD. North, Lois. WSA; SR, SS, CtyCl.

Dolliver, James. WSA; GCOS, S Ct.

Evans, Daniel J. "Inaugural Address to the Legislature." 1/15/69. Olympia: Office of the Governor, 1969.

_____. The Linfield Papers. Seattle: Private Printing, 1969.

_____. Lessons in Leadership. Seattle: The Agora Foundation, 1999.

_____. Twelve Years: A Report to the Citizens of Washington State on the Administration of Governor Daniel J. Evans, 1965-1977. Olympia: Office of the Governor, 1/77.

Gettings, Robert M. "Hidden Impediments to Deinstitutionalization." SG 43 (Autumn 1970): 214-19.

"Governor's Commission on the Status of Women. "Final Report." Olympia: Office of the Governor, 1965.

Governor's Council on Urban Affairs. "Urban Washington: Apathy or Action?" Olympia: The Council, 1968.

Governor's Select Panel on the Department of Social and Health Services. "Report to the Governor." Olympia: The Panel 1977.

Hughes, John C. "Slade Gorton: A Half Century in Politics." Olympia, OSOS, 2011.

McCall, Governor Thomas and Steve Neal. Tom McCall: Maverick. Portland: Bindfords and Mort, 1977.

Office of the Governor. "Report of the Council for the Reorganization of Washington State Government." 1967.

__________________. "Report of the Constitutional Advisory Council." 12/66.

Prior, Harry Jr., and Associates. "Report of Survey of the Office of the Governor." Seattle: 1966.

Ransone, Coleman, B. Jr. "The American Governor in the '70's: A Symposium." PAR 30 (1-2/70): 1-42.

Reed, Sam S. "An Analysis of the Factional Struggle in the Republican Party of Washington State from 1962 to 1967." MA, WASU, 1968.

Scott, George W. "Politics in the Blood: The Rise of Daniel Jackson Evans." C 40 (Spring 1998): 40-44.

Snow, Mary A., and Tammie K. Wilson, "Finance Reform in Washington State 1970-1995: Where Do We Go From Here?" MPAs, TESC, 1995.

Van Asselt, Karl A. "The House of Representatives Coalition in the 1963 Washington Legislature." MA, WASU, 1964. Voorhees, Melvin B. "Once More, Out of the West comes a Blond Young Man." [re: Richard Christensen]. A, 9/28/62, 1, 10.

Walth, Brent, Fire at Heaven's Gate: Tom McCall: Tom McCall and the Oregon Story. Portland: OHSP, 1994.

Warren, James. "The Pioneer Roots of Daniel Jackson Evans." Portage 10 (Spring, 1989): 9, 12, 39.

Warren, Robert, and James T. Best. "The 1968 Elections in Washington." WPQ 22 (9/69): 536-45.

Weeks, George. "A Statehouse Hall of Fame: Ten Outstanding Governors of the Twentieth Century." SG 55 (3 1982): 67-73.

Goldsworthy, Robert. WSA; SR.

Gorton, Slade. WSA, UWASC; SR (ML), AG, USS.

Grant, Gary. WSA; SR, SS.

*Hurley, Margaret. WSA;SR, SS.

*Kinnear, George. SR(ML), DD.

*McCaffree, Mary Ellen. SR, DD.

Moriarity, Charles. UWASC; SR, SS.

Pritchard, Joel. WSA, UW; SR, SS, USR, LtG.

Scott, George W. SR, SS. Sub cited as: bf (book file), rf (research file), SF(subject file), and*NTM (Notes to Myself).

Smith, Sam. SR, CC.

Stern, Bernice. CtyC. (Scrapbooks). In his possession, 1/65 to 7/76. (Microfilm), UWA.

*Tollefson, Thor, WSA; USR, DD.; WSA.

Washington Citizens for Abortion Reform.

Whetzel, Jonathan A., SR, SS.

WSL, "Governors Collection," (Clipping file), DJE.

**VIII. Dixy Lee Ray**

Ray, Dixy Lee. Trashing the Planet: How Science Can Help Us Deal with Acid Rain, Depletion of the Ozone, and Nuclear Waste. Washington, D.C., Henry Regnery Gateway; Lanham, M.D. University Press of America, 1990.

Scammon, Richard M. The Real Majority. New York: Coward-McCann, 1970.

Schaefer, Kim K. "Right in the Eye: The Political Style of Dixy Lee Ray." PNQ 93 (Spring 2002): 81-93.

Adlum, Merle, [Washington Committee for a Responsible Environmental Policy] [1970-1972]

Odegaard, Gary, SS.

Bailey, Robert. WSA; SS.

Ray, Dixy Lee, WSA ; The Hoover Institution, Stanford University.

___________, WSA.

Bagnariol, John, WSA, NARA (Seattle); SR (Spkr).

Berentson, Duane SR(Spkr). WSA

Chandler, Rod, SR.

Wallgren, Gordon, WSA; SR, SS (ML).

Ehlers, Wayne, SR (Spkr).

Clarke, George, SR, SS.

Goltz, Barney, SS.

### IX. John D. Spellman

Adams, Kathleen. A Changing Federalism: The Condition of the States. Denver: ECS, 1982.

Beyle, Thad, ed. Gubernatorial Transitions: The 1983 and 1984 Elections. Durham, N.C.: Duke University Press, 1985.

Dolbeare, Kenneth. Economic Development and Jobs in Washington: A Citizen's Guide. Olympia: TESC, 1983.

Drew, Elizabeth. Portrait of an Election: The 1980 Presidential Campaign. New York: Simon and Schuster, 1981.

Lipset, Seymour, ed. Party Coalitions in the 1980's. San Francisco: Institute for Contemporary Studies, 1981.

Thurow, Lester C. The Zero-Sum Solution: An Economic and Political Agenda for the Eighties. New York: Simon and Schuster, 1985.

Beyle, Thad L. "New Governors in Hard Economic Times." In Beyle, ed. Governors and Hard Times. Washington, D.C.: CQP, 1992. 1-14.

Broder, David. "The New Face of State Politics." CQ, 9/8/83.

Gross, Donald. "Governors and Economic Development Policy." PSJ 17 (4): 764-87.

Kinney, Patrick J. "The Effect of Economic Conditions on the Vote for Governor." SSQ 64 (83): 154-61.

Lowry, David, and Lee Sigelman. "Understanding the Tax Revolt: Eight Explanations." APSR 76 (12/81): 963-74.

Pilcher, Dan. "The Puzzle of Block Grants." SL (July/August 1981): 9-21.

Shannon, John. "The Return to Fend-for-Yourself Federalism: The Reagan Mark." Intergovernmental Perspective 13 (Fall 1987): 34-37.

Office of the Governor. "Washington's Water. Recommendations and Possible Changes for the Future." Olympia: Governor's Cabinet Task Force on Water Resources, 1983.

Spellman, John D. "Address to the Forty-Seventh Washington State Legislature, 1982 Regular Session." 1/11/82. Olympia: State Printer, 1982.

_________. Governor's Mid-Term Report. Good Government in Hard Times. Olympia: Office of the Governor; Interview of Governor Spellman by Denny

Heck, 5/22/2000.

WSRC. "Agenda for the Eighties: The Forces Shaping Washington's Future: Perspectives on Public Education." Olympia: WSRC, 1980.

Old, Steven D. State and Federal Fiscal Relations in the Early 1980's. Washington D.C: Urban Institute, 1983.

Seeberger, Ed. "Switches." Unpublished Mss. on the

1981-83 legislative sessions. AP.

Bauer, Al. WSA. SR, SS.

Bone, Hugh A.

McDonald Dan. SR, SS.

McGavick, Joseph L. WSA. SR, Cty DD.

Sommers, Helen, SR.

Spellman, John D. KCA; CtyCl, CtyEx, G.

Thompson, Alan. SR, (ML), SS.

**X. Booth Gardner**

Beyle, Thad. Gubernatorial Transitions: The 1983 and 1984 Elections. Durham, N.C.: Duke University Press, 1989.

Brown, Lawrence D., James W. Fossett, and Kenneth T. Palmer. The Changing Politics of Federal Grants. Washington, D.C.: Brookings Institution, 1984.

Hughes, John C. "Booth Who? A Biography of Booth Gardner" Olympia: OSOS, 2010

Gardner, Booth. "State of the State Transcript." 1/13/87.

_______. "Environment 2010 Speech." WSA, BG, 8, govs. offc., press.

_______. The Gardner Years: Washington State Governor 1985-1993. Olympia: Office of the Governor, 1993.

NCSL. The President's 1991 Budget: Impact on the States. Washington, D.C., NCSL, 1990.

NGA. Time for Results: The Governor's 1991 Report on Education. Chicago: NGA, 1991.

Office of the Governor. "Agenda 1990: A Summary of Executive Policy Proposals." Olympia: The Office, 1989.

____________________. Governor's Timber Team. "Forestry and Community-Economic Benefits-Washington State." Olympia: The Team, 1992.

____________________. "Governor's Committee on Washington's Financial Future: A Financial Plan for Washington. Olympia: The Committee, 1989.

Roettig, Terry, et al. "Log Export Restrictions: Cost and Benefits." Olympia: OFM, 1992.

Riveland, Chase. "Gubernatorial Styles: Is There a Right One?" JSG 62 (4), 136-39.

Bauer, Al. WSA SR, SS.

Ehlers, Wayne. WSA; SR (Spkr).

Gardner, Booth. WSA; Pierce County Archives; SS, CtyE, G.

*Heck, Denny, WSA; SR, GCOS.

Riveland, Mary. DD(3).

Thompson, Richard, WSA; DD.

Wang, Art P.

### XI. Mike Lowry

Washington State, Governors Task Force on Regulatory Reform: Final Report. Olympia: The Task Force, 1997.

_______________. Governors Task Force on Hunger. Hunger in Washington State: A Report. Spokane: The Task Force, 1988.

_______________. Washington State Governors Task Force on Regulatory Reform: Final Report." Olympia: The Task Force, 1994.

Washington State, [and Roundtable Associates]. Washington State Retail Liquor Sales Task Force. Final Report. Olympia: The Task Force, 1997.

Adams, Brock. UWASC, LOC: USR, USS.

Ehlers, Wayne Spkr.

*Hine, Lorraine. WSA; SR (ML), GCOS.

Lowry, Mike. WSA, LOC; UWASC, (Congressional); CtyC, USR, G.

### XII. Gary Locke

Robbins, William G., "The World of Columbia River Salmon: Nature, Culture and the Great River of the West." In Joseph Cone and Sandy Redlington, eds. *The Northwest Salmon Crisis: A Documentary History*. Corvallis: OSUP, 1996.

Governor's Affirmative Action Policy Committee. *Report to Governor Gary Locke on Affirmative Action in State Government*. Olympia: OFM, 1997.

Governors' Task Force on Higher Education. *Final Report of the Governors' Task Force on Higher Education*. Olympia: The Task Force, 1996.

Locke, Gary, WSA, UWASC; SR, CtyE, G.

Republican State Central Committee of Washington, Records.(1993 ff). WASUSC.

## E. Statewide Areas and Issues of Ongoing Import

### 1. Agriculture

Crawford, Harriet A. The Washington State Grange, 1889-1924: A Romance of Democracy. Portland: Binfords and Mort, 1940.

McGregor, Alexander Campbell, Counting Sheep: From Open Range to Agribusiness on the Columbia Plateau. Seattle, UWAP, 1982.

Meinig, Donald. The Great Columbia Plain: a Historical Geography, 1805-1910. Seattle: UWAP, 1968.

Meinig, Donald. "Environment and Settlement in the Palouse, 1868-1910." MA, UWA, 1950.

Nesbit, Robert C., and Charles M. Gates, "Agriculture in Eastern Washington, 1890-1910." PNQ 37 (10/46): 279-302.

Olsen, Michael L. "The Beginnings of Agriculture in Western Oregon and Western Washington." Ph.D., UWA, 1970.

Watkins, Marilyn. Family Farmers and Politics in Western Washington, 1890-1925. Ithaca: Syracuse University Press, 1995.

Worster, Donald. River of Empire: Water, Aridity, and the Growth of the American West. New York: Oxford University Press, 1985.

### 2. The Bureaucracy

Cunningham, Robert B., and Dorothy Olshfsk. "Interpreting State Administrator-Legislator Relationships." WPQ 39 (3/86): 104-17.

Elling, Richard, "State Bureaucrats as Policy Shapers." In *Politics in the American States,* edited by Virginia Gray, H. Jacob, and K. N. Vines. Boston: Little Brown, 1988.

Hammond, Susan W. "Legislative Staffs." LSQ 9 (5/84): 271-317.

Scott, George W. "Insiders: The Staff and Bureaucracy." In Scott, *A Majority of One.* Seattle: Civitas Press, 2005. 289-306.

Connally, James K. "Administrative Reorganization of Washington State Government, 1889-1957." MA, WASU, 1959.

### 3. The Courts

Canon, Bradley C., and Charles A. Johnson. *Judicial Politics: Implementation and Impact.* 2nd ed., Washington, D.C.: CQP, 1999.

Legal Foundation of Washington. *Of Shoes and Ships and Ceiling Wax: Historic Encounters with the Washington State Supreme Court and the United States Supreme Court.* Olympia: LFW, 1989.

Lopeman, Charles S. *The Activist Advocate: Policy Making in State Supreme Courts.* Westport, CT., Praeger, 1999.

Sheldon, Charles H. *The Washington High Bench: A Biographical History of the State Supreme Court, 1889-1991.* Pullman: WSUP, 1992.

________. *A Century of Judging: A Political History of the Washington State Supreme Court.* Seattle: UWAP, 1988.

Dolliver, Justice James. "The Washington Constitution and 'State Action': The View of the Framers." WLR 102: 445-58.

Hunter, Justice Robert. "The Practice of Judging with the Superior and Supreme Court of Washington." PNF 2: 2-23.

Henschen, Beth M., "Judicial Use of Legislative History and Intent in Statutory Interpretation." LSQ 10 (8/68): 353-72.

Utter, Justice Robert, and Hugh Spitzer. *The Washington State Constitution: A Reference Guide.* Westport, CT: Greenwood Press, 2000.

Beardsley, Arthur, papers. WSA.

### 4. Culture

Bloom, Leonard. Removal and Return: The Socio-Economic Effects of the War on Japanese Americans. Berkeley: UCABP, 1949.

Brewster, David, and David Buerge. Washingtonians: A Biographical Portrait of the State. Seattle: Sasquatch Press, 1988.

Daniels, Roger. Asian America: Chinese and Japanese in the United States Since 1850. Seattle: UWAP, 1988.

Findlay, John M. Magic Lands and Western Cityscapes: American Culture After 1940. Berkeley: UCAPB, 1992.

Fiset, Louis, and Gail M. Nomura, eds. Nikkei in the Pacific Northwest: Japanese Americans and Japanese Canadians in the Twentieth Century. Seattle: Center for the Study of the Pacific Northwest in Association with the UWAP, 2005.

Gastil, Raymond O., "The Pacific as a Cultural Region." PNQ 64, (10/73): 147-62.

McWhorter, L.V. Hear Me My Chiefs!: Nez Perce History and Legend. Caldwell, ID: Caxton Printers, 1952.

Rasmussen, Janet E., Scandinavian Immigrants to the Pacific Northwest. Seattle: UWAP, 1993.

Taylor, Quintard, and Shelly Ann Wilson Moore, eds. African-American Women Confront the West, 1600-2000. Boulder: University of Colorado Press, 2003.

_____. The Forging of a Black Community: Seattle's Central District from 1870 Through the Civil Rights Era. Seattle: UWAP, 1994.

White, Sid, and S.E. Solberg, eds. Peoples of Washington: Perspectives of Cultural Diversity. Pullman: WSUP, 1989.

Campbell, Robert A. "Blacks and the Coal Mines of Western Washington, 1888-1896." PNQ 73 (10/82): 146-55.

Droker, Howard. "Seattle Race Relations During the Second World War." PNQ 67 (10/76): 163-74.

Gamboa, Ernest. "Mexican Labor in the Pacific Northwest, 1843-1947." PNQ 73 (10/82): 175-81.

Laurie, Clayton D. "The United States Army and the Anti-Chinese Riots in Washington Territory, 1885-1886." PNQ 81 (1/90): 22-29.

Ptolemy, Charles A. "The Evacuation of Japanese Americans from Washington State During World War II: A Study in Race Discrimination." MA, CWASC, 1965.

Sari, Kay E. "Demographic and Racial Changes in Seattle: 1950-1975." MA, UWA, 1976.

### 5. Disclosure/Ethics

Bone, Hugh A., and Cindy M. Fey. The People's Right to Know: An Analysis of the Washington State Public Disclosure Law. Seattle: IPPR, 1978.

Malbin, Michael J. Parties, Interest Groups, and Campaign Finance Laws. Washington, D.C.: American Enterprise Institute, 1980.

Noonan, John T. Bribes. New York: Macmillan, 1984.

Rosenthal, Alan. The Third House: Lobbyists and Lobbying in the States. Washington, D.C.: CQP, 1993.

Unsoeld, Jolene. "Who Gave, Who Got, How Much?" Olympia: The PDC, 1977.

Washington State, Public Disclosure Commission. 1998 Election Financing Factbook. Olympia: The PDC. Annual.

### 6. The Economy and the Private Sector

Appleton, John B., "Migration and Economic Opportunity in the Pacific Northwest." *Geographical Review* 21 (1/1941): 46-62.

Bourque, Phillip J. "The Washington Economy: An Input-Output Study." (Graduate School of Business Administration, UWA). Olympia: Department of Commerce and Economic Development, 1967.

Clarke, M.K. *Revitalizing State Economics: A Review of State Economic Development Policies and Programs.* Washington, D.C.: NGC Press, 1986.

Dolbeare, Kenneth. *Economic Development and Jobs in Washington: A Citizen's Guide.*

Olympia: TESC, 1983.

Gates, Charles M. "A Historical Sketch of the State of Washington of the Economic Development of Washington Since Statehood." PNQ 79 (7/48): 214-32.

Miller, Charles J. "A Foreign Trade Zone for Puget Sound: Its Economic Desirability and Feasibility." Seattle: Port of Seattle, and the Division of Progress and Industry Development of the State of Washington, 1/47.

Tattersall, James. "The Economic Development of the Pacific Northwest to 1920." Ph.D., UWA, 1960.

### 7. Education/Higher Education

Kink, Steve, and John Cahill. Class Wars: The Story of the Washington Education Association, 1965-2004. Federal Way, WA: The WEA, 2004.

Rosenthal, Alan. Pedagogues and Power: Teacher Groups in School Politics. Syracuse: Syracuse University Press, 1969.

Garms, Walter, and Michael Kirst. "The Political Environment of School Finance Politics in the 1980's." In James W. Guthrie ed. A Decade of Conflict. Cambridge, MA: Ballinger Pub., 1980.

Laderle, John W. "Governors in Higher Education." In Thad Beyle and Williams eds. The American Governor in Behavioral Perspective. New York: Harper and Row, 1972.

Lipset, Seymour M. "Academia and Politics in Modern America." In T. J. Nossiter, A. H. Hanson, and Stein Rokkan, eds. Imagination and Precision in the Social Sciences: Essays in Honor of Peter Nettl. London: Faber and Faber, 1972.

Halperin, Samuel. "Bridging the Gap Between Educators and Politicians." CPT (2/72): 30-31.

Raymer, Robert G. "Educational Development in the Territory and the State of Washington, 1883-1908." WHQ 18 (7/27), 163-80.

Salisbury, Robert H. "State Politics and Education." In Herbert Jacob and Kenneth N. Vines eds. Politics in the American States, 2nd ed. Boston: Little Brown, 1971.

Scully, Malcolm H. "State Support of Colleges: A New Way to Analyze It." Boulder: WICHE, 1981.

Miller, Wallace, and Associates, "Common School Financing and Reform: A Report to the Select Educational Study Coordinating Committee of the Washington State Legislature." WSL (9/75).

Washington State, Governor's Task Force on Higher Education. Final Report of the Governor's Task Force on Higher Education. Olympia: The Task Force, 1986.

Washington State, Governor's 20/20 Commission on the Future of Post-Secondary Education. Olympia: Governor's Executive Policy Office, 1998.

### 8.The Environment/Natural Resources

Dietrich, William. *Northwest Passage*. New York: Simon and Schuster, 1995.

Ficken, Robert E. *Rufus Woods, the Columbia Riviera and the Building of Modern Washington*. Pullman: WSUP, 1995.

______. *The Forested Land: A History of Lumbering in Western Washington*. Seattle: UWAP, 1987.

Petulla, Joseph M. *American Environmental History: The Exploitation and Conservation of Natural Resources*. San Francisco: Boyd and Frazier, 1977.

Richardson, Elmo. *Dams, Parks and Politics: Resource Development and Preservation in the Truman-Eisenhower Era*. Lexington: The University Press of Kentucky, 1973.

Taylor, Joseph E. III. *Making Salmon: An Environmental History of the Northwest Fisheries Crisis*. Seattle: UWAP, 1999.

Washington State Growth Strategies Commission. *A Growth Strategy for Washington State*. Seattle: The Commission, 1990.

White Richard. *The Organic Machine: The Remaking of the Columbia River*. New York, Hill and Wang, 1995

Wyman, Mark. *Hard Rock Epic: Western Miners and the Industrial Revolution*. Berkeley: UCAPB, 1979.

Medler, Jerry F. "Governors and Environmental Policy." PSJ 17 (4): 895-908.

Swain, Donald C. "The Bureau of Reclamation and the New Deal 1933-1940." PNQ 61 (7/70): 137-46.

"Proposals for a Columbia Valley Authority." In Charles McKinley. *Uncle Sam in the Northwest: Federal Management of Natural Resources on the Columbia*. Berkeley: UCAPB, 1952, 443-566.

Lindeman, Edward B., Chair, Alternatives for Washington. Statewide Citizen Task Force Washington. "Pathways to 1985." Olympia: OPP&FM, 1975.

Seattle First National Bank. "The Hanford Works." *Pacific Northwest Industries* (12/48): 1-8.

### 9. Federal-State Relations

Kaplan, Marshall, and Sue O'Brien eds. *The Governors and the New Federalism*. Boulder, CO: Westview Press, 1991. 94-112.

Grady, D.O. "American Governors and State–Federal Relations: Attitudes and Activities, 1960-1980." SG 57 (3): 106-12.

Walker, David B., and Albert J. Richter, "States and the Impact of Federal Grants." SG 50 (Spring 1977): 83-88.

### 10. Initiatives and Referenda

Broder, David. The Derailing of Democracy: Initiative Campaigns and the Power of Money. New York: Hillcrest Books, 2000.

Cronin, Thomas. Direct Democracy: The Politics of Initiative, Referendum, and Recall. Cambridge: HUP, 1904.

Schumaker, Waldo. "Thirty Years of People's Rule in Oregon: An Analysis." PSQ 47 (6/1932): 242-58.

Chasan, Dan. "Ultimate Democracy," in Scott, George W., ed. Turning Points in Washington's Public Life. Seattle: Civitas Press, 2011.

### 11. Labor

Chaplin, Ralph. Wobbly, The Rough-and-Tumble Story of an American Radical. Chicago: UCP, 1948.

Ficken, Robert E. Lumber and Politics: The Career of Mark E. Reed. Santa Cruz: Forest History Society, 1979.

Hyman, Harold M. Soldiers and Spruce: Origins of the Loyal Legion of Loggers and Lumbermen. Los Angeles: Berkeley: UCAPB, 1963.

Schwantes, Carlos. Radical Heritage: Labor, Socialism, and Reform in Washington and British Columbia, 1885-1917. Seattle: UWAP, 1979.

Dembo, Jonathan, "Dave Beck and the Transportation Revolution in the West. 1917-1944."In Thomas G. Edwards and Carlos Schwantes eds. Experiences in A Promised Land. Seattle: UWAP, 1986, 339-52.

Washington State Federation of Labor. Final Legislative Report. 1967, ff.

Ames, William E., and Roger A. Samson, Unionism or Hearst: The Seattle Post-Intelligencer Strike of 1926. Seattle: Pacific Northwest Labor History Association, 1978.

Dembo, Jonathan. "A History of the Washington State Labor Movement, 1885-1935." Ph.D., UWA, 1978.

**12. The Legislature**

Clynch, Edward J., and Thomas P. Lauth, eds. *Governors, Legislatures and Budgets: Diversity Across the American States.* New York: Greenwood Press, 1991.

Cox, Gary W., and Samuel Kernell eds. *The Politics of Divided Government.* Boulder: Westview Press, 1991.

Barber, James D. *The Lawmakers: Recruitment and Adaptation to Legislative Life.* New Haven: Yale University Press, 1965.

Citizen's Conference on State Legislatures. *The Sometime Governments.* New York: Bantam Books, 1971.

Heard, Alexander, ed. *State Legislatures in American Politics.* Englewood Cliffs: Prentice-Hall, 1966.

Rosenthal, Alan. *The Decline of Representative Democracy, Process, Participation and Power in State Legislatures.* Washington, D.C.: CQP, 1998.

Seeberger, Ed.. *Toward Sine Die: A Guide to the Washington State Legislative Process.* 2nd ed., Seattle: UWAP, 1997.

Beckett, Paul L. and Celeste Sunderlund, "Washington State's Law Makers: Some

Personnel Factions in [the] Washington State Legislature." WPQ (3/57): 180-202.

Francis, Wayne L., "Leadership, Party Caucuses, and Committees in U.S. State Legislatures." LSQ 10 (5/85): 243-58.

Johnson, Claudius O., "Washington's Blanket Primary Revisited." PNQ 12, (10/52): 113-19.

Loftus, Tom. "Branches of State Government: The Separation of Unequal Powers," in Loftus, *The Art of Legislative Politics.* Washington, D.C.: CQP, 1994, 61-75.

Pomeroy, Earl S. "The American Colonial Office." MVHR, 29, (1944): 531-32.

Rockman, Bert A. "Legislative-Executive Relations and Legislative Oversight." LSQ 9 (8/84): 384-87.

Sharkansky, Ira. "Agency Requests, Gubernatorial Support, and Budget Success in the State Legislature." APSR 62 (12/68): 1220-31.

Skok, James E "Federal Funds and State Legislature: Executive-Legislative Conflict in State Government." PAR 6, (11-12/80): 561-67.

Wright, Gerald C., Jr., Robert S. Erickson, and John R. McIver. "Public Opinion and

Policy Liberalism in the American States." AJPS 31 (11/87): 980-1001.

### 13. Local government

Washington State Local Governance Study Commission. "A History of Washington's Local Governments." V. (Final Report). Olympia: The Commission, and the Institute of Public Policy, TESC, 1988.

Washington State Research Council. *A Handbook for Washington's Governments*, 5th ed., Olympia: The WSRC, 1981.

Abbott, Newton C. "The Evolution of Washington Counties." MA, UW, 1927.

### 14. The Media

Cook, Timothy. Governing with the News: The News Media as a Political Institution. 2nd ed. Chicago: UCP, 2005.

CSG, The Governor and Public Information: Selected Methods Employed by Governors' Offices in Communicating with the Public. Chicago: CSG, 1961.

Halberstam, David. The Powers That Be: Technology of Communications in Politics. New York: Knopf, 1979.

Kovach, Bill, and Tom Rosenstiel. The Elements of Journalism: What News people Should Know and What the Public Should Expect. Berkeley: UCAPB, 1975.

McConaghy, Lorraine, and Sharon Boswell. Raise Hell and Sell Newspapers. Seattle: UWAP, 1996.

McCombs, Maxwell, and Donald Shaw, "The Agenda-Setting Function of the Mass Media." POQ (Summer 1971): 176-87.

### 15. Redistricting

Baker, Gordon. *The Politics of Redistricting in Washington State*. New York: Holt, Rhinehart, and Winston, 1960.

Washington State, Redistricting Commission. "The 2000 Redistricting." The Commission, at WWW// WA. gov.

Gorton, Slade. "New Methods Urged: Washington State Legislator Discouraged by Partisan Wrangles, Offers Alternatives." NMR (4/64), 176-81.

McCurdy, Howard, "Redistricting Wars," in Scott, George W., ed., *Turning Points in Washington's Public Life*. Seattle: Civitas Press, 2011]

McCombs, Maxwell, and Donald Shaw. "The Agenda-Setting Function of the Mass Media." POQ 35 (Summer, 1971): 176-87.

McDermott, William B. "The Impact of Baker v Carr in the State of Washington. The Relationship of Constituency to Compliance." Ph.D., UWA, 1966.

### 16. State Government

Clayton, Cornell, Lance LeLoup, and Nicholas P. Loverich, *Washington State Government and Politics*. Pullman: WSUP, 2004.

Dorpat, Paul, and Genevieve McCoy. *Building Washington: A History of Washington State Public Works*. Seattle: Tartu Press, 1998.

Ogden Daniel. *Washington Politics*. New York: New York University Press, 1960.

Osborne, David. *Laboratories of Democracy*. Cambridge: HUP, 1998.

**17. Taxation**

Burrows, Don."A Progressive State with RegressiveTaxes." In *Turning Points in Washingtons Public Life*. Seattle: Civitas Press, 2011.

Pascall, Glenn R. "Washington's Tax System: Choices for the Future." Paper # 17. Seattle: IPPM, UWA, (7/82).

State of Washington, Department of Efficiency. *Financial History of the State of Washington for the Period Statehood to March 31, 1921*. Olympia: The Department, 1921.

Office of Program Planning and Fiscal Management. *Pocket Data Book*. Olympia: State Printer, 1970, ff.

Cheng, Yung-Ping. "A Historical of the General Property Tax in the State of Washington." MA, UWA, 1957.

**18. The Third House/Ethics**

Berry, Jeffery. Lobbying for the People: The Political Behavior of Public Interest Groups. Princeton: Princeton University Press, 1977.

Carter, Stephen. Civility: Manners, Morals and the Etiquette of Democracy. New York: Basic Books, 1998.

Dobel, E. Patrick. Pork Barrel Politics. Stanford: Stanford University Press, 1974.

Noonan, John. Bribes. New York: Macmillan, 1984.

Rosenthal, Alan. Lobbyists and Lobbying in the States. Washington, D.C.: CQP. 2007.

The Ethics Process in State Legislatures: Disciplining Members in a Public Forum. Denver: State Legislative Leaders Foundation/National Conference of State Legislators, 1999.

Peterson, Walfred. "Interest Groups and Lobbies in Washington State Government." In Thor Swanson, et. al., Political Life in Washington: Governing the Evergreen State. Pullman: WSUP, 1985.

Sell, T.M. "Riding the Milk Wagon: The Effect of Money on the Outcomes of Legislative Campaigns in Washington State, 1974-1982," Olympia: PDC, 1988.

Unsoeld, Jolene. Who Gave? Who Got? How Much? Everett: Working Press, 1976.

Washington State Public Disclosure Commission. Annual Report. Olympia: The PDC, 1974, ff..

Ray, Randy, and Megan Mardesich. Perceptions: Corporate Political Involvement in the Washington State Legislature. Olympia: TESC, 1976.

**19. Transportation**

Lewty, Peter J. To the Columbia Gateway: The Oregon Railway and the Northern Pacific, 1889-1894. Pullman: WSUP Press, 1987.

Malone, Michael P. James J. Hill: Empire Builder of the Northwest. Norman: UOKP, 1996.

Newell, Gordon, ed. The H.W. McCurdy Marine History of the Pacific Northwest, 1966-1976. Seattle: The Superior Company, 1977.

Schwantes, Carlos A. Going Places: Transportation Redefines the Twentieth-Century West. Bloomington: INUP, 2003.

Schwantes, Carlos. Railroad Signatures Across the Northwest. Seattle: UWAP, 1998.

Mills, Randall V. "A History of Transportation in the Pacific Northwest." OHQ, 65 (9/1946): 281-312.

Washington State, Department of Transportation. A History of Highways and TransportationWashington State Transportation Commission 1951-1993. Olympia: The Commission, 1993.

**20. Requisite Documents Applicable to all Administrations**

Agency director's files 1922, ff., WSA.

Governor's Office, Central Files, 1957, ff., WSA.

Hitchcock, Henry-Russell, and William Seale. *Temples of Democracy: The State Capitols of the USA.* New York: Brace Jovanovich, 1976.

*Journal of the United States House of Representatives*, 1853, ff.

*Journal of the United States Senate*, 1853, ff.

*Journal of the State House of Representatives*, 1889, ff.

*Journal of the Washington State Senat*e, 1889, ff.

*OSOS. Washington State Yearbook.* Sammamish, WA: Electronic Handbook Publishers, 1980, ff.

_____. *Abstract[s] of Votes Primary and General Elections.* Olympia: State Printer, 1889, ff.

*Washington Public Documents.* Olympia: State Printer, 1941-68. WSA.

Washington State Efficiency Commission. *Annual Report.* 1889-1909(?).

Washington State Legislature, Office of the Code Reviser. *Session Laws.* 1889, ff.

Washington State Legislature. *Final Legislative Report. Olympia.* Annual since 1967.

Washington State Legislature. *Legislative Manual.* 1949, ff.

Washington State Democratic Central Committee, WSUSP. (1960s-80s).

## F. Acronyms

### 1. General Lexigraphy

*AP*. Author's possession.

*AWB*. Association of Washington Business.

*BGRS*. Bureau of Governmental Research and Services, UWA.

*Cabinet*. Now the directors of 30 departments, divided into "large, and "small" agencies, which are appointed by and report to the governor.

*Capital Budget*. That for facilities and repairs.

*Caucus*. The basic organization of the members of each party in each house, who convene in private during session to discuss issues and tactics.

*Central Staff*. Senior specialists in the governor's office reporting directly to the GCOS.

*Commissioner of Public Lands*. One of nine statewide elected officials. In charge of timber grant lands held by the State.

*Conference Committee*. Appointed by the leaders of the two houses of the legislature to resolve legislative differences between them. (See Free Conference Committee).

*Council of State Governments*. A joint organization subscribed to by all the states for research and services needed by all.

*CWU, EWU, WWU.* The regional universities at Ellensburg, Cheney, and Bellingham.

*Dedicated Fund.* Proceeds from a tax specified by statute or the constitution and reserved for an single purpose.

*DNC.* Democratic National Committee.

*DOL* Department of Licenses.

*DSCC.* The Democratic State Central Committee.

*DSHS.* The Department of Social and Health Services.

*DTED* Department of Trade and Economic Development.

*ECS.* Education Commission of the States.

*Executive Order.* The limited power of the governor to effect necessary administrative and budgetary revisions within the provisions of a statute. E.g., Revision the budget into balance on a quarterly basis.

*Free Conference Committee.* One made up equally of House and Senate members according to partisan strength, and empowered to make unlimited changes to any bill in dispute between the houses, then voted "up" or "down."

*General Election.* One held every year, statewide.

*IGR.* Institute for Governmental Research (UWA).

*Legislative Budget Committee.* (Now JLARC, Joint Legislative Assessment and Review Committeee). Composed of senior members of the financial committees to "performance audit" agencies.

*Legislative Digest.* A history of official actions on bills, by session.

*Legislative Manual.* (aka, "The Red Book," or "The legislator's Bible"), containing the U.S. and State Constitutions, parliamentary law, and the rules and joint rules of the houses. Revised annually.

*Legislative Report.* Issued at the end of each session, summarizing legislation that has become law, and vetoes.

*Merit System.* "Civil Service."

*MIS.* Management Information System. The computer based subsidiary of the legislature for investigation and statistical research.

*NCSL.* The National Conference of State Legislators.

*NGC* National Governors Conference. (Now the National Governors association).

*OFM.* (Previously OPP and FM). The Office of Financial Management. The budget making, policy, and supervisory arm of the Office of the Governor.

*PAC.* Political Action Committee. Formed by lobbies to dispense funds.

*PDC.* Public Disclosure Commission. Enacted by initiative in 1973.

*Redistricting.* The constitutional mandate, now carried out by a gubernatorially appointed commission, to redraw legislative and congressional districts lines after every decennial census to make them equal in size.

RNC. Republican National Committee.

RSCC. Republican State Central Committee.

*Special Election.* Generally called in the spring of odd numbered years to sanction special measures. (E.g., school "special" levies, or bonds).

*TESC*. The Evergreen State College

*Veto*. Originally the power of the governor to veto any item in any bill passed by the legislature, subject to a two-thirds legislative override in both houses. Now limited to a paragraph or more.

*WICHE*. The Western Interstate Commission for Higher Education, (Denver).

*Third House*. The lobbies.

*WFSEA*. The Washington Association of State Employees (Union).

*WBA*. Washington Association of Business.

*WSL*. Washington State legislature.

*WSLC*. Washington State Labor Council, AFL-CIO.

*WEA*. Washington [State] Education Association.

**2. Acronyms for Governors**

| | | | |
|---|---|---|---|
| *ADR* | Albert D. Rosellini | *GL* | Gary Locke |
| *ABL* | Arthur B. Langlie | *JDS* | John D. Spellman |
| *BG* | Booth Gardner | *MCW* | Monrad C. Wallgren |
| *DJE* | Daniel J Evans | *ML* | Mike Lowry |
| *DLR* | Dixie Lee Ray | RHR | Roland H. Hartley |

**3. Journals/Publications**

| | |
|---|---|
| AAAPS | Annals of the American Academy of Political Science. |
| AGB | AGB Reports (Higher Education). |
| AHR | American Historical Review. |
| AJPR | American Journal of Political Science. |
| APQ | American Politics Quarterly. |
| APSR | American Political Science Review. |
| AM | American Magazine. |
| AmCR | American Civil Liberties Review. |
| AJP | American Journal of Political Science (formerly MWJP). |
| APQ | American Political Quarterly. |
| AR | Antioch Review. |
| A | Argus (Seattle). |
| AT | Atlantic Monthly. |
| BW | Business Week. |
| ChHED | The Chronicle of Higher Education. |
| CJ | California Journal. |
| CJR | Columbia Journalism Review. |
| CMR | California Management Review. |
| C | Columbia. |
| CQ | Congressional Quarterly. |

| | |
|---|---|
| CQP | Congressional Quarterly Press. |
| CQS | Congressional Quarterly Service. |
| Cpt | Compact (Higher Education). |
| CS | Common Sense. |
| ECS | Education Commission of the States. |
| F | Fortune. |
| FRB | Federal Reserve Bank of San Francisco Business Review. |
| HBR | Harvard Business Review. |
| IGP | Intergovernmental Perspective (National Advisory Commission on Intergovernmental Relations). |
| IGR | Intergovernmental Review |
| IW | Industry Week. |
| J | Judicature. |
| JEH | Journal of Economic History. |
| JFK | John F. Kennedy School of Government. |
| HUM | Harvard University Magazine. |
| JHE | Journal of Higher Education. |
| JIH | Journal of the House of the State of Washington. |
| JlS | Journal of the Senate of the State of Washington. |
| JPH | Journal of Policy History. |
| JOP | Journal of Politics. |
| JSG | Journal of State Government. |
| JW | Journal of the West. |
| LSQ | Legislative Studies Quarterly. |
| MJPS | Midwest Journal of Political Science. |
| MVHR | The Mississippi Valley Historical Review. |
| N | The Nation. |
| NCR | National Civic Review. |
| NR | New Republic. |
| NW | Newsweek. |
| OHQ | Oregon Historical Quarterly. |
| P | Pacific Magazine. |
| PAR | Public Administration Review. |
| PAJ | Political Studies Journal. |
| PHR | Pacific Historical Review. |
| PNF | Pacific Northwest Forum. |
| PNQ | Pacific Northwest Quarterly. |
| POQ | Public Opinion Quarterly. |
| PS | Puget Soundings (Seattle). |

| | |
|---|---|
| PSJ | Policy Studies Journal. |
| PSQ | Political Science Quarterly. |
| RF | The Ripon Forum. |
| SG | State Government. |
| SL | State Legislatures. |
| SLPR | State Legislatures Progress Reporter. |
| SQ | Sociological Quarterly. |
| SSQ | Social Science Quarterly. |
| T | Time. |
| TJF | The Journal of Federalism. |
| USNWR | U.S. News and World Report. |
| UWALR | University of Washington Law Review. |
| UWR | University of Washington Report. |
| WPPN | Washington Public Policy Notes (Bureau of Research and Services, University of Washington). |
| IPPM | Institute for Public Policy Management, (University of Washington). |
| WH | Western History. |
| WLR | Washington Law Review. |
| WHQ | Washington Historical Quarterly. |
| WICHE | Western Interstate Compact for Higher Education. |
| WLR | University of Washington Law Review. |
| WPQ | Western Political Quarterly. |
| WQ | Wilson Quarterly. |
| WSBN | Washington State Bar News. |
| WSRC | Washington State Research Council, (Monthly Report). |

**4. Elective and Appointive Offices**

| | |
|---|---|
| AAG | Assistant Attorney General. |
| AG | (State) Attorney General |
| CC | City Councilman |
| CCH | Chief Clerk of the House |
| CPL | (State) Commissioner of Public Lands |
| CtyC | County Councilman |
| CtyE | County Executive |
| DD | Department Director |
| G | Governor |
| GCOS | Governor's Chief of Staff |
| GCS | Governor's central staff |
| LB | Liquor Board |

| | |
|---|---|
| LL | Legislative Liaison of the Governor's office. |
| LtG | Lieutenant Governor |
| M | Mayor |
| ML | Majority Leader |
| MNL | Minority Leader |
| PA | Prosecuting Attorney |
| PUDC | Public Utility District Commissioner |
| OSOS | Office of the Secretary of State |
| SPI | (State) Superintendent of Public Instruction |
| SR | State Representative |
| SPR | Speaker of the House |
| IIIH | Third House (lobbyists) |
| SSCt | Washington State Supreme Court |
| USC | United states Congressman |
| USR | United States Representative |
| USS | United States Senator |

**5. Oft-Cited Publishers**

| | |
|---|---|
| BYUP | Brigham Young University Press, Provo, UT. |
| CQP | Congressional Quarterly Press, Washington, D.C. |
| CSG | Council of State Governments. |
| HUP | Harvard University Press, Cambridge, MA. |
| INUP | Indiana University Press, Bloomington. |
| OHSP | Oregon Historical Society Press. |
| ORUP | Oregon State University Press, Corvallis. |
| OUP | Oxford University Press, New York, and London. |
| UCAPB | University of California Press, Berkeley. |
| UCP | University of Chicago Press, Chicago. |
| UIDP | University of Idaho Press, Moscow. |
| UKAP | University of Kansas Press, Lawrence, KS. |
| UNEP | University of Nebraska Press, Lincoln. |
| UOKP | University of Oklahoma Press, Norman. |
| UNMP | University of New Mexico Press, Albuquerque. |
| UORP | University of Oregon Press, Eugene. |
| UPAP | University of Pennsylvania Press, Philadelphia. |
| UWAP | University of Washington Press, Seattle and London. |
| UWIP | University of Wisconsin Press, Madison. |
| WSUP | Washington State University Press, Pullman. |

**6. Institutional Repositories**

| | |
|---|---|
| CSAS | California State Archives, Sacramento. |
| DDEPL | Dwight D. Eisenhower Presidential Library, Abilene, KS. |
| DLRM | (Governor) Dixy Lee Ray Museum, Fox Island, WA. |
| EPLA | Everett Public Library, Archives. |
| EWSHS | Eastern Washington State Historical Society, Cheney. |
| HISU | Hoover Institute, Stanford University. |
| HSTPL | Harry S. Truman Presidential Library, Independence, MO. |
| IDSHS | Idaho State Historical Society (and State Archives), Boise, ID. |
| KCA | King County Archives, Seattle. |
| LOC | Library of Congress, Washington, D.C. |
| NARA-S | National Archives and Records Administration Regional Office, Seattle. |
| NARA-1 | Original depository, Washington, D.C. |
| NARA-2 | Depository at College Park, M.D. |
| PLUSSC | Pacific Lutheran University, Scandinavian Special Collections Division, Parkland. |
| RMNPL | Richard M. Nixon Presidential Library, Yorba Linda, CA. |
| SMRL | Seattle Municipal Reference Library. (Now part of SPL). |
| SpL | Spokane Public Library. |
| SUSC | Stanford University, Special Collections, Palo Alto. |
| SPL | Seattle Public Library, Archives Division. |
| TPLA | Tacoma Public Library and Archives. |
| TCL | Tri Cities Public Library. |
| UCBSC | University of California Berkeley, Special Collections. |
| UCLAA | University of Southern California Archives. |
| UOSC | University of Oregon, Special Collections, Salem. |
| UPSSC | University of Puget Sound, Special Collections, Tacoma. |
| UWASC | University of Washington Library, Special Collections, Seattle. |
| UWAGL | University of Washington, Gallagher Law Library, Seattle. |
| UWL | University of Washington Library, Seattle. |
| WCA | Whitman College Archives, Walla Walla. |
| WSA | Washington State Archives, Olympia; |
| (-B), | Bellingham, |
| (-C) | Cheney, |
| (-E), | Ellensburg. |
| WSHSA | Washington State Historical Society Archives, Tacoma. |
| WSL | Washington State Library, Tumwater. |
| WSUSC | Washington State University Library, Special Collections, Pullman. |
| WWUA | Western Washington State University Archives, Bellingham. |

| | |
|---|---|
| YPL | Yakima Public Library. |

**7. Newspapers**

| | |
|---|---|
| ADW | Aberdeen Daily World. |
| AGN | Auburn Globe News. |
| ANJ | Auburn News Journal. |
| Ad | The Advocate (The Third House, Olympia). |
| A | Seattle Argus. |
| BH | Bellingham Herald. |
| BS | Bremerton Sun. |
| Col | The Columbian (Vancouver). |
| DO | The Daily Olympian. |
| EVH | The Everett Herald. |
| JA | The Journal-American, Bellevue (Now the Eastside Journal). |
| KCLS | King County Labor Council, Scanner. |
| LCS | Lake City Star (Seattle). |
| NJ | Northgate Journal (Seattle). |
| MN | Municipal News (Seattle). |
| NB | New Beginnings. (The Republican State Central Committee of Washington. 1981, ff.). |
| O | The Olympian. |
| ON | Olympia News. |
| PI | The Post-Intelligencer (Seattle). |
| SDC | Spokane Daily Chronicle. |
| SR | The Spokesman-Review (Spokane). |
| SS | Seattle Star. |
| ST | The Seattle Times. |
| SuT | The Suburban Times (King County). |
| TCH | Tri City Herald (Richland-Pasco-Kennewick). |
| TNT | Tacoma News Tribune. |
| UFWN | United For Washington Newsletter (An adjunct of the Association of Washington Business), Olympia. |
| WB | Washington Business (The Association of Washington Business, Olympia). |
| UWD | The University of Washington Daily |
| WDW | The Wenatchee Daily World. |
| WEA | Action. (Washington Education Association, Federal Way/Olympia). |
| Wkly | The Weekly (Seattle). |
| WPPN | Washington Public Policy Notes (University of Washington). |
| WS | The Washington Standard (Olympia). |

WSE. The Washington State Employee (Olympia).

WSLCR Washington State Labor Council Reports (Olympia).

WT The Washington Teamster (Seattle).

WWUB Walla Walla Union Bulletin.

YHR Yakima Herald Republic.

### 8. Out of State Newspapers

CSM The Christian Science Monitor.

LMT Lewiston (ID) Morning Tribune.

NYT The New York Times.

NYTM The New York Times Magazine.

OR The Oregonian (Portland).

PO The Portland, (OR) Oregonian.

WP The Washington Post.

WSJ The Wall Street Journal.

## G. Oral Histories (by the author).

### 1. "Governor Arthur B. Langlie Persona Oral Histories," 1970. WSA.

Frederick Baker.

Ralph Davis. DD.

Charles Frankland.

William Fitzgerald. Seattle Fire Chief.

Dr. Roger Freeman. GCS.

Charles Hodde. SR (Spkr), DD (X3).

Judge Frederick Hamley. SSCt, Ninth U.S. District Court.

Harold Van Eaton. DD.

Arthur Sheridan Langlie. Son.

Hugh B. Mitchell. USC, USS.

Albert D. Rosellini. SS, G.

### 2. Legislative Oral History Project I ("LOHP I"), 1989-90. WSA (810 pp).

Ken Billington. WA PUD Association.

Duane Berenston. SR (Co-spkr), DD.

Warren Bishop. GCOS/DD.

Willliam Bugge. DD.

Gordon Clinton. M.

Arthur Comfort. SR.

Joe Davis. President, WSFL.

James Dolliver. GCOS, Justice.

Daniel J. Evans. (2) SR (Mel, ML), G, USS.

Steve Excel. LL, OSOS.

William A. Ginsberg. SS.

Robert Goldsworthy. SR.

Jack Gorrie. GCOS.

R.R. "Bob" Grieve. SS, CtyC.

Leroy Hittle. ST, LB.

Charles Hodde. SR (Spkr), DD.

Robert Hollister. DD.

Karen Rahm. DD.

Albert D. Rosellini. (2) SS, G.

Warren F. Reid. COS.

Jim Ryan. DD.

Norm Schut. ED, WFSE, TH.

John D. Spellman. CtyC, CtyE, G.

**3 "LOHP II"; 2005-2006. WSA, UW, WSU, Special Collections. (804 pp).**

Marlin Appelwick. SR (MNL).

Clyde Ballard. SR (MnL, Spkr).

Everett Billingsley. GCS.

Marty Brown. CCH, DD, LL, GCOS.

Don Brunell. President, Association of Washington Industries.

Dick Davis. President, Washington State Research Council.

Joe Dear. DD (Unemployment Security), GCOS.

Wayne Ehlers. SR (MnL, Spkr), LL.

Tom Fitzsimmons. DD (Ecology), GCOS.

Dean Foster. CCH, GCOS.

Mary Faulk. DD (Lottery, Ecology, Licenses).

Booth Gardner. SS, CtyE, G.

Denny Heck. SR (MnL), GCOS.

Lorraine Hine. SR (MnL), LL, GCOS.

Dennis Karras. DD (Personnel).

Fred Kiga, DD. GCOS.

Gary Locke. SR, CtyE, G.

Mike Lowry. CtyC, USR, G.

Dan McDonald. SR, SS (MNL, ML).

Lyle Quasim. DD (Social and Health Services).

Chase Riveland. DD (Institutions).

Mary Riveland. DD (Ecology, Lottery, Licenses).

Mike Ryherd. TH.

Helen Sommers. SR.

Art Wang. SR, Chief Judge, Office of Administrative Appeals.

Richard Thompson. DD (Community Affairs, OFM, DSHS), GCOS.

**4. Other Oral Histories by the Author (at UWASP). Various dates.**

Stewart Bledsoe. SR (ML).

Gordon Clinton. M (Seattle).

Don Eldridge. SR (Spkr).

Kinnear, George SR (ML); DD.

Mort Frayn. SR (Spkr).

Larry Kenney President, WSFL.

David Levine. CC (Seattle).

Ralph B. Potts.

Alan Thompson. SR, (ML), SS, CCH.

Pearl Wanamaker. SR, SS, SPI.

**5. Oral histories by Others. OSOS, Legislative Oral History Project, WSA.**

Don Eldridge. SR (Spkr).

James Dolliver. GCOS.

William Gissberg. SS.

Robert Goldsworthy. SR.

Margaret Hurley. SR, SS.

Wilbur E. Hallauer. SR, SS, DD.

August P. Mardesich. SR (ML), SS (ML).

Mary Ellen McCaffree. SR, DD.

Joel M. Pritchard. SR, SS, USR, LtG.

Albert D. Rosellini SS, G.

**6. Oral Histories by the DDEPL, (Abilene, KS), and Columbia University.**

George Kinnear. SR (ML), DD.

Thor Tollefson. USR, DD.

Walter Williams Sr., Chair RSCC, Citizens for Eisenhower,

Undersecretary of Commerce.

# *Index*

**A**



**B**

C

## D